USA TODAY SPORTS BASEBALLHQ.COM'S 2018

MINOR LEAGUE BASEBALL ANALYST

ROB GORDON AND JEREMY DELONEY | BRENT HERSHEY, EDITOR | 13TH EDITION

TRIUMPH BOOKS

This book is available in quantity at special discounts for your group or organization. For further information, contact:

Triumph Books LLC
814 North Franklin Street
Chicago, Illinois 60610
(312) 337-0747
www.triumphbooks.com

Printed in U.S.A.
ISBN: 978-1-62937-482-6

Data provided by TheBaseballCube.com and Baseball Info Solutions

Cover design by Brent Hershey
Front cover photograph by Kim Klement/USA TODAY Sports Images

Acknowledgments

Jeremy Deloney:

This is my 9th—and final—year of the *Minor League Baseball Analyst* and it has been a source of pride and accomplishment. I have thoroughly enjoyed my time with BaseballHQ.com.

My wife Amy is a true inspiration to me. She supports me and allows me to pursue my creative outlets. I look at her with awe and admiration for her selfless nature and unconditional love.

My kids (Owen, Ethan, Madeline) allow me to look at life from a different perspective. They teach this old-timer so many things and they provide the type of joy that I crave.

My parents—Bill and Nancy—and my brothers—BJ and Andy—have always been a source of support. They are all phenomenal human beings who do things the right way. I look up to all of them.

And thank you to the readers, all of you. Thank you for allowing me to do what I do.

In my parting words, I'd like to share my appreciation for the opportunity I've been given by the great people at BaseballHQ. Thank you to Deric McKamey, Ron Shandler, Brent Hershey, Ray Murphy, and Rob Gordon. Those are some big names in this industry and I appreciate all you have done for me. To be able to write and analyze baseball with you has been a tremendous honor for me.

Despite my 13+ year tenure, I've never really considered myself to be a writer. I can spell. I can write in complete sentences. I can use appropriate punctuation (I think). I'm simply a fan of baseball who has been given an opportunity to write about the game I love. Now, I can sit back and watch.

With deepest gratitude, I bid adieu.

Rob Gordon:

In 2003 Ron Shandler and Deric McKamey gave me the opportunity to do something I always wanted to do—write about baseball. Ron and Deric showed me the ropes, and explained what scouts look for. Deric's total recall of the most obscure minor league players still amazes me. They have both moved on to bigger and better things, but their imprint on the structure of this book lives on.

Jeremy and I are now in our ninth edition of the *Minor League Baseball Analyst*. Over the past couple of years we have gotten invaluable help from the rest of the BaseballHQ.com minor league team: Brent Hershey, Chris Blessing, and Alec Dopp. I would especially like to thank Brent who has been the glue that holds this project together.

Many other baseball people provided invaluable support and encouragement over the years. They include Jeff Barton, Jim Callis, John Sickels, Ray Murphy, Rick Wilton, Patrick Davitt, Todd Zola, Jason Grey, Joe Sheehan, Jeff Erickson, Kimball Crossley, Steve Moyer, Phil Hertz, Jock Thompson and Doug Dennis among others.

Someday someone will write a story about Baseball Unlimited. Until then I'll just have to thank the boys—Michael Hartman, Kegan Hartman, Steve Hartman, Michael Cooney, Bob Hathaway, Doug Hathaway, Derald Cook, Dave Dannemiller, Ted Maizes, Randy Jones, Duncan Hathaway, and John Mundelius.

My oldest son Bobby had a blast playing varsity baseball for Dearborn High and the coaches—Kyle Jenks, Eric Jenks, and Matt McKay did a great job with the boys as did his travel baseball coaches Rob Stockman, John Schneider, and Rob Septor. Also a big thank you to the guys at Michigan Strategy Baseball—Craig Cotter, Rob Fay, and Ryan Gilbert.

I would especially like to thank my family. My two boys—Bobby and Jimmy—make the sky bluer, the sun brighter, and the crack of the bat all the more sweet. My sister Susan Arntson helped raise me and tried to keep me out of trouble—mostly. Thanks to the Arntson clan—Jeff, Rachel, Josh, Marissa, and Jake. My mother Sandra Gordon took me on an annual birthday trip to see the Cubs play and my father Robert W. Gordon III who has shared my passion for the game of baseball. Finally, a huge thank you to my amazing and beautiful wife Paula—stay strong!

Finally, I want to acknowledge my partner is this effort over the past nine years, Jeremy Deloney. I was crushed to find out that this will be Jeremy's final year co-authoring the MLBA and truth be told, I'm not sure how we are going to replace his exhaustive knowledge of the minor leagues, his attention to detail, and the tireless effort he puts into making this book possible. Jeremy sees tons of minor league games, has detailed knowledge of even the most obscure prospects, and has extensive contact with scouts, analysts, the media, and player personal folks. Finally, Jeremy organizes all of the positional rankings at the back of the book, helps to proofread all of the player write-ups, and has been the driving force behind this entire project.

Jeremy, it has been a pleasure working with you over the past nine years and I can't thank you enough for all of your hard work and support over that time.

Table of Contents

Growing Edges

by Brent Hershey

This game.

One of the tenets of prospect evaluation is that there's always something to learn. The prospects that we examine—okay, maybe "obsess over" is a more accurate term—are still-developing human beings who continue to evolve in their baseball skills, physiques, abilities, all as they negotiate adulthood. The offseason provides time to evaluate and then rank them, as if we can reach some nebulous goal of quintessential prospect card-reading. But we're fooling ourselves if we don't remember that this offseason evaluation of players is always, always, always one thing:

In-progress.

To treat our recommendations as anything else is silly, short-sighted, and in many cases just downright arrogant. We'll never get it 100% right (just look at our Top 100 archives in this book for instance (starting on page 132)), but the push to improve in our evaluation process is the allure that keeps us coming back. While it's arrogant to act like one *knows* how player X will adjust to major-league pitching, or be able to improve his feel for a change-up, it's very good practice to always be looking back, trying to add some small sliver of knowledge or perspective to our ever-expanding evaluation toolbox.

Enter Rhys Hoskins and The Quality At-bat. Though there's no metric (beyond pitches per plate appearance, by which Hoskins fared very well in 2017) to quantify it, we'll still try to define it. A quality at-bat is an at-bat where a batter (among other things): 1) sees a lot of pitches; 2) establishes good ball-strike recognition and ability to take a walk; 3) shows the ability to not swing at pitches out of the strike zone; 4) demonstrates he can foul off, or spoil, quality strikes; and ultimately 5) crushes pitches that he can handle or that the pitcher missed his spot on. That last element is important, because no matter how patient a hitter is (or how adept the hitter is at fouling off a pitcher's pitch, etc.), if he isn't able to punish a mistake with frequency, he's less likely to be noticed or feared in the lineup.

Hoskins, of course, did all these during most of his two-month debut, in which he hit 11 HR in his first 18 games, firmly implanting himself as a power-hitting center of a rebuilding Phillies lineup. While it's still a small sample size, and Hoskins still has much to prove, the kernel of something special is there, both in real life and in fantasy circles.

Some history on Hoskins, and how I came to realize the importance of quality at-bats. Hoskins was drafted in the 5th round in 2014 from Sacramento State University. As a right-handed hitting college first baseman, Hoskins faced an uphill battle to the majors from the start. Why? There are just not many MLB starting first basemen who were right-handed hitting college first basemen. A quick and informal scan of MLB depth charts as of January 2018 revealed just two, in fact: Paul Goldschmidt (1B, ARI) and C.J. Cron (1B, LAA).

One is a superstar, the other, a youngish player whose MLB future is far from decided. The point is just two out of 30 fit Hoskins' profile. So when you hear the adage that right-handed hitting first base prospects have to be exceptional hitters—this is what we mean.

Now let's examine how this publication covered Hoskins during his time in the minors. (Disclosure: As the writer of the comments on the Phillies prospects for several seasons, almost all of the following is my own work).

After signing his pro contract in 2014, Hoskins was placed in short-season Williamsport of the New York Penn League (NYPL), where he hit .237/.297/.408. He did have 9 HR in 245 AB, but on the whole the debut was nondescript. Hoskins didn't get his own box in the 2015 edition of this book (meaning we didn't feel like he was among the Phillies top 30 or so prospects for 2015), but did earn a mention in the 2014 Draft Recap as a "reliable hitter at Sacramento State, though he struggled in the NYPL."

Hoskins moved up to Low-A Lakewood in 2015. With a better contact rate and a bit more patience, he slugged another 9 HR in 255 AB, but upped his slashline to an impressive .322/.384/.525, earning him a mid-season promotion to High-A Clearwater. This was not yet out of line for an established collegiate hitter, and the mid-season promotion clearly was to challenge him at the next level. The stat results in High-A were similar—243 AB, 8 HR, .317/.390/.510. He then appeared in the 2016 edition of the book, with this description:

> *"As RH college 1B, the bar is high, but rose to occasion in first full season. Long swing, great extension, but without normal huge holes. No noticeable platoon split, but speed not part of his game. Good agility around the bag on defense. Has surprised with hitting acumen so far, but upper-level arms will be the true test."*

We gave him a 7C grade—an MLB regular's ceiling, but our concerns about production at the high minors enough to hedge our bets with the "C" (50% chance of reaching that ceiling).

In 2016, Hoskins advanced to AA-Reading, and he took off, battling teammate Dylan Cozens for the minor-league HR crown that Cozens eventually won. But in 498 AB, Hoskins went deep 38 times, while showing improved patience (12% walk rate) and career-high OPS (.937) from a .281/.371/.566 line. The caveat was that the Reading ballpark is a known hitters paradise, a combination of great sightlines for hitters and often-favorable wind conditions. Home run figures there typically inflate a player's power numbers. So even though Hoskins did fine with his first taste of upper-level pitching, we still stayed skeptical, as noted in his commentary in the 2017 edition of the book:

> *"Has continued to hit—and with power—at each step. Some stiffness to his swing, is pull-happy, and has trouble tracking quality breaking stuff. But is patient enough to get into FB counts, will take a walk, and has light-tower strength. Lack of speed and only average defense limits his overall projection, so he'll need to keep producing in the box."*

We moved Hoskins into our Phillies top 15 (#14) for 2017, but we left his grade at 7C. Of course he had no trouble with Triple-A pitching in 2017 (29 HR in 475 AB; .284/.385/.581), was promoted on August 11, and that magical two-month run was off and running.

In addition to assigning the grades and writing the commentary, I also got to see Hoskins in person at various levels of his minor-league career. I too was surprised to his initial success, but as I watched him handling himself more like a polished veteran than a green-cheeked rookie, I was curious to look back at my game notes at the different stages of his development. And I soon came upon something I obviously sidestepped in my evaluation of Hoskins: his repeated ability to put together quality at-bats.

I first saw Hoskins in person in May of 2015 in Lakewood. He went 2-for-5 with a walk; with several hard-hit balls. "Strong, and saw a good number of pitches," my notes read. "Will need to lay off soft stuff." In 2016 and 2017, my high-minors looks increased.

And in almost in every viewing, he continued to run deep counts and wait for his pitch to hit. He logged a number of six-, seven- and eight-pitch at-bats over this time. A representative note from August 2016: "Worked it; nice AB" as he drew a walk on pitch number nine after fouling off three pitches. "Good patience" my notes read in 2017 as he let a just-outside 96 mph fastball go by for ball four.

That characteristic stayed with Hoskins all the way to the majors. His MLB AB were marked by all the characteristicis of a "good at-bat" above—only this time, it was against world-class pitching. The challenge will be to sustain that focus over a whole season. But in looking back—granted, with a bit of 20/20 hindsight—one can see these attributes in his minors AB, even if I didn't recognize them at that point.

Of course, this is not to say that every player who puts together good at-bats in the minors will be able to find success early-on in their MLB career. But from a player evaluation standpoint, it's fair to say that from this experience with Hoskins, I have added an awareness of the fuzzily-defined "good at-bat" to my list of characteristics to be keenly aware of.

•

Long-time readers of the *Minor League Baseball Analyst* will no doubt recognize most of the elements of the pages that follow in this 13th Edition. For both new and old, let's run through the features and structure.

The Insights section provides some narrative details and tools you can use as you prepare for getting the most out of your farm system and the rookies that will emerge during the 2018 baseball season. All the essays are designed to help you assemble your teams, as well as give you some food for thought on the prospect landscape, delving into building a fantasy farm system; the top international players; reviews of the 2017 Arizona Fall League, the Rule 5 Draft, and the First Year Player Draft; and a preview of the 2018 college baseball season. If the past is any indication, no doubt many of these players mentioned in the essays will soon be fantasy cornerstones. It's time to get on board.

Up next is the HQ100—our signature list of the top 100 fantasy baseball prospects for 2018. The HQ100 is a compilation of six individual lists (Jeremy Deloney, Rob Gordon, Chris Blessing, Alec Dopp, Brent Hershey, as well as BaseballHQ.com prospect-savvy writers Jock Thompson, Nick Richards and Matthew St-Germain). This list is ranked by overall fantasy value, in an attempt to balance raw skill level, level of polish/refinement, risk in terms of age/level, and overall potential impact value. And then Dopp suggests 12 more "Sleepers" just outside the HQ100, young players who could make the jump to the list in 2019.

While the HQ100 is a collaborative exercise, the player profiles—including the skills grades, commentaries and player ratings—are the primary work of one analyst. Assignments are divided up by organization, so that our analysts get to know an MLB team's system from top to bottom. The roster is Deloney (the entire AL except for CHW and HOU, as well as SF); Gordon (MIA, PIT, STL, CHC, LA, COL); Blessing (ATL, NYM, CIN, MIL, ARI, CHW); Dopp (HOU, SD); and Hershey (PHI, WAS). Given our emphasis on seeing players in person—and the daunting task when the book covers 1000+ players—we did share information and insights with each other, tapping the strength of our team. In addition, each writer filled in the gaps with the various scouting and front-office contacts.

As noted at the beginning of the Batters and Pitchers sections, our Potential Ratings have two parts. The first is on upside, graded on a 10-1 scale, with 10 being Hall of Fame potential; 1 is minor league roster filler. A "6" (platoon MLBer) is the lowest grade you'll find in the book, as these are the least likely players to have an impact on your fantasy team.

But potential and actualization are two different things, and the A-E letter grades attempt to assess the likelihood of reaching that potential. It's a proxy for risk, which may or may not include age, ability and/or willingness to improve, current grasp of fundamental skills (fastball command, strike zone judgement), experience, and success in the high minors, among other factors.

In the end, these Potential Ratings are carefully considered by the author, and there is no one "correct" grade. One can make the argument that in a sense, an 8B player can at the same time be a 9D—higher ceiling, but much less likely to reach it. It is up to the author to decide which rating will give the clearest picture of this prospect at this point in time. The most valuable information to fantasy players cannot be encapsulated in one rating, but in the combination of skills grades, statistics, biographical information and commentary that the MLBA provides.

Though the player profiles make up the bulk of the book, don't miss the tools that follow: the Major League Equivalencies; the Organization Grades; the Top Prospects by organization, by position, and by specific skills; the Top 75 prospects for 2018 only; an archive of our Top 100 lists; the glossary and a list of minor league affiliates. Whew … there's a lot of information in these pages.

One final note: as mentioned in the Acknowledgements, this is Jeremy Deloney's last project after nine years authoring the book. His attention to detail, thoroughness and love of the game and prospect evaluation will be greatly missed. It will be new territory for me to put together next year's version of this book without Jeremy's assistance. Best to you, Jeremy ... thank you for all of your contributions over the years.

But for now—if you have a suggestion to share, email us at support@baseballhq.com. Otherwise, grab a shovel and dig in. A better fantasy farm system awaits.

Building a Successful Fantasy Farm System

by Chris Blessing

You've prepared for this upcoming dynasty draft for months. If you pre-ordered your *Baseball Forecaster* copy, you've been combing through data since before Thanksgiving. You have your Forecaster handy, along with your own copious notes, printed copies of BHQ's Top 15 organizational prospect lists, BaseballHQ.com pulled up on one computer screen, spreadsheets pulled up on another and a beverage of your choice by your side, ready to tackle and own your dynasty draft. Are you really ready? Sure, you have a game plan for your main roster. But, do you have a game plan for your available minor league slots?

The owners who go into the draft strategizing the minor league portion are most likely the owners contending every September for the championship. These owners are not just reviewing prospect lists. They're embracing the prospect draft with clearly defined expectations. They've developed their strategy by managing risk, identifying player pool inefficiencies and strengths, assessing prospect opportunities and trade potential throughout the season, defining the parameters of their league and exploiting the biases of fellow owners.

How to do it? Read on ...

Defined Expectations

No matter the format, successful farm system construction starts with defining expectations.

Essentially, what are you trying to accomplish? If it's to guess which players are tomorrow's superstar fantasy contributors, you are probably doing it wrong. It's not a sound strategy, especially in smaller formats where taking on greater risk can have catastrophic consequences. An appropriate defined expectation can be as simple as you want to make it—like acquiring assets to contend or maintaining a competitive advantage over the league's other owners. Whatever the expectation, there are some sound strategies to consider when tackling farm system construction.

Risk Evaluation

Level of risk varies based on factors such as format, player pool size, league rules and eligibility. In shallow formats, there is no need to assume too much risk acquiring prospects with a variable degree of outcomes. Don't make bold statements. An owner shouldn't want to use one of their limited roster spots on a player like Reds outfielder Jose Siri, who had a terrific 2017 as an older prospect in the Midwest League. His MLB impact won't be for another two or three years and there is a variable amount of risk that 2017 was more fluke than actual player. Instead, a shallow format owner should target a player with less boom-or-bust risk, like Yankees pitching prospect Chance Adams. Vastly underrated by prospect media, Adams has dominated each minor league level, including Triple-A last season. Adams is close to contributing and at worst is an injury away from a rotation spot while someone like Siri has more heralded prospects like Taylor Trammell and Jesse Winker ahead of him on the Reds OF depth chart.

Even though Adams is a pitcher, which is an unreliable position set, he also carries curb appeal for owners using prospects to acquire veterans to make a championship run. Opposing owners tend to know the names of Yankees prospects like Adams, Justus Sheffield, Clint Frazier and Miguel Andujar because their media coverage is greater than teams like the Reds, even if Adams has been unheralded. Siri has curb appeal too. He made headlines in 2017 for his 39-game hit streak. If other owners in your league don't do a lot of minor league research and go by name recognition, Siri may be a guy a with some name recognition.

In deeper formats, an owner should manage a farm system like a financial portfolio, breaking down risk by identifying short-term, medium-term and long-term assets.

Short-term assets are prospects who are 0-to-2 years away from making a fantasy impact (which is different than 0-to-2 years from making their debut). These players may already be in the big leagues; just not having a fantasy impact yet. In formats with 15 or more slots available for prospects, owners should allocate 25%-to-40% of their farm system to short-term assets. Prospects such as Adams, Rays prospect Brent Honeywell, Rangers prospect Willie Calhoun and Reds prospect Nick Senzel are great examples of short-term assets. Each player has a clear path towards playing time and should hold their own as rookies. There are other short-term assets to consider too. Guys like Rays prospect Jake Bauers and Brewers prospect Mauricio Dubon are unheralded players with solid track records, who lack curb appeal and a clear path towards playing time unless opportunity arises through trade or injury.

Medium-term assets are prospects who are 2-to-3 years away from making a fantasy impact. In fantasy, medium-term assets should make up the bulk of your farm system portfolio because most Top 100 prospects fall into the medium-term asset category. These assets should make up 50% of your portfolio. Each player in this category should have a greater than 50% chance of becoming a solid fantasy contributor and greater than 30% chance of becoming a fantasy all-star. For higher impact guys, names such as Blue Jays prospect Vladimir Guerrero Jr and Phillies prospect Sixto Sanchez should be considered part of this category. Owners should also try to find steady High-A and Double-A pitchers who may lack top-of-the-rotation upside but have solid potential to become mid-rotation starters or late-inning relievers. Think guys like Padres prospect Cal Quantrill, Tigers prospect Beau Burrows and Dodgers prospect Mitchell White. This is where owners should stash recently drafted college bats like Brewers prospect Keston Hiura and Diamondbacks prospect Pavin Smith.

Long-term assets are prospects who are 4 or more years away from making a fantasy impact. These types of assets should only account for 5%-to-25% of your portfolio. Made up of mostly teenaged players, this category is reserved for prospects with high ceilings and low floors. In other words, speculative stocks. A good philosophy is to target standout short-season performers, especially teenaged pitching since it's the most speculative market. It is easy to find the prep guys who recently debuted for their organizations, like Reds prospect Hunter Greene and Padres prospect MacKenzie Gore. It's harder to find international teenaged prospects to target. This book can help you find those players. The next great pitching prospect will be debuting in full-season ball next season. It could be Greene, Gore or someone not mentioned yet, like Athletics prospect Jesus Luzardo.

Player Pool Inefficiencies and Strengths

Identifying player pool inefficiencies and strengths gives owners a distinct advantage over the competition, especially in shallow formats. These inefficiencies and strengths can be positional, category-driven or skill-driven. For instance, third base continues to be a weak player pool on the MLB level, even with Jose Ramirez having a breakout season and Rafael Devers making his MLB debut. While other infield positions go 12-to-15 deep in the player pool, 3B goes about 10 deep. In a 12-team format, two or three teams are stuck with an average-to-subpar regular at 3B. Loading up on 3B prospects is a solid strategy to control a weak player pool. Having 3B prospects like Nick Senzel, Marlins prospect Brian Anderson and White Sox prospect Jake Burger at your disposal could help mitigate trades with less fortunate owners and/or improve your depth.

Speed is the ultimate lacking quality in fantasy. If a prospect has exhibited a proficiency stealing bases, he's probably worth targeting. There are few upper level prospects showcasing big SB numbers, like Athletics prospect Jorge Mateo and Blue Jays prospect Anthony Alford. Identifying speed prospects early is ideal, especially working in deeper prospect formats. Guys like the aforementioned Reds prospects Siri and Trammell and Braves prospect Cristian Pache are good examples of riskier big SB potential guys to target who are further away from the big leagues.

Other Factors

Every dynasty league plays by its own set of rules and behaviors. Some leagues allow you to keep a small number of minor league players each year while others allow owners to keep a slew of minor leaguers. If your league allows only a couple of keepers a season, target top prospects only for those keeper spots and load up on short-term assets in the draft to help get you through the season. In these sort of leagues, minor league eligibility is an ongoing issue since most of the farm system is dedicated to short-term assets. In these cases, it is important to monitor the waiver wire for prospects to fill newly created minor league slots.

Often overlooked in a fantasy farm system is bias within farm system development. We've all been in leagues where an owner's bias, whether towards a certain type of player or a specific team, can easily be identified. Don't be that owner. It is easy to take advantage of owners that let their bias bleed out, especially in trade discussion. Some of the best fantasy owners have clearly defined biases. Don't underestimate this and use this to your advantage.

Finally, adjust your farm system strategy every off-season to best compete for a league title. Do you need prospects to fill holes on your roster to compete this season or do you need to build up your farm system to compete in the future? Determine where your roster is at and make the necessary adjustments to your farm system strategy. The goal for farm system construction should always be to sustain fantasy success. The mission statement should change regularly.

Top 20 International Prospects for 2018

by Jeremy Deloney

Over the last several years, Major League Baseball has made tweaks and implemented changes to the signing of international players, some in part for the purposes of leveling the playing field. There have been numerous discussions about making international players available for a draft. Listed below are various international prospects who inked contracts during the international signing period in 2017 or have yet to sign, but are eligible to do so. Because of the uncertainty of defections and eligibility, some top Cuban prospects are not profiled below.

Please note that some players eligible for this list who have already signed contracts with major league organizations have player boxes in this book. For the purposes of space, those players aren't profiled here. Such prospects include: Wander Franco (SS, TAM), Julio Rodriguez (OF, SEA), and Ynmanol Marinez (SS, MIA).

In alphabetical order:

Aaron Bracho (SS, CLE)

One of the younger signees in this class, the switch-hitter doesn't turn 17 until April 2018. Bracho doesn't have the flashiest tools around, but he is fundamentally sound and uses an advanced approach at the plate. His quick, level swing path produces hard line drives and he is able and willing to use the entire field. Though he only exhibits average power potential at most, he has enough strength to keep defenses honest. His future position is up in the air. Some see him sticking at shortstop due to his fluid actions while others see a move to 2B where his average arm and range are more suitable.

Signing bonus/status: Signed for $1.5 million
MLB debut: 2024

Roberto Chirinos (SS, NYY)

The quick, athletic 17-year-old is all about agility, fluidity and defense at present. He possesses quick, sure hands while displaying fundamental footwork. His range may be a little short, but his arm strength would be an asset at 3B, 2B, or possibly the outfield. His feel for the game is advanced for his age. As a hitter, Chirinos has exemplary bat speed and some pull power. He focuses on putting the ball in play with a compact stroke. He is more likely to hit for BA than he is for HR when he reaches full maturity.

Signing bonus/status: Signed for $900,000
MLB debut: 2024

Trent Deveaux (OF, LAA)

The Angels quickly fell in love with the 17-year-old's speed and believe he has the projectable build to turn into a well-rounded player. Deveaux has elite wheels which help him to cover a ton of ground in CF. His reads and routes are a bit crude right now, but with polish, he could become a premium defender down the road. His lean frame could add significant strength and he could hit for a modicum of power at his peak. Deveaux has a keen understanding of the strike zone and he generally keeps the ball on the ground to use his speed.

Signing bonus/status: Signed for $1.2 million
MLB debut: 2024

Danny Diaz (SS, BOS)
The 17-year-old can really put a charge in the ball and has a chance to evolve into a middle-of-the-order run producer. He's quite slender now, but with his bat speed and swing path, he has well above average power potential. Diaz has the ability to use the entire field with hard contact and is able to differentiate between balls and strikes. He has a chance to hit for both BA and power. As a defender, he's likely to move to 3B or the outfield because of his size and cannon arm. He isn't the most proficient defensively, though he exhibits good instincts.
Signing bonus/status: Signed for $1.6 million
MLB debut: 2023

Larry Ernesto (OF, MIL)
There are a number of scouts who have already heaped effusive praise on the 17-year-old. Ernesto, a switch-hitter, is an electric and projectable athlete who projects to all five tools. While he is extremely fast now, he's likely to slow down as he matures, but he'll still be a stolen base threat. He owns a very disciplined approach at the plate and has above average raw power to all fields. Once he grows into his frame, he could be an ideal #3 hitter in the lineup. Defensively, he needs work on his routes and jumps, but he tracks down balls in the gaps and has a strong arm.
Signing bonus/status: Signed for $1.8 million
MLB debut: 2024

Luis Garcia (SS, PHI)
The 17-year-old is one of the more fundamentally-sound signees from this international class. The Phillies signed him based mostly on his potential plus defensive skills. He is a smooth defender with the range, footwork, and arm to be a signficant contributor with the glove. Garcia makes both spectacular and routine plays look easy. As a hitter, he'll likely never be much of a power threat, but he makes consistent contact from both sides of the plate and can use the entire field with his approach. His plate patience is also admirable and could lead to a potentially high OBP.
Signing bonus/status: Signed for $2.5 million
MLB debut: 2024

Adrian Hernandez (OF, NYM)
Though he won't turn 17 until February 2018, Hernandez already looks the part of a big leaguer. He has an athletic, strong frame and owns plus speed. He needs to add significant polish to his crude plate approach and swing mechanics, but the natural talent is there. The right-handed hitter has lightning-quick bat speed and owns plus, raw power as a result. He tends to swing at everything right now and has trouble reading spin. Hernandez profiles very well in RF, though he's currently a CF due to his strong arm. If he reaches his potential, he could hit in the middle of the lineup.
Signing bonus/status: Signed for $1.5 million
MLB debut: 2023

Miguel Hilardo (SS, TOR)
The 17-year-old is a natural hitter who could potentially hit at the top of the lineup with high BA and OBP upside. His swing mechanics are clean and quick while his batting eye is keen. Hilardo likes to use the entire field with his line drive approach and use his speed to leg out extra base hits. As he continues to grow and read pitches better, his power could escalate to at least average status. A troublesome spot at this point is his defense. He plays SS now, but is likely to slide over to 3B or 2B eventually. While he has quick hands and smooth actions, his arm and range would be better elsewhere.
Signing bonus/status: Signed for $750,000
MLB debut: 2024

Jelfry Marte (SS, TAM)
The Twins originally were all-in on the 16-year-old and signed him to a $3 million bonus. However, they later voided the contract due to concern with his physical, and then the Rays picked him up. Though some see him as more of a light-hitting shortstop; others envision a switch-hitter who could grow into average power. His short, lean frame needs significant muscle to realize any power, but his bat control and plate coverage are advanced for his age. Marte is a true shortstop who should stay at that position long-term. All of his tools play up due to his innate feel for the game.
Signing bonus/status: Signed for $800,000
MLB debut: 2025

Ronny Mauricio (SS, NYM)
The Mets project the 16-year-old to be a potential All-Star shortstop. Mauricio is very lean and offers outstanding agility and body control for his age. His long and thin frame needs to add good weight for him to realize his offensive upside and he will be given time to develop. He has a high baseball IQ and makes good contact from both sides of the plate. He hits a lot of doubles now and those should turn into HR as he grows. As a defender, he ranges well to both sides and has the plus arm to make throws from deep in the hole.
Signing bonus/status: Signed for $2.1 million
MLB debut: 2023

Eric Pardinho (RHP, TOR)
The Blue Jays didn't sign the 17-year-old due to his size – he's only 5'10 155 pounds – or his projection, but for his advanced pitchability and quality secondary offerings. From Brazil, Pardinho can pound the strike zone with a solid-average 88-93 mph fastball. He generates his average velocity with a loose, clean arm and he's able to repeat his mechanics. His sharp curveball is his best breaking ball and he can miss bats with it. He'll also mix in a slider and change-up. His lack of size could be a long-term concern, but he could still throw harder with mechanical adjustments.
Signing bonus/status: Signed for $1.4 million
MLB debut: 2023

Everson Pereira (OF, NYY)
The 16-year-old has a terrific array of talents on both sides of the ball. The right-handed hitter has excellent bat speed, advanced pitch recognition, and the ability to put bat to ball with relative ease. He's more of a gap hitter with merely average power potential, but he uses the entire field and makes loud contact. He's been tough to get out due to his patient approach. Defensively, he is a solid CF with polished instincts and above average range. Pereira runs well and could be an ideal top-of-the-order hitter.
Signing bonus/status: Signed for $1.5 million
MLB debut: 2024

Juan Querecuto (SS, SEA)
Long and lean at 6'2" 175 pounds, the 17-year-old has significant projection and has the instincts to play above his existing, average tools. Querecuto doesn't have one standout talent, but he does everything relatively well. He is likely to move off shortstop as he continues to grow and his strong arm could be ideal for 3B. He has quick hands and nimble feet as well. As a hitter, he offers above average bat speed and a line drive swing that allows him to slash balls to the gaps. In time, his power should get to at least average and possibly more.
Signing bonus/status: Signed for $1.225 million
MLB debut: 2024

Kristian Robinson (OF, ARI)
The 17-year-old signed one of the more lucrative deals in the international class when the Diamondbacks inked him to a large bonus. There are valid reasons why. For one, Robinson is an incredible athlete with a strong frame that projects to well above average power potential. His speed is currently elite which allows him to steal bases and cover a lot of ground in CF. His right-handed bat is a bit raw, however. He has trouble with pitch recognition and he lacks big game experience. Over time, Robinson could become the best player in this class.
Signing bonus/status: Signed for $2.55 million
MLB debut: 2023

Carlos Rodriguez (OF, MIL)
If one is looking for an ideal leadoff hitter, then the 17-year-old Rodriguez could be the guy. He has an innate feel for the strike zone and is willing to work deep counts to get on base. His level swing path and easy bat speed make good contact and he likes to use all fields in his approach. Though not blessed with great size or strength, he exhibits some power potential due to his bat control and whippy swing. Rodriguez should be able to stick in CF despite a below average arm. He runs very well and has excellent range with efficient routes.
Signing bonus/status: Signed for $1.355 million
MLB debut: 2024

Ronny Rojas (SS, NYY)
One of the youngest signed prospects in the class, Rojas won't turn 17 until August 2018. He may not be very big or strong now, but he has above average raw pop and an ability to make consistent, hard contact. As a switch hitter, he has a nice swing from both sides and has a patient eye. Because of his hitting instincts, he should be able to hit for a solid BA in the future. Defensively, Rojas possesses ideal quickness for the middle infield and a strong enough arm that could work at 3B or an outfield corner. His upside isn't as high as others in this class, but he has a higher floor than others as well.
Signing bonus/status: Signed for $1 million
MLB debut: 2025

Raimfer Salinas (OF, NYY)
The toolsy outfielder from Venezula has the potential to hit in the middle of a big league lineup one day. His athleticism oozes from his lean 6'0" 170 pound frame and has the projection to grow significantly over the coming years. As a hitter, he focuses on line drives with hard contact to the gaps. Though Salinas doesn't have much present pop, his bat speed and swing path should lead to future power. There is some swing-and-miss to his game, however. With plus speed and advanced instincts, he should be able to stick in CF over the long haul.
Signing bonus/status: Unknown
MLB debut: 2025

Florencio Serrano (RHP, CHC)
He may not have gotten a bigger signing bonus as anticipated, but the 18-year-old has a mature frame and offers nice upside. Serrano has a strong, quick arm that is able to hit 94 mph with his fastball. It features late, heavy life generally in the 88-93 mph range and he commands it well. His secondary offerings need polish and more precision, but they at least have average potential. He has some feel for a curveball and his change-up exhibits good depth. Due to the effort in his delivery, some see a move to the bullpen over the long-term.
Signing bonus/status: Signed for $300,000
MLB debut: 2023

Ezequiel Tovar (SS, COL)
With a patient approach and high OBP potential, the 17-year-old could hit at the top of a lineup, though adding more strength and muscle to his slender frame will be required. He focuses on making consistent contact with his quick, compact stroke. He has enough bat speed to hit line drives, but his frame isn't strong enough to reach the seats at present. Though not a standout defender, he makes the routine plays with good quickness and footwork. Tovar is likely to move over to 2B as a pro.
Signing bonus/status: Unknown
MLB debut: 2024

George Valera (OF, CLE)
Armed with all five tools, the 17-year-old could turn into a big-time player. He has a very athletic frame that should add good weight as he ages. Valera is already a natural hitter with keen bat-to-ball skills and a discerning eye. His power development will ultimately dictate how productive of a player he becomes. He is a swift runner who gets on base and can steal bags. Once he fully matures, he is likely to move from CF to RF to take advantage of his above average arm strength. The Indians are in need of an upgrade in their system and Valera should be a key component.
Signing bonus/status: Signed for $1.3 million
MLB debut: 2023

2017 Arizona Fall League Risers/Fallers

by Alec Dopp

For more than 25 years, the Arizona Fall League (AFL) has been a critical tool for scouts and evaluators to assess prospects at the end of the minor league season and heading into the Winter Meetings. As First-Pitch Arizona attendees know, though, it can also be a valuable means for fantasy owners to gain a first-hand perspective on future contributors. Though small sample size caveats apply, here are several prospects whose fantasy stocks were most positively or negatively affected by their AFL performance.

Risers

Ronald Acuna (OF, ATL): After stockpiling 21 HR, 44 SB and a .325 BA in the upper minors in 2017, Acuna solidified his fantasy stock by leading the fall league in HR (7) alongside a 1.088 OPS. The 19-year-old is one of the most exciting talents the minors has to offer, owning easy plus raw power to all fields and projecting to be valuable HR source at the next level. His quality athleticism should enable him to rack up a fair amount of stolen bases, and he has adept contact skills and should be a solid BA contributor. He could reach the majors by midseason.

Justus Sheffield (LHP, NYY): Acquired by New York from Cleveland in 2016, Sheffield posted a 3.18 ERA, 7.9 Dom and 3.2 Ctl in Double-A in 2017. The 21-year-old truly turned heads in Arizona, however, mustering a 0.84 WHIP and 7.33 Cmd in five starts. Sheffield has three above-average pitches at his disposal, including a 91-93 mph fastball that he will cut, a low-80s slider and a changeup that he sells with good arm speed. A smallish frame and iffy command have been the biggest knocks against him, but he has potential to be a quality #3 starter.

Monte Harrison (OF, MIL): Harrison had a full breakout in 2017—21 HR, 27 SB between Low/High-A—and carried his momentum to Arizona, hitting .283 with 5 HR/5 SB in 13 games. The 22-year-old is a plus all-around athlete who was a touted football prospect in high school with quick-twitch actions required for center field and a strong arm required for right. Though he employs an aggressive approach, his quick hands and strong upper body lend themselves to bat speed and intriguing power and he should be a valuable stolen base chip long-term.

Max Fried (LHP, ATL): Fried made his debut with Atlanta last September, posting a 3.81 ERA across 26 innings split between the bullpen and rotation. He parlayed a successful 2017 with a stellar fall league showing, leading the AFL in strikeouts (32) alongside a 1.73 ERA and 0.88 WHIP in six starts. Fried's fastball sits 90-93 mph and he'll complement it with a plus curveball and average changeup. Fried's biggest hurdle has been command and control of his stuff (4.2 Ctl in five seasons as a pro) but he posted a 2.8 Ctl in Arizona and things are now looking up.

Eric Filia (OF, SEA): One of the older prospects on the fall league circuit, Filia, 25, parlayed a successful 2017 campaign with High-A Modesto into a stellar Arizona performance, leading his AFL counterparts in BA (.408) and OPS (1.088). Filia's strengths include superb bat-to-ball skills (91.3% ct% as a pro) and plate discipline (1.64 Eye), and he should be considered a future BA/OBP asset. He doesn't produce much power from his crouched stance or slap-oriented hitting style, but he remains a name who could soon have value in deeper formats.

Fallers

Bobby Bradley (1B, CLE): Bradley owns some of the best raw power in the minors, tabbing 23 HR with a 44% extra-base hit percentage (x/h%) in Double-A in 2017. The question has been whether or not he'll make enough contact for the power to play consistently. While he improved his contact skills this past season, his AFL performance did not inspire a ton of confidence that those issues have been fully resolved (.230 BA, 56% ct%, 0.06 Eye in 77 PA). Bradley remains an intriguing future source of HR/RBI at first base, but a BA in the .230-.250 range would limit his overall value.

Sandy Alcantara (RHP, MIA): Alcantara broke through to the majors with St. Louis' bullpen as a 21-year-old last September, though an uneven Fall League showing (4.20 ERA, 4.8 Ctl) suggests he may need more developmental time before grabbing a meaningful role. (Alcantara was subsequently shipped to Miami in the Marcell Ozuna trade.) He owns a lively 96-99 mph fastball, flashes of a plus changeup and an average curveball, though the issue remains a lack of control. Alcantara's stuff is good, and a career 8.9 Dom shows he has some upside, but he'll need to find the zone more consistently before owners should take on the risk.

Tanner Scott (LHP, BAL): Another prospect who debuted last September, Scott, 23, has yet to rectify the control issues that have stalled his development as a high-upside arm. The former sixth-round pick posted a 6.0 Ctl in 24 starts in Double-A in 2017 before shipping off to Arizona, where he issued 11 walks to just seven strikeouts in 9.1 innings. Scott's raw stuff is impressive, owning a true elite fastball that will touch 100 mph and a hard slider that shows potential to miss bats in late relief. An obvious and recurring lack of strikes will cap his fantasy value, however.

Henry Owens (LHP, LA): Previously graded an '8A' prospect in the 2015 version of this book, Owens' fantasy stock has since tumbled, and there appears no end in sight. The 25-year-old posted a 8.86 ERA and 6.3 Dom/5.5 Ctl tandem in six starts for Peoria after managing a 8.2 Ctl across 126 innings in the upper minors in 2017. The elite swing-and-miss stuff simply isn't there anymore for Owens; his fastball now sits 89-91 mph and his curve, slider and change all grade as average. Significant improvement will be required for Owens to regain fantasy relevance; he was put on waivers twice in December and was claimed by the Diamondbacks, and then the Dodgers.

The 2017 Rule 5 Draft Recap

by Jeremy Deloney

The 2017 MLB Winter Meetings concluded with the annual Rule 5 Draft. The unique aspect of this annual player movement exercise is that a handful of minor league players who just months ago were buried in one organization, now have a shot to make an Opening Day MLB roster with a new club. Of course, some of these players will not secure a roster spot, in which case they will get returned to their original organization. But given the opportunity for the players below to be fantasy-eligible come March, here's a short primer on players selected, their potential 2018 and long-term impacts. (Note that some of these players were traded during and after the draft; we list only the current and original teams.)

Victor Reyes (OF, DET); selected from Arizona
Profile: Reyes, a switch-hitting, contact-first OF, became more of a gap-to-gap hitter in Double-A. The 23-year-old grinds at-bats from both sides and handles velocity, using his hand-to-eye coordination superbly. Doesn't have much HR power—his career-high in HR was 6 in 2016. A solid athlete with average speed, Reyes can handle all OF positions, but is most effective in the corners.
2018 Fantasy Impact: Reyes has yet to play above Double-A, but will be given an opportunity in Detroit. If he makes the team, he would likely serve as a bench piece who could provide BA/SB.
Long-term Impact: About the same. In the right situation, he profiles as an ideal 4th outfielder who supplies credible defense and solid bat-to-ball skills.

Julian Fernandez (RHP, SF); selected from Colorado
Profile: Despite never pitching above Low-A, the 22-year-old has among the best pure arms in all of baseball. Fernandez was in the Rockies organization for five years and only pitched in full-season ball for the first time in 2017. The reliever is all about velocity and he regularly exceeds 100 mph. He improved his control, but still lacks a dependable secondary offering.
2018 Fantasy Impact: A long shot to make the team, he could be stashed for low-leverage situations. This is the type of Rule 5 pick that could pitch minimally this year and return to the minors in 2019.
Long-term Impact: The upside is as high as any pick in the Rule 5 draft with the potential to be a dominating, late-inning reliever. That upside is far from a sure thing, however.

Nick Burdi (RHP, PIT); selected from Minnesota
Profile: The 24-year-old has an elite arm, but underwent Tommy John surgery in May 2017. He's only pitched 20 innings the past two seasons. When healthy, Burdi is tough to hit based upon his power arsenal and arm slot. He throws downhill due to his height and he gets nasty sinking action on his mid-to-high 90s fastball. He owns a slider that can be downright filthy.
2018 Fantasy Impact: Very little, as he's unlikely to pitch in game action until late in the season. The Pirates are expected to hold onto him and then send him on a 30-day rehab assignment.
Long-term Impact: Burdi must improve his command and control, but he could be a dyanmic late-inning reliever. The injury history is a concern and he won't make an impact until 2019 or beyond.

Carlos Tocci (OF, TEX); selected from Philadelphia
Profile: The 22-year-old has been a decent prospect for years, but hasn't developed much power. His lean frame could use muscle, but he offers value with his bat-handling and defense. A fluid athlete with long limbs, he has bat-to-ball skills that give his hit tool promise. The lack of strength and his level swing path mean power is unlikely to materialize. He is an excellent defender in CF.
2018 Fantasy Impact: Tocci has a good chance at earning a reserve spot, especially because of his ability to play CF. He's unlikely to have much of a fantasy impact, as he won't hit HR or steal bases.
Long-term Impact: If he can at least develop 10+ HR power, then he could be a contributor. If not, then he'll be a BA-only 4th outfielder.

Brad Keller (RHP, KC); selected from Arizona
Profile: Took a step back in 2017 as his stuff and control both regressed. Keller's FB only sat 89-92 mph for most of the year, but remains a heavy, sinking offering that is effective at lower velocities. He compensated by nit-picking around the strike zone with a below average SL. Keller has a solid change-up that flashes plus.
2018 Fantasy Impact: The Royals may opt to move Keller to the bullpen, which would increase his odds of making the team. Perhaps his stuff and velocity would play up in shorter stings.
Long-term Impact: He has started 75 games and pitched 407.2 innings over the last three seasons and has the look and arsenal of a back-end, innings-eating starter. It will be intriguing to see how he fares if he is converted to a reliever.

Burch Smith (RHP, KC); selected from Tampa Bay
Profile: Smith will be 28 in mid-April, but he isn't a journeyman. After reaching the majors in 2013 with the Padres, he missed most of the next three seasons due to arm ailments. Though rusty upon his return in 2017, he flashed plus stuff, including a 94-97 mph fastball, curveball, and dynamite change-up. He pitched briefly in the minors before mowing down hitters in the AFL.
2018 Fantasy Impact: It is uncertain how the Royals will utilize him, but he is almost assured of making the club. They may opt to ease him back by using him in low-leverage relief situations.
Long-term Impact: If Smith was five years younger, then his profile would scream mid-rotation starter. The injury history is a concern, but a permanent move to the bullpen could yield save opportunities and a high strikeout rate.

Anyelo Gomez (RHP, ATL); selected from New York Yankees
Profile: Though not at the same level as the elite Atlanta arms, Gomez can hold his own with a plus fastball that reaches the high-90s. He was mostly a starter before the Yankees moved him to the bullpen at midseason in 2016 while in Low-A. Since then, he's taken off, though he could use a better slider and cleaner delivery.
2018 Fantasy Impact: It will be difficult for him to make the team and even if he did, he would slot in as a middle innings guy. If he can match his 2017 success, then he could have a brighter future than originally thought.
Long-term Impact: Gomez has a reliever profile and could become a setup option if he can maintain his fastball command and velocity. It is hard to envision him as anything more than a potential set-up guy.

Jordan Milbrath (RHP, PIT); selected from Cleveland
Profile: The 26-year-old reliever found his niche when moved to the bullpen in 2016, and became even more effective when he lowered his arm slot in 2017. Milbrath sits in the mid-90s with natural sinking action on his pitches. The 6'6" 215 pounder needs to improve his control and find a dependable secondary offering.
2018 Fantasy Impact: Milbrath will compete for bullpen role in spring training. The Pirates could decide to keep him because of his unusual delivery and pitch mix.
Long-term Impact: At best, Milbrath could become a setup reliever or an arm that can come in to register a strikeout or groundball. His strikeout rate has been much better as a reliever.

Nestor Cortes (LHP, BAL); selected from New York Yankees
Profile: The 23-year-old has enjoyed a stellar career since being a 36th-round pick (2013). Cortes has started and relieved and performed in both roles in 2017 at Double-A and Triple-A. He works with a sneaky 87-93 mph fastball and complements it with a fringy curveball and change-up. All of his pitches play up due to his deception and he changes speeds well.
2018 Fantasy Impact: He will compete for a back-end rotation spot or one as a low-leverage reliever. Cortes won't be a viable fantasy option, however, as his stuff may not be good enough to retire big league hitters.
Long-term Impact: He lacks size and stuff, but the ability to change speeds and keep hitters off-guard might have minimal value.

Elieser Hernandez (RHP, MIA); selected from Houston
Profile: The 22-year-old has flown under the radar, has never pitched above High-A, and struggled at that level the past two seasons. He started to put things together at mid-season last year when he showed improved sequencing. He works with an 87-92 mph fastball and mixes in a solid-average CB and CU.
2018 Fantasy Impact: His arsenal may not be good enough for the majors. Expect him to have little to no fantasy impact in 2018.
Long-term Impact: At best, Hernandez could evolve into a back-end starter at the major league level. He doesn't throw with great velocity and his secondary offerings are only average.

Mike Ford (1B, SEA); selected from New York Yankees
Profile: The 25-year-old established career-highs in HR and doubles in 2017. Ford is a bat-only prospect who has walked more than he's struck out in his career. The rest of his profile is limited: He rarely steals bases (4 in career) and is a sub-par defender at 1B.
2018 Fantasy Impact: The increase in his power was a pleasant surprise and the Mariners hope it wasn't a fluke. He has his work cut out for him to make the team as he has to hit to survive.
Long-term Impact: Mostly a fringe prospect, Ford can provide a long-term boost if he can sustain his power growth.

Luke Bard (RHP, LAA); selected from Minnesota
Profile: Bard was a supplemental first round pick in 2012 and was beset by a number of maladies early on, including shoulder surgery. Fully healthy the last three years, he has thrived with a mid-90s fastball and hard slider. Bard's strikeout rate increased dramatically in 2017.
2018 Fantasy Impact: Unless he upgrades his control and command, Bard will likely only pitch in the middle innings if he makes the team. Because he can miss bats, he still could have value in that role.
Long-term Impact: It is difficult to project Rule 5 relievers due to the few save opportunities in the majors. Bard has the fastball and good enough secondary offering in his slider to be potent.

Tyler Kinley (RHP, MIN); selected from Miami
Profile: The 27-year-old is a hard-thrower with an ideal pitcher's frame. He dominated High-A in 2017 with surprising control and a 94-98 mph fastball before being promoted to Double-A. At his best, Kinley can work entirely off his electric fastball that not only exhibits velocity, but late movement. The lack of command has been his career-long bugaboo.
2018 Fantasy Impact: The Twins have a need for bullpen arms and Kinley will be given a chance. It is difficult to see him making the jump from Double-A to a prominent role in the majors.
Long-term Impact: Already 27 and never having pitched above Double-A, it's a rough road ahead. If he can show the stuff and control that made him dominant in High-A, he could have a chance to be a setup reliever.

Albert Suarez (RHP, ARI); selected from San Francisco
Profile: The 29-year-old is the rare pick who no longer qualifies for rookie status. Suarez has pitched 115 innings in the majors, all with the Giants. He has 12 starts to his name, though his best chance of sticking in 2018 could be as a reliever. Suarez generally works with a low-90s sinking fastball and average secondary offerings, including a slider, curveball, and change-up.
2018 Fantasy Impact: Given his previous succcess as a reliever, he has a chance as a middle innings guy. His increased strikeout rate in shorter stints is intriguing and he could provide value with his control.
Long-term Impact: The ceiling is low, but the floor is high. His ability to throw consistent strikes and keep the ball on the ground are his best attributes.

Anthony Gose (LHP/OF, HOU); selected from Texas
Profile: After toiling in major league outfields for four years, the 27-year-old decided to give pitching a shot in 2017. With a fastball that touches 100 mph and a vicious slider, he began his pitching career at High-A Lakeland in May. He didn't fare well before ending his season with a minor elbow injury. This could be one of the most interesting Rule 5 picks in history.
2018 Fantasy Impact: With only 10.2 innings of pro pitching under his belt, Gose faces a steep, uphill climb to pitch in the majors. He could make the team and provide a unique hitter-pitcher role while the Astros cultivate the live arm on the side.
Long-term Impact: This is the biggest question mark of any of the Rule 5 picks. Because of his plus arm strength, he will be a commodity for any organization, but he must progress quickly.

2017 First-Year Player Draft Recap

by Jeremy Deloney (AL) and Rob Gordon (NL)

AMERICAN LEAGUE

BALTIMORE ORIOLES

The Orioles generally are conservative with their draft picks and this year was no different. On the other hand, four of their top six picks were from the prep ranks, including the top two in LHP D.L. Hall (1) and SS Adam Hall (2) who both received seven-figure bonuses. With Hall and RHP Michael Baumann (3) in the mix, the Orioles added two power arms with intriguing upsides. On the flip side, LHP Zac Lowther (S-2) was a safe, low ceiling/ high floor pick who could pay dividends in the short-term. They saved money with safe college picks from rounds six through ten before opening the wallet for a few picks in the later rounds, most notably LHP Cameron Bishop (26) who signed for $605,000.

Sleeper: LHP Tucker Baca (12) was selected from a tiny NAIA school, but impressed with his pure arm strength and solid fastball/slider combination. He profiles as a late-inning reliever if he can improve his command.

Grade: B-

BOSTON RED SOX

With a diverse mix of picks from both the college and high school ranks as well as multiple positions of need, the Red Sox had a well-rounded draft. The two best products from this class could be RHP Tanner Houck (1) and RHP Alex Scherff (5). Houck was the 24th overall pick from Missouri and could reach the majors quickly. Scherff, from a high school in Texas, will take time to develop, but has very high upside. RHP Jake Thompson (4) gives the Red Sox another strong arm on which to build. As for the position players, none of the picks have significantly high ceilings, but OF Cole Brannen (2) and OF Tyler Esplin (7) were prep picks who could become everyday outfielders in several years.

Sleeper: OF David Durden (20) was among the better athletes in the high school draft class and has the potential to be a stud. He needs significant work with his plate approach and swing, but he possesses all five tools.

Grade: B-

CHICAGO WHITE SOX

The White Sox added to an already-deep farm system by signing their first 34 picks, only one of which was a prep player. Their first three picks were position players. Without question, the highlights of the draft were the top two – 3B Jake Burger (1) and 1B Gavin Sheets (2). Both offer natural hitting skills with above average power. The only high school player selected in the first 34 rounds was 1B Sam Abbott (8) who also provides plenty of wallop from his long, strong frame. The first two pitchers selected were college closers – RHPs Lincoln Henzman (4) and Tyler Johnson (5). All in all, it wasn't the best draft class, but it was a safe draft with a handful of players who could reach the majors.

Sleeper: 3B Justin Yurchak (12) isn't a great athlete or defender, but he is a terrific hitter who puts bat to ball with ease and has enough strength to reach the seats. He can play either corner infield spot.

Grade: C

CLEVELAND INDIANS

With no first round pick, the Indians did not sign a player for a seven-figure bonus. However, they stocked up on three high school position players with their first three picks and didn't select a pitcher until round 7. Prep OFs Quentin Holmes (2) and Johnathan Rodriguez (3) have the highest ceilings of all Indians draftees, but have a long way to go to fulfill that promise. Holmes is more of a speedy, athletic player whereas Rodriguez relies on his natural power. SS Tyler Freeman (S-2) is a pure hitter with a chance to stick at shortstop. The best arm selected by the Indians may be RHP James Karinchak (9), though the vast majority of pitchers are command-oriented guys with average fastballs.

Sleeper: RHP Eli Morgan (8) had one of the best pro debuts of any draftee (1.03 ERA, 14.9 Dom) based mostly on his plus change-up. The stats aren't likely to be sustained, but he is fun to watch.

Grade: C-

DETROIT TIGERS

There has been a concerted effort in recent years to shore up the catching depth in the organization. The Tigers added two top backstops among their first five picks. C Joey Morgan (3) and C Sam McMillan (5) both have legitimate potential. Morgan's glove is ahead of his bat while McMillan has an advanced bat for a prep player. RHP Alex Faedo (1) is the top prospect in the Tigers draft class and it isn't even close. He has two plus pitches and could evolve into a #2 or #3 starter within the next few seasons. College players were the norm, as usual, for the Tigers. Of their 31 signed picks, 30 were from college. Only McMillan was signed out of high school.

Sleeper: OF Garrett McCain (10) is a multi-talented outfielder who can play all three positions. He brings an advanced approach to the plate and has enough bat speed and strength to hit for power.

Grade: B-

HOUSTON ASTROS

With five of the first 91 picks in the draft, the Astros had an opportunity to add to its solid organizational depth. RHPs J.B. Bukauskas (1) and Corbin Martin (2) were both signed to seven-figure bonuses and carry with them impressive arsenals. Bukauskas owns good velocity and a slider that could evolve to double-plus. The position players aren't nearly as strong, but there are some good hitters in the lot, led by 2B J.J. Matijevic (S-2). Keep an eye on 3B Joe Perez (2) , a high school hitter who showcases power to all fields. It is customary for teams to take low-bonus college players in rounds 6 thru 10 (bonuses of less than $10,000), but the Astros took very solid collegiate players with those picks (all six-figure bonuses).

Sleeper: OF Jake Meyers (13) fits the Astros mold of players who work counts and get on base at a high clip. He doesn't have great power, but he offers above average speed and solid-average CF defense.

Grade: A-

KANSAS CITY ROYALS

After inking their top two picks, both prep position players, to seven-figure bonuses, the Royals also signed a few more high school players in the later rounds. 1B Nick Pratto (1) is a very advanced hitter with a beautiful swing and a discerning eye at the plate. Catcher M.J. Melendez (2) is already a solid defender for a catcher this young and has a powerful punch in his lefty stroke. With their next two picks, the Royals opted for pitchers from junior college, LHP Evan Steele (S-2) and LHP Daniel Tillo (3). OF Michael Gigliotti (4) had the best debut of anyone from this Royals class and he has already exceeded expectations. Though none of the arms are sure things, there are some very intriguing ones such as RHP Charlie Neuweiler (5).

Sleeper: OF Brewer Hicklen (7) is a premium athlete with amazing speed and strength. He's a bit raw on the diamond, but the Royals will be more than patient as he adds significant polish to his tools.

Grade: B+

LOS ANGELES ANGELS

The Angels feasted on two things—high school players and pitchers, particularly right-handers. Four of the first five picks were from the high school ranks—they signed three of those. Pitchers comprised nine of the top 12 picks as well. In an improving system, this draft class adds even more talent. Few draftees can match the upside of OF Jo Adell (1) who has incredible tools and the potential to hit in the middle of a lineup some day. OF Jacob Pearson (3) has a solid all-around game, but was traded to Minnesota in December. RHP Griffin Canning (2) has a deep pitch mix and should be counted on to move up the organizational ladder quickly.

Sleeper: LHP Jerryell Rivera (11) is all about projection, but he has advanced pitchability for his age. If he can bump his fastball into the low-to-mid 90s, then he could be a real find for an organization in need of arms.

Grade: B

MINNESOTA TWINS

With the first overall pick in the draft, the Twins opted for high school SS Royce Lewis (1) who ended the year in Low-A as an 18-year-old. He exhibited all five tools and he immediately becomes a legitimate top 100 prospect. In addition to Lewis, the Twins took two other high schoolers among their top four picks, including RHPs Landon Leach (2) and Blayne Enlow (3). Add Mississippi State OF Brent Rooker (S-1) to the mix and the Twins gave four players a seven-figure signing bonus. There was also a focus on prep stars as the Twins selected four among their top seven picks. There is a lot to be excited about with this draft class with a diverse group of pitchers and position players.

Sleeper: LHP Ryley Widell (7) is a projectable junior college arm who thrives with an average fastball and above average change-up. He posted a 12.4 Dom in the Appalachian League and he could add more ticks to his heater.

Grade: A-

NEW YORK YANKEES

Already blessed with one of the deepest farm systems in baseball, the Yankees capitalized on a draft filled with impressive young arms. They went with pitchers with ten of their first 11 selections, including nine from the college ranks. Some of the draftees will stay as starters while others could be fast-moving relievers. RHP Clarke Schmidt (1) likely would have been drafted earlier if not for Tommy John surgery. RHP Trevor Stephan (3) and RHP Glenn Otto (5) were terrific in their pro debuts and could cruise thru the lower minors in short order. The best arm among draftees could be RHP Matt Sauer (2) from a California high school. As for position players, OF Canaan Smith (4) is a high upside prep pick with incredible plate patience and impressive raw power.

Sleeper: 1B Eric Wagaman (13) looks more like a football player with his physique, but he punishes baseballs with a strong righty stroke. He has swing-and-miss in his game, but he's a solid overall hitter.

Grade: B+

OAKLAND ATHLETICS

After focusing on pitching in the 2016 draft, the Athletics did the complete opposite for 2017. They drafted all position players, including two shortstops, with their first six picks. Four of those players received seven-figure signing bonuses, which left little draft pool for later-round finds. That's OK, however, as they signed some potential everyday players. OF Austin Beck (1) is the cream of the crop and the prep star should be among the fastest movers among high school picks. SS Nick Allen (3) and C Santis Sanchez (5) were also prep picks who were highly coveted. SS Kevin Merrell (S-1), OF Greg Deichmann (2) and 3B Will Toffey (4) add to the impressive mix of position players already in the system.

Sleeper: RHP Wyatt Marks (13) posted the highest strikeout rate in Division 1 baseball and is surely to be a reliever as a pro. He has an average fastball at best, but owns a power curveball that misses a ton of bats.

Grade: A-

SEATTLE MARINERS

A pitching-heavy draft was in order and the Mariners drafted and signed a number of arms, particularly relievers. With their first pick, however, they chose Kentucky 1B Evan White (1) who was among the better natural hitters. He's also a nifty defender who can play the outfield. C David Banuelos (5) was a shrewd pick from the college ranks after an All-American season and he is very solid defensively, but was traded to Minnesota. The pitcher with the highest upside is high school RHP Sam Carlson (2) who has a chance to be a power-armed starter in the middle of the rotation. Two college relievers were popped early. RHP Wyatt Mills (3) and RHP Seth Elledge (4) have late-inning pedigrees and could reach the majors quickly.

Sleeper: LHP Jorge Benitez (9) was young for the draft class and offers a ton of projection in his long, lean frame. His pro debut didn't go well, but he has the ingredients to be a special pitcher with a lively fastball and hard breaking ball.

Grade: C+

TAMPA BAY RAYS

College pitchers appeared to be highly coveted by the Rays and they selected a slew of mature arms in the top 15 rounds. With 15 of the top 16 picks being from college or the JC ranks, the Rays are hoping some of them could advance quickly. The 4th overall pick 1B/LHP Brendan McKay (1) is the jewel of the draft class, signing for a whopping $7 million bonus. Only two other draftees received more than $500,000. McKay could play both ways for the near-term, though he's likely to settle in as a 1B. The Rays really like RHP Michael Mercado (2), one of their few prep draftees, and he has a ton of projection. They didn't sign their supplemental first round selection (RHP Drew Rasmussen) due to a failed physical. Unless McKay and/or Mercado pan out, this class was quite thin.
Sleeper: RHP Alex Valverde (22) had an impressive pro debut and has the ability to locate his fastball and secondary offerings. If he adds a few ticks to his heater, he could become one of the Rays better draft picks.
Grade: C

TEXAS RANGERS

The Rangers had one of the most impressive draft hauls in 2017. They injected the system with high upside players, including four high school picks among their first five selections. Furthermore, they drafted and signed a handful of intriguing players after round 10. They had two first round picks and selected OF Bubba Thompson (1) and SS Chris Seise (1). Both immediately become two of the system's best prospects. Add in high school arms RHP Hans Crouse (2) and RHP Ryan Dease (4) and there is reason for optimism. In particular, Crouse had a spectacular debut and showed better stuff after signing. C Matt Whatley (3) from Oral Roberts has plenty of skill with both bat and glove.
Sleeper: RHP Ricky Vanasco (15) is a young, projectable pitcher who needs to upgrade his secondary offerings, but his arm strength and deceptive delivery give him a lot of promise. He'll need plenty of development time, however.
Grade: A

TORONTO BLUE JAYS

With the benefit of two first round selections and an apparent focus on up-the-middle position players, the Jays signed an impressive haul. SS Logan Warmoth (1) and SS Kevin Smith (4) were solid college infielders and both could move in tandem thru the minors. Of course, one may have to move to 2B, but both have instincts and talent. Two catchers were selected early, Hagen Danner (2) and Riley Adams (3). Already with a solid stable of backstops in the minors, both will be given time to develop. The most dynamic arm in the draft could belong to RHP Nate Pearson (1) who had a terrific pro debut and surpassed expectations with his feel for pitching and improved command. As usual, the focus was also on college players, with the exception of Danner.
Sleeper: OF D.J. Neal (26) is an exciting athlete who looks the part of a football player with his size and strength. He has raw baseball skills, but he could be a fast, middle-of-the-order run producer if all goes according to wishes.
Grade: B+

NATIONAL LEAGUE

ARIZONA DIAMONDBACKS

The Diamondbacks had the 7th pick in the draft and landed 1B Pavin Smith (1). Widely seen as the most advanced collegiate hitter in the class, he has the tools to hit for power and average while drawing plenty of walks. The Snakes also added Louisville 3B Drew Ellis (2), a fringe defender, but with above-average power and a good approach at the plate. C Daulton Varsho (S-2) has good raw power, runs well for a catcher, but has a below-average arm. The team went over-slot for high school RHP Matt Tabor (3). Tabor is projectable and could be a steal. The haul here was solid with four players cracking the Diamondbacks top 15 prospect list, but that speaks as much to the scarcity of talent in the organization.
Sleeper: RHP Matt Brill (12) was relatively unknown in college, but has a plus 94-97 mph fastball that bumps 99 mph. He mixes in an inconsistent slider and below-average control and could develop into an excellent bullpen arm.
Grade: A-

ATLANTA BRAVES

The Braves were thrilled to land Vanderbilt RHP Kyle Wright (1) with the 5th pick. He uses a plus four-pitch mix to dominate and has the size and stuff to be a front-of-the-rotation starter. The Braves also snagged prep OF Drew Waters (2) and high school RHP Freddy Tarnok (3) who signed for $1.5 million, more than double his allotted bonus. Waters is a plus runner with an advanced understanding of the strike zone and had a solid debut. JuCo RHP Troy Bacon (4) is raw, but has a plus 93-97 mph heater. The Braves came into the draft with one of the better systems in baseball and did an excellent job of adding to that depth.
Sleeper: C/3B Drew Lugbauer (11) split time at 3B and behind the plate. He has plus raw power and a patient approach at the plate. He does have some swing-and-miss and could develop into a nice backup catcher/utility player down the road.
Grade: A-

CHICAGO CUBS

Not surprisingly, the Cubs went pitching-heavy in this draft with 10 of their first 12 picks being hurlers. After winning the World Series in 2016, the Cubs had to wait until the end of round one to land Florida JuCo LHP Brandon Little (1) and followed that up three picks later with LSU RHP Alex Lange (1). Both Lange and Little made the Cubs top 15 prospect list (Lange at #3 and Little at #6), but profile more as mid-rotation starters. RHP Cory Abbott (2), RHP Keegan Thompson (3), and RHP Erich Uelman (4) all had impressive pro debuts. While the Cubs don't have any true frontline starters, this draft class, along with their international signings, has quickly bolstered an organization that was in desperate need of pitching depth.
Sleeper: Ben Hecht (12) has good size and some projection left. Working exclusively in relief, he struck out 30 in 20 IP, but also walked 13 so there is still some work to do.
Grade: A-

CINCINNATI REDS

The Reds had the second pick in the draft and were elated when top ranked RHP Hunter Greene (1) fell to them after the Twins took SS Royce Lewis. Greene is a phenomenal athlete and was the best two-way player in the draft, with some scouts projecting 25-30 HR potential. He already has a 97-100 mph fastball and owns excellent mechanics and the potential to be a true #1 starter. The Reds used their Competitive Balance pick to land high school SS Jeter Downs (S-1) and then added Wake Forest OF Stuart Fairchild (2). Both had solid pro debuts. The club went over slot to land Florida prep SS Cash Case (4) who has an excellent glove but not the range needed to stick at short.

Sleeper: RHP John Ghyzel (18) is a big reliever with a big-time 94-97 mph fastball, but lacks a quality secondary offering. Ghyzel posted a 5.73 ERA in 22 IP, but also struck out 26 and has a chance to reach the majors in a relief role.

Grade: A-

COLORADO ROCKIES

The Rockies forfeited their 1st round pick to the Rangers as compensation for signing Ian Desmond. When the Rockies finally picked at #48, they landed Oklahoma prep 3B Ryan Vilade (2) . He has an advanced approach at the plate and slashed .308/.438/.496 with 5 HR and 27BB/31K in 117 AB. The club's next three picks were RHPs Tommy Doyle (S-2), Will Gaddis (3), and Pearson McMahan (4), none of whom project to be impact starters though Doyle does have a plus 91-93 mph fastball that tops out at 96 mph in relief. All told, the Rockies spent just north of $5 million on the entire draft and this paltry haul shows it.

Sleeper: OF Casey Golden (20) has plus raw power and had an excellent pro debut, hitting .288/.372/.654 with 14 doubles and 20 home runs in 208 AB in the Pioneer League. At 22 he was old for this level, but the power is legit.

Grade: D

LOS ANGELES DODGERS

The Dodgers were able to land one of the more exciting but divisive players in the draft when they picked Vanderbilt OF Jeren Kendall at #23. Coming into 2017, he was widely seen as a likely top 10 pick, but an inconsistent junior season and concerns about his ability to make consistent contact caused him to slide. Kendall has top-shelf speed and is an excellent CF. The Dodgers added Texas RHP Morgan Cooper (2), Houston catcher Connor Wong (3), and Florida high school RHP James Marinan (4) with their next picks. Wong had the best debut of the bunch, hitting .276/.333/.490 in the Low-A Midwest League. Kendall's development will be key to this draft class and for now, the jury is still out.

Sleeper: 3B Rylan Bannon (8) is undersized at 5-10, 180 but has solid all-around skills and had an impressive pro debut. He's a plus defender with average to above-average speed and should be able to stick at 3B.

Grade: B

MIAMI MARLINS

The Marlins came into the draft with one of the thinner farm systems in baseball and opted to bolster their pitching when they took high school LHP Trevor Rogers (1). At 6-6, 185 he was one of the more projectable pitchers in the draft and already owns a plus 90-94 mph fastball that tops out at 97 mph from a low ¾ arm slot. He has yet to make his pro debut. The Marlins added North Carolina CF Brian Miller (S-1). North Carolina State 3B Joe Dunand (2) has above-average power and blasted 18 HR for the Wolfpack. They also added Kentucky 2B Riley Mahan (3), Stanford RHP Colton Hock (4), and UC Riverside RHP Ryan Lillie (5) all of whom are legitimate prospects. This was a solid haul for the Marlins, but only Rogers profiles as an impact prospect.

Sleeper: RHP Matt Givin (20) fell out of the top rounds due to concerns about his signability. At 6-3, 180 he has some projection left and already features a good low-90s fastball and a power curve.

Grade: B

MILWAUKEE BREWERS

Over the past several years the Brewers have quietly developed a nice group of position players and they added to that when they landed UC-Irvine 2B Keston Hiura (1) and high school OF Tristen Lutz (S-1). Hiura was widely viewed as one of the more polished bats in the draft and he might have had the best debut of any player in the draft. At 6-3, 210 Lutz is already physically mature and shows above-average to plus raw power with a right field arm. The Brewers also added RHP Caden Lemons (2) a 6-6 Alabama prep hurler who has been clocked as high as 97 mph and Oregon State backstop K.J. Harrison (3). Overall this was an impressive draft for the Brewers, though Lemons was the only potential impact arm in the group.

Sleeper: RHP Justin Bullock (16) was an early and strong commit to NC State. He works off a low-90s fastball and needs to develop his secondary offerings, but he held his own in his debut.

Grade: A-

NEW YORK METS

Given the injuries to their starting rotation and their lack of pitching depth, it wasn't surprising that the Mets prioritized pitching, taking hurlers with nine of their first 13 picks including LHP David Peterson (1). At 6-6, 240, he has ideal size and comes after hitters with a plus fastball/slider mix. He gives the Mets a solid mid-rotation lefty who should move up quickly. Although light on position players, the Mets did add several intriguing bats including high school 3B Mark Vientos (2) and Stanford teammates OF Quinn Brodey (3) and OF Matt Winaker (5). Vientos was one of the younger players in the draft and didn't turn 18 until December. The Mets didn't break the bank with this draft, rarely going above slot money, but they did add arm some nice collegiate arms.

Sleeper: RHP Connor O'Neil (7) served as the closer for Cal State Northridge and notched a school record 39 saves. He owns a low-90s fastball that sets up his plus hard slider and mixes in a curve and change-up.

Grade: B

PHILADELPHIA PHILLIES

The Phillies have an underrated farm system and they added to that depth, landing one of the better two-way players in the country in Virginia OF Adam Haseley (1). He doesn't project to have above-average power, but he does everything else well and is able to play all three OF slots. Given that the Phillies went above-slot and gave Haseley $5.1 million to sign, he needs to meet expectations for this draft to be a success. The Phillies saved money with below-slot Cal Poly RHP Spencer Howard (2) and then grabbed Cal State Fullerton RHP Connor Seabold (3), Houston 3B Jake Scheiner (4), and high school LHP Ethan Lindow (5). Howard saw his fastball velocity sit at 94-96 mph in his debut and struck out 40 in just 28.1 IP (12.7 Dom).

Sleeper: SS Jake Holmes (11) has above-average speed and raw power and should be able to stick at shortstop. He is a toolsy player worth watching.

Grade: B-

PITTSBURGH PIRATES

The Pirates drafted high school RHP Shane Baz at #12 and then took advantage of having three picks in round two of the draft, adding three prep players—RHP Steven Jennings (2), OF Calvin Mitchell (2), and OF Conner Uselton (S-2) before taking their first collegiate player in 3B Dylan Busby (4). Baz is physically mature and has a plus fastball that sits at 92-96 mph, topping out at 98 mph, with a cutter and plus breaking ball. He has the stuff to be a frontline starter. At 6-3, 185 Uselton has good bat speed and plus raw power, though scouts are mixed on whether he makes enough contact to hit for both average and power. Mitchell also profiles to have above-average power with a pretty left-handed swing, but is a below-average runner with fringe defense.

Sleeper: OF Mason Martin (17) is a strong, physically mature OF with plus raw power. He had an excellent debut hitting .307/.457/.630 with 8 doubles and 11 home runs in just 127 AB.

Grade: A-

SAN DIEGO PADRES

The Padres have not had a lot of success in the draft over the past several decades, but are hopeful that will change with the addition of high school LHP MacKenzie Gore (1). He dominated in high school and has a good 90-94 mph fastball, a plus 1-7 power curve, slider, and above-average change. He's polished at a very young age and was lights-out in his pro debut. The Padres then added two high school catchers Luis Campusano (2) and Blake Hunt (S-2) and didn't take a collegiate player until round six with LHP Aaron Leasher (6). High school OF Mason House (3) has above-average power and posted a .293/.354/.463 line in his debut. There isn't much to write home about, but Gore was dazzling in his debut and could finally give the Padres a home-grown impact starter.

Sleeper: RHP Chandler Newman (11) has a plus mid-90s heater that has been clocked as high as 100 mph. What kept him out of the early round of the draft is his inability to throw strikes.

Grade: B

SAN FRANCISCO GIANTS

Coming into the draft the Giants were thin on position players who have the tools to make an impact in the majors. They addressed that need when they picked high school OF Heloit Ramos (1). He is unproven with wood bats and is raw in some aspects of his game, but he shows an intriguing power/speed mix that the Giants lack. The Giants then added high school OF Jacob Gonzalez (2) for below-slot. The son of five-time all-star Luis Gonzalez also impressed in his debut and has a mature approach at the plate. The club went prep heavy early in the draft, not taking a collegiate player until RHP Garrett Cave (4). He struck out 29 in 20 IP and has a plus 94-96 mph fastball. Ramos is a high-risk, high-reward prospect, but the upside is huge.

Sleeper: OF Aaron Bond (12) is a big and projectable with a long swing and aggressive approach at the plate, but also has big-time power. He slashed .306/.368/.565 with 8 doubles and 8 HR in Rookie ball.

Grade B+

ST. LOUIS CARDINALS

The Cardinals had to wait longer than any other team before making a selection, having lost their first three picks of the draft (one for signing Dexter Fowler as a free agent and two as compensation to the Astros for the data breach). When they did finally pick they stayed the college route taking OF Scott Hurst (3). He is a bit undersized but has a mature approach at the plate with above-average speed. He lacks the power needed to be an impact player in the majors. They also added LSU SS Kramer Robertson (5) who has a solid bat and plus speed, but questions about his ability to stick at SS and OF Chase Pinder (7). It was always going to be tough for the Cardinals to do much with this draft and at this point there are no clear major league regulars in this group.

Sleeper: 3B Evan Mendoza (11) moved from the mound to 3B and showed a mature, patient approach. A slow start in his junior year caused him to slide, but the Cardinals liked his bat well enough and he ended up winning the NYPL batting title.

Grade: D-

WASHINGTON NATIONALS

After an impressive run of landing impact draft picks the Nationals are realizing it is hard to keep the streak going when having to wait until the back-end of round one. The Nationals went heavy on pitching, taking just one position player and no prep players in the first 10 rounds. The Nationals landed Houston LHP Seth Romero (1) and signed him to an over-slot deal. He has a good 92-95 mph fastball, a plus late-breaking slider, and a serviceable change-up. South Carolina RHP Wil Crowe (2) could be a steal and has a plus fastball that tops at 97 mph and a good four-pitch mix. The club also added hard throwing LHP Nick Raquet (3) before taking LSU 2B Cole Freeman (4) and Texas A&M RHP Brigham Hill (5). Considering their draft position, the Nationals managed to land some interesting power arms.

Sleeper: LHP Alex Troop (9) is tall and projectable and has a fastball that sits at 88-91 mph for now, but he could add some velocity once he fills out his lean 6-5, 200 pound frame. He held his own at three stops in his debut.

Grade: B

College Players to Watch in 2018

by Chris Lee

Familiarity with the top draft-eligible college players is a great way to get a kick-start on your fantasy farm system. If history serves, some of the players below will soon reside on their future MLB team's top prospect list as well as future HQ100s.

Two notes about the 2018 college draft class: First, this is a deep class for potential fantasy contributors; there are easily a dozen players worth discussing. And second, identifying separation within the list is a challenge.

Pay close attention to that uncertainty. The best way to utilize this list is to not get hung up on the order, but follow player progress during the season, even the "more to watch" list. The college season gets under way in mid-February, and leads up to the 2018 MLB draft in early June.

All stats are from 2017 unless noted.

1. Nick Madrigal, SS — *Oregon St., R/R, 5-7, 160*
Madrigal draws Jose Altuve comps due to his size, Eye (1.69) ct% (93), speed (16 SB) and on-base ability (.449). Power (4 HR) is the issue, but he hits the ball hard. There's no guarantee he's a star, but he's the lowest-risk player on the list, and offers the best chance at the rare high-average/high steals combination.

2. Brady Singer, RHP — *Florida, RHP, 6-5, 180*
Singer was last seen throwing a 12-strikeout masterpiece, operating low in the zone and hitting corners with precision, in winning Game 1 of the 2017 College World Series finals. He's most experts' choice at No. 1 overall thanks to his four-pitch mix, a mid-90s fastball and a fantastic slider that he used to a 9.2 Dom with 4.0 Cmd. A highly emotional pitcher, he'll have to keep that in check and show another great season after a mediocre freshman campaign.

3. Jeremy Eierman, SS — *Missouri St., R/R, 6-1, 195*
Eierman hit .313 with 23 HR, 17 SB and an 0.67 Eye. The power looks legit and his defense projects on the left side. Two cautions: there's been too much swing-and-miss to his game (71 and 75 ct% in 2016 and 2017) and did it against middle-of-the-road collegiate competition. In 40 summer at-bats for Team USA, he hit just .125/182/.225, though maybe a .167 BABIP was to blame. But, the potential speed/power combo is enticing.

4. Casey Mize, RHP — *Auburn, R/R, 6-3, 208*
Mize was nowhere on draft radar in high school, but reinvented himself with added strength and better mechanics in the last two years. Arm injuries and fatigue are concerning, but he was electric (11.7 Dom, with reports of him touching 100 mph in 2017) in 83.1 IP and owns a nasty splitter. We need to see a repeat, but it's exceptionally rare to see that combination of high strikeouts and elite control (12.1 K/BB) at the highest levels of college baseball.

5. Shane McClanahan, LHP — *South Florida, L/L, 6-1, 173*
He drew Chris Sale comparisons with lights-out Dom (12.6) in 74 IP after missing 2016 with Tommy John surgery. He has top-five overall upside with his ability to hold velocity, but sample size, injury history and Ctl (4.3) are significant risks.

6. Travis Swaggerty, OF — *South Alabama, L/L, 5-11, 180*
Swaggerty showed power (11 HR, .571 Slg) and speed (19 SB, after 20 in 2016) supported by a solid approach (1.09 Eye). He followed up with a good summer with Team USA (.328/.449/.406 in 64 AB) though 79% ct% needs some work. May be a double-digit HR and SB guy in the bigs, though the homer total projects on the low end.

7. Jake McCarthy, OF — *Virginia, L/L, 6-2, 195*
McCarthy barely played as a freshman, then hit .338/.425/.506 in 2017 with good ct% (85%). He has little power, but has drawn some Jacoby Ellsbury comps (27 SB). We need to see more, but he's the type that offers tons of fantasy value if it sticks.

8. Griffin Conine, OF — *Duke, L/R, 6-1, 195*
Jeff Conine's son was a non-factor as a freshman before hitting .298/.425/.546 with 13 HR and 9 SB and an 0.91 Eye, and then hit 9 HR in the summer Cape Cod League. His tools are decent across the board, but his fantasy contributions are likely in the power categories and he should stick in the outfield.

9. Luken Baker, 1B — *Texas Christian, R/R, 6-4, 265*
Baker can't run, but can hit (20 bb%, 1.11 Eye) and has power (8 HR in 161 AB). It also remains to be seen how he recovers from an on-field collision that resulted in torn ligaments and a hairline fracture in his left (non-throwing) arm. He was said to be fully healthy in the fall. There's massive power here—if he can hit for an okay average.

10. Seth Beer, 1B — *Clemson, L/R, 6-2, 195*
There was once some thought Beer could go No. 1 overall in 2018 after hitting .369/.535/.700 as a freshman. Now, some think he's not a first rounder after he dipped to .298/.478/.606 and had another poor summer with the wooden bat (.208/.344/.287 in two years with Team USA). The peripherals are great (23 bb%, 84 ct%, 1.83 Eye) but his speed and defensive grades are awful. His real position may be "batter's box," making the highest risk/reward candidate on the list.

11. Logan Gilbert, RHP — *Stetson, R/R, 6-5, 195*
The Atlantic Sun Pitcher of the Year (10.8 Dom, 4.1 Cmd) offers athleticism with a four-pitch mix highlighted by a mid-90s fastball out of a three-quarters arm slot. In 31.1 innings of Cape Cod League work, he struck out 31 and walked four.

12. Tristan Pompey, OF — *Kentucky, S/R, 6-4, 200*
Dalton Pompey's brother had a good all-around season (.364, 10 HR, 9 SB). He's a potential power-speed guy with improving Eye (0.82) and ct% (79), but issues in the Cape (.230/.284/.345) dampen expectations a bit.

More to watch:
Greyson Jenista, OF, Wichita St.
Steele Walker, OF, Oklahoma
Alec Bohm, 3B, Wichita St.
Ryan Rollison, LHP, Ole Miss
Jackson Kowar, RHP, Florida

2018's Top Fantasy Prospects

1	Ronald Acuna	OF	ATL
2	Victor Robles	OF	WAS
3	Vladimir Guerrero Jr.	3B	TOR
4	Eloy Jimenez	OF	CHW
5	Gleyber Torres	SS	NYY
6	Brendan Rodgers	SS	COL
7	Nick Senzel	3B	CIN
8	Alex Reyes	RHP	STL
9	Walker Buehler	RHP	LA
10	Michael Kopech	RHP	CHW
11	Fernando Tatis Jr.	SS	SD
12	Kyle Tucker	OF	HOU
13	Bo Bichette	SS	TOR
14	Lewis Brinson	OF	MIL
15	Brent Honeywell	RHP	TAM
16	MacKenzie Gore	LHP	SD
17	Forrest Whitley	RHP	HOU
18	Willy Adames	SS	TAM
19	Leody Taveras	OF	TEX
20	Royce Lewis	SS	MIN
21	Mitch Keller	RHP	PIT
22	Francisco Mejia	C	CLE
23	Kyle Wright	RHP	ATL
24	A.J. Puk	LHP	OAK
25	Sixto Sanchez	RHP	PHI
26	Hunter Greene	RHP	CIN
27	Franklin Barreto	SS	OAK
28	Juan Soto	OF	WAS
29	Triston McKenzie	RHP	CLE
30	Luiz Gohara	LHP	ATL
31	Alex Verdugo	OF	LA
32	Franklin Perez	RHP	DET
33	Luis Robert	OF	CHW
34	Keston Hiura	2B	MIL
35	Ryan McMahon	1B	COL
36	Scott Kingery	2B	PHI
37	Mike Soroka	RHP	ATL
38	Willie Calhoun	OF	TEX
39	Kolby Allard	LHP	ATL
40	Austin Hays	OF	BAL
41	Jack Flaherty	RHP	STL
42	J.P. Crawford	SS	PHI
43	Anthony Alford	OF	TOR
44	Austin Meadows	OF	PIT
45	Brendan McKay	1B/LHP	TAM
46	Luis Urias	2B/SS	SD
47	Kyle Lewis	OF	SEA
48	Taylor Trammell	OF	CIN
49	Yadier Alvarez	RHP	LA
50	Estevan Florial	OF	NYY
51	Jay Groome	LHP	BOS
52	Cal Quantrill	RHP	SD
53	Nick Gordon	SS	MIN
54	Jesus Sanchez	OF	TAM
55	Chance Adams	RHP	NYY
56	Jorge Mateo	SS	OAK
57	Ian Anderson	RHP	ATL
58	Michel Baez	RHP	SD
59	Alec Hansen	RHP	CHW
60	Monte Harrison	OF	MIL
61	Keibert Ruiz	C	LA
62	Carson Kelly	C	STL
63	Kevin Maitan	3B	LAA
64	Riley Pint	RHP	COL
65	Anderson Espinoza	RHP	SD
66	Matt Manning	RHP	DET
67	Austin Beck	OF	OAK
68	Dylan Cease	RHP	CHW
69	Jorge Alfaro	C	PHI
70	Justus Sheffield	LHP	NYY
71	Blake Rutherford	OF	CHW
72	Chance Sisco	C	BAL
73	Ryan Mountcastle	3B	BAL
74	Corbin Burnes	RHP	MIL
75	Jake Bauers	OF/1B	TAM
76	Pavin Smith	1B	ARI
77	Adonis Medina	RHP	PHI
78	Jon Duplantier	RHP	ARI
79	Heliot Ramos	OF	SF
80	Adrian Morejon	LHP	SD
81	Dustin Fowler	OF	OAK
82	Mickey Moniak	OF	PHI
83	Shane Baz	RHP	PIT
84	Yusniel Diaz	OF	LA
85	Jesse Winker	OF	CIN
86	Stephen Gonsalves	LHP	MIN
87	Isan Diaz	2B	MIL
88	Joey Wentz	LHP	ATL
89	Tyler O'Neill	OF	STL
90	Alex Faedo	RHP	DET
91	Jo Adell	OF	LAA
92	Austin Riley	3B	ATL
93	Corey Ray	OF	MIL
94	Brandon Woodruff	RHP	MIL
95	Mitchell White	RHP	LA
96	Yordan Alvarez	1B	HOU
97	Michael Chavis	3B	BOS
98	Jose De Leon	RHP	TAM
99	Christian Arroyo	3B	TAM
100	Chris Shaw	1B	SF

Sleepers Outside the HQ100

by Alec Dopp

Each year the BaseballHQ.com minors team spends precious hours scouting players, evaluating tools, researching metrics and analyzing video before debating which prospects will end up on the annual HQ100 prospect list.

Equally as important as the HQ100 itself, however, is the process of identifying prospects who didn't make the top 100, but who could shoot up rankings lists in the near future. In past years, we've identified many such prospects—Adonis Medina (RHP, PHI) and Luiz Gohara (LHP, ATL) from 2017 are two examples—who have joined the list in subsequent seasons, and this search has become a valued and essential practice for the BaseballHQ minors team.

Continuing that tradition, here are 12 "sleeper" prospects who didn't make the cut for this year's HQ100, but who could ascend to that level in 2018 and could be available for owners in long-term keeper and dynasty formats.

Lazaro Armenteros (OF, OAK): Plucked from the Cuban ranks for $3 million as a 17-year-old in 2016, Armenteros made his stateside debut in the rookie Arizona League this summer and hit .288 with 10 SB in just shy of 200 plate trips, with 38% of his hits going for extra bases (x/h%). Despite his age, Armenteros is already a physical specimen with plus speed who should make SB impact as an outfielder. There is work to be done with his aggressive approach, especially against quality breaking balls as he moves up the minor league ladder, but his bat speed combined with natural strength makes him a high-upside bat with both future BA/HR value.

Lucas Erceg (3B, MIL): A two-way star in college, Erceg hit .327 in his pro debut in 2016 before moving to High-A in 2017, where he clubbed 15 HR with a .256 BA and 39% x/h%. Lean with wiry strength, Erceg will have a chance to hit for at least average power via a leveraged swing and has above-average bat speed from the left side of the plate. His swing can get long at times and he will need to improve against quality breaking balls, but he has the contact ability and overall bat-to-ball skills to hit for a solid average. He is instinctual and has just enough range for third base, and a plus-plus arm should allow him to stick there long-term.

Akil Baddoo (OF, MIN): Drafted by Minnesota in the second round in 2016, Baddoo moved up two levels in 2017 and displayed growth each step of the way, hitting a combined .323 with 4 HR, 9 SB and 36/32 BB/K between the the Gulf Coast League (GCL) and Appalachian League. Athletic and compact at 5-foot-11, Baddoo's best tool is his plus speed, but he also possesses some bat speed and has strong pitch recognition ability for future BA/OBP. His power is predominantly limited to right field at present, but should grow to become an average overall tool. Baddoo will need ample time to develop, but he could offer versatility as an everyday outfielder.

Peter Alonso (1B, NYM): A physical specimen at 6-foot-3, 245 pounds, Alonso has mashed ever since being taken in the second round back in 2016, slashing .297/.364/.539 with 23 HR and an 80% ct% across 123 pro games spanning three different levels. Alonso's best chance for impact as an everyday first baseman will be with his near plus-plus raw power, as he generates a ton of fly-ball contact via a leveraged stroke without sacrificing much contact. While a .300 BA long-term may be a stretch, Alonso has the overall skills for a .275-ish BA. The talent pool at first base is saturated at the big-league level, but Alonso should have value in deep NL formats.

Jeisson Rosario (OF, SD): A July 2 signee from the Dominican in 2016, Rosario made waves in his pro debut that included a .299/.404/.369 slash with 8 SB and 33 BB/36 K ratio in the rookie Arizona League. The 18-year-old stands out for his approach, hand-eye coordination and bat speed, each of which allow him to make quality contact and get on base at a high clip. His power is presently limited to the gaps, but he is young and will have a chance to add strength to his lean frame. Defensively, he reads the ball well off the bat and glides almost effortlessly in centerfield, and will be a plus defender at that position down the road.

Carter Kieboom (SS, WAS): A late-first-round draftee back in 2016, Kieboom spent most of his 2017 campaign abusing South Atlantic League arms to the tune of a .296/.400/.497 slash line with 8 HR and a 0.70 Eye in 48 games. The 20-year-old combines true plus bat speed from the right side of the plate with a mature approach and significant pull-side power. He'll need to learn to use the entire field in order to become a more complete hitter, as well as become a more consistent defender at short, but his potential for above-average returns in BA/HR at either shortstop or third base is exciting.

Adbert Alzolay (RHP, CHC): Capping a solid 2017 campaign between A+ and AA—2.99 ERA, 8.5 Dom, 2.7 Ctl in 22 starts—with a stint in the AFL, Alzolay has swiftly become a coveted arm in dynasty formats. The 22-year-old maintains 93-96 mph on his plus fastball and shows aptitude for throwing a hard-breaking 81-83 mph slider. Alzolay's change-up still requires some work, but should become a useable, average third pitch. He has made significant strides with his control as a pro, and his quality athleticism should allow it to get better. He has the look of a solid mid-rotation starter with above-average Dom ability as a moderate-risk investment.

Jesus Luzardo (LHP, OAK): Acquired from Washington last July in the Sean Doolittle and Ryan Madson trade, Luzardo opened eyes in his pro debut, posting a 1.66 ERA and 9.6 Cmd across 43.1 innings in the low minors. Luzardo displays advanced control for his age and shows an ability to effectively mix speeds with a plus fastball and changeup. His curveball should be an average third pitch, giving him three weapons with which to rack up whiffs as a #2/3 type starter. Luzardo's biggest obstacle will be handling 150-plus innings—he missed all of 2016 after undergoing Tommy John—and he'll get a chance to prove it in Low-A ball this year.

Hans Crouse (RHP, TEX): Texas's second-round pick last summer, Crouse was one of the most exciting arms in the rookie Arizona League in 2017, harboring a 0.45 ERA with 30 strikeouts in just 20 innings split between the bullpen and rotation. Tall and lean, Crouse requires physical projection but already has premium stuff, wielding a lively plus fastball in the mid-90s that can touch 98 mph. His breaking ball blends between slider and curve and has potential to miss bats, but his change-up will need work. There's some funk and deception to Crouse's delivery that portends a future power reliever, but he'll be developed as a starter.

Freicer Perez (RHP, NYY): One of the largest pitchers you'll find in the minors—he stands 6-foot-8, 190 pounds—Perez attacks hitters with a double-plus fastball that sits 94-96 mph and will touch 99 mph on occasion, which enabled him to overpower less-advanced hitters and post a 8.5 Dom in his full-season debut. The Dominican righty will mix in mid-80s slider and raw change-up around 86-87 mph, though he'll require time to develop feel for his secondaries to stay in the rotation. There's some concern as to whether Perez's command will grow to become even average, though if it doesn't, his stuff could play as a Dom-heavy, late-inning arm.

Griffin Canning (RHP, LAA): Drafted and signed by the Angels in the second round last summer, Canning has yet to make his pro debut but was dominant collegiately, collecting a 2.34 ERA and 10.6 Dom in 100-plus innings as a junior at UCLA. The 21-year-old has a chance to move quickly given his above-average control and solid four-pitch mix that includes a low-90s fastball capable of hitting 95 mph. He keeps hitters guessing with a changeup that features tumble and fade around 82-84 mph, and he'll throw in an average curveball and slider. The upside here isn't sky-high, but this could be a valued #3/4 starter.

Braxton Garrett (LHP, MIA): A top-10 pick from 2016, Garrett's pro debut was derailed before it had the chance to gain any momentum, as he required Tommy John surgery last July after just four starts with Low-A Greensboro. The 20-year-old righty has can't-miss stuff when he's on, showing command of a 90-94 mph fastball and setting up hitters with a plus curveball thrown with depth required for empty hacks. He'll also maintain arm speed well for an above-average changeup that could be another legitimate weapon. There's a lot of risk involved with any arm post-TJS, and while perhaps making the 2018 HQ100 is a stretch, his solid foundation will give him a chance to be a quality #2/3 starter and a visit to the list once he's back at full speed.

POSITIONS: Up to four positions are listed for each batter and represent those for which he appeared (in order) the most games at in 2016. Positions are shown with their numeric designation (2=CA, 3=1B, 7=LF, 0=DH, etc.)

BATS: Shows which side of the plate he bats from—right (R), left (L) or switch-hitter (S).

AGE: Player's age, as of April 1, 2018.

DRAFTED: The year, round, and school that the player performed at as an amateur if drafted, or where the player was signed from, if a free agent.

EXP MLB DEBUT: The year a player is expected to debut in the major leagues.

H/W: The player's height and weight.

FUT: The role that the batter is expected to have for the majority of his major league career, not necessarily his greatest upside.

SKILLS: Each skill a player possesses is graded and designated with a "+", indicating the quality of the skills, taking into context the batter's age and level played. An average skill will receive three "+" marks.

- **PWR:** Measures the player's ability to drive the ball and hit for power.
- **BAVG:** Measures the player's ability to hit for batting average and judge the strike zone.
- **SPD:** Measures the player's raw speed and base-running ability.
- **DEF:** Measures the player's overall defense, which includes arm strength, arm accuracy, range, agility, hands, and defensive instincts.

PLAYER STAT LINES: Player statistics for the last five teams that he played for (if applicable), including college and the major leagues.

TEAM DESIGNATIONS: Each team that the player performed for during a given year is included.

LEVEL DESIGNATIONS: The level for each team a player performed is included. "AAA" means Triple-A, "AA" means Double-A, "A+" means high Class-A, "A-" means low Class-A, and "Rk" means rookie level.

SABERMETRIC CATEGORIES: Descriptions of all the sabermetric categories appear in the glossary.

CAPSULE COMMENTARIES: For each player, a brief an... of their skills/statistics, and their future potential is provided.

ELIGIBILITY: Eligibility for inclusion is the standard for which Major League Baseball adheres to; 130 at-bats or 45 days on the 25-man roster, not including the month of September.

POTENTIAL RATINGS: The Potential Ratings are a two-part system in which a player is assigned a number rating based on his upside potential (1-10) and a letter rating based on the probability of reaching that potential (A-E).

Potential

10:	Hall of Famer	5:	MLB reserve
9:	Elite player	4:	Top minor leaguer
8:	Solid regular	3:	Average minor leaguer
7:	Average regular	2:	Minor league reserve
6:	Platoon player	1:	Minor league roster filler

Probability Rating

A: 90% probability of reaching potential
B: 70% probability of reaching potential
C: 50% probability of reaching potential
D: 30% probability of reaching potential
E: 10% probability of reaching potential

SKILLS: Scouts usually grade a player's skills on the 20-80 scale, and while most of the grades are subjective, there are grades that can be given to represent a certain hitting statistic or running speed. These are indicated on this chart:

Scout Grade	HR	BA	Speed (L)	Speed (R)
80	39+	.320+	3.9	4.0
70	32-38	.300-.319	4.0	4.1
60	25-31	.286-.299	4.1	4.2
50 (avg)	17-24	.270-.285	4.2	4.3
40	11-16	.250-.269	4.3	4.4
30	6-10	.220-.249	4.4	4.5
20	0-5	.219-	4.5	4.6

CATCHER POP TIMES: Catchers are timed (in seconds) from the moment the pitch reaches the catcher's mitt until the time that the middle infielder receives the baseball at second base. This number assists both teams in assessing whether a base-runner should steal second base or not.

1.85	+
1.95	MLB average
2.05	–

Abreu,Osvaldo | 6 | Washington

EXP MLB DEBUT: 2019 | H/W: 6-0 170 | FUT: Reserve SS | 6B

Bats R Age 23	Year	Lev	Team	AB	R	H	HR	RBI	Avg	OB	Slg	OPS	bb%	ct%	Eye	SB	CS	x/h%	Iso	RC/G
2012 FA (DR)	2013	Rk	GCL Nationals	147	24	42	0	24	286	367	381	748	11	84	0.79	16	6	31	95	5.12
Pwr ++	2014	A-	Auburn	210	31	48	1	15	229	260	305	565	4	80	0.22	10	6	23	76	2.35
BAvg ++	2015	A	Hagerstown	442	74	121	6	47	274	348	412	759	10	80	0.56	30	11	37	138	5.10
Spd ++	2016	A+	Potomac	497	86	123	6	52	247	322	346	669	10	78	0.51	18	10	27	99	3.88
Def +++	2017	AA	Harrisburg	431	40	106	5	42	246	290	336	627	6	75	0.25	1	6	24	90	3.10

Energetic player whose aggressiveness can get the better of him in the batters box. Iffy contact rate, a bit of doubles power, and speed on the decline. Value comes from stellar defense; is smooth and athletic around the bag and enough ability to stick at SS, but trending towards reserve IF status.

Acuna,Ronald | 789 | Atlanta

EXP MLB DEBUT: 2018 | H/W: 6-0 180 | FUT: Starting OF | 10D

Bats R Age 20	Year	Lev	Team	AB	R	H	HR	RBI	Avg	OB	Slg	OPS	bb%	ct%	Eye	SB	CS	x/h%	Iso	RC/G
2014 FA (VZ)	2016	Rk	GCL Braves	6	1	2	0	1	333	429	333	762	14	83	1.00	0	0	0	0	5.32
Pwr ++++	2016	A	Rome	148	27	46	4	18	311	386	432	818	11	81	0.64	14	7	17	122	5.71
BAvg ++++	2017	A+	Florida	115	21	33	3	19	287	333	478	812	7	65	0.20	14	3	33	191	6.08
Spd ++++	2017	AA	Mississippi	221	29	72	9	30	326	377	520	897	8	75	0.32	19	11	33	195	6.66
Def ++++	2017	AAA	Gwinnett	221	38	76	9	33	344	391	548	938	7	78	0.35	11	6	33	204	7.05

Quick-twitch athlete exploded on the scene, making Triple-A debut at 19. Combines advanced approach with lightning quick hands and wrists, pounds pitches with a short, compact swing. Raw plus power popped up in-game. Still more power in physical profile and swing. Not yet physically mature, will likely bulk up off CF. High SB IQ plays up run tool.

Adames,Willy | 6 | Tampa Bay

EXP MLB DEBUT: 2018 | H/W: 6-0 200 | FUT: Starting SS | 8A

Bats R Age 22	Year	Lev	Team	AB	R	H	HR	RBI	Avg	OB	Slg	OPS	bb%	ct%	Eye	SB	CS	x/h%	Iso	RC/G
2012 FA (DR)	2014	A	West Michigan	353	40	95	6	50	269	342	428	770	10	73	0.41	3	6	34	159	5.31
Pwr +++	2014	A	Bowling Green	97	15	27	2	11	278	375	433	808	13	69	0.50	3	0	33	155	6.08
BAvg ++++	2015	A+	Charlotte	396	51	102	4	46	258	347	379	725	12	69	0.44	10	1	33	121	4.88
Spd +++	2016	AA	Montgomery	486	89	133	11	57	274	370	430	800	13	75	0.61	13	6	36	156	5.77
Def ++++	2017	AAA	Durham	506	74	140	10	62	277	359	415	774	11	74	0.49	11	5	32	138	5.35

Advanced INF who has moved one level per year and continues to improve. Mostly played SS, but saw action at 2B. Lot of strikeouts, but still profiles well for BA due to plate discipline, plus bat speed, and pitch recognition. Has solid raw power and should hit for doubles and HR in time. Owns plus range at SS and arm strength among best around.

Adams,Riley | 2 | Toronto

EXP MLB DEBUT: 2020 | H/W: 6-4 225 | FUT: Starting C | 7C

Bats R Age 21	Year	Lev	Team	AB	R	H	HR	RBI	Avg	OB	Slg	OPS	bb%	ct%	Eye	SB	CS	x/h%	Iso	RC/G
2017 (3) San Diego																				
Pwr ++++																				
BAvg ++																				
Spd +	2017	NCAA	San Diego	202	45	63	13	47	312	409	564	973	14	72	0.58	2	0	40	252	8.06
Def ++	2017	A-	Vancouver	203	26	62	3	35	305	362	438	800	8	75	0.36	1	1	32	133	5.54

Strong, physical CA with advanced feel for bat and offers plus power to all fields. Can be pitched to as he will expand strike zone and subject to high K totals. Needs time to develop with glove. Shows promise with plus arm and quick release, but nuances of blocking and receiving aren't yet present.

Adell,Jo | 789 | Los Angeles (A)

EXP MLB DEBUT: 2021 | H/W: 6-2 195 | FUT: Starting OF | 9E

Bats R Age 18	Year	Lev	Team	AB	R	H	HR	RBI	Avg	OB	Slg	OPS	bb%	ct%	Eye	SB	CS	x/h%	Iso	RC/G
2017 (1) HS (KY)																				
Pwr +++																				
BAvg +++																				
Spd ++++	2017	Rk	Orem	85	25	32	1	9	376	404	518	922	4	80	0.24	3	2	25	141	6.76
Def ++	2017	Rk	AZL Angels	118	18	34	4	21	288	344	542	886	8	73	0.31	5	0	47	254	6.81

Athletic, lanky OF with big-time upside predicated on elite speed and hitting potential. Makes hard contact, but will expand strike zone at times. May take time to hit for power, but has strength and bat speed. Has chance to be standout defender with plus range and double plus arm, though all of his game needs development time.

Ademan,Aramis | 6 | Chicago (N)

EXP MLB DEBUT: 2021 | H/W: 5-11 160 | FUT: Starting SS | 7B

Bats L Age 19	Year	Lev	Team	AB	R	H	HR	RBI	Avg	OB	Slg	OPS	bb%	ct%	Eye	SB	CS	x/h%	Iso	RC/G
2015 FA (DR)																				
Pwr ++																				
BAvg ++++																				
Spd +++	2017	A-	Eugene	161	23	46	4	27	286	343	466	809	8	81	0.47	10	6	37	180	5.54
Def +++	2017	A	South Bend	127	13	31	3	15	244	267	378	645	3	81	0.17	4	2	32	134	3.20

Short, athletic Dominican has solid all-around tools. Uses a compact left-handed stroke and did launch a surprising 7 HR in 288 AB. Power is limited due to small frame but could grow to average. Uses plus instincts to go along with average range and arm. Should be able to stick at SS over the long-term.

Adolfo,Micker | 79 | Chicago (A)

EXP MLB DEBUT: 2020 | H/W: 6-3 200 | FUT: Starting OF | 9E

Bats R Age 21	Year	Lev	Team	AB	R	H	HR	RBI	Avg	OB	Slg	OPS	bb%	ct%	Eye	SB	CS	x/h%	Iso	RC/G
2013 FA (DR)	2014	Rk	AZL White Sox	179	27	39	5	21	218	275	380	654	7	53	0.16	0	0	44	162	4.47
Pwr ++++	2015	Rk	AZL White Sox	83	14	21	0	10	253	303	313	617	7	70	0.24	3	2	19	60	3.07
BAvg +++	2016	Rk	AZL White Sox	16	2	4	1	2	250	294	563	857	6	50	0.13	0	0	75	313	8.68
Spd +++	2016	A	Kannapolis	247	30	54	5	21	219	261	340	601	5	64	0.16	0	1	35	121	2.79
Def ++++	2017	A	Kannapolis	424	60	112	16	68	264	314	453	767	7	65	0.21	2	0	41	189	5.30

Strong OF finally remained healthy, improved immensely in 2017. Shortened up swing, becoming less pull happy. Pitch recognition skills got better as season wore on. Raw power is massive. Hedging bets with 30-HR projection due to swing-and-miss issues. Solid runner, will likely lose foot speed as body matures. Big arm profiles in RF.

Alcantara,Sergio | 6 | Detroit

EXP MLB DEBUT: 2019 | H/W: 5-9 168 | FUT: Starting SS | 7C

Bats B Age 21	Year	Lev	Team	AB	R	H	HR	RBI	Avg	OB	Slg	OPS	bb%	ct%	Eye	SB	CS	x/h%	Iso	RC/G
2012 FA (DR)	2016	A-	Hillsboro	47	12	15	0	8	319	439	362	800	18	79	1.00	4	2	13	43	6.04
Pwr +	2016	A	Kane County	180	15	48	1	16	267	320	328	647	7	86	0.54	3	2	17	61	3.59
BAvg +++	2016	A+	Visalia	15	2	4	0	0	267	389	333	722	17	87	1.50	0	1	25	67	5.14
Spd +++	2017	A+	Visalia	340	44	95	3	28	279	345	362	707	9	83	0.60	11	10	21	82	4.36
Def ++++	2017	A+	Lakeland	126	18	29	0	7	230	307	278	585	10	82	0.61	4	3	17	48	2.93

Small, quick SS who plays game with mature skills. Doesn't project for much power, but makes easy, consistent contact from both sides with short stroke. Needs to drive ball more to keep defense honest. Runs very well and can steal bases, but is caught often. Stands out with incredible arm strength and smooth actions.

Alemais,Stephen | 6 | Pittsburgh

EXP MLB DEBUT: 2019 | H/W: 6-0 190 | FUT: Starting SS | 7C

Bats B Age 22	Year	Lev	Team	AB	R	H	HR	RBI	Avg	OB	Slg	OPS	bb%	ct%	Eye	SB	CS	x/h%	Iso	RC/G
2016 (3) Tulane	2016	NCAA	Tulane	212	37	66	1	28	311	371	401	772	9	86	0.69	19	5	24	90	5.18
Pwr +	2016	A	West Virginia	37	2	7	0	2	189	231	270	501	5	70	0.18	1	3	29	81	1.44
BAvg +++	2017	Rk	GCL Pirates	27	6	7	0	2	259	355	370	725	13	81	0.80	0	0	43	111	4.92
Spd +++	2017	A	West Virginia	121	14	27	3	12	223	254	380	634	4	74	0.16	5	3	41	157	3.12
Def ++++	2017	A+	Bradenton	101	10	32	1	20	317	400	406	806	12	86	1.00	5	2	22	89	5.78

Plus defender with good range, soft hands, and strong, accurate arm. Started slow at Low-A, but looked comfortable when moved up to High-A. Makes consistent contact with good strike zone awareness and a line-drive approach, but swing can get big despite below average power. Has the chops to stick at SS.

Alfaro,Jorge | 2 | Philadelphia

EXP MLB DEBUT: 2016 | H/W: 6-2 225 | FUT: Starting C | 8C

Bats R Age 24	Year	Lev	Team	AB	R	H	HR	RBI	Avg	OB	Slg	OPS	bb%	ct%	Eye	SB	CS	x/h%	Iso	RC/G
2010 FA (CB)	2015	AA	Frisco	190	22	48	5	21	253	286	432	718	5	68	0.15	2	1	46	179	4.45
Pwr ++++	2016	AA	Reading	404	68	115	15	67	285	322	458	780	5	74	0.21	3	2	33	173	4.99
BAvg ++	2016	MLB	Philadelphia	16	0	2	0	0	125	176	125	301	6	50	0.13	0	0	0	0	-2.23
Spd +++	2017	AAA	Lehigh Valley	324	34	78	7	43	241	276	358	634	5	65	0.14	1	1	28	117	3.23
Def ++	2017	MLB	Philadelphia	107	12	34	5	14	318	336	514	850	3	69	0.09	0	0	32	196	5.98

Owns impressive all-fields power for both gap doubles and long HR. But shaky plate approach both in ball/strike recognition and contact issues will cap his short-term results. Struggles with off-speed pitches, especially low and away. Despite cannon arm and quick release, overall defense and game-calling also need significant polish.

Alford,Anthony | 789 | Toronto

EXP MLB DEBUT: 2017 | H/W: 6-1 215 | FUT: Starting CF | 8B

Bats R Age 23	Year	Lev	Team	AB	R	H	HR	RBI	Avg	OB	Slg	OPS	bb%	ct%	Eye	SB	CS	x/h%	Iso	RC/G
2012 (3) HS (MS)	2016	A+	Dunedin	339	53	80	9	44	236	339	378	717	14	65	0.45	18	6	35	142	4.75
Pwr +++	2017	A+	Dunedin	21	1	3	0	2	143	143	143	286	0	62	0.00	1	0	0	0	-2.23
BAvg +++	2017	AA	New Hampshire	245	41	76	5	24	310	396	429	825	13	82	0.78	18	3	25	118	5.96
Spd ++++	2017	AAA	Buffalo	12	1	4	0	0	333	385	417	801	8	83	0.50	0	0	25	83	5.48
Def +++	2017	MLB	Toronto	8	0	1	0	0	125	125	250	375	0	63	0.00	0	0	100	125	-0.48

Premium athlete who missed two months w/ broken wrist. Combines plate discipline with natural strength and bat speed to produce BA and current gap power. Should evolve into HR pop in time. Top-of-order guy due to high OBP and should steal loads of bases. Has potential to become elite CF, but needs more reps.

Allen,Austin — 2 — San Diego

EXP MLB DEBUT: 2019 | H/W: 6-4 225 | FUT: Starting 1B | 7D

Bats L Age 24
2015 (4) Florida Tech

- Pwr +++
- BAvg +++
- Spd +
- Def ++

Year	Lev	Team	AB	R	H	HR	RBI	Avg	OB	Slg	OPS	bb%	ct%	Eye	SB	CS	x/h%	Iso	RC/G
2015	A-	Tri-City	196	23	47	2	34	240	313	332	645	10	81	0.55	1	2	28	92	3.61
2016	A	Fort Wayne	409	52	131	7	61	320	365	425	791	7	83	0.42	0	0	22	105	5.17
2016	AA	San Antonio	11	1	3	1	1	273	273	545	818	0	100		0	0	33	273	4.93
2017	A+	Lake Elsinore	463	71	131	22	81	283	345	497	842	9	76	0.40	0	1	41	214	5.92

Tall, strong CA who led High-A backstops in HR and xbh Owns plus raw power to pull side via slight uppercut swing and good bat speed. Has decent bat-to-ball skills and will make enough contact for solid BA. Average arm strength behind plate, but still needs work on receiving and blocking skills to remain CA long-term. A move to 1B appears likely.

Allen,Greg — 8 — Cleveland

EXP MLB DEBUT: 2017 | H/W: 6-0 175 | FUT: Starting OF | 7B

Bats B Age 25
2014 (6) San Diego St

- Pwr +
- BAvg +++
- Spd ++++
- Def ++++

Year	Lev	Team	AB	R	H	HR	RBI	Avg	OB	Slg	OPS	bb%	ct%	Eye	SB	CS	x/h%	Iso	RC/G
2016	AA	Akron	145	26	42	3	13	290	372	441	813	12	81	0.70	7	6	31	152	5.81
2017	Rk	AZL Indians	15	3	5	0	2	333	333	333	667	0	93	0.00	3	0	0	0	3.43
2017	AA	Akron	258	37	68	2	24	264	321	357	678	8	79	0.40	21	2	28	93	3.92
2017	MLB	Cleveland	35	7	8	1	6	229	270	343	613	5	77	0.25	1	0	25	114	2.80

Fast, lean OF who missed time with broken hand, but reached CLE for first time. Outstanding CF who tracks balls well and has plus range. Possesses strong, accurate arm and takes efficient routes. Has limited pop, but knows limitations. Contact-oriented stroke who can line balls to gaps. Exhibits plus speed on base and is threat to steal.

Allen,Nick — 6 — Oakland

EXP MLB DEBUT: 2022 | H/W: 5-9 155 | FUT: Starting SS | 7C

Bats R Age 19
2017 (3) HS (CA)

- Pwr +
- BAvg +++
- Spd ++++
- Def ++++

Year	Lev	Team	AB	R	H	HR	RBI	Avg	OB	Slg	OPS	bb%	ct%	Eye	SB	CS	x/h%	Iso	RC/G
2017	Rk	AZL Athletics	138	26	35	1	14	254	318	326	644	9	80	0.46	7	3	17	72	3.51

Small, instinctual SS who impresses with fundamental approach to game. Already standout defender with plus speed. Hands and arm work well while exhibiting nimble footwork. Body control is asset. Leadoff hitter with compact stroke and advanced knowledge of K zone. Power not part of game, though can punch line drives to gaps.

Almanzar,Luis — 56 — San Diego

EXP MLB DEBUT: 2020 | H/W: 6-0 180 | FUT: Starting 3B | 8E

Bats R Age 19
2016 FA (DR)

- Pwr ++
- BAvg +++
- Spd +++
- Def +++

Year	Lev	Team	AB	R	H	HR	RBI	Avg	OB	Slg	OPS	bb%	ct%	Eye	SB	CS	x/h%	Iso	RC/G
2017	A-	Tri-City	261	36	60	2	21	230	297	299	596	9	67	0.29	10	5	22	69	2.80

Young, toolsy INF with quality overall skillset and chance to be a versatile contributor. Employs fluid, level stroke and sprays line drives to the gaps. Has aggressive approach and will need to improve vs. off-speed. Power isn't there yet, but could become average as he fills out. Signed as SS, but build portends a move to 3B with his strong arm.

Alonso,Peter — 3 — New York (N)

EXP MLB DEBUT: 2019 | H/W: 6-3 245 | FUT: Starting 1B | 9D

Bats R Age 23
2016 (2) Florida

- Pwr ++++
- BAvg +++
- Spd +
- Def +++

Year	Lev	Team	AB	R	H	HR	RBI	Avg	OB	Slg	OPS	bb%	ct%	Eye	SB	CS	x/h%	Iso	RC/G
2016	NCAA	Florida	211	51	79	14	60	374	455	659	1113	13	85	1.00	2	0	41	284	9.25
2016	A-	Brooklyn	109	20	35	5	21	321	383	587	970	9	80	0.50	0	1	51	266	7.60
2017	A+	St. Lucie	308	45	88	16	58	286	339	516	856	8	79	0.39	3	4	44	231	5.96
2017	AA	Binghamton	45	7	14	2	5	311	340	578	918	4	84	0.29	0	0	50	267	6.54

Big-bodied, powerful RH slugger flourished in full season debut. Tightened up swing in college, now short and compact, which allowed HRs to flourish in pitcher friendly FSL. Has limited his strikeouts considerably, yet still needs to learn to take a walk. Raw plus-plus power is calling card. A 1B only defender, he's solid around the base.

Alvarez,Yordan — 37 — Houston

EXP MLB DEBUT: 2020 | H/W: 6-5 225 | FUT: Starting 1B | 8C

Bats L Age 20
2016 FA (CU)

- Pwr +++
- BAvg ++++
- Spd ++
- Def ++

Year	Lev	Team	AB	R	H	HR	RBI	Avg	OB	Slg	OPS	bb%	ct%	Eye	SB	CS	x/h%	Iso	RC/G
2017	A	Quad Cities	111	26	40	9	33	360	470	658	1128	17	68	0.64	2	0	38	297	10.74
2017	A+	Buies Creek	224	19	62	3	36	277	333	393	726	8	82	0.46	6	1	27	116	4.52

Natural-hitting prospect who excelled in Cuba and hit .300 in two Class-A stops in 2017. Sprays ball to all fields with smooth LH stroke and possesses advanced strike-zone discipline. Still tapping into his power, but long levers, ct% skills, bat speed point to HR upside. Not much of a runner; likely relegated to 1B/LF. A name to watch for in 2018.

Anderson,Brian — 5 — Miami

EXP MLB DEBUT: 2017 | H/W: 6-3 185 | FUT: Starting 3B | 8C

Bats R Age 24
2014 (3) Arkansas

- Pwr +++
- BAvg +++
- Spd ++
- Def ++++

Year	Lev	Team	AB	R	H	HR	RBI	Avg	OB	Slg	OPS	bb%	ct%	Eye	SB	CS	x/h%	Iso	RC/G
2016	A+	Jupiter	182	27	55	3	25	302	377	440	817	11	79	0.58	3	0	31	137	5.84
2016	AA	Jacksonville	301	38	73	8	40	243	323	359	682	11	80	0.61	0	0	25	116	4.01
2017	AA	Jacksonville	311	53	78	14	55	251	329	450	779	10	77	0.51	1	1	40	199	5.17
2017	AAA	New Orleans	118	21	40	8	26	339	400	602	1002	9	77	0.44	0	1	38	263	7.89
2017	MLB	Miami	84	11	22	0	8	262	340	369	709	11	67	0.36	0	0	36	107	4.74

Has been one of the Marlins top hitting prospects since 2014 and finally made his MLB debut. Strong frame generates above-average power that finally showed up in game action, but mostly to pull-side. Moves well at 3B with a plus arm, but speed is not part of his game. Profiles as a solid producer, but with limited upside.

Andrade,Greifer — 7 — Seattle

EXP MLB DEBUT: 2020 | H/W: 6-0 170 | FUT: Starting OF | 7D

Bats R Age 21
2013 FA (VZ)

- Pwr ++
- BAvg +++
- Spd ++
- Def +++

Year	Lev	Team	AB	R	H	HR	RBI	Avg	OB	Slg	OPS	bb%	ct%	Eye	SB	CS	x/h%	Iso	RC/G
2016	Rk	AZL Mariners	82	17	28	3	16	341	379	549	928	6	79	0.29	2	2	29	207	6.84
2016	A-	Everett	6	1	0	0	0	0	0	0	0	0	50	0.00	1	0		0	-7.85
2017	A-	Everett	207	28	61	5	35	295	311	420	732	2	72	0.09	0	0	26	126	4.27

Athletic prospect who has yet to appear in full season. Showcases pure hitting ability with quality hand-eye coordination and barrel control. Rarely walks due to extreme contact approach. Compact stroke with some quickness and may reach 10+ HR. Has quality range in corners despite fringy speed. Exhibits arm for RF, but will need to hit to stick.

Andujar,Miguel — 5 — New York (A)

EXP MLB DEBUT: 2017 | H/W: 6-0 215 | FUT: Starting 3B | 8D

Bats R Age 23
2011 FA (DR)

- Pwr +++
- BAvg +++
- Spd ++
- Def ++

Year	Lev	Team	AB	R	H	HR	RBI	Avg	OB	Slg	OPS	bb%	ct%	Eye	SB	CS	x/h%	Iso	RC/G
2016	A+	Tampa	230	34	65	10	41	283	335	474	809	7	87	0.60	1	3	34	191	5.36
2016	AA	Trenton	282	28	75	2	42	266	317	358	675	7	85	0.50	2	1	27	92	3.92
2017	AA	Trenton	253	30	79	7	52	312	343	494	837	5	85	0.32	2	3	39	182	5.61
2017	AAA	Scranton/WB	227	36	72	9	30	317	365	502	867	7	85	0.52	3	0	32	185	6.02
2017	MLB	NY Yankees	7	0	4	0	4	571	625	857	1482	13	100		1	0	50	286	13.29

Aggressive hitter who continues to produce and improve. Had best year of career with highs in BA, doubles, and HR. Uses level swing to make easy, hard contact. Started to be more patient with better pitch recognition. Still can be too aggressive early in count. Improved footwork has led to better glovework with strong arm. Could move to RF.

Antuna,Yasel — 56 — Washington

EXP MLB DEBUT: 2022 | H/W: 6-0 170 | FUT: Starting SS | 8D

Bats B Age 18
2016 FA (DR)

- Pwr +++
- BAvg +++
- Spd ++
- Def ++

Year	Lev	Team	AB	R	H	HR	RBI	Avg	OB	Slg	OPS	bb%	ct%	Eye	SB	CS	x/h%	Iso	RC/G
2017	Rk	GCL Nationals	173	25	52	1	17	301	383	399	781	12	83	0.79	5	5	23	98	5.48

Showed outstanding strike zone judgement as 17-year-old in first pro exposure, and flexed line drive as well as gap power. Pop should continue to grow as body fills out. Scouts split on his defense; some point to throwing mistakes that might move him to 3B; others laud the smooth actions and plus arm. Lots of development time left.

Aparicio,Miguel — 78 — Texas

EXP MLB DEBUT: 2021 | H/W: 6-0 165 | FUT: Starting OF | 8D

Bats L Age 19
2015 FA (VZ)

- Pwr ++
- BAvg +++
- Spd ++
- Def +++

Year	Lev	Team	AB	R	H	HR	RBI	Avg	OB	Slg	OPS	bb%	ct%	Eye	SB	CS	x/h%	Iso	RC/G
2017	A-	Spokane	294	47	86	4	33	293	329	395	724	5	87	0.41	2	8	22	102	4.35
2017	A	Hickory	85	6	15	0	9	176	239	247	486	8	79	0.39	1	2	27	71	1.54

Advanced, lean OF who began year in Low-A before demotion to short-season. Has good potential in all facets of game, including power. Has short, compact stroke to make high contact and focuses on line drives. Not the best athlete, but has quickness and ability to play CF. Needs lot of seasoning and TEX will be patient.

Aquino,Aristides — 9 — Cincinnati

EXP MLB DEBUT: 2019 | H/W: 6-4 220 | FUT: Starting OF | 8E

Bats R Age 23 — 2011 FA (DR)
Pwr ++++ / BAvg + / Spd ++++ / Def ++++

Year	Lev	Team	AB	R	H	HR	RBI	Avg	OB	Slg	OPS	bb%	ct%	Eye	SB	CS	x/h%	Iso	RC/G
2014	Rk	Billings	284	48	83	16	64	292	328	577	905	5	77	0.23	21	5	53	285	6.57
2015	Rk	Billings	52	7	16	2	13	308	333	558	891	4	83	0.22	0	1	38	250	6.24
2015	A	Dayton	231	25	54	5	27	234	269	364	632	5	77	0.21	6	1	31	130	3.10
2016	A+	Daytona	484	69	132	23	79	273	320	519	839	7	79	0.33	11	7	46	246	5.78
2017	AA	Pensacola	459	54	99	17	56	216	277	397	674	8	68	0.27	9	3	43	181	3.80

Toolsy RH OF watched hit tool plummet in 2017. Struggled mightily with long and lumbering swing. Hitch in load, hands not direct to ball; too much soft contact. 30-HR potential in frame if can straighten out swing. Plus-plus, game changing arm in RF. Plus runner with solid base running instincts.

Arauz,Jonathan — 6 — Houston

EXP MLB DEBUT: 2020 | H/W: 6-0 150 | FUT: Starting SS | 7D

Bats B Age 19 — 2014 FA (PN)
Pwr + / BAvg +++ / Spd +++ / Def +++

Year	Lev	Team	AB	R	H	HR	RBI	Avg	OB	Slg	OPS	bb%	ct%	Eye	SB	CS	x/h%	Iso	RC/G
2016	Rk	Greeneville	201	26	50	2	18	249	314	338	652	9	78	0.42	1	3	26	90	3.60
2017	A-	Tri City	121	16	32	1	11	264	331	364	694	9	76	0.41	1	0	28	99	4.19
2017	A	Quad Cities	127	23	28	0	4	220	327	276	602	14	86	1.11	0	1	18	55	3.49

Switch-hitting SS known more for glove than bat. Combines athleticism, feel and strong arm necessary for above-average defensive profile at SS. Has quality bat-to-ball skills and line-drive stroke for solid BA down the road; power is more gap-oriented and will not be big HR threat at next level. Still young with time to grow into his lean frame.

Arias,Gabriel — 56 — San Diego

EXP MLB DEBUT: 2021 | H/W: 6-1 185 | FUT: Starting SS | 9E

Bats R Age 18 — 2016 FA (VZ)
Pwr ++ / BAvg +++ / Spd +++ / Def ++++

Year	Lev	Team	AB	R	H	HR	RBI	Avg	OB	Slg	OPS	bb%	ct%	Eye	SB	CS	x/h%	Iso	RC/G
2017	Rk	AZL Padres 2	153	18	42	0	13	275	319	353	672	6	67	0.20	4	6	21	78	3.94
2017	A	Fort Wayne	62	8	15	0	4	242	266	258	524	3	74	0.13	1	0	7	16	1.56

Young Venezuelan SS who signed for $1.9 million in 2016. Works middle and opposite side of the field with fluid, level stroke for future BA value. Lean, wiry frame does not produce much power and is likely a gap-to-gap type bat. Has range, instincts and arm for SS but could move to 3B as he fills out.

Armenteros,Lazaro — 78 — Oakland

EXP MLB DEBUT: 2022 | H/W: 6-0 185 | FUT: Starting OF | 9E

Bats R Age 18 — 2016 FA (CU)
Pwr +++ / BAvg +++ / Spd ++++ / Def ++

Year	Lev	Team	AB	R	H	HR	RBI	Avg	OB	Slg	OPS	bb%	ct%	Eye	SB	CS	x/h%	Iso	RC/G
2017	Rk	AZL Athletics	156	24	45	4	22	288	355	474	829	9	69	0.33	10	1	38	186	6.21

Athletic OF who dazzled in U.S. debut. Was high-profile signee in 2016 and showcased plus tools in 2017. Owns incredible bat speed and fluidity to hit for both power and BA. Chases breaking balls and swing can get long. Needs polish, but upside is huge. Exhibits plus speed on base and in OF. Has work to do with routes and arm is only average.

Arozarena,Randy — 789 — St. Louis

EXP MLB DEBUT: 2019 | H/W: 5-11 170 | FUT: Starting OF | 8D

Bats R Age 23 — 2016 FA (CU)
Pwr +++ / BAvg +++ / Spd +++ / Def +++

Year	Lev	Team	AB	R	H	HR	RBI	Avg	OB	Slg	OPS	bb%	ct%	Eye	SB	CS	x/h%	Iso	RC/G
2017	A+	Palm Beach	265	38	73	8	40	275	309	472	781	5	80	0.25	10	4	45	196	5.00
2017	AA	Springfield	163	34	41	3	9	252	358	380	738	14	79	0.79	8	3	34	129	4.99

Short, athletic Cuban player was solid if not spectacular in his state-side debut, showing good power and speed—32 doubles, 11 HR, and 18 SB. Quick bat with above-average power and speed give him the tools to be a top-of-the-order hitter who could move up quickly, but aggressive approach can be exploited.

Arraez,Luis — 4 — Minnesota

EXP MLB DEBUT: 2020 | H/W: 5-10 155 | FUT: Starting 2B | 7D

Bats L Age 20 — 2013 FA (VZ)
Pwr + / BAvg ++++ / Spd ++ / Def +++

Year	Lev	Team	AB	R	H	HR	RBI	Avg	OB	Slg	OPS	bb%	ct%	Eye	SB	CS	x/h%	Iso	RC/G
2015	Rk	GCL Twins	206	23	63	0	19	306	367	388	756	9	95	2.00	8	8	25	83	5.24
2016	A	Cedar Rapids	475	67	165	3	66	347	387	444	832	6	89	0.61	3	3	22	97	5.70
2017	A+	Fort Myers	13	1	5	0	1	385	385	538	923	0	100		0	0	20	154	6.39

Undersized INF who ended season after three games due to torn ACL in knee. Not a power guy or flashy hitter, but controls bat as well as any in organization. Makes extreme contact and willing to use all fields. Offers very little over-wall pop, but can line to the gaps. Should hit for high BA. Speed and arm a bit short, but makes routine plays with few errors.

Arroyo,Christian — 456 — Tampa Bay

EXP MLB DEBUT: 2017 | H/W: 6-1 180 | FUT: Starting 3B | 8C

Bats R Age 22 — 2013 (1) HS (FL)
Pwr ++ / BAvg ++++ / Spd ++ / Def +++

Year	Lev	Team	AB	R	H	HR	RBI	Avg	OB	Slg	OPS	bb%	ct%	Eye	SB	CS	x/h%	Iso	RC/G
2014	A	Augusta	118	10	24	1	14	203	230	271	501	3	81	0.18	1	2	21	68	1.51
2015	A+	San Jose	381	48	116	9	42	304	338	459	797	5	81	0.26	5	3	34	155	5.16
2016	AA	Richmond	474	57	130	3	49	274	316	373	690	6	85	0.40	1	1	31	99	4.03
2017	AAA	Sacramento	91	18	36	4	16	396	433	604	1037	6	87	0.50	2	0	31	209	7.89
2017	MLB	SF Giants	125	9	24	3	14	192	241	304	545	6	74	0.25	1	2	33	112	1.94

Instinctual INF who reached SF, but broke left hand and missed most of season after May. Played mostly 3B and has chance to be plus defender with strong, accurate arm. Uses compact stroke to produce doubles power, yet has strength to pull balls out of park. Not many walks in approach, but has plus hand-eye coordination and bat control for high BA.

Austin,Tyler — 379 — New York (A)

EXP MLB DEBUT: 2016 | H/W: 6-2 220 | FUT: Starting 1B | 7B

Bats R Age 26 — 2010 (13) HS (GA)
Pwr ++++ / BAvg +++ / Spd ++ / Def ++

Year	Lev	Team	AB	R	H	HR	RBI	Avg	OB	Slg	OPS	bb%	ct%	Eye	SB	CS	x/h%	Iso	RC/G
2016	MLB	NY Yankees	83	7	20	5	12	241	300	458	758	8	57	0.19	1	0	40	217	5.62
2017	AA	Trenton	14	5	6	0	1	429	500	786	1286	13	86	1.00	0	0	50	357	11.94
2017	AAA	Scranton/WB	171	29	47	10	32	275	344	544	888	10	70	0.35	0	0	53	269	6.85
2017	MLB	NY Yankees	40	4	9	2	8	225	295	425	720	9	58	0.24	0	0	44	200	5.00

Bat-first prospect who missed most of season with broken ankle and bad hamstring. Spent most of last 3 yrs in AAA. Mostly 1B in 2017, but has arm and passable glove for corner OF. Will swing and miss, but possesses all fields pop with double-plus bat speed. Swings under control and has feel for hitting breakers. Can be inconsistent in approach.

Avelino,Abiatal — 456 — New York (A)

EXP MLB DEBUT: 2018 | H/W: 5-11 205 | FUT: Starting MIF | 7D

Bats R Age 23 — 2011 FA (DR)
Pwr ++ / BAvg +++ / Spd +++ / Def +++

Year	Lev	Team	AB	R	H	HR	RBI	Avg	OB	Slg	OPS	bb%	ct%	Eye	SB	CS	x/h%	Iso	RC/G
2016	A+	Tampa	357	54	95	6	34	266	321	375	697	8	82	0.46	20	13	26	109	4.11
2016	AA	Trenton	127	15	31	0	14	244	299	331	630	7	85	0.53	1	2	35	87	3.48
2017	A+	Tampa	32	1	7	0	2	219	265	250	515	6	84	0.40	4	0	14	31	1.93
2017	AA	Trenton	230	35	62	3	28	270	311	396	707	6	86	0.42	4	0	31	126	4.23
2017	AAA	Scranton/WB	61	5	13	0	6	213	273	262	535	8	84	0.50	3	1	15	49	2.27

Strong, versatile INF who is on cusp of majors due to all-around skills. Played all INF spots but 1B in 2017 and has ideal range and arm strength. Exhibits first-step quickness and smooth actions, though makes careless errors. Has never hit double-digit HR and has seen SB rapidly decline. Owns steady stroke and BA ability due to barrel control.

Azocar,Jose — 89 — Detroit

EXP MLB DEBUT: 2020 | H/W: 5-11 165 | FUT: Starting CF | 8E

Bats R Age 21 — 2012 FA (VZ)
Pwr + / BAvg ++ / Spd ++++ / Def +++

Year	Lev	Team	AB	R	H	HR	RBI	Avg	OB	Slg	OPS	bb%	ct%	Eye	SB	CS	x/h%	Iso	RC/G
2016	A	West Michigan	501	56	141	0	51	281	316	335	651	5	76	0.21	14	5	13	54	3.39
2017	A+	Lakeland	431	38	95	3	37	220	245	292	537	3	72	0.11	12	6	20	72	1.77

Exciting, aggressive OF with limited power, but has traits of RF. Owns plus speed on base and in OF where he ranges well and has cannon for arm. Has high ceiling, but he needs significant polish. Had big drop off in BA and doesn't hit for any power. Walk rate is very poor and needs to be more disciplined. Needs to get on base more to use wheels.

Baddoo,Akil — 8 — Minnesota

EXP MLB DEBUT: 2021 | H/W: 5-11 185 | FUT: Starting OF | 8E

Bats L Age 19 — 2016 (S-2) HS (GA)
Pwr +++ / BAvg ++ / Spd +++ / Def ++

Year	Lev	Team	AB	R	H	HR	RBI	Avg	OB	Slg	OPS	bb%	ct%	Eye	SB	CS	x/h%	Iso	RC/G
2016	Rk	GCL Twins	107	15	19	2	15	178	296	271	567	14	66	0.50	8	1	21	93	2.45
2017	Rk	Elizabethton	126	39	45	3	19	357	471	579	1050	18	85	1.42	5	4	44	222	9.14
2017	Rk	GCL Twins	75	18	20	1	10	267	345	440	785	11	83	0.69	4	0	40	173	5.52

Emerging OF who added serious strength and starting to realize natural power potential. Drew more walks than Ks and has leadoff type skills. Swings fast bat and nifty approach to put ball in play. Can be pull happy at times. Possesses average speed and will likely move to LF. Instincts a bit short and will need better reads.

Bader,Harrison — 789 — St. Louis

EXP MLB DEBUT: 2017 | H/W: 6-0 195 | FUT: Starting OF | 8C

Bats R Age 23
2015 (3) Florida

- Pwr + + +
- BAvg + + +
- Spd + + +
- Def + + +

Year	Lev	Team	AB	R	H	HR	RBI	Avg	OB	Slg	OPS	bb%	ct%	Eye	SB	CS	x/h%	Iso	RC/G
2015	A	Peoria	206	34	62	9	28	301	348	505	853	7	79	0.34	15	6	35	204	5.92
2016	AA	Springfield	318	48	90	16	41	283	335	497	832	7	71	0.27	11	10	36	214	5.88
2016	AAA	Memphis	147	22	34	3	17	231	285	354	639	7	74	0.29	2	3	32	122	3.28
2017	AAA	Memphis	431	74	122	20	55	283	335	469	804	7	73	0.29	15	9	32	186	5.40
2017	MLB	St. Louis	85	10	20	3	10	235	278	376	654	6	72	0.21	2	1	30	141	3.32

Above-average tools across the board but none that standout as plus. Aggressive approach at the plate with good bat speed and average power resulted in a solid season at Triple-A Memphis, but was exploited once he reached the majors, striking out 24 times in 85 AB. Should see plenty of PT in 2018.

Baldwin,Roldani — 2 — Boston

EXP MLB DEBUT: 2020 | H/W: 5-11 175 | FUT: Starting C | 7E

Bats R Age 22
2013 FA (DR)

- Pwr + +
- BAvg + + +
- Spd +
- Def + +

Year	Lev	Team	AB	R	H	HR	RBI	Avg	OB	Slg	OPS	bb%	ct%	Eye	SB	CS	x/h%	Iso	RC/G
2015	Rk	GCL Red Sox	156	18	45	3	25	288	347	397	744	8	88	0.74	1	1	24	109	4.78
2015	A-	Lowell	7	0	2	0	0	286	286	429	714	0	86	0.00	0	0	50	143	4.08
2016	A-	Lowell	95	10	29	1	14	305	347	442	789	6	78	0.29	0	0	34	137	5.26
2016	A	Greenville	225	26	56	3	23	249	278	342	620	4	75	0.16	1	1	27	93	2.89
2017	A	Greenville	368	45	101	14	66	274	310	489	799	5	80	0.26	1	0	50	215	5.20

Offense-first backstop who repeated Low-A and finished 2nd in SAL in doubles and SLG. Hit for significantly more HR and doubles while showing better bat control. Not much for seeing pitches and has typical catcher speed. Defense is below average, but could become better in time. Has worked hard on release and receiving.

Banks,Nick — 79 — Washington

EXP MLB DEBUT: 2020 | H/W: 6-1 215 | FUT: Starting OF | 7C

Bats L Age 23
2016 (4) Texas A&M

- Pwr + + +
- BAvg + +
- Spd + + +
- Def + + +

Year	Lev	Team	AB	R	H	HR	RBI	Avg	OB	Slg	OPS	bb%	ct%	Eye	SB	CS	x/h%	Iso	RC/G
2016	NCAA	Texas A&M	239	48	67	9	49	280	346	473	819	9	80	0.51	7	0	37	192	5.65
2016	A-	Auburn	231	18	64	0	19	277	310	320	630	5	84	0.30	7	2	14	43	3.20
2017	A	Hagerstown	440	52	111	7	58	252	301	373	674	7	80	0.34	14	7	32	120	3.78

Simple, quiet swing with some uppercut that produced better power numbers. Likes to go to the opposite field, often at the expense of driving pitches to his pull side. Can struggle with velocity. Some SB, but not huge straight-line speed. Corner outfielder with enough tools for RF currently.

Bannon,Rylan — 5 — Los Angeles (N)

EXP MLB DEBUT: 2020 | H/W: 5-10 180 | FUT: Starting 3B | 8D

Bats R Age 21
2017 (8) Xavier

- Pwr + + +
- BAvg + + +
- Spd + +
- Def + + + +

Year	Lev	Team	AB	R	H	HR	RBI	Avg	OB	Slg	OPS	bb%	ct%	Eye	SB	CS	x/h%	Iso	RC/G
2017	NCAA	Xavier	221	45	75	15	50	339	436	633	1070	15	79	0.83	17	0	43	294	9.07
2017	Rk	Ogden	149	39	50	10	30	336	411	591	1001	11	81	0.66	5	0	36	255	7.88

Had a monster pro debut in rookie ball. Plus defender at 3B with good hands and a strong arm. Above-average power plays up due to balanced, aggressive swing with high leg kick and good understanding of the strike zone. Continues to exceed expectations.

Banuelos,David — 2 — Minnesota

EXP MLB DEBUT: 2020 | H/W: 6-0 205 | FUT: Starting C | 7C

Bats R Age 21
2017 (5) Long Beach St

- Pwr + +
- BAvg + +
- Spd + +
- Def + + + +

Year	Lev	Team	AB	R	H	HR	RBI	Avg	OB	Slg	OPS	bb%	ct%	Eye	SB	CS	x/h%	Iso	RC/G
2017	NCAA	Long Beach St	201	31	58	7	29	289	344	468	812	8	78	0.38	5	2	33	179	5.52
2017	A-	Everett	127	24	30	4	26	236	322	394	715	11	69	0.40	1	1	40	157	4.54

Defensive-oriented backstop who thrives with leadership skills and excellent receiving. Possesses strong arm and is tough to run on thanks to quick release. Textbook footwork aids in blocking and calls efficient game. Needs work as hitter. Has strong swing, but too many Ks. Will work deep counts and could develop some power with modified approach.

Barley,Jordy — 6 — San Diego

EXP MLB DEBUT: 2022 | H/W: 6-0 175 | FUT: Starting SS | 8E

Bats R Age 18
2016 FA (DR)

- Pwr + +
- BAvg + +
- Spd + + + +
- Def + + +

Year	Lev	Team	AB	R	H	HR	RBI	Avg	OB	Slg	OPS	bb%	ct%	Eye	SB	CS	x/h%	Iso	RC/G
2017	Rk	AZL Padres	182	34	44	4	28	242	285	434	719	6	64	0.17	7	2	48	192	4.76

Young, athletic glove-first prospect who covers ground and has plus arm required for SS. Runs well and should be considered valuable SB chip. Approach remains unrefined and smaller, leaner frame project mostly gap power. Shows some feel for hitting and could be a decent BA source.

Barreto,Franklin — 46 — Oakland

EXP MLB DEBUT: 2017 | H/W: 5-10 190 | FUT: Starting MIF | 8A

Bats R Age 22
2012 FA (VZ)

- Pwr + + +
- BAvg + + + +
- Spd + + +
- Def + + +

Year	Lev	Team	AB	R	H	HR	RBI	Avg	OB	Slg	OPS	bb%	ct%	Eye	SB	CS	x/h%	Iso	RC/G
2015	A+	Stockton	338	50	102	13	47	302	331	500	831	4	80	0.22	8	3	37	198	5.51
2016	AA	Midland	462	63	130	10	50	281	333	413	747	7	81	0.40	30	15	29	132	4.68
2016	AAA	Nashville	17	2	6	1	3	353	353	647	1000	0	76	0.00	0	2	33	294	7.45
2017	AAA	Nashville	469	63	136	15	54	290	329	456	785	5	70	0.19	15	8	30	166	5.26
2017	MLB	Oakland	71	10	14	2	6	197	250	352	602	7	54	0.15	2	0	36	155	3.38

Productive MIF who was youngest position player in PCL and set career high in HR . Presents good power for size, though can expand zone at times. Owns high BA potential due to bat speed, hard contact, and instincts. SB declined but runs well. Split time between 2B and SS and is average defender at both. No obvious weakness in game.

Basabe,Luis Alexander — 789 — Chicago (A)

EXP MLB DEBUT: 2019 | H/W: 6-0 160 | FUT: Starting OF | 8D

Bats B Age 21
2012 FA (VZ)

- Pwr + + +
- BAvg + +
- Spd + + + +
- Def + + + +

Year	Lev	Team	AB	R	H	HR	RBI	Avg	OB	Slg	OPS	bb%	ct%	Eye	SB	CS	x/h%	Iso	RC/G
2014	Rk	DSL Red Sox	148	38	42	0	26	284	404	480	884	17	76	0.83	13	2	43	196	7.38
2015	A-	Lowell	222	36	54	7	23	243	339	401	739	13	70	0.48	15	4	33	158	4.91
2016	A	Greenville	403	61	104	12	52	258	325	447	772	9	71	0.34	25	5	42	189	5.27
2016	A+	Salem	22	5	8	0	1	364	391	545	937	4	86	0.33	0	0	38	182	6.96
2017	A+	Winston-Salem	375	52	83	5	36	221	311	320	631	12	72	0.47	17	6	27	99	3.40

Switch hitter took a step back after breakout 2016 due to decline in K-rate and hard contact rate. Owns quick-twitch swing but lacks pitch recognition skills. Still projected for solid power despite HR drop off. Athletic and brings plus speed in CF and on bases.

Bauers,Jake — 379 — Tampa Bay

EXP MLB DEBUT: 2018 | H/W: 6-1 195 | FUT: Starting 1B | 8C

Bats L Age 22
2013 (7) HS (CA)

- Pwr + + +
- BAvg + + +
- Spd + +
- Def + +

Year	Lev	Team	AB	R	H	HR	RBI	Avg	OB	Slg	OPS	bb%	ct%	Eye	SB	CS	x/h%	Iso	RC/G
2014	A	Fort Wayne	406	59	120	8	64	296	374	414	788	11	80	0.64	5	6	24	118	5.42
2015	A+	Charlotte	217	33	58	6	38	267	354	433	787	12	85	0.88	2	3	38	166	5.47
2015	AA	Montgomery	257	36	71	5	36	276	331	405	736	8	84	0.51	6	3	32	128	4.61
2016	AA	Montgomery	493	79	135	14	78	274	367	420	787	13	82	0.82	10	6	32	146	5.49
2017	AAA	Durham	486	79	128	13	63	263	365	412	777	14	77	0.70	20	3	35	148	5.42

Patient, natural hitter who continues to draw ton of walks while exhibiting doubles pop to gaps. Hits LHP with plus bat control and clean swing mechanics. Shows plus raw pop, but hasn't developed as much as hoped because of flatter bat path. Split time between 1B and OF corners and exhibits near-average speed and range. Not a liability with glove.

Bautista,Rafael — 789 — Washington

EXP MLB DEBUT: 2017 | H/W: 6-2 165 | FUT: Reserve OF | 6A

Bats R Age 25
2012 FA (DR)

- Pwr +
- BAvg + +
- Spd + + + + +
- Def + + +

Year	Lev	Team	AB	R	H	HR	RBI	Avg	OB	Slg	OPS	bb%	ct%	Eye	SB	CS	x/h%	Iso	RC/G
2015	A+	Potomac	206	23	56	0	8	272	309	325	634	5	89	0.50	23	4	16	53	3.44
2016	AA	Harrisburg	543	77	153	4	39	282	337	341	677	8	83	0.48	56	10	13	59	3.89
2017	Rk	GCL Nationals	44	7	13	0	3	295	367	386	754	10	89	1.00	2	1	23	91	5.17
2017	AAA	Syracuse	176	23	44	0	11	250	286	313	599	5	85	0.35	7	4	23	63	2.93
2017	MLB	Washington	25	2	4	0	0	160	222	160	382	7	80	0.40	0	0	0	0	0.16

Slight OF who makes lots of contact due to quick hands/wrists, but whose lack of strength limits him from driving the ball. Rarely turns on pitches; can be beaten inside. Average plate patience gives him a chance of solid OBP, which would unlock his SB. Can close gaps on defense.

Beaty,Matt — 345 — Los Angeles (N)

EXP MLB DEBUT: 2019 | H/W: 6-0 210 | FUT: Utility player | 7C

Bats L Age 24
2015 (12) Belmont

- Pwr + + +
- BAvg + + +
- Spd + +
- Def + +

Year	Lev	Team	AB	R	H	HR	RBI	Avg	OB	Slg	OPS	bb%	ct%	Eye	SB	CS	x/h%	Iso	RC/G
2015	NCAA	Belmont	238	53	91	12	76	382	456	668	1124	12	93	1.88	12	2	44	286	9.26
2015	Rk	Ogden	25	3	12	0	3	480	519	520	1039	7	88	0.67	2	2	8	40	8.06
2015	A	Great Lakes	246	37	73	4	25	297	352	390	742	8	89	0.75	2	1	18	93	4.74
2016	A+	Rancho Cuca	489	66	145	11	88	297	350	425	775	8	85	0.54	6	1	28	129	5.05
2017	AA	Tulsa	438	61	143	15	69	326	376	505	881	7	88	0.65	3	3	33	178	6.24

Underrated corner IF continued to rake at Double-A. Quick left-handed bat, average power, and excellent bat to ball skills resulted in 47 extra base hits. Below average speed and defense and is being groomed as a utility player, seeing action at 3B, 1B, 2B, and DH.

Becerra,Wuilmer

379 | New York (N) | EXP MLB DEBUT: 2019 | H/W: 6-3 243 | FUT: Reserve OF | 6B

Bats R Age 23
2011 FA (VZ)

- Pwr ++
- BAvg ++
- Spd +++
- Def +++

Year	Lev	Team	AB	R	H	HR	RBI	Avg	OB	Slg	OPS	bb%	ct%	Eye	SB	CS	x/h%	Iso	RC/G
2013	Rk	GCL Mets	173	21	42	1	25	243	321	295	616	10	65	0.33	5	6	17	52	3.17
2014	Rk	Kingsport	207	37	62	7	29	300	344	469	812	6	73	0.25	7	3	31	169	5.53
2015	A	Savannah	449	67	130	9	63	290	338	423	761	7	79	0.34	16	8	30	134	4.87
2016	A+	St. Lucie	247	27	77	1	34	312	336	393	729	4	79	0.17	7	1	23	81	4.30
2017	A+	St. Lucie	469	49	125	4	44	267	319	335	654	7	72	0.27	16	5	18	68	3.51

Strong-bodied, injury-prone OF had 2nd consecutive down season. Explosiveness in swing hasn't returned since shoulder surgery. Raw power almost completely gone in game. Swing plane designed for hard, line drive contact. Swing lacks loft and produces heavy topspin. Can play all 3 OF positions, better suited for corners.

Bechtold,Andrew

5 | Minnesota | EXP MLB DEBUT: 2020 | H/W: 6-1 185 | FUT: Starting 3B | 8D

Bats R Age 21
2017 (5) Chipola JC

- Pwr +++
- BAvg +++
- Spd ++
- Def ++

Year	Lev	Team	AB	R	H	HR	RBI	Avg	OB	Slg	OPS	bb%	ct%	Eye	SB	CS	x/h%	Iso	RC/G
2017	NCAA	Chipola College	210	81	88	12	65	419	529	676	1205	19	79	1.11	24	4	33	257	11.18
2017	Rk	Elizabethton	144	33	43	2	19	299	409	424	833	16	72	0.68	0	0	30	125	6.47

Athletic INF who played 3B in debut and could see action at 2B, SS, and OF in future. Uses short, compact stroke to advantage with average power and BA ability. Likes to use opposite field with sufficient plate coverage and bat control. Bat speed is quite impressive. Hands and arm good enough for 3B, but lacks speed and quickness.

Beck,Austin

8 | Oakland | EXP MLB DEBUT: 2022 | H/W: 6-1 200 | FUT: Starting CF | 9D

Bats R Age 19
2017 (1) HS (NC)

- Pwr +++
- BAvg +++
- Spd +++
- Def +++

Year	Lev	Team	AB	R	H	HR	RBI	Avg	OB	Slg	OPS	bb%	ct%	Eye	SB	CS	x/h%	Iso	RC/G
2017	Rk	AZL Athletics	152	23	32	2	28	211	290	349	639	10	66	0.33	7	1	41	138	3.58

Toolsy, impressive OF who started slow in debut, but finished well. Has explosive bat speed which enhances offensive potential. Should hit for plus pop at peak with moderate to high BA. Runs well and has All-Star potential. Reads and routes in CF need polish, but could be above average defender in time.

Beltre,Kelvin

4 | San Francisco | EXP MLB DEBUT: 2020 | H/W: 5-11 170 | FUT: Starting 2B | 7D

Bats R Age 21
2013 FA (DR)

- Pwr +++
- BAvg ++
- Spd +++
- Def ++

Year	Lev	Team	AB	R	H	HR	RBI	Avg	OB	Slg	OPS	bb%	ct%	Eye	SB	CS	x/h%	Iso	RC/G
2015	Rk	AZL Giants	46	5	11	1	3	239	352	348	700	15	63	0.47	3	2	27	109	4.60
2016	Rk	AZL Giants	24	3	8	0	5	333	360	583	943	4	83	0.25	1	0	63	250	7.21
2016	A	Augusta	192	29	48	4	22	250	308	406	714	8	67	0.25	7	4	42	156	4.55
2017	A	Augusta	423	65	107	6	37	253	328	362	689	10	77	0.49	15	6	30	109	4.14

Short, lean INF who has flown under radar. Needs a lot of polish and strength, but good upside. Swings very fast bat and exhibits plus raw power. Has tendency to expand strike zone and needs to recognize pitches better. Low BA in career, but shows promise with improving eye. Most of time at 2B where he profiles well. Owns enough range and arm.

Beltre,Michael

79 | Cincinnati | EXP MLB DEBUT: 2020 | H/W: 6-3 180 | FUT: Reserve OF | 6C

Bats B Age 22
2013 FA (DR)

- Pwr ++
- BAvg ++
- Spd +++
- Def ++

Year	Lev	Team	AB	R	H	HR	RBI	Avg	OB	Slg	OPS	bb%	ct%	Eye	SB	CS	x/h%	Iso	RC/G
2015	Rk	AZL Reds	82	6	18	1	7	220	264	293	557	6	67	0.19	5	1	22	73	2.09
2016	Rk	Billings	81	14	25	3	13	309	417	531	948	16	84	1.15	4	1	48	222	7.65
2016	Rk	AZL Reds	106	23	31	0	10	292	359	443	802	9	76	0.44	9	0	32	151	5.80
2017	A	Dayton	407	51	97	3	36	238	320	324	644	11	78	0.55	9	9	24	86	3.63

Toolsy, switch-hitting OF struggled in first taste of full-season ball. An older prospect, has been brought along slowly. Has solid bat-to-ball skills and an improving approach. Strength hasn't materialized to power in BP or game. An athletic beast, speed carries tool shed.

Benedetti,Carmen

79 | Houston | EXP MLB DEBUT: 2019 | H/W: 6-2 215 | FUT: Starting OF | 7C

Bats L Age 23
2016 (12) Michigan

- Pwr ++
- BAvg +++
- Spd ++
- Def ++

Year	Lev	Team	AB	R	H	HR	RBI	Avg	OB	Slg	OPS	bb%	ct%	Eye	SB	CS	x/h%	Iso	RC/G
2016	NCAA	Michigan	193	44	63	3	33	326	454	492	946	19	85	1.55	6	1	38	166	7.95
2016	A-	Tri City	165	22	51	1	19	309	367	364	730	8	76	0.38	0	0	14	55	4.56
2017	A	Quad Cities	241	49	80	4	32	332	449	465	913	17	80	1.09	1	0	30	133	7.45
2017	A+	Buies Creek	82	9	22	1	9	268	341	415	755	10	74	0.43	1	0	41	146	5.11

Michigan product performed admirably in full-season debut. Has quick line-drive stroke conducive to plus contact and gap power to all fields; won't be a HR threat. Identifies spin well, works walks and will be OBP asset. Doesn't run well or have range for CF, but has good enough arm for RF, which is where he profiles best long-term.

Benson,Will

9 | Cleveland | EXP MLB DEBUT: 2021 | H/W: 6-5 225 | FUT: Starting OF | 8D

Bats L Age 19
2016 (1) HS (GA)

- Pwr ++++
- BAvg ++
- Spd +++
- Def +++

Year	Lev	Team	AB	R	H	HR	RBI	Avg	OB	Slg	OPS	bb%	ct%	Eye	SB	CS	x/h%	Iso	RC/G
2016	Rk	AZL Indians	158	31	33	6	27	209	306	424	730	12	62	0.37	10	2	58	215	5.09
2017	A-	Mahoning Val	202	29	48	10	36	238	339	475	814	13	60	0.39	7	1	48	238	6.53

Premium power prospect with electric bat and plus pop to all fields. Hasn't yet played in full-season, but has been menace in short-season with vicious hacks. Very long swing results in Ks and may need to revise stroke to hit for BA. Gets fooled by LHP. Sound defender with strong arm and average speed and range.

Bichette,Bo

46 | Toronto | EXP MLB DEBUT: 2019 | H/W: 6-0 200 | FUT: Starting SS | 8A

Bats R Age 20
2016 (2) HS (FL)

- Pwr +++
- BAvg +++++
- Spd +++
- Def ++

Year	Lev	Team	AB	R	H	HR	RBI	Avg	OB	Slg	OPS	bb%	ct%	Eye	SB	CS	x/h%	Iso	RC/G
2016	Rk	GCL Blue Jays	82	21	35	4	36	427	466	732	1198	7	79	0.35	3	0	43	305	10.33
2017	A	Lansing	284	60	109	10	51	384	439	623	1062	9	81	0.51	12	3	41	239	8.74
2017	A+	Dunedin	164	28	53	4	23	323	376	463	840	8	84	0.54	10	4	26	140	5.83

Pure-hitting INF who led minors in BA. Posted incredible numbers and showed advanced bat skills. Reads spin and controls bat like wily veteran. Can work deep counts, yet hit with two strikes. Swings aggressively at pitches and owns above average power potential. Secondary skills are average at best. Plays mostly SS, but has seen action at 2B.

Biggio,Cavan

45 | Toronto | EXP MLB DEBUT: 2019 | H/W: 6-1 203 | FUT: Utility player | 6B

Bats L Age 22
2016 (5) Notre Dame

- Pwr ++
- BAvg ++
- Spd +++
- Def ++

Year	Lev	Team	AB	R	H	HR	RBI	Avg	OB	Slg	OPS	bb%	ct%	Eye	SB	CS	x/h%	Iso	RC/G
2016	NCAA	Notre Dame	196	43	61	4	28	311	460	454	914	22	84	1.69	14	0	30	143	7.66
2016	A-	Vancouver	202	24	57	0	21	282	372	366	739	13	86	1.04	9	3	25	84	5.09
2016	A	Lansing	36	3	8	0	5	222	300	250	550	10	81	0.57	2	0	13	28	2.43
2017	A+	Dunedin	463	75	108	11	60	233	339	363	702	14	70	0.53	11	7	31	130	4.45

Smart, fundamentally-sound INF who grinds out at bats with selective eye and level stroke. Gets beaten by good fastballs and may not have bat speed to catch up. Could be ideal leadoff hitter and will occasionally pull ball over fence. Limited athleticism limits him to 2B. Has seen some action at 3B, but arm and quickness better at 2B.

Bishop,Braden

78 | Seattle | EXP MLB DEBUT: 2018 | H/W: 6-1 190 | FUT: Starting OF | 8D

Bats R Age 24
2015 (3) Washington

- Pwr ++
- BAvg +++
- Spd ++++
- Def ++++

Year	Lev	Team	AB	R	H	HR	RBI	Avg	OB	Slg	OPS	bb%	ct%	Eye	SB	CS	x/h%	Iso	RC/G
2015	A-	Everett	219	34	70	2	22	320	335	393	728	2	85	0.15	13	3	16	73	4.15
2016	A	Clinton	248	38	72	1	21	290	355	331	686	9	81	0.52	6	1	10	40	4.05
2016	A+	Bakersfield	166	19	41	2	22	247	294	319	613	6	77	0.28	2	0	20	72	2.91
2017	A+	Modesto	355	71	105	2	32	296	375	400	775	11	82	0.69	16	4	29	104	5.38
2017	AA	Arkansas	125	18	42	1	11	336	407	448	855	11	88	1.00	6	1	26	112	6.31

Speedy, athletic OF who hit over .300 in breakout campaign. Best attributes involve speed—can chase down any ball in CF and steal bases. Improved walk rate to go along with enough bat speed to drive ball to gaps. HR aren't part of game, but will hit loads of doubles. True CF with plus range and great jumps.

Blandino,Alex

456 | Cincinnati | EXP MLB DEBUT: 2018 | H/W: 6-0 190 | FUT: Starting 2B | 7C

Bats R Age 25
2014 (1) Stanford

- Pwr ++
- BAvg +++
- Spd ++
- Def +++

Year	Lev	Team	AB	R	H	HR	RBI	Avg	OB	Slg	OPS	bb%	ct%	Eye	SB	CS	x/h%	Iso	RC/G
2015	AA	Pensacola	115	15	27	3	18	235	338	374	712	14	82	0.86	2	2	37	139	4.60
2016	AA	Pensacola	401	52	93	8	37	232	325	337	661	12	72	0.48	14	5	28	105	3.78
2017	AA	Pensacola	197	31	51	6	31	259	362	462	824	14	75	0.65	3	4	55	203	6.14
2017	AAA	Louisville	196	29	53	6	20	270	373	444	817	14	81	0.86	1	3	40	173	5.93

Former 1st rd pick enjoyed success in 2017 after down in 2016. Shortened up swing and perfected approach, becoming an on-base machine. Pull HR power, but best when using gaps to pepper extra base hits. A solid athlete despite limited foot speed. Has soft hands and has transitioned to 2B effortlessly.

Blankenhorn,Travis

45 | Minnesota | EXP MLB DEBUT: 2019 | H/W: 6-2 208 | FUT: Starting 2B | 8D

Bats L Age 21 — 2015 (3) HS (PA) — Pwr +++ | BAvg +++ | Spd ++ | Def ++

Year	Lev	Team	AB	R	H	HR	RBI	Avg	OB	Slg	OPS	bb%	ct%	Eye	SB	CS	x/h%	Iso	RC/G
2015	Rk	GCL Twins	49	6	12	0	3	245	339	408	747	13	78	0.64	2	0	50	163	5.25
2015	Rk	Elizabethton	144	14	35	3	20	243	297	326	623	7	78	0.34	1	0	17	83	3.03
2016	Rk	Elizabethton	138	30	41	9	29	297	336	558	894	5	76	0.24	3	0	41	261	6.33
2016	A	Cedar Rapids	91	11	26	1	12	286	343	418	761	8	69	0.29	2	1	31	132	5.22
2017	A	Cedar Rapids	438	68	110	13	69	251	324	441	764	10	73	0.39	13	2	42	189	5.15

Pure-hitting INF who split time between 2B/3B while ending season on fire. Has potential with both BA and power, though needs to improve against LHP. Has patient approach and will likely see K rate drop as he recognizes pitches better. Owns average arm for 3B, but has poor hands. Will leg out xbh more on instincts than speed.

Boldt,Ryan

789 | Tampa Bay | EXP MLB DEBUT: 2019 | H/W: 6-2 210 | FUT: Starting OF | 7B

Bats L Age 23 — 2016 (2) Nebraska — Pwr ++ | BAvg +++ | Spd +++ | Def +++

Year	Lev	Team	AB	R	H	HR	RBI	Avg	OB	Slg	OPS	bb%	ct%	Eye	SB	CS	x/h%	Iso	RC/G
2016	NCAA	Nebraska	257	48	74	5	30	288	339	416	756	7	86	0.56	20	9	28	128	4.84
2016	A-	Hudson Valley	170	17	37	1	15	218	261	276	538	6	86	0.42	8	9	19	59	2.24
2017	A+	Charlotte	440	60	130	5	62	295	353	407	760	8	80	0.44	23	6	25	111	4.96

Impressive OF who bypassed Low-A and finished 3rd in FSL in BA. Got better each month with consistent, hard contact and gap power. Has frame and strength for pop, but focuses more on line drives with level swing. Can hit LHP and reads spin well. Very good defender at all OF spots and takes efficient routes. Solid average arm works well in corners.

Boswell,Bret

4 | Colorado | EXP MLB DEBUT: 2020 | H/W: 6-1 180 | FUT: Starting 2B | 7D

Bats L Age 23 — 2017 (8) Texas — Pwr +++ | BAvg ++ | Spd +++ | Def +++

Year	Lev	Team	AB	R	H	HR	RBI	Avg	OB	Slg	OPS	bb%	ct%	Eye	SB	CS	x/h%	Iso	RC/G
2017	NCAA	Texas	198	34	54	7	33	273	379	444	824	15	80	0.87	5	0	37	172	6.01
2017	A-	Boise	229	46	67	11	42	293	336	515	851	6	76	0.27	3	3	36	223	5.92

8th round pick out of Texas had an impressive pro debut. Mature hitter has plus raw power and put it into action in the NWL. Does have length to swing and posted a 22% K rate. Covers ground well and should be able to stick at 2B as he moves up.

Boyd,B.J.

789 | Oakland | EXP MLB DEBUT: 2018 | H/W: 5-11 230 | FUT: Reserve OF | 6B

Bats L Age 24 — 2012 (4) HS (CA) — Pwr ++ | BAvg +++ | Spd +++ | Def ++

Year	Lev	Team	AB	R	H	HR	RBI	Avg	OB	Slg	OPS	bb%	ct%	Eye	SB	CS	x/h%	Iso	RC/G
2014	A	Beloit	464	57	105	6	38	226	299	319	618	9	80	0.51	15	9	25	93	3.21
2015	A+	Stockton	458	67	127	5	52	277	337	389	725	8	81	0.46	18	5	26	111	4.54
2016	A+	Stockton	413	48	119	8	58	288	342	395	737	8	82	0.46	8	6	21	107	4.57
2016	AAA	Nashville	30	2	8	0	1	267	313	267	579	6	90	0.67	0	0	0	0	2.85
2017	AA	Midland	533	82	172	5	56	323	363	428	791	6	86	0.46	16	5	23	105	5.21

Compact, strong OF who had best season of career, finishing 3rd in TL in BA and doubles. Focuses on hard contact with smooth, short stroke. Has strength to line balls to gaps, but has never hit more than 8 HR in season. Tough on RHP and could be leadoff hitter due to speed and eye. Mostly played CF and has the speed to track down balls in gaps.

Bradley,Bobby

3 | Cleveland | EXP MLB DEBUT: 2019 | H/W: 6-1 225 | FUT: Starting 1B | 8D

Bats L Age 21 — 2014 (3) HS (MS) — Pwr ++++ | BAvg ++ | Spd + | Def ++

Year	Lev	Team	AB	R	H	HR	RBI	Avg	OB	Slg	OPS	bb%	ct%	Eye	SB	CS	x/h%	Iso	RC/G
2014	Rk	AZL Indians	155	39	56	8	50	361	421	652	1073	9	77	0.44	3	0	45	290	9.04
2015	A	Lake County	401	62	108	27	92	269	359	529	888	12	63	0.38	3	0	43	259	7.30
2015	A+	Lynchburg	8	0	0	0	0	0	111	0	111	11	75	0.50	0	0		0	-3.61
2016	A+	Lynchburg	485	82	114	29	102	235	338	466	803	13	65	0.44	3	0	46	231	5.90
2017	AA	Akron	467	66	117	23	89	251	330	465	794	11	74	0.45	3	3	44	214	5.42

Massively-strong 1B who has hit at least 23 HR in each full season as pro. Comes at the cost of a ton of Ks, but can crush ball when contact made. Needs to improve against LHP (.177 BA) and can get overly pull-conscious. Has benefited from patient approach. Speed and defense are substandard. Limited to 1B with average arm and poor hands.

Brannen,Cole

8 | Boston | EXP MLB DEBUT: 2022 | H/W: 6-0 170 | FUT: Starting CF | 8E

Bats L Age 19 — 2017 (2) HS (GA) — Pwr ++ | BAvg ++ | Spd ++++ | Def +++

Year	Lev	Team	AB	R	H	HR	RBI	Avg	OB	Slg	OPS	bb%	ct%	Eye	SB	CS	x/h%	Iso	RC/G
2017	Rk	GCL Red Sox	134	23	31	0	7	231	372	246	618	18	72	0.81	9	1	6	15	3.48
2017	A-	Lowell	9	0	1	0	1	111	385	333	718	31	56	1.00	1	1	100	222	5.63

Speedy CF with mature approach to game. Uses short stroke and has discerning eye to draw walks and post high OBP. Bat speed lacks a bit and struck out far too often in pro debut. Lack of extra base hits was slightly concerning, though controls bat well and offers some power potential. Needs to add strength. A true CF with range.

Brigman,Bryson

46 | Seattle | EXP MLB DEBUT: 2019 | H/W: 5-11 180 | FUT: Starting 2B | 7D

Bats R Age 22 — 2016 (3) San Diego — Pwr + | BAvg ++ | Spd +++ | Def +++

Year	Lev	Team	AB	R	H	HR	RBI	Avg	OB	Slg	OPS	bb%	ct%	Eye	SB	CS	x/h%	Iso	RC/G
2016	NCAA	San Diego	191	31	71	0	22	372	420	424	844	8	90	0.84	17	7	13	52	5.95
2016	A-	Everett	265	51	69	0	19	260	359	291	650	13	84	0.95	17	12	10	30	3.95
2017	A	Clinton	463	55	109	2	36	235	302	296	598	9	84	0.59	16	8	18	60	3.07

Short, spry INF who got off to decent start, but faded down stretch. Spent more time at 2B and showed quick actions and ability to make plays. No plus tool in arsenal and has limited offensive upside. Lacks punch in short stroke, but puts bat to ball and uses above average speed well. Some hope for him to revise swing for gap power.

Brinson,Lewis

789 | Milwaukee | EXP MLB DEBUT: 2017 | H/W: 6-3 195 | FUT: Starting CF | 9C

Bats R Age 23 — 2012 (1) HS (FL) — Pwr ++++ | BAvg +++ | Spd ++++ | Def ++++

Year	Lev	Team	AB	R	H	HR	RBI	Avg	OB	Slg	OPS	bb%	ct%	Eye	SB	CS	x/h%	Iso	RC/G
2016	Rk	AZL Rangers	13	3	3	0	1	231	333	308	641	13	85	1.00	2	0	33	77	3.93
2016	AA	Frisco	304	46	72	11	40	237	277	431	708	5	79	0.27	11	4	43	194	4.08
2016	AAA	Col Springs	89	14	34	4	20	382	396	618	1014	2	76	0.10	4	2	38	236	7.78
2017	AAA	Col Springs	299	66	99	13	48	331	396	562	958	10	79	0.52	11	5	39	231	7.45
2017	MLB	Milwaukee	47	2	5	2	3	106	222	277	499	13	64	0.41	1	0	60	170	1.20

Athletic, all-around solid RHH OF struggled in MLB debut. Has cleaned up swing mechanics tremendously since earlier in pro career w/o compromising bat speed or power. Bat path smooth to the contact zone. Power in swing trajectory and frame, mostly to the pull side and CF. Potential perennial 20/20 skills. Rangy defender, will stick in CF.

Brito,Daniel

4 | Philadelphia | EXP MLB DEBUT: 2021 | H/W: 6-1 155 | FUT: Starting 2B | 8D

Bats L Age 20 — 2014 FA (VZ) — Pwr ++ | BAvg +++ | 4.26 Spd +++ | Def +++

Year	Lev	Team	AB	R	H	HR	RBI	Avg	OB	Slg	OPS	bb%	ct%	Eye	SB	CS	x/h%	Iso	RC/G
2016	Rk	GCL Phillies	190	35	54	2	25	284	355	421	777	10	86	0.78	7	2	31	137	5.35
2017	A	Lakewood	447	54	107	6	32	239	292	318	609	7	79	0.35	12	9	21	78	2.92

Hit ground running in April, but production tailed off noticeably as aggressive approach got the best of him. Can sting a FB with nice barrel control, and has a live body, but got himself out against soft stuff. Some added strength would be a welcome addition. Athletic defender with great lateral first step; enough arm to turn DP.

Brito,Ronny

46 | Los Angeles (N) | EXP MLB DEBUT: 2021 | H/W: 6-0 165 | FUT: Starting SS | 8E

Bats B Age 19 — 2015 FA (DR) — Pwr ++ | BAvg ++ | Spd ++++ | Def ++++

Year	Lev	Team	AB	R	H	HR	RBI	Avg	OB	Slg	OPS	bb%	ct%	Eye	SB	CS	x/h%	Iso	RC/G
2017	Rk	AZL Dodgers	54	10	13	2	12	241	281	444	725	5	65	0.16	0	0	54	204	4.66
2017	Rk	Ogden	63	12	15	1	7	238	262	349	611	3	65	0.09	6	0	27	111	2.87

Switch-hitting shortstop is a plus-plus defender with excellent range, good hands, and a strong arm. At the plate there is lots of work to do. Average bat speed, below-average power, and poor pitch recognition raise doubts about whether he will ever hit, though he could improve as he matures and fills out his skinny frame.

Brito,Socrates

789 | Arizona | EXP MLB DEBUT: 2016 | H/W: 6-2 205 | FUT: Starting OF | 7B

Bats L Age 25 — 2010 FA (DR) — Pwr ++ | BAvg +++ | Spd +++ | Def ++++

Year	Lev	Team	AB	R	H	HR	RBI	Avg	OB	Slg	OPS	bb%	ct%	Eye	SB	CS	x/h%	Iso	RC/G
2016	Rk	AZL Dbacks	7	0	1	0	2	143	143	143	286	0	57	0.00	0	0	0	0	-2.36
2016	A+	Visalia	9	1	1	1	2	111	111	444	556	0	78	0.00	0	0	100	333	1.54
2016	AAA	Reno	303	46	89	6	39	294	323	439	762	4	80	0.22	7	6	27	145	4.72
2016	MLB	Arizona	95	10	17	4	12	179	196	358	554	2	76	0.09	2	0	47	179	1.88
2017	AAA	Reno	292	43	85	5	44	291	341	449	789	7	78	0.34	6	1	33	158	5.31

Athletic, injury prone LH OF missed two months to start '17 with dislocated finger. Continues to refine approach, taking more pitches and better working counts. Raw athleticism still hasn't translated to game action. Above-average power and speed hasn't appeared in stat line. Has 15-20 HR potential at projection. Plus defensively in CF.

Brodey,Quinn

78 | New York (N) | EXP MLB DEBUT: 2020 | H/W: 6-1 200 | FUT: Starting OF | 7E

Bats L Age 22
2017 (3) Stanford
Pwr +++
BAvg +++
Spd ++
Def +++

Year	Lev	Team	AB	R	H	HR	RBI	Avg	OB	Slg	OPS	bb%	ct%	Eye	SB	CS	x/h%	Iso	RC/G
2017	A-	Columbia	35	4	8	1	7	229	308	400	708	10	89	1.00	0	0	38	171	4.53
2017	A	Brooklyn	210	20	54	2	30	257	304	348	651	6	77	0.29	10	3	24	90	3.46

Offensively skilled LH OF stood out in Cape Cod league in 2016 but struggled in college before draft. Contact swing with solid pull-side power potential. Struggled with velocity and expanding zone during pro debut. Stocky lower half provides good base for HR potential. Swing trajectory conducive to power improvement. Arm limits to LF.

Brujan,Vidal

4 | Tampa Bay | EXP MLB DEBUT: 2021 | H/W: 5-9 155 | FUT: Starting 2B | 7D

Bats B Age 20
2014 FA (DR)
Pwr +
BAvg +++
Spd ++++
Def +++

Year	Lev	Team	AB	R	H	HR	RBI	Avg	OB	Slg	OPS	bb%	ct%	Eye	SB	CS	x/h%	Iso	RC/G
2016	Rk	GCL Rays	202	41	57	1	8	282	329	406	735	6	93	0.93	8	5	32	124	4.80
2016	A-	Hudson Valley	8	1	0	0	0	0	111	0	111	11	88	1.00	2	0		0	-2.31
2017	A-	Hudson Valley	260	51	74	3	20	285	367	415	783	12	86	0.94	16	8	31	131	5.51

Short-framed INF who profiles as leadoff hitter thanks to willingness to work counts. Has been very tough out with short, level swing path and discerning eye. Hits for good BA from both sides of plate. Has yet to see full season action and lacks any semblance of power projection. Runs very well and could play CF. Has good quickness and footwork.

Brusa,Gio

7 | San Francisco | EXP MLB DEBUT: 2019 | H/W: 6-3 235 | FUT: Starting OF | 7E

Bats B Age 24
2016 (6) Pacific
Pwr ++++
BAvg ++
Spd ++
Def ++

Year	Lev	Team	AB	R	H	HR	RBI	Avg	OB	Slg	OPS	bb%	ct%	Eye	SB	CS	x/h%	Iso	RC/G
2016	NCAA	Pacific	202	38	68	14	46	337	412	614	1026	11	80	0.63	1	2	41	277	8.24
2016	A-	Salem-Keizer	220	36	58	10	42	264	299	495	794	5	69	0.16	1	1	48	232	5.42
2017	A+	San Jose	426	58	101	17	55	237	292	432	724	7	71	0.27	1	2	47	195	4.43

Muscular OF who can hit for mammoth power, but may not have the feel for hitting to tap into it consistently. Had solid 1st full year in minors in power only. Chases pitches out of zone and has trouble reading spin. Big swing and miss profile. Below average runner and is limited to LF with fringy range and average arm.

Burger,Jake

5 | Chicago (A) | EXP MLB DEBUT: 2019 | H/W: 6-2 210 | FUT: Starting 3B | 8C

Bats R Age 21
2017 (1) Missouri St
Pwr ++++
BAvg +++
Spd ++
Def +++

Year	Lev	Team	AB	R	H	HR	RBI	Avg	OB	Slg	OPS	bb%	ct%	Eye	SB	CS	x/h%	Iso	RC/G
2017	NCAA	Missouri State	247	69	81	22	65	328	428	648	1075	15	85	1.13	3	1	43	320	8.80
2017	Rk	AZL White Sox	13	4	2	1	2	154	214	462	676	7	85	0.50	0	0	100	308	3.70
2017	A	Kannapolis	181	21	49	4	27	271	320	409	728	7	85	0.46	0	1	31	138	4.47

Physically strong, bashed his way to 11th overall pick in 2017 by employing unorthodox approach. Patient hitter, will hit for average and slug for power at projection. His solid bat speed and swing plane could result in plus-plus power long term. Decent athlete despite bulky physique. Soft hands, quick reactions and plus arm.

Burks,Charcer

789 | Chicago (N) | EXP MLB DEBUT: 2018 | H/W: 6-0 170 | FUT: Reserve OF | 7D

Bats R Age 23
2013 (9) HS (TX)
Pwr ++
BAvg ++
Spd ++++
Def ++++

Year	Lev	Team	AB	R	H	HR	RBI	Avg	OB	Slg	OPS	bb%	ct%	Eye	SB	CS	x/h%	Iso	RC/G
2014	Rk	AZL Cubs	65	14	20	1	10	308	338	446	784	4	69	0.15	9	1	30	138	5.34
2014	A-	Boise	128	25	40	0	20	313	409	391	800	14	76	0.68	4	3	20	78	5.91
2015	A	South Bend	435	63	112	3	44	257	335	347	683	10	81	0.61	28	9	26	90	4.15
2016	A+	Myrtle Beach	445	71	110	11	43	247	344	407	751	13	74	0.57	23	7	40	160	5.10
2017	AA	Tennessee	456	67	123	10	40	270	366	395	760	13	77	0.64	16	12	28	125	5.18

Plus runner who covers tons of ground and should stick in CF. Solid offensive approach offers some fantasy appeal and continues to make progress. Contact can be an issue as he searches for pitches he can drive, but he also has shown he can take walks and could be a useful 4th OF.

Cabrera,Oswaldo

456 | New York (A) | EXP MLB DEBUT: 2021 | H/W: 5-10 145 | FUT: Starting SS | 7E

Bats R Age 19
2015 FA (VZ)
Pwr +
BAvg +++
Spd ++
Def ++

Year	Lev	Team	AB	R	H	HR	RBI	Avg	OB	Slg	OPS	bb%	ct%	Eye	SB	CS	x/h%	Iso	RC/G
2016	Rk	GCL Yankees	33	9	15	2	6	455	471	818	1289	3	94	0.50	1	1	53	364	10.25
2017	A-	Staten Island	90	12	26	0	16	289	319	344	664	4	88	0.36	2	1	15	56	3.67
2017	A	Charleston (Sc)	318	37	77	4	37	242	299	314	614	8	86	0.57	6	0	19	72	3.18

Small, lean INF with advanced instincts. Struggled in A- and sent to short-season before returning. Has feel for strike zone and can hit for BA with solid OBP. Limited strength and bat speed hinder power development. Needs to drive gaps to have bat value. Versatile defender, but not master of any INF spot. Range and arm a bit short for SS.

Calhoun,Willie

47 | Texas | EXP MLB DEBUT: 2017 | H/W: 5-8 187 | FUT: Starting OF | 8B

Bats L Age 23
2015 (4) Yavapai JC
Pwr ++++
BAvg +++
Spd ++
Def ++

Year	Lev	Team	AB	R	H	HR	RBI	Avg	OB	Slg	OPS	bb%	ct%	Eye	SB	CS	x/h%	Iso	RC/G
2015	A+	Rancho Cuca	73	11	24	3	14	329	388	548	935	9	82	0.54	0	0	42	219	7.04
2016	AA	Tulsa	503	75	128	27	88	254	316	469	785	8	87	0.69	0	0	41	215	5.10
2017	AAA	Round Rock	113	16	35	8	26	310	345	566	911	5	89	0.50	1	0	34	257	6.23
2017	AAA	Oklahoma City	373	64	111	23	67	298	359	574	933	9	87	0.73	3	2	47	276	6.86
2017	MLB	Texas	34	3	9	1	4	265	306	353	658	6	79	0.29	0	0	11	88	3.34

Short OF who finished 5th in minors in HR, yet makes very easy contact. Consistent run producer with feel for bat and plate coverage. Differentiates between balls and strikes and has balanced stroke to hit behind in count. Plus pop is best tool. Not very quick and seems poised to move to LF full time. Only an average athlete with limited speed.

Call,Alex

789 | Chicago (A) | EXP MLB DEBUT: 2019 | H/W: 6-0 188 | FUT: Starting OF | 7E

Bats R Age 23
2016 (3) Ball St
Pwr +++
BAvg +++
Spd +++
Def ++

Year	Lev	Team	AB	R	H	HR	RBI	Avg	OB	Slg	OPS	bb%	ct%	Eye	SB	CS	x/h%	Iso	RC/G
2016	Rk	Great Falls	107	19	33	3	17	308	413	439	852	15	83	1.06	4	4	21	131	6.40
2016	A	Kannapolis	185	23	57	3	18	308	360	449	809	8	78	0.38	10	2	35	141	5.55
2017	Rk	AZL White Sox	51	8	3	0	6	59	172	78	251	12	90	1.40	1	0	33	20	-0.40
2017	A	Kannapolis	145	24	36	3	22	248	323	386	709	10	77	0.48	2	2	36	138	4.38
2017	A+	Winston-Salem	41	2	10	0	5	244	295	366	661	7	73	0.27	2	1	40	122	3.79

Limited to 61 games due to chest strain in '17. Fundamentally sound, maxed out tool shed. Grinder, works counts and pitchers to maximize abilities. Line drive hitter with average power struggled making consistent hard contact between levels. Heady base runner, maximizing average foot speed to be a small threat on bases. Arm can play, not a CF.

Cameron,Daz

8 | Detroit | EXP MLB DEBUT: 2020 | H/W: 6-2 185 | FUT: Starting OF | 8D

Bats R Age 21
2015 (S-1) HS (GA)
Pwr +++
BAvg +++
Spd +++
Def +++

Year	Lev	Team	AB	R	H	HR	RBI	Avg	OB	Slg	OPS	bb%	ct%	Eye	SB	CS	x/h%	Iso	RC/G
2015	Rk	GCL Astros	70	13	15	0	6	214	304	243	547	11	76	0.53	12	4	13	29	2.31
2016	A-	Tri City	79	13	22	2	14	278	329	418	747	7	67	0.23	8	2	27	139	4.92
2016	A	Quad Cities	77	5	11	0	6	143	224	221	444	9	57	0.24	4	3	36	78	0.58
2017	A	West Michigan	8	1	2	0	1	250	455	250	705	27	50	0.75	0	1	0	0	5.68
2017	A	Quad Cities	446	79	121	14	73	271	338	466	804	9	76	0.42	32	12	42	195	5.60

Athletic OF who rebounded in big way from disastrous '16. Becoming more complete player with keen approach and ability to make hard contact. Using solid-average speed well on base and in CF. Swings aggressively at hittable balls and has been menace to LHH. Offers average power and BA potential. Not a dynamic player, but does everything well.

Campos,Alexander

6 | Oakland | EXP MLB DEBUT: 2022 | H/W: 6-0 178 | FUT: Starting SS | 8E

Bats R Age 18
2016 FA (VZ)
Pwr ++
BAvg +++
Spd +++
Def +++

Year	Lev	Team	AB	R	H	HR	RBI	Avg	OB	Slg	OPS	bb%	ct%	Eye	SB	CS	x/h%	Iso	RC/G
2017		*Did not play in US*																	

Versatile, athletic INF who has yet to make U.S. debut. Can be full-time SS due to quick, smooth actions and terrific arm. Has feel for contact with some gap power, but has long ways to go to realize offensive potential. Uses disciplined eye to get on base where he can use his plus speed for SB.

Campusano,Luis

2 | San Diego | EXP MLB DEBUT: 2021 | H/W: 6-0 195 | FUT: Starting C | 8D

Bats R Age 19
2017 (2) HS (GA)
Pwr +++
BAvg +++
Spd +
Def +++

Year	Lev	Team	AB	R	H	HR	RBI	Avg	OB	Slg	OPS	bb%	ct%	Eye	SB	CS	x/h%	Iso	RC/G
2017	Rk	AZL Padres 2	13	1	2	0	1	154	154	154	308	0	92	0.00	0	0	0	0	-0.30
2017	Rk	AZL Padres	121	7	34	4	24	281	360	413	774	11	80	0.63	0	2	24	132	5.13

Young CA drafted in 2nd round with chance to hit and stick behind the plate. Stocky, strong build produces good bat speed and slight uppercut plane could allow him to hit for some HR power. Will need to smooth out load and improve ability to stay back on breaking balls, but shows decent barrel control. Has plus arm and decent blocking skills.

Cancel,Gabriel — 4 — Kansas City

EXP MLB DEBUT: 2020 | H/W: 6-1 185 | FUT: Starting 2B | **7C**

Bats R Age 21
2015 (7) HS (PR)

- Pwr +++
- BAvg +++
- Spd ++
- Def ++

Year	Lev	Team	AB	R	H	HR	RBI	Avg	OB	Slg	OPS	bb%	ct%	Eye	SB	CS	x/h%	Iso	RC/G
2016	Rk	Burlington	172	28	50	5	26	291	348	494	842	8	81	0.47	1	2	48	203	5.95
2017	A	Lexington	401	70	111	14	49	277	316	466	782	5	75	0.23	9	8	41	190	5.07

Offensive-minded 2B who exhibited consistent pop in first full year as pro. Destroyed LHP with natural strength and bat speed. Has some power upside, but could hit for decent BA with slight mechanical adjustments. K rate too high and should see more pitches. Lacks ideal foot speed and quickness for 2B. Hands are soft and makes routine plays.

Capel,Conner — 789 — Cleveland

EXP MLB DEBUT: 2020 | H/W: 6-1 185 | FUT: Starting OF | **7C**

Bats L Age 20
2016 (5) HS (TX)

- Pwr +++
- BAvg ++
- Spd +++
- Def +++

Year	Lev	Team	AB	R	H	HR	RBI	Avg	OB	Slg	OPS	bb%	ct%	Eye	SB	CS	x/h%	Iso	RC/G
2016	Rk	AZL Indians	138	22	29	0	13	210	268	290	558	7	86	0.55	10	3	28	80	2.66
2017	A	Lake County	439	73	108	22	61	246	313	478	792	9	75	0.40	15	10	47	232	5.31

Young, improving OF who finished 3rd in MWL in HR in first full season. Got off to slow start, but finished strong. Power output raised eyebrows, though has natural loft and leverage in strong stroke. Gets behind in count often and can flail against breaking balls. Has athletic actions and quickness which help him in RF. Owns plus arm.

Caratini,Victor — 23 — Chicago (N)

EXP MLB DEBUT: 2017 | H/W: 6-1 215 | FUT: Starting C | **7C**

Bats B Age 24
2013 (2) Miami-Dade JC

- Pwr +++
- BAvg +++
- Spd +
- Def ++

Year	Lev	Team	AB	R	H	HR	RBI	Avg	OB	Slg	OPS	bb%	ct%	Eye	SB	CS	x/h%	Iso	RC/G
2014	A	Kane County	53	7	14	0	13	264	316	377	693	7	81	0.40	0	0	36	113	4.19
2015	A+	Myrtle Beach	393	39	101	4	53	257	339	372	711	11	81	0.65	0	0	36	115	4.55
2016	AA	Tennessee	412	57	120	6	47	291	373	405	779	12	81	0.68	2	1	28	114	5.38
2017	AAA	Iowa	292	50	100	10	61	342	398	558	956	8	84	0.56	1	0	40	216	7.30
2017	MLB	Chi Cubs	59	6	15	1	2	254	302	356	658	6	78	0.31	0	0	27	102	3.50

Offensive-minded backstop put up monster numbers at Triple-A Iowa and then held his own in his MLB debut. Switch-hitter uses a smooth stroke to shoot balls to all fields and posted a career best 11 HR with more power to come. Below-average defender will have to work hard to stick behind the dish.

Carlson,Dylan — 789 — St. Louis

EXP MLB DEBUT: 2021 | H/W: 6-3 195 | FUT: Starting OF | **8D**

Bats B Age 19
2016 (1) HS (CA)

- Pwr +++
- BAvg +++
- Spd ++
- Def ++

Year	Lev	Team	AB	R	H	HR	RBI	Avg	OB	Slg	OPS	bb%	ct%	Eye	SB	CS	x/h%	Iso	RC/G
2016	Rk	GCL Cardinals	183	30	46	3	22	251	312	404	716	8	72	0.31	4	2	41	153	4.51
2017	A	Peoria	383	63	92	7	42	240	331	347	678	12	70	0.45	6	6	28	107	4.06

2016 1st rounder has yet to find his footing as a pro, but was one of the youngest players in the MWL. Strong, physically mature player lacks the bat speed to develop plus power, but should hit 20+ HR at maturity. Switch-hitter has good approach at the plate and is a hard worker with solid across-the-board tools.

Carpio,Luis — 46 — New York (N)

EXP MLB DEBUT: 2020 | H/W: 5-11 190 | FUT: Starting MIF | **7D**

Bats R Age 20
2013 FA (VZ)

- Pwr +
- BAvg +++
- Spd +++
- Def ++++

Year	Lev	Team	AB	R	H	HR	RBI	Avg	OB	Slg	OPS	bb%	ct%	Eye	SB	CS	x/h%	Iso	RC/G
2015	Rk	Kingsport	181	31	55	0	22	304	364	359	723	9	81	0.50	9	7	18	55	4.54
2016	Rk	GCL Mets	31	3	9	0	2	290	313	387	700	3	65	0.09	0	0	22	97	4.37
2016	A-	Brooklyn	43	4	6	0	1	140	275	186	461	16	77	0.80	0	0	33	47	1.39
2017	A	Columbia	474	53	110	3	36	232	309	302	611	10	80	0.56	17	5	22	70	3.19

Hard-working, MIF prospect struggled in first full season back from shoulder surgery. Pre-surgery explosiveness missing from swing. A contact-oriented RH hitter, just couldn't get the bat head through the zone quick enough to produce hard contact. Not HR hitter. Rangy defender.

Castro,Willi — 6 — Cleveland

EXP MLB DEBUT: 2020 | H/W: 6-1 165 | FUT: Starting SS | **7B**

Bats B Age 20
2013 FA (DR)

- Pwr ++
- BAvg +++
- Spd +++
- Def +++

Year	Lev	Team	AB	R	H	HR	RBI	Avg	OB	Slg	OPS	bb%	ct%	Eye	SB	CS	x/h%	Iso	RC/G
2014	Rk	AZL Indians	155	31	37	2	11	239	267	348	615	4	79	0.18	9	4	27	110	2.90
2015	A-	Mahoning Val	273	34	72	1	25	264	290	330	619	4	89	0.32	20	7	18	66	3.15
2016	A	Lake County	518	68	134	7	49	259	285	371	656	4	81	0.20	16	11	27	112	3.41
2016	A+	Lynchburg	9	0	2	0	0	222	222	222	444	0	78	0.00	0	1	0	0	0.46
2017	A+	Lynchburg	469	69	136	11	58	290	330	424	754	6	81	0.31	19	9	28	134	4.67

Well-rounded SS who continues to evolve in all aspects of game. Set high in HR while walking more. Has stolen at least 16 bases each season as pro and is threat to run when on base. Mostly doubles power and should grow into more HR pop. Has strength and quickness in hands which serve him well at SS. Commits lot of errors, but has tantalizing tools.

Cave,Jake — 789 — New York (A)

EXP MLB DEBUT: 2018 | H/W: 6-0 200 | FUT: Reserve OF | **6B**

Bats L Age 25
2011 (6) HS (VA)

- Pwr +++
- BAvg +++
- Spd ++
- Def +++

Year	Lev	Team	AB	R	H	HR	RBI	Avg	OB	Slg	OPS	bb%	ct%	Eye	SB	CS	x/h%	Iso	RC/G
2015	AAA	Scranton/WB	24	4	11	0	2	458	519	667	1185	11	67	0.38	0	0	36	208	12.13
2016	AA	Trenton	104	12	30	3	17	288	351	510	860	9	73	0.36	3	4	47	221	6.48
2016	AAA	Scranton/WB	322	47	84	5	38	261	316	401	717	7	76	0.33	3	3	35	140	4.41
2017	AA	Trenton	128	19	34	5	18	266	319	516	834	7	74	0.30	1	0	59	250	5.97
2017	AAA	Scranton/WB	278	47	90	15	38	324	365	554	919	6	71	0.22	1	3	34	230	7.03

Consistent OF who set easy high in HR. Was better in AAA upon promotion and showed knack for using whole field. Can swing aggressively early in count and may need to be more patient. Speed is fringy at best, but can play all OF spots well. No one tool stands out, though none are glaring weakness. Fits 4th OF profile.

Cecchini,Gavin — 46 — New York (N)

EXP MLB DEBUT: 2016 | H/W: 6-2 196 | FUT: Utility player | **6B**

Bats R Age 24
2012 (1) HS (LA)

- Pwr ++
- BAvg +++
- Spd +++
- Def +++

Year	Lev	Team	AB	R	H	HR	RBI	Avg	OB	Slg	OPS	bb%	ct%	Eye	SB	CS	x/h%	Iso	RC/G
2015	AA	Binghamton	439	64	139	7	51	317	376	442	818	9	87	0.76	3	4	27	125	5.70
2016	AAA	Las Vegas	446	71	145	8	55	325	391	448	839	10	88	0.87	4	1	26	123	5.98
2016	MLB	NY Mets	6	2	2	0	2	333	333	667	1000	0	67	0.00	0	0	100	333	9.06
2017	AAA	Las Vegas	453	68	121	6	39	267	327	380	706	8	87	0.66	5	4	30	113	4.37
2017	MLB	NY Mets	77	4	16	1	7	208	247	273	520	5	75	0.21	0	1	19	65	1.60

Solid MIF, but misses tool to set him apart from pack. Advanced hitter, works pitchers like veteran hitter. Contact bat that doesn't produce enough hard contact. Cheats against higher velocity, making him susceptible to soft stuff. Skinnier frame, all power generated by leverage in swing. Capped at 10 HR potential. Smart base runner.

Cedrola,Lorenzo — 89 — Boston

EXP MLB DEBUT: 2021 | H/W: 5-11 170 | FUT: Starting OF | **7C**

Bats R Age 20
2015 FA (VZ)

- Pwr ++
- BAvg +++
- Spd ++++
- Def +++

Year	Lev	Team	AB	R	H	HR	RBI	Avg	OB	Slg	OPS	bb%	ct%	Eye	SB	CS	x/h%	Iso	RC/G
2016	Rk	GCL Red Sox	214	33	62	2	21	290	324	393	717	5	87	0.39	9	4	27	103	4.30
2017	A	Greenville	354	47	101	4	34	285	307	387	694	3	86	0.23	19	7	25	102	3.88

Short, athletic OF with extreme contact approach. Doesn't work counts and needs to get on base more to use plus speed. Hit for BA, especially against LHP, in first full season, though physically limited to hit HR. Has slashing bat to hit line drives and offers BA potential. Spent most of time in CF and can play RF with plus range and avg arm.

Celestino,Gilberto — 789 — Houston

EXP MLB DEBUT: 2020 | H/W: 6-0 170 | FUT: Starting OF | **8E**

Bats R Age 19
2015 FA (DR)

- Pwr ++
- BAvg +++
- Spd +++
- Def +++

Year	Lev	Team	AB	R	H	HR	RBI	Avg	OB	Slg	OPS	bb%	ct%	Eye	SB	CS	x/h%	Iso	RC/G
2016	Rk	GCL Astros	55	7	11	0	2	200	302	291	592	13	71	0.50	6	1	36	91	3.01
2017	Rk	Greeneville	235	38	63	4	24	268	331	379	709	9	75	0.37	10	2	25	111	4.31

Makes tons of contact and has advanced feel for strike zone; knows how to draw walks and get on base; picks spots well and will steal some bases at the next level. Lean, wiry frame produces bat speed and athleticism required for plus range in CF with quality arm for RF. If and when the power comes, could be a name worth watching.

Cespedes,Ricardo — 789 — Miami

EXP MLB DEBUT: 2021 | H/W: 6-1 205 | FUT: Reserve OF | **7D**

Bats L Age 20
2013 FA (DR)

- Pwr ++
- BAvg ++
- Spd +++
- Def +++

Year	Lev	Team	AB	R	H	HR	RBI	Avg	OB	Slg	OPS	bb%	ct%	Eye	SB	CS	x/h%	Iso	RC/G
2016	Rk	Kingsport	227	30	73	1	16	322	347	374	722	4	84	0.25	7	7	11	53	4.19
2017	Rk	GCL Mets	15	0	3	0	0	200	200	200	400	0	80	0.00	0	0	0	0	0.01
2017	A-	Brooklyn	80	3	18	1	12	225	262	263	524	5	80	0.25	1	1	6	38	1.72
2017	A-	Batavia	79	4	15	0	4	190	200	215	415	1	73	0.05	0	1	13	25	0.07
2017	A	Columbia	12	1	5	0	3	417	417	500	917	0	75	0.00	0	0	20	83	6.55

Dominican OF was traded from the Mets as part of the A.J. Ramos deal in 2017. Cespedes has above-average tools, but none that profile as plus. Difficulties with pitch recognition and an aggressive approach have resulted in poor contact, but he does have a quick left-handed bat and should develop more power as he matures.

Chang,Yu-Cheng | 6 | Cleveland

EXP MLB DEBUT: 2018 | H/W: 6-1 175 | FUT: Starting SS | 7B

Bats R Age 22
2013 FA (TW)
Pwr ++++
BAvg ++
Spd +++
Def ++

Year	Lev	Team	AB	R	H	HR	RBI	Avg	OB	Slg	OPS	bb%	ct%	Eye	SB	CS	x/h%	Iso	RC/G
2014	Rk	AZL Indians	159	39	55	6	25	346	412	566	978	10	82	0.64	6	1	35	220	7.68
2015	A	Lake County	393	52	91	9	52	232	281	361	642	6	74	0.26	5	6	32	130	3.29
2016	A+	Lynchburg	417	78	108	13	70	259	331	463	794	10	74	0.41	11	3	47	204	5.55
2017	AA	Akron	440	72	97	24	66	220	303	461	764	11	70	0.39	11	4	55	241	5.11

Improving INF who revised swing for more power. Also led to higher Ks (3rd in EL), but set easy career high in HR while getting on base consistently. Owns plus bat speed with slight uppercut. Only a .249 BA for career and has little feel for hitting spin. Exhibits above average speed and strong arm. Defense should get better with more reps.

Chatham,C.J. | 6 | Boston

EXP MLB DEBUT: 2019 | H/W: 6-4 185 | FUT: Starting SS | 7C

Bats R Age 23
2016 (2) Florida Atlantic
Pwr +++
BAvg ++
Spd +++
Def +++

Year	Lev	Team	AB	R	H	HR	RBI	Avg	OB	Slg	OPS	bb%	ct%	Eye	SB	CS	x/h%	Iso	RC/G
2016	NCAA	Florida Atlantic	249	48	89	8	50	357	412	554	966	8	86	0.64	2	1	33	197	7.36
2016	Rk	GCL Red Sox	24	2	4	1	2	167	167	375	542	0	71	0.00	0	0	75	208	1.68
2016	A-	Lowell	108	19	28	4	19	259	310	426	736	7	81	0.40	0	1	32	167	4.46
2017	Rk	GCL Red Sox	16	5	5	1	3	313	389	500	889	11	94	2.00	0	0	20	188	6.43
2017	A	Greenville	3	0	1	0	2	333	333	333	667	0	100		0	1	0	0	3.67

Tall, lanky SS who missed most of season due to lingering hamstring issues. Has fundamental, instinctual approach, plus body control and positioning and a solid arm. Should stick at SS despite height. Might hit for BA with above average contact and average pull power. Not great upside, but has consistent skills and production.

Chavis,Michael | 5 | Boston

EXP MLB DEBUT: 2018 | H/W: 5-10 210 | FUT: Starting 3B | 7B

Bats R Age 22
2014 (1) HS (GA)
Pwr ++++
BAvg +++
Spd ++
Def ++

Year	Lev	Team	AB	R	H	HR	RBI	Avg	OB	Slg	OPS	bb%	ct%	Eye	SB	CS	x/h%	Iso	RC/G
2015	A	Greenville	435	56	97	16	58	223	272	405	676	6	67	0.20	8	5	47	182	3.83
2016	A	Greenville	279	30	68	8	35	244	299	391	690	7	73	0.30	3	1	32	147	3.95
2016	A+	Salem	25	5	4	0	1	160	222	160	382	7	72	0.29	1	0	0	0	-0.25
2017	A+	Salem	223	50	71	17	55	318	372	641	1013	8	74	0.33	1	0	51	323	8.13
2017	AA	Portland	248	39	62	14	39	250	306	492	798	7	77	0.36	1	0	52	242	5.24

Compact, strong INF who was promoted to AA in June and finished 5th in minors in HR. Lot of power to all fields, though holes in swing can be exploited. BA potential in question due to swing path; struggles against breakers. Improving defender at 3B, but saw action at 1B in AFL. Owns average arm strength.

Chisholm,Jasardo | 6 | Arizona

EXP MLB DEBUT: 2021 | H/W: 5-11 165 | FUT: Starting SS | 8C

Bats L Age 20
2015 FA (BM)
Pwr +++
BAvg +++
Spd +++
Def +++

Year	Lev	Team	AB	R	H	HR	RBI	Avg	OB	Slg	OPS	bb%	ct%	Eye	SB	CS	x/h%	Iso	RC/G
2016	Rk	Missoula	249	42	70	9	37	281	332	446	778	7	71	0.26	13	4	31	165	5.16
2017	A	Kane County	109	14	27	1	12	248	311	358	669	8	64	0.26	3	0	30	110	4.04

Athletic, thin prospect missed much of 2017 with buckle-handle tear in his meniscus. Quick hands and wrists guide hit tool, but needs to refine approach. Much more powerful than frame suggests; generates significant drive from lower half and trajectory of swing. 20-HR potential. A solid defender with average speed.

Ciuffo,Nick | 2 | Tampa Bay

EXP MLB DEBUT: 2018 | H/W: 6-1 205 | FUT: Reserve C | 6B

Bats L Age 23
2013 (1) HS (SC)
Pwr ++
BAvg ++
Spd ++
Def ++++

Year	Lev	Team	AB	R	H	HR	RBI	Avg	OB	Slg	OPS	bb%	ct%	Eye	SB	CS	x/h%	Iso	RC/G
2014	Rk	Princeton	192	25	43	4	20	224	287	333	620	8	77	0.38	2	1	28	109	3.08
2015	A	Bowling Green	356	30	92	1	32	258	273	326	599	2	85	0.13	2	3	24	67	2.71
2016	Rk	GCL Rays	15	1	1	0	0	67	176	67	243	12	87	1.00	0	0	0	0	-0.84
2016	A+	Charlotte	229	16	60	0	15	262	290	297	587	4	80	0.20	2	3	13	35	2.54
2017	AA	Montgomery	371	42	91	7	42	245	322	385	707	10	74	0.44	2	0	41	140	4.40

Advanced backstop who set career-high in HR while increasing walk rate. Far from polished hitter as he strikes out a lot and struggles with LHP. Has more doubles pop than HR and has hitch in swing that limits upside. Shows off above average arm strength with quick release and is adept at blocking and receiving. Needs to hit to play every day.

Clement,Ernie | 46 | Cleveland

EXP MLB DEBUT: 2020 | H/W: 6-0 170 | FUT: Utility player | 6B

Bats R Age 22
2017 (4) Virginia
Pwr +
BAvg +++
Spd +++
Def ++

Year	Lev	Team	AB	R	H	HR	RBI	Avg	OB	Slg	OPS	bb%	ct%	Eye	SB	CS	x/h%	Iso	RC/G
2017	NCAA	Virginia	254	56	80	2	34	315	348	366	714	5	97	1.86	14	2	10	51	4.46
2017	A-	Mahoning Val	175	32	49	0	13	280	304	343	647	3	93	0.50	6	2	20	63	3.59

Extreme contact hitter who is tough out and controls bat as well as any in organization. Has little thunder in bat, though puts ball in play and has speed to keep defense honest. Doesn't walk much as he covers plate well. Has lean frame and little strength, but owns average arm that works at SS or 2B. Probable 2B long-term due to hands and limited range.

Collins,Gavin | 5 | Cleveland

EXP MLB DEBUT: 2020 | H/W: 5-11 205 | FUT: Starting 3B | 7D

Bats R Age 22
2016 (13) Mississippi St
Pwr +++
BAvg +++
Spd ++
Def ++

Year	Lev	Team	AB	R	H	HR	RBI	Avg	OB	Slg	OPS	bb%	ct%	Eye	SB	CS	x/h%	Iso	RC/G
2016	NCAA	Mississippi St	215	43	65	10	39	302	388	516	904	12	85	0.91	0	0	38	214	6.80
2016	A-	Mahoning Val	173	19	45	0	19	260	344	318	662	11	84	0.79	0	0	20	58	4.01
2017	A	Lake County	141	23	38	8	19	270	335	489	825	9	79	0.47	0	0	37	220	5.60
2017	A+	Lynchburg	142	18	39	4	35	275	335	472	807	8	68	0.29	1	1	51	197	5.90

Short, fundamental INF who split season between two levels and was equally good at both. Lacks a frontline tool in repertoire, but puts ball in play and has strength for average power. There are concerns about injury history and speed isn't part of his game. Has the arm to stick at 3B, though he lacks first-step quickness and range.

Collins,Zack | 2 | Chicago (A)

EXP MLB DEBUT: 2019 | H/W: 6-3 220 | FUT: Starting C | 8C

Bats L Age 23
2016 (1) Miami
Pwr +++
BAvg +++
Spd ++
Def ++

Year	Lev	Team	AB	R	H	HR	RBI	Avg	OB	Slg	OPS	bb%	ct%	Eye	SB	CS	x/h%	Iso	RC/G
2016	NCAA	Miami	190	54	69	16	59	363	549	668	1217	29	72	1.47	1	3	38	305	12.25
2016	Rk	AZL White Sox	11	1	1	0	0	91	91	91	182	0	36	0.00	0	0	0	0	-4.52
2016	A+	Winston-Salem	120	24	31	6	18	258	418	467	885	22	68	0.85	0	0	42	208	7.38
2017	A+	Winston-Salem	341	63	76	17	48	223	365	443	807	18	65	0.64	0	2	50	220	6.17
2017	AA	Birmingham	34	7	8	2	5	235	422	471	893	24	68	1.00	0	0	50	235	7.50

Was expected to fly through development, but struggled immensely after changing swing plane to maximize power potential. K-rate skyrocketed. Still employs advanced approach, taking pitches and working counts. A bat-first catcher, has improved somewhat behind the plate. A below-average runner.

Contreras,Mc Gregory | 79 | Toronto

EXP MLB DEBUT: 2022 | H/W: 6-1 170 | FUT: Starting OF | 7E

Bats R Age 19
2015 FA (VZ)
Pwr ++
BAvg +++
Spd +++
Def ++

Year	Lev	Team	AB	R	H	HR	RBI	Avg	OB	Slg	OPS	bb%	ct%	Eye	SB	CS	x/h%	Iso	RC/G
2017	Rk	Bluefield	190	36	53	5	33	279	322	421	743	6	71	0.22	4	3	28	142	4.66

Sleeper prospect with very athletic profile and advanced skills for age. Plays game under control and makes it look easy. Combines patient approach with ability to use entire field to give him BA upside. Can be inconsistent in approach, though, and sell out for power. Has impressive set of tools, but development time awaits.

Cooper,Garrett | 3 | Miami

EXP MLB DEBUT: 2017 | H/W: 6-6 230 | FUT: Starting 1B | 7D

Bats R Age 27
2013 (6) Auburn
Pwr +++
BAvg +++
Spd +
Def ++

Year	Lev	Team	AB	R	H	HR	RBI	Avg	OB	Slg	OPS	bb%	ct%	Eye	SB	CS	x/h%	Iso	RC/G
2016	AAA	Col Springs	127	17	35	5	20	276	328	433	762	7	84	0.50	0	0	29	157	4.77
2017	AA	Trenton	20	5	8	1	2	400	478	600	1078	13	70	0.50	0	0	25	200	9.71
2017	AAA	Scranton/WB	7	0	0	0	0	0	0	0	0	0	86	0.00	0	0		0	-4.14
2017	AAA	Col Springs	279	64	102	17	82	366	433	652	1085	11	83	0.69	0	0	45	287	8.89
2017	MLB	NY Yankees	43	3	14	0	6	326	341	488	829	2	72	0.08	0	0	43	163	5.92

Tall, slugging 1B who set high in HR and reached majors. Has hit over .300 for career with disciplined approach and level swing path. Hits HR due to strength, but focuses more on bat to ball. Very poor speed, but is fairly athletic for size and is adequate defender with soft hands.

Cordell,Ryan | 5789 | Chicago (A)

EXP MLB DEBUT: 2018 | H/W: 6-4 195 | FUT: Utility player | 7C

Bats R Age 26
2013 (11) Liberty
Pwr +++
BAvg +++
Spd +++
Def +++

Year	Lev	Team	AB	R	H	HR	RBI	Avg	OB	Slg	OPS	bb%	ct%	Eye	SB	CS	x/h%	Iso	RC/G
2014	A+	Myrtle Beach	62	12	19	5	19	306	377	645	1022	10	79	0.54	3	1	47	339	8.13
2015	A+	High Desert	286	58	89	13	57	311	373	528	901	9	81	0.53	10	5	35	217	6.59
2015	AA	Frisco	221	26	48	5	18	217	258	335	592	5	67	0.16	10	1	27	118	2.57
2016	AA	Frisco	405	69	107	19	70	264	318	484	802	7	76	0.33	12	4	43	220	5.35
2017	AAA	Col Springs	261	49	74	10	45	284	346	506	852	9	75	0.38	9	4	45	222	6.20

Versatile player with super-utility potential. Back injury has slowed ascent to big leagues. Solid hand-to-eye skills. Improved discipline, laying off more balls out of zone than ever before. Below-average power enhanced by pull approach. A solid athlete, has ability to play across infield and outfield. Foot speed also asset on base paths.

Cordero,Franchy
789 | San Diego | EXP MLB DEBUT: 2017 | H/W: 6-3 175 | FUT: Starting OF | 8E

Bats L Age 23
2011 FA (DR)
Pwr +++
BAvg ++
Spd ++++
Def +++

Year	Lev	Team	AB	R	H	HR	RBI	Avg	OB	Slg	OPS	bb%	ct%	Eye	SB	CS	x/h%	Iso	RC/G
2016	A+	Lake Elsinore	297	47	85	5	35	286	329	444	774	6	72	0.23	11	8	34	158	5.19
2016	AA	San Antonio	245	31	75	6	19	306	351	478	829	6	73	0.25	12	6	29	171	5.89
2016	AAA	El Paso	13	1	1	0	0	77	250	77	327	19	69	0.75	0	0	0	0	-0.97
2017	AAA	El Paso	390	68	127	17	64	326	363	603	966	6	70	0.19	15	4	44	277	7.93
2017	MLB	San Diego	92	15	21	3	9	228	276	424	699	6	52	0.14	1	1	43	196	5.38

Dominican OF who debuted with San Diego in 2017. Is one of the best athletes in the system, with plus speed required for moderate SB impact and enough range/arm for CF or RF. Chance to hit for average power when all said and done. Swing can get long and is over-aggressive at times; could be BA/OBP burden. Has intriguing tools, but comes with risk.

Cozens,Dylan
9 | Philadelphia | EXP MLB DEBUT: 2018 | H/W: 6-6 235 | FUT: Reserve OF | 8D

Bats L Age 23
2012 (2) HS (AZ)
Pwr +++++
BAvg +
Spd +++
Def ++

Year	Lev	Team	AB	R	H	HR	RBI	Avg	OB	Slg	OPS	bb%	ct%	Eye	SB	CS	x/h%	Iso	RC/G
2015	Rk	GCL Phillies	15	1	3	0	4	200	200	267	467	0	73	0.00	0	0	33	67	0.78
2015	A+	Clearwater	365	52	103	5	46	282	330	411	741	7	78	0.33	18	5	31	129	4.65
2015	AA	Reading	40	6	14	3	9	350	395	625	1020	7	83	0.43	2	1	36	275	7.71
2016	AA	Reading	521	106	144	40	125	276	352	591	943	10	64	0.33	21	1	56	315	8.01
2017	AAA	Lehigh Valley	476	68	100	27	75	210	296	418	714	11	59	0.30	8	3	42	208	4.72

Strikeouts have continued to mount, but all-fields power is among the best in the minors. Though pitch recognition skills have improved a bit, holes in his swing are monstrous and he's feeble against LHP. OK defender with good arm and some speed, but bat meeting ball is job #1. Absolute best-case scenario is Joey Gallo; likelihood is far less.

Craig,Will
3 | Pittsburgh | EXP MLB DEBUT: 2019 | H/W: 6-3 212 | FUT: Starting 1B | 8D

Bats R Age 23
2016 (1) Wake Forest
Pwr +++
BAvg +++
Spd +
Def ++

Year	Lev	Team	AB	R	H	HR	RBI	Avg	OB	Slg	OPS	bb%	ct%	Eye	SB	CS	x/h%	Iso	RC/G
2016	NCAA	Wake Forest	182	53	69	16	66	379	507	731	1237	21	81	1.34	0	1	46	352	11.42
2016	A-	West Virginia	218	28	61	2	23	280	394	362	756	16	83	1.11	2	0	23	83	5.37
2017	A+	Bradenton	458	59	124	6	61	271	358	371	729	12	77	0.58	1	3	27	100	4.75

Pedestrian season for 22nd overall pick in '16. Huge frame and plus raw power failed to show up in game action in the FSL. Plus plate discipline and contact ability should allow him to hit for power and average once he figures things out. Below-average runner and defender is limited to 1B.

Crawford,J.P.
6 | Philadelphia | EXP MLB DEBUT: 2017 | H/W: 6-2 180 | FUT: Starting SS | 8B

Bats L Age 23
2013 (1) HS (CA)
Pwr +++
BAvg ++++
Spd +++
Def ++++

Year	Lev	Team	AB	R	H	HR	RBI	Avg	OB	Slg	OPS	bb%	ct%	Eye	SB	CS	x/h%	Iso	RC/G
2015	AA	Reading	351	53	93	5	34	265	355	407	762	12	87	1.09	7	2	35	142	5.33
2016	AA	Reading	136	23	36	3	13	265	398	390	787	18	85	1.43	5	3	31	125	5.84
2016	AAA	Lehigh Valley	336	40	82	4	30	244	328	318	646	11	82	0.71	7	4	20	74	3.70
2017	AAA	Lehigh Valley	474	75	115	15	63	243	351	405	756	14	80	0.81	5	4	36	162	5.15
2017	MLB	Philadelphia	70	8	15	0	6	214	360	300	660	19	69	0.73	1	0	33	86	4.19

Lost some prospect luster due to lethargic first half (.211/.328/.330 with inconsistent defense). Looked much better in July/August, when he was driving the ball into gaps, and earned his MLB debut in Sept. At his best, owns excellent batting eye, doubles power, some speed and premium SS defense. Could take some time to adjust to MLB pitching.

Cruz,Derian
46 | Atlanta | EXP MLB DEBUT: 2021 | H/W: 6-1 180 | FUT: Starting OF | 7E

Bats B Age 19
2015 FA (DR)
Pwr ++
BAvg +++
Spd ++++
Def +

Year	Lev	Team	AB	R	H	HR	RBI	Avg	OB	Slg	OPS	bb%	ct%	Eye	SB	CS	x/h%	Iso	RC/G
2016	Rk	GCL Braves	110	11	34	2	16	309	321	445	767	2	85	0.13	4	1	29	136	4.62
2016	Rk	Danville	104	10	19	0	5	183	206	279	484	3	73	0.11	3	2	37	96	1.20
2017	Rk	Danville	213	32	50	2	22	235	282	315	596	6	71	0.23	11	5	24	80	2.70
2017	A	Rome	114	14	19	0	13	167	188	237	425	3	69	0.09	3	2	37	70	0.25

Athletic, switch-hitting MIF overmatched by full-season assignment. Raw from both sides of plate, especially LH side. Aggressive approach. Struggles reading spin. Plus-plus runner with raw baserunning instincts. Rangy defender with poor footwork and hands. Could move to outfield where athleticism plays up.

Cruz,Oneil
56 | Pittsburgh | EXP MLB DEBUT: 2022 | H/W: 6-6 175 | FUT: Starting OF | 8E

Bats R Age 19
2015 FA (DR)
Pwr ++
BAvg +++
Spd +++
Def +++

Year	Lev	Team	AB	R	H	HR	RBI	Avg	OB	Slg	OPS	bb%	ct%	Eye	SB	CS	x/h%	Iso	RC/G
2017	A	Great Lakes	342	51	82	8	36	240	297	342	639	8	68	0.25	8	7	22	102	3.29
2017	A	West Virginia	55	9	12	2	8	218	317	400	717	13	60	0.36	0	0	42	182	4.96

Projectable Dominican OF has tons of raw potential, but struggled in his state-side debut slashing .237/.297/.350 with 132 K. At his size, unlikely to stick on the dirt. Has the size and bat speed to develop above-average power. Moves well for his size with a strong, accurate arm, but needs to grow into his body.

Cuevas,Noel
789 | Colorado | EXP MLB DEBUT: 2018 | H/W: 6-2 210 | FUT: Reserve OF | 6B

Bats R Age 26
2010 (21) HS (PR)
Pwr +++
BAvg ++
Spd +++
Def +++

Year	Lev	Team	AB	R	H	HR	RBI	Avg	OB	Slg	OPS	bb%	ct%	Eye	SB	CS	x/h%	Iso	RC/G
2014	AA	Chattanooga	425	50	98	7	44	231	283	351	633	7	78	0.34	6	3	29	120	3.27
2015	AA	New Britain	406	47	107	4	51	264	293	355	648	4	79	0.20	31	12	25	91	3.30
2016	AA	Hartford	194	28	66	2	27	340	360	474	834	3	86	0.22	4	4	29	134	5.52
2016	AAA	Albuquerque	137	13	32	1	8	234	276	328	604	6	80	0.29	4	2	25	95	2.90
2017	AAA	Albuquerque	493	79	154	15	79	312	346	487	832	5	79	0.25	16	3	29	174	5.60

21st round pick has made it to the brink of the show and had his best season yet. Average tools across the board, but none are plus. At 26 it is hard to see a path to FT AB in Coors, but could carve out a bench role.

Cumberland,Brett
2 | Atlanta | EXP MLB DEBUT: 2019 | H/W: 5-11 205 | FUT: Starting C | 7C

Bats B Age 22
2016 (S-2) California
Pwr +++
BAvg ++
Spd ++
Def ++

Year	Lev	Team	AB	R	H	HR	RBI	Avg	OB	Slg	OPS	bb%	ct%	Eye	SB	CS	x/h%	Iso	RC/G
2016	NCAA	California	180	46	62	16	51	344	459	678	1136	17	78	0.95	5	0	44	333	10.03
2016	Rk	Danville	162	11	35	3	30	216	278	340	618	8	70	0.29	0	4	40	123	3.07
2017	A	Rome	175	34	46	10	48	263	374	531	905	15	65	0.51	1	0	57	269	7.64
2017	A+	Florida	182	14	49	1	21	269	335	363	698	9	66	0.29	0	2	29	93	4.44

Stocky switch-hitting bat-first catcher advanced to High-A in 2017. Advanced approach from both sides of plate, will work pitchers. Hit tool is hurt by elongated swing plane, causing bat speed to be fringy. Power is real and to all fields. Very powerful lower half. Footwork, arm and release need work but frames pitches well behind plate.

Dalbec,Bobby
5 | Boston | EXP MLB DEBUT: 2019 | H/W: 6-4 225 | FUT: Starting 3B | 8E

Bats R Age 22
2016 (4) Arizona
Pwr ++++
BAvg ++
Spd +
Def +++

Year	Lev	Team	AB	R	H	HR	RBI	Avg	OB	Slg	OPS	bb%	ct%	Eye	SB	CS	x/h%	Iso	RC/G
2016	NCAA	Arizona	231	42	60	7	40	260	360	429	788	13	63	0.42	7	3	38	169	6.00
2016	A-	Lowell	132	25	51	7	33	386	426	674	1100	6	75	0.27	2	2	43	288	9.30
2017	Rk	GCL Red Sox	27	3	7	0	2	259	375	296	671	16	67	0.56	1	0	14	37	4.21
2017	A	Greenville	284	48	70	13	39	246	331	437	768	11	57	0.29	4	5	40	190	5.97

Huge-framed 3B with significant power potential who missed time w/ broken wrist. Almost half of AB led to Ks and all-or-nothing approach can be exploited. Sells out for power and has difficulty repeating swing. Well above average bat speed and strength leads to double-plus pop. Can be solid defender at times with cannon for arm.

Danner,Hagen
2 | Toronto | EXP MLB DEBUT: 2022 | H/W: 6-2 185 | FUT: Starting C | 8E

Bats R Age 19
2017 (2) HS (CA)
Pwr ++
BAvg ++
Spd ++
Def +++

Year	Lev	Team	AB	R	H	HR	RBI	Avg	OB	Slg	OPS	bb%	ct%	Eye	SB	CS	x/h%	Iso	RC/G
2017	Rk	GCL Blue Jays	125	10	20	2	20	160	192	248	440	4	71	0.14	3	1	35	88	0.42

Raw hitter, but advanced defender for age. Has excellent agility and mobility behind plate and could be premium backstop in time. Plus arm strength keeps baserunners at bay. Too much swing and miss, though exhibits plus power to pull side. Bat speed a little short and can be pull conscious. Needs major time to develop.

Davis,Brendon
456 | Texas | EXP MLB DEBUT: 2020 | H/W: 6-4 185 | FUT: Starting MIF | 8E

Bats R Age 20
2015 (5) HS (CA)
Pwr ++
BAvg ++
Spd ++
Def +++

Year	Lev	Team	AB	R	H	HR	RBI	Avg	OB	Slg	OPS	bb%	ct%	Eye	SB	CS	x/h%	Iso	RC/G
2015	Rk	AZL Dodgers	90	14	25	0	14	278	309	322	631	4	71	0.15	2	0	12	44	3.10
2016	A	Great Lakes	398	51	96	5	49	241	293	334	627	7	70	0.25	8	3	26	93	3.15
2017	A	Hickory	77	8	14	2	6	182	292	273	565	13	64	0.43	0	0	21	91	2.30
2017	A	Great Lakes	310	39	76	8	35	245	345	403	748	13	65	0.44	3	7	39	158	5.26
2017	A+	Rancho Cuca	30	2	6	1	8	200	273	400	673	9	57	0.23	0	0	67	200	4.46

Lean, wiry INF who repeated Low-A and saw jump in power production and walk rate. Has ton of projection, but still needs to add strength. Too many Ks for little power and needs better barrel control. Plays all INF spots but 1B and is good at all. Quick first step and body control are assets and arm is strong. High ceiling, but could go bust.

Davis,J.D.

35	Houston	EXP MLB DEBUT: 2017	H/W: 6-3 225	FUT: Starting 3B	7A

Bats R Age 24
2014 (3) Cal St Fullerton
Pwr ++++
BAvg ++
Spd +
Def ++

Year	Lev	Team	AB	R	H	HR	RBI	Avg	OB	Sig	OPS	bb%	ct%	Eye	SB	CS	x/h%	Iso	RC/G
2015	A+	Lancaster	485	93	140	26	101	289	360	520	880	10	68	0.34	5	2	41	231	6.85
2016	AA	Corpus Christi	485	61	130	23	81	268	330	485	815	8	71	0.31	1	3	45	216	5.74
2017	AA	Corpus Christi	351	49	98	21	60	279	338	510	848	8	74	0.34	5	2	40	231	5.93
2017	AAA	Fresno	61	10	18	5	18	295	386	623	1009	13	70	0.50	0	0	56	328	8.54
2017	MLB	Houston	62	8	14	4	7	226	273	484	757	6	68	0.20	1	1	57	258	4.83

Muscular 3B with track record for power in minors. Strong forearms, lower half produce hard line-drive contact to all fields and will have HR impact at next level. Downside is aggressive approach and below-average contact skills and will likely be a BA/OBP burden. Plus arm fits him well at 3B, but build and lack of range figures to land him as DH.

Dawson,Ronnie

79	Houston	EXP MLB DEBUT: 2019	H/W: 6-2 225	FUT: Starting OF	7C

Bats L Age 22
2016 (2) Ohio St
Pwr +++
BAvg ++
Spd ++
Def +++

Year	Lev	Team	AB	R	H	HR	RBI	Avg	OB	Sig	OPS	bb%	ct%	Eye	SB	CS	x/h%	Iso	RC/G
2016	NCAA	Ohio State	257	55	85	13	51	331	415	611	1026	13	83	0.86	21	4	49	280	8.38
2016	A-	Tri City	244	41	55	7	36	225	337	373	710	14	73	0.62	12	6	38	148	4.53
2017	A	Quad Cities	438	81	119	14	62	272	353	438	791	11	77	0.54	17	8	34	167	5.45
2017	A+	Buies Creek	52	7	17	0	5	327	375	423	798	7	83	0.44	1	3	24	96	5.43

Big-bodied OF who flaunted pop, speed, contact at Ohio State. Has plus raw power, creates loft in swing and should have modest HR upside. Makes enough contact to hit for solid average, but struggles to square up LHP. Tried to run in pro debut and wasn't successful; large frame suggests he won't have SB value. Lack of range limits him to RF/LF.

De La Guerra,Chad

46	Boston	EXP MLB DEBUT: 2019	H/W: 5-11 190	FUT: Utility player	6B

Bats L Age 25
2015 (17) Grand Canyon
Pwr ++
BAvg +++
Spd ++
Def ++

Year	Lev	Team	AB	R	H	HR	RBI	Avg	OB	Sig	OPS	bb%	ct%	Eye	SB	CS	x/h%	Iso	RC/G
2015	NCAA	Grand Canyon	215	49	74	11	51	344	392	544	936	7	86	0.55	7	2	27	200	6.77
2015	A-	Lowell	223	28	59	2	29	265	328	381	709	9	79	0.46	4	3	32	117	4.39
2016	A	Greenville	240	40	60	1	20	250	336	329	665	11	76	0.54	7	2	22	79	3.93
2017	A+	Salem	218	47	64	5	36	294	366	463	830	10	82	0.63	5	2	38	170	5.94
2017	AA	Portland	196	34	53	4	23	270	347	408	755	11	76	0.48	2	1	36	138	5.02

Consistent, capable INF who split time between SS and 2B in best pro year. Set highs in HR and doubles, though still better with BA than power. Gets on base at high clip due to pitch recognition and patient eye. Can hit LHP and has enough strength for gap power. Uses quick, clean hands to make routine plays, but range may be a tad short for SS.

De Leon,Michael

6	Texas	EXP MLB DEBUT: 2019	H/W: 6-1 160	FUT: Starting SS	7C

Bats B Age 21
2013 FA (DR)
Pwr ++
BAvg ++
Spd ++
Def +++

Year	Lev	Team	AB	R	H	HR	RBI	Avg	OB	Sig	OPS	bb%	ct%	Eye	SB	CS	x/h%	Iso	RC/G
2014	A+	Myrtle Beach	24	5	7	1	6	292	370	542	912	11	83	0.75	0	0	57	250	6.94
2014	AA	Frisco	3	1	1	0	0	333	333	667	1000	0	67	0.00	0	0	100	333	9.06
2015	A	Hickory	306	29	68	1	29	222	277	281	558	7	85	0.49	1	1	21	59	2.53
2016	A+	High Desert	454	54	121	9	54	267	303	385	689	5	87	0.42	7	5	29	119	3.94
2017	AA	Frisco	394	29	88	2	35	223	257	284	542	4	88	0.38	3	2	22	61	2.30

Instinctual SS who has advanced one level per year and is consistently young for level. Adding strength to wiry frame. Has plus hand-eye coordination and puts bat to ball frequently, but swings early in count. Big drop in HR, though hits doubles. Not the greatest runner despite quick first step at SS. Has smooth actions and accurate arm.

Dean,Austin

79	Miami	EXP MLB DEBUT: 2018	H/W: 6-1 190	FUT: Reserve OF	7E

Bats R Age 24
2012 (4) HS (TX)
Pwr +++
BAvg ++
Spd ++
Def +++

Year	Lev	Team	AB	R	H	HR	RBI	Avg	OB	Sig	OPS	bb%	ct%	Eye	SB	CS	x/h%	Iso	RC/G
2014	A	Greensboro	403	67	124	9	58	308	367	444	812	9	82	0.53	4	4	27	136	5.56
2015	A+	Jupiter	519	67	139	5	52	268	319	366	685	7	85	0.51	18	10	28	98	4.04
2016	AA	Jacksonville	480	60	114	11	67	238	307	375	682	9	77	0.44	1	2	34	138	3.96
2017	Rk	GCL Marlins	17	3	7	1	7	412	412	706	1118	0	88	0.00	0	0	43	294	8.27
2017	AA	Jacksonville	234	29	66	4	30	282	323	427	750	6	80	0.30	3	1	33	145	4.70

Thick, strong bodied OF missed the first half of the season with injury. Aggressive approach results in power that is a tick above-average but at the price of less contact. Sets up tall in the batter's box with hands low and drives the ball up the middle. He has average speed but that isn't going to be part of his game as he moves up.

DeCarlo,Joe

23	Seattle	EXP MLB DEBUT: 2019	H/W: 5-10 210	FUT: Starting C	7E

Bats R Age 24
2012 (2) HS (PA)
Pwr +++
BAvg ++
Spd +
Def +

Year	Lev	Team	AB	R	H	HR	RBI	Avg	OB	Sig	OPS	bb%	ct%	Eye	SB	CS	x/h%	Iso	RC/G
2014	A-	Everett	9	2	2	0	1	222	300	333	633	10	44	0.20	0	0	50	111	5.39
2014	A	Clinton	268	29	66	5	42	246	336	381	716	12	69	0.43	0	1	38	134	4.67
2015	A	Clinton	384	47	78	10	37	203	326	333	659	15	68	0.57	2	1	36	130	3.86
2016	A+	Bakersfield	377	58	100	14	54	265	365	454	818	14	71	0.54	1	0	39	188	6.05
2017	A+	Modesto	325	45	78	13	46	240	327	415	742	11	70	0.42	1	2	37	175	4.86

Short, stocky prospect who was moved to catcher in 2017. Repeated High-A due to change and was very good late in year. Also saw action at 1B to get bat into lineup. Works counts with disciplined approach and exhibits average power, mostly to pull side. Has very little speed. Defense has a ways to go, but has promise due to strong arm.

Deichmann,Greg

9	Oakland	EXP MLB DEBUT: 2020	H/W: 6-2 190	FUT: Starting OF	7C

Bats L Age 22
2017 (2) Louisiana St
Pwr +++
BAvg ++
Spd +++
Def +++

Year	Lev	Team	AB	R	H	HR	RBI	Avg	OB	Sig	OPS	bb%	ct%	Eye	SB	CS	x/h%	Iso	RC/G
2017	NCAA	LSU	266	54	82	19	73	308	420	579	999	16	77	0.82	7	3	41	271	8.24
2017	A-	Vermont	164	31	45	8	30	274	380	530	911	15	76	0.70	4	1	49	256	7.22

Exceeded expectations in pro debut. Swings quick bat and can go to opposite field. Has good two-strike approach and willing to go deep into counts. Power grades as solid-average and could grow into more with swing tweaks. BA upside only moderate as he can sell out for power. Average speed assists with some SB and is decent corner OF with OK arm.

DeLuzio,Ben

789	Arizona	EXP MLB DEBUT: 2019	H/W: 6-3 190	FUT: Reserve OF	6C

Bats R Age 23
2016 FA (Florida State)
Pwr +
BAvg +++
Spd ++++
Def +++

Year	Lev	Team	AB	R	H	HR	RBI	Avg	OB	Sig	OPS	bb%	ct%	Eye	SB	CS	x/h%	Iso	RC/G
2016	NCAA	Florida State	198	40	47	1	25	237	326	333	659	12	81	0.70	15	3	32	96	3.96
2016	Rk	AZL Dbacks	11	1	4	0	1	364	364	364	727	0	82	0.00	0	0	0	0	3.89
2016	A-	Hillsboro	80	23	25	0	7	313	389	388	776	11	81	0.67	14	2	16	75	5.39
2017	A	Kane County	186	20	59	0	18	317	362	425	787	7	82	0.39	13	7	29	108	5.27
2017	A+	Visalia	117	20	41	0	8	350	377	402	779	4	82	0.24	12	1	12	51	4.90

Speedy RH OF who has hit at every level, albeit old for each league. Heady, he uses a short, compact swing to hit ball to all fields and use his best attribute, a plus run tool. Has trouble laying off breaking balls and doesn't have much power, despite frame. Plays a rangy OF with enough arm to play RF. Will steal bases.

Demeritte,Travis

45	Atlanta	EXP MLB DEBUT: 2018	H/W: 6-0 180	FUT: Starting 2B	7C

Bats R Age 23
2013 (1) HS (GA)
Pwr +++
BAvg ++
Spd +++
Def ++++

Year	Lev	Team	AB	R	H	HR	RBI	Avg	OB	Sig	OPS	bb%	ct%	Eye	SB	CS	x/h%	Iso	RC/G
2015	A-	Spokane	20	0	3	0	0	150	227	150	377	9	45	0.18	0	2	0	0	-0.70
2015	A	Hickory	170	27	41	5	19	241	338	412	750	13	59	0.36	10	1	44	171	5.62
2016	A+	High Desert	331	73	90	25	59	272	352	583	935	11	62	0.33	13	3	54	311	8.12
2016	A+	Carolina	124	21	31	3	11	250	380	476	856	17	60	0.52	4	1	55	226	7.67
2017	AA	Mississippi	458	62	106	15	45	231	306	402	707	10	71	0.37	5	7	40	170	4.33

Glove-glove caliber 2B struggled mightily offensively in 2017. Always a big power bat with contact concerns, struggled with adjustments and was caught in between swings. Despite swing-and-miss issues, brings advanced approach to plate. Power regressed and hard contact rate declined. Defensively gifted at 2B, arm profiles at 3B.

Denton,Bryce

79	St. Louis	EXP MLB DEBUT: 2021	H/W: 6-0 190	FUT: Starting OF	7D

Bats R Age 20
2015 (2) HS (TN)
Pwr ++
BAvg +++
Spd ++
Def ++

Year	Lev	Team	AB	R	H	HR	RBI	Avg	OB	Sig	OPS	bb%	ct%	Eye	SB	CS	x/h%	Iso	RC/G
2015	Rk	GCL Cardinals	155	21	30	1	14	194	247	245	492	7	79	0.34	3	0	13	52	1.49
2016	Rk	Johnson City	202	34	57	4	26	282	347	376	723	9	82	0.54	2	1	19	94	4.46
2017	A-	State College	213	27	57	2	21	268	322	352	674	7	74	0.30	2	2	19	85	3.81
2017	A	Peoria	70	2	11	1	4	157	203	257	460	5	74	0.22	2	1	45	100	0.87

2nd round pick struggled in his full season debut and was demoted to short season ball. Shows feel for hitting with raw power, but aggressive approach results in sub-par contact. Moved from 3B to OF where he has decent range and enough arm strength to play either corner. Was just 19 so there is still time.

DeVito,Chris

3	Kansas City	EXP MLB DEBUT: 2020	H/W: 6-2 220	FUT: Starting 1B	7E

Bats L Age 23
2016 (8) New Mexico
Pwr ++++
BAvg ++
Spd +
Def ++

Year	Lev	Team	AB	R	H	HR	RBI	Avg	OB	Sig	OPS	bb%	ct%	Eye	SB	CS	x/h%	Iso	RC/G
2016	NCAA	New Mexico	232	49	87	16	65	375	444	685	1130	11	87	0.94	0	0	44	310	9.29
2016	Rk	Burlington	218	34	57	9	50	261	353	445	798	12	79	0.69	2	0	39	183	5.53
2017	A	Lexington	121	25	42	11	38	347	378	702	1080	5	74	0.19	0	1	50	355	8.82
2017	A+	Wilmington	387	38	93	10	53	240	283	382	665	6	76	0.25	0	0	35	142	3.55

Slugging 1B who is all about HR with leveraged stroke. Power comes as result of natural strength as opposed to bat speed. FB-only hitter who struggles with breakers and LHP. Will sell out for power, but can hit ball long way when contact made. Took advantage of lower level pitching and struggled in High-A. Lacks speed, athleticism, and defense.

Dewees,Donnie

78 | **Kansas City** | EXP MLB DEBUT: 2018 | H/W: 5-11 204 | FUT: Starting OF | **7C**

Bats L | Age 24 | 2015 (2) North Florida

Pwr ++ | BAvg +++ | Spd ++++ | Def ++

Year	Lev	Team	AB	R	H	HR	RBI	Avg	OB	Sig	OPS	bb%	ct%	Eye	SB	CS	x/h%	Iso	RC/G
2015	NCAA	North Florida	251	88	106	18	68	422	484	749	1233	11	94	1.88	23	3	36	327	10.21
2015	A-	Eugene	282	42	75	5	30	266	301	376	677	5	81	0.26	19	7	27	110	3.68
2016	A	South Bend	365	65	103	3	54	282	335	414	749	7	86	0.57	17	5	29	132	4.87
2016	A+	Myrtle Beach	149	25	43	2	19	289	333	423	756	6	76	0.28	14	0	33	134	4.87
2017	AA	NW Arkansas	464	67	126	9	52	272	337	407	745	9	83	0.57	20	8	31	136	4.80

Steady OF who heated up at midseason and is on cusp of majors. Best attribute is well above average speed which allows him to steal bases and range well in OF. Could become better defender with improved routes and jumps, though arm is very short. Can hit for moderate pop and draws walks. Bat control allows for decent BA.

Diaz,Edwin

456 | **Oakland** | EXP MLB DEBUT: 2020 | H/W: 6-2 195 | FUT: Starting 3B | **7E**

Bats R | Age 22 | 2013 (15) HS (PR)

Pwr ++ | BAvg ++ | Spd + | Def ++++

Year	Lev	Team	AB	R	H	HR	RBI	Avg	OB	Sig	OPS	bb%	ct%	Eye	SB	CS	x/h%	Iso	RC/G
2015	Rk	AZL Athletics	76	10	13	2	6	171	250	276	526	10	71	0.36	0	0	31	105	1.72
2015	A	Beloit	140	9	14	0	13	100	149	157	306	5	65	0.16	0	0	57	57	-1.57
2016	A	Beloit	296	31	70	5	34	236	298	331	629	8	66	0.26	4	2	26	95	3.25
2017	A	Beloit	302	49	77	10	45	255	348	414	762	12	70	0.47	0	0	32	159	5.22
2017	A+	Stockton	45	2	4	0	3	89	163	133	297	8	67	0.27	0	0	25	44	-1.62

Emerging INF who repeated Low-A to better results. Has spent the better part of last three years there. Shows elite defense with smooth, easy actions and strong arm. Hands are very quick and can work at 2B or 3B as well. Hits LHP well, but lacks punch with flat swing path. A revised swing could be in the offing to take advantage of bat speed.

Diaz,Isan

46 | **Milwaukee** | EXP MLB DEBUT: 2019 | H/W: 5-10 185 | FUT: Starting MIF | **9E**

Bats L | Age 21 | 2014 (S-2) HS (MA)

Pwr ++++ | BAvg +++ | Spd +++ | Def +++

Year	Lev	Team	AB	R	H	HR	RBI	Avg	OB	Sig	OPS	bb%	ct%	Eye	SB	CS	x/h%	Iso	RC/G
2014	Rk	AZL Dbacks	182	22	34	3	21	187	285	330	615	12	69	0.45	6	5	44	143	3.23
2015	Rk	Missoula	272	58	98	13	51	360	431	640	1071	11	76	0.52	12	7	45	279	9.20
2016	A	Wisconsin	507	71	134	20	75	264	356	469	825	12	71	0.49	11	8	44	205	6.11
2017	A+	Carolina	383	59	85	13	54	222	330	376	706	14	68	0.51	9	3	39	154	4.47

Middle infielder had down year at High-A, where his aggressive swing was victimized by pitchers. Solid approach but swings out of his shoes and struggles staying back on off-speed pitches. Continues to add strength to short, stocky frame. Projects for plus power at maturity. Solid runner, won't be big factor in running game. Likely 2B long term.

Diaz,Lewin

3 | **Minnesota** | EXP MLB DEBUT: 2020 | H/W: 6-3 180 | FUT: Starting 1B | **8D**

Bats L | Age 21 | 2013 FA (DR)

Pwr ++++ | BAvg +++ | Spd + | Def ++

Year	Lev	Team	AB	R	H	HR	RBI	Avg	OB	Sig	OPS	bb%	ct%	Eye	SB	CS	x/h%	Iso	RC/G
2015	Rk	GCL Twins	111	12	29	1	15	261	344	369	713	11	78	0.58	2	0	31	108	4.56
2015	Rk	Elizabethton	48	7	8	3	5	167	216	375	591	6	65	0.18	0	0	50	208	2.37
2016	Rk	Elizabethton	174	26	54	9	37	310	355	575	930	6	80	0.34	0	0	48	264	6.86
2017	A	Cedar Rapids	466	47	136	12	68	292	328	444	772	5	83	0.31	2	1	34	152	4.86

Strong, bat-only 1B who led MWL in doubles in first year above rookie ball. Makes ton of contact for power approach and some hope for BA as he can hit LHP and breaking balls. Has little care for drawing walks and generally is pull-only hitter. Not very fast and will only be average defender at best. Owns strong arm, though.

Diaz,Yusniel

789 | **Los Angeles (N)** | EXP MLB DEBUT: 2019 | H/W: 6-1 195 | FUT: Starting OF | **8D**

Bats R | Age 21 | 2015 FA (CU)

Pwr +++ | BAvg +++ | Spd ++++ | Def +++

Year	Lev	Team	AB	R	H	HR	RBI	Avg	OB	Sig	OPS	bb%	ct%	Eye	SB	CS	x/h%	Iso	RC/G
2016	Rk	AZL Dodgers	14	2	2	1	3	143	143	357	500	0	79	0.00	0	0	50	214	0.98
2016	A+	Rancho Cuca	316	47	86	8	54	272	333	418	751	8	78	0.41	7	8	27	146	4.81
2017	A+	Rancho Cuca	331	42	92	8	39	278	347	414	761	10	78	0.48	7	9	28	136	4.99
2017	AA	Tulsa	108	15	36	3	13	333	390	491	881	8	73	0.34	2	5	31	157	6.62

Cuban OF signed in 2015 and is just now starting to tap into his impressive raw tools. High leg kick and aggressive approach results in swing-and-miss, but quick bat and ability to barrel the ball gets results. Plus speed should result in double-digit SB and can play all three OF spots.

Downs,Jeter

6 | **Cincinnati** | EXP MLB DEBUT: 2021 | H/W: 5-11 180 | FUT: Starting SS | **8E**

Bats R | Age 19 | 2017 (S-1) HS (FL)

Pwr +++ | BAvg +++ | Spd +++ | Def +++

Year	Lev	Team	AB	R	H	HR	RBI	Avg	OB	Sig	OPS	bb%	ct%	Eye	SB	CS	x/h%	Iso	RC/G
2017	Rk	Billings	172	31	46	6	29	267	367	424	791	14	81	0.84	8	5	26	157	5.53

Athletic RH SS displayed advanced hitting skills in rookie ball debut. A solid, line drive hitter. Uses quick wrists and a compact swing to barrel balls gap-to-gap. Swing trajectory geared towards gaining loft on line drives. Already showcasing raw plus pull power. A terrific athlete with high baseball IQ, gets most out of range and run tool.

Dozier,Hunter

359 | **Kansas City** | EXP MLB DEBUT: 2016 | H/W: 6-4 220 | FUT: Starting 3B | **7B**

Bats R | Age 26 | 2013 (1) Steph F Austin

Pwr +++ | BAvg +++ | Spd ++ | Def ++

Year	Lev	Team	AB	R	H	HR	RBI	Avg	OB	Sig	OPS	bb%	ct%	Eye	SB	CS	x/h%	Iso	RC/G
2016	AA	NW Arkansas	95	14	29	8	21	305	394	642	1037	13	76	0.61	4	0	55	337	8.59
2016	MLB	KC Royals	19	4	4	0	1	211	286	263	549	10	58	0.25	0	0	25	53	2.32
2017	A+	Wilmington	11	1	4	0	1	364	417	455	871	8	55	0.20	0	0	25	91	8.41
2017	AA	NW Arkansas	16	4	4	0	0	250	400	313	713	20	50	0.50	0	0	25	63	6.03
2017	AAA	Omaha	84	11	19	4	12	226	301	464	765	10	56	0.24	1	1	58	238	6.07

Injury-prone prospect who missed most of season with sprained oblique and fractured wrist. Exhibits natural hitting ways with strong, compact stroke. Should hit for solid BA with bat speed, pitch recognition, and use of whole field. Can also hit for power due to leverage. Not polished with glove, but plays variety of positions. Could win 3B job.

Dubon,Mauricio

46 | **Milwaukee** | EXP MLB DEBUT: 2018 | H/W: 6-0 160 | FUT: Starting MIF | **8C**

Bats R | Age 23 | 2013 (26) HS (CA)

Pwr ++ | BAvg +++ | Spd ++++ | Def +++

Year	Lev	Team	AB	R	H	HR	RBI	Avg	OB	Sig	OPS	bb%	ct%	Eye	SB	CS	x/h%	Iso	RC/G
2015	A+	Salem	237	27	65	1	18	274	338	325	663	9	84	0.61	12	3	15	51	3.83
2016	A+	Salem	235	53	72	0	29	306	392	379	771	12	89	1.32	24	4	19	72	5.49
2016	AA	Portland	251	48	85	6	40	339	366	538	904	4	86	0.31	6	3	38	199	6.41
2017	AA	Biloxi	268	34	74	2	24	276	338	351	689	9	84	0.60	31	9	22	75	4.13
2017	AAA	Col Springs	224	40	61	6	33	272	315	420	735	6	85	0.41	7	6	34	147	4.47

Athletic, contact bat ready to contribute in MIF utility role. Short, compact swing with up-the-middle approach. Solid bat-to-ball skills. Aggressive at plate, will expand zone. Has pull-side power on middle-in pitches. Smart baserunner, gets most out of plus run tool. Solid defender at 2B & SS. Athletic enough to play multiple positions.

Duenez,Samir

3 | **Kansas City** | EXP MLB DEBUT: 2018 | H/W: 6-1 195 | FUT: Starting 1B | **7C**

Bats L | Age 21 | 2012 FA (VZ)

Pwr ++ | BAvg +++ | Spd ++ | Def +++

Year	Lev	Team	AB	R	H	HR	RBI	Avg	OB	Sig	OPS	bb%	ct%	Eye	SB	CS	x/h%	Iso	RC/G
2015	A	Lexington	361	47	96	1	37	266	312	332	644	6	91	0.73	11	5	19	66	3.68
2016	A	Lexington	265	30	72	6	49	272	311	419	730	5	85	0.38	14	2	33	147	4.41
2016	A+	Wilmington	213	30	64	7	42	300	358	479	837	8	84	0.56	10	2	34	178	5.80
2016	AA	NW Arkansas	54	4	15	0	9	278	339	370	709	8	78	0.42	2	0	33	93	4.42
2017	AA	NW Arkansas	523	65	132	17	75	252	302	402	703	7	78	0.32	10	3	32	149	4.04

Athletic 1B who set new high in HR, but K rate rose dramatically as well. Inconsistent approach, particularly against LHP, and should work more counts. Power not ideal for 1B, but uses smooth stroke with sufficient bat speed for BA potential. Can steal bases despite fringy speed. Instinctual defender with good footwork and average arm strength.

Duggar,Steven

89 | **San Francisco** | EXP MLB DEBUT: 2018 | H/W: 6-2 195 | FUT: Starting OF | **7B**

Bats L | Age 24 | 2015 (6) Clemson

Pwr ++ | BAvg +++ | Spd ++++ | Def +++

Year	Lev	Team	AB	R	H	HR	RBI	Avg	OB	Sig	OPS	bb%	ct%	Eye	SB	CS	x/h%	Iso	RC/G
2016	A+	San Jose	264	43	75	9	30	284	386	462	848	14	75	0.67	6	7	33	178	6.41
2016	AA	Richmond	243	35	78	1	24	321	391	432	823	10	79	0.55	9	7	27	111	5.96
2017	Rk	AZL Giants	3	0	0	0	0	0	400	0	400	40	100		0	0		0	3.26
2017	A+	San Jose	115	22	31	4	20	270	364	470	833	13	63	0.40	7	0	48	200	6.69
2017	AAA	Sacramento	46	7	12	2	6	261	370	413	783	15	74	0.67	3	2	25	152	5.42

All-around talent who missed most of 2017 with hip and elbow ailments. Uses all fields in line drive approach and has patience to draw walks and use above average speed on base. Outstanding athlete with quickness and is solid-average defender in CF. Plus arm is true asset. Could add more power but would need more loft to stroke. Knows strike zone.

Dunand,Joe

5 | **Miami** | EXP MLB DEBUT: 2021 | H/W: 6-2 205 | FUT: Starting 3B | **7C**

Bats R | Age 22 | 2017 (2) North Carolina St

Pwr ++++ | BAvg +++ | Spd + | Def ++

Year	Lev	Team	AB	R	H	HR	RBI	Avg	OB	Sig	OPS	bb%	ct%	Eye	SB	CS	x/h%	Iso	RC/G
2017	NCAA	NC State	209	42	60	18	51	287	346	632	978	8	78	0.42	2	0	55	344	7.45
2017	Rk	GCL Marlins	16	4	6	1	3	375	474	750	1224	16	75	0.75	0	0	67	375	11.63
2017	A+	Jupiter	11	1	4	0	1	364	462	545	1007	15	64	0.50	0	1	50	182	9.94

2nd rounder is a nephew of Alex Rodriguez and had solid pro debut. Drafted as a SS, but profiles better at 3B with plus raw power and a strong arm. Swing can get long, but worked hard to keep stroke short. Good hands and a strong arm, but fringe range at SS.

Edman,Tommy — 6 — St. Louis

EXP MLB DEBUT: 2019 | H/W: 5-10 180 | FUT: Starting SS | 7D

Bats B Age 22
2016 (6) Stanford
Pwr +
BAvg + + +
Spd + + +
Def + + + +

Year	Lev	Team	AB	R	H	HR	RBI	Avg	OB	Slg	OPS	bb%	ct%	Eye	SB	CS	x/h%	Iso	RC/G
2016	NCAA	Stanford	213	35	61	0	24	286	361	371	732	11	92	1.56	8	1	23	85	5.03
2016	A-	State College	255	61	73	4	33	286	399	427	827	16	89	1.66	19	3	32	141	6.32
2017	A	Peoria	155	24	44	2	18	284	347	439	786	9	88	0.79	8	2	34	155	5.41
2017	A+	Palm Beach	70	7	18	1	11	257	325	357	682	9	74	0.39	0	1	22	100	3.97
2017	AA	Springfield	219	20	54	2	26	247	298	347	645	7	84	0.47	5	2	30	100	3.55

Has the chops to stick at SS, but poor power limits his fantasy appeal. Contact-oriented approach with above-average speed give him some value and held his own across three levels. Plus defender with good range and a strong arm.

Ellis,Drew — 5 — Arizona

EXP MLB DEBUT: 2020 | H/W: 6-3 210 | FUT: Starting 3B | 8C

Bats R Age 22
2017 (2) Louisville
Pwr + + + +
BAvg + + +
Spd + +
Def + +

Year	Lev	Team	AB	R	H	HR	RBI	Avg	OB	Slg	OPS	bb%	ct%	Eye	SB	CS	x/h%	Iso	RC/G
2017	NCAA	Louisville	231	56	82	20	61	355	450	701	1151	15	83	1.00	6	0	48	346	9.85
2017	A-	Hillsboro	181	35	41	8	23	227	317	403	720	12	75	0.53	3	1	39	177	4.45

Power-first INF took significant step forward leading up to 2017 draft. Led Louisville in BA & HR. Swing is conducive to hard fly ball contact. Uses leverage in swing to drive the ball, but also works pitchers and will take walks. Somewhat limited defensively. Scouts are split on whether he is a 1B or 3B moving forward due to limited range.

Enright,Kole — 45 — Texas

EXP MLB DEBUT: 2021 | H/W: 6-1 175 | FUT: Starting 2B | 7D

Bats B Age 20
2016 (3) HS (FL)
Pwr + +
BAvg + +
Spd + +
Def + +

Year	Lev	Team	AB	R	H	HR	RBI	Avg	OB	Slg	OPS	bb%	ct%	Eye	SB	CS	x/h%	Iso	RC/G
2016	Rk	AZL Rangers	150	22	47	1	17	313	372	420	792	9	78	0.42	3	1	30	107	5.44
2017	A-	Spokane	232	29	54	3	20	233	305	323	628	9	76	0.44	4	2	24	91	3.28

Quick-swinging INF who split time between 2B and 3B in short-season ball. Has yet to see advanced pitching, yet struggled to find consistent stroke. Swing may need revision and is better from right. Has gap power now and could evolve into average pop. Contact issues limit BA upside as swing gets long. Probable 2B with average footwork and arm.

Erceg,Lucas — 5 — Milwaukee

EXP MLB DEBUT: 2019 | H/W: 6-3 200 | FUT: Starting 3B | 8C

Bats L Age 22
2016 (2) Menlo
Pwr + + + +
BAvg + + +
Spd + + +
Def + + +

Year	Lev	Team	AB	R	H	HR	RBI	Avg	OB	Slg	OPS	bb%	ct%	Eye	SB	CS	x/h%	Iso	RC/G
2016	Rk	Helena	105	17	42	2	22	400	442	552	995	7	85	0.50	8	1	26	152	7.64
2016	A	Wisconsin	167	17	47	7	29	281	330	497	827	7	77	0.32	1	3	40	216	5.65
2017	A+	Carolina	496	66	127	15	81	256	305	417	722	7	81	0.37	2	3	39	161	4.33
2017	AAA	Col Springs	10	2	4	0	2	400	455	600	1055	9	90	1.00	0	0	50	200	8.61

Athletic, power hitting LHH 3B has a high offensive ceiling. Solid approach, doesn't strike out much despite fringe bat speed. Has struggled against advanced velocity. Power completely to pull side. Using solid base and swing trajectory to produce carry. Will stick at 3B long term. Plus arm.

Ervin,Phillip — 789 — Cincinnati

EXP MLB DEBUT: 2017 | H/W: 5-10 207 | FUT: Starting OF | 7C

Bats R Age 25
2013 (1) Samford
Pwr + +
BAvg + +
Spd + + + +
Def + + +

Year	Lev	Team	AB	R	H	HR	RBI	Avg	OB	Slg	OPS	bb%	ct%	Eye	SB	CS	x/h%	Iso	RC/G
2015	A+	Daytona	405	68	98	12	63	242	330	375	705	12	80	0.64	30	7	31	133	4.33
2015	AA	Pensacola	51	7	12	2	8	235	391	412	802	20	71	0.87	4	3	42	176	6.05
2016	AA	Pensacola	419	71	100	13	45	239	341	399	739	13	79	0.74	36	10	38	160	4.89
2017	AAA	Louisville	363	46	93	7	40	256	325	380	705	9	77	0.45	23	6	31	124	4.28
2017	MLB	Cincinnati	58	8	15	3	10	259	306	448	755	6	74	0.27	4	1	33	190	4.62

A maddening prospect with plus tool shed, finally made it to MLB. Hit and power tools likely at projection. Covers two-thirds of plate, with bad habit of trying to hit ball over the fence. Stocky frame packs incredible punch during BP, struggles to bring to game. Excellent athlete and SB threat. Better suited for LF but can play all 3 OF positions.

Estevez,Omar — 46 — Los Angeles (N)

EXP MLB DEBUT: 2020 | H/W: 5-10 168 | FUT: Starting 2B | 7D

Bats R Age 20
2015 FA (CU)
Pwr + +
BAvg + + +
Spd + + +
Def + + +

Year	Lev	Team	AB	R	H	HR	RBI	Avg	OB	Slg	OPS	bb%	ct%	Eye	SB	CS	x/h%	Iso	RC/G
2016	A	Great Lakes	471	46	120	9	61	255	294	389	682	5	74	0.21	3	6	36	134	3.81
2017	A+	Rancho Cuca	457	56	117	4	47	256	306	348	654	7	79	0.34	2	2	26	92	3.55

Cuban infielder has solid across-the-board tools. Looked overmatched at times in the CAL, but has a good all-fields approach and should be able to hit for average with moderate power. Good range with soft hands and an average arm. Might be pressed at SS, but profiles nicely at 2B.

Estrada,Thairo — 46 — New York (A)

EXP MLB DEBUT: 2018 | H/W: 5-10 185 | FUT: Starting SS | 7C

Bats R Age 22
2012 FA (VZ)
Pwr + +
BAvg + + +
Spd + + +
Def + + +

Year	Lev	Team	AB	R	H	HR	RBI	Avg	OB	Slg	OPS	bb%	ct%	Eye	SB	CS	x/h%	Iso	RC/G
2014	A-	Staten Island	59	11	16	0	2	271	338	288	627	9	88	0.86	8	1	6	17	3.53
2015	A-	Staten Island	247	37	66	2	23	267	330	360	690	9	88	0.77	8	3	29	93	4.25
2016	A	Charleston (Sc)	140	11	40	5	19	286	324	429	753	5	85	0.38	11	3	23	143	4.56
2016	A+	Tampa	315	52	92	3	30	292	352	375	726	8	85	0.63	7	5	21	83	4.58
2017	AA	Trenton	495	72	149	6	48	301	346	392	738	6	89	0.61	8	11	19	91	4.62

Emerging, consistent INF who shines with contact profile and solid glovework. Does everything relatively well and could hit double-digit HR. Exhibits plus speed, though gets caught stealing often. Bat control is steady and smooth. May lack the range for SS, but makes plays with instincts and plus arm. Could be solid 2B over long-term.

Evans,Phillip — 4567 — New York (N)

EXP MLB DEBUT: 2017 | H/W: 5-10 223 | FUT: Reserve IF | 6B

Bats R Age 25
2011 (15) HS (CA)
Pwr + +
BAvg + +
Spd + +
Def + + +

Year	Lev	Team	AB	R	H	HR	RBI	Avg	OB	Slg	OPS	bb%	ct%	Eye	SB	CS	x/h%	Iso	RC/G
2015	A+	St. Lucie	252	19	59	0	32	234	301	313	614	9	83	0.55	2	2	29	79	3.29
2016	A+	St. Lucie	28	3	4	0	2	143	273	143	416	15	89	1.67	0	0	0	0	1.51
2016	AA	Binghamton	361	50	121	8	39	335	368	485	853	5	83	0.32	1	1	31	150	5.83
2017	AAA	Las Vegas	466	58	130	11	56	279	339	418	757	8	83	0.53	2	3	31	139	4.88
2017	MLB	NY Mets	33	4	10	0	1	303	378	364	742	11	76	0.50	0	0	20	61	4.93

Stocky IF made MLB debut in 2017. Hit well in cup of coffee, likely unsustainable. A patient hitter with an understanding of zone, relies on a short, compact arm-heavy swing. Can be beaten by velocity. Strength in frame, struggles transferring lower half energy into swing. Still, could hit 10+ HR w/ solid playing time.

Fabian,Sandro — 9 — San Francisco

EXP MLB DEBUT: 2021 | H/W: 6-1 180 | FUT: Starting OF | 8D

Bats R Age 20
2014 FA (DR)
Pwr + + +
BAvg + + +
Spd + +
Def + + +

Year	Lev	Team	AB	R	H	HR	RBI	Avg	OB	Slg	OPS	bb%	ct%	Eye	SB	CS	x/h%	Iso	RC/G
2016	Rk	AZL Giants	159	30	54	2	35	340	367	522	889	4	82	0.25	3	1	37	182	6.37
2017	A	Augusta	480	51	133	11	61	277	292	408	700	2	82	0.11	5	4	31	131	3.80

Projectable OF with sound hitting skills. Exhibits plus bat speed and combines with hand-eye coordination to project to high BA. Struggles with breakers and free-swinging ways need to be tamed. Should hit for at least average pop with his natural strength. Doesn't run well, but gets good jumps and takes efficient routes in RF. Strong, accurate arm.

Fairchild,Stuart — 789 — Cincinnati

EXP MLB DEBUT: 2020 | H/W: 6-0 190 | FUT: Starting OF | 8E

Bats R Age 22
2017 (2) Wake Forest
Pwr + + +
BAvg + + +
Spd + + + +
Def + + +

Year	Lev	Team	AB	R	H	HR	RBI	Avg	OB	Slg	OPS	bb%	ct%	Eye	SB	CS	x/h%	Iso	RC/G
2017	NCAA	Wake Forest	261	65	94	17	67	360	428	636	1064	11	79	0.57	21	5	39	276	8.72
2017	Rk	Billings	204	36	62	3	23	304	363	412	775	9	83	0.54	12	4	19	108	5.13

Athletic RH OF enjoyed successful pro debut. An inconsistent performer in college, found himself as a hitter in his junior season by utilizing a more compact, uppercut swing. Power in frame and swing. Should hit for 15-20 HRs at maturity; 20/20 potential also present. Will stick in CF, although arm is fringy.

Farmer,Kyle — 2345 — Los Angeles (N)

EXP MLB DEBUT: 2017 | H/W: 6-0 214 | FUT: Utility player | 6C

Bats R Age 27
2013 (8) Georgia
Pwr + +
BAvg + + + +
Spd + +
Def + +

Year	Lev	Team	AB	R	H	HR	RBI	Avg	OB	Slg	OPS	bb%	ct%	Eye	SB	CS	x/h%	Iso	RC/G
2016	Rk	AZL Dodgers	17	4	5	2	4	294	333	647	980	6	94	1.00	0	0	40	353	6.80
2016	AA	Tulsa	266	31	68	5	31	256	320	395	714	9	83	0.57	2	0	37	139	4.44
2017	AA	Tulsa	124	21	42	3	18	339	414	468	882	11	90	1.23	1	0	24	129	6.56
2017	AAA	Oklahoma City	223	32	68	7	38	305	343	480	823	6	84	0.36	0	4	35	175	5.47
2017	MLB	LA Dodgers	20	1	6	0	2	300	300	350	650	0	85	0.00	0	0	17	50	3.15

Offensive-minded backstop finally made it to the majors at 26 and played well in 20 G. Position versatility and contact-oriented approach at the plate are his best tools. Puts the ball in play regularly and has a minor league career .297 BA. Below-average power and fringe defense behind the plate limit him to a utility role in the majors.

Feliciano,Mario

2 | **Milwaukee** | EXP MLB DEBUT: 2020 | H/W: 6-1 195 | FUT: Starting C | **7C**

Bats R Age 19
2016 (S-2) HS (PR)

Pwr ++
BAvg +++
Spd +++
Def ++

Year	Lev	Team	AB	R	H	HR	RBI	Avg	OB	Slg	OPS	bb%	ct%	Eye	SB	CS	x/h%	Iso	RC/G
2016	Rk	AZL Brewers	117	16	31	0	16	265	306	359	665	6	84	0.37	2	2	26	94	3.77
2017	A	Wisconsin	402	47	101	4	36	251	310	331	640	8	82	0.47	10	2	22	80	3.46

Athletic, hit-first RHH catcher made defensive strides to stick at position. Solid hitting approach at plate. Drives ball up the middle with compact swing. Has pull power but stays within self. Has solid foot speed, using smarts to steal bases. Has worked hard on catching footwork but still lacks framing skills.

Ferguson,Drew

789 | **Houston** | EXP MLB DEBUT: 2018 | H/W: 5-11 180 | FUT: Starting OF | **7D**

Bats R Age 25
2015 (19) Belmont

Pwr ++
BAvg +++
Spd +++
Def +++

Year	Lev	Team	AB	R	H	HR	RBI	Avg	OB	Slg	OPS	bb%	ct%	Eye	SB	CS	x/h%	Iso	RC/G
2015	A	Quad Cities	174	23	50	1	21	287	347	374	721	8	82	0.50	10	4	24	86	4.51
2016	A+	Lancaster	326	70	102	14	69	313	396	531	927	12	75	0.55	28	9	40	218	7.34
2016	AA	Corpus Christi	52	14	17	3	7	327	397	615	1012	10	75	0.46	2	0	47	288	8.35
2017	AA	Corpus Christi	312	55	91	8	32	292	381	426	807	13	75	0.58	15	5	29	135	5.77
2017	AAA	Fresno	103	11	23	1	9	223	304	320	625	10	80	0.57	3	1	35	97	3.39

Short, slender OF with good-but-not-great tools across the board. Works counts well and draws plenty of walks; likes to run and could be an SB asset. Makes solid contact with simple RH stroke. Not a major HR threat and power is limited to pull side. Best chance for impact is BA/SB as fourth-OF type.

Fisher,Jameson

7 | **Chicago (A)** | EXP MLB DEBUT: 2019 | H/W: 6-2 200 | FUT: Reserve OF | **6C**

Bats L Age 24
2016 (4) SE Louisiana

Pwr ++
BAvg +++
Spd ++
Def ++

Year	Lev	Team	AB	R	H	HR	RBI	Avg	OB	Slg	OPS	bb%	ct%	Eye	SB	CS	x/h%	Iso	RC/G
2016	NCAA	SE Louisiana	198	49	84	11	66	424	548	692	1240	21	84	1.74	15	0	35	268	11.55
2016	Rk	Great Falls	187	39	64	4	25	342	425	487	912	13	77	0.63	13	7	28	144	7.18
2017	A	Kannapolis	223	35	60	3	36	269	358	417	775	12	74	0.53	2	2	37	148	5.50
2017	A+	Winston-Salem	235	33	52	7	32	221	302	387	689	10	77	0.49	3	4	46	166	4.09

Smooth-swinging OF is a one-dimensional prospect. Hit tool carries profile despite High-A struggle. Works counts, makes solid contact. Power improved in High-A but BA crashed. Had shoulder surgery in college, limiting his defensive profile to LF. Already a below-average runner, likely profiles as bench or platoon bat in LF.

Fletcher,David

46 | **Los Angeles (A)** | EXP MLB DEBUT: 2018 | H/W: 5-10 175 | FUT: Starting SS | **7C**

Bats R Age 23
2015 (6) Loyola Marymount

Pwr ++
BAvg +++
Spd +++
Def +++

Year	Lev	Team	AB	R	H	HR	RBI	Avg	OB	Slg	OPS	bb%	ct%	Eye	SB	CS	x/h%	Iso	RC/G
2015	A	Burlington	120	18	34	1	10	283	348	358	707	9	89	0.92	6	1	18	75	4.48
2016	A+	Inland Empire	324	42	89	3	31	275	321	346	666	6	87	0.51	15	3	18	71	3.77
2016	AA	Arkansas	80	10	24	0	6	300	325	375	700	4	84	0.23	1	0	25	75	4.01
2017	AA	Mobile	243	32	67	1	22	276	333	354	687	8	88	0.70	12	5	24	78	4.19
2017	AAA	Salt Lake	205	27	52	2	17	254	275	322	597	3	88	0.24	8	1	17	68	2.78

Fundamentally-sound MIF who has hit at each level of minors, though not likely to be offensive threat. Very limited pop, but makes easy contact. Used speed to set high in SB and plays above tools due to instincts. Very solid defender at both 2B and SS and has quickness and range for either. Tied a career high with three HR.

Florial,Estevan

8 | **New York (A)** | EXP MLB DEBUT: 2019 | H/W: 6-1 185 | FUT: Starting OF | **9D**

Bats L Age 20
2015 FA (HT)

Pwr +++
BAvg +++
Spd ++++
Def +++

Year	Lev	Team	AB	R	H	HR	RBI	Avg	OB	Slg	OPS	bb%	ct%	Eye	SB	CS	x/h%	Iso	RC/G
2016	Rk	Pulaski	236	36	53	7	25	225	307	364	671	11	67	0.36	10	2	34	140	3.89
2016	A	Charleston (Sc)	20	4	6	1	5	300	364	550	914	9	75	0.40	0	0	33	250	6.97
2016	A+	Tampa	8	0	1	0	0	125	125	125	250	0	75	0.00	0	0	0	0	-2.09
2017	A	Charleston (Sc)	344	64	102	11	43	297	371	483	854	11	64	0.33	17	7	36	186	6.91
2017	A+	Tampa	76	13	23	2	14	303	376	461	837	11	68	0.38	6	1	26	158	6.36

Advanced OF who was 3rd in SAL in OBP and SLG in first full pro season. Best present tool is double-plus speed and has makings of becoming middle-of-order producer. Works long counts to find pitches to hit hard, though can be too passive at times. Lot of swing and miss with two strikes. Very good CF with plus range. Upside, but not without risk.

Foster,Jared

789 | **Los Angeles (A)** | EXP MLB DEBUT: 2019 | H/W: 6-1 200 | FUT: Starting OF | **7C**

Bats R Age 25
2015 (5) Louisiana St

Pwr +++
BAvg ++
Spd +++
Def +++

Year	Lev	Team	AB	R	H	HR	RBI	Avg	OB	Slg	OPS	bb%	ct%	Eye	SB	CS	x/h%	Iso	RC/G
2015	Rk	Orem	232	36	60	6	38	259	306	392	699	6	82	0.38	13	5	30	134	4.03
2016	A	Burlington	267	26	71	5	33	266	317	412	729	7	82	0.42	3	8	38	146	4.51
2016	A+	Inland Empire	160	23	47	4	23	294	311	438	748	2	79	0.12	6	2	28	144	4.41
2017	Rk	AZL Angels	9	2	1	0	2	111	200	111	311	10	89	1.00	1	0	0	0	0.04
2017	A+	Inland Empire	138	15	38	4	18	275	320	428	747	6	79	0.31	4	2	32	152	4.60

Athletic OF who missed time with injury, but exhibits solid-average tools when healthy. Impresses with raw power, but may not get to at higher levels unless he becomes more patient with swing-happy approach. Has raw feel for bat, but can beat out groundballs with pure speed. Crude routes in OF, yet has chance to stick in CF due to plus range.

Fowler,Dustin

789 | **Oakland** | EXP MLB DEBUT: 2017 | H/W: 6-0 195 | FUT: Starting OF | **8C**

Bats L Age 23
2013 (18) HS (GA)

Pwr +++
BAvg +++
Spd ++++
Def ++++

Year	Lev	Team	AB	R	H	HR	RBI	Avg	OB	Slg	OPS	bb%	ct%	Eye	SB	CS	x/h%	Iso	RC/G
2014	A	Charleston (Sc)	257	33	66	9	41	257	293	459	752	5	79	0.25	3	2	42	202	4.62
2015	A	Charleston (Sc)	241	35	74	4	31	307	337	419	756	4	80	0.23	18	7	22	112	4.63
2015	A+	Tampa	246	29	71	1	39	289	330	370	699	6	83	0.35	12	6	21	81	4.10
2016	AA	Trenton	541	67	152	12	88	281	309	458	767	4	84	0.26	25	11	38	177	4.81
2017	AAA	Scranton/WB	297	49	87	13	43	293	327	542	869	5	79	0.24	13	5	46	249	6.09

Improving OF who was having career year prior to knee injury in MLB debut. Set career high in HR despite missed time and exhibits plus speed on base and in CF. Good power for size, but can go gap-to-gap with line drive approach. Strikeout rate rose and could stand to be more patient. Quality defender with ample range, but arm may move him to LF.

Fox,Lucius

6 | **Tampa Bay** | EXP MLB DEBUT: 2020 | H/W: 6-1 175 | FUT: Starting SS | **8D**

Bats B Age 20
2015 FA (BM)

Pwr +
BAvg +++
Spd ++++
Def +++

Year	Lev	Team	AB	R	H	HR	RBI	Avg	OB	Slg	OPS	bb%	ct%	Eye	SB	CS	x/h%	Iso	RC/G
2016	A	Augusta	285	46	59	2	16	207	298	277	575	11	73	0.49	25	7	20	70	2.65
2017	A	Bowling Green	302	45	84	2	27	278	349	361	710	10	74	0.41	27	10	21	83	4.44
2017	A+	Charlotte	115	19	27	1	12	235	307	287	594	9	71	0.36	3	3	15	52	2.75

Premium athlete who returned to Low-A and fared well before jump to High-A. Has incredible quickness and fluid actions to project as above average defender at SS. Hands and arm work well together. Not much power yet, but controls bat with line drive stroke. Double-plus speed is best present attribute. High upside.

Franco,Anderson

35 | **Washington** | EXP MLB DEBUT: 2021 | H/W: 6-3 190 | FUT: Starting 3B | **7C**

Bats R Age 20
2013 FA (DR)

Pwr +++
BAvg ++
Spd +
Def ++

Year	Lev	Team	AB	R	H	HR	RBI	Avg	OB	Slg	OPS	bb%	ct%	Eye	SB	CS	x/h%	Iso	RC/G
2015	Rk	GCL Nationals	153	19	43	4	19	281	341	412	753	8	83	0.54	2	3	26	131	4.80
2015	A-	Auburn	40	0	9	0	4	225	340	300	640	15	95	3.50	0	0	22	75	4.42
2016	Rk	GCL Nationals	83	9	23	1	9	277	310	349	660	5	87	0.36	1	0	17	72	3.55
2017	A	Hagerstown	408	57	82	11	63	201	274	348	622	9	75	0.41	3	1	44	147	3.15

Struggled in first taste of full-season, which included lots of strikeouts and only moderate power. Primarily gap-to-gap hitter now with some barrel control and hard-hit contact that give hints of potential future production. An adequate fielder at 3B, also spent time at first. Taking it slow for now.

Franco,Wander

6 | **Tampa Bay** | EXP MLB DEBUT: 2022 | H/W: 5-10 160 | FUT: Starting SS | **9E**

Bats B Age 17
2017 FA (DR)

Pwr ++
BAvg +++
Spd +++
Def +++

Year	Lev	Team	AB	R	H	HR	RBI	Avg	OB	Slg	OPS	bb%	ct%	Eye	SB	CS	x/h%	Iso	RC/G
2017		*Did not play in the US*																	

Short, polished INF who was high profile signee and very advanced for age. Will likely stay at SS due to easy, quick actions, range, and average arm. Uses compact stroke from both sides along with plus bat speed to make consistent, hard contact. Recognizes pitches and possesses above average raw power. Very high upside.

Freeman,Tyler

46 | **Cleveland** | EXP MLB DEBUT: 2022 | H/W: 6-0 170 | FUT: Starting 2B | **7D**

Bats R Age 18
2017 (S-2) HS (CA)

Pwr ++
BAvg +++
Spd +++
Def ++

Year	Lev	Team	AB	R	H	HR	RBI	Avg	OB	Slg	OPS	bb%	ct%	Eye	SB	CS	x/h%	Iso	RC/G
2017	Rk	AZL Indians	128	19	38	2	14	297	333	414	747	5	91	0.58	5	1	29	117	4.69

Instinctual, savvy INF who may not have eye-popping tools, but succeeds with contact approach. Uses level swing path to make hard contact and is difficult to strike out. Power profile isn't there, but can reach seats on occasion. Quick, soft hands work well at SS, though may move to 2B due to arm and range. Could advance quickly for HS draftee.

Friedl,TJ — 8 — Cincinnati

EXP MLB DEBUT: 2019 | H/W: 5-10 170 | FUT: Starting OF | 7C

Bats L Age 22
2016 (NDFA) Nevada
Pwr ++
BAvg ++
Spd ++++
Def +++

Year	Lev	Team	AB	R	H	HR	RBI	Avg	OB	Sig	OPS	bb%	ct%	Eye	SB	CS	x/h%	Iso	RC/G
2016	NCAA	Nevada	222	68	89	3	35	401	476	563	1039	13	88	1.23	13	5	24	162	8.58
2016	Rk	Billings	121	24	42	3	17	347	410	545	956	10	79	0.52	7	2	38	198	7.55
2017	A	Dayton	250	47	71	5	25	284	358	472	830	10	82	0.63	14	8	44	188	6.01
2017	A+	Daytona	179	15	46	2	13	257	296	346	643	5	78	0.26	2	1	22	89	3.29

Athletic, quick-twitch LHH OF had solid full-season debut in Single-A. Promoted to High-A, didn't fare as well. Hit tool very raw despite advanced approach. Swing has length and is beaten by velocity. Trajectory of swing lends to some power in bat. A plus runner, uses tool to get on base and disrupt. Raw base stealer. Can cover ground in CF.

Galindo,Wladimir — 35 — Chicago (N)

EXP MLB DEBUT: 2020 | H/W: 6-3 210 | FUT: Reserve 1B | 7D

Bats R Age 21
2013 FA (VZ)
Pwr +++
BAvg ++
Spd +
Def ++

Year	Lev	Team	AB	R	H	HR	RBI	Avg	OB	Sig	OPS	bb%	ct%	Eye	SB	CS	x/h%	Iso	RC/G
2016	A-	Eugene	247	46	60	9	40	243	332	462	794	12	67	0.41	3	0	53	219	5.83
2017	A	South Bend	162	21	47	4	19	290	347	432	779	8	75	0.35	1	1	32	142	5.17

Strong, physically mature infielder has above-average power due more to physical strength than bat speed. Is stiff at the plate but does use the whole field. Below-average runner has the arm for 3B but not the range and he split time at 1B, which is a likely long-term destination.

Gallagher,Cam — 2 — Kansas City

EXP MLB DEBUT: 2017 | H/W: 6-3 230 | FUT: Reserve C | 6B

Bats R Age 25
2011 (2) HS (PA)
Pwr ++
BAvg ++
Spd +
Def ++++

Year	Lev	Team	AB	R	H	HR	RBI	Avg	OB	Sig	OPS	bb%	ct%	Eye	SB	CS	x/h%	Iso	RC/G
2014	A+	Wilmington	312	24	71	5	34	228	309	333	643	11	88	0.97	1	0	32	106	3.80
2015	A+	Wilmington	253	24	62	5	23	245	320	364	684	10	87	0.82	0	0	32	119	4.18
2016	AA	NW Arkansas	301	23	78	4	24	259	340	359	699	11	83	0.71	2	2	27	100	4.36
2017	AAA	Omaha	260	26	76	5	37	292	338	400	738	6	87	0.55	0	1	24	108	4.57
2017	MLB	KC Royals	24	2	6	1	5	250	333	417	750	11	83	0.75	0	0	33	167	4.85

Defense-first catcher who is progressing nicely, but doesn't hit for much pop despite hulking frame. Not adept at drawing walks and modest bat speed can be beaten with good fastballs. Could show more power if he tweaked swing. Very good receiver with strong, accurate arm. Has leadership ability and calls efficient game.

Gamboa,Arquimedes — 6 — Philadelphia

EXP MLB DEBUT: 2021 | H/W: 6-0 175 | FUT: Starting SS | 8E

Bats B Age 20
2014 FA (VZ)
Pwr ++
BAvg +++
4.19 Spd +++
Def ++++

Year	Lev	Team	AB	R	H	HR	RBI	Avg	OB	Sig	OPS	bb%	ct%	Eye	SB	CS	x/h%	Iso	RC/G
2016	A-	Williamsport	130	15	26	2	15	200	252	292	544	6	78	0.32	5	1	31	92	2.09
2017	A	Lakewood	307	44	80	6	29	261	332	378	710	10	83	0.63	8	0	26	117	4.40

Very good defender at SS featuring excellent range and a strong arm. Some projection left in his body, but has solid bat-on-ball skills, can take a walk and steal a base. Improvements and growth in power and against LHP necessary to become MLB starter.

Garcia,Aramis — 23 — San Francisco

EXP MLB DEBUT: 2018 | H/W: 6-2 220 | FUT: Starting C | 7C

Bats R Age 25
2014 (2) Florida Intl
Pwr +++
BAvg +++
Spd ++
Def ++

Year	Lev	Team	AB	R	H	HR	RBI	Avg	OB	Sig	OPS	bb%	ct%	Eye	SB	CS	x/h%	Iso	RC/G
2015	A+	San Jose	75	10	17	0	5	227	310	280	590	11	71	0.41	1	0	24	53	2.83
2016	Rk	AZL Giants	22	1	5	0	4	227	227	273	500	0	95	0.00	0	0	20	45	1.93
2016	A+	San Jose	144	20	37	2	20	257	323	340	663	9	71	0.33	1	0	22	83	3.70
2017	A+	San Jose	324	43	88	17	65	272	304	497	801	4	77	0.21	0	0	43	225	5.11
2017	AA	Richmond	78	11	22	0	8	282	356	436	792	10	73	0.43	0	0	55	154	5.80

Tall, strong CA who uses physical frame to advantage. Starting to realize power potential with highs in HR and doubles. Has been good hitter at every level. Has very aggressive approach and draws few walks. Owns plus arm behind plate, but is fringy defender with limited athleticism and receiving skills. Has played some 1B.

Garcia,Dermis — 35 — New York (A)

EXP MLB DEBUT: 2021 | H/W: 6-3 200 | FUT: Starting 1B | 8E

Bats R Age 20
2014 FA (DR)
Pwr ++++
BAvg ++
Spd +
Def +

Year	Lev	Team	AB	R	H	HR	RBI	Avg	OB	Sig	OPS	bb%	ct%	Eye	SB	CS	x/h%	Iso	RC/G
2016	Rk	Pulaski	194	31	40	13	24	206	319	454	772	14	59	0.41	0	2	55	247	5.71
2017	Rk	Pulaski	115	24	31	9	25	270	396	565	961	17	66	0.62	6	0	48	296	8.31
2017	A	Charleston (Sc)	110	12	25	8	20	227	315	518	833	11	62	0.33	0	0	60	291	6.49

Power-hitting INF who began year in Rookie ball before elevation to A- in August. Has tremendous size and natural strength to produce all-fields power. Mature frame already and could have double-plus pop at peak. Typical slugger profile—lot of Ks and low BA. Speed and defense are well below average and needs to improve raw glove.

Garcia,Jose Adolis — 89 — St. Louis

EXP MLB DEBUT: 2018 | H/W: 6-1 180 | FUT: Starting OF | 8C

Bats R Age 25
2017 FA (CU)
Pwr +++
BAvg +++
Spd ++++
Def ++++

Year	Lev	Team	AB	R	H	HR	RBI	Avg	OB	Sig	OPS	bb%	ct%	Eye	SB	CS	x/h%	Iso	RC/G
2017	AA	Springfield	309	43	88	12	55	285	340	476	816	8	75	0.34	12	8	40	191	5.61
2017	AAA	Memphis	136	21	41	3	10	301	336	478	814	5	77	0.23	3	1	39	176	5.50

Athletic Cuban OF had a solid pro debut, hitting .290/.340/.476 between AA/AAA. Has plus speed and average power with an aggressive approach at the plate and a quick bat. Struggles against off-speed stuff, but has the tools to be an everyday RF with an outstanding arm.

Garcia,Julio — 56 — Los Angeles (A)

EXP MLB DEBUT: 2021 | H/W: 6-0 175 | FUT: Starting SS | 7D

Bats R Age 20
2014 FA (DR)
Pwr +
BAvg ++
Spd ++
Def +++

Year	Lev	Team	AB	R	H	HR	RBI	Avg	OB	Sig	OPS	bb%	ct%	Eye	SB	CS	x/h%	Iso	RC/G
2015	Rk	AZL Angels	58	5	13	0	6	224	250	259	509	3	72	0.13	4	0	15	34	1.39
2016	Rk	AZL Angels	47	2	7	0	7	149	216	213	428	8	72	0.31	1	0	43	64	0.54
2017	Rk	Orem	70	13	23	0	11	329	356	457	813	4	73	0.16	0	1	39	129	5.70
2017	Rk	AZL Angels	159	31	45	1	23	283	367	415	782	12	79	0.62	3	2	33	132	5.53

Improving INF who has yet to see full season, but bat starting to come around. Driving ball more to gaps while showing more consistent swing path. Could develop BA skills with added strength. Power not part of equation. Split time between SS and 3B and has range and plus arm for both. Glove instincts a bit short.

Garcia,Luis — 46 — Washington

EXP MLB DEBUT: 2022 | H/W: 6-0 190 | FUT: Starting 2B | 8D

Bats L Age 17
2016 FA (DR)
Pwr ++
BAvg ++++
Spd ++++
Def ++++

Year	Lev	Team	AB	R	H	HR	RBI	Avg	OB	Sig	OPS	bb%	ct%	Eye	SB	CS	x/h%	Iso	RC/G
2017	Rk	GCL Nationals	199	25	60	1	22	302	332	387	719	4	84	0.28	11	2	20	85	4.24

One of the headliners from 2016 international class, he hit as 17 year old, using very good hand-eye coordination and a flat, contact-oriented swing. Physical projection left for additional power, and has excellent instincts and confidence. Plus runner with SB potential. Can play all three IF spots, but likely settles at 2B.

Garrett,Stone — 789 — Miami

EXP MLB DEBUT: 2021 | H/W: 6-2 195 | FUT: Starting OF | 8E

Bats R Age 22
2014 (8) HS (TX)
Pwr +++
BAvg ++
Spd +++
Def ++

Year	Lev	Team	AB	R	H	HR	RBI	Avg	OB	Sig	OPS	bb%	ct%	Eye	SB	CS	x/h%	Iso	RC/G
2014	Rk	GCL Marlins	148	17	35	0	11	236	271	270	541	5	79	0.23	4	1	11	34	2.00
2015	A-	Batavia	222	36	66	11	46	297	353	581	934	8	73	0.32	8	5	53	284	7.35
2016	Rk	GCL Marlins	7	1	1	0	0	143	333	143	476	22	57	0.67	1	0	0	0	0.93
2016	A	Greensboro	197	21	42	6	16	213	255	371	625	5	64	0.15	1	2	40	157	3.15
2017	A+	Jupiter	373	37	79	4	29	212	254	314	567	5	66	0.17	8	1	37	102	2.32

Physical athlete has been a bust as a pro with a career .235 BA. Tends to hit off his front foot, but has plus bat speed and raw, projectable power if he can fix his lower half. Plus raw power, but it doesn't translate to game action. Needs to make more consistent contact to fully tap into his considerable raw talent.

Garver,Mitch — 237 — Minnesota

EXP MLB DEBUT: 2017 | H/W: 6-1 220 | FUT: Starting C | 7C

Bats R Age 27
2013 (9) New Mexico
Pwr +++
BAvg ++
Spd +
Def ++

Year	Lev	Team	AB	R	H	HR	RBI	Avg	OB	Sig	OPS	bb%	ct%	Eye	SB	CS	x/h%	Iso	RC/G
2015	A+	Fort Myers	433	46	106	4	58	245	349	333	681	14	81	0.84	5	3	27	88	4.29
2016	AA	Chattanooga	358	44	92	11	66	257	337	419	756	11	76	0.50	1	3	39	162	4.98
2016	AAA	Rochester	76	6	25	1	8	329	386	434	820	8	72	0.33	0	0	24	105	5.87
2017	AAA	Rochester	320	56	93	17	45	291	386	541	927	14	73	0.59	2	0	49	250	7.42
2017	MLB	Minnesota	46	5	9	0	3	196	288	348	636	12	67	0.40	0	0	44	152	3.75

Versatile, steady prospect who set high in HR while providing value at multiple positions. Originally a catcher, but has played 1B and LF. Improving receiver with average arm. Not a standout with glove and may not have enough skill for full-time catching job. Draws walks in consistent approach and offers good pop to pull side.

Gasparini,Marten

78 | **Kansas City** | EXP MLB DEBUT: 2020 | H/W: 6-0 195 | FUT: Starting OF | **8E**

Bats B Age 20 — 2013 FA (IT)

- Pwr ++
- BAvg ++
- Spd ++++
- Def +++

Year	Lev	Team	AB	R	H	HR	RBI	Avg	OB	Slg	OPS	bb%	ct%	Eye	SB	CS	x/h%	Iso	RC/G
2014	Rk	Burlington	68	11	13	0	1	191	225	250	475	4	53	0.09	4	1	23	59	1.20
2015	Rk	Idaho Falls	197	36	51	2	25	259	342	411	754	11	59	0.31	26	9	31	152	5.86
2016	A	Lexington	382	35	75	7	42	196	257	293	550	8	65	0.23	14	10	28	97	2.04
2017	A	Lexington	406	48	92	9	50	227	275	355	630	6	70	0.22	18	11	34	128	3.13

Raw prospect who was moved to OF in '17. Repeated Low-A and wasn't much better after disastrous 2016. Showed promise, though, with high in HR. Has good gap power and could grow into average HR pop at peak. Has plus speed and could steal more bases with better approach and OBP. Very solid OF with surprisingly advanced range and jumps.

Gassaway,Randolph

7 | **Baltimore** | EXP MLB DEBUT: 2019 | H/W: 6-4 210 | FUT: Starting OF | **7E**

Bats R Age 22 — 2013 (16) HS (GA)

- Pwr ++
- BAvg +++
- Spd ++
- Def ++

Year	Lev	Team	AB	R	H	HR	RBI	Avg	OB	Slg	OPS	bb%	ct%	Eye	SB	CS	x/h%	Iso	RC/G
2015	A-	Aberdeen	227	22	62	0	22	273	313	335	647	5	79	0.27	0	2	23	62	3.41
2016	A-	Aberdeen	18	1	8	0	4	444	500	778	1278	10	78	0.50	0	1	63	333	12.24
2016	A	Delmarva	182	21	60	7	17	330	374	511	885	7	80	0.36	2	0	32	181	6.28
2017	A+	Frederick	431	48	114	5	58	265	302	348	650	5	81	0.28	3	3	22	84	3.38
2017	AA	Bowie	27	4	5	0	3	185	313	185	498	16	93	2.50	0	0	0	0	2.68

Late-blooming OF with strong, physical frame. Starting to turn raw tools into production. Offers good bat speed and some power, but still focuses more on line drives to gaps. Can be free-swinger at times, though covers plate well. Has limited speed and is improving defender, albeit still below average. Takes crude routes and has below average arm.

Gatewood,Jake

35 | **Milwaukee** | EXP MLB DEBUT: 2019 | H/W: 6-5 190 | FUT: Starting 1B | **8E**

Bats R Age 22 — 2014 (S-1) HS (CA)

- Pwr ++++
- BAvg ++
- Spd +++
- Def +++

Year	Lev	Team	AB	R	H	HR	RBI	Avg	OB	Slg	OPS	bb%	ct%	Eye	SB	CS	x/h%	Iso	RC/G
2015	Rk	Helena	212	38	58	6	41	274	330	476	807	8	68	0.26	3	5	52	203	5.90
2015	A	Wisconsin	177	16	37	4	16	209	267	316	583	7	63	0.22	5	0	27	107	2.54
2016	A	Wisconsin	496	70	119	14	64	240	267	391	658	4	72	0.13	3	2	39	151	3.38
2017	A+	Carolina	420	66	113	11	53	269	337	438	775	9	69	0.33	7	5	42	169	5.42
2017	AA	Biloxi	92	9	22	4	9	239	300	457	757	8	68	0.28	3	0	45	217	5.01

Tall, athletic 1B with considerable swing-and-miss in profile despite plus bat speed. Doesn't recognize spin well and struggles with velocity. Takes awhile to get trigger going, which regulates bat speed. Power in frame and upper-cut swing, struggles getting bat out in front to take advantage of power. A solid defender, has moved to 1B long term.

Gerber,Michael

89 | **Detroit** | EXP MLB DEBUT: 2018 | H/W: 6-0 190 | FUT: Starting OF | **7B**

Bats L Age 25 — 2014 (15) Creighton

- Pwr +++
- BAvg +++
- Spd ++
- Def +++

Year	Lev	Team	AB	R	H	HR	RBI	Avg	OB	Slg	OPS	bb%	ct%	Eye	SB	CS	x/h%	Iso	RC/G
2016	A+	Lakeland	351	52	99	14	60	282	342	481	824	8	68	0.29	2	3	39	199	6.00
2016	AA	Erie	153	17	40	4	20	261	347	431	778	12	73	0.49	6	0	38	170	5.42
2017	A+	Lakeland	18	3	8	0	2	444	500	667	1167	10	61	0.29	0	0	38	222	12.73
2017	AA	Erie	350	62	102	13	45	291	362	477	840	10	76	0.46	10	6	36	186	6.03
2017	AAA	Toledo	17	4	7	1	3	412	444	706	1150	6	65	0.17	0	0	43	294	11.06

Well-rounded, fundamentally-sound prospect who flies under radar due to lack of impact tool. Yet, produces with moderate power and sweet, line drive stroke. Reads pitches well and works counts to advantage. Possesses ability to play CF, though probably will end up in corner. Can shorten swing with two strikes.

Gettys,Michael

8 | **San Diego** | EXP MLB DEBUT: 2019 | H/W: 6-1 203 | FUT: Starting OF | **8D**

Bats R Age 22 — 2014 (2) HS (GA)

- Pwr +++
- BAvg ++
- Spd ++++
- Def ++++

Year	Lev	Team	AB	R	H	HR	RBI	Avg	OB	Slg	OPS	bb%	ct%	Eye	SB	CS	x/h%	Iso	RC/G
2014	Rk	Azl Padres	213	29	66	3	38	310	355	437	792	7	69	0.23	14	2	24	127	5.56
2015	A	Fort Wayne	494	62	114	6	44	231	272	346	618	5	67	0.17	20	10	34	115	3.07
2016	A	Fort Wayne	257	37	78	3	27	304	349	416	765	7	73	0.26	24	10	23	113	5.03
2016	A+	Lake Elsinore	248	40	76	9	33	306	351	468	819	6	69	0.22	9	6	29	161	5.77
2017	A+	Lake Elsinore	457	84	116	17	51	254	322	431	753	9	58	0.24	22	8	37	177	5.62

Toolsy OF who lacks polish but has upside if everything comes together. Is quality athlete and plus runner with impact SB potential. Owns one of minors' best arms and covers plenty of ground in CF. Ct% has been an issue, though he became more patient in 2017. Has strong wrists and bat speed for moderate HR impact, but strikeout woes are worrisome.

Gigliotti,Michael

8 | **Kansas City** | EXP MLB DEBUT: 2020 | H/W: 6-1 180 | FUT: Starting CF | **7C**

Bats L Age 21 — 2017 (4) Lipscomb

- Pwr ++
- BAvg +++
- Spd ++++
- Def +++

Year	Lev	Team	AB	R	H	HR	RBI	Avg	OB	Slg	OPS	bb%	ct%	Eye	SB	CS	x/h%	Iso	RC/G
2017	NCAA	Lipscomb	202	60	58	3	17	287	431	411	842	20	80	1.24	31	5	31	124	6.68
2017	Rk	Burlington	155	30	51	3	30	329	444	477	921	17	86	1.52	15	5	27	148	7.48
2017	A	Lexington	86	14	26	1	8	302	362	419	780	9	77	0.40	7	5	27	116	5.27

Lean, athletic OF with terrific pro debut. Gets on base consistently with selective eye and takes clean swings at hittable pitches. Focuses on putting ball in play and has enough punch to line gaps. Power isn't part of game, though isn't a slouch. Has excellent speed and tracks balls well in CF. Not a high upside guy, but good instincts for game.

Gillaspie,Casey

3 | **Chicago (A)** | EXP MLB DEBUT: 2018 | H/W: 6-4 240 | FUT: Starting 1B | **7D**

Bats B Age 25 — 2014 (1) Wichita St

- Pwr ++++
- BAvg ++
- Spd +
- Def +++

Year	Lev	Team	AB	R	H	HR	RBI	Avg	OB	Slg	OPS	bb%	ct%	Eye	SB	CS	x/h%	Iso	RC/G
2015	A+	Charlotte	41	3	6	1	4	146	222	268	491	9	78	0.44	0	0	33	122	1.48
2016	AA	Montgomery	293	51	79	11	41	270	390	454	844	17	73	0.73	5	1	41	184	6.48
2016	AAA	Durham	179	27	55	7	23	307	383	520	903	11	79	0.58	0	1	40	212	6.85
2017	AAA	Durham	353	45	80	9	44	227	298	357	655	9	78	0.47	1	1	33	130	3.60
2017	AAA	Charlotte	105	17	22	6	18	210	303	429	731	12	78	0.61	0	0	50	219	4.54

Big, lumbering switch-hitter struggled in Triple-A. Had difficulty making consistent hard contact. Hand-to-eye coordination is solid and will work pitchers. However, lacks bat speed to handle velocity. Power comes from frame, not swing. A poor athlete, 1B or DH is long term home.

Gimenez,Andres

6 | **New York (N)** | EXP MLB DEBUT: 2020 | H/W: 5-11 176 | FUT: Starting SS | **9D**

Bats L Age 19 — 2015 FA (VZ)

- Pwr ++
- BAvg ++++
- Spd ++++
- Def ++++

Year	Lev	Team	AB	R	H	HR	RBI	Avg	OB	Slg	OPS	bb%	ct%	Eye	SB	CS	x/h%	Iso	RC/G
2017	A	Columbia	347	49	92	4	31	265	320	349	669	7	82	0.46	14	8	18	84	3.78

Toolsy SS handled aggressive full season assignment to Single-A. Advanced hitter, still learning zone. Good bat-to-ball contact skills. Gets bat head out in front of plate on contact. Slight build, uses leverage to drive ball over strength. Likely 10-15 HR at projection. Plus runner with good instincts. Can steal a base. Has glove and arm for SS.

Gomez,Miguel

4 | **San Francisco** | EXP MLB DEBUT: 2017 | H/W: 5-10 185 | FUT: Reserve IF | **6B**

Bats B Age 25 — 2011 FA (DR)

- Pwr ++
- BAvg ++++
- Spd +
- Def ++

Year	Lev	Team	AB	R	H	HR	RBI	Avg	OB	Slg	OPS	bb%	ct%	Eye	SB	CS	x/h%	Iso	RC/G
2015	A-	Salem-Kaizer	276	30	88	6	52	319	331	442	773	2	91	0.21	0	1	24	123	4.68
2016	A	Augusta	267	41	99	8	43	371	398	532	930	4	91	0.48	3	2	26	161	6.54
2016	A+	San Jose	172	25	46	9	24	267	300	500	800	4	84	0.29	1	0	43	233	5.06
2017	AA	Richmond	308	43	94	8	38	305	331	458	789	4	88	0.33	0	0	31	153	4.99
2017	MLB	SF Giants	33	3	8	0	2	242	242	303	545	0	82	0.00	0	0	25	61	1.92

Fast-rising 2B who reached SF based upon easy BA and pure-hitting ways. Had drop off in power, but has ideal bat control and plate coverage. Doesn't walk much and puts ball in play early in count. Could hit for more pop if he changed approach. Very poor foot speed and is well below average defender. Possesses limited range and only average arm.

Gonzalez,Brayan

4 | **Philadelphia** | EXP MLB DEBUT: 2022 | H/W: 5-11 172 | FUT: Starting 2B | **8E**

Bats R Age 18 — 2016 FA (VZ)

- Pwr +++
- BAvg +++
- Spd +++
- Def ++++

Year	Lev	Team	AB	R	H	HR	RBI	Avg	OB	Slg	OPS	bb%	ct%	Eye	SB	CS	x/h%	Iso	RC/G
2017	Rk	GCL Phillies	134	23	36	2	24	269	329	388	717	8	75	0.36	6	0	33	119	4.42

Teenager with an innate feel for the game, he was signed as a SS but played first season at 2B, where his good arm and MIF actions translated well. Compactly built, he made fair contact with a solid approach and a simple swing. Currently has gap power and some SB ability, but is a long way from the majors.

Gonzalez,Jacob

5 | **San Francisco** | EXP MLB DEBUT: 2021 | H/W: 6-3 190 | FUT: Starting 3B | **8D**

Bats R Age 19 — 2017 (2) HS (AZ)

- Pwr ++
- BAvg +++
- Spd ++
- Def ++

Year	Lev	Team	AB	R	H	HR	RBI	Avg	OB	Slg	OPS	bb%	ct%	Eye	SB	CS	x/h%	Iso	RC/G
2017	Rk	AZL Giants	168	23	57	1	21	339	397	458	855	9	86	0.70	0	1	30	119	6.19

Advanced hitter who had terrific pro debut. Shows uncanny plate discipline and feel for strike zone. Uses clean swing to make good contact and has size and strength to project to at least average power. Limited speed and athleticism. Lacks range at 3B, but owns plus arm and soft hands. Could eventually move to 1B, but would need to add pop.

Gonzalez,Oscar

79 | **Cleveland** | EXP MLB DEBUT: 2022 | H/W: 6-2 180 | FUT: Starting OF | **8E**

Bats R Age 20
2014 FA (DR)

- Pwr ++++
- BAvg ++
- Spd ++
- Def +

Year	Lev	Team	AB	R	H	HR	RBI	Avg	OB	Slg	OPS	bb%	ct%	Eye	SB	CS	x/h%	Iso	RC/G
2016	Rk	AZL Indians	145	30	44	8	26	303	340	566	905	5	61	0.14	4	0	45	262	7.75
2016	A-	Mahoning Val	3	0	0	0	0	0	250	0	250	25	67	1.00	0	0		0	-2.42
2017	A-	Mahoning Val	237	20	67	3	34	283	298	388	686	2	74	0.08	0	0	28	105	3.69

Tall, slender OF with high upside based upon solid tools. Approach at plate needs significant work and fails to recognize spin. Long swing results in load of Ks. Exhibits well above average power potential and should grow to plus with continued maturation. Uses whole field and is close to average speed. Profiles well as RF with strong arm.

Gonzalez,Pedro

8 | **Texas** | EXP MLB DEBUT: 2021 | H/W: 6-5 190 | FUT: Starting OF | **9E**

Bats R Age 20
2014 FA (DR)

- Pwr +++
- BAvg +++
- Spd +++
- Def +++

Year	Lev	Team	AB	R	H	HR	RBI	Avg	OB	Slg	OPS	bb%	ct%	Eye	SB	CS	x/h%	Iso	RC/G
2016	Rk	Grand Junction	226	32	52	2	19	230	275	394	669	6	66	0.18	6	7	48	164	4.02
2017	Rk	Grand Junction	187	28	60	3	28	321	380	519	899	9	72	0.34	11	6	42	198	7.17
2017	A-	Spokane	17	2	0	0	0	0	105	0	105	11	53	0.25	0	0		0	-5.99

Projectable OF who had best year to date, though hasn't played in full season ball. Has significant ceiling based upon speed and plus power potential. Has added strength, but needs to fill out more. Bat speed should result in solid BA, though has holes in swing that can be exploited. Possesses true CF actions, but could move to corner if needed.

Gordon,Nick

6 | **Minnesota** | EXP MLB DEBUT: 2018 | H/W: 6-0 160 | FUT: Starting MIF | **8B**

Bats L Age 22
2014 (1) HS (FL)

- Pwr ++
- BAvg +++
- Spd +++
- Def +++

Year	Lev	Team	AB	R	H	HR	RBI	Avg	OB	Slg	OPS	bb%	ct%	Eye	SB	CS	x/h%	Iso	RC/G
2014	Rk	Elizabethton	235	46	69	1	28	294	325	366	691	4	81	0.24	11	7	16	72	3.89
2015	A	Cedar Rapids	481	79	133	1	58	277	331	360	690	8	82	0.44	25	8	23	83	4.11
2016	A+	Fort Myers	461	56	134	3	52	291	324	386	710	5	81	0.26	19	13	24	95	4.16
2017	AA	Chattanooga	519	80	140	9	66	270	337	408	746	9	74	0.40	13	7	33	139	4.89

Fundamentally-sound INF who has advanced one level per year, but wore down at end of 2017. Has exemplary barrel control with disciplined approach. Hits hard line drives to gaps and uses average speed well. Set high in HR and could be ideal table-setter. Saw K rate rise and didn't steal as many bags. Can play either MIF spot with plus arm strength.

Granite,Zack

8 | **Minnesota** | EXP MLB DEBUT: 2017 | H/W: 6-1 175 | FUT: Starting OF | **7C**

Bats L Age 25
2013 (14) Seton Hall

- Pwr ++
- BAvg +++
- Spd ++++
- Def +++

Year	Lev	Team	AB	R	H	HR	RBI	Avg	OB	Slg	OPS	bb%	ct%	Eye	SB	CS	x/h%	Iso	RC/G
2015	A+	Fort Myers	381	59	95	1	26	249	322	304	627	10	83	0.65	21	12	16	55	3.46
2016	AA	Chattanooga	526	86	155	4	52	295	347	382	729	7	92	0.98	56	14	19	87	4.70
2017	A+	Fort Myers	19	2	7	0	1	368	429	526	955	10	89	1.00	3	0	29	158	7.48
2017	AAA	Rochester	284	46	96	5	29	338	390	475	865	8	88	0.71	15	6	26	137	6.16
2017	MLB	Minnesota	93	14	22	1	13	237	324	290	614	11	90	1.33	2	2	14	54	3.59

Steady, progressing CF who reached MIN after showing offensive consistency in AAA. Set high in HR, though more of contact, all-fields hitter. Can hit at top of order with level swing path and easy contact. Tough to fan and has solid two-strike approach. Plays all OF positions with average arm. Plus speed accentuates range.

Greiner,Grayson

2 | **Detroit** | EXP MLB DEBUT: 2018 | H/W: 6-6 220 | FUT: Starting C | **7D**

Bats R Age 25
2014 (3) South Carolina

- Pwr +++
- BAvg ++
- Spd +
- Def +++

Year	Lev	Team	AB	R	H	HR	RBI	Avg	OB	Slg	OPS	bb%	ct%	Eye	SB	CS	x/h%	Iso	RC/G
2016	A+	Lakeland	109	14	34	0	12	312	380	367	747	10	76	0.46	0	0	18	55	4.93
2016	AA	Erie	208	20	60	7	30	288	321	462	783	5	74	0.18	1	0	32	173	5.05
2016	AAA	Toledo	4	0	0	0	0	0	0	0	0	0	50	0.00	0	0		0	-7.85
2017	AA	Erie	328	34	79	14	42	241	320	436	756	10	78	0.53	0	0	44	195	4.89
2017	AAA	Toledo	14	0	2	0	2	143	250	214	464	13	79	0.67	0	0	50	71	1.45

Tall, agile backstop who repeated AA and set career-high in HR. Doesn't wow with any particular skill, yet continues to have value. Defense is ahead of bat and has strong, accurate arm as asset. Blocks and receives well and provides big target for pitchers. BA ability in question as he can lunge at balls in aggressive approach.

Grier,Anfernee

78 | **Arizona** | EXP MLB DEBUT: 2020 | H/W: 6-1 180 | FUT: Starting OF | **7E**

Bats R Age 22
2016 (S-1) Auburn

- Pwr ++
- BAvg ++
- Spd ++++
- Def ++++

Year	Lev	Team	AB	R	H	HR	RBI	Avg	OB	Slg	OPS	bb%	ct%	Eye	SB	CS	x/h%	Iso	RC/G
2016	NCAA	Auburn	238	56	87	12	41	366	441	576	1016	12	77	0.58	19	5	26	210	8.33
2016	Rk	Missoula	14	2	3	1	2	214	214	500	714	0	64	0.00	0	0	67	286	4.18
2016	A-	Hillsboro	75	8	18	1	6	240	269	307	576	4	72	0.14	9	2	17	67	2.24
2017	A	Kane County	475	69	119	4	36	251	332	331	663	11	76	0.51	30	11	23	80	3.83

Athletically gifted LF-only prospect. Hit tool is raw. Plus bat speed but needs to refine swing path. Patient hitter, will work pitchers and take walks. Some power in frame but swing path doesn't suggest high HR totals. Has speed and is a heady base runner. Can cover ground in OF. Arm profiles in LF.

Grisham,Trent

789 | **Milwaukee** | EXP MLB DEBUT: 2019 | H/W: 6-0 205 | FUT: Starting OF | **9E**

Bats L Age 21
2015 (S-1) HS (TX)

- Pwr +++
- BAvg ++
- Spd ++++
- Def +++

Year	Lev	Team	AB	R	H	HR	RBI	Avg	OB	Slg	OPS	bb%	ct%	Eye	SB	CS	x/h%	Iso	RC/G
2015	Rk	Helena	42	5	13	1	5	310	431	381	812	18	81	1.13	5	3	8	71	6.01
2015	Rk	AZL Brewers	165	34	51	1	16	309	415	442	858	15	78	0.83	20	5	27	133	6.74
2016	A	Wisconsin	221	27	51	2	24	231	341	344	685	14	69	0.54	5	10	37	113	4.36
2017	A+	Carolina	457	78	102	8	45	223	360	348	708	18	69	0.70	37	5	34	125	4.74

Athletic OF stayed healthy, struggled with contact in '17. Exceptional approach, working counts and pitchers with high BB%. Quick, explosive LHH swing, produces hard contact to all fields. Despite approach, struggles with spin recognition, contributing to high K% and low BA, but gains power in lower half and swing. Potential 20/20; arm suited for LF.

Guaimaro,Albert

789 | **Miami** | EXP MLB DEBUT: 2019 | H/W: 6-0 180 | FUT: Reserve OF | **7D**

Bats R Age 19
2015 FA (VZ)

- Pwr +++
- BAvg +
- Spd +++
- Def +++

Year	Lev	Team	AB	R	H	HR	RBI	Avg	OB	Slg	OPS	bb%	ct%	Eye	SB	CS	x/h%	Iso	RC/G
2017	Rk	GCL Marlins	154	24	36	1	16	234	298	370	668	8	79	0.44	8	4	39	136	3.92

Aggressive Venezuelan OF is a good athlete with plus tools, but has yet to hit his stride. Quick, compact line-drive stroke with good bat speed, but needs to be more selective at the plate. Average to above speed with enough arm to play CF or RF. Will make his full-season debut in 2018.

Guerrero,Gregory

46 | **New York (N)** | EXP MLB DEBUT: 2021 | H/W: 6-0 186 | FUT: Starting SS | **8E**

Bats R Age 19
2015 FA (DR)

- Pwr +++
- BAvg +++
- Spd ++
- Def +++

Year	Lev	Team	AB	R	H	HR	RBI	Avg	OB	Slg	OPS	bb%	ct%	Eye	SB	CS	x/h%	Iso	RC/G
2017	Rk	GCL Mets	143	17	31	0	12	217	253	252	505	5	81	0.26	1	3	13	35	1.63

Toolsy athletic MIF with MLB bloodlines struggled in US debut; still extremely raw. Physically, should grow into power. Hit tool dependent on corraling wicked quick bat speed. Defensively, rangy at SS. However, body may grow out of position. Because of positional depth, has played 2B & 3B as pro too.

Guerrero,Vladimir

5 | **Toronto** | EXP MLB DEBUT: 2019 | H/W: 6-1 200 | FUT: Starting 3B | **9B**

Bats R Age 19
2015 FA (QC)

- Pwr ++++
- BAvg ++++
- Spd ++
- Def ++

Year	Lev	Team	AB	R	H	HR	RBI	Avg	OB	Slg	OPS	bb%	ct%	Eye	SB	CS	x/h%	Iso	RC/G
2016	Rk	Bluefield	236	32	64	8	46	271	361	449	810	12	85	0.94	15	5	36	178	5.74
2017	A	Lansing	269	53	85	7	45	316	405	480	884	13	87	1.18	6	2	34	164	6.72
2017	A+	Dunedin	168	31	56	6	31	333	451	494	945	18	83	1.29	2	2	25	161	7.69

Mega prospect who led minors in OBP in spectacular season. Hits for easy BA due to explosive bat speed, knowledge of strike zone, and plate coverage. Reads pitches well and rarely fans. Well above average raw power yet to surface in games, but has 30+ HR potential. Below average defender now, though possesses average range.

Guillorme,Luis

456 | **New York (N)** | EXP MLB DEBUT: 2018 | H/W: 5-9 199 | FUT: Starting MIF | **7C**

Bats L Age 23
2013 (10) HS (FL)

- Pwr +
- BAvg +++
- Spd +++
- Def ++++

Year	Lev	Team	AB	R	H	HR	RBI	Avg	OB	Slg	OPS	bb%	ct%	Eye	SB	CS	x/h%	Iso	RC/G
2014	Rk	Kingsport	238	38	67	0	17	282	329	324	653	7	88	0.61	6	4	15	42	3.70
2014	A	Savannah	9	2	3	0	0	333	400	333	733	10	100		0	0	0	0	5.15
2015	A	Savannah	446	67	142	0	55	318	392	354	746	11	84	0.77	18	8	11	36	4.96
2016	A+	St. Lucie	441	47	116	1	46	263	329	315	644	9	86	0.68	4	2	16	52	3.67
2017	AA	Binghamton	481	70	136	1	43	283	376	331	707	13	89	1.31	4	3	15	48	4.74

Contact-oriented, defensively sound MIF continues to defy expectations with the bat. Advanced hitter with good hand-eye skills and understanding of zone. Uses all fields, takes what the pitcher gives him with a flick of his wrists. Uses lower body to drive ball to gaps more, but still no HR power to speak of. Defensively skilled at 2B and SS.

Gurriel,Lourdes — 46 — Toronto

EXP MLB DEBUT: 2018 | H/W: 6-2 185 | FUT: Starting 3B | **7B**

Bats R Age 24
2016 FA (CU)

- Pwr + + +
- BAvg + + +
- Spd + + +
- Def + +

Year	Lev	Team	AB	R	H	HR	RBI	Avg	OB	Slg	OPS	bb%	ct%	Eye	SB	CS	x/h%	Iso	RC/G
2017	A+	Dunedin	66	6	13	1	8	197	221	258	478	3	80	0.15	1	0	15	61	1.10
2017	AA	New Hampshire	170	20	41	4	28	241	283	371	654	6	82	0.33	2	0	34	129	3.46

Thin, athletic INF who started late due to hamstring issue. Lingered for most of season, but showed above average tools. Split time between 2B and SS, though was exclusively SS in AFL. Likely to move to 3B with strong arm and range. Knows strike zone with advanced approach and has power to be asset. Swing can get long and needs polish with glove.

Gushue,Taylor — 2 — Washington

EXP MLB DEBUT: 2019 | H/W: 6-1 215 | FUT: Reserve C | **7D**

Bats B Age 24
2014 (4) Florida

- Pwr + + +
- BAvg + +
- Spd + +
- Def + +

Year	Lev	Team	AB	R	H	HR	RBI	Avg	OB	Slg	OPS	bb%	ct%	Eye	SB	CS	x/h%	Iso	RC/G
2014	A-	Jamestown	199	25	48	5	29	241	332	402	734	12	81	0.73	0	1	42	161	4.82
2015	A	West Virginia	360	35	83	5	47	231	281	342	622	6	78	0.32	1	2	31	111	3.12
2016	A+	Bradenton	328	42	74	8	38	226	276	357	633	7	79	0.33	0	0	35	131	3.21
2017	A+	Potomac	323	38	78	18	67	241	327	437	763	11	73	0.47	0	0	35	195	4.95
2017	AA	Harrisburg	12	0	1	0	0	83	154	83	237	8	92	1.00	0	0	0	0	-0.66

Repeated Hi-A with new organization, and had best power year as a pro. Thick, strong frame and powerful lower half got good raw power to show up in games. Hitting LHP, making contact, only average bat speed are still shortcomings. Defense adequate but not standout. Strikeouts might keep him from showcasing natural pop.

Gutierrez,Kelvin — 5 — Washington

EXP MLB DEBUT: 2019 | H/W: 6-3 185 | FUT: Reserve 3B | **7C**

Bats R Age 23
2013 FA (DR)

- Pwr +
- BAvg + +
- Spd +
- Def + +

Year	Lev	Team	AB	R	H	HR	RBI	Avg	OB	Slg	OPS	bb%	ct%	Eye	SB	CS	x/h%	Iso	RC/G
2016	A-	Auburn	31	5	10	0	6	323	382	419	802	9	84	0.60	4	0	30	97	5.59
2016	A	Hagerstown	377	58	113	3	48	300	350	406	756	7	83	0.45	19	7	25	106	4.87
2016	A+	Potomac	38	7	9	1	2	237	293	342	635	7	87	0.60	2	2	22	105	3.38
2017	Rk	GCL Nationals	33	6	7	0	1	212	297	364	661	11	79	0.57	2	0	57	152	4.04
2017	A+	Potomac	222	34	64	2	16	288	344	414	759	8	73	0.32	3	0	28	126	5.06

High energy player with enough athleticism/size that give him a chance. There's some feel to hit, and patience needs to improve, but power so far has been almost non-existent, which is problematic for a corner infielder. Adjusting swing to get more balls in the air would be a start. Makes the plays on defense.

Guzman,Jeison — 6 — Kansas City

EXP MLB DEBUT: 2022 | H/W: 6-2 180 | FUT: Starting SS | **8E**

Bats B Age 19
2015 FA (DR)

- Pwr + +
- BAvg + + +
- Spd + +
- Def + + +

Year	Lev	Team	AB	R	H	HR	RBI	Avg	OB	Slg	OPS	bb%	ct%	Eye	SB	CS	x/h%	Iso	RC/G
2016	Rk	AZL Royals	188	35	49	1	19	261	325	378	703	9	77	0.41	5	3	31	117	4.35
2017	Rk	Burlington	193	21	40	0	15	207	285	249	534	10	77	0.47	3	3	15	41	2.12

Smooth, mature SS with big upside predicated on bat potential and knowledge of game. Not particularly flashy with glove, but makes plays with quick actions and average arm. Could move to OF or 3B if needed. Exhibits average, raw pop and sweet, level swing from both sides. Uses all fields and gap power could turn to HR.

Guzman,Jonathan — 6 — Philadelphia

EXP MLB DEBUT: 2022 | H/W: 6-0 156 | FUT: Starting SS | **8D**

Bats R Age 18
2015 FA (DR)

- Pwr + +
- BAvg + + +
- Spd + + +
- Def + + + +

Year	Lev	Team	AB	R	H	HR	RBI	Avg	OB	Slg	OPS	bb%	ct%	Eye	SB	CS	x/h%	Iso	RC/G
2017	Rk	GCL Phillies	153	17	38	1	13	248	299	320	619	7	84	0.46	5	1	18	72	3.21
2017	A-	Williamsport	19	2	5	1	2	263	391	421	812	17	84	1.33	0	1	20	158	5.87
2017	A+	Clearwater	3	0	0	0	0	0	0	0	0	0	0	0.00	0	0		0	

Currently a defense-above-hit SS, he is just 18 years old and shows some impressive traits with the stick. He makes very good contact with bat speed and already has a knack for discerning balls and strikes. Needs to add strength, but has the frame to do so. More usable foundational skills than many international teenagers.

Guzman,Ronald — 3 — Texas

EXP MLB DEBUT: 2018 | H/W: 6-5 205 | FUT: Starting 1B | **7A**

Bats L Age 23
2011 FA (DR)

- Pwr + + +
- BAvg + + +
- Spd +
- Def + +

Year	Lev	Team	AB	R	H	HR	RBI	Avg	OB	Slg	OPS	bb%	ct%	Eye	SB	CS	x/h%	Iso	RC/G
2015	A	Hickory	97	10	30	3	14	309	350	433	783	6	85	0.40	2	0	20	124	4.93
2015	A+	High Desert	422	54	117	9	73	277	321	434	754	6	76	0.27	3	0	35	156	4.79
2016	AA	Frisco	375	51	108	15	56	288	346	477	823	8	78	0.40	2	1	33	189	5.64
2016	AAA	Round Rock	88	9	19	1	11	216	266	330	596	6	74	0.26	0	1	37	114	2.76
2017	AAA	Round Rock	470	78	140	12	62	298	362	434	796	9	82	0.55	4	1	26	136	5.37

Tall, natural-hitting 1B who has advanced one level per year and is on verge of majors. Destroys RHP with simple swing and advanced pitch recognition. Uses entire field in improved approach and makes good contact. Power may not be enough for typical 1B, but should hit for high BA. Not much athleticism and speed is below average.

Hall,Adam — 6 — Baltimore

EXP MLB DEBUT: 2021 | H/W: 6-0 170 | FUT: Starting SS | **8E**

Bats R Age 18
2017 (2) HS (ON)

- Pwr + +
- BAvg + + +
- Spd + + +
- Def + +

Year	Lev	Team	AB	R	H	HR	RBI	Avg	OB	Slg	OPS	bb%	ct%	Eye	SB	CS	x/h%	Iso	RC/G
2017	Rk	GCL Orioles	9	4	6	0	2	667	667	1000	1667	0	78	0.00	1	0	33	333	16.18

Pure-hitting SS with nice upside, but raw tools. Will need time to revamp swing and can be pitched inside. Impresses by making hard contact and use of whole field. Plus bat speed and natural strength mean plus power could be in offing. Knows balls and strikes. Runs well at present and has quick hands and range. Actions and timing need work at SS.

Hampson,Garrett — 46 — Colorado

EXP MLB DEBUT: 2020 | H/W: 5-11 185 | FUT: Starting 2B | **8C**

Bats R Age 23
2016 (3) Long Beach St

- Pwr + +
- BAvg + + + +
- Spd + + + +
- Def + + +

Year	Lev	Team	AB	R	H	HR	RBI	Avg	OB	Slg	OPS	bb%	ct%	Eye	SB	CS	x/h%	Iso	RC/G
2016	NCAA	Long Beach St	245	55	75	2	26	306	380	400	780	11	84	0.74	23	8	23	94	5.36
2016	A-	Boise	256	43	77	2	44	301	411	441	853	16	78	0.86	36	4	31	141	6.69
2017	A+	Lancaster	533	113	174	8	70	326	390	462	852	10	86	0.73	51	14	25	135	6.16

Athletic player with an advanced hit tool and plus speed. Patient at the plate and barrels the ball consistently. Split time between SS and 2B and has the arm to play either spot. 51 SB were tops in the system.

Hansen,Mitch — 79 — Los Angeles (N)

EXP MLB DEBUT: 2020 | H/W: 6-4 210 | FUT: Starting OF | **8D**

Bats L Age 21
2015 (2) HS (TX)

- Pwr + + + +
- BAvg + +
- Spd + + +
- Def + +

Year	Lev	Team	AB	R	H	HR	RBI	Avg	OB	Slg	OPS	bb%	ct%	Eye	SB	CS	x/h%	Iso	RC/G
2015	Rk	AZL Dodgers	149	23	30	0	17	201	274	282	556	9	66	0.29	6	1	30	81	2.35
2016	Rk	Ogden	293	55	91	11	50	311	359	491	850	7	76	0.31	11	4	27	181	5.97
2017	Rk	Ogden	140	27	46	7	33	329	397	614	1012	10	79	0.55	4	3	48	286	8.20
2017	A	Great Lakes	263	32	52	5	25	198	285	312	597	11	71	0.43	11	3	33	114	2.85

Mixed results in first attempt at full-season leagues. Dreadful start at Low-A resulted in a demotion to rookie ball where he posted a 1.007 OPS. Long lefty swing results in contact issues, but above-average power gives him potential. Runs well for his size and split time at both corners.

Harrison, KJ — 2 — Milwaukee

EXP MLB DEBUT: 2020 | H/W: 6-0 208 | FUT: Starting C | **8E**

Bats R Age 21
2017 (3) Oregon St

- Pwr + + +
- BAvg + +
- Spd + +
- Def + +

Year	Lev	Team	AB	R	H	HR	RBI	Avg	OB	Slg	OPS	bb%	ct%	Eye	SB	CS	x/h%	Iso	RC/G
2017	Rk	Helena	185	38	57	10	33	308	385	546	931	11	70	0.42	0	0	42	238	7.48

Handled introduction to pro ball with flying colors. Bat-first RHH catching with solid feel for hitting, has long, lumbering swing that struggles against velocity. Has power in frame and swing trajectory, mainly to pull-side. Profiles only at CA, where he struggles defensively. Was a DH DH most of college season.

Harrison,Monte — 789 — Milwaukee

EXP MLB DEBUT: 2019 | H/W: 6-3 220 | FUT: Starting OF | **9D**

Bats R Age 22
2014 (2) HS (MO)

- Pwr + + + +
- BAvg + + +
- Spd + + + +
- Def + +

Year	Lev	Team	AB	R	H	HR	RBI	Avg	OB	Slg	OPS	bb%	ct%	Eye	SB	CS	x/h%	Iso	RC/G
2016	Rk	AZL Brewers	19	4	4	0	1	211	348	368	716	17	79	1.00	0	0	50	158	5.07
2016	A	Wisconsin	267	34	59	6	37	221	275	337	612	7	64	0.21	8	3	31	116	3.00
2017	A	Wisconsin	223	32	59	11	32	265	349	475	825	12	69	0.41	11	3	41	211	6.06
2017	A+	Carolina	230	41	64	10	35	278	320	487	807	6	70	0.20	16	1	42	209	5.54

Athletic, potential five-tool RHH star took tremendous step forward in 2017. Healthy, hit for power, flashing potential 30/30 production. Has shortened up swing, still struggles with pitch recognition issues that lead to high K%. Power in frame and swing, mainly to pull-side and CF. Rangy defender with a solid arm.

Haseley,Adam — 78 — Philadelphia

EXP MLB DEBUT: 2020 | H/W: 6-1 195 | FUT: Starting OF | 8C

Bats L Age 21
2017 (1) Virginia
Pwr ++
BAvg +++
Spd +++
Def +++

Year	Lev	Team	AB	R	H	HR	RBI	Avg	OB	Slg	OPS	bb%	ct%	Eye	SB	CS	x/h%	Iso	RC/G
2017	NCAA	Virginia	223	68	87	14	56	390	491	659	1150	16	91	2.10	10	4	36	269	9.83
2017	Rk	GCL Phillies	12	3	7	0	4	583	643	833	1476	14	75	0.67	1	1	29	250	15.42
2017	A-	Williamsport	137	18	37	2	18	270	338	380	717	9	80	0.50	5	3	30	109	4.46
2017	A	Lakewood	66	15	17	1	6	258	319	379	698	8	80	0.46	0	1	29	121	4.19

Two-way player at UVA, looked worn down by end of 2017. Makes up for unconventional swing mechanics with bat speed, but crouch-and-fire setup could limit power. Shows patience, contact and some foot speed, though fringy routes and average arm might move him to a corner OF. Well-rounded, but lacks a standout tool of many first rounders.

Hawkins,Courtney — 79 — Chicago (A)

EXP MLB DEBUT: 2018 | H/W: 6-3 245 | FUT: Reserve OF | 6E

Bats R Age 24
2012 (1) HS (TX)
Pwr ++++
BAvg +
Spd ++
Def ++

Year	Lev	Team	AB	R	H	HR	RBI	Avg	OB	Slg	OPS	bb%	ct%	Eye	SB	CS	x/h%	Iso	RC/G
2015	AA	Birmingham	300	39	73	9	41	243	291	410	701	6	67	0.20	1	4	41	167	4.24
2016	AA	Birmingham	418	35	85	12	60	203	253	349	603	6	67	0.20	0	3	44	146	2.76
2017	A	Kannapolis	28	2	10	0	1	357	400	500	900	7	61	0.18	0	1	40	143	8.09
2017	A+	Winston-Salem	18	3	4	2	5	222	222	556	778	0	78	0.00	0	0	50	333	4.25
2017	AA	Birmingham	295	33	56	10	27	190	244	325	569	7	64	0.20	0	0	34	136	2.22

Have we come to the end of the road for this former 1st round pick? 3rd shot at Double-A was much like round 1 and 2: disappointing. Inability to make consistent contact has derailed career. Still, power potential gives the slightest glimmer of hope. Could the 4th time in Double-A be the charm?

Hayes,Ke'Bryan — 5 — Pittsburgh

EXP MLB DEBUT: 2020 | H/W: 6-1 210 | FUT: Starting 3B | 8C

Bats R Age 21
2015 (1) HS (TX)
Pwr +++
BAvg +++
Spd +++
Def +++

Year	Lev	Team	AB	R	H	HR	RBI	Avg	OB	Slg	OPS	bb%	ct%	Eye	SB	CS	x/h%	Iso	RC/G
2015	Rk	GCL Pirates	144	24	48	0	13	333	422	375	797	13	83	0.92	7	1	10	42	5.73
2015	A-	West Virginia	41	8	9	0	7	220	319	244	563	13	83	0.86	1	1	11	24	2.82
2016	Rk	GCL Pirates	5	0	2	0	0	400	500	600	1100	17	80	1.00	0	0	50	200	10.07
2016	A	West Virginia	247	27	65	6	37	263	308	393	701	6	79	0.31	6	5	29	130	4.02
2017	A+	Bradenton	421	66	117	2	43	278	342	363	705	9	82	0.54	27	5	21	86	4.36

Had a solid campaign at High-A despite getting off to a slow start with a broken rib. Professional approach at the plate has resulted in a career .281 BA and he should continue to hit as he moves up. Power should develop once he learns how to turn on pitches and he was one of the youngest players in the FSL.

Hays,Austin — 89 — Baltimore

EXP MLB DEBUT: 2017 | H/W: 6-1 195 | FUT: Starting OF | 9C

Bats R Age 22
2016 (3) Jacksonville
Pwr ++++
BAvg ++++
Spd +++
Def +++

Year	Lev	Team	AB	R	H	HR	RBI	Avg	OB	Slg	OPS	bb%	ct%	Eye	SB	CS	x/h%	Iso	RC/G
2016	A-	Aberdeen	140	14	47	4	21	336	384	514	898	7	77	0.34	4	3	32	179	6.66
2017	A+	Frederick	262	42	86	16	41	328	358	592	949	4	85	0.30	4	6	40	263	6.75
2017	AA	Bowie	261	39	86	16	54	330	361	594	955	5	83	0.29	1	1	41	264	6.89
2017	MLB	Baltimore	60	4	13	1	8	217	242	317	559	3	73	0.13	0	0	31	100	2.04

Strong OF with huge breakout year. Consistently good and finished 2nd in minors in HR. Plus set of tools and should hit for BA and power. Terrific bat speed and leverage leads to plus pop to all fields. Revised swing and covers plate well. Not very patient, but makes good contact and uses whole field. Improving OF who can play CF with plus arm.

Heineman,Scott — 789 — Texas

EXP MLB DEBUT: 2018 | H/W: 6-1 215 | FUT: Reserve OF | 6B

Bats R Age 25
2015 (11) Oregon
Pwr ++
BAvg +++
Spd +++
Def +++

Year	Lev	Team	AB	R	H	HR	RBI	Avg	OB	Slg	OPS	bb%	ct%	Eye	SB	CS	x/h%	Iso	RC/G
2016	A+	High Desert	525	96	159	17	80	303	373	505	878	10	77	0.49	30	14	40	202	6.58
2017	AA	Frisco	468	82	133	9	44	284	353	427	781	10	74	0.41	12	9	32	143	5.36

Heady OF who had similar success from A+ in '16. Plays all OF spots and has effective grinding approach. Exhibits nice arm that is playable in corner. Speed is average and enhances range. SB output dropped, though not a concern. Uses patient approach to get on base, but swing mechanics conducive to high K totals. Can hit for BA, but not many HR.

Herbert,Lucas — 2 — Atlanta

EXP MLB DEBUT: 2020 | H/W: 6-0 200 | FUT: Starting C | 7E

Bats R Age 21
2015 (2) HS (CA)
Pwr +++
BAvg ++
Spd +
Def ++++

Year	Lev	Team	AB	R	H	HR	RBI	Avg	OB	Slg	OPS	bb%	ct%	Eye	SB	CS	x/h%	Iso	RC/G
2015	Rk	GCL Braves	4	1	2	1	1	500	500	1250	1750	0	75	0.00	0	0	50	750	16.26
2016	A	Rome	335	29	62	6	30	185	227	278	504	5	71	0.19	2	4	29	93	1.33
2017	A	Rome	375	40	91	8	50	243	292	368	660	6	80	0.35	3	0	33	125	3.57

Physically-mature, glove-first catcher with power potential. Wasn't over-matched as much 2nd time through Single-A. Still, raw hit tool. Solid hand-eye coordination, struggles expanding zone. Strength in frame and swing. Very hard contact when squares up pitches. Potential plus defender behind plate. Needs to be lighter on feet. Plus throwing arm.

Heredia,Starling — 789 — Los Angeles (N)

EXP MLB DEBUT: 2020 | H/W: 6-2 200 | FUT: Starting OF | 9E

Bats R Age 19
2015 FA (DR)
Pwr ++++
BAvg +++
Spd +++
Def +++

Year	Lev	Team	AB	R	H	HR	RBI	Avg	OB	Slg	OPS	bb%	ct%	Eye	SB	CS	x/h%	Iso	RC/G
2017	Rk	AZL Dodgers	28	8	12	2	9	429	500	857	1357	13	75	0.57	0	0	50	429	13.23
2017	Rk	Ogden	82	21	35	4	17	427	489	732	1221	11	71	0.42	5	4	46	305	11.75
2017	A	Great Lakes	99	14	21	1	8	212	284	323	608	9	62	0.26	5	1	38	111	3.18

Toolsy Dominican OF generates mixed reviews from scouts. Bigger than his listed frame, he has plus bat speed and raw strength generates above-average power. Overly aggressive approach can be swing-and-miss, but hit combined .325 on the year with a .952 OPS. Moves well in the OF with a strong arm. High risk/high reward.

Hermosillo,Michael — 789 — Los Angeles (A)

EXP MLB DEBUT: 2018 | H/W: 5-11 190 | FUT: Reserve OF | 6B

Bats R Age 23
2013 (28) HS (IL)
Pwr ++
BAvg ++
Spd ++++
Def +++

Year	Lev	Team	AB	R	H	HR	RBI	Avg	OB	Slg	OPS	bb%	ct%	Eye	SB	CS	x/h%	Iso	RC/G
2016	A	Burlington	138	22	45	2	22	326	404	442	846	12	84	0.82	4	3	24	116	6.20
2016	A+	Inland Empire	149	36	46	4	17	309	376	490	866	10	80	0.53	6	7	33	181	6.35
2017	A+	Inland Empire	53	5	17	0	2	321	419	434	853	15	72	0.60	5	2	35	113	6.84
2017	AA	Mobile	278	40	69	4	26	248	343	353	695	13	74	0.55	21	9	28	104	4.33
2017	AAA	Salt Lake	115	20	33	5	16	287	328	487	815	6	76	0.25	9	2	36	200	5.44

Emerging prospect who set highs in SB and HR in breakout year. Sets tone with plus speed and has patient approach to get on base consistently. Helps in all OF spots as he possesses solid arm. Power isn't part of game, though starting to drive ball more. Not a great baserunner, but speed makes up for lack of instincts.

Hernandez,Brayan — 789 — Miami

EXP MLB DEBUT: 2022 | H/W: 6-2 175 | FUT: Starting CF | 8D

Bats B Age 20
2014 FA (VZ)
Pwr ++
BAvg +++
Spd ++++
Def ++++

Year	Lev	Team	AB	R	H	HR	RBI	Avg	OB	Slg	OPS	bb%	ct%	Eye	SB	CS	x/h%	Iso	RC/G
2016	Rk	AZL Mariners	130	13	37	1	19	285	321	400	721	5	72	0.19	9	3	30	115	4.43
2017	Rk	GCL Marlins	8	2	2	0	0	250	333	375	708	11	75	0.50	0	0	50	125	4.62
2017	A-	Everett	103	9	26	2	15	252	300	408	708	6	75	0.27	4	1	31	155	4.24
2017	A-	Batavia	59	9	16	0	3	271	295	407	702	3	76	0.14	0	0	31	136	4.14
2017	AAA	Tacoma	5	0	2	0	0	400	400	400	800	0	100		1	0	0	0	4.93

Athletic Venezuelan OF come over from Mariners in Phelps trade. Plus speed and arm are best tools. Quick bat and decent contact skills make for an above-average hit tool, but slender frame is built more for speed than power. Needs time, but has tools to be starting CF.

Hernandez,Ronaldo — 2 — Tampa Bay

EXP MLB DEBUT: 2021 | H/W: 6-1 185 | FUT: Starting C | 7C

Bats R Age 20
2014 FA (CB)
Pwr ++
BAvg +++
Spd +
Def +++

Year	Lev	Team	AB	R	H	HR	RBI	Avg	OB	Slg	OPS	bb%	ct%	Eye	SB	CS	x/h%	Iso	RC/G
2017	Rk	Princeton	223	42	74	5	40	332	377	507	883	7	83	0.41	2	2	38	175	6.36

Solid hitter and defender and exhibited quality skills in first year in U.S. Uses smooth swing to make average contact and offers some power potential with natural strength. Ultimate HR production is big question. Has advanced receiving skills that couple well with cannon arm. No major weakness in game, but no eye popping tools other than arm.

Hernandez,Yadiel — 79 — Washington

EXP MLB DEBUT: 2018 | H/W: 5-9 185 | FUT: Reserve OF | 7D

Bats L Age 30
2016 FA (CU)
Pwr +++
BAvg ++++
4.46 Spd ++
Def ++

Year	Lev	Team	AB	R	H	HR	RBI	Avg	OB	Slg	OPS	bb%	ct%	Eye	SB	CS	x/h%	Iso	RC/G
2017	AA	Harrisburg	397	57	116	12	59	292	380	441	820	12	83	0.85	5	2	29	149	5.85

Older Cuban defector who signed before 2017 season. Short but pure hitter who squares up pitches consistently with a balanced stroke. Patient and disciplined at the plate, works his way into hitters counts and makes solid contact with some power. Handled AA with no problem, could make MLB debut as a bench bat as soon as 2018.

Hill,Derek — 8 — Detroit

EXP MLB DEBUT: 2019 | H/W: 6-2 195 | FUT: Starting CF | 8D

Bats R Age 22
2014 (1) HS (CA)
Pwr + +
BAvg + + +
Spd + + + +
Def + + + +

Year	Lev	Team	AB	R	H	HR	RBI	Avg	OB	Slg	OPS	bb%	ct%	Eye	SB	CS	x/h%	Iso	RC/G
2015	A	West Michigan	210	33	50	0	16	238	304	314	619	9	79	0.45	25	7	22	76	3.27
2016	A	West Michigan	384	66	102	1	31	266	309	349	658	6	73	0.23	35	6	24	83	3.59
2017	Rk	GCL Tigers	49	11	8	1	7	163	305	286	591	17	69	0.67	7	0	38	122	2.92
2017	A	West Michigan	144	28	41	1	21	285	356	444	801	10	74	0.42	12	5	37	160	5.82
2017	A+	Lakeland	31	3	6	0	2	194	306	226	531	14	68	0.50	9	0	17	32	2.01

Athletic, fast OF who returned from Tommy John surgery in July. Was very good late in year and showing signs of bat breakout. Working counts more in order to get on base and use double-plus speed. Could stand to make more contact. Has leadoff potential if he improves selectivity. Terrific CF with plus range. Arm strength should return to normal soon.

Hilliard,Sam — 79 — Colorado

EXP MLB DEBUT: 2020 | H/W: 6-5 225 | FUT: Starting OF | 8D

Bats L Age 24
2015 (15) Wichita St
Pwr + + + +
BAvg + +
Spd + + + +
Def + + +

Year	Lev	Team	AB	R	H	HR	RBI	Avg	OB	Slg	OPS	bb%	ct%	Eye	SB	CS	x/h%	Iso	RC/G
2015	Rk	Grand Junction	222	45	68	7	42	306	403	532	935	14	75	0.65	12	4	41	225	7.65
2016	A	Asheville	461	71	123	17	83	267	346	449	795	11	67	0.37	30	12	37	182	5.73
2017	A+	Lancaster	536	95	161	21	92	300	360	487	847	9	71	0.32	37	17	32	187	6.18

Former 15th rounder had a breakout season, putting up big HR/SB numbers. Huge left-handed hitter has plus raw power and athleticism with 20/20 potential. Moves well in the OF with a plus arm and a was two-way player at Wichita State. Some swing and miss; will need to prove he can hit for average as he moves up.

Hinojosa,C.J. — 456 — San Francisco

EXP MLB DEBUT: 2018 | H/W: 5-10 175 | FUT: Starting 2B | 7D

Bats R Age 23
2015 (11) Texas
Pwr + +
BAvg + + +
Spd + +
Def + + +

Year	Lev	Team	AB	R	H	HR	RBI	Avg	OB	Slg	OPS	bb%	ct%	Eye	SB	CS	x/h%	Iso	RC/G
2015	NCAA	Texas	211	26	51	7	30	242	316	403	719	10	88	0.92	4	0	35	161	4.57
2015	A-	Salem-Kaizer	189	24	56	5	19	296	325	481	806	4	92	0.53	2	3	43	185	5.30
2016	A+	San Jose	260	45	77	6	34	296	382	442	824	12	82	0.78	1	4	30	146	5.94
2016	AA	Richmond	226	27	56	3	19	248	309	336	645	8	81	0.47	1	0	21	88	3.50
2017	AA	Richmond	373	47	99	4	35	265	322	340	662	8	89	0.74	5	4	20	75	3.86

Extreme contact hitter who can play any INF position. Uses level swing path to put ball in play and is very difficult to strike out. Can hit for BA, though not much punch in bat. Can chase balls out of zone, though makes contact. More of instinctual defender than tool-oriented and makes routine plays look easy. Strong arm is benefit at any spot.

Hiura,Keston — 4 — Milwaukee

EXP MLB DEBUT: 2019 | H/W: 5-11 190 | FUT: Starting 2B | 9C

Bats R Age 21
2017 (1) UC-Irvine
Pwr + + +
BAvg + + + + +
Spd + + +
Def + +

Year	Lev	Team	AB	R	H	HR	RBI	Avg	OB	Slg	OPS	bb%	ct%	Eye	SB	CS	x/h%	Iso	RC/G
2017	NCAA	UC Irvine	199	48	88	8	42	442	554	693	1248	20	81	1.32	9	6	38	251	11.87
2017	Rk	AZL Brewers	62	18	27	4	18	435	485	839	1324	9	79	0.46	0	2	44	403	12.12
2017	A	Wisconsin	105	14	35	0	15	333	375	476	851	6	77	0.29	2	0	37	143	6.20

Hard-hitting, contact oriented RHH 2B with spectacular hit tool; one of top hit tools in the game. Unorthodox swing produces loud, hard contact and he uses all fields. Power in frame and swing trajectory; played very little in field in 2017 due to Tommy John surgery but expected to recover. Likely 2B or LF future.

Holmes,Quentin — 8 — Cleveland

EXP MLB DEBUT: 2022 | H/W: 6-3 175 | FUT: Starting CF | 8D

Bats R Age 18
2017 (2) HS (NY)
Pwr + +
BAvg + +
Spd + + + +
Def + +

Year	Lev	Team	AB	R	H	HR	RBI	Avg	OB	Slg	OPS	bb%	ct%	Eye	SB	CS	x/h%	Iso	RC/G
2017	Rk	AZL Indians	159	22	29	2	15	182	222	289	511	5	62	0.13	5	4	34	107	1.50

Young OF who stands out with double-plus speed. Offense needs polish and time to develop. Raw approach at plate and likes to swing aggressively early in count. Has whippy swing to produce fringy power now, but should grow to average. Has BA potential as well with clean stroke. Making great strides in CF and has plus potential with better instincts.

House,Mason — 789 — San Diego

EXP MLB DEBUT: 2021 | H/W: 6-3 190 | FUT: Starting OF | 8D

Bats L Age 19
2017 (3) HS (TX)
Pwr + + +
BAvg + + +
Spd + + +
Def + + +

Year	Lev	Team	AB	R	H	HR	RBI	Avg	OB	Slg	OPS	bb%	ct%	Eye	SB	CS	x/h%	Iso	RC/G
2017	Rk	AZL Padres 2	164	28	48	2	33	293	345	463	808	7	59	0.19	3	0	33	171	6.78

Switch-hitting OF who turned heads in pro debut among rookie AZL ranks. Lean athlete who produces great bat head speed through zone and should hit for above-average power from both sides. Can be impatient hitter and consistency of contact will be a sticking point in his development. Good athlete who will have moderate SB value as an everyday RF/LF.

Howard,Ryan — 56 — San Francisco

EXP MLB DEBUT: 2019 | H/W: 6-2 195 | FUT: Utility player | 6B

Bats R Age 23
2016 (5) Missouri
Pwr + +
BAvg + + +
Spd + +
Def + +

Year	Lev	Team	AB	R	H	HR	RBI	Avg	OB	Slg	OPS	bb%	ct%	Eye	SB	CS	x/h%	Iso	RC/G
2016	NCAA	Missouri	217	40	64	5	27	295	378	433	811	12	85	0.88	10	0	30	138	5.76
2016	Rk	AZL Giants	8	1	2	0	0	250	400	250	650	20	100		0	0	0	0	5.05
2016	A-	Salem-Keizer	224	33	61	4	31	272	312	371	683	5	89	0.54	2	2	23	98	3.93
2017	A+	San Jose	526	59	161	9	50	306	335	397	732	4	85	0.28	7	2	19	91	4.30

Instinctual INF who hit .300 each month except August. Possesses decent tools and focuses on making contact with very short stroke. Rarely works counts and OBP entirely predicated on BA. Not much pop in bat and likely to hit at bottom of order. Has quick, strong arm playable on left side of infield, though range is limited. Fringy speed at best.

Huff,Sam — 2 — Texas

EXP MLB DEBUT: 2021 | H/W: 6-4 215 | FUT: Starting C | 8E

Bats R Age 20
2016 (7) HS (AZ)
Pwr + + +
BAvg + +
Spd +
Def + + +

Year	Lev	Team	AB	R	H	HR	RBI	Avg	OB	Slg	OPS	bb%	ct%	Eye	SB	CS	x/h%	Iso	RC/G
2016	Rk	AZL Rangers	97	19	32	1	17	330	425	485	909	14	70	0.55	0	0	38	155	7.67
2017	Rk	AZL Rangers	197	34	49	9	31	249	330	452	782	11	66	0.36	3	2	41	203	5.53

Tall, strong backstop who increased power production in solid all-around campaign. Increase in K rate could hinder BA development, though owns average raw power. More strength than bat speed and will need to recognize pitches better. Solid tools behind plate, highlighted by strong arm. Release and footwork need additional work.

Hunt,Blake — 2 — San Diego

EXP MLB DEBUT: 2020 | H/W: 6-3 185 | FUT: Starting C | 7D

Bats R Age 19
2017 (S-2) HS (CA)
Pwr + +
BAvg + + +
Spd + +
Def + + + +

Year	Lev	Team	AB	R	H	HR	RBI	Avg	OB	Slg	OPS	bb%	ct%	Eye	SB	CS	x/h%	Iso	RC/G
2017	Rk	AZL Padres	28	7	6	1	4	214	290	393	683	10	54	0.23	0	0	50	179	4.84
2017	Rk	AZL Padres 2	144	28	34	3	23	236	290	403	693	7	62	0.20	1	0	47	167	4.49

Defensively skilled CA whose upside is limited, but could grow into an average regular. Owns plus arm and smothers balls in the dirt efficiently. Hitch in load prevents him from fully tapping into his power, but stays short and simple for potentially average BA output. Good athlete behind the plate, but won't be a base stealer.

Hurst,Scott — 8 — St. Louis

EXP MLB DEBUT: 2020 | H/W: 5-10 175 | FUT: Reserve OF | 7D

Bats L Age 22
2017 (3) Cal St Fullerton
Pwr + +
BAvg + +
Spd + + +
Def + + +

Year	Lev	Team	AB	R	H	HR	RBI	Avg	OB	Slg	OPS	bb%	ct%	Eye	SB	CS	x/h%	Iso	RC/G
2017	NCAA	CalSt Fullerton	247	56	81	12	40	328	411	575	986	12	85	0.97	7	1	40	247	7.81
2017	A-	State College	213	36	60	3	21	282	349	432	781	9	73	0.38	6	4	33	150	5.45

3rd round pick out of Fullerton is undersized but has plus speed and is a grinder. Has some swing and miss to his game, but has good plate discipline and posted solid OBP. Covers ground well in the OF and should be able to stick in CF.

Ibanez,Andy — 4 — Texas

EXP MLB DEBUT: 2018 | H/W: 5-10 170 | FUT: Starting 2B | 7C

Bats R Age 25
2015 FA (CU)
Pwr + + +
BAvg + + +
Spd + +
Def + +

Year	Lev	Team	AB	R	H	HR	RBI	Avg	OB	Slg	OPS	bb%	ct%	Eye	SB	CS	x/h%	Iso	RC/G
2016	A	Hickory	185	28	60	7	35	324	416	546	962	14	85	1.04	10	8	43	222	7.66
2016	AA	Frisco	307	39	80	6	31	261	316	391	707	8	85	0.53	5	2	33	130	4.28
2017	AA	Frisco	310	33	82	8	29	265	319	400	719	7	85	0.52	6	1	29	135	4.37

Short, offense-first INF who puts ball in play with short, compact stroke. Returned to AA and posted similar numbers. Missed about six weeks due to finger injury, but still continued to hit. Understands balls and strikes and rarely misses ball. Has double-digit HR potential. Not a great athlete and has limited speed. Relegated to 2B with fringy arm.

Ice,Logan — 2 — Cleveland

EXP MLB DEBUT: 2019 | H/W: 5-10 195 | FUT: Starting C | 7D

Bats B Age 22 — 2016 (S-2) Oregon St

Pwr ++ | BAvg ++ | Spd ++ | Def ++++

Year	Lev	Team	AB	R	H	HR	RBI	Avg	OB	Sig	OPS	bb%	ct%	Eye	SB	CS	x/h%	Iso	RC/G
2016	NCAA	Oregon State	174	42	54	7	39	310	431	563	994	18	86	1.48	2	0	46	253	8.33
2016	A-	Mahoning Val	126	13	25	2	8	198	322	302	624	15	70	0.61	0	0	36	103	3.40
2017	A	Lake County	316	38	72	11	42	228	318	370	689	12	77	0.57	1	1	31	142	4.07

Sound defensive backstop with short, strong frame. Receives well and has agility to block balls. Possesses accurate, average arm. Considered good leader and calls mature game. Has posted very low BA in both pro seasons and doesn't project well. Draws walks in simple approach and offers fringe-average power to pull side. Bat development is key.

Jackson,Alex — 2 — Atlanta

EXP MLB DEBUT: 2019 | H/W: 6-2 215 | FUT: Starting C | 8C

Bats R Age 22 — 2014 (1) HS (CA)

Pwr ++++ | BAvg ++ | Spd ++ | Def ++

Year	Lev	Team	AB	R	H	HR	RBI	Avg	OB	Sig	OPS	bb%	ct%	Eye	SB	CS	x/h%	Iso	RC/G
2015	A-	Everett	163	31	39	8	25	239	326	466	792	11	63	0.34	2	4	51	227	5.94
2015	A	Clinton	108	10	17	0	13	157	202	213	415	5	68	0.17	1	1	35	56	0.11
2016	A	Clinton	333	43	81	11	55	243	313	408	722	9	69	0.33	2	1	40	165	4.55
2017	A+	Florida	257	44	70	14	45	272	307	502	809	5	71	0.18	0	1	44	230	5.42
2017	AA	Mississippi	110	12	28	5	20	255	317	427	744	8	71	0.31	0	0	32	173	4.66

Strong, RHH converted OF hit offensive stride after moving behind the plate. Average swing speed with a hitch in load, reacts poorly to breaking pitches. Swing trajectory and body crafted for big power, 25-plus HRs at projection. Work-in-progress defensively blocking pitches and framing zone. Can stop running game with throwing arm.

Jackson,Drew — 456 — Los Angeles (N)

EXP MLB DEBUT: 2019 | H/W: 6-2 200 | FUT: Reserve SS | 6B

Bats R Age 24 — 2015 (5) Stanford

Pwr + | BAvg ++ | Spd ++++ | Def ++++

Year	Lev	Team	AB	R	H	HR	RBI	Avg	OB	Sig	OPS	bb%	ct%	Eye	SB	CS	x/h%	Iso	RC/G
2015	A-	Everett	226	64	81	2	26	358	434	447	880	12	85	0.86	47	4	19	88	6.63
2016	A+	Bakersfield	524	87	135	6	47	258	322	345	668	9	80	0.48	16	8	24	88	3.81
2017	Rk	AZL Dodgers	10	1	2	0	4	200	273	600	873	9	60	0.25	0	0	100	400	8.45
2017	A+	Rancho Cuca	252	48	64	8	30	254	343	429	771	12	73	0.51	14	6	41	175	5.29
2017	AA	Tulsa	111	22	26	1	10	234	303	324	628	9	75	0.39	7	2	27	90	3.28

Plus athlete from Stanford has the tools to stick at short. Plus runner with a plus, plus arm, and soft hands. Poor power and issues making consistent contact limit his offensive upside; career SLG is just .385 making it likely his future is as a late-inning replacement.

Jackson,Zach — 2 — St. Louis

EXP MLB DEBUT: 2022 | H/W: 6-3 215 | FUT: Starting C | 7D

Bats L Age 19 — 2017 (6) HS (FL)

Pwr ++++ | BAvg ++ | Spd ++ | Def ++

Year	Lev	Team	AB	R	H	HR	RBI	Avg	OB	Sig	OPS	bb%	ct%	Eye	SB	CS	x/h%	Iso	RC/G
2017	Rk	GCL Cardinals	41	2	4	0	5	98	275	98	372	20	51	0.50	0	0	0	0	-1.20

Big-bodied high school catcher is an offensive-minded backstop. He gets plus raw power from his 6-3 frame. Uses a compact upper-cut swing to generate power and loft. Has a plus arm and good offensive potential, but is not nimble or athletic and will need to work hard to stick behind the dish.

Jansen,Danny — 2 — Toronto

EXP MLB DEBUT: 2018 | H/W: 6-2 225 | FUT: Starting C | 7C

Bats R Age 22 — 2013 (16) HS (WI)

Pwr ++ | BAvg +++ | Spd ++ | Def +++

Year	Lev	Team	AB	R	H	HR	RBI	Avg	OB	Sig	OPS	bb%	ct%	Eye	SB	CS	x/h%	Iso	RC/G
2016	Rk	GCL Blue Jays	9	0	2	0	2	222	300	222	522	10	78	0.50	0	0	0	0	1.94
2016	A+	Dunedin	188	18	41	1	23	218	300	271	571	10	79	0.55	7	1	20	53	2.66
2017	A+	Dunedin	122	19	45	5	18	369	408	541	949	6	89	0.57	0	0	24	172	6.83
2017	AA	New Hampshire	179	23	52	2	20	291	368	419	787	11	89	1.16	1	0	35	128	5.57
2017	AAA	Buffalo	67	8	22	3	10	328	423	552	975	14	90	1.57	0	0	36	224	7.77

Tall CA who had surprising breakout year at three levels. Set easy high in 2B and HR while making good contact and drawing more walks than Ks. Works counts and hits hard line drives to gaps. Solid receiver who blocks well, though needs polish with game calling and framing. Has been injury prone, but profiles as every day catcher.

Javier,Wander — 6 — Minnesota

EXP MLB DEBUT: 2021 | H/W: 6-1 165 | FUT: Starting SS | 9E

Bats R Age 19 — 2015 FA (DR)

Pwr +++ | BAvg ++++ | Spd ++++ | Def +++

Year	Lev	Team	AB	R	H	HR	RBI	Avg	OB	Sig	OPS	bb%	ct%	Eye	SB	CS	x/h%	Iso	RC/G
2017	Rk	Elizabethton	157	34	47	4	22	299	375	471	846	11	69	0.39	4	3	38	172	6.52

Toolsy, talented INF with electric bat ability and could become mega offensive producer. Can expand zone at times with erratic swing, but puts charge into ball with extreme bat speed and wiry strength. Has above average speed and strong arm now, but needs polish with throwing accuracy and SS actions. Very high upside.

Jimenez,Anthony — 89 — Seattle

EXP MLB DEBUT: 2020 | H/W: 5-11 165 | FUT: Starting OF | 8D

Bats R Age 22 — 2013 FA (VZ)

Pwr ++ | BAvg +++ | Spd ++++ | Def +++

Year	Lev	Team	AB	R	H	HR	RBI	Avg	OB	Sig	OPS	bb%	ct%	Eye	SB	CS	x/h%	Iso	RC/G
2016	Rk	AZL Mariners	186	30	58	1	22	312	354	441	794	6	77	0.28	14	6	29	129	5.39
2017	Rk	AZL Mariners	9	1	3	0	1	333	333	667	1000	0	78	0.00	0	0	67	333	8.05
2017	A	Clinton	228	43	68	7	33	298	352	482	835	8	68	0.26	24	10	38	184	6.23

Unheralded OF who had solid first year in full season ball before June injury ended season. All about speed and athleticism as he steals lots of bases and ranges well at all OF spots. Needs more mature eye at plate to get on base and has too much swing and miss in game. But has hit as pro with a very fast bat and fringy power.

Jimenez,Eloy — 79 — Chicago (A)

EXP MLB DEBUT: 2018 | H/W: 6-4 205 | FUT: Starting OF | 9B

Bats R Age 21 — 2013 FA (DR)

Pwr +++++ | BAvg ++++ | Spd ++ | Def +++

Year	Lev	Team	AB	R	H	HR	RBI	Avg	OB	Sig	OPS	bb%	ct%	Eye	SB	CS	x/h%	Iso	RC/G
2015	A-	Eugene	232	36	66	7	33	284	328	418	746	6	81	0.35	3	2	26	134	4.53
2016	A	South Bend	432	65	142	14	81	329	365	532	898	5	78	0.27	8	3	40	204	6.52
2017	A+	Winston-Salem	110	20	38	8	26	345	410	682	1092	10	81	0.57	0	2	53	336	8.97
2017	A+	Myrtle Beach	155	23	42	8	32	271	347	490	837	10	77	0.51	0	0	38	219	5.90
2017	AA	Birmingham	68	11	24	3	7	353	397	559	956	7	76	0.31	1	1	33	206	7.30

The centerpiece in the Jose Quintana trade, RHH OF improved on breakout 2016 campaign. Showed no ill effects from shoulder injury early in season, increasing his HR-to-fly ball ratio between two levels after trade. Has matured into disciplined hitter, chasing at a far lesser clip. Profiles as RF long term due to strong throwing arm.

Johnson,Bryce — 78 — San Francisco

EXP MLB DEBUT: 2019 | H/W: 6-2 180 | FUT: Starting OF | 7D

Bats B Age 22 — 2017 (6) Sam Houston St

Pwr + | BAvg +++ | Spd ++++ | Def ++++

Year	Lev	Team	AB	R	H	HR	RBI	Avg	OB	Sig	OPS	bb%	ct%	Eye	SB	CS	x/h%	Iso	RC/G
2017	NCAA	Sam Houston St	263	63	92	0	43	350	424	433	858	11	84	0.83	33	7	18	84	6.41
2017	A-	Salem-Keizer	222	41	73	0	16	329	377	369	746	7	77	0.33	25	10	10	41	4.72

Aggressive, fast OF who stands out for double-plus speed and terrific defense. Plays game with aggressive nature, both on base and in OF. Tracks down balls with good jumps and instincts and has average arm. Gets on base consistently, but slap approach doesn't project well for pop. Could steal ton of bases.

Johnson,Daniel — 789 — Washington

EXP MLB DEBUT: 2020 | H/W: 5-10 185 | FUT: Starting OF | 8D

Bats L Age 22 — 2016 (5) New Mexico St

Pwr +++ | BAvg ++ | Spd +++ | Def ++

Year	Lev	Team	AB	R	H	HR	RBI	Avg	OB	Sig	OPS	bb%	ct%	Eye	SB	CS	x/h%	Iso	RC/G
2016	NCAA	New Mexico St	246	67	94	12	50	382	424	630	1054	7	88	0.62	29	4	32	248	8.13
2016	A-	Auburn	245	25	65	1	14	265	286	347	633	3	83	0.17	13	3	22	82	3.13
2017	A	Hagerstown	327	61	98	17	52	300	344	529	873	6	79	0.31	12	9	38	229	6.11
2017	A+	Potomac	170	22	50	5	20	294	344	459	803	7	82	0.43	10	2	36	165	5.35

Raised stock with a 20/20 season across two levels. Undersized but strong, has above average raw power and the speed to be a MLB SB threat. But questions about his hit tool and ability to handle offspeed stuff remain, despite ample bat speed and quick-twitch actions. Reads and routes still need work, though strong enough arm for an OF corner.

Jones,Jahmai — 8 — Los Angeles (A)

EXP MLB DEBUT: 2019 | H/W: 6-0 215 | FUT: Starting CF | 8B

Bats R Age 20 — 2015 (2) HS (GA)

Pwr +++ | BAvg +++ | Spd ++++ | Def +++

Year	Lev	Team	AB	R	H	HR	RBI	Avg	OB	Sig	OPS	bb%	ct%	Eye	SB	CS	x/h%	Iso	RC/G
2015	Rk	AZL Angels	160	28	39	2	20	244	316	344	660	10	79	0.52	16	7	26	100	3.77
2016	Rk	Orem	196	49	63	3	20	321	387	459	846	10	85	0.72	19	6	29	138	6.10
2016	A	Burlington	62	8	15	1	10	242	299	306	605	7	79	0.38	1	0	13	65	2.85
2017	A	Burlington	346	54	94	9	30	272	333	425	758	8	82	0.51	18	7	33	153	4.90
2017	A+	Inland Empire	172	32	52	5	17	302	351	488	840	7	75	0.30	9	6	37	186	5.97

Strongly-built OF who had great year in 1st full season as pro. Promoted to A+ in July. Power emerged throughout year and he showed a more discerning eye. Natural athlete with plus speed and instincts. Owns plus bat speed and should turn doubles into HR over time. Solid CF with keen routes and average arm. Has chance to impact game with bat and glove.

Jones,Nolan — 5 — Cleveland

EXP MLB DEBUT: 2020 | H/W: 6-4 185 | FUT: Starting 3B | 8D

Bats L Age 19
2016 (2) HS (PA)

- Pwr +++
- BAvg +++
- Spd ++
- Def ++

Year	Lev	Team	AB	R	H	HR	RBI	Avg	OB	Slg	OPS	bb%	ct%	Eye	SB	CS	x/h%	Iso	RC/G
2016	Rk	AZL Indians	109	10	28	0	9	257	386	339	726	17	55	0.47	3	1	25	83	5.82
2017	A-	Mahoning Val	218	41	69	4	33	317	429	482	911	16	72	0.72	1	0	36	165	7.61

Tall, natural-hitting 3B who led NYP in OBP. Offers good size and should continue to add muscle to lean frame. Projects to plus power with clean, quick stroke and keen pitch recognition. Runs well for size, though may slow down. Current glovework is shoddy, though still new to 3B and owns fantastic arm strength. Needs to be better against LHP.

Jones,Thomas — 789 — Miami

EXP MLB DEBUT: 2021 | H/W: 6-4 195 | FUT: Starting OF | 8E

Bats R Age 20
2016 (3) HS (SC)

- Pwr ++
- BAvg ++
- Spd ++++
- Def +++

Year	Lev	Team	AB	R	H	HR	RBI	Avg	OB	Slg	OPS	bb%	ct%	Eye	SB	CS	x/h%	Iso	RC/G
2016	Rk	GCL Marlins	64	11	15	0	6	234	347	313	659	15	69	0.55	6	2	27	78	4.03
2017	A-	Batavia	238	31	43	2	21	181	283	282	565	13	61	0.36	7	6	37	101	2.55

Athletic two-sport star in HS had a horrendous season, striking out 94 times in 238 AB. Excellent speed, but ineffencient SB% and remains raw at the plate. Does have a quick RH bat, but has a flat swing, which gets long. Plus-plus runner with a strong arm and can play all three OF slots.

Justus,Connor — 6 — Los Angeles (A)

EXP MLB DEBUT: 2019 | H/W: 6-0 190 | FUT: Utility player | 6B

Bats R Age 23
2016 (5) Georgia Tech

- Pwr ++
- BAvg ++
- Spd +++
- Def ++++

Year	Lev	Team	AB	R	H	HR	RBI	Avg	OB	Slg	OPS	bb%	ct%	Eye	SB	CS	x/h%	Iso	RC/G
2016	NCAA	Georgia Tech	247	62	80	6	37	324	420	486	906	14	85	1.08	9	3	31	162	7.08
2016	Rk	Orem	93	19	32	0	23	344	450	430	881	16	80	0.95	0	2	22	86	7.06
2016	A	Burlington	139	19	32	2	9	230	301	309	610	9	76	0.41	1	2	19	79	2.99
2017	A+	Inland Empire	411	52	83	5	34	202	305	299	604	13	73	0.55	15	6	33	97	3.10

Defensive-oriented INF who hasn't been potent with stick. Has plus instincts with glove and quick, soft hands to match. Ranges well to both sides and has average arm. Looks like SS with easy actions. Very poor hitter with limited power and BA ability. Swings and misses often and stroke is stiff. Will draw walks, though.

Kelly,Carson — 2 — St. Louis

EXP MLB DEBUT: 2016 | H/W: 6-2 220 | FUT: Starting C | 7B

Bats R Age 23
2012 (2) HS (OR)

- Pwr +++
- BAvg ++
- Spd ++
- Def ++++

Year	Lev	Team	AB	R	H	HR	RBI	Avg	OB	Slg	OPS	bb%	ct%	Eye	SB	CS	x/h%	Iso	RC/G
2016	AA	Springfield	216	29	62	6	18	287	330	403	733	6	79	0.30	0	1	21	116	4.36
2016	AAA	Memphis	113	14	33	0	14	292	355	381	735	9	85	0.65	0	0	30	88	4.80
2016	MLB	St. Louis	13	1	2	0	1	154	154	231	385	0	85	0.00	0	0	50	77	0.23
2017	AAA	Memphis	244	37	69	10	41	283	368	459	827	12	84	0.83	0	2	33	176	5.85
2017	MLB	St. Louis	69	5	12	0	6	174	230	217	447	7	84	0.45	0	0	25	43	1.20

Plus defensive backstop had his best season as a pro in Triple-A, but struggled when called up to fill in for Yadier Molina. Premium defender with a cannon behind the plate, but power is likely to settle in at the 12-15 HR range and might need a trade to get regular PT in the majors.

Kemmer,Jon — 79 — Houston

EXP MLB DEBUT: 2018 | H/W: 6-2 230 | FUT: Starting OF | 7C

Bats L Age 27
2013 (21) Brewton-Parker

- Pwr +++
- BAvg +++
- Spd +
- Def +++

Year	Lev	Team	AB	R	H	HR	RBI	Avg	OB	Slg	OPS	bb%	ct%	Eye	SB	CS	x/h%	Iso	RC/G
2014	A	Quad Cities	180	29	52	4	17	289	360	450	810	10	78	0.51	3	1	38	161	5.70
2014	A+	Lancaster	153	32	45	12	33	294	312	608	920	3	78	0.12	0	1	51	314	6.39
2015	AA	Corpus Christi	364	67	119	18	65	327	401	574	975	11	76	0.51	9	1	42	247	7.87
2016	AAA	Fresno	407	53	108	18	69	265	328	477	805	9	69	0.30	8	10	43	211	5.71
2017	AAA	Fresno	304	68	91	16	57	299	388	533	921	13	69	0.46	6	2	40	234	7.52

Older prospect who reworked swing/approach en route to bounce-back 2017 in PCL. Strong frame, forearms generate good bat speed and power to all fields. Learned to work counts deeper and can get on base; hits both LH/RH well. Decent athlete, but fringe speed and range limit his defensive home to 1B or LF, which hinder his overall value.

Kendall,Jeren — 789 — Los Angeles (N)

EXP MLB DEBUT: 2020 | H/W: 6-0 190 | FUT: Starting CF | 8D

Bats L Age 22
2017 (1) Vanderbilt

- Pwr +++
- BAvg +++
- Spd ++++
- Def ++++

Year	Lev	Team	AB	R	H	HR	RBI	Avg	OB	Slg	OPS	bb%	ct%	Eye	SB	CS	x/h%	Iso	RC/G
2017	NCAA	Vanderbilt	261	59	80	15	53	307	365	556	920	8	72	0.32	20	4	38	249	7.11
2017	Rk	Ogden	22	5	10	1	7	455	455	727	1182	0	86	0.00	4	0	30	273	9.11
2017	A	Great Lakes	140	21	31	2	18	221	288	400	688	8	70	0.31	5	8	45	179	4.24

23rd overall pick is a plus athlete with great arm and enough speed to track down anything in the air. Pretty left-handed swing and a quick bat should allow him to hit for average with moderate power. Pitch recognition and contact ability developed in college and will need to extend to the pros.

Kieboom,Carter — 6 — Washington

EXP MLB DEBUT: 2020 | H/W: 6-2 190 | FUT: Starting SS | 9D

Bats R Age 20
2016 (1) HS (GA)

- Pwr +++
- BAvg +++
- Spd ++
- Def +++

Year	Lev	Team	AB	R	H	HR	RBI	Avg	OB	Slg	OPS	bb%	ct%	Eye	SB	CS	x/h%	Iso	RC/G
2016	Rk	GCL Nationals	135	22	33	4	25	244	306	452	758	8	68	0.28	1	2	48	207	5.19
2017	Rk	GCL Nationals	11	1	5	0	5	455	571	727	1299	21	100		0	0	60	273	12.25
2017	A-	Auburn	28	4	7	1	4	250	276	393	669	3	93	0.50	1	0	29	143	3.68
2017	A	Hagerstown	179	36	53	8	26	296	391	497	889	14	78	0.70	2	2	38	201	6.77

Off to fantastic start in first full season before hamstring injury felled him for several months. Lean body type with room to fill out; current bat speed matched with patient plate approach hints at future middle-of-the-order potential. Good actions at SS, though average range may push him to 3B eventually.

Kiner-Falefa,Isiah — 245 — Texas

EXP MLB DEBUT: 2018 | H/W: 5-10 176 | FUT: Utility player | 6B

Bats R Age 23
2013 (4) HS (HI)

- Pwr +
- BAvg +++
- Spd +++
- Def ++

Year	Lev	Team	AB	R	H	HR	RBI	Avg	OB	Slg	OPS	bb%	ct%	Eye	SB	CS	x/h%	Iso	RC/G
2015	A	Hickory	125	16	34	0	13	272	345	336	681	10	82	0.64	7	3	21	64	4.15
2015	A+	High Desert	233	38	72	0	27	309	335	343	678	4	88	0.32	4	3	10	34	3.75
2016	Rk	AZL Rangers	10	2	1	0	1	100	100	100	200	0	90	0.00	1	0	0	0	-1.59
2016	AA	Frisco	402	55	103	0	27	256	325	286	611	9	87	0.80	6	6	10	30	3.35
2017	AA	Frisco	513	58	148	5	48	288	341	390	731	7	86	0.57	17	6	26	101	4.61

Versatile prospect who repeated AA and led TL in doubles. Hit first career HRs in '17, though has little power upside. Improved across board by taking harder hacks and driving ball. Has decent approach and will get on base. Exhibits average speed and upped SB totals. No defensive home, but has value in playing multiple positions, including C.

King,Jose — 6 — Detroit

EXP MLB DEBUT: 2022 | H/W: 6-0 160 | FUT: Starting SS | 7E

Bats L Age 19
2015 FA (DR)

- Pwr +
- BAvg +++
- Spd ++++
- Def ++

Year	Lev	Team	AB	R	H	HR	RBI	Avg	OB	Slg	OPS	bb%	ct%	Eye	SB	CS	x/h%	Iso	RC/G
2017	Rk	GCL Tigers	112	18	36	0	6	321	356	366	722	5	74	0.21	8	9	11	45	4.32
2017	Rk	AZL Dbacks	46	7	12	0	9	261	306	348	654	6	57	0.15	2	2	17	87	4.25

Lean, athletic INF who is ready for full-season ball. Plays small ball at present with well above average speed and quick actions. Smooth defender with soft hands, though arm strength may lead him to 2B. Strikes out a lot for limited pop and needs to focus more on contact. Has stroke to put bat to ball, but is inconsistent in swing path.

Kingery,Scott — 4 — Philadelphia

EXP MLB DEBUT: 2018 | H/W: 5-10 180 | FUT: Starting 2B | 9D

Bats R Age 23
2015 (2) Arizona

- Pwr +++
- BAvg +++
- Spd ++++ (4.18)
- Def ++++

Year	Lev	Team	AB	R	H	HR	RBI	Avg	OB	Slg	OPS	bb%	ct%	Eye	SB	CS	x/h%	Iso	RC/G
2015	A	Lakewood	252	43	63	3	21	250	300	337	637	7	83	0.42	11	1	22	87	3.37
2016	A+	Clearwater	375	60	110	3	28	293	350	411	761	8	86	0.61	26	5	32	117	5.04
2016	AA	Reading	156	16	39	2	18	250	273	333	607	3	77	0.14	4	2	23	83	2.68
2017	AA	Reading	278	62	87	18	44	313	376	608	984	9	82	0.55	19	3	47	295	7.58
2017	AAA	Lehigh Valley	265	41	78	8	21	294	327	449	776	5	78	0.22	10	2	28	155	4.87

Increased strength led to across-board-improvement. Features a simple swing that peppers the whole field, but now able to turn on drivable pitches, which fueled power boost. Can still expand zone, but top-of-the-order potential with good speed and instincts that point to SB. Excellent defender with exceptional range, steady glove and strong arm.

Kirilloff,Alex — 9 — Minnesota

EXP MLB DEBUT: 2021 | H/W: 6-2 195 | FUT: Starting OF | 8C

Bats L Age 20
2016 (1) HS (PA)

- Pwr +++
- BAvg ++++
- Spd +++
- Def ++

Year	Lev	Team	AB	R	H	HR	RBI	Avg	OB	Slg	OPS	bb%	ct%	Eye	SB	CS	x/h%	Iso	RC/G
2016	Rk	Elizabethton	216	33	66	7	33	306	339	454	793	5	85	0.34	0	1	26	148	5.02
2017		*Did not play - injured*																	

Natural-hitting OF who missed all season after Tommy John surgery. Brings quality approach and clean swing which leads to ample contact. Should realize power potential with more pull-oriented approach and adding strength with age. Probably a corner OF at maturity and can play 1B.

Knizner,Andrew — 2 — St. Louis

EXP MLB DEBUT: 2020 | H/W: 6-1 200 | FUT: Starting C | 7C

Bats R Age 23 — 2016 (7) North Carolina St

Pwr +++ · BAvg +++ · Spd + · Def +++

Year	Lev	Team	AB	R	H	HR	RBI	Avg	OB	Slg	OPS	bb%	ct%	Eye	SB	CS	x/h%	Iso	RC/G
2016	NCAA	NC State	240	40	70	6	30	292	349	388	736	8	85	0.58	3	0	16	96	4.55
2016	Rk	Johnson City	185	35	59	6	42	319	388	492	880	10	89	1.00	0	0	32	173	6.44
2017	A	Peoria	179	18	50	8	29	279	314	480	794	5	88	0.41	1	1	38	201	5.04
2017	AA	Springfield	182	27	59	4	22	324	372	462	834	7	85	0.52	0	1	29	137	5.72

Converted backstop is still learning the tools of the trade, but has solid offensive potential. Plus strike zone awareness and contact ability backed by average to above power. Moves well for his size with good hands, a strong arm, and solid receiving skills.

Kramer,Kevin — 5 — Pittsburgh

EXP MLB DEBUT: 2019 | H/W: 6-0 190 | FUT: Starting 2B | 7D

Bats L Age 24 — 2015 (2) UCLA

Pwr ++ · BAvg +++ · Spd ++ · Def +++

Year	Lev	Team	AB	R	H	HR	RBI	Avg	OB	Slg	OPS	bb%	ct%	Eye	SB	CS	x/h%	Iso	RC/G
2015	A	West Virginia	50	9	12	0	3	240	309	320	629	9	84	0.63	3	0	25	80	3.53
2016	A+	Bradenton	444	56	123	4	57	277	348	378	726	10	86	0.76	3	9	28	101	4.70
2017	Rk	GCL Pirates	2	0	0	0	1	0	0	0	0	0	50	0.00	0	0		0	-7.85
2017	A-	West Virginia	13	1	3	0	2	231	231	231	462	0	85	0.00	1	0	0	0	0.92
2017	AA	Altoona	202	31	60	6	27	297	352	500	852	8	75	0.34	7	2	43	203	6.18

Polished hitter with a line-drive, gap-to-gap approach. Broken hand limited him to just 217 AB. Good strike zone judgement and contact ability, but below-average power and speed limit upside. Good hands and an average arm, but range limits him to 2B.

Krause,Kevin — 9 — Pittsburgh

EXP MLB DEBUT: 2019 | H/W: 6-2 200 | FUT: Reserve OF | 6C

Bats R Age 25 — 2014 (9) Stony Brook

Pwr ++ · BAvg ++ · Spd +++ · Def ++

Year	Lev	Team	AB	R	H	HR	RBI	Avg	OB	Slg	OPS	bb%	ct%	Eye	SB	CS	x/h%	Iso	RC/G
2014	NCAA	Stony Brook	198	46	70	8	51	354	429	551	979	12	86	0.93	8	3	33	197	7.66
2014	A-	Jamestown	134	22	37	7	32	276	353	560	913	11	79	0.57	6	2	54	284	6.96
2016	A-	West Virginia	176	34	48	3	20	273	393	369	763	17	85	1.35	10	4	21	97	5.48
2017	A+	Bradenton	283	36	78	10	43	276	365	459	825	12	83	0.85	7	4	38	184	5.91

Fringe catching prospect has dealt with injuries and spent most of 2017 in the OF. Solid bat-on-ball skills with above-average power and a short compact stroke give him some value, but at 24 he was old for High-A. Has yet to log more than 300 AB in any pro season and now looks like a 4th OF.

Krieger,Tyler — 4 — Cleveland

EXP MLB DEBUT: 2018 | H/W: 6-2 170 | FUT: Utility player | 6B

Bats B Age 24 — 2015 (4) Clemson

Pwr ++ · BAvg ++ · Spd +++ · Def +++

Year	Lev	Team	AB	R	H	HR	RBI	Avg	OB	Slg	OPS	bb%	ct%	Eye	SB	CS	x/h%	Iso	RC/G
2016	A	Lake County	262	51	82	3	35	313	381	427	809	10	75	0.44	15	8	24	115	5.77
2016	A+	Lynchburg	220	33	62	2	23	282	363	405	767	11	76	0.54	6	7	31	123	5.30
2017	AA	Akron	418	55	94	6	43	225	296	337	633	9	74	0.39	12	6	35	112	3.35

Lean INF who fits utility profile. Has semblance of bat control with knowledge of strike zone, but had big drop in BA. Can be beaten with good velocity. Draws walks with discerning eye. Not much offensive thump—hit career-high 6 HR in 2017. Hits line drives to all fields and uses speed well on base. Possesses range, but owns below average arm.

Laureano,Ramon — 89 — Oakland

EXP MLB DEBUT: 2018 | H/W: 5-11 185 | FUT: Starting OF | 7C

Bats R Age 23 — 2014 (16) NE Oklahoma A&M

Pwr ++ · BAvg +++ · Spd ++++ · Def +++

Year	Lev	Team	AB	R	H	HR	RBI	Avg	OB	Slg	OPS	bb%	ct%	Eye	SB	CS	x/h%	Iso	RC/G
2014	Rk	Greeneville	53	8	10	1	2	189	283	245	529	12	70	0.44	4	0	10	57	1.78
2015	A	Quad Cities	287	43	76	4	34	265	315	415	730	7	71	0.25	18	3	36	150	4.67
2016	A+	Lancaster	293	69	93	10	60	317	417	519	936	15	71	0.58	33	11	37	201	7.86
2016	AA	Corpus Christi	124	20	40	5	13	323	417	548	965	14	73	0.61	10	3	40	226	8.06
2017	AA	Corpus Christi	463	65	105	11	55	227	288	369	658	8	76	0.36	24	5	36	143	3.59

Short, athletic OF who broke out in 2016 but struggled in second Double-A stint. Plus runner who will be SB source and shows aptitude for OBP. Stays compact, produces low line-drives for BA value, but should tab double-digit HR. Was over-aggressive in '17, which got him into trouble and could be obstacle. Enough range for CF but profiles better at LF/RF.

LaValley,Gavin — 3 — Cincinnati

EXP MLB DEBUT: 2019 | H/W: 6-3 235 | FUT: Starting 1B | 7D

Bats R Age 23 — 2014 (4) HS (OK)

Pwr ++++ · BAvg ++ · Spd + · Def ++

Year	Lev	Team	AB	R	H	HR	RBI	Avg	OB	Slg	OPS	bb%	ct%	Eye	SB	CS	x/h%	Iso	RC/G
2015	A	Dayton	469	52	125	4	53	267	337	358	695	10	76	0.44	4	1	27	92	4.22
2016	A	Dayton	19	2	4	0	0	211	318	263	581	14	63	0.43	0	0	25	53	2.81
2016	A+	Daytona	338	50	93	11	61	275	332	470	803	8	79	0.40	0	0	45	195	5.45
2017	A+	Daytona	236	38	68	15	45	288	331	538	869	6	79	0.31	0	0	43	250	5.96
2017	AA	Pensacola	247	24	62	3	34	251	305	352	657	7	73	0.28	0	0	31	101	3.57

Big-bodied, slow-footed RHH 1B struggled in his Double-A debut. Cut down on swing since pro debut. Takes time to get trigger going. Massive physical power in frame. Struggled with velocity and consistent hard contact. 20-25 HR potential. 1B-only profile. Would work best in platoon.

Lee,Khalil — 89 — Kansas City

EXP MLB DEBUT: 2020 | H/W: 5-10 170 | FUT: Starting OF | 8D

Bats L Age 19 — 2016 (3) HS (VA)

Pwr +++ · BAvg +++ · Spd +++ · Def ++

Year	Lev	Team	AB	R	H	HR	RBI	Avg	OB	Slg	OPS	bb%	ct%	Eye	SB	CS	x/h%	Iso	RC/G
2016	Rk	AZL Royals	182	43	49	6	29	269	381	484	865	15	69	0.58	8	4	43	214	6.99
2017	A	Lexington	451	71	107	17	61	237	333	430	763	13	62	0.38	20	18	44	193	5.60

Athletic OF who was 2nd in SAL in HR, but also 1st in Ks. Owns passive approach and lets hittable pitches pass. Should improve with experience as he owns plus raw power and electric bat speed. Has speed for SB, though not polished baserunner. Split time between RF and CF and should become playable at both. Has very good tools that project well.

Lewis,Kyle — 8 — Seattle

EXP MLB DEBUT: 2019 | H/W: 6-4 210 | FUT: Starting OF | 9D

Bats R Age 22 — 2016 (1) Mercer

Pwr ++++ · BAvg ++++ · Spd ++ · Def +++

Year	Lev	Team	AB	R	H	HR	RBI	Avg	OB	Slg	OPS	bb%	ct%	Eye	SB	CS	x/h%	Iso	RC/G
2016	NCAA	Mercer	223	70	88	20	72	395	533	731	1264	23	78	1.38	6	5	38	336	12.05
2016	A-	Everett	117	26	35	3	26	299	383	530	913	12	81	0.73	3	0	46	231	7.16
2017	Rk	AZL Mariners	38	9	10	1	7	263	333	447	781	10	63	0.29	1	0	40	184	5.84
2017	A+	Modesto	149	20	38	6	24	255	323	403	726	9	74	0.39	2	1	26	148	4.39

Elite athlete who began year late due to knee surgery in 2016. Assigned to AFL, but only played few games due to lingering soreness. Has chance to be perennial All-Star thanks to instincts and plus tools. Has plus power to all fields and combines patient approach with feel for hitting to allow for high BA. Usually runs well, but knee may curtail.

Lewis,Royce — 6 — Minnesota

EXP MLB DEBUT: 2021 | H/W: 6-2 188 | FUT: Starting SS | 9D

Bats R Age 18 — 2017 (1) HS (CA)

Pwr ++ · BAvg ++++ · Spd ++++ · Def ++++

Year	Lev	Team	AB	R	H	HR	RBI	Avg	OB	Slg	OPS	bb%	ct%	Eye	SB	CS	x/h%	Iso	RC/G
2017	Rk	GCL Twins	133	38	36	3	17	271	362	414	775	13	87	1.12	15	2	31	143	5.42
2017	A	Cedar Rapids	71	16	21	1	10	296	351	394	745	8	77	0.38	3	1	19	99	4.71

Athletic SS who put on show in pro debut. Has plus tools and polish for age and could be quick riser. Bat speed is unmatched and should hit for high BA/OBP. Power may take longer to develop, but could grow to plus. Has advanced eye at plate and makes easy contact. No weakness in game, including defense with quickness and plus arm.

Leyba,Domingo — 46 — Arizona

EXP MLB DEBUT: 2018 | H/W: 5-11 160 | FUT: Starting 2B | 7C

Bats B Age 22 — 2012 FA (DR)

Pwr ++ · BAvg +++ · Spd +++ · Def +++

Year	Lev	Team	AB	R	H	HR	RBI	Avg	OB	Slg	OPS	bb%	ct%	Eye	SB	CS	x/h%	Iso	RC/G
2015	A+	Visalia	514	60	122	2	43	237	274	309	583	5	82	0.29	10	6	23	72	2.65
2016	A+	Visalia	340	48	100	6	40	294	350	426	776	8	82	0.47	5	1	32	132	5.12
2016	AA	Mobile	156	21	47	4	20	301	370	436	806	10	86	0.77	4	2	26	135	5.55
2017	A-	Hillsboro	28	4	8	1	6	286	375	429	804	13	93	2.00	0	0	25	143	5.75
2017	AA	Jackson	58	11	16	2	9	276	333	448	782	8	90	0.83	0	0	38	172	5.18

Aggressive MIF spent much of 2017 on DL with shoulder injury that needed surgery in July. When healthy, tremendous hand-eye coordination but ultra-aggressive at plate. Has power, especially to pull side. Gets by at SS but is likely a 2B long term. Average runner, has slowed down as he added bulk.

Liberato,Luis — 789 — Seattle

EXP MLB DEBUT: 2019 | H/W: 6-1 175 | FUT: Starting OF | 8E

Bats L Age 22 — 2012 FA (DR)

Pwr ++ · BAvg ++ · Spd +++ · Def ++++

Year	Lev	Team	AB	R	H	HR	RBI	Avg	OB	Slg	OPS	bb%	ct%	Eye	SB	CS	x/h%	Iso	RC/G
2015	A	Clinton	30	3	4	0	0	133	188	233	421	6	67	0.20	1	0	50	100	0.31
2015	AA	Jackson	10	0	0	0	0	0	0	0	0	0	80	0.00	0	0		0	-4.74
2016	A	Clinton	372	65	96	2	29	258	341	368	710	11	73	0.47	4	2	30	110	4.57
2017	A	Clinton	191	34	44	6	22	230	313	445	758	11	73	0.45	5	4	45	215	5.13
2017	A+	Modesto	257	41	66	8	28	257	313	432	745	8	69	0.26	7	4	36	175	4.86

Wiry, athletic OF who entices with solid tools, but frustrates with inconsistency. Established easy high in HR and has speed for double-digit SB. Drives balls to gaps with average power potential, but struggles to hit for BA and hit under .150 against LHP. Outstanding defender with pure speed and tracking ability.

Lin,Tzu-Wei

4568 | Boston | EXP MLB DEBUT: 2017 | H/W: 5-9 155 | FUT: Utility player | 6A

- Bats L Age 24
- 2012 FA (TW)
- Pwr +
- BAvg + +
- Spd + + +
- Def + + +

Year	Lev	Team	AB	R	H	HR	RBI	Avg	OB	Slg	OPS	bb%	ct%	Eye	SB	CS	x/h%	Iso	RC/G
2015	AA	Portland	173	21	35	0	14	202	270	266	536	8	84	0.59	8	3	23	64	2.38
2016	AA	Portland	372	39	83	2	27	223	288	293	581	8	85	0.62	10	7	20	70	2.90
2017	AA	Portland	159	31	48	5	19	302	380	491	870	11	83	0.74	8	2	35	189	6.43
2017	AAA	Pawtucket	141	12	32	2	9	227	283	319	602	7	80	0.39	2	4	25	92	2.90
2017	MLB	Boston	56	7	15	0	2	268	369	339	709	14	70	0.53	1	1	13	71	4.71

Short, lithe INF who had Double-A breakout with bat and reached BOS. Played multiple positions for versatility, including CF. Became better overall hitter with more hard contact, though power is not part of game. Best when using middle of field and focusing on bat to ball. Strong arm highlights defense and has polished feel for game.

Lindsay,Desmond

8 | New York (N) | EXP MLB DEBUT: 2020 | H/W: 5-11 196 | FUT: Starting OF | 8E

- Bats R Age 21
- 2015 (2) HS (FL)
- Pwr + + +
- BAvg + + +
- Spd + + + +
- Def + +

Year	Lev	Team	AB	R	H	HR	RBI	Avg	OB	Slg	OPS	bb%	ct%	Eye	SB	CS	x/h%	Iso	RC/G
2015	Rk	GCL Mets	69	10	21	1	6	304	400	464	864	14	70	0.52	3	2	33	159	6.97
2015	A-	Brooklyn	45	3	9	0	7	200	308	267	574	13	58	0.37	0	1	33	67	2.83
2016	Rk	GCL Mets	10	3	4	0	0	400	600	500	1100	33	50	1.00	0	0	25	100	14.55
2016	A-	Brooklyn	111	18	33	4	17	297	405	450	855	15	77	0.77	3	1	27	153	6.46
2017	A	Columbia	214	40	47	8	30	220	324	388	712	13	64	0.43	4	2	40	168	4.64

Athletic, RH OF having trouble staying healthy. Constant hamstring issues have stunted development and ulnar nerve transposition surgery in elbow has put career in doubt. When healthy, a quick twitch swing and strong forearms aid hit tool. Pitch recognition skills lag behind. Strength and swing leverage aids power tool; is an average runner.

Long,Shed

4 | Cincinnati | EXP MLB DEBUT: 2019 | H/W: 5-8 180 | FUT: Starting 2B | 8D

- Bats L Age 22
- 2013 (12) HS (AL)
- Pwr + + +
- BAvg + + +
- Spd + + +
- Def + +

Year	Lev	Team	AB	R	H	HR	RBI	Avg	OB	Slg	OPS	bb%	ct%	Eye	SB	CS	x/h%	Iso	RC/G
2015	A	Dayton	152	22	43	6	16	283	359	474	833	11	80	0.58	2	3	35	191	5.89
2016	A	Dayton	335	47	94	11	45	281	364	457	821	12	75	0.52	16	3	38	176	5.92
2016	A+	Daytona	143	22	46	4	30	322	366	503	870	7	76	0.29	5	1	30	182	6.31
2017	A+	Daytona	247	37	77	13	36	312	380	543	922	10	74	0.43	6	3	39	231	7.09
2017	AA	Pensacola	141	13	32	3	14	227	319	362	680	12	78	0.61	3	1	34	135	4.10

Short-statured converted catcher broke out in High-A. Offensive-minded LHH 2B in mold of TEX Willie Calhoun. Quick bat, longish swing works. Lots of power in frame. Hit 16 HR between two levels. Gets most out of tool shed. Below-average run tool plays up because of aggressiveness and smarts. Will not win accolades as defender.

Longhi,Nick

379 | Cincinnati | EXP MLB DEBUT: 2018 | H/W: 6-2 205 | FUT: Utility player | 7C

- Bats R Age 22
- 2013 (30) HS (FL)
- Pwr + +
- BAvg + + + +
- Spd + +
- Def + + +

Year	Lev	Team	AB	R	H	HR	RBI	Avg	OB	Slg	OPS	bb%	ct%	Eye	SB	CS	x/h%	Iso	RC/G
2014	A-	Lowell	109	19	36	0	10	330	392	440	832	9	80	0.50	0	3	31	110	6.03
2015	A	Greenville	442	52	124	7	62	281	332	403	735	7	80	0.39	2	0	30	122	4.57
2016	A+	Salem	471	56	133	2	77	282	351	393	744	10	77	0.47	2	3	34	110	4.92
2017	AA	Portland	237	26	62	6	33	262	300	401	701	5	83	0.33	0	1	34	139	4.01
2017	AA	Pensacola	19	2	6	1	7	316	409	526	935	14	74	0.60	0	0	33	211	7.47

Fundamentally-sound RHH with limited projection due to power limitations in level swing. Has hit for BA and OBP at every level. Adapts well to velocity and adapt at hitting to all fields. Advanced approach. Swing generates tons of top spin, depressing power potential. Limited defensively to 1B and corner OF, but possible starter in the right lineup.

Longo,Mitch

79 | Cleveland | EXP MLB DEBUT: 2020 | H/W: 6-0 185 | FUT: Starting OF | 7D

- Bats L Age 23
- 2016 (14) Ohio
- Pwr + +
- BAvg + + +
- Spd + + +
- Def + +

Year	Lev	Team	AB	R	H	HR	RBI	Avg	OB	Slg	OPS	bb%	ct%	Eye	SB	CS	x/h%	Iso	RC/G
2016	NCAA	Ohio	214	36	77	3	22	360	427	467	894	10	91	1.32	12	5	22	107	6.69
2016	A-	Mahoning Val	137	21	42	1	15	307	345	409	754	6	88	0.47	4	0	26	102	4.78
2017	A	Lake County	202	37	73	4	25	361	427	530	956	10	83	0.66	18	1	33	168	7.49
2017	A+	Lynchburg	16	8	9	0	3	563	650	688	1338	20	88	2.00	2	0	22	125	12.83

Unheralded OF who missed most of first half of season after hand surgery. Has pure hitting ability, highlighted by smooth, sweet stroke. Likely won't develop much pop based upon swing path, but can smoke doubles to all fields. More BA than power. Runs well and can steal bases, but has crude actions in OF corner. Arm strength is suspect.

Lopez,Nicky

46 | Kansas City | EXP MLB DEBUT: 2019 | H/W: 5-11 175 | FUT: Starting SS | 7C

- Bats L Age 23
- 2016 (5) Creighton
- Pwr +
- BAvg + + +
- Spd + + +
- Def + + +

Year	Lev	Team	AB	R	H	HR	RBI	Avg	OB	Slg	OPS	bb%	ct%	Eye	SB	CS	x/h%	Iso	RC/G
2016	NCAA	Creighton	196	35	60	2	22	306	387	444	831	12	93	2.00	11	2	30	138	6.21
2016	Rk	Burlington	231	54	65	6	29	281	376	429	805	13	87	1.17	24	4	26	147	5.78
2017	A+	Wilmington	285	42	84	2	27	295	374	407	781	11	92	1.57	14	8	25	112	5.58
2017	AA	NW Arkansas	232	26	60	0	11	259	306	293	600	6	88	0.55	7	4	12	34	3.06

Athletic SS who plays game under control and has proven to be tough out with bat speed and level swing path. Reached AA in first full season and could get to the KC quickly. Not much punch due to lack of size and strength, but puts ball in play and uses average speed effectively. Has plus arm strength and body control to play either MIF spot.

Lowe,Brandon

4 | Tampa Bay | EXP MLB DEBUT: 2018 | H/W: 6-0 185 | FUT: Starting 2B | 7B

- Bats L Age 23
- 2015 (3) Maryland
- Pwr + + +
- BAvg + + +
- Spd + +
- Def + +

Year	Lev	Team	AB	R	H	HR	RBI	Avg	OB	Slg	OPS	bb%	ct%	Eye	SB	CS	x/h%	Iso	RC/G
2016	A	Bowling Green	379	67	94	5	42	248	351	343	694	14	80	0.78	6	3	24	95	4.39
2017	A+	Charlotte	315	62	98	9	46	311	401	524	924	13	79	0.72	6	3	47	213	7.34
2017	AA	Montgomery	95	8	24	2	12	253	268	389	658	2	73	0.08	1	1	33	137	3.33

Offensive-minded 2B who had breakout year by leading FSL in doubles and SLG. Stalled in AA with aggressive approach, but offers moderate BA potential along with average power. Hangs in against LHP with slightly-revised swing path. Not a great defender, but makes routine plays with modest range and OK footwork.

Lowe,Joshua

8 | Tampa Bay | EXP MLB DEBUT: 2020 | H/W: 6-4 205 | FUT: Starting OF | 9D

- Bats L Age 20
- 2016 (1) HS (GA)
- Pwr + + +
- BAvg + + +
- Spd + + +
- Def + + +

Year	Lev	Team	AB	R	H	HR	RBI	Avg	OB	Slg	OPS	bb%	ct%	Eye	SB	CS	x/h%	Iso	RC/G
2016	Rk	Princeton	80	11	19	3	11	238	371	400	771	18	60	0.53	1	1	26	163	5.91
2016	Rk	GCL Rays	93	14	24	2	15	258	389	409	798	18	71	0.74	1	1	38	151	6.04
2017	A	Bowling Green	456	60	122	8	55	268	329	386	715	8	68	0.29	22	8	30	118	4.51

Tall and toolsy, he moved from 3B to OF in first full season. Has innate understanding of strike zone and starting to leverage bat speed and strength to hit for power. Has very high upside with bat and smokes line drives all over field. Possesses above average speed now and solid instincts on base. Has relative polish in CF with plus arm.

Lugo,Dawel

5 | Detroit | EXP MLB DEBUT: 2018 | H/W: 6-0 190 | FUT: Starting 3B | 7B

- Bats R Age 23
- 2011 FA (DR)
- Pwr + + +
- BAvg + + +
- Spd + +
- Def + +

Year	Lev	Team	AB	R	H	HR	RBI	Avg	OB	Slg	OPS	bb%	ct%	Eye	SB	CS	x/h%	Iso	RC/G
2015	A+	Dunedin	260	16	57	2	21	219	245	292	538	3	81	0.18	1	3	23	73	1.96
2016	A+	Visalia	315	61	99	13	42	314	345	514	860	5	87	0.37	2	1	32	200	5.78
2016	AA	Mobile	173	24	53	4	20	306	322	451	773	2	91	0.27	1	1	28	145	4.75
2017	AA	Jackson	341	40	96	7	43	282	323	428	751	6	85	0.41	1	0	33	147	4.71
2017	AA	Erie	175	18	47	6	22	269	316	417	733	6	88	0.57	2	1	28	149	4.46

Stocky, strong INF who has grown into frame and developed consistent pop. Improved approach, but still has work to do with pitch selection. Swings quick bat and makes nimble contact thanks to hand-eye coordination. Lacks foot speed, though offers quick hands and actions at 3B. Becoming better defender with plus arm strength.

Lund,Brennon

79 | Los Angeles (A) | EXP MLB DEBUT: 2019 | H/W: 5-10 185 | FUT: Starting OF | 7D

- Bats R Age 23
- 2016 (11) Brigham Young
- Pwr + +
- BAvg + + +
- Spd + + +
- Def + +

Year	Lev	Team	AB	R	H	HR	RBI	Avg	OB	Slg	OPS	bb%	ct%	Eye	SB	CS	x/h%	Iso	RC/G
2016	Rk	Orem	73	15	29	2	11	397	450	521	971	9	85	0.64	7	2	17	123	7.36
2016	A	Burlington	181	19	49	1	19	271	316	359	675	6	82	0.36	8	1	24	88	3.83
2017	A	Burlington	173	25	53	2	18	306	391	428	819	12	85	0.92	14	3	25	121	5.95
2017	A+	Inland Empire	196	26	63	3	23	321	373	423	796	8	79	0.39	5	4	22	102	5.32
2017	AA	Mobile	122	17	35	1	6	287	304	336	640	2	73	0.09	1	2	11	49	3.03

Improving prospect who has been quick mover and ended in Double-A in first full year as pro. Consistent producer with grinder approach and can lead lineup. No highlight tools in repertoire, but maximizes ability. Has bat speed and barrel control for decent contact and can draw walks. Plays OF corners, but arm strength a little short.

Luplow,Jordan

789 | Pittsburgh | EXP MLB DEBUT: 2017 | H/W: 6-1 195 | FUT: Reserve OF | 7C

- Bats R Age 24
- 2014 (3) Fresno St
- Pwr + + +
- BAvg + + +
- Spd + +
- Def + +

Year	Lev	Team	AB	R	H	HR	RBI	Avg	OB	Slg	OPS	bb%	ct%	Eye	SB	CS	x/h%	Iso	RC/G
2015	A	West Virginia	390	74	103	12	67	264	361	465	825	13	83	0.88	11	2	50	200	6.02
2016	A+	Bradenton	354	63	90	10	54	254	362	421	783	14	78	0.77	6	2	40	167	5.55
2017	AA	Altoona	254	45	73	16	37	287	360	535	896	10	82	0.64	1	3	42	248	6.50
2017	AAA	Indianapolis	160	29	52	7	19	325	386	513	899	9	78	0.44	4	1	29	188	6.64
2017	MLB	Pittsburgh	78	6	16	3	11	205	262	385	647	7	72	0.27	0	1	44	179	3.33

Breakout season for former Fresno State standout resulting in career highs in HR and BA. Simple stroke allows him to barrel the ball consistently with above-average power. Range and arm limit him to LF and despite the breakout his future is as a 4th OF.

Lutz,Tristen — 78 — Milwaukee

EXP MLB DEBUT: 2020 | H/W: 6-3 210 | FUT: Starting OF | 8C

Bats R Age 19 — 2017 (S-1) HS (TX)

Pwr ++++ | BAvg +++ | Spd +++ | Def ++++

Year	Lev	Team	AB	R	H	HR	RBI	Avg	OB	Slg	OPS	bb%	ct%	Eye	SB	CS	x/h%	Iso	RC/G
2017	Rk	Helena	93	23	31	6	16	333	410	559	969	11	77	0.57	2	4	26	226	7.55
2017	Rk	AZL Brewers	68	12	19	3	11	279	319	559	878	6	69	0.19	1	0	53	279	6.75

Athletic CF with plus bat speed and power potential. Employs solid approach at plate. Swing is a bit long but wrist strength and hand speed make up for it. May have trouble later with velocity if swing mechanics not worked out. Big power potential in swing. Ball jumps off bat. Rangy in CF despite average speed.

Lux,Gavin — 46 — Los Angeles (N)

EXP MLB DEBUT: 2019 | H/W: 6-2 190 | FUT: Starting SS | 8D

Bats L Age 20 — 2016 (1) HS (WI)

Pwr +++ | BAvg +++ | Spd +++ | Def ++++

Year	Lev	Team	AB	R	H	HR	RBI	Avg	OB	Slg	OPS	bb%	ct%	Eye	SB	CS	x/h%	Iso	RC/G
2016	Rk	Ogden	31	7	12	0	3	387	441	484	925	9	74	0.38	1	0	25	97	7.36
2016	Rk	AZL Dodgers	192	34	53	0	18	276	359	380	740	12	78	0.58	1	0	28	104	5.00
2017	A	Great Lakes	434	68	106	7	39	244	331	362	692	11	80	0.64	27	10	27	118	4.27

20th overall pick in 2016 struggled in his full-season debut, though collected a pile of SB. Quick left-handed stroke should play as he moves up, but power grades out as fringe-average. A plus defender, he moves well with a strong arm and should be able stick at shortstop.

Machado,Jonathan — 8 — St. Louis

EXP MLB DEBUT: 2022 | H/W: 5-9 155 | FUT: Starting CF | 7B

Bats L Age 19 — 2016 FA (CU)

Pwr + | BAvg +++ | Spd +++++ | Def ++++

Year	Lev	Team	AB	R	H	HR	RBI	Avg	OB	Slg	OPS	bb%	ct%	Eye	SB	CS	x/h%	Iso	RC/G
2017	Rk	GCL Cardinals	124	27	40	2	20	323	364	435	799	6	90	0.62	8	2	25	113	5.29

Speedy Cuban was solid in state-side debut with excellent speed but below-average power. True CF with plus range and good reads, but arm is fringe. Potential lead-off hitter with game-changing speed.

Maciel,Gabriel — 78 — Arizona

EXP MLB DEBUT: 2021 | H/W: 5-10 170 | FUT: Starting CF | 7E

Bats B Age 19 — 2015 FA (BR)

Pwr ++ | BAvg +++ | Spd ++++ | Def ++++

Year	Lev	Team	AB	R	H	HR	RBI	Avg	OB	Slg	OPS	bb%	ct%	Eye	SB	CS	x/h%	Iso	RC/G
2016	Rk	Missoula	79	15	21	0	4	266	310	291	601	6	76	0.26	11	1	10	25	2.75
2016	Rk	AZL Dbacks	149	28	43	0	10	289	342	309	650	7	85	0.55	11	4	7	20	3.61
2017	Rk	Missoula	217	40	70	3	25	323	390	438	828	10	84	0.71	9	8	26	115	5.88

Young, Brazilian OF with leadoff hitter upside. Primary tool is his plus-plus speed. However, don't sleep on his switch-hitting contact ability. Advanced approach at plate, capable of adjustments during ABs. There may be some power in short frame. Very raw route runner in CF. Needs every bit of speed to make up for rawness.

Mahan,Riley — 4 — Miami

EXP MLB DEBUT: 2020 | H/W: 6-3 185 | FUT: Starting OF | 7C

Bats L Age 22 — 2017 (3) Kentucky

Pwr +++ | BAvg ++ | Spd ++ | Def +++

Year	Lev	Team	AB	R	H	HR	RBI	Avg	OB	Slg	OPS	bb%	ct%	Eye	SB	CS	x/h%	Iso	RC/G
2017	NCAA	Kentucky	262	58	88	15	67	336	387	618	1006	8	79	0.39	9	3	47	282	7.91
2017	A	Greensboro	27	4	7	1	4	259	259	407	667	0	74	0.00	0	0	29	148	3.19

Has a smooth left-handed stroke with above-average power. Good bat-to-ball skills give him a chance to hit for power and average. Runs well for size with an above-average arm. Profiles best as a corner OF or 1B.

Maitan,Kevin — 56 — Los Angeles (A)

EXP MLB DEBUT: 2021 | H/W: 6-2 190 | FUT: Starting 3B | 9E

Bats B Age 18 — 2016 FA (VZ)

Pwr ++++ | BAvg ++++ | Spd ++ | Def +++

Year	Lev	Team	AB	R	H	HR	RBI	Avg	OB	Slg	OPS	bb%	ct%	Eye	SB	CS	x/h%	Iso	RC/G
2017	Rk	Danville	127	10	28	2	15	220	272	323	595	7	69	0.23	1	0	29	102	2.68
2017	Rk	GCL Braves	35	5	11	0	3	314	351	400	751	5	71	0.20	1	0	27	86	4.89

Switch-hitting phenom struggled in US debut. Bulked up considerably. Scouts believe struggles were combination of culture shock and getting acclimated to new physique. Quick bat, quicker from RH box, with good swing plane from both sides of plate. Raw power off the charts, especially from LH side. Tapped out physically at SS. Likely 3B at maturity.

Marinez,Ynmanol — 6 — Miami

EXP MLB DEBUT: 2022 | H/W: 6-0 170 | FUT: Starting SS | 8D

Bats R Age 16 — 2017 FA (DR)

Pwr ++ | BAvg +++ | Spd +++ | Def ++++

Year	Lev	Team	AB	R	H	HR	RBI	Avg	OB	Slg	OPS	bb%	ct%	Eye	SB	CS	x/h%	Iso	RC/G
2017	*Did not play in the US*																		

16-year-old Dominican shortstop signed for $1.2 million in June. Average runner with good range, instincts, and a plus arm. Line-drive approach at the plate, but should add power as he matures and fills out his lean frame. Has yet to make his state-side debut.

Marlette,Tyler — 2 — Seattle

EXP MLB DEBUT: 2018 | H/W: 5-11 195 | FUT: Starting C | 7D

Bats R Age 25 — 2011 (5) HS (FL)

Pwr +++ | BAvg ++ | Spd ++ | Def ++

Year	Lev	Team	AB	R	H	HR	RBI	Avg	OB	Slg	OPS	bb%	ct%	Eye	SB	CS	x/h%	Iso	RC/G
2015	A+	Bakersfield	148	17	32	5	20	216	275	365	640	8	76	0.34	2	1	34	149	3.25
2015	AA	Jackson	178	15	46	3	12	258	298	393	691	5	83	0.32	0	0	37	135	3.96
2016	A+	Bakersfield	326	42	89	14	53	273	334	472	807	8	75	0.37	5	3	40	199	5.50
2016	AA	Jackson	50	4	15	1	6	300	340	400	740	6	78	0.27	1	0	20	100	4.46
2017	AA	Arkansas	368	47	90	11	65	245	303	405	708	8	76	0.35	0	1	39	160	4.21

Short CA with decent all-around skills, but hasn't seen time above AA. Has nice approach at plate and improved strength has led to average power. Bat control not up to snuff for BA as he swings and misses. Best hope for offense is power. Has improved catching skills, but receiving still needs attention. Owns above average arm with quick release.

Marmolejos,Jose — 37 — Washington

EXP MLB DEBUT: 2018 | H/W: 6-1 185 | FUT: Reserve OF | 7C

Bats L Age 25 — 2011 FA (DR)

Pwr ++ | BAvg +++ | Spd ++ | Def ++

Year	Lev	Team	AB	R	H	HR	RBI	Avg	OB	Slg	OPS	bb%	ct%	Eye	SB	CS	x/h%	Iso	RC/G
2014	A-	Auburn	234	30	62	1	31	265	344	385	728	11	79	0.56	0	1	37	120	4.79
2015	A	Hagerstown	468	63	145	11	87	310	358	485	843	7	81	0.39	3	1	38	175	5.90
2016	A+	Potomac	378	72	108	11	59	286	382	495	877	14	78	0.70	2	3	48	209	6.78
2016	AA	Harrisburg	127	15	38	2	15	299	326	417	743	4	77	0.17	0	0	29	118	4.48
2017	AA	Harrisburg	400	68	115	14	66	288	358	458	816	10	80	0.56	0	2	31	170	5.64

Natural hitter who has put up solid BA every step up the ladder. Balanced swing, can use the whole field, but HR power is mainly limited to pull side. Can easily be fooled and out on front foot by offspeed stuff. Very little foot speed and only an average defender. Without plus power, most likely future is as a bench bat or up-and-down guy.

Marsh,Brandon — 89 — Los Angeles (A)

EXP MLB DEBUT: 2020 | H/W: 6-4 210 | FUT: Starting OF | 8D

Bats L Age 20 — 2016 (2) HS (GA)

Pwr +++ | BAvg +++ | Spd ++++ | Def +++

Year	Lev	Team	AB	R	H	HR	RBI	Avg	OB	Slg	OPS	bb%	ct%	Eye	SB	CS	x/h%	Iso	RC/G
2016	*Did not play - injured*																		
2017	Rk	Orem	177	47	62	4	44	350	382	548	930	5	80	0.26	10	2	35	198	6.88

Tall, physical OF who impressed in pro debut after DNP in 2016 due to back injury. Started hot and showed polish with bat and exhibited all tools. Should continue to develop more power, but needs to tame aggressive attack. Has plus speed and may slow down, but is shrewd runner. Solid instincts in OF with plus arm and ample range.

Martin,Jason — 789 — Houston

EXP MLB DEBUT: 2018 | H/W: 5-11 190 | FUT: Starting OF | 7C

Bats L Age 22 — 2013 (8) HS (CA)

Pwr +++ | BAvg +++ | 4.17 Spd +++ | Def +++

Year	Lev	Team	AB	R	H	HR	RBI	Avg	OB	Slg	OPS	bb%	ct%	Eye	SB	CS	x/h%	Iso	RC/G
2014	A-	Tri City	81	7	18	1	2	222	284	321	605	8	84	0.54	5	3	28	99	3.10
2015	A	Quad Cities	396	65	107	8	57	270	348	396	744	11	81	0.64	14	15	25	126	4.86
2016	A+	Lancaster	400	74	108	23	75	270	358	533	891	12	73	0.51	20	12	48	263	6.84
2017	A+	Buies Creek	174	34	50	7	29	287	361	494	855	10	76	0.48	9	5	40	207	6.25
2017	AA	Corpus Christi	300	38	82	11	37	273	317	483	800	6	73	0.23	7	6	46	210	5.43

Shorter, athletic OF with well-rounded skills but lacks standout tool. Uses compact swing to make solid contact and sprays balls to all fields. More power than body lets on; lifts ball enough for 15-ish HR. Plus runner who will be SB asset. Lacks arm for RF and will be average defensively in CF. Chance to be an average contributor offensively.

Martin,Mason

39 | **Pittsburgh** | EXP MLB DEBUT: 2022 | H/W: 6-0 201 | FUT: Starting 1B | **7D**

Bats L Age 18
2017 (17) HS (WA)

- Pwr ++++
- BAvg ++
- Spd +
- Def +

Year	Lev	Team	AB	R	H	HR	RBI	Avg	OB	Slg	OPS	bb%	ct%	Eye	SB	CS	x/h%	Iso	RC/G
2017	Rk	GCL Pirates	127	37	39	11	22	307	447	630	1076	20	68	0.78	2	2	49	323	10.03

Bought out from a college commitment, he delivered in pro debut. Plus bat speed and raw power were the highlights. Aggressive approach results in lots of strikeouts but also draws plenty of walks. Below average runner and defender limits him to 1B.

Martin,Richie

6 | **Oakland** | EXP MLB DEBUT: 2018 | H/W: 5-11 190 | FUT: Starting SS | **7C**

Bats R Age 23
2015 (1) Florida

- Pwr ++
- BAvg ++
- Spd ++++
- Def ++++

Year	Lev	Team	AB	R	H	HR	RBI	Avg	OB	Slg	OPS	bb%	ct%	Eye	SB	CS	x/h%	Iso	RC/G
2015	A-	Vermont	190	31	45	2	16	237	326	342	668	12	75	0.53	7	7	27	105	3.95
2016	A+	Stockton	330	46	76	3	31	230	306	312	618	10	78	0.49	12	8	25	82	3.22
2016	AA	Midland	15	1	5	0	7	333	444	533	978	17	87	1.50	2	1	40	200	8.35
2017	A+	Stockton	94	16	25	1	6	266	324	383	707	8	78	0.38	1	1	24	117	4.29
2017	AA	Midland	286	43	64	3	27	224	284	315	599	8	80	0.42	12	3	27	91	2.92

Athletic, quick SS who stands out more for glove than bat. Can be plus defender due to great range, quick hands, strong arm and polished instincts. Hasn't hit for BA as he swings early in count with sub-par plate coverage. Has potential with stick as he has fast bat and plus speed. Not much of a power hitter, but is good enough with glove to stick.

Martinez,Eddy

789 | **Chicago (N)** | EXP MLB DEBUT: 2020 | H/W: 6-1 195 | FUT: Reserve OF | **7D**

Bats R Age 23
2015 FA (CU)

- Pwr ++
- BAvg ++
- Spd +++
- Def ++++

Year	Lev	Team	AB	R	H	HR	RBI	Avg	OB	Slg	OPS	bb%	ct%	Eye	SB	CS	x/h%	Iso	RC/G
2016	A	South Bend	460	72	117	10	67	254	327	380	708	10	75	0.44	8	5	31	126	4.33
2017	A+	Myrtle Beach	464	59	113	14	61	244	291	366	657	6	83	0.40	6	6	24	123	3.49

Cuban OF signed for $3 million, but has been slow to develop and after two years in the U.S. looks less dynamic. Only plus tool is strong arm, everything else grades out as average to a tick above. Power tool is average though he did hit a career high HR at A+. Runs well, but isn't a base-stealing threat. Solid 4th OF.

Mateo,Jorge

468 | **Oakland** | EXP MLB DEBUT: 2018 | H/W: 6-0 190 | FUT: Starting SS | **8B**

Bats R Age 22
2012 FA (DR)

- Pwr +++
- BAvg +++
- Spd +++++
- Def +++

Year	Lev	Team	AB	R	H	HR	RBI	Avg	OB	Slg	OPS	bb%	ct%	Eye	SB	CS	x/h%	Iso	RC/G
2015	A+	Tampa	84	15	27	0	7	321	374	452	826	8	79	0.39	11	2	30	131	5.92
2016	A+	Tampa	464	65	119	8	48	256	306	381	687	7	77	0.31	36	15	28	125	3.94
2017	A+	Tampa	275	39	66	4	11	240	282	400	682	5	71	0.20	28	3	42	160	3.97
2017	AA	Trenton	120	26	36	4	26	300	378	525	903	11	73	0.47	11	7	44	225	7.13
2017	AA	Midland	137	25	40	4	20	292	336	518	854	6	76	0.27	13	3	40	226	6.16

Speedy, rangy SS whose power starting to emerge. Set high in 2B while continuing to steal 50+ bases. Exciting prospect with all-around tools, but also strikes out a lot. Offensive game needs polish, particularly approach. Elite speed is best tool and has plus range and strong arm at SS. Could also move to CF.

Mathias,Mark

456 | **Cleveland** | EXP MLB DEBUT: 2019 | H/W: 6-0 200 | FUT: Utility player | **6B**

Bats R Age 23
2015 (3) Cal Poly

- Pwr +
- BAvg +++
- Spd +++
- Def ++

Year	Lev	Team	AB	R	H	HR	RBI	Avg	OB	Slg	OPS	bb%	ct%	Eye	SB	CS	x/h%	Iso	RC/G
2015	NCAA	Cal Poly	202	42	72	1	28	356	422	436	858	10	91	1.21	9	4	15	79	6.30
2015	A-	Mahoning Val	245	38	69	2	32	282	371	408	780	13	85	0.97	5	4	35	127	5.55
2016	A+	Lynchburg	427	70	117	5	60	274	347	405	753	10	80	0.55	9	1	38	131	5.02
2016	AA	Akron	15	1	1	0	1	67	125	133	258	6	60	0.17	0	0	100	67	-2.51
2017	AA	Akron	104	17	22	1	13	212	299	308	607	11	67	0.38	4	0	32	96	3.08

Compact INF who missed most of season due to shoulder injury. Very versatile defensively with ideal body control and strong arm. Not the quickest guy around and can hold own with routine plays. Best position is 2B. Swings steady, consistent bat and mostly focuses on gaps. Has good hitting instincts, though little power.

Mathisen,Wyatt

5 | **Pittsburgh** | EXP MLB DEBUT: 2018 | H/W: 6-0 227 | FUT: Reserve 3B | **6C**

Bats R Age 24
2012 (2) HS (TX)

- Pwr ++
- BAvg +++
- Spd ++
- Def ++

Year	Lev	Team	AB	R	H	HR	RBI	Avg	OB	Slg	OPS	bb%	ct%	Eye	SB	CS	x/h%	Iso	RC/G
2013	A	West Virginia	119	13	22	0	9	185	242	210	452	7	82	0.41	1	0	14	25	1.12
2014	A	West Virginia	375	48	105	3	42	280	338	360	698	8	86	0.61	6	2	21	80	4.24
2015	A+	Bradenton	403	46	106	4	34	263	334	342	677	10	82	0.60	0	1	20	79	4.00
2016	A+	Bradenton	115	13	34	1	18	296	357	409	766	9	82	0.52	0	1	32	113	5.10
2017	AA	Altoona	375	43	102	5	31	272	348	365	714	11	80	0.59	3	2	23	93	4.47

Bounce-back season for former 2nd round pick. Has a good understanding of the strike zone, but power has never developed. Move to 3B is a work in progress and for now his footwork and range are below-average. Needs to show more power and was skipped over in Rule 5 draft.

Matias,Seuly

89 | **Kansas City** | EXP MLB DEBUT: 2022 | H/W: 6-3 200 | FUT: Starting OF | **9E**

Bats R Age 19
2015 FA (DR)

- Pwr ++++
- BAvg ++
- Spd +++
- Def +++

Year	Lev	Team	AB	R	H	HR	RBI	Avg	OB	Slg	OPS	bb%	ct%	Eye	SB	CS	x/h%	Iso	RC/G
2016	Rk	AZL Royals	172	32	43	8	29	250	335	477	812	11	58	0.30	2	4	49	227	6.73
2017	Rk	Burlington	222	27	54	7	36	243	294	423	718	7	68	0.22	2	1	43	180	4.48

Young, toolsy OF with ideal RF profile with plus-plus raw power and cannon arm. Needs lot of development time, particularly with bat approach. More of a free swinger now who chases pitches out of zone. Struggles with spin as well. Runs very well for size and able to track down balls. Played exclusively CF and will likely move to RF. Huge upside.

Matijevic,J.J.

7 | **Houston** | EXP MLB DEBUT: 2020 | H/W: 6-0 206 | FUT: Starting OF | **7C**

Bats L Age 22
2017 (S-2) Arizona

- Pwr ++
- BAvg +++
- Spd +++
- Def ++

Year	Lev	Team	AB	R	H	HR	RBI	Avg	OB	Slg	OPS	bb%	ct%	Eye	SB	CS	x/h%	Iso	RC/G
2017	NCAA	Arizona	240	57	92	10	65	383	437	633	1071	9	84	0.61	9	1	43	250	8.64
2017	A-	Tri City	200	34	48	6	27	240	303	400	703	8	70	0.30	11	3	42	160	4.23
2017	A	Quad Cities	24	2	3	1	4	125	160	250	410	4	63	0.11	0	1	33	125	-0.39

Stocky, strong OF who was collegiate standout at Arizona. Employs simple, quick stroke for line-drive contact and solid BA. Lacks loft in swing and power is mostly gap-oriented and to pull side; likely not a HR threat. Fringe-avg runner who won't be an SB threat long-term; lacks ideal range for OF position and may be relegated to LF.

Mazeika,Patrick

23 | **New York (N)** | EXP MLB DEBUT: 2019 | H/W: 6-3 208 | FUT: Starting C | **7C**

Bats L Age 24
2015 (8) Stetson

- Pwr ++
- BAvg +++
- Spd +
- Def +++

Year	Lev	Team	AB	R	H	HR	RBI	Avg	OB	Slg	OPS	bb%	ct%	Eye	SB	CS	x/h%	Iso	RC/G
2015	NCAA	Stetson	202	43	62	7	53	307	404	485	889	14	92	2.06	1	0	34	178	6.84
2015	Rk	Kingsport	226	44	80	5	48	354	416	540	956	10	88	0.92	1	0	40	186	7.36
2016	A	Columbia	239	34	73	3	35	305	401	402	802	14	84	0.97	2	0	23	96	5.80
2017	A+	St. Lucie	352	45	101	7	50	287	373	406	779	12	85	0.91	2	2	28	119	5.39
2017	AA	Binghamton	21	3	7	0	5	333	391	571	963	9	71	0.33	0	0	71	238	8.32

Unheralded LH hitter continues to hit at every stop. Advanced approach with understanding of zone, uses short, compact swing to spray ball around the field. Not known for power but will turn on middle-in pitches, pulling occasional HRs. Has made strides defensively. Still, bat-first. Tireless worker.

McCarthy,Joe

379 | **Tampa Bay** | EXP MLB DEBUT: 2018 | H/W: 6-3 225 | FUT: Starting OF | **7C**

Bats L Age 24
2015 (5) Virginia

- Pwr ++
- BAvg +++
- Spd +++
- Def ++

Year	Lev	Team	AB	R	H	HR	RBI	Avg	OB	Slg	OPS	bb%	ct%	Eye	SB	CS	x/h%	Iso	RC/G
2015	NCAA	Virginia	112	19	22	2	11	196	338	277	615	18	82	1.20	3	0	23	80	3.59
2015	A-	Hudson Valley	184	24	51	0	21	277	342	337	679	9	88	0.78	18	3	18	60	4.15
2016	A	Bowling Green	153	31	44	3	29	288	414	425	839	18	80	1.10	11	2	34	137	6.48
2016	A+	Charlotte	198	20	56	5	31	283	372	434	806	12	81	0.74	8	3	30	152	5.72
2017	AA	Montgomery	454	76	129	7	56	284	403	434	836	17	79	0.96	20	5	36	150	6.45

Sound hitter who led SL in walks and was 2nd in OBP and 3rd in doubles. Brings very patient approach to plate and controls strike zone with disciplined eye. Can put bat to ball consistently with compact stroke. Has size and strength, but not much long ball punch. Runs well for size. Plays 1B and OF corners, but may not have enough range or arm.

McGuire,Reese

2 | **Toronto** | EXP MLB DEBUT: 2018 | H/W: 5-11 215 | FUT: Starting C | **7C**

Bats L Age 23
2013 (1) HS (WA)

- Pwr ++
- BAvg +++
- Spd ++
- Def ++++

Year	Lev	Team	AB	R	H	HR	RBI	Avg	OB	Slg	OPS	bb%	ct%	Eye	SB	CS	x/h%	Iso	RC/G
2016	AA	New Hampshire	53	5	12	0	5	226	317	264	581	12	85	0.88	2	2	17	38	3.07
2016	AA	Altoona	266	29	69	1	37	259	332	346	678	10	90	1.12	4	4	28	86	4.30
2017	Rk	GCL Blue Jays	22	4	9	0	7	409	480	500	980	12	95	3.00	0	1	22	91	7.86
2017	A+	Dunedin	12	1	3	0	1	250	308	333	641	8	83	0.50	0	0	33	83	3.58
2017	AA	New Hampshire	115	19	32	6	20	278	366	496	862	12	83	0.84	2	1	38	217	6.25

Defensive-oriented C who missed most of year due to knee injury. Started to pick up pace with bat by showing more power. Can hit for BA with level swing path and feel for contact. Willing to work counts to get on base. Key to future will be power development. Very good defender behind plate with plus agility and average, accurate arm.

McKay,Brendan | 3 | Tampa Bay | EXP MLB DEBUT: 2019 | H/W: 6-2 212 | FUT: Starting 1B | 8C

Bats L Age 22
2017 (1) Louisville
Pwr +++
BAvg +++
Spd +++
Def +++

Year	Lev	Team	AB	R	H	HR	RBI	Avg	OB	Slg	OPS	bb%	ct%	Eye	SB	CS	x/h%	Iso	RC/G
2017	NCAA	Louisville	223	57	76	18	57	341	451	659	1111	17	83	1.15	2	0	45	318	9.50
2017	A-	Hudson Valley	125	16	29	4	22	232	342	376	718	14	74	0.64	2	0	31	144	4.61

Solid two-way player who is pure hitter with easy swing and plus raw power. Has advanced instincts and barrel control to hit for BA while drawing high number of walks. Uses whole field with level stroke, but will likely add loft for pop. Solid-average 1B with soft, quick hands and agility. Plus arm is a highlight.

McKinney,Billy | 79 | New York (A) | EXP MLB DEBUT: 2018 | H/W: 6-1 205 | FUT: Starting OF | 7D

Bats L Age 23
2013 (1) HS (TX)
Pwr ++
BAvg +++
Spd ++
Def ++

Year	Lev	Team	AB	R	H	HR	RBI	Avg	OB	Slg	OPS	bb%	ct%	Eye	SB	CS	x/h%	Iso	RC/G
2015	AA	Tennessee	274	29	78	3	39	285	349	420	769	9	83	0.57	0	0	38	135	5.17
2016	AA	Trenton	128	15	30	3	13	234	300	375	675	9	77	0.41	2	2	37	141	3.85
2016	AA	Tennessee	298	37	75	1	31	252	354	322	676	14	77	0.69	2	4	21	70	4.18
2017	AA	Trenton	232	34	58	6	29	250	336	431	767	11	81	0.67	2	1	45	181	5.22
2017	AAA	Scranton/WB	209	32	64	10	35	306	335	541	876	4	77	0.18	0	0	41	234	6.12

Natural hitting OF who got off to very slow start, but heated up in June. Has mostly doubles pop now and may never develop HR power. Hits LHP and can read spin. Has hand-eye coordination and ability to discern balls from strikes. Willing to work counts to get on base. Below average speed and arm limit defense and saw action at 1B in AFL.

McMahon,Ryan | 345 | Colorado | EXP MLB DEBUT: 2017 | H/W: 6-2 185 | FUT: Starting 1B | 9C

Bats L Age 23
2013 (2) HS (CA)
Pwr ++++
BAvg +++
Spd ++
Def +++

Year	Lev	Team	AB	R	H	HR	RBI	Avg	OB	Slg	OPS	bb%	ct%	Eye	SB	CS	x/h%	Iso	RC/G
2015	A+	Modesto	496	85	149	18	75	300	363	520	883	9	69	0.32	6	13	45	220	6.94
2016	AA	Hartford	466	49	113	12	75	242	322	399	722	11	65	0.34	11	6	39	157	4.78
2017	AA	Hartford	181	28	59	6	32	326	393	536	929	10	78	0.51	7	0	41	210	7.19
2017	AAA	Albuquerque	289	46	108	14	56	374	416	612	1029	7	82	0.40	4	3	36	239	8.00
2017	MLB	Colorado	19	2	3	0	1	158	333	211	544	21	74	1.00	0	0	33	53	2.57

Bounce-back season proved his offensive chops were legit and that 2016 was an injury-related fluke. Smooth LH stroke generates loft and natural power. Reduced K% rate from 30% to 17% in 2017. Split time at 2B, 3B, and 1B in preparation for UT role until a permanent opening becomes available.

McMillan,Sam | 2 | Detroit | EXP MLB DEBUT: 2022 | H/W: 6-1 195 | FUT: Starting C | 8E

Bats R Age 19
2017 (5) HS (FL)
Pwr ++
BAvg +++
Spd ++
Def +++

Year	Lev	Team	AB	R	H	HR	RBI	Avg	OB	Slg	OPS	bb%	ct%	Eye	SB	CS	x/h%	Iso	RC/G
2017	Rk	GCL Tigers	111	24	32	3	25	288	392	432	825	15	85	1.12	1	1	28	144	6.07

Despite youth, advanced catcher with both bat and glove. Has mature approach at plate and uses quick, compact stroke to put ball in play to all fields. May not have much power projection due to swing path. Has solid defensive tools, highlighted by deft receiving ability. Strong arm is good, but needs to improve accuracy.

Meadows,Austin | 789 | Pittsburgh | EXP MLB DEBUT: 2018 | H/W: 6-3 200 | FUT: Starting OF | 9D

Bats L Age 22
2013 (1) HS (GA)
Pwr ++++
BAvg ++++
Spd +++
Def +++

Year	Lev	Team	AB	R	H	HR	RBI	Avg	OB	Slg	OPS	bb%	ct%	Eye	SB	CS	x/h%	Iso	RC/G
2016	AA	Altoona	167	33	52	6	23	311	372	611	982	9	81	0.50	9	3	58	299	7.84
2016	AAA	Indianapolis	126	16	27	6	24	214	298	460	758	11	73	0.44	8	2	59	246	5.03
2017	Rk	GCL Pirates	13	3	7	1	7	538	571		1648	7	85	0.50	0	0	57	538	15.44
2017	A-	West Virginia	21	2	5	0	3	238	333	286	619	13	86	1.00	0	0	20	48	3.61
2017	AAA	Indianapolis	284	48	71	4	36	250	308	359	668	8	82	0.48	11	3	32	109	3.80

Another lost season for this highly touted prospect. Hamstring and oblique injuries limited him to 81 game and when he was healthy he scuffled, posting a.707 OPS. Five tools remain intact and he is still just 22, but needs to stay healthy and prove he is ready for the rigors of a full season.

Mejia,Francisco | 2 | Cleveland | EXP MLB DEBUT: 2017 | H/W: 5-10 180 | FUT: Starting C | 8C

Bats B Age 22
2012 FA (DR)
Pwr +++
BAvg ++++
Spd ++
Def ++

Year	Lev	Team	AB	R	H	HR	RBI	Avg	OB	Slg	OPS	bb%	ct%	Eye	SB	CS	x/h%	Iso	RC/G
2015	A	Lake County	391	45	95	9	53	243	310	345	655	9	80	0.49	4	1	23	102	3.58
2016	A	Lake County	239	41	83	7	51	347	386	531	917	6	84	0.38	1	0	33	184	6.64
2016	A+	Lynchburg	168	22	56	4	29	333	381	488	869	7	86	0.54	1	2	30	155	6.15
2017	AA	Akron	347	52	103	14	52	297	342	490	832	6	85	0.45	7	2	36	193	5.60
2017	MLB	Cleveland	13	1	2	0	1	154	214	154	368	7	77	0.33	0	0	0	0	-0.20

Switch-hitting CA who makes extreme contact with improving pop. Pure hitter with balanced swing and pitch recognition. Doesn't walk much due to bat-to-ball skill. Starting to use all fields and smash hard line drives to gaps. Exhibits cannon arm which neutralizes runners. Sub-par defender, though getting better with improved footwork and release.

Melendez,M.J. | 2 | Kansas City | EXP MLB DEBUT: 2022 | H/W: 6-1 185 | FUT: Starting C | 8D

Bats L Age 19
2017 (2) HS (FL)
Pwr +++
BAvg ++
Spd ++
Def +++

Year	Lev	Team	AB	R	H	HR	RBI	Avg	OB	Slg	OPS	bb%	ct%	Eye	SB	CS	x/h%	Iso	RC/G
2017	Rk	AZL Royals	168	25	44	4	30	262	361	417	777	13	64	0.43	4	2	34	155	5.81

Agile, mobile CA who could become solid prospect with bat and glove. Owns athleticism with quick feet and soft hands. Receives and blocks well for age. Has very strong arm, but needs to improve accuracy. Exhibits above average raw power to all fields, but Ks need to be curbed. Can be pull happy with long stroke and needs to improve against LHP.

Mercado,Oscar | 8 | St. Louis | EXP MLB DEBUT: 2019 | H/W: 6-2 175 | FUT: Starting CF | 8D

Bats R Age 23
2013 (2) HS (FL)
Pwr ++
BAvg ++
Spd ++++
Def ++++

Year	Lev	Team	AB	R	H	HR	RBI	Avg	OB	Slg	OPS	bb%	ct%	Eye	SB	CS	x/h%	Iso	RC/G
2013	Rk	GCL Cardinals	163	18	34	1	14	209	283	307	590	9	76	0.44	12	4	29	98	2.87
2014	Rk	Johnson City	245	41	55	3	25	224	283	306	589	8	85	0.54	26	7	24	82	2.89
2015	A	Peoria	472	70	120	4	44	254	289	341	630	5	87	0.38	50	19	25	87	3.29
2016	A+	Palm Beach	442	50	95	0	27	215	286	271	558	9	84	0.62	33	20	25	57	2.64
2017	AA	Springfield	477	76	137	13	46	287	332	428	760	6	77	0.29	38	19	27	140	4.78

Fleet-footed OF had a solid season at Double-A, raising hopes for more to come. Moved from SS to CF where he is now a plus defender with good range and a strong arm. Power remains a tick below average and an aggressive approach at the plate makes him a fringe regular, but the move to CF raises his profile.

Mercedes,Yermin | 23 | Chicago (A) | EXP MLB DEBUT: 2018 | H/W: 5-11 175 | FUT: Starting C | 7E

Bats R Age 25
2011 FA (DR)
Pwr +++
BAvg +++
Spd +
Def +

Year	Lev	Team	AB	R	H	HR	RBI	Avg	OB	Slg	OPS	bb%	ct%	Eye	SB	CS	x/h%	Iso	RC/G
2015	A	Delmarva	239	33	65	8	42	272	304	456	760	4	83	0.27	1	0	40	184	4.67
2016	A	Delmarva	340	58	120	14	60	353	412	579	991	9	81	0.54	1	1	37	226	7.77
2016	A+	Frederick	107	20	34	6	17	318	376	542	918	9	82	0.53	0	0	35	224	6.68
2017	A+	Frederick	336	48	92	15	55	274	339	458	797	9	82	0.56	4	3	35	185	5.28
2017	AA	Bowie	44	5	13	1	7	295	326	432	758	4	82	0.25	1	0	31	136	4.64

Natural-hitting CA who has been somewhat old for each level of minors and is career .302 batter. Hits for pop and is willing to go to opposite field. Drives ball well and has solid two-strike approach. Has limited utility with glove and has seen action at both C and 1B. Not a particularly good blocker or receiver.

Merrell,Kevin | 6 | Oakland | EXP MLB DEBUT: 2020 | H/W: 6-1 180 | FUT: Starting SS | 7C

Bats L Age 22
2017 (S-1) South Florida
Pwr ++
BAvg +++
Spd ++++
Def ++

Year	Lev	Team	AB	R	H	HR	RBI	Avg	OB	Slg	OPS	bb%	ct%	Eye	SB	CS	x/h%	Iso	RC/G
2017	NCAA	South Florida	216	48	83	7	36	384	457	569	1027	12	86	0.94	19	4	27	185	8.29
2017	A-	Vermont	125	27	40	2	9	320	366	424	790	7	82	0.41	10	3	20	104	5.17

Consistent, steady INF with athletic, quick actions. Should be able to stick at SS despite fringy arm as footwork and hands work well. Could likely play CF due to double-plus speed. Not much power forthcoming, but makes easy contact with hand-eye coordination. Can fly on basepaths and could stand to draw more walks. Needs to hit for BA.

Michalczewski,Trey | 5 | Chicago (A) | EXP MLB DEBUT: 2019 | H/W: 6-3 210 | FUT: Reserve 3B | 6C

Bats B Age 23
2013 (7) HS (OK)
Pwr +++
BAvg ++
Spd ++
Def +++

Year	Lev	Team	AB	R	H	HR	RBI	Avg	OB	Slg	OPS	bb%	ct%	Eye	SB	CS	x/h%	Iso	RC/G
2014	A+	Winston-Salem	72	5	14	0	5	194	284	222	506	11	71	0.43	1	0	14	28	1.61
2015	A+	Winston-Salem	474	59	123	7	75	259	330	395	725	10	76	0.44	4	3	37	135	4.62
2016	AA	Birmingham	487	62	110	11	59	226	306	363	669	10	69	0.37	4	0	36	138	3.89
2017	A+	Winston-Salem	68	12	20	4	12	294	351	559	910	8	72	0.32	1	0	45	265	6.95
2017	AA	Birmingham	368	40	86	9	38	234	307	356	663	10	66	0.31	8	1	29	122	3.78

Switch-hitting 3B who has continued to struggle at the plate. Was sent back to High-A to work on swing mechanics and was a little better in Double-A during 2nd half. Struggles with a consistent swing plane and is susceptible to balls out of zone. Running out of chances. A solid runner and defender.

Mieses,Johan — 789 — Los Angeles (N)

EXP MLB DEBUT: 2019 | H/W: 6-2 185 | FUT: Starting OF | 8E

Bats R Age 22 — 2013 FA (DR)
- Pwr ++++
- BAvg +
- Spd +++
- Def +++

Year	Lev	Team	AB	R	H	HR	RBI	Avg	OB	Slg	OPS	bb%	ct%	Eye	SB	CS	x/h%	Iso	RC/G
2015	A	Great Lakes	166	16	46	5	20	277	322	440	762	6	81	0.35	7	4	35	163	4.79
2015	A+	Rancho Cuca	196	35	48	6	19	245	292	439	731	6	71	0.23	3	1	52	194	4.58
2016	A+	Rancho Cuca	461	72	114	28	78	247	302	510	812	7	68	0.24	3	7	54	262	5.71
2017	A+	Rancho Cuca	116	25	41	8	27	353	405	707	1112	8	67	0.26	0	0	61	353	10.30
2017	AA	Tulsa	294	34	47	16	36	160	231	347	577	8	61	0.23	0	0	49	187	2.34

Athletic Dominican OF started well back at High-A in the CAL but imploded when moved up to Double-A Tulsa, striking out 116 times in 294 AB. Plus raw power and good bat speed, but aggressive at the plate and poor pitch recognition results in unsustainable contact rate. Good speed for his size with a plus arm and profiles best in RF.

Miller,Anderson — 789 — Kansas City

EXP MLB DEBUT: 2018 | H/W: 6-3 208 | FUT: Starting OF | 7D

Bats L Age 23 — 2015 (3) W Kentucky
- Pwr +++
- BAvg +++
- Spd +++
- Def +++

Year	Lev	Team	AB	R	H	HR	RBI	Avg	OB	Slg	OPS	bb%	ct%	Eye	SB	CS	x/h%	Iso	RC/G
2015	A	Lexington	169	15	44	2	21	260	317	355	672	8	83	0.50	0	1	25	95	3.86
2016	A	Lexington	155	24	44	3	18	284	373	432	805	12	67	0.43	3	1	36	148	6.09
2016	A+	Wilmington	144	18	29	3	16	201	263	361	624	8	65	0.24	5	0	48	160	3.27
2017	A+	Wilmington	269	37	78	7	37	290	374	439	812	12	78	0.60	15	2	28	149	5.78
2017	AA	NW Arkansas	213	17	49	2	19	230	261	296	557	4	74	0.16	3	2	20	66	2.05

Athletic OF who has tools that profile well at next level. Set highs in HR and SB. Rarely chases pitches and hangs in against LHP. Approach is fine, but has fanned over 100 times each of last two years. Swing can get long and will sell out for power. Plays all OF spots and likely to move to corner. Owns strong arm and offers average speed.

Miller,Brian — 789 — Miami

EXP MLB DEBUT: 2020 | H/W: 6-1 186 | FUT: Starting CF | 8D

Bats L Age 22 — 2017 (S-1) North Carolina
- Pwr ++
- BAvg +++
- Spd ++++
- Def +++

Year	Lev	Team	AB	R	H	HR	RBI	Avg	OB	Slg	OPS	bb%	ct%	Eye	SB	CS	x/h%	Iso	RC/G
2017	NCAA	North Carolina	271	61	93	7	49	343	424	502	926	12	87	1.09	24	6	28	159	7.15
2017	A	Greensboro	233	42	75	1	28	322	383	416	799	9	85	0.66	21	6	25	94	5.53

Supplemental 1st round pick has solid across-the-board tools. Quick lefty bat with contact ability and plus strike zone judgement (23 BB/35 K). Good range and speed in CF and profiles as top-of-the-order hitter. Below-average power and arm are only negatives. Swiped 21 bags in 57 games in his pro debut.

Miller,Ian — 78 — Seattle

EXP MLB DEBUT: 2018 | H/W: 6-0 175 | FUT: Reserve OF | 6B

Bats L Age 26 — 2013 (14) Wagner
- Pwr +
- BAvg ++
- Spd ++++
- Def +++

Year	Lev	Team	AB	R	H	HR	RBI	Avg	OB	Slg	OPS	bb%	ct%	Eye	SB	CS	x/h%	Iso	RC/G
2015	A+	Bakersfield	159	20	47	0	6	296	337	352	689	6	79	0.29	21	5	15	57	3.95
2015	AA	Jackson	347	40	88	0	23	254	311	320	631	8	85	0.55	29	13	20	66	3.47
2016	AA	Jackson	430	64	109	0	28	253	324	305	629	9	87	0.83	49	3	14	51	3.61
2017	AA	Arkansas	344	63	112	4	29	326	376	430	807	8	80	0.41	30	4	22	105	5.48
2017	AAA	Tacoma	168	22	45	0	6	268	289	315	604	3	80	0.15	13	1	13	48	2.73

Short, lean OF who was 2nd in TL in BA, OBP, and SB. Spent 2 1/2 years in AA before promotion to AAA where he struggled. Has little loft in swing and offers limited power, even to pull side. Uses entire field with extreme contact approach. Has been consistent 25+ SB producer thanks to plus speed. Can be average CF with good range and average arm.

Miller,Jalen — 46 — San Francisco

EXP MLB DEBUT: 2020 | H/W: 5-11 190 | FUT: Starting 2B | 7E

Bats R Age 21 — 2015 (3) HS (GA)
- Pwr ++
- BAvg +
- Spd +++
- Def +++

Year	Lev	Team	AB	R	H	HR	RBI	Avg	OB	Slg	OPS	bb%	ct%	Eye	SB	CS	x/h%	Iso	RC/G
2015	Rk	AZL Giants	174	28	38	0	13	218	288	259	547	9	76	0.40	11	2	16	40	2.22
2016	A	Augusta	457	65	102	5	44	223	265	322	587	5	77	0.24	11	5	29	98	2.59
2017	A+	San Jose	431	61	98	6	44	227	279	346	625	7	77	0.31	6	4	36	118	3.16

Quick INF with tools to be sound defensive player. Can play both MIF spots with soft hands and ample range. Arm strength better at 2B. Hasn't developed with bat, but has been young for levels. Posted low BA each month and fans too much for limited pop. Can slash doubles to gaps and has speed to beat out grounders. More of a slap approach than hard contact.

Miranda,Jose — 4 — Minnesota

EXP MLB DEBUT: 2020 | H/W: 6-2 180 | FUT: Starting 2B | 7C

Bats R Age 19 — 2016 (S-2) HS (PR)
- Pwr +++
- BAvg +++
- Spd ++
- Def ++

Year	Lev	Team	AB	R	H	HR	RBI	Avg	OB	Slg	OPS	bb%	ct%	Eye	SB	CS	x/h%	Iso	RC/G
2016	Rk	GCL Twins	185	14	42	1	20	227	299	292	591	9	81	0.53	4	5	21	65	2.92
2017	Rk	Elizabethton	223	43	63	11	43	283	331	484	815	7	89	0.67	2	3	33	202	5.38

Vastly-improving INF with drastic uptick in power while maintaining contact ability. Has chance to grow into above average pop with strong, compact stroke. Could become offensive-minded 2B or potential 3B due to average arm. Doesn't run well and has limited range. One to keep an eye on long-term.

Mitchell,Calvin — 789 — Pittsburgh

EXP MLB DEBUT: 2022 | H/W: 6-0 190 | FUT: Starting OF | 8E

Bats L Age 19 — 2017 (2) HS (CA)
- Pwr +++
- BAvg +++
- Spd ++
- Def ++

Year	Lev	Team	AB	R	H	HR	RBI	Avg	OB	Slg	OPS	bb%	ct%	Eye	SB	CS	x/h%	Iso	RC/G
2017	Rk	GCL Pirates	159	17	39	2	20	245	344	352	696	13	78	0.69	2	3	33	107	4.41

2nd rounder has interesting tools, but might not be able to hit for both power and average. Sold out for power in senior season pulling everything and saw his draft stock drop. Average speed and arm limit him to LF. Showed an ability to barrel the ball to all fields in the past so the upside is legit.

Moniak,Mickey — 8 — Philadelphia

EXP MLB DEBUT: 2020 | H/W: 6-2 185 | FUT: Starting CF | 8E

Bats L Age 19 — 2016 (1) HS (CA)
- Pwr ++
- BAvg +++
- Spd ++ (4.43)
- Def +++

Year	Lev	Team	AB	R	H	HR	RBI	Avg	OB	Slg	OPS	bb%	ct%	Eye	SB	CS	x/h%	Iso	RC/G
2016	Rk	GCL Phillies	176	27	50	1	28	284	326	409	735	6	80	0.31	10	4	32	125	4.60
2017	A	Lakewood	466	53	110	5	44	236	279	341	621	6	77	0.26	11	7	30	105	3.06

Disappointing season for former 1-1 pick, and not just the laggard stat line. Consistently struggled to square up pitches, often off-balance and lunging at breaking balls, and LHP ate him up (.484 OPS). Still young with some physical projection remaining; was an adequate defender in CF. But needs to improve pitch recognition and quality of contact.

Montano,Daniel — 9 — Colorado

EXP MLB DEBUT: 2022 | H/W: 6-1 170 | FUT: Starting OF | 7C

Bats L Age 19 — 2015 FA (VZ)
- Pwr +++
- BAvg +++
- Spd +++
- Def +++

Year	Lev	Team	AB	R	H	HR	RBI	Avg	OB	Slg	OPS	bb%	ct%	Eye	SB	CS	x/h%	Iso	RC/G
2017		*Did not play in the US*																	

Projectable, athletic OF has yet to make his state-side debut despite a solid season in the Dominican Summer League: .270/.355/.423. Does have some swing and miss, but also has good pitch recognition and is patient at the plate. Above-average power and speed potential make him worth watching.

Montero,Elehuris — 5 — St. Louis

EXP MLB DEBUT: 2022 | H/W: 6-3 195 | FUT: Starting 3B | 8D

Bats R Age 19 — 2014 FA (DR)
- Pwr +++
- BAvg +++
- Spd ++
- Def ++

Year	Lev	Team	AB	R	H	HR	RBI	Avg	OB	Slg	OPS	bb%	ct%	Eye	SB	CS	x/h%	Iso	RC/G
2017	Rk	GCL Cardinals	173	30	48	5	36	277	359	468	827	11	81	0.67	0	2	46	191	5.95

Tall, athletic Dominican 3B had a solid state-side debut in the GCL. Quick bat, plus raw power, and a slight upper-cut stroke give him the potential to develop into an impact hitter. Shows solid discipline at the plate and posted an impressive OPS and Eye as an 18-year-old.

Montgomery,Troy — 789 — Detroit

EXP MLB DEBUT: 2019 | H/W: 5-10 185 | FUT: Starting OF | 7E

Bats L Age 23 — 2016 (8) Ohio State
- Pwr ++
- BAvg ++
- Spd +++
- Def +++

Year	Lev	Team	AB	R	H	HR	RBI	Avg	OB	Slg	OPS	bb%	ct%	Eye	SB	CS	x/h%	Iso	RC/G
2016	Rk	Orem	88	16	30	4	17	341	437	557	994	15	77	0.75	10	4	30	216	8.25
2016	A	Burlington	142	15	37	3	13	261	335	401	737	10	79	0.53	3	2	32	141	4.75
2017	A	Burlington	43	6	11	2	4	256	418	465	883	22	91	3.00	2	1	36	209	7.20
2017	A+	Inland Empire	262	41	74	6	31	282	347	443	790	9	78	0.45	9	5	31	160	5.39
2017	AA	Mobile	68	15	16	0	3	235	333	265	598	13	82	0.83	4	0	13	29	3.24

Short, aggressive OF who ended season in August due to shoulder but played in AFL. Plays all OF spots and is sound defender with keen isntincts. Runs well, but not a burner. Has contact skills and will go gap to gap with fringy power. Has ability to hit LHP. Has nice tools and can play CF, but not standout in any phase of game.

Morales,Roy — 2 — Miami

EXP MLB DEBUT: 2019 | H/W: 6-2 195 | FUT: Starting C | 7C

Bats R Age 22 — 2014 (12) HS (PR)
Pwr ++ | BAvg +++ | Spd +++ | Def +++

Year	Lev	Team	AB	R	H	HR	RBI	Avg	OB	Slg	OPS	bb%	ct%	Eye	SB	CS	x/h%	Iso	RC/G
2014	Rk	GCL Marlins	76	11	17	0	7	224	280	263	544	7	97	3.00	0	2	18	39	2.97
2015	A-	Batavia	122	7	38	0	14	311	364	352	716	8	89	0.77	0	1	11	41	4.50
2015	A	Greensboro	44	2	8	0	0	182	234	227	461	6	89	0.60	0	0	25	45	1.58
2016	A	Greensboro	205	26	59	1	21	288	357	341	698	10	89	0.96	2	0	15	54	4.41
2017	A+	Jupiter	104	12	30	1	15	288	368	356	723	11	88	1.08	4	1	17	67	4.76

Tall, athletic backstop is starting to make an impact. Moves well behind the plate with an above-average arm and nailed 33% of runners. Line-drive approach with plus bat-on-ball skills (54 BB/55 K in career), but below-average power. Should be able to stick behind the plate.

Moran,Colin — 35 — Houston

EXP MLB DEBUT: 2016 | H/W: 6-4 204 | FUT: Starting 1B | 7A

Bats L Age 25 — 2013 (1) North Carolina
Pwr +++ | BAvg +++ | Spd + | Def ++

Year	Lev	Team	AB	R	H	HR	RBI	Avg	OB	Slg	OPS	bb%	ct%	Eye	SB	CS	x/h%	Iso	RC/G
2016	AAA	Fresno	459	50	119	10	69	259	328	368	696	9	73	0.38	3	2	24	109	4.13
2016	MLB	Houston	23	1	3	0	2	130	167	174	341	4	65	0.13	0	0	33	43	-1.10
2017	A	Quad Cities	10	0	1	0	2	100	250	200	450	17	60	0.50	0	0	100	100	0.72
2017	AAA	Fresno	302	53	93	18	63	308	372	543	915	9	82	0.56	0	3	37	235	6.69
2017	MLB	Houston	11	3	4	1	3	364	417	818	1235	8	91	1.00	0	0	50	455	10.16

Former 1st-round pick bounced back from down 2016, hit .300 against PCL arms. Combines terrific plate skills with great feel for the barrel and contact. Has plus power to pull side, but likely a strong shift candidate at next level. Strong arm for 3B but lacks athleticism for the position. Future home is 1B, which limits his overall value.

Morgan,Gareth — 79 — Seattle

EXP MLB DEBUT: 2020 | H/W: 6-4 220 | FUT: Starting OF | 8E

Bats R Age 21 — 2014 (S-2) HS (ON)
Pwr ++++ | BAvg + | Spd +++ | Def ++

Year	Lev	Team	AB	R	H	HR	RBI	Avg	OB	Slg	OPS	bb%	ct%	Eye	SB	CS	x/h%	Iso	RC/G
2014	Rk	AZL Mariners	155	15	23	2	12	148	228	252	480	9	53	0.22	4	1	48	103	1.20
2015	Rk	AZL Mariners	222	31	50	5	30	225	265	383	648	5	60	0.13	5	1	42	158	3.78
2016	Rk	AZL Mariners	125	17	27	1	11	216	263	344	607	6	54	0.14	5	1	37	128	3.67
2016	A+	Bakersfield	13	3	5	0	4	385	385	615	1000	0	46	0.00	0	0	60	231	13.26
2017	A	Clinton	405	55	93	17	61	230	319	422	741	12	54	0.29	14	5	44	193	5.79

Big OF who is starting to leverage natural strength to realize power potential. Led MWL in Ks and will always struggle with contact due to swing-at-anything approach and uppercut stroke. Power is unmatched in system and is starting to work deeper counts and draw walks. Runs well for size and could steal some bases in future. Needs to improve defense.

Morgan,Joey — 2 — Detroit

EXP MLB DEBUT: 2020 | H/W: 6-0 185 | FUT: Starting C | 7D

Bats R Age 21 — 2017 (3) Washington
Pwr ++ | BAvg ++ | Spd ++ | Def +++

Year	Lev	Team	AB	R	H	HR	RBI	Avg	OB	Slg	OPS	bb%	ct%	Eye	SB	CS	x/h%	Iso	RC/G
2017	NCAA	Washington	182	28	59	5	45	324	420	500	920	14	81	0.86	1	0	36	176	7.28
2017	A-	Connecticut	112	14	28	1	10	250	306	321	627	7	78	0.36	0	0	21	71	3.19

Strong backstop with excellent catch-and-throw skills and relatively polished with glovework. Has above average agility and mobility with quick feet. Should be able to catch in majors soon. Bat needs work, though, and has limited upside. Could hit for BA with all-fields approach and more selective eye. Power doesn't project.

Morgan,Josh — 26 — Texas

EXP MLB DEBUT: 2019 | H/W: 5-11 185 | FUT: Starting C | 8E

Bats R Age 22 — 2014 (3) HS (CA)
Pwr ++ | BAvg +++ | Spd ++ | Def ++

Year	Lev	Team	AB	R	H	HR	RBI	Avg	OB	Slg	OPS	bb%	ct%	Eye	SB	CS	x/h%	Iso	RC/G
2014	Rk	AZL Rangers	113	26	38	0	10	336	432	372	803	14	88	1.46	2	2	8	35	5.95
2014	A-	Spokane	89	11	27	0	9	303	374	315	688	10	89	1.00	1	1	4	11	4.30
2015	A	Hickory	351	59	101	3	36	288	369	362	731	11	85	0.85	9	4	19	74	4.81
2016	A+	High Desert	470	74	141	7	64	300	360	394	754	9	87	0.72	4	2	20	94	4.90
2017	A+	Down East	408	56	110	6	45	270	313	380	693	6	87	0.48	3	0	27	110	4.07

Versatile prospect who repeated High-A and continued to see time at catcher. Has produced good BA with short stroke and use of whole field. Recognizes spin and is tough to fan. Walk rate in decline and hasn't stolen many bases. Limited pop at present, though could increase with swing change. Has arm for C, though needs polish with release and blocking.

Mountcastle,Ryan — 56 — Baltimore

EXP MLB DEBUT: 2019 | H/W: 6-3 195 | FUT: Starting OF | 8B

Bats R Age 21 — 2015 (1) HS (FL)
Pwr +++ | BAvg ++++ | Spd ++ | Def ++

Year	Lev	Team	AB	R	H	HR	RBI	Avg	OB	Slg	OPS	bb%	ct%	Eye	SB	CS	x/h%	Iso	RC/G
2015	Rk	GCL Orioles	163	21	51	3	14	313	349	411	760	5	78	0.25	10	4	20	98	4.70
2015	A-	Aberdeen	33	2	7	1	5	212	212	303	515	0	70	0.00	0	1	14	91	1.13
2016	A	Delmarva	455	53	128	10	51	281	319	426	745	5	79	0.26	5	4	33	145	4.57
2017	A+	Frederick	360	63	113	15	47	314	340	542	881	4	83	0.23	8	2	45	228	6.05
2017	AA	Bowie	153	18	34	3	15	222	237	366	603	2	77	0.09	0	0	47	144	2.65

Natural-hitting INF who led minors in doubles while leading CAR in BA, SLG, and OPS. Young for level, but has advanced bat. Reads breaking balls and knows strike zone, but doesn't draw many walks. Plus bat speed and has above average pop potential. Played SS in High-A and 3B in AA. Prob move to OF due to poor arm. Bat will have to carry him.

Mullins,Cedric — 8 — Baltimore

EXP MLB DEBUT: 2018 | H/W: 5-8 175 | FUT: Starting CF | 7C

Bats B Age 23 — 2015 (13) Campbell
Pwr +++ | BAvg ++ | Spd ++++ | Def ++++

Year	Lev	Team	AB	R	H	HR	RBI	Avg	OB	Slg	OPS	bb%	ct%	Eye	SB	CS	x/h%	Iso	RC/G
2015	NCAA	Campbell	235	59	80	4	23	340	378	549	926	6	85	0.39	23	4	43	209	6.86
2015	A-	Aberdeen	277	34	73	2	32	264	318	375	693	7	88	0.67	17	4	30	112	4.26
2016	A	Delmarva	517	79	141	14	55	273	321	464	786	7	80	0.37	30	6	43	191	5.19
2017	AA	Bowie	309	53	82	13	37	265	324	460	784	8	81	0.47	9	7	40	194	5.11

Short OF who bypassed High-A and continued to showcase bat while exhibiting potential for at least average pop. Needs to make more contact from right side and can play small ball due to plus speed and instincts. Doesn't steal many bags despite wheels, but is plus CF with innate tracking and range. Nagging hamstring limited time in 2017.

Mundell,Brian — 3 — Colorado

EXP MLB DEBUT: 2019 | H/W: 6-3 230 | FUT: Starting 1B | 7C

Bats R Age 24 — 2015 (7) Cal Poly
Pwr +++ | BAvg +++ | Spd + | Def +

Year	Lev	Team	AB	R	H	HR	RBI	Avg	OB	Slg	OPS	bb%	ct%	Eye	SB	CS	x/h%	Iso	RC/G
2015	NCAA	Cal Poly	170	24	48	5	34	282	378	447	825	13	84	0.96	0	2	35	165	5.99
2015	A-	Boise	244	35	67	4	36	275	359	410	769	12	82	0.71	7	1	36	135	5.27
2016	A	Asheville	537	94	168	14	83	313	378	503	881	9	85	0.67	7	8	43	190	6.48
2017	A+	Lancaster	264	44	79	12	59	299	381	504	885	12	83	0.80	0	1	37	205	6.54
2017	AA	Hartford	172	30	52	3	19	302	391	424	815	13	85	0.96	1	1	29	122	5.89

Stocky, broad-shouldered 1B prospect has a surprisingly advanced approach at the plate. Average to above power, but is very selective, choosing to hit line drives into the gaps instead of selling out for power. Below-average speed and arm limit him to 1B where his power profile might be a bit short.

Munoz,Yairo — 4568 — St. Louis

EXP MLB DEBUT: 2018 | H/W: 6-1 165 | FUT: Starting MIF | 7B

Bats R Age 23 — 2012 FA (DR)
Pwr +++ | BAvg ++ | Spd +++ | Def +++

Year	Lev	Team	AB	R	H	HR	RBI	Avg	OB	Slg	OPS	bb%	ct%	Eye	SB	CS	x/h%	Iso	RC/G
2015	A	Beloit	369	48	87	9	48	236	279	363	642	6	83	0.35	10	2	30	127	3.33
2015	A+	Stockton	150	21	48	4	26	320	366	480	846	7	87	0.55	1	1	33	160	5.84
2016	AA	Midland	387	44	93	9	39	240	283	367	650	6	80	0.30	6	7	30	127	3.38
2017	AA	Midland	190	35	60	6	26	316	350	532	882	5	82	0.29	12	1	43	216	6.23
2017	AAA	Nashville	256	30	74	7	42	289	318	414	732	4	82	0.24	10	4	23	125	4.26

Consistent prospect who had best pro season to date with career high in SB and HR. Very versatile defender with ability to play all spots but C. Much improved bat from 2016 and shows good contact with steady punch. Strength and bat speed are assets. Runs well but would benefit from more patience. Hands and range are sufficient while arm is plus.

Murphy,Sean — 2 — Oakland

EXP MLB DEBUT: 2019 | H/W: 6-3 215 | FUT: Starting C | 7B

Bats R Age 23 — 2016 (3) Wright St
Pwr +++ | BAvg ++ | Spd ++ | Def +++

Year	Lev	Team	AB	R	H	HR	RBI	Avg	OB	Slg	OPS	bb%	ct%	Eye	SB	CS	x/h%	Iso	RC/G
2016	NCAA	Wright State	136	38	39	6	34	287	398	507	905	16	87	1.39	6	0	36	221	7.05
2016	Rk	AZL Athletics	3	1	0	0	0	0	0	0	0	0	100		0	0		0	-2.66
2016	A-	Vermont	76	10	18	2	7	237	318	329	647	11	84	0.75	1	0	17	92	3.62
2017	A+	Stockton	165	22	49	9	26	297	341	527	868	6	80	0.33	0	0	41	230	6.00
2017	AA	Midland	191	25	40	4	22	209	288	309	597	10	82	0.62	0	0	28	99	2.98

Big, durable backstop who had outstanding first full season. Showcases plus arm along with blocking and receiving skills. Calls good game. BA potential muted by inconsistent stroke, but has bat speed and hand-eye coordination for contact. Has strength and leverage in stroke to produce at least average pop. Some upside.

Murphy,Tom — 2 — Colorado

EXP MLB DEBUT: 2015 | H/W: 6-1 220 | FUT: Starting C | 7C

Bats R Age 27 — 2012 (3) Buffalo
Pwr +++ | BAvg ++ | Spd ++ | Def ++

Year	Lev	Team	AB	R	H	HR	RBI	Avg	OB	Slg	OPS	bb%	ct%	Eye	SB	CS	x/h%	Iso	RC/G
2015	MLB	Colorado	35	5	9	3	9	257	333	543	876	10	71	0.40	0	0	44	286	6.37
2016	AAA	Albuquerque	303	53	99	19	59	327	361	647	1007	5	74	0.21	1	1	53	320	8.03
2016	MLB	Colorado	44	8	12	5	13	273	333	659	992	8	57	0.21	1	0	58	386	9.43
2017	AAA	Albuquerque	141	22	36	4	19	255	300	426	726	6	60	0.16	0	0	42	170	5.00
2017	MLB	Colorado	24	1	1	0	1	42	115	83	199	6	63	0.22	0	0	100	42	-3.39

Offensive-minded backstop was on the verge of extended action in the majors when he broke his arm in spring training. Was out of action until mid-June and then never found his rhythm. Still has plus raw power and a track-record of hitting for average, though his ct% remains a red flag. Should get another shot in 2018.

Naylor,Josh

3 | **San Diego** | EXP MLB DEBUT: 2019 | H/W: 6-0 225 | FUT: Starting 1B | **7B**

Bats L Age 20
2015 (1) HS (ON)
Pwr +++
BAvg +++
Spd +
Def +++

Year	Lev	Team	AB	R	H	HR	RBI	Avg	OB	Slg	OPS	bb%	ct%	Eye	SB	CS	x/h%	Iso	RC/G
2015	Rk	GCL Marlins	98	8	32	1	16	327	353	418	771	4	89	0.36	1	0	19	92	4.83
2016	A	Greensboro	342	42	92	9	54	269	313	430	743	6	82	0.35	10	3	38	161	4.58
2016	A+	Lake Elsinore	139	17	35	3	21	252	268	353	620	2	84	0.14	1	1	23	101	2.86
2017	A+	Lake Elsinore	283	41	84	8	45	297	358	452	810	9	83	0.56	7	1	31	155	5.53
2017	AA	San Antonio	156	18	39	2	19	250	320	346	666	9	77	0.44	2	1	28	96	3.79

Former 1st round pick who was one of the youngest hitters to appear at AA. Projected 1B given thick, top-heavy build and fringy athletic actions. Chance for average BA/HR output at peak with plus bat speed and good raw power. Aggressive and prone to lunging at off-speed; often falls behind in counts. Lack of defensive versatility limits his value.

Nelson,James

5 | **Miami** | EXP MLB DEBUT: 2021 | H/W: 6-2 180 | FUT: Starting 3B | **8D**

Bats R Age 20
2016 (15) Cisco JC
Pwr ++++
BAvg +++
Spd +++
Def ++

Year	Lev	Team	AB	R	H	HR	RBI	Avg	OB	Slg	OPS	bb%	ct%	Eye	SB	CS	x/h%	Iso	RC/G
2016	Rk	GCL Marlins	162	26	46	1	24	284	341	364	705	8	81	0.47	7	3	24	80	4.27
2017	A	Greensboro	395	41	122	7	59	309	352	456	807	6	73	0.25	6	2	34	147	5.58

Strong, physically mature 3B had an impressive full-season debut, posting an .800 OPS as 19-year-old at Low-A. Quick, upper-cut stroke generates plus power, but can be overly aggressive and strikes out too much. Above-average speed and arm strength, but poor footwork and throws make for a below-average defender.

Netzer,Brett

4 | **Boston** | EXP MLB DEBUT: 2020 | H/W: 6-0 195 | FUT: Starting 2B | **7D**

Bats L Age 21
2017 (3) Charlotte
Pwr ++
BAvg +++
Spd +++
Def ++

Year	Lev	Team	AB	R	H	HR	RBI	Avg	OB	Slg	OPS	bb%	ct%	Eye	SB	CS	x/h%	Iso	RC/G
2017	NCAA	Charlotte	234	50	80	5	44	342	414	509	923	11	88	1.07	5	2	31	167	7.07
2017	A-	Lowell	82	11	26	0	14	317	385	390	775	10	76	0.45	0	3	23	73	5.33
2017	A	Greenville	100	15	26	0	13	260	321	300	621	8	76	0.38	5	1	15	40	3.16

Offensive-minded 2B with good athleticism and feel for hitting. Hangs in against LHP and uses fast bat to lace doubles to gaps. Has consistent swing path and can read spin. Projects to only average pop at best. Runs bases with good speed, but lacks quick actions at 2B.

Neuse,Sheldon

56 | **Oakland** | EXP MLB DEBUT: 2019 | H/W: 6-0 195 | FUT: Starting 3B | **7C**

Bats R Age 23
2016 (2) Oklahoma
Pwr +++
BAvg ++++
Spd ++
Def ++

Year	Lev	Team	AB	R	H	HR	RBI	Avg	OB	Slg	OPS	bb%	ct%	Eye	SB	CS	x/h%	Iso	RC/G
2016	NCAA	Oklahoma	198	42	73	10	48	369	473	646	1119	16	78	0.91	12	2	41	278	10.01
2016	A-	Auburn	126	16	29	1	11	230	302	341	643	9	79	0.50	2	2	31	111	3.61
2017	A	Hagerstown	292	40	85	9	51	291	347	469	816	8	77	0.38	12	5	36	178	5.62
2017	A+	Stockton	83	21	32	7	22	386	446	675	1120	10	70	0.36	2	0	31	289	9.93
2017	AA	Midland	67	9	25	0	6	373	425	433	857	8	69	0.29	0	0	16	60	6.61

Polished hitter who hit over .300 with good power in first full season that ended in AA. Short stroke leads to acceptable contact and has charge in bat to create average pop. More power could be forthcoming, but more adept at BA with use of whole field. Fringy quickness and range limit defensive skills, but is capable.

Nevin,Tyler

35 | **Colorado** | EXP MLB DEBUT: 2021 | H/W: 6-4 200 | FUT: Starting 1B | **8D**

Bats R Age 20
2015 (S-1) HS (CA)
Pwr +++
BAvg +++
Spd ++
Def ++

Year	Lev	Team	AB	R	H	HR	RBI	Avg	OB	Slg	OPS	bb%	ct%	Eye	SB	CS	x/h%	Iso	RC/G
2015	Rk	Grand Junction	189	29	50	2	18	265	362	386	749	13	78	0.69	3	7	36	122	5.14
2016	A-	Boise	1	1	1	0	0	1000			3000	0	100		0	0	100	1000	27.71
2017	A-	Boise	30	4	7	1	5	233	233	433	667	0	70	0.00	0	1	57	200	3.44
2017	A	Asheville	298	45	91	7	47	305	363	456	819	8	81	0.48	10	5	31	151	5.65

Son of former big leaguer Phil Nevin, his injuries have limited him to just 328 AB over the last two seasons. When healthy, he has good bat speed and above-average power. He's a solid if not spectacular defender, but long-term fits better at 1B, especially in Colorado.

Newman,Kevin

6 | **Pittsburgh** | EXP MLB DEBUT: 2018 | H/W: 6-1 180 | FUT: Starting 2B | **7B**

Bats R Age 24
2015 (1) Arizona
Pwr +
BAvg ++++
Spd +++
Def +++

Year	Lev	Team	AB	R	H	HR	RBI	Avg	OB	Slg	OPS	bb%	ct%	Eye	SB	CS	x/h%	Iso	RC/G
2015	A	West Virginia	98	14	30	0	8	306	364	367	732	8	92	1.13	6	1	17	61	4.82
2016	A+	Bradenton	164	24	60	3	24	366	425	494	919	9	93	1.42	4	1	23	128	6.89
2016	AA	Altoona	233	41	67	2	28	288	359	378	737	10	90	1.08	6	3	22	90	4.91
2017	AA	Altoona	343	42	89	4	30	259	304	359	663	6	88	0.55	4	2	27	99	3.77
2017	AAA	Indianapolis	166	23	47	0	11	283	312	373	686	4	87	0.32	7	1	28	90	3.94

Ability to make consistent contact and above-average speed are his best tools, but below average power limits his fantasy appeal. Solid defender with good range, soft hands, and a strong arm. A move to 2B seems likely as Cole Tucker has the higher upside.

Nido,Tomas

2 | **New York (N)** | EXP MLB DEBUT: 2017 | H/W: 6-0 210 | FUT: Starting C | **7C**

Bats R Age 23
2012 (8) HS (FL)
Pwr ++
BAvg ++
Spd +
Def +++

Year	Lev	Team	AB	R	H	HR	RBI	Avg	OB	Slg	OPS	bb%	ct%	Eye	SB	CS	x/h%	Iso	RC/G
2014	A-	Brooklyn	188	20	52	1	21	277	327	335	662	7	78	0.34	2	2	15	59	3.62
2015	A	Savannah	317	39	82	6	40	259	286	372	658	4	73	0.14	1	1	27	114	3.38
2016	A+	St. Lucie	344	38	110	7	46	320	355	459	815	5	88	0.45	0	1	29	140	5.40
2017	AA	Binghamton	367	41	85	8	60	232	290	354	644	8	83	0.48	0	0	33	123	3.47
2017	MLB	NY Mets	10	0	3	0	3	300	300	400	700	0	80	0.00	0	0	33	100	3.81

Polarizing prospect made MLB debut after struggling offensively in Double-A following strides the previous season. Hard contact rate plummeted back to 2015 levels. Trying to curb aggressiveness left in-between many swings. Raw power but doesn't create loft. Solid defensively. Pitchers love throwing to target.

Noda,Ryan

39 | **Toronto** | EXP MLB DEBUT: 2020 | H/W: 6-3 217 | FUT: Starting OF | **7D**

Bats L Age 22
2017 (15) Cincinnati
Pwr +++
BAvg +++
Spd ++
Def ++

Year	Lev	Team	AB	R	H	HR	RBI	Avg	OB	Slg	OPS	bb%	ct%	Eye	SB	CS	x/h%	Iso	RC/G
2017	NCAA	Cincinnati	178	43	42	9	30	236	355	478	833	16	62	0.49	9	2	55	242	6.77
2017	Rk	Bluefield	214	62	78	7	39	364	502	575	1077	22	72	0.98	7	4	36	210	10.23

Strong prospect who led Appy in BA, OBP, and SLG in pro debut. Surprised with natural hitting ability and approach. Draws ton of walks with keen eye and finds pitches to drive to gaps. BA and power are only average, but good enough to warrant attention. Can play OF corners with average speed and arm. Probably will stick at 1B long-term.

Norwood,John

89 | **Miami** | EXP MLB DEBUT: 2018 | H/W: 6-1 185 | FUT: Reserve OF | **7D**

Bats R Age 25
2014 (NDFA) Vanderbilt
Pwr +++
BAvg +
Spd +++
Def +++

Year	Lev	Team	AB	R	H	HR	RBI	Avg	OB	Slg	OPS	bb%	ct%	Eye	SB	CS	x/h%	Iso	RC/G
2014	NCAA	Vanderbilt	218	32	65	3	32	298	368	404	771	10	77	0.47	17	8	25	106	5.20
2014	A-	Batavia	78	4	20	0	6	256	284	295	579	4	68	0.12	0	0	10	38	2.37
2015	A	Greensboro	446	53	104	16	55	233	299	392	692	9	75	0.37	34	14	36	159	3.98
2016	A+	Jupiter	469	68	127	9	50	271	340	397	736	9	75	0.42	14	12	29	126	4.71
2017	AA	Jacksonville	473	68	135	19	62	285	365	459	823	11	72	0.44	4	4	30	173	5.93

Undrafted out of college, he has established himself as a viable prospect. Above-average power and speed are his best tools. Aggressive approach at the plate results in swing-and-miss and could limit to a backup role in the majors.

Nottingham,Jacob

23 | **Milwaukee** | EXP MLB DEBUT: 2018 | H/W: 6-2 230 | FUT: Starting C | **7E**

Bats R Age 23
2013 (6) HS (CA)
Pwr +++
BAvg ++
Spd +
Def ++

Year	Lev	Team	AB	R	H	HR	RBI	Avg	OB	Slg	OPS	bb%	ct%	Eye	SB	CS	x/h%	Iso	RC/G
2015	A	Quad Cities	230	34	75	10	46	326	375	543	918	7	78	0.35	1	2	39	217	6.82
2015	A+	Stockton	164	25	49	3	22	299	347	409	755	7	77	0.32	1	0	24	110	4.77
2015	A+	Lancaster	71	14	23	4	14	324	351	606	957	4	86	0.30	0	0	48	282	6.87
2016	AA	Biloxi	415	46	97	11	37	234	284	347	631	7	67	0.21	9	2	26	113	3.13
2017	AA	Biloxi	325	37	68	9	48	209	290	369	659	10	73	0.43	7	3	47	160	3.70

Offensive-minded catcher continues to struggle with hit tool and defense in upper minors. Has underachieved despite solid bat-to-ball skills. Slow bat struggles getting to the hit zone, resulting in a lot of soft contact. Raw plus power, generated from frame not bat. A poor athlete, has struggled with footwork blocking and receiving.

Nova,Freudis

6 | **Houston** | EXP MLB DEBUT: 2021 | H/W: 6-1 180 | FUT: Starting SS | **8E**

Bats R Age 18
2016 FA (DR)
Pwr +++
BAvg +++
Spd ++++
Def +++

Year	Lev	Team	AB	R	H	HR	RBI	Avg	OB	Slg	OPS	bb%	ct%	Eye	SB	CS	x/h%	Iso	RC/G
2017		*Did not play in the US*																	

Wiry and athletic, his strong tools are headlined by plus speed and quality defensive range and arm to stick at SS. Added bonus of bat speed and fluid RH stroke conducive to contact and at least average power. Still a long ways from reaching his potential, but skills make for an intriguing profile worth monitoring.

Nunez,Dom — 2 — Colorado

EXP MLB DEBUT: 2018 | H/W: 6-0 175 | FUT: Starting C | 7D

Bats L Age 23
2013 (6) HS (CA)
Pwr +++
BAvg ++
Spd ++
Def +++

Year	Lev	Team	AB	R	H	HR	RBI	Avg	OB	Slg	OPS	bb%	ct%	Eye	SB	CS	x/h%	Iso	RC/G
2013	Rk	Grand Junction	195	24	39	3	23	200	268	323	591	8	83	0.53	11	8	44	123	2.94
2014	Rk	Grand Junction	176	30	55	8	40	313	386	517	903	11	84	0.75	5	7	36	205	6.68
2015	A	Asheville	373	61	105	13	53	282	371	448	819	12	85	0.96	7	7	34	166	5.83
2016	A+	Modesto	390	44	94	10	51	241	326	362	687	11	77	0.54	8	1	27	121	4.07
2017	AA	Hartford	297	37	60	11	28	202	323	354	676	15	72	0.64	7	1	37	152	4.01

Solid defensive backstop has strong arm and moves well behind the plate, but poor footwork leads to too many passed balls. Regressed at the plate, with a career-low OPS, which raises concerns about his ability to be a full-time regular.

Nunez,Renato — 57 — Oakland

EXP MLB DEBUT: 2016 | H/W: 6-1 220 | FUT: Starting 3B | 8D

Bats R Age 24
2010 FA (VZ)
Pwr ++++
BAvg ++
Spd +
Def ++

Year	Lev	Team	AB	R	H	HR	RBI	Avg	OB	Slg	OPS	bb%	ct%	Eye	SB	CS	x/h%	Iso	RC/G
2015	AA	Midland	381	62	106	18	61	278	328	480	808	7	83	0.42	1	0	39	202	5.29
2016	AAA	Nashville	505	61	115	23	75	228	272	412	684	6	76	0.26	2	0	39	184	3.70
2016	MLB	Oakland	15	0	2	0	1	133	133	133	267	0	80	0.00	0	0	0	0	-1.57
2017	AAA	Nashville	473	74	118	32	78	249	317	518	835	9	70	0.33	2	1	52	268	5.95
2017	MLB	Oakland	15	1	3	1	3	200	250	400	650	6	47	0.13	0	0	33	200	4.66

Slugging prospect who finished 2nd in minors in HR. Exhibits plus power to all fields and has elite strength and bat speed. Strikeouts and pull happy approach mute BA potential, but will work counts. Possesses little to no speed and is sub-par defender at 3B and LF. Would be ideal DH or 1B where plus-plus power would play.

Ockimey,Josh — 3 — Boston

EXP MLB DEBUT: 2019 | H/W: 6-1 215 | FUT: Starting 1B | 7C

Bats L Age 22
2014 (5) HS (PA)
Pwr ++++
BAvg ++
Spd +
Def ++

Year	Lev	Team	AB	R	H	HR	RBI	Avg	OB	Slg	OPS	bb%	ct%	Eye	SB	CS	x/h%	Iso	RC/G
2014	Rk	GCL Red Sox	112	17	21	0	10	188	278	232	510	11	67	0.38	1	0	19	45	1.63
2015	A-	Lowell	199	30	53	4	38	266	348	422	770	11	61	0.32	2	2	38	156	5.90
2016	A	Greenville	407	60	92	18	62	226	364	425	789	18	68	0.68	3	1	48	199	5.79
2017	A+	Salem	349	56	96	11	63	275	390	438	829	16	68	0.60	1	4	34	163	6.41
2017	AA	Portland	103	12	28	3	11	272	375	427	802	14	68	0.52	0	0	36	155	5.98

Big-framed slugger who got off to hot start and finished 2nd in CAR in OBP and 3rd in OPS. More doubles pop than HR at present, though swing and strength should lead to more HR. Uses all fields, but struggles to make consistent contact. Can be pull conscious and has well below average speed. OK defender, but does not stand out.

O'Hearn,Ryan — 37 — Kansas City

EXP MLB DEBUT: 2018 | H/W: 6-3 200 | FUT: Starting 1B | 7C

Bats L Age 24
2014 (8) Sam Houston St
Pwr ++++
BAvg ++
Spd +
Def ++

Year	Lev	Team	AB	R	H	HR	RBI	Avg	OB	Slg	OPS	bb%	ct%	Eye	SB	CS	x/h%	Iso	RC/G
2015	A+	Wilmington	161	14	38	8	21	236	317	447	764	11	66	0.35	0	0	47	211	5.21
2016	A+	Wilmington	88	13	31	7	18	352	406	670	1077	8	69	0.30	0	0	45	318	9.39
2016	AA	NW Arkansas	414	49	107	15	60	258	335	437	773	10	68	0.37	3	5	39	179	5.35
2017	AA	NW Arkansas	66	7	17	4	11	258	355	485	840	13	70	0.50	0	0	35	227	6.21
2017	AAA	Omaha	413	48	104	18	53	252	325	450	776	10	71	0.38	1	0	43	199	5.23

Power-hitting 1B/OF who started in AAA before demotion to AA in August. Has as much raw pop as any in org with lots of load and leverage in stroke. Has patient approach, though K rate remains high. BA in decline at upper levels and exhibits below average speed. Saw time in OF corners and should become average defender in time.

Okey,Chris — 2 — Cincinnati

EXP MLB DEBUT: 2019 | H/W: 5-11 195 | FUT: Starting C | 7C

Bats R Age 23
2016 (2) Clemson
Pwr +++
BAvg ++
Spd ++
Def +++

Year	Lev	Team	AB	R	H	HR	RBI	Avg	OB	Slg	OPS	bb%	ct%	Eye	SB	CS	x/h%	Iso	RC/G
2016	NCAA	Clemson	239	61	81	15	74	339	455	611	1066	18	77	0.94	4	3	41	272	9.30
2016	Rk	Billings	37	5	6	0	1	162	184	189	373	3	78	0.13	0	0	17	27	-0.20
2016	A	Dayton	148	21	36	6	21	243	309	432	741	9	67	0.29	5	0	42	189	4.85
2017	A+	Daytona	325	27	60	3	28	185	258	249	507	9	68	0.31	2	1	23	65	1.48

Athletic RH catcher struggled in full-season debut. Slow trigger and reaction skills took away from advanced eye at plate. Was beaten by velocity due to slow bat. Power generated from frame, not swing. Hasn't materialized in game. High marks behind plate. Pitchers love throwing to him. Will stick as a regular if bat comes along.

Olivares,Edward — 789 — Toronto

EXP MLB DEBUT: 2019 | H/W: 6-2 186 | FUT: Starting OF | 7D

Bats R Age 22
2014 FA (VZ)
Pwr +++
BAvg +++
Spd +++
Def +++

Year	Lev	Team	AB	R	H	HR	RBI	Avg	OB	Slg	OPS	bb%	ct%	Eye	SB	CS	x/h%	Iso	RC/G
2015	Rk	GCL Blue Jays	116	21	23	3	10	198	268	362	630	9	77	0.41	14	2	52	164	3.29
2016	Rk	Bluefield	55	8	15	1	6	273	333	418	752	8	78	0.42	1	2	33	145	4.87
2017	A	Lansing	426	82	118	17	65	277	313	500	813	5	81	0.27	18	7	44	223	5.35
2017	A+	Dunedin	68	11	15	0	7	221	303	265	567	11	75	0.47	2	2	13	44	2.56

Athletic OF who surpassed expectations in first full season. Broke out with big increase in pop by driving ball to all fields. Can hit breaking balls with compact stroke. Approach doesn't lead to many walks and free-swinging ways should get better. Good range in OF with average speed and has knack for getting solid jumps.

Ona,Jorge — 79 — San Diego

EXP MLB DEBUT: 2020 | H/W: 6-0 220 | FUT: Starting OF | 8D

Bats R Age 21
2016 FA (CU)
Pwr +++
BAvg ++
Spd +++
Def +++

Year	Lev	Team	AB	R	H	HR	RBI	Avg	OB	Slg	OPS	bb%	ct%	Eye	SB	CS	x/h%	Iso	RC/G
2017	A	Fort Wayne	415	54	115	11	64	277	341	405	745	9	72	0.35	8	2	26	128	4.77

Stocky, athletic OF with strong midsection and a lower half that creates plus bat speed and solid-average game power. Hunts fastballs and can expand zone against off-speed. Has fringe-average running ability but will pick spots for moderate SB impact. Owns good arm for RF and likely profiles there best long-term.

O'Neill,Tyler — 789 — St. Louis

EXP MLB DEBUT: 2018 | H/W: 5-11 210 | FUT: Starting OF | 8C

Bats R Age 22
2013 (3) HS (BC)
Pwr ++++
BAvg ++
Spd ++
Def +++

Year	Lev	Team	AB	R	H	HR	RBI	Avg	OB	Slg	OPS	bb%	ct%	Eye	SB	CS	x/h%	Iso	RC/G
2014	A	Clinton	219	31	54	13	38	247	310	466	775	8	64	0.25	5	0	41	219	5.36
2015	A+	Bakersfield	407	68	106	32	87	260	310	558	867	7	66	0.21	16	5	52	297	6.49
2016	AA	Jackson	492	68	144	24	102	293	372	508	880	11	70	0.41	12	2	38	215	6.82
2017	AAA	Tacoma	349	54	85	19	56	244	328	479	807	11	69	0.41	9	2	49	235	5.76
2017	AAA	Memphis	146	23	37	12	39	253	301	548	849	6	71	0.23	5	0	49	295	5.92

Traded for Marco Gonzales in July and has the best raw power in the system. Blasted 30 HR for the second time in 2017. Uses an ultra aggressive approach at the plate, which resulted in a troubling contact rate, 151 punch-outs, and a combined .246 BA. Moves well in the field with a plus arm needed for RF. Power will be his carrying tool.

Ortega,Irving — 46 — Baltimore

EXP MLB DEBUT: 2021 | H/W: 6-2 165 | FUT: Starting SS | 7E

Bats R Age 21
2014 FA (DR)
Pwr +
BAvg ++
Spd +++
Def ++++

Year	Lev	Team	AB	R	H	HR	RBI	Avg	OB	Slg	OPS	bb%	ct%	Eye	SB	CS	x/h%	Iso	RC/G
2016	Rk	GCL Orioles	134	25	36	0	12	269	324	336	660	8	81	0.44	4	0	22	67	3.74
2016	A-	Aberdeen	29	1	6	0	0	207	281	241	523	9	79	0.50	1	1	17	34	2.03
2017	A-	Aberdeen	111	14	24	1	11	216	281	324	605	8	75	0.36	3	0	29	108	2.99
2017	A	Delmarva	54	5	9	0	0	167	224	185	409	7	59	0.18	0	0	11	19	-0.17

Long, lean SS with nifty athleticism and good feel for game. Stat line doesn't do his upside justice. Will take time to develop, but has instinctual approach at plate. Won't draw many walks, though makes easy contact. Power not part of the equation for foreseeable future. Has great range and strong, accurate arm to stick at SS long-term.

Ortiz,Jhailyn — 9 — Philadelphia

EXP MLB DEBUT: 2021 | H/W: 6-3 215 | FUT: Starting OF | 9C

Bats R Age 19
2015 FA (DR)
Pwr ++++
BAvg +++
Spd ++
Def ++

Year	Lev	Team	AB	R	H	HR	RBI	Avg	OB	Slg	OPS	bb%	ct%	Eye	SB	CS	x/h%	Iso	RC/G
2016	Rk	GCL Phillies	173	29	40	8	27	231	300	434	734	9	69	0.32	8	2	45	202	4.63
2017	A-	Williamsport	159	27	48	8	30	302	373	560	933	10	70	0.38	5	1	50	258	7.54

Physically developed for teenager, uses broad shoulders and thick trunk for easy all-fields power. Can be too aggressive, reaching for pitches he can't handle, but also takes walks and hit tool much better than anticipated. Though body will need monitoring, surprised with agility in RF and even stole a couple bases. Power, youth equals big upside.

Pache,Cristian — 8 — Atlanta

EXP MLB DEBUT: 2020 | H/W: 6-2 185 | FUT: Starting OF | 8D

Bats R Age 19
2015 FA (DR)
Pwr +
BAvg +++
Spd ++++
Def ++++

Year	Lev	Team	AB	R	H	HR	RBI	Avg	OB	Slg	OPS	bb%	ct%	Eye	SB	CS	x/h%	Iso	RC/G
2016	Rk	GCL Braves	106	16	30	0	11	283	321	377	699	5	90	0.55	7	3	20	94	4.25
2016	Rk	Danville	114	12	38	0	10	333	372	404	775	6	89	0.54	4	2	13	70	5.06
2017	A	Rome	469	60	132	0	42	281	337	343	680	8	78	0.38	32	14	16	62	3.94

Contact-oriented, quick-twitch speedster had successful full-season debut. An advanced approach at the plate, employs a short, compact swing to litter diamond with hard line drives. Swing trajectory generates tons of top spin, depressing loft and power potential. Plus-plus foot speed, still learning the art of SB. Has plus range and arm in CF.

Padlo,Kevin

5	Tampa Bay	EXP MLB DEBUT: 2019	H/W: 6-2 205	FUT: Starting 3B	7D

Bats R Age 21
2014 (5) HS (CA)

Pwr	+++
BAvg	++
Spd	++
Def	+++

Year	Lev	Team	AB	R	H	HR	RBI	Avg	OB	Slg	OPS	bb%	ct%	Eye	SB	CS	x/h%	Iso	RC/G
2015	A-	Boise	255	44	75	9	46	294	400	502	902	15	76	0.73	33	5	44	208	7.19
2015	A	Asheville	83	11	12	2	7	145	268	277	545	14	69	0.54	2	1	58	133	2.15
2016	A	Bowling Green	414	71	95	16	66	229	353	413	766	16	68	0.59	14	9	43	184	5.45
2017	Rk	GCL Rays	17	3	2	0	1	118	250	235	485	15	94	3.00	1	0	50	118	2.75
2017	A+	Charlotte	220	28	49	6	34	223	329	391	720	14	73	0.58	4	5	45	168	4.70

Tall, strong INF who has positive tools and natural skills, but has trouble putting all together. Has contact issues due to long, exploitable swing. Can see too many pitches and fails to recognize spin. Can drive ball long way with plus leverage and loft. Gets on base via walk and has above average bat speed. Very capable defender with strong arm.

Palacios,Jermaine

6	Minnesota	EXP MLB DEBUT: 2019	H/W: 6-0 155	FUT: Starting SS	7D

Bats R Age 21
2013 FA (VZ)

Pwr	++
BAvg	+++
Spd	+++
Def	++

Year	Lev	Team	AB	R	H	HR	RBI	Avg	OB	Slg	OPS	bb%	ct%	Eye	SB	CS	x/h%	Iso	RC/G
2015	Rk	GCL Twins	95	13	40	1	14	421	471	589	1061	9	88	0.82	4	2	30	168	8.54
2015	Rk	Elizabethton	140	23	47	2	23	336	350	507	857	2	86	0.15	5	2	38	171	5.75
2016	A	Cedar Rapids	261	34	58	1	28	222	272	287	560	6	85	0.46	3	4	21	65	2.54
2017	A	Cedar Rapids	259	52	83	11	39	320	351	544	895	4	82	0.26	9	8	36	224	6.26
2017	A+	Fort Myers	245	30	66	2	28	269	298	359	657	4	78	0.19	11	7	21	90	3.43

Offensive-minded INF who set easy career-highs in HR, doubles, and SB. Brings steady approach to plate, but can often sell out for power. Has very lithe frame and could use strength, but may slow down. Has very strong arm for any INF spot and may move off SS due to limited range. Has solid overall skills and will need significant polish.

Palacios,Joshua

789	Toronto	EXP MLB DEBUT: 2020	H/W: 6-1 193	FUT: Starting OF	7C

Bats L Age 22
2016 (4) Aurburn

Pwr	++
BAvg	++++
Spd	+++
Def	+++

Year	Lev	Team	AB	R	H	HR	RBI	Avg	OB	Slg	OPS	bb%	ct%	Eye	SB	CS	x/h%	Iso	RC/G
2016	NCAA	Auburn	143	34	55	5	23	385	457	608	1065	12	81	0.70	12	5	33	224	8.93
2016	Rk	GCL Blue Jays	49	10	13	0	4	265	308	327	634	6	88	0.50	4	1	23	61	3.46
2016	A-	Vancouver	110	15	39	0	13	355	427	473	900	11	85	0.82	4	2	26	118	6.96
2016	A	Lansing	38	2	13	0	1	342	359	421	780	3	92	0.33	0	2	23	79	4.93
2017	A	Lansing	368	65	103	2	39	280	354	361	715	10	79	0.54	12	6	22	82	4.52

Pure-hitting OF who got off to slow start, but hit .333 in 2nd half. Exhibits ideal barrel control for contact and has solid understanding of strike zone. Power could emerge, but not part of present game. Likes to slap ball and use speed to leg out xbh. Has struggled with LHP. Plays all OF spots and should find way to LF due to iffy arm strength.

Palka,Daniel

79	Chicago (A)	EXP MLB DEBUT: 2018	H/W: 6-2 220	FUT: Starting OF	7D

Bats L Age 26
2013 (3) Georgia Tech

Pwr	++++
BAvg	++
Spd	++
Def	++

Year	Lev	Team	AB	R	H	HR	RBI	Avg	OB	Slg	OPS	bb%	ct%	Eye	SB	CS	x/h%	Iso	RC/G
2015	A+	Visalia	511	95	143	29	90	280	351	532	883	10	68	0.34	24	7	48	252	6.89
2016	AA	Chattanooga	300	42	81	21	65	270	352	547	899	11	67	0.38	7	4	46	277	7.16
2016	AAA	Rochester	203	31	47	13	25	232	294	483	777	8	58	0.21	2	1	53	251	5.89
2017	Rk	GCL Twins	18	4	5	1	2	278	350	444	794	10	94	2.00	1	0	20	167	5.39
2017	AAA	Rochester	332	47	91	11	42	274	329	431	759	8	76	0.34	1	2	30	157	4.83

Slugging OF who missed 2 months with broken finger. All about power and dominates LHP with leverage and strength. All or nothing approach curbs BA, but will work counts from time to time. Becoming serviceable defender in OF corner, but doesn't run well. Strong arm is best asset outside of power.

Papi,Mike

79	Cleveland	EXP MLB DEBUT: 2018	H/W: 6-3 215	FUT: Starting OF	7E

Bats L Age 25
2014 (S-1) Virginia

Pwr	+++
BAvg	++
Spd	++
Def	+++

Year	Lev	Team	AB	R	H	HR	RBI	Avg	OB	Slg	OPS	bb%	ct%	Eye	SB	CS	x/h%	Iso	RC/G
2015	A+	Lynchburg	416	53	98	4	45	236	360	356	716	16	72	0.69	6	7	41	120	4.86
2016	A+	Lynchburg	140	22	33	7	18	236	371	450	821	18	70	0.71	0	1	48	214	6.17
2016	AA	Akron	259	33	59	8	40	228	333	398	731	14	72	0.57	4	0	44	170	4.82
2017	AA	Akron	296	50	79	10	37	267	373	412	785	14	79	0.82	5	2	29	145	5.48
2017	AAA	Columbus	119	20	28	2	18	235	345	328	673	14	79	0.80	1	1	25	92	4.11

Tall, patient OF who draws ton of walks with keen batting eye. Has struggled to hit for BA as his bat speed is a bit short. Uses level swing path and saw K rate drop. Exhibits average power, mostly to pull side. Can play all OF spots, but mostly corner positions with strong arm. Range is lacking as his foot speed is on slow side.

Paredes,Isaac

6	Detroit	EXP MLB DEBUT: 2020	H/W: 5-11 175	FUT: Starting SS	8D

Bats R Age 19
2015 FA (MX)

Pwr	+++
BAvg	+++
Spd	++
Def	+++

Year	Lev	Team	AB	R	H	HR	RBI	Avg	OB	Slg	OPS	bb%	ct%	Eye	SB	CS	x/h%	Iso	RC/G
2016	Rk	AZL Cubs	167	23	51	1	26	305	356	443	799	7	88	0.65	4	0	35	138	5.48
2016	A	South Bend	12	0	2	0	0	167	167	167	333	0	83	0.00	0	0	0	0	-0.59
2017	A	West Michigan	115	16	25	4	21	217	297	348	645	10	89	1.00	0	0	28	130	3.70
2017	A	South Bend	337	49	89	7	49	264	322	401	723	8	84	0.54	2	1	36	136	4.48

Improving SS who put himself on map after impressive season. Young for level, yet showed advanced ability to put bat to ball. Recognizes pitches and has patient eye to find pitches to drive. Has above average power potential in strong, compact frame. Also could hit for high BA. Not much speed, but has clean actions at SS with above average arm.

Park,Hoy Jun

46	New York (A)	EXP MLB DEBUT: 2019	H/W: 6-1 175	FUT: Starting SS	7D

Bats L Age 21
2014 FA (KR)

Pwr	++
BAvg	++
Spd	++++
Def	+++

Year	Lev	Team	AB	R	H	HR	RBI	Avg	OB	Slg	OPS	bb%	ct%	Eye	SB	CS	x/h%	Iso	RC/G
2016	A	Charleston (Sc)	435	60	98	2	34	225	329	329	657	13	72	0.56	32	3	30	103	3.94
2017	A	Charleston (Sc)	324	53	85	6	34	262	342	367	709	11	81	0.62	18	7	20	105	4.40
2017	A+	Tampa	94	20	20	1	5	213	308	330	638	12	85	0.93	7	0	40	117	3.81

Lean, quick SS who repeated A- to better results. Needs to fill out frame in order to become bat threat, though has some pull-side pop. Puts barrel of bat on ball consistently and gets on base with keen approach. Split time between 2B and SS and is comfortable at both. Owns strong, erratic arm and can make routine plays. Best tool is plus speed.

Patterson,Jordan

379	Colorado	EXP MLB DEBUT: 2016	H/W: 6-4 215	FUT: Starting OF	7C

Bats L Age 26
2013 (4) South Alabama

Pwr	++++
BAvg	++
Spd	+++
Def	+++

Year	Lev	Team	AB	R	H	HR	RBI	Avg	OB	Slg	OPS	bb%	ct%	Eye	SB	CS	x/h%	Iso	RC/G
2015	A+	Modesto	303	62	92	10	43	304	345	568	912	6	71	0.22	9	6	52	264	7.21
2015	AA	New Britain	185	26	53	7	32	286	327	503	829	6	77	0.26	9	4	49	216	5.66
2016	AAA	Albuquerque	427	75	125	14	61	293	363	480	843	10	72	0.40	10	0	36	187	6.22
2016	MLB	Colorado	18	1	8	0	2	444	474	500	974	5	94	1.00	0	1	13	56	7.14
2017	AAA	Albuquerque	484	78	137	26	92	283	333	539	872	7	74	0.28	3	5	47	256	6.34

Professional hitter continues to put up impressive numbers in hitter-friendly parks, but lacks the speed and athleticism to win a starting role. Quick left-handed bat combined with aggressive approach resulted in 65 extra base hits but also a lot of strikeouts.

Pearson,Jacob

7	Minnesota	EXP MLB DEBUT: 2022	H/W: 6-1 185	FUT: Starting OF	8E

Bats L Age 19
2017 (3) HS (LA)

Pwr	++
BAvg	++
Spd	+++
Def	++

Year	Lev	Team	AB	R	H	HR	RBI	Avg	OB	Slg	OPS	bb%	ct%	Eye	SB	CS	x/h%	Iso	RC/G
2017	Rk	AZL Angels	155	20	35	0	13	226	294	284	578	9	76	0.41	5	3	23	58	2.67

Multi-talented OF with high upside, but has long development time ahead. Could become legitimate power/speed threat with feel for bat. Goes to gaps now with line drive approach, but has leverage and load in stroke. Has to improve against breaking balls and LHP. Needs more time in OF and poor arm needs attention. Likely relegated to LF long-term.

Pentecost,Max

23	Toronto	EXP MLB DEBUT: 2018	H/W: 6-2 195	FUT: Starting C	8D

Bats R Age 25
2014 (1) Kennesaw St

Pwr	+++
BAvg	+++
Spd	++
Def	++

Year	Lev	Team	AB	R	H	HR	RBI	Avg	OB	Slg	OPS	bb%	ct%	Eye	SB	CS	x/h%	Iso	RC/G
2015		*Did not play - injured*																	
2016	A	Lansing	239	36	75	7	34	314	369	490	859	8	79	0.41	4	2	33	176	6.15
2016	A+	Dunedin	49	6	12	3	7	245	288	469	758	6	65	0.18	1	1	42	224	4.91
2017	Rk	GCL Blue Jays	2	0	0	0	0	0	0	0	0	0	100		0	0		0	-2.66
2017	A+	Dunedin	286	34	79	9	54	276	330	434	764	7	78	0.37	0	1	32	157	4.87

Athletic C who can't stay healthy. Three shoulder surgeries since 2014 and missed time in 2017. Saw action at C, 1B, and DH. When healthy, shows offensive talent with bat speed, short stroke, and contact ability. Exhibits above average raw power with leverage. Has chance to be solid backstop, but needs work to return to catch-and-throw skills.

Perez,Delvin

6	St. Louis	EXP MLB DEBUT: 2021	H/W: 6-3 175	FUT: Starting SS	8D

Bats R Age 19
2016 (1) HS (PR)

Pwr	++
BAvg	+++
Spd	++++
Def	++++

Year	Lev	Team	AB	R	H	HR	RBI	Avg	OB	Slg	OPS	bb%	ct%	Eye	SB	CS	x/h%	Iso	RC/G
2016	Rk	GCL Cardinals	163	19	48	0	19	294	343	393	735	7	83	0.43	12	1	25	98	4.67
2017	Rk	GCL Cardinals	42	7	10	0	5	238	319	357	676	11	76	0.50	2	1	30	119	4.15
2017	Rk	Johnson City	76	7	14	0	4	184	295	224	519	14	82	0.86	3	4	14	39	2.28

Toolsy, athletic 1st rounder had a disastrous campaign, hitting .203/.314/.271 with only 5 extra base hits. Remains an elite defender with a plus arm and speed to burn. Good bat on ball skills, but poor pitch recognition led to tons of weak contact and needs to add bulk to his skinny frame.

Perez,Joe

59 | **Houston** | EXP MLB DEBUT: 2021 | H/W: 6-3 210 | FUT: Starting 3B | **7C**

Bats R Age 18
2017 (2) HS (FL)

Tool	Grade
Pwr	+++
BAvg	+++
Spd	++
Def	++

Year	Lev	Team	AB	R	H	HR	RBI	Avg	OB	Slg	OPS	bb%	ct%	Eye	SB	CS	x/h%	Iso	RC/G
2017		*Did not play*																	

Tall, strong 3B who has yet to make his pro debut but has intriguing tools. Combines bat speed, natural loft and ease of action at the plate for potential plus raw power. Uses entire field and makes solid-average contact. Subpar overall athlete, but has plus-plus arm ideal for 3B/RF profile. A long way off, but BA/HR potential is tantalizing.

Perez,Yanio

359 | **Texas** | EXP MLB DEBUT: 2019 | H/W: 6-2 205 | FUT: Starting 3B | **8D**

Bats R Age 22
2016 FA (CU)

Tool	Grade
Pwr	+++
BAvg	+++
Spd	+++
Def	++

Year	Lev	Team	AB	R	H	HR	RBI	Avg	OB	Slg	OPS	bb%	ct%	Eye	SB	CS	x/h%	Iso	RC/G
2017	A	Hickory	180	27	58	9	30	322	384	533	917	9	81	0.53	3	0	33	211	6.76
2017	A+	Down East	281	31	71	5	36	253	302	370	672	7	77	0.30	3	1	30	117	3.73

Strong prospect who may not have a defensive home, but he sure can hit. Possesses natural hitting instincts with bat control, plate coverage, and hand-eye coordination. Showcases above average raw power and runs well for size. Can be too pull conscious and sell out for power at times. Plays INF and OF corners, though sub-par at present.

Perkins,Blake

8 | **Washington** | EXP MLB DEBUT: 2020 | H/W: 6-1 165 | FUT: Starting CF | **7C**

Bats B Age 21
2015 (2) HS (AZ)

Tool	Grade
Pwr	++
BAvg	++
4.10 Spd	++++
Def	++++

Year	Lev	Team	AB	R	H	HR	RBI	Avg	OB	Slg	OPS	bb%	ct%	Eye	SB	CS	x/h%	Iso	RC/G
2015	Rk	GCL Nationals	166	21	35	1	12	211	268	283	551	7	78	0.36	4	5	23	72	2.27
2016	A-	Auburn	209	31	49	1	16	234	316	282	599	11	81	0.64	10	3	14	48	3.08
2016	A	Hagerstown	25	4	5	0	2	200	333	200	533	17	76	0.83	0	1	0	0	2.31
2017	A	Hagerstown	482	105	123	8	48	255	352	378	730	13	76	0.61	31	8	32	122	4.82

Slightly built CFer whose game is built on speed and defense. Has taken to switch-hitting well, and provided unexpected power boost in 2017. Some contact issues, but has a patient approach that pads OBP and SB total. Improving his hit tool will determine whether he's a top-of-the-order starter or 4th OF.

Peter,Jake

457 | **Los Angeles (N)** | EXP MLB DEBUT: 2018 | H/W: 6-1 185 | FUT: Utility player | **7C**

Bats L Age 25
2014 (7) Creighton

Tool	Grade
Pwr	++
BAvg	+++
Spd	+++
Def	+++

Year	Lev	Team	AB	R	H	HR	RBI	Avg	OB	Slg	OPS	bb%	ct%	Eye	SB	CS	x/h%	Iso	RC/G
2015	A+	Winston-Salem	497	76	129	3	57	260	331	348	679	10	82	0.60	23	3	26	89	4.08
2016	AA	Birmingham	253	27	77	4	29	304	380	407	787	11	79	0.60	5	1	23	103	5.42
2016	AAA	Charlotte	228	30	59	2	24	259	310	342	652	7	81	0.39	3	1	25	83	3.54
2017	AA	Birmingham	285	35	77	4	21	270	331	361	693	8	72	0.33	9	4	22	91	4.09
2017	AAA	Charlotte	178	28	52	9	28	292	347	506	853	8	75	0.34	2	2	35	213	6.01

Line drive hitting 2B sold out for power in second half. Hit 13 HRs between Double-A & Triple-A at the expense of contact rate. Still worked gaps and maintained patient approach despite upswing in K-rate. A versatile athlete, best suited for super-utility role. A solid threat on the bases. Traded to the Dodgers in the offseason.

Peters,DJ

789 | **Los Angeles (N)** | EXP MLB DEBUT: 2019 | H/W: 6-6 225 | FUT: Starting OF | **8D**

Bats R Age 22
2016 (4) Western Nevada JC

Tool	Grade
Pwr	++++
BAvg	++
Spd	+++
Def	+++

Year	Lev	Team	AB	R	H	HR	RBI	Avg	OB	Slg	OPS	bb%	ct%	Eye	SB	CS	x/h%	Iso	RC/G
2016	Rk	Ogden	262	63	92	13	48	351	428	615	1042	12	75	0.53	5	3	43	263	8.88
2017	A+	Rancho Cuca	504	91	139	27	82	276	357	514	871	11	63	0.34	3	3	44	238	7.18

Huge, athletic OF has plus raw power. Bat speed is only average and long levers result in lots of swing-and-miss. Sells out for power resulting in 189 K. Runs well for his size with a plus arm that plays well in RF.

Peterson,Dustin

79 | **Atlanta** | EXP MLB DEBUT: 2018 | H/W: 6-2 210 | FUT: Starting OF | **7D**

Bats R Age 23
2013 (2) HS (AZ)

Tool	Grade
Pwr	+++
BAvg	++
Spd	+++
Def	+++

Year	Lev	Team	AB	R	H	HR	RBI	Avg	OB	Slg	OPS	bb%	ct%	Eye	SB	CS	x/h%	Iso	RC/G
2013	Rk	AZL Padres	157	20	46	0	18	293	331	344	675	5	79	0.27	3	0	17	51	3.74
2014	A	Fort Wayne	527	64	123	10	79	233	268	361	629	5	74	0.18	1	3	36	127	3.06
2015	A+	Carolina	446	58	112	8	62	251	318	348	666	9	80	0.48	6	3	22	96	3.75
2016	AA	Mississippi	524	65	148	12	88	282	339	431	770	8	81	0.45	4	1	35	149	5.04
2017	AAA	Gwinnett	314	35	78	1	30	248	308	318	626	8	75	0.35	1	2	24	70	3.24

Promising OF bat struggled returning from hand surgery in spring. Injury sapped bat speed and power. Despite issues, approach at plate continued to improve, taking pitches and working pitchers. A solid runner, speed not a part of offensive game. Defensively, a corner OF going forward.

Phillips,Brett

789 | **Milwaukee** | EXP MLB DEBUT: 2017 | H/W: 6-0 185 | FUT: Starting CF | **8B**

Bats L Age 23
2012 (6) HS (FL)

Tool	Grade
Pwr	++++
BAvg	+++
Spd	++++
Def	++++

Year	Lev	Team	AB	R	H	HR	RBI	Avg	OB	Slg	OPS	bb%	ct%	Eye	SB	CS	x/h%	Iso	RC/G
2015	AA	Corpus Christi	134	22	43	0	18	321	359	463	822	6	81	0.31	7	2	30	142	5.65
2015	AA	Biloxi	80	14	20	0	6	250	362	413	774	15	63	0.47	2	1	50	163	6.21
2016	AA	Biloxi	441	60	101	16	62	229	331	397	728	13	65	0.44	12	7	36	168	4.86
2017	AAA	Col Springs	383	79	117	19	78	305	379	567	945	11	66	0.35	9	1	44	261	8.06
2017	MLB	Milwaukee	87	9	24	4	12	276	344	448	792	9	61	0.26	5	0	29	172	5.92

Athletic, LHH CF re-discovered hit tool en route to solid MLB cup-of-coffee. Short, compact explosive swing was able to catch, breathe and develop. Showed aptitude to hit to opposite field. Big power, mainly pull-side and to the gaps. Swing trajectory conducive to big HR numbers. Fast runner, not a big SB guy. Plus range and exceptional arm.

Plummer,Nick

789 | **St. Louis** | EXP MLB DEBUT: 2021 | H/W: 5-10 200 | FUT: Starting OF | **8E**

Bats L Age 21
2015 (1) HS (MI)

Tool	Grade
Pwr	+++
BAvg	++
Spd	+++
Def	+++

Year	Lev	Team	AB	R	H	HR	RBI	Avg	OB	Slg	OPS	bb%	ct%	Eye	SB	CS	x/h%	Iso	RC/G
2015	Rk	GCL Cardinals	180	43	41	1	22	228	365	344	710	18	69	0.70	8	6	34	117	4.89
2016		*Did not play - injured*																	
2017	A	Peoria	278	36	55	4	17	198	326	288	614	16	61	0.49	8	9	29	90	3.32

Former 1st rounder has been a complete bust, piling up 109 strikeouts in 278 Low-A AB. Injuries cost him critical development time, yet the tools remain intriguing. Quick left-handed bat, raw strength, and above-average speed give him potential, but lack of plate discipline and pitch recognition must be corrected—soon.

Polo,Tito

78 | **Chicago (A)** | EXP MLB DEBUT: 2019 | H/W: 5-10 195 | FUT: Starting OF | **7D**

Bats R Age 23
2012 FA (CB)

Tool	Grade
Pwr	++
BAvg	+++
Spd	++++
Def	+++

Year	Lev	Team	AB	R	H	HR	RBI	Avg	OB	Slg	OPS	bb%	ct%	Eye	SB	CS	x/h%	Iso	RC/G
2016	A+	Tampa	8	2	2	0	1	250	333	250	583	11	100		0	0	0	0	3.73
2016	A+	Bradenton	214	40	59	4	28	276	340	346	686	9	78	0.45	17	7	12	70	3.93
2017	A+	Tampa	233	42	66	4	20	283	329	429	759	6	73	0.26	19	5	30	146	4.94
2017	AA	Trenton	55	14	21	1	17	382	443	545	988	10	85	0.75	7	1	29	164	7.79
2017	AA	Birmingham	72	10	20	0	7	278	325	389	714	6	79	0.33	7	3	30	111	4.40

Aggressive hitter with terrific hand-eye coordination. Has never seen a pitch he wouldn't swing at. Makes a lot of soft-contact and can luck into hit due to plus foot speed. Has hit for some power but doesn't project as HR hitter in MLB. Speed is best tool. Was 34 for 44 in SB attempts. Not good route runner for CF.

Potts,Hudson

5 | **San Diego** | EXP MLB DEBUT: 2020 | H/W: 6-3 205 | FUT: Starting 3B | **8C**

Bats R Age 19
2016 (1) HS (TX)

Tool	Grade
Pwr	+++
BAvg	+++
Spd	++
Def	+++

Year	Lev	Team	AB	R	H	HR	RBI	Avg	OB	Slg	OPS	bb%	ct%	Eye	SB	CS	x/h%	Iso	RC/G
2016	Rk	AZL Padres	183	35	54	1	21	295	328	399	727	5	81	0.26	8	4	28	104	4.39
2016	A-	Tri-City	60	7	14	0	6	233	333	267	600	13	78	0.69	2	1	7	33	3.16
2017	A	Fort Wayne	491	67	124	20	69	253	286	438	724	4	71	0.16	0	1	38	185	4.27

Tall, strong 3B with scintillating raw power but a fair amount of swing-and-miss to his game. Drives ball well to pull side and produces fly-ball contact with leveraged swing. Can be over-aggressive early, will lunge at off-speed. Has range and arm strength required of a solid defender at 3B. Strong 2H (.290 BA, 13 HR) could carry into 2018 breakout.

Pratto,Nick

3 | **Kansas City** | EXP MLB DEBUT: 2021 | H/W: 6-1 195 | FUT: Starting 1B | **8C**

Bats L Age 19
2017 (1) HS (CA)

Tool	Grade
Pwr	+++
BAvg	+++
Spd	++
Def	++++

Year	Lev	Team	AB	R	H	HR	RBI	Avg	OB	Slg	OPS	bb%	ct%	Eye	SB	CS	x/h%	Iso	RC/G
2017	Rk	AZL Royals	198	25	49	4	34	247	329	414	743	11	71	0.41	10	4	45	167	5.01

Pure-hitting, instinctual 1B with beautiful swing and advanced pitch recognition. Covers plate with smooth stroke and should hit for high BA with at least average pop. Focuses more on contact than HR, but exhibits natural bat speed and strength. Not the fleetest afoot, but is terrific defender with agility and fundamental skills.

Pullin,Andrew — 7 — Philadelphia

EXP MLB DEBUT: 2018 | H/W: 6-0 190 | FUT: Reserve OF | 7C

Bats L Age 24 — 2012 (5) HS (WA)

Tools	Year	Lev	Team	AB	R	H	HR	RBI	Avg	OB	Slg	OPS	bb%	ct%	Eye	SB	CS	x/h%	Iso	RC/G
Pwr +++	2015	A+	Clearwater	493	55	127	14	73	258	292	396	688	5	85	0.32	1	5	28	138	3.81
BAvg +++	2016	A+	Clearwater	147	21	43	4	19	293	316	476	792	3	87	0.26	0	0	40	184	5.03
Spd ++	2016	AA	Reading	188	32	65	10	32	346	388	559	947	6	81	0.36	0	0	31	213	6.92
Def +	2017	AA	Reading	266	40	82	14	46	308	361	556	918	8	84	0.51	2	0	45	248	6.67
	2017	AAA	Lehigh Valley	238	22	55	6	23	231	271	412	683	5	79	0.26	3	1	53	181	3.84

Natural hitter with pure LH stroke and ability to go the other way, even with moderate power. Has improved in handling breaking balls from earlier in career. Defensive questions limit his upside as poor arm, questionable routes and lack of speed make LF the only option. Most likely a bench bat in the majors.

Quinn,Heath — 79 — San Francisco

EXP MLB DEBUT: 2019 | H/W: 6-2 190 | FUT: Starting OF | 7D

Bats R Age 22 — 2016 (3) Samford

Tools	Year	Lev	Team	AB	R	H	HR	RBI	Avg	OB	Slg	OPS	bb%	ct%	Eye	SB	CS	x/h%	Iso	RC/G
Pwr ++++	2016	NCAA	Samford	242	62	83	21	77	343	444	682	1126	15	77	0.80	4	2	47	339	9.82
BAvg ++	2016	Rk	AZL Giants	5	4	3	0	0	600	714	800	1514	29	80	2.00	0	0	33	200	16.58
Spd ++	2016	A-	Salem-Keizer	205	37	69	9	34	337	411	571	982	11	76	0.52	3	0	42	234	8.01
Def +++	2016	A+	San Jose	17	2	6	0	0	353	421	412	833	11	59	0.29	0	0	17	59	7.15
	2017	A+	San Jose	272	24	62	10	29	228	281	371	652	7	68	0.23	0	0	31	143	3.38

Tall OF who suffered hamate injury early in year and struggled after. Has good power to all fields, based more on natural strength than bat speed. Doesn't read spin well and is mostly free-swinger. Long swing can be exploited, particularly inside. Doesn't run well, but very sound defender with sufficient range and above average arm.

Quinn,Roman — 8 — Philadelphia

EXP MLB DEBUT: 2016 | H/W: 5-10 170 | FUT: Starting CF | 7C

Bats B Age 24 — 2011 (2) HS (FL)

Tools	Year	Lev	Team	AB	R	H	HR	RBI	Avg	OB	Slg	OPS	bb%	ct%	Eye	SB	CS	x/h%	Iso	RC/G
Pwr ++	2015	AA	Reading	232	44	71	4	15	306	356	435	791	7	82	0.43	29	10	23	129	5.26
BAvg +++	2016	Rk	GCL Phillies	22	6	11	0	0	500	522	591	1113	4	86	0.33	5	1	18	91	8.76
3.87 Spd +++++	2016	AA	Reading	286	58	82	6	25	287	354	441	795	9	76	0.44	31	8	32	154	5.51
Def +++	2016	MLB	Philadelphia	57	10	15	0	6	263	354	333	687	12	67	0.42	5	1	27	70	4.39
	2017	AAA	Lehigh Valley	175	24	48	2	13	274	342	389	731	9	72	0.37	10	4	27	114	4.73

Energetic player with top-shelf speed but just cannot stay healthy. 2017 season ended in late May with an elbow injury. Has CF skills and some punch with the bat; has also shown ability to take a walk. Once on base, SB usually follow. Major health risk, but is nearly MLB ready and could win reserve job in spring.

Raley,Luke — 379 — Los Angeles (N)

EXP MLB DEBUT: 2020 | H/W: 6-3 220 | FUT: Starting OF | 7C

Bats L Age 23 — 2016 (7) Lake Erie

Tools	Year	Lev	Team	AB	R	H	HR	RBI	Avg	OB	Slg	OPS	bb%	ct%	Eye	SB	CS	x/h%	Iso	RC/G
Pwr +++	2016	Rk	Ogden	24	6	10	1	5	417	440	792	1232	4	96	1.00	0	0	50	375	9.88
BAvg +++	2016	Rk	AZL Dodgers	16	4	10	1	2	625	667	875	1542	11	88	1.00	0	0	20	250	13.96
Spd +++	2016	A	Great Lakes	200	24	49	2	17	245	298	370	668	7	77	0.32	4	4	35	125	3.77
Def +++	2017	A+	Rancho Cuca	478	102	141	14	62	295	353	473	826	8	74	0.35	9	1	33	178	5.86

Large, athletic OF had a breakout season at High-A, setting career highs across the board. Above-average power and a quick left-handed stroke results in gap power and has the potential to hit 20+ in the majors. Range limits him to a corner slot, but arm is enough for RF.

Ramirez,Harold — 79 — Toronto

EXP MLB DEBUT: 2018 | H/W: 5-10 220 | FUT: Reserve OF | 6B

Bats R Age 23 — 2011 FA (CB)

Tools	Year	Lev	Team	AB	R	H	HR	RBI	Avg	OB	Slg	OPS	bb%	ct%	Eye	SB	CS	x/h%	Iso	RC/G
Pwr ++	2014	A	West Virginia	204	30	63	1	24	309	344	402	746	5	83	0.31	12	3	25	93	4.63
BAvg ++	2015	A+	Bradenton	306	45	103	4	47	337	387	458	844	8	84	0.52	22	15	22	121	5.92
Spd +++	2016	AA	New Hampshire	4	2	3	0	1	750	800		1800	20	100		0	0	33	250	17.38
Def ++	2016	AA	Altoona	379	58	116	2	49	306	343	401	744	5	83	0.32	7	10	22	95	4.61
	2017	AA	New Hampshire	444	46	118	6	53	266	315	358	673	7	85	0.49	5	3	23	92	3.84

Short, stout OF who seems to be regressing after promising start to career. Makes very easy contact and has feel for bat control. Can swing aggressively early in count and doesn't have selective eye. Power is below average, though can go to opposite field. Runs well, but rarely steals bases. Patrols OF corners with limited arm strength and routes.

Ramirez,Juan — 8 — Houston

EXP MLB DEBUT: 2022 | H/W: 5-9 160 | FUT: Starting CF | 8E

Bats L Age 18 — 2015 FA (DR)

Tools	Year	Lev	Team	AB	R	H	HR	RBI	Avg	OB	Slg	OPS	bb%	ct%	Eye	SB	CS	x/h%	Iso	RC/G
Pwr +																				
BAvg +++																				
Spd +++																				
Def +++	2017	Rk	GCL Tigers	163	30	49	0	10	301	377	362	739	11	91	1.43	11	7	16	61	5.07

Short, lean OF with no full season exposure yet. Extreme contact approach and difficult to fan due to ability to put bat to ball. Plays small ball with aplomb and draws more walks than Ks. Has little strength and needs to drive ball to keep defense honest. At best when on base and using speed. Solid CF defender.

Ramirez,Tyler — 79 — Oakland

EXP MLB DEBUT: 2019 | H/W: 5-9 185 | FUT: Reserve OF | 6B

Bats L Age 23 — 2016 (7) North Carolina

Tools	Year	Lev	Team	AB	R	H	HR	RBI	Avg	OB	Slg	OPS	bb%	ct%	Eye	SB	CS	x/h%	Iso	RC/G
	2016	NCAA	North Carolina	189	46	63	8	47	333	473	540	1012	21	71	0.93	10	3	33	206	9.17
Pwr ++	2016	Rk	AZL Athletics	28	5	8	0	8	286	310	536	846	3	64	0.10	1	0	63	250	7.01
BAvg +++	2016	A-	Vermont	150	22	33	2	15	220	308	327	634	11	74	0.49	5	0	33	107	3.45
Spd ++	2017	A+	Stockton	279	51	84	7	39	301	398	434	832	14	71	0.56	5	2	25	133	6.28
Def ++	2017	AA	Midland	208	29	64	4	24	308	390	428	818	12	75	0.53	3	3	25	120	5.93

Short, compact OF who hit over .300 in first full season as pro. Draws lot of walks with very mature approach. Lot of Ks despite lack of power and can allow good pitches to go by. Performed consistently with level, smooth stroke and showed ability to hit LHP. Plays all OF spots, though arm strength a bit short and routes are crude.

Ramos,Heliot — 8 — San Francisco

EXP MLB DEBUT: 2021 | H/W: 6-2 185 | FUT: Starting OF | 8C

Bats R Age 18 — 2017 (1) HS (PR)

Tools	Year	Lev	Team	AB	R	H	HR	RBI	Avg	OB	Slg	OPS	bb%	ct%	Eye	SB	CS	x/h%	Iso	RC/G
Pwr +++																				
BAvg ++++																				
Spd ++++																				
Def ++	2017	Rk	AZL Giants	138	33	48	6	27	348	392	645	1037	7	65	0.21	10	2	48	297	9.53

Advanced young OF who amazed in pro debut with better tools than advertised. Uses plus bat speed and barrel control to make easy, hard contact. Can expand strike zone at times and has some holes in swing. Offers plus raw power and could realize pop potential very quickly. Runs extremely well which makes up for crude jumps and routes in CF.

Ramos,Milton — 56 — Baltimore

EXP MLB DEBUT: 2020 | H/W: 5-11 193 | FUT: Starting SS | 7D

Bats R Age 22 — 2014 (3) HS (FL)

Tools	Year	Lev	Team	AB	R	H	HR	RBI	Avg	OB	Slg	OPS	bb%	ct%	Eye	SB	CS	x/h%	Iso	RC/G
	2015	Rk	Kingsport	164	22	52	1	24	317	345	415	760	4	82	0.23	3	6	25	98	4.72
Pwr ++	2015	Rk	GCL Mets	36	3	7	0	3	194	216	222	438	3	75	0.11	1	2	14	28	0.49
BAvg ++	2016	A	Columbia	363	31	80	0	35	220	284	273	556	8	76	0.36	5	4	21	52	2.33
Spd +++	2017	A	Delmarva	180	16	43	2	17	239	267	322	590	4	76	0.16	6	3	23	83	2.50
Def +++	2017	A	Columbia	181	19	41	0	18	227	271	276	547	6	77	0.27	9	0	20	50	2.13

Flashy, quick INF whose glove is ahead of bat at this point. Repeated Low-A and got off to sluggish start. Has little to no approach at plate and struggles to make consistent contact. Still has potential with some gap power and BA ability. Has smooth, quick actions at SS and ranges well to both sides. Solid average arm also sufficient for 3B.

Randolph,Corneilus — 7 — Philadelphia

EXP MLB DEBUT: 2020 | H/W: 5-11 205 | FUT: Starting OF | 7D

Bats L Age 20 — 2015 (1) HS (GA)

Tools	Year	Lev	Team	AB	R	H	HR	RBI	Avg	OB	Slg	OPS	bb%	ct%	Eye	SB	CS	x/h%	Iso	RC/G
Pwr +++	2015	Rk	GCL Phillies	172	35	52	1	24	302	412	442	854	16	81	1.00	7	5	37	140	6.68
BAvg +++	2016	Rk	GCL Phillies	12	1	1	0	0	83	214	83	298	14	75	0.67	0	0	0	0	-1.03
Spd +	2016	A	Lakewood	241	33	66	2	27	274	345	357	701	10	76	0.46	5	4	23	83	4.29
Def ++	2017	A+	Clearwater	440	47	110	13	55	250	333	402	736	11	72	0.44	7	3	33	152	4.77

Still young, but progressing slower than expected. Sprays singles to all fields, but extra-base pop is mainly restricted to his pull side, though did adjust swing for more power in 2017. Has sufficient bat speed, but expands the zone often and struggles with LHP. Arm and questionable route-running limit him to LF.

Ray,Corey — 89 — Milwaukee

EXP MLB DEBUT: 2019 | H/W: 5-11 185 | FUT: Starting OF | 8E

Bats L Age 23 — 2016 (1) Louisville

Tools	Year	Lev	Team	AB	R	H	HR	RBI	Avg	OB	Slg	OPS	bb%	ct%	Eye	SB	CS	x/h%	Iso	RC/G
Pwr +++	2016	NCAA	Louisville	268	55	83	15	60	310	391	545	936	12	85	0.88	44	0	39	235	7.10
BAvg ++	2016	A	Wisconsin	12	2	1	0	0	83	267	83	350	20	67	0.75	1	1	0	0	-0.79
Spd ++++	2016	A+	Brevard County	231	24	57	5	17	247	307	385	692	8	77	0.37	9	5	35	139	4.05
Def ++++	2017	A+	Carolina	449	56	107	7	48	238	312	367	679	10	65	0.31	24	10	37	129	4.17

Athletic former 1st rd pick struggled with swing-and-miss issues in '17. Solid approach, struggles identifying spin. Doesn't make in-game adjustments. Swing is compact but struggles with consistent swing plane. Raw plus power in BP, will struggle to reach power potential due to hit tool issues. Plus runner & defender.

Read,Raudy

2 | Washington | EXP MLB DEBUT: 2017 | H/W: 6-0 170 | FUT: Starting C | 7C

Bats R Age 24
2011 FA (DR)

- Pwr +++
- BAvg +++
- Spd +
- Def +++

Year	Lev	Team	AB	R	H	HR	RBI	Avg	OB	Slg	OPS	bb%	ct%	Eye	SB	CS	x/h%	Iso	RC/G
2015	A	Hagerstown	295	38	72	5	36	244	303	369	673	8	83	0.50	4	3	36	125	3.88
2015	A+	Potomac	18	1	7	0	5	389	450	500	950	10	83	0.67	0	0	29	111	7.47
2016	A+	Potomac	386	54	101	9	51	262	317	415	731	7	86	0.58	6	3	40	153	4.58
2017	AA	Harrisburg	411	44	109	17	61	265	311	455	765	6	81	0.34	2	0	39	190	4.78
2017	MLB	Washington	11	1	3	0	0	273	273	273	545	0	73	0.00	0	0	0	0	1.63

Made big strides in power; used strong uppercut swing to notch career high in HR. Mostly uses pull side in game, though consistently hits the ball hard. Ambushes FBs, but susceptible to soft stuff down/away. Strong arm behind the plate, but questionable blocking, receiving and gamecalling.

Reed,Buddy

8 | San Diego | EXP MLB DEBUT: 2020 | H/W: 6-4 210 | FUT: Reserve OF | 7D

Bats B Age 22
2016 (2) Florida

- Pwr ++
- BAvg ++
- Spd ++++
- Def ++++

Year	Lev	Team	AB	R	H	HR	RBI	Avg	OB	Slg	OPS	bb%	ct%	Eye	SB	CS	x/h%	Iso	RC/G
2016	NCAA	Florida	256	57	67	4	32	262	359	395	754	13	76	0.63	24	0	30	133	5.18
2016	A-	Tri-City	205	31	52	0	13	254	326	337	663	10	74	0.42	15	5	25	83	3.86
2017	A	Fort Wayne	316	48	74	6	35	234	286	396	682	7	69	0.24	12	8	42	161	4.02

Long, lean CF who has athletic tools but needs offensive polish. Covers plenty of real estate and possesses plus arm for any OF position. Quick to full speed out of box; long, fluid strides underway. Started tapping into power in 2017, but likely a gap-oriented hitter from both sides. Approach still requires work; lacks OBP for leadoff profile.

Reinheimer,Jack

456 | Arizona | EXP MLB DEBUT: 2017 | H/W: 6-1 185 | FUT: Reserve INF | 6B

Bats R Age 25
2013 (5) East Carolina

- Pwr +
- BAvg ++
- Spd ++++
- Def +++

Year	Lev	Team	AB	R	H	HR	RBI	Avg	OB	Slg	OPS	bb%	ct%	Eye	SB	CS	x/h%	Iso	RC/G
2015	AA	Mobile	283	39	75	4	26	265	350	371	721	12	81	0.69	9	5	27	106	4.65
2015	AA	Jackson	202	25	56	1	16	277	324	351	676	6	81	0.36	12	1	21	74	3.82
2016	AAA	Reno	500	64	144	2	48	288	350	384	734	9	81	0.52	20	11	26	96	4.73
2017	AAA	Reno	482	87	134	4	56	278	342	351	693	9	82	0.55	12	8	19	73	4.16
2017	MLB	Arizona	5	0	0	0	0	0	0	0	0	0	40	0.00	0	0		0	-8.89

Solid MIF made MLB debut in '17, good on both sides of ball, real grinder. Contact bat, and uses all fields. Power limited due to size and swing. More quick than fast, can be a double digit base stealing threat in a likely bench role. Is sound defensively.

Reyes,Jomar

5 | Baltimore | EXP MLB DEBUT: 2019 | H/W: 6-3 220 | FUT: Starting 1B | 8D

Bats R Age 21
2014 FA (DR)

- Pwr ++++
- BAvg ++
- Spd +
- Def ++

Year	Lev	Team	AB	R	H	HR	RBI	Avg	OB	Slg	OPS	bb%	ct%	Eye	SB	CS	x/h%	Iso	RC/G
2015	Rk	GCL Orioles	16	2	4	0	4	250	333	375	708	11	69	0.40	1	0	50	125	4.71
2015	A	Delmarva	309	36	86	5	44	278	318	440	758	6	76	0.25	1	0	42	162	4.87
2016	A+	Frederick	464	53	106	10	51	228	268	336	604	5	78	0.25	3	0	26	108	2.74
2017	Rk	GCL Orioles	28	6	13	0	4	464	483	500	983	3	89	0.33	0	0	8	36	7.06
2017	A+	Frederick	182	28	55	4	21	302	332	434	766	4	83	0.26	1	0	27	132	4.72

Hulking slugger who repeated High-A, but missed most of season due to broken finger after punching wall. Has ideal size and strength to evolve into massive pop. Improved contact at plate could lead to better BA and has ability to drive ball to gaps. Inconsistent approach and swing mechanics hinder. Lack of speed and agility may move him to 1B.

Reyes,Victor

789 | Detroit | EXP MLB DEBUT: 2018 | H/W: 6-3 170 | FUT: Starting OF | 7C

Bats L Age 23
2011 FA (VZ)

- Pwr ++
- BAvg +++
- Spd +++
- Def +++

Year	Lev	Team	AB	R	H	HR	RBI	Avg	OB	Slg	OPS	bb%	ct%	Eye	SB	CS	x/h%	Iso	RC/G
2013	Rk	Danville	81	12	26	0	4	321	345	358	703	4	89	0.33	0	0	12	37	4.04
2014	A	Rome	332	32	86	0	34	259	309	298	607	7	83	0.41	12	7	15	39	3.02
2015	A	Kane County	424	57	132	2	59	311	345	389	734	5	86	0.38	13	4	18	78	4.48
2016	A+	Visalia	469	62	142	6	54	303	349	416	764	7	83	0.42	20	8	20	113	4.91
2017	AA	Jackson	479	59	140	4	51	292	330	399	729	5	83	0.34	18	9	27	106	4.44

Switch-hitting, contact-first OF became more of a gap-to-gap hitter in Double-A. Grinds at-bats from both sides of plate. Handles velocity well, using his hand-to-eye coordination to ruin pitcher's offerings. Lacks HR power. A solid athlete, can handle all OF positions. Arm limits RF exposure. Solid utility OF. Selected from ARI in Rule 5.

Reynolds,Bryan

789 | San Francisco | EXP MLB DEBUT: 2018 | H/W: 6-3 205 | FUT: Starting OF | 8C

Bats B Age 23
2016 (2) Vanderbilt

- Pwr +++
- BAvg ++++
- Spd +++
- Def +++

Year	Lev	Team	AB	R	H	HR	RBI	Avg	OB	Slg	OPS	bb%	ct%	Eye	SB	CS	x/h%	Iso	RC/G
2016	NCAA	Vanderbilt	224	59	74	13	57	330	451	603	1053	18	74	0.84	8	5	43	272	9.36
2016	A-	Salem-Keizer	154	28	48	5	30	312	358	500	858	7	73	0.27	2	0	38	188	6.21
2016	A	Augusta	63	11	20	1	8	317	348	444	793	5	68	0.15	1	0	30	127	5.49
2017	A+	San Jose	491	72	153	10	63	312	360	462	822	7	78	0.35	5	3	29	151	5.67

Pure hitting OF with across-the-board tools but no obvious shortcoming. Uses whole field and works counts to get pitches to drive. Very athletic and possesses average pop and speed. Should hit for high BA with loose swing and plate coverage. Plays all OF spots and ranges well while owning sufficient arm strength.

Reynolds,Sean

3 | Miami | EXP MLB DEBUT: 2022 | H/W: 6-7 205 | FUT: Starting 1B/RF | 8E

Bats L Age 19
2016 (4) HS (CA)

- Pwr ++++
- BAvg +
- Spd ++
- Def ++

Year	Lev	Team	AB	R	H	HR	RBI	Avg	OB	Slg	OPS	bb%	ct%	Eye	SB	CS	x/h%	Iso	RC/G
2016	Rk	GCL Marlins	148	17	23	0	11	155	265	196	461	13	57	0.34	3	3	17	41	0.78
2017	Rk	GCL Marlins	103	19	22	1	14	214	308	311	618	12	57	0.32	1	1	32	97	3.56
2017	A-	Batavia	74	11	13	4	10	176	218	405	623	5	45	0.10	2	0	62	230	4.77

Looked overmatched as pro, hitting combined .198 with 85 K in 177 AB. Huge 6-7 frame gives him the potential for plus power, but needs to work on making more contact. Plus arm with above-average speed should play well in RF, but played exclusively 1B in 2017. Tons of work to be done.

Riley,Austin

5 | Atlanta | EXP MLB DEBUT: 2018 | H/W: 6-3 220 | FUT: Starting 3B | 8C

Bats R Age 21
2015 (S-1) HS (MS)

- Pwr ++++
- BAvg +++
- Spd ++
- Def +++

Year	Lev	Team	AB	R	H	HR	RBI	Avg	OB	Slg	OPS	bb%	ct%	Eye	SB	CS	x/h%	Iso	RC/G
2015	Rk	GCL Braves	106	18	27	7	21	255	331	500	831	10	65	0.32	2	1	44	245	6.17
2015	Rk	Danville	111	18	39	5	19	351	424	586	1010	11	75	0.50	0	1	38	234	8.41
2016	A	Rome	495	68	134	20	80	271	324	479	803	7	70	0.27	3	3	46	208	5.58
2017	A+	Florida	306	43	77	12	47	252	304	408	712	7	76	0.31	0	2	30	157	4.13
2017	AA	Mississippi	178	28	56	8	27	315	384	511	895	10	72	0.40	2	0	32	197	6.86

Big-bodied RHH 3B spent part of 20-year-old season succeeding at Double-A. He's a gritty power hitter with an advanced approach who grinds out ABs, makes adjustments pitch-by-pitch beyond years. Lots of hard contact despite below-average swing speed. Power in frame and swing. Will stick at 3B.

Rincon,Carlos

79 | Los Angeles (N) | EXP MLB DEBUT: 2021 | H/W: 6-3 190 | FUT: Starting OF | 8E

Bats R Age 20
2015 FA (DR)

- Pwr ++++
- BAvg +
- Spd +++
- Def +++

Year	Lev	Team	AB	R	H	HR	RBI	Avg	OB	Slg	OPS	bb%	ct%	Eye	SB	CS	x/h%	Iso	RC/G
2016	Rk	AZL Dodgers	103	13	31	7	23	301	314	621	936	2	71	0.07	0	2	52	320	7.08
2017	Rk	Ogden	51	8	14	3	13	275	288	529	818	2	69	0.06	0	0	50	255	5.54
2017	A	Great Lakes	334	41	66	18	48	198	268	404	672	9	57	0.22	6	1	48	207	4.15

Big, athletic Dominican OF looked over-matched as 19-year-old at Low-A, but found his groove when demoted to rookie ball. Plus raw power and all-or-nothing approach resulted in 21 HR and 159 K in 385 AB. Average runner with a good arm could land him in RF if he can figure out how to hit.

Ring,Jake

79 | Baltimore | EXP MLB DEBUT: 2019 | H/W: 5-11 175 | FUT: Reserve OF | 6B

Bats L Age 23
2016 (31) Missouri

- Pwr +++
- BAvg +++
- Spd +++
- Def +++

Year	Lev	Team	AB	R	H	HR	RBI	Avg	OB	Slg	OPS	bb%	ct%	Eye	SB	CS	x/h%	Iso	RC/G
2016	Rk	GCL Orioles	169	24	47	0	21	278	361	337	699	12	73	0.49	15	3	19	59	4.39
2016	A	Delmarva	12	2	2	0	1	167	167	250	417	0	75	0.00	0	0	50	83	0.23
2017	A	Delmarva	464	69	126	14	65	272	325	457	782	7	70	0.26	17	6	43	185	5.38
2017	A+	Frederick	8	1	1	1	2	125	222	500	722	11	88	1.00	1	0	100	375	4.20

Short, fundamentally-sound OF enjoyed solid first full pro season. Got off to hot start, but faded late. Smokes a ton of doubles to pull side and uses solid-average speed well. Has instincts and wheels to steal bags and offers good range in OF corners. Has tendency to overswing and try to pull everything. K totals are a big concern.

Rios,Edwin

357 | Los Angeles (N) | EXP MLB DEBUT: 2018 | H/W: 6-3 220 | FUT: Starting 1B | 7C

Bats L Age 23
2015 (6) Florida Intl

- Pwr ++++
- BAvg ++
- Spd ++
- Def +

Year	Lev	Team	AB	R	H	HR	RBI	Avg	OB	Slg	OPS	bb%	ct%	Eye	SB	CS	x/h%	Iso	RC/G
2016	A	Great Lakes	119	17	30	6	13	252	299	487	787	6	63	0.18	3	1	50	235	5.67
2016	A+	Rancho Cuca	177	37	65	16	46	367	395	712	1106	4	80	0.23	0	0	43	345	8.65
2016	AA	Tulsa	122	14	31	5	17	254	300	434	734	6	75	0.26	0	0	39	180	4.42
2017	AA	Tulsa	306	47	97	15	62	317	353	533	886	5	77	0.25	1	1	37	216	6.24
2017	AAA	Oklahoma City	169	23	50	9	29	296	364	533	896	10	75	0.43	0	1	44	237	6.71

Tall, powerfully built corner infielder uses raw strength and an aggressive approach to launch missiles and blasted 24 HR in 475 AB. Low BB% moderated by ability to make consistent contact. Absent speed and below-average glove likely limit him to 1B, meaning he has to mash to stay relevant. So far, so good.

Rivas,Leonardo

6 | **Los Angeles (A)** | EXP MLB DEBUT: 2021 | H/W: 5-10 150 | FUT: Starting SS | **7C**

Bats B Age 20
2014 FA (VZ)

- Pwr +
- BAvg ++
- Spd ++++
- Def +++

Year	Lev	Team	AB	R	H	HR	RBI	Avg	OB	Sig	OPS	bb%	ct%	Eye	SB	CS	x/h%	Iso	RC/G
2016	Rk	AZL Angels	91	22	23	1	4	253	364	341	705	15	82	1.00	6	3	26	88	4.66
2017	Rk	Orem	137	37	41	2	29	299	455	445	900	22	84	1.77	11	0	29	146	7.57
2017	A	Burlington	90	24	24	0	7	267	400	322	722	18	76	0.91	8	1	21	56	5.03

Steady MIF who makes game look easy with fundamental defensive ability and simple offensive approach. Makes most of size by working counts and getting on base. Has leadoff ability, but lacks the strength and swing to generate power. Runs well underway and should steal bases. Uses strong arm to make plays, but not a toolsy prospect.

Rivera,Emmanuel

5 | **Kansas City** | EXP MLB DEBUT: 2020 | H/W: 6-2 195 | FUT: Starting 3B | **8E**

Bats R Age 21
2015 (19) Univers Inter JC

- Pwr +++
- BAvg +++
- Spd ++
- Def +++

Year	Lev	Team	AB	R	H	HR	RBI	Avg	OB	Sig	OPS	bb%	ct%	Eye	SB	CS	x/h%	Iso	RC/G
2016	Rk	Burlington	217	25	54	2	27	249	315	373	688	9	80	0.48	7	3	35	124	4.16
2017	A	Lexington	464	60	144	12	72	310	354	468	821	6	81	0.36	8	10	31	157	5.53

Consistent, steady 3B who led SAL in BA in first full season. Focuses on spraying ball to all fields and offers average power, mostly to pull side. Swing conducive to doubles, though may need to tweak approach to become more disciplined. Crude baserunner with near-average speed. Owns soft hands and plus arm at 3B.

Rivera,Reynaldo

39 | **Detroit** | EXP MLB DEBUT: 2020 | H/W: 6-6 250 | FUT: Starting OF | **7C**

Bats L Age 20
2017 (2) Chipola JC

- Pwr ++++
- BAvg ++
- Spd ++
- Def ++

Year	Lev	Team	AB	R	H	HR	RBI	Avg	OB	Sig	OPS	bb%	ct%	Eye	SB	CS	x/h%	Iso	RC/G
2017	NCAA	Chipola College	192	74	84	20	77	438	534	865	1399	17	78	0.93	4	2	49	427	13.52
2017	A-	Connecticut	182	16	34	2	26	187	260	280	540	9	70	0.33	3	1	35	93	2.02

Huge-framed prospect who is all bat right now. Takes vicious hacks at ball, yet has some semblance of bat control. Has power to reach any part of park, but has lot of swing and miss in game. May need to shorten stroke to put more balls in play. Runs well for size, though not much of threat. Has played mostly RF with strong arm and some time at 1B.

Rizzo,Joe

5 | **Seattle** | EXP MLB DEBUT: 2020 | H/W: 5-9 195 | FUT: Starting 3B | **8E**

Bats L Age 20
2016 (2) HS (NJ)

- Pwr ++
- BAvg ++
- Spd ++
- Def +

Year	Lev	Team	AB	R	H	HR	RBI	Avg	OB	Sig	OPS	bb%	ct%	Eye	SB	CS	x/h%	Iso	RC/G
2016	Rk	AZL Mariners	148	21	43	2	21	291	364	392	756	10	76	0.47	2	1	23	101	5.02
2017	A	Clinton	410	47	104	7	50	254	353	346	699	13	72	0.56	3	1	23	93	4.38
2017	A+	Modesto	20	1	4	0	1	200	238	300	538	5	60	0.13	0	0	25	100	2.12

Short, thick 3B who highlighted patient approach in first full season. Despite strength and leverage, produced disappointing pop and may only project to average. Can hit LHP and has feel for contact and will draw walks. Not much athleticism in profile and is sub-par defender. Needs all-around work, but some hope due to instincts for game.

Robert,Luis

8 | **Chicago (A)** | EXP MLB DEBUT: 2020 | H/W: 6-3 185 | FUT: Starting CF | **9D**

Bats R Age 20
2017 FA (CU)

- Pwr ++++
- BAvg +++
- Spd +++
- Def +++

Year	Lev	Team	AB	R	H	HR	RBI	Avg	OB	Sig	OPS	bb%	ct%	Eye	SB	CS	x/h%	Iso	RC/G
2017		*Did not play in the US*																	

Quick-twitch athlete yet to make US debut due to visa issues. Electrifying bat speed and significant power potential. Solid runner and defender. Profiles now as a CF. As body matures, may lose some foot speed and off CF. Plus arm makes him candidate for RF.

Robertson,Kramer

6 | **St. Louis** | EXP MLB DEBUT: 2020 | H/W: 5-10 166 | FUT: Utility player | **6C**

Bats R Age 23
2017 (4) Louisiana St

- Pwr +
- BAvg +++
- Spd +++
- Def ++

Year	Lev	Team	AB	R	H	HR	RBI	Avg	OB	Sig	OPS	bb%	ct%	Eye	SB	CS	x/h%	Iso	RC/G
2017	NCAA	LSU	290	85	89	8	43	307	383	472	856	11	89	1.13	9	3	33	166	6.26
2017	A	Peoria	215	34	58	3	13	270	335	367	702	9	83	0.58	10	4	26	98	4.28

4th round pick out of LSU has a contact orientated approach at the plate and should continue to hit as he moves up. Above-average speed, solid range, and good hands should allow him to stay up the middle as pro. Below average power limits his fantasy appeal and will have to work hard to carve out a starting role.

Robles,Victor

8 | **Washington** | EXP MLB DEBUT: 2017 | H/W: 6-0 185 | FUT: Starting CF | **9A**

Bats R Age 20
2013 FA (DR)

- Pwr +++
- BAvg ++++
- 4.15 Spd +++++
- Def ++++

Year	Lev	Team	AB	R	H	HR	RBI	Avg	OB	Sig	OPS	bb%	ct%	Eye	SB	CS	x/h%	Iso	RC/G
2016	A	Hagerstown	233	48	71	5	30	305	355	459	814	7	84	0.47	19	8	28	155	5.53
2016	A+	Potomac	168	24	44	3	11	262	319	387	706	8	81	0.44	18	5	30	125	4.23
2017	A+	Potomac	291	49	84	7	33	289	345	495	840	8	79	0.40	16	7	46	206	6.01
2017	AA	Harrisburg	139	24	45	3	14	324	377	489	867	8	84	0.55	11	3	36	165	6.22
2017	MLB	Washington	24	2	6	0	4	250	250	458	708	0	75	0.00	0	1	50	208	4.24

Mature hit tool via lightning hands that deliver the barrel to ball in any part of the zone. Top-shelf speed turns tappers and grounders into singles and outfield singles into doubles. Current pull-side power, with more to come. Great range and arm more than enough to keep him in CF. Impact talent.

Robson,Jacob

789 | **Detroit** | EXP MLB DEBUT: 2019 | H/W: 5-10 175 | FUT: Reserve OF | **7D**

Bats L Age 23
2016 (8) Mississippi St

- Pwr ++
- BAvg +++
- Spd +++
- Def +++

Year	Lev	Team	AB	R	H	HR	RBI	Avg	OB	Sig	OPS	bb%	ct%	Eye	SB	CS	x/h%	Iso	RC/G
2016	Rk	GCL Tigers	101	16	27	0	5	267	368	347	714	14	78	0.73	14	4	22	79	4.74
2016	A-	Connecticut	76	14	25	1	6	329	440	461	900	16	74	0.75	1	2	28	132	7.42
2017	A	West Michigan	228	38	75	1	27	329	409	395	804	12	74	0.53	5	9	16	66	5.82
2017	A+	Lakeland	224	27	62	2	18	277	344	388	733	9	74	0.39	16	9	27	112	4.75

Grinding OF who maximizes limited tools. Split season evenly between A- and A+ and showed progress. Works counts in disciplined approach and is particularly tough on RHP. Won't hit many HR due to frame and swing path, but can use whole field. Strikes out too much for lack of punch. Plays all OF positions with solid-average speed and range.

Rodgers,Brendan

6 | **Colorado** | EXP MLB DEBUT: 2018 | H/W: 6-0 180 | FUT: Starting SS | **9C**

Bats R Age 21
2015 (1) HS (FL)

- Pwr ++++
- BAvg +++
- Spd +++
- Def +++

Year	Lev	Team	AB	R	H	HR	RBI	Avg	OB	Sig	OPS	bb%	ct%	Eye	SB	CS	x/h%	Iso	RC/G
2015	Rk	Grand Junction	143	22	39	3	20	273	342	420	761	9	74	0.41	4	3	33	147	5.08
2016	A	Asheville	442	73	124	19	73	281	333	480	813	7	78	0.36	6	3	40	199	5.46
2017	A+	Lancaster	222	44	86	12	47	387	404	671	1075	3	84	0.17	2	1	42	284	8.17
2017	AA	Hartford	150	20	39	6	17	260	297	413	711	5	76	0.22	0	2	28	153	3.99

Top SS prospect in the NL blitzed through A+ with a 1.078 OPS, earning a mid-season jump to AA. Hand injury cost him three weeks in August and was only blemish. Features plus bat speed and above-average power, but can tend to be pull happy. Plus arm and good hands should keep him at SS for now.

Rodriguez,Alfredo

6 | **Cincinnati** | EXP MLB DEBUT: 2019 | H/W: 6-0 190 | FUT: Starting SS | **8E**

Bats R Age 23
2016 FA (CU)

- Pwr ++
- BAvg ++
- Spd ++++
- Def ++++

Year	Lev	Team	AB	R	H	HR	RBI	Avg	OB	Sig	OPS	bb%	ct%	Eye	SB	CS	x/h%	Iso	RC/G
2017	A+	Daytona	483	52	122	2	36	253	289	294	583	5	84	0.32	11	9	13	41	2.63

Athletic glove-first Cuban SS struggled with hard contact rate in 2017. Solid hand-eye coordination but aggressive approach. Doesn't read spin well but adapts and makes soft contact. Will chase pitches out of zone. Power in frame but doesn't drive ball, even in BP. Great athlete. Plus runner and defender. Arm sticks at SS too.

Rodriguez,Johnathan

9 | **Cleveland** | EXP MLB DEBUT: 2022 | H/W: 6-3 180 | FUT: Starting OF | **8E**

Bats B Age 18
2017 (3) HS (PR)

- Pwr +++
- BAvg ++
- Spd ++
- Def ++

Year	Lev	Team	AB	R	H	HR	RBI	Avg	OB	Sig	OPS	bb%	ct%	Eye	SB	CS	x/h%	Iso	RC/G
2017	Rk	AZL Indians	96	13	24	0	11	250	385	333	718	18	76	0.91	0	1	25	83	5.00

Long, projectable OF who has intriguing tools, but will take time to develop. Swing mechanics are crude and choppy and may strike out in bunches without better control. Has room for added strength in order to realize plus raw power. Can take too many hittable pitches. Outstanding arm, but limited range at present.

Rodriguez,Julio — 9 — Seattle

EXP MLB DEBUT: 2023 | H/W: 6-3 205 | FUT: Starting OF | 9E

Bats R Age 17
2017 FA (DR)

Pwr + + + +
BAvg + + +
Spd + + +
Def + +

Year	Lev	Team	AB	R	H	HR	RBI	Avg	OB	Slg	OPS	bb%	ct%	Eye	SB	CS	x/h%	Iso	RC/G
2017		*Did not play in the US*																	

High-profile signee with tantalizing upside. Could become offensive behemoth once he grows into frame and adds strength. Possesses well above average power at present. Some length to swing, but has the instincts and barrel awareness to project to solid BA. Runs well for size and is ideal RF. Long-termer worth watching.

Rogers,Jake — 2 — Detroit

EXP MLB DEBUT: 2019 | H/W: 6-1 190 | FUT: Starting C | 7B

Bats R Age 22
2016 (3) Tulane

Pwr + + +
BAvg + +
Spd + +
Def + + + +

Year	Lev	Team	AB	R	H	HR	RBI	Avg	OB	Slg	OPS	bb%	ct%	Eye	SB	CS	x/h%	Iso	RC/G
2016	A-	Tri City	87	11	22	2	12	253	350	425	775	13	79	0.72	0	2	45	172	5.42
2016	A	Quad Cities	72	7	15	1	4	208	288	319	607	10	65	0.32	1	0	33	111	3.05
2017	A	Quad Cities	102	17	26	6	15	255	315	520	835	8	73	0.32	1	0	54	265	5.90
2017	A+	Lakeland	7	0	1	0	0	143	250	143	393	13	71	0.50	0	0	0	0	0.02
2017	A+	Buies Creek	313	43	83	12	55	265	356	457	813	12	77	0.61	13	8	40	192	5.77

Athletic backstop who had breakout with bat in impressive season. Exhibited surprising pop with improved, more leveraged stroke. Can also shorten swing to use whole field. Has discerning eye at plate, though can struggle with good velocity. Runs well for catcher and is standout defender with plus, accurate arm. One to watch.

Rondon,Adrian — 5 — Tampa Bay

EXP MLB DEBUT: 2021 | H/W: 6-1 190 | FUT: Starting 3B | 8D

Bats R Age 19
2014 FA (DR)

Pwr + + +
BAvg + +
Spd + +
Def + + +

Year	Lev	Team	AB	R	H	HR	RBI	Avg	OB	Slg	OPS	bb%	ct%	Eye	SB	CS	x/h%	Iso	RC/G
2015	Rk	GCL Rays	145	3	24	0	11	166	253	234	488	10	61	0.30	0	2	38	69	1.28
2016	Rk	Princeton	193	29	48	7	36	249	296	430	726	6	70	0.22	1	5	40	181	4.46
2017	A	Bowling Green	394	53	87	9	48	221	281	330	611	8	67	0.26	4	2	26	109	2.91

Rangy INF who had disappointing first full season, but has very exciting tools. Growing into frame and starting to show natural power. Drives ball well with fast bat. Needs to be more selective and long swing can be exploited. Chases too many pitches. Profiles as very good defender at 3B with strong, accurate arm.

Rondon,Jose — 46 — San Diego

EXP MLB DEBUT: 2016 | H/W: 6-1 195 | FUT: Starting MIF | 7C

Bats R Age 24
2011 FA (VZ)

Pwr +
BAvg + + +
Spd + + +
Def + + + +

Year	Lev	Team	AB	R	H	HR	RBI	Avg	OB	Slg	OPS	bb%	ct%	Eye	SB	CS	x/h%	Iso	RC/G
2016	MLB	San Diego	25	1	3	0	1	120	154	120	274	4	84	0.25	0	0	0	0	-1.04
2017	Rk	AZL Padres 2	5	4	3	1	3	600	750		1950	38	80	3.00	1	0	33	600	21.70
2017	Rk	AZL Padres	17	5	6	2	7	353	476	706	1182	19	82	1.33	1	0	33	353	10.26
2017	AA	San Antonio	215	30	63	4	28	293	342	433	775	7	80	0.37	2	1	30	140	5.05
2017	AAA	El Paso	85	9	24	1	14	282	330	412	741	7	81	0.38	1	0	38	129	4.67

Made his debut in 2016; has exemplary contact skills via quick hands, level bat path, ability to spray ball to all fields. Should be a good BA source. Lacks leverage in swing and power will be limited to the gaps. Good instincts help his range up the middle and he should man an above-average SS or 2B long-term.

Rooker,Brent — 37 — Minnesota

EXP MLB DEBUT: 2019 | H/W: 6-3 215 | FUT: Starting 1B | 7B

Bats R Age 23
2017 (S-1) Mississippi St

Pwr + + + +
BAvg + + +
Spd + +
Def + +

Year	Lev	Team	AB	R	H	HR	RBI	Avg	OB	Slg	OPS	bb%	ct%	Eye	SB	CS	x/h%	Iso	RC/G
2017	NCAA	Mississippi St	248	60	96	23	82	387	486	810	1297	16	77	0.83	18	5	58	423	12.28
2017	Rk	Elizabethton	85	19	24	7	17	282	365	588	953	11	75	0.52	2	2	50	306	7.39
2017	A+	Fort Myers	143	23	40	11	35	280	352	552	905	10	67	0.34	0	0	43	273	7.08

Advanced prospect who feasted upon pitching in pro debut. Brings ton of power to game and can reach seats to all fields. Natural loft and strength bring pop, but has long swing. Draws walks in patient approach, though Ks part of profile. Arm is limited in OF corner, but has playable speed. Makes plays at 1B, but far from polished with glove.

Rortvedt,Ben — 2 — Minnesota

EXP MLB DEBUT: 2020 | H/W: 5-10 190 | FUT: Starting C | 7C

Bats L Age 20
2016 (2) HS (WI)

Pwr + +
BAvg + +
Spd + +
Def + +

Year	Lev	Team	AB	R	H	HR	RBI	Avg	OB	Slg	OPS	bb%	ct%	Eye	SB	CS	x/h%	Iso	RC/G
2016	Rk	GCL Twins	59	3	12	0	3	203	266	254	520	8	86	0.63	0	0	25	51	2.23
2016	Rk	Elizabethton	40	2	10	0	7	250	333	250	583	11	95	2.50	0	0	0	0	3.46
2017	A	Cedar Rapids	308	33	69	4	30	224	276	315	591	7	81	0.37	1	0	29	91	2.75

Raw, compact catcher who was passable in first full season. Got off to slow start with bat, though was fine after May. Very mobile and agile backstop with average arm. Still crude with footwork and throwing mechanics. Has short stroke to make good contact and has average raw power. BA could be issue as he can be free swinger.

Rosario,Jeisson — 8 — San Diego

EXP MLB DEBUT: 2021 | H/W: 6-1 175 | FUT: Starting CF | 8C

Bats L Age 18
2016 FA (DR)

Pwr + +
BAvg + + +
Spd + + +
Def + + + +

Year	Lev	Team	AB	R	H	HR	RBI	Avg	OB	Slg	OPS	bb%	ct%	Eye	SB	CS	x/h%	Iso	RC/G
2017	Rk	AZL Padres	187	31	56	1	24	299	405	369	774	15	81	0.92	8	6	20	70	5.53

Ultra-lean, wiry athlete with well-rounded skillset and intriguing upside. Loose hands and quick wrists lend themselves to bat speed and plus contact. Advanced approach for young age. Mostly gap power at present but could develop average game power. Above average speed underway. Reads ball well off the bat and routes are efficient; will be plus CF.

Ruiz,Esteury — 4 — San Diego

EXP MLB DEBUT: 2021 | H/W: 6-0 150 | FUT: Starting 2B | 9E

Bats R Age 19
2015 FA (DR)

Pwr + + +
BAvg + + +
Spd + + + +
Def + + +

Year	Lev	Team	AB	R	H	HR	RBI	Avg	OB	Slg	OPS	bb%	ct%	Eye	SB	CS	x/h%	Iso	RC/G
2017	Rk	AZL Royals	86	22	36	3	23	419	444	779	1224	4	77	0.20	9	0	53	360	10.94
2017	Rk	AZL Padres	120	23	36	1	16	300	349	475	824	7	72	0.26	17	6	42	175	6.07

Young 2B acquired in trade from KC who has well-rounded skillset and high upside. Ultra lean, wiry frame produces big-time bat speed and potential for both BA/HR value. Employs aggressive approach and will need to improve spin recognition. Quality athlete who will be legitimate SB source and play an above-average 2B for the long haul.

Ruiz,Keibert — 2 — Los Angeles (N)

EXP MLB DEBUT: 2020 | H/W: 6-0 200 | FUT: Starting C | 8B

Bats B Age 19
2014 FA (VZ)

Pwr + +
BAvg + + + +
Spd + +
Def + + + +

Year	Lev	Team	AB	R	H	HR	RBI	Avg	OB	Slg	OPS	bb%	ct%	Eye	SB	CS	x/h%	Iso	RC/G
2016	Rk	Ogden	189	28	67	2	33	354	393	503	896	6	88	0.52	0	0	33	148	6.45
2016	Rk	AZL Dodgers	33	5	16	0	15	485	528	667	1194	8	88	0.75	0	0	31	182	10.14
2017	A	Great Lakes	227	34	72	2	24	317	367	423	790	7	87	0.60	0	0	26	106	5.30
2017	A+	Rancho Cuca	149	24	47	6	27	315	346	497	843	4	85	0.30	0	0	30	181	5.56

Switch-hitting backstop had an impressive breakout. Features a quick bat combined with contact-orientated approach that results in career .330 BA, but below-average power. Solid defender with an average to above arm and should stick behind the dish as he moves up.

Rutherford,Blake — 789 — Chicago (A)

EXP MLB DEBUT: 2020 | H/W: 6-3 195 | FUT: Starting OF | 8D

Bats L Age 20
2016 (1) HS (CA)

Pwr + + +
BAvg + + + +
Spd + + +
Def + +

Year	Lev	Team	AB	R	H	HR	RBI	Avg	OB	Slg	OPS	bb%	ct%	Eye	SB	CS	x/h%	Iso	RC/G
2016	Rk	Pulaski	89	13	34	2	9	382	439	618	1057	9	73	0.38	0	2	38	236	9.27
2017	A	Charleston (Sc)	274	41	77	2	30	281	341	391	732	8	80	0.45	9	4	31	109	4.66
2017	A	Kannapolis	122	11	26	0	5	213	289	254	543	10	83	0.62	1	0	19	41	2.43

The best hit tool in the 2016 draft had a so-so Single-A debut. Trying to tap into his raw power, NYY worked on improving swing trajectory, but then traded him to CHW in July. Natural LHH line drive swing, generates tons of top spin, which will depress HR totals. A solid runner and defender, arm projects best in LF.

Sanchez,Ali — 2 — New York (N)

EXP MLB DEBUT: 2020 | H/W: 6-1 196 | FUT: Reserve C | 6C

Bats R Age 21
2013 FA (VZ)

Pwr +
BAvg + +
Spd + +
Def + + + +

Year	Lev	Team	AB	R	H	HR	RBI	Avg	OB	Slg	OPS	bb%	ct%	Eye	SB	CS	x/h%	Iso	RC/G
2015	Rk	Kingsport	11	2	2	0	3	182	182	182	364	0	82	0.00	0	0	0	0	-0.33
2015	Rk	GCL Mets	162	20	45	0	17	278	328	315	642	7	84	0.46	2	0	13	37	3.48
2016	A-	Brooklyn	171	15	37	0	11	216	260	275	535	6	85	0.38	2	0	27	58	2.21
2017	A	Columbia	182	20	42	1	15	231	282	264	546	7	86	0.50	2	3	10	33	2.34

Glove-first catcher with solid hand-eye coordination at plate. Hit tool downgraded due to continued issues producing hard contact. Extends zone. Hasn't improved BB rate. Gap-to-gap power in BP, but hasn't translated to games. All future value tied in glove and throwing ability.

Sanchez,Jesus — 79 — Tampa Bay

EXP MLB DEBUT: 2020 | H/W: 6-3 210 | FUT: Starting OF | 9D

Bats L Age 20
2014 FA (DR)
Pwr +++
BAvg ++++
Spd +++
Def +++

Year	Lev	Team	AB	R	H	HR	RBI	Avg	OB	Slg	OPS	bb%	ct%	Eye	SB	CS	x/h%	Iso	RC/G
2016	Rk	GCL Rays	164	25	53	4	31	323	347	530	878	4	81	0.19	1	5	34	207	6.15
2016	Rk	Princeton	49	8	17	3	8	347	385	612	997	6	76	0.25	1	0	41	265	7.76
2017	A	Bowling Green	475	81	145	15	82	305	349	478	827	6	81	0.35	7	2	33	173	5.59

Tall, athletic OF who took big step forward with highs in HR and doubles. Makes easy contact, hit .300+ each month except one, and was 2nd in MWL in BA. Covers plate with nice swing and has ability to hit LHP. Should get to above average pop, but could stand to work more counts. Solid mix of tools, including average work in OF corners w/ strong arm.

Sanchez,Lolo — 8 — Pittsburgh

EXP MLB DEBUT: 2021 | H/W: 6-0 150 | FUT: Starting CF | 8D

Bats R Age 18
2015 FA (DR)
Pwr ++
BAvg +++
Spd +++++
Def ++++

Year	Lev	Team	AB	R	H	HR	RBI	Avg	OB	Slg	OPS	bb%	ct%	Eye	SB	CS	x/h%	Iso	RC/G
2017	Rk	GCL Pirates	204	42	58	4	20	284	351	417	768	9	91	1.11	14	7	29	132	5.20

Athletic OF has game-changing speed but needs to refine his approach on the bases. Line-drive approach at the plate with an advanced understanding of the strike zone and walked more than he struck out in stateside debut. Below-average power, but showed surprising pop for his frame. Covers ground well and should stick in CF as he moves up.

Sanchez,Santis — 2 — Oakland

EXP MLB DEBUT: 2022 | H/W: 6-1 199 | FUT: Starting C | 7E

Bats R Age 19
2017 (5) HS (PR)
Pwr ++
BAvg ++
Spd +
Def +++

Year	Lev	Team	AB	R	H	HR	RBI	Avg	OB	Slg	OPS	bb%	ct%	Eye	SB	CS	x/h%	Iso	RC/G
2017	Rk	AZL Athletics	99	10	25	0	10	253	308	313	622	7	69	0.26	0	1	24	61	3.18

Athletic, quick backstop with as strong of an arm as any in minors. Has ton of agility and mobility, but needs polish with nuances of catching. Offense lags far behind, but has promising tools. Could hit for average power at peak due to natural strength. Can be pull happy at times and sell out for power. Should get to majors on basis of glove.

Sands,Donny — 2 — New York (A)

EXP MLB DEBUT: 2020 | H/W: 6-2 190 | FUT: Starting C | 7D

Bats R Age 21
2015 (8) HS (AZ)
Pwr ++
BAvg +++
Spd ++
Def ++

Year	Lev	Team	AB	R	H	HR	RBI	Avg	OB	Slg	OPS	bb%	ct%	Eye	SB	CS	x/h%	Iso	RC/G
2016	Rk	GCL Yankees	52	3	14	0	3	269	283	327	610	2	92	0.25	1	0	21	58	3.07
2016	Rk	Pulaski	60	7	18	2	10	300	364	417	780	9	85	0.67	1	0	17	117	5.09
2017	A	Charleston (Sc)	286	31	77	2	45	269	319	350	669	7	81	0.40	0	5	25	80	3.76
2017	A+	Tampa	62	9	19	2	10	306	358	484	842	7	84	0.50	1	1	37	177	5.82

Improving C who reached A+ in first full season. Moved to C in '16 and has made strides with footwork and throwing. Still has lot to work on, but tools are there. Possesses quick hands at bat and has stroke and strength to hit for OK pop down road. Mostly line drive contact now. Swings and misses and will need to be curbed to keep hitting for BA.

Santana,Cristian — 345 — Los Angeles (N)

EXP MLB DEBUT: 2020 | H/W: 6-2 175 | FUT: Starting 3B | 8D

Bats R Age 21
2014 FA (DR)
Pwr +++
BAvg +++
Spd +++
Def +++

Year	Lev	Team	AB	R	H	HR	RBI	Avg	OB	Slg	OPS	bb%	ct%	Eye	SB	CS	x/h%	Iso	RC/G
2016	Rk	AZL Dodgers	172	26	44	8	24	256	277	453	730	3	73	0.11	0	1	36	198	4.20
2017	Rk	Ogden	41	18	22	5	16	537	596		1596	13	85	1.00	0	0	36	463	14.74
2017	A	Great Lakes	174	18	56	5	25	322	341	460	801	3	76	0.12	0	1	25	138	5.08

A free swinger, but had a breakout in 2017, even in an injury shortened season. Aggressive approach is mitigated by good bat-to-ball skills, but could be exploited as he moves up. Needs to quiet his approach in the box, but should add power as he matures. Above-average defender at 3B with a strong arm.

Santander,Anthony — 79 — Baltimore

EXP MLB DEBUT: 2017 | H/W: 6-2 190 | FUT: Starting OF | 7C

Bats B Age 23
2011 FA (VZ)
Pwr +++
BAvg +++
Spd ++
Def ++

Year	Lev	Team	AB	R	H	HR	RBI	Avg	OB	Slg	OPS	bb%	ct%	Eye	SB	CS	x/h%	Iso	RC/G
2015	A	Lake County	248	46	68	10	42	274	323	460	783	7	79	0.34	4	2	38	185	5.04
2016	A+	Lynchburg	500	90	145	20	95	290	359	494	853	10	76	0.46	10	5	43	204	6.18
2017	A+	Frederick	5	0	2	0	0	400	400	400	800	0	80	0.00	0	0	0	0	4.75
2017	AA	Bowie	50	13	19	5	14	380	456	780	1236	12	82	0.78	0	0	53	400	10.72
2017	MLB	Baltimore	30	1	8	0	2	267	267	367	633	0	73	0.00	0	0	38	100	3.03

Injury-prone OF who missed most of season after offseason shoulder surgery and other injuries. Can be terrific offensive producer with above average power and solid eye. Swings hard and fast and has chance to hit for BA and power. Rest of tools are ordinary at best. Not a strong defender and may be relegated to LF with sub-par arm and range.

Schrock,Max — 4 — St. Louis

EXP MLB DEBUT: 2019 | H/W: 5-8 180 | FUT: Starting 2B | 7C

Bats L Age 23
2015 (13) South Carolina
Pwr ++
BAvg ++++
Spd ++
Def ++

Year	Lev	Team	AB	R	H	HR	RBI	Avg	OB	Slg	OPS	bb%	ct%	Eye	SB	CS	x/h%	Iso	RC/G
2016	A	Hagerstown	270	46	88	4	39	326	377	459	836	8	93	1.10	15	3	30	133	5.89
2016	A+	Stockton	9	0	1	0	0	111	111	111	222	0	100		0	0	0	0	-0.55
2016	A+	Potomac	232	30	79	5	29	341	365	453	818	4	91	0.41	7	2	20	112	5.28
2016	AA	Midland	23	3	9	0	3	391	391	435	826	0	100		0	1	11	43	5.26
2017	AA	Midland	417	55	134	7	46	321	373	422	795	8	90	0.81	4	2	20	101	5.33

Instinctual hitter with career .326 BA. Finished 3rd in TL in OBP and hit at least .314 every month but one. Can be very tough out and is difficult to fan. Uses simple swing and strike zone knowledge to spray line dives to gaps, but below average power limits profile. Has fringe speed and defensive skills are sub-par, limiting him to 2B.

Seise,Chris — 6 — Texas

EXP MLB DEBUT: 2021 | H/W: 6-2 175 | FUT: Starting SS | 8C

Bats R Age 19
2017 (1) HS (FL)
Pwr +++
BAvg +++
Spd +++
Def +++

Year	Lev	Team	AB	R	H	HR	RBI	Avg	OB	Slg	OPS	bb%	ct%	Eye	SB	CS	x/h%	Iso	RC/G
2017	Rk	AZL Rangers	116	23	39	3	27	336	384	509	893	7	74	0.30	5	0	28	172	6.71
2017	A-	Spokane	99	10	22	0	9	222	252	273	525	4	70	0.13	1	1	18	51	1.65

Pure, natural SS with athletic actions and quickness. Has chance to be special defender with soft hands, nimble feet, and plus arm. Solid hitter who uses all fields with level swing path and ability to recognize pitches. Offers good power and should hit for BA. Doesn't have elite speed, but runs well.

Senzel,Nick — 5 — Cincinnati

EXP MLB DEBUT: 2018 | H/W: 6-1 205 | FUT: Starting 3B | 9B

Bats R Age 22
2016 (1) Tennessee
Pwr ++++
BAvg ++++
Spd +++
Def ++++

Year	Lev	Team	AB	R	H	HR	RBI	Avg	OB	Slg	OPS	bb%	ct%	Eye	SB	CS	x/h%	Iso	RC/G
2016	NCAA	Tennessee	210	57	74	8	59	352	456	595	1051	16	90	1.90	25	4	46	243	8.85
2016	Rk	Billings	33	3	5	0	4	152	282	182	464	15	85	1.20	3	0	20	30	1.84
2016	A	Dayton	210	38	69	7	36	329	417	567	984	13	77	0.65	15	7	48	238	8.22
2017	A+	Daytona	246	41	75	4	31	305	364	476	840	9	78	0.43	9	2	43	171	6.07
2017	AA	Pensacola	209	40	71	10	34	340	413	560	973	11	79	0.60	5	4	35	220	7.66

Athletic RH 3B continued rise through farm system. Combines an advanced approach with quick, compact bat, dominated after mid-season promotion to Double-A. Tapped into raw power; potential for 25-30 HRs at projection. A solid runner, uses good jumps to be a 15-20 SB threat. A rangy defender, will stick at 3B.

Sepulveda,Carlos — 4 — Chicago (N)

EXP MLB DEBUT: 2020 | H/W: 5-10 170 | FUT: Utility player | 6B

Bats L Age 21
2014 FA (MX)
Pwr +
BAvg +++
Spd ++
Def +++

Year	Lev	Team	AB	R	H	HR	RBI	Avg	OB	Slg	OPS	bb%	ct%	Eye	SB	CS	x/h%	Iso	RC/G
2016	A	South Bend	332	55	103	1	24	310	360	373	734	7	88	0.63	4	11	17	63	4.65
2017	Rk	AZL Cubs	37	6	12	0	4	324	390	378	769	10	89	1.00	0	1	17	54	5.25
2017	A+	Myrtle Beach	112	13	22	0	7	196	268	214	483	9	83	0.58	0	1	9	18	1.64

Started 2017 red-hot, but cratered when moved up to High-A. Solid defender with good hands, but below average speed and arm limit him to 2B. Smooth lefty stroke at the plate results in gap-to-gap line drives, but below average power limits his long-term fantasy appeal.

Seymour,Anfernee — 789 — Atlanta

EXP MLB DEBUT: 2019 | H/W: 5-11 165 | FUT: Reserve OF | 6C

Bats B Age 22
2014 (7) HS (FL)
Pwr +
BAvg +++
Spd +++++
Def ++

Year	Lev	Team	AB	R	H	HR	RBI	Avg	OB	Slg	OPS	bb%	ct%	Eye	SB	CS	x/h%	Iso	RC/G
2015	A-	Batavia	238	39	65	0	14	273	329	349	678	8	78	0.38	29	6	22	76	3.96
2016	A	Rome	82	11	23	0	5	280	314	293	607	5	73	0.18	7	1	4	12	2.71
2016	A	Greensboro	409	61	103	1	26	252	290	306	596	5	77	0.23	36	12	17	54	2.68
2017	A	Rome	108	17	31	0	6	287	330	352	682	6	80	0.32	8	3	19	65	3.90
2017	A+	Florida	307	45	86	1	18	280	340	358	699	8	71	0.31	17	17	21	78	4.28

Quicked-footed switch-hitting converted SS excelled as lead off hitter in '17. Advanced approach, though struggles with breaking-ball recognition. Uses slashing approach at plate, keeping the ball on a line or on the ground. No power in frame or swing. Exceptional run tool plays up, though has some makeup concerns.

Shaw,Chris | 37 | San Francisco

EXP MLB DEBUT: 2018 | H/W: 6-4 235 | FUT: Starting OF | 8B

Bats L Age 24	Year	Lev	Team	AB	R	H	HR	RBI	Avg	OB	Slg	OPS	bb%	ct%	Eye	SB	CS	x/h%	Iso	RC/G
2015 (1) Boston Col	2015	A-	Salem-Kaizer	178	22	51	12	30	287	355	551	906	10	77	0.46	0	0	45	264	6.68
Pwr ++++	2016	A+	San Jose	270	47	77	16	55	285	352	544	897	9	74	0.40	0	0	49	259	6.73
BAvg +++	2016	AA	Richmond	232	26	57	5	30	246	306	414	719	8	76	0.36	0	0	44	168	4.46
Spd +	2017	AA	Richmond	133	16	40	6	29	301	384	511	895	12	80	0.69	0	0	40	211	6.73
Def ++	2017	AAA	Sacramento	336	42	97	18	50	289	329	530	858	6	68	0.19	0	0	45	241	6.32

Productive prospect who set career high in HR, doubles, and BA. Knows strike zone and covers plate with long arms. Will swing and miss, but makes hard contact to all fields. Can hit LHP and hangs in against solid breakers. Played LF exclusively in AAA after mostly 1B in past. Not stellar defender, but passable. Strong arm suitable for the outfield.

Sheets,Gavin | 3 | Chicago (A)

EXP MLB DEBUT: 2020 | H/W: 6-4 230 | FUT: Starting 1B | 8C

Bats L Age 21	Year	Lev	Team	AB	R	H	HR	RBI	Avg	OB	Slg	OPS	bb%	ct%	Eye	SB	CS	x/h%	Iso	RC/G
2017 (2) Wake Forest																				
Pwr ++++																				
BAvg +++	2017	NCAA	Wake Forest	240	57	76	21	84	317	427	629	1056	16	85	1.24	1	0	42	313	8.65
Spd +	2017	Rk	AZL White Sox	12	3	6	1	3	500	600	917	1517	20	100		0	0	50	417	13.90
Def +++	2017	A	Kannapolis	192	16	51	3	25	266	335	365	699	9	82	0.59	0	0	25	99	4.25

Power-first prospect with MLB bloodlines, he had solid professional debut. Advanced approach, works pitchers and can spray power to all fields. Some length to swing but not susceptible to swing-and-miss. A shortened swing will allow for consistent harder contact. A slug out of the box, profiles as 1B defensively.

Sierra,Magneuris | 8 | Miami

EXP MLB DEBUT: 2017 | H/W: 5-11 160 | FUT: Starting CF | 8D

Bats L Age 21	Year	Lev	Team	AB	R	H	HR	RBI	Avg	OB	Slg	OPS	bb%	ct%	Eye	SB	CS	x/h%	Iso	RC/G
2012 FA (DR)	2015	A	Peoria	178	19	34	1	7	191	222	247	469	4	71	0.13	4	5	15	56	0.83
Pwr +	2016	A	Peoria	524	78	161	3	60	307	335	395	730	4	81	0.23	31	17	22	88	4.35
BAvg +++	2017	A+	Palm Beach	81	16	22	0	9	272	330	407	737	8	81	0.47	3	5	32	136	4.82
Spd ++++	2017	AA	Springfield	327	32	88	1	35	269	311	352	663	6	82	0.34	17	5	25	83	3.67
Def ++++	2017	MLB	St. Louis	60	10	19	0	5	317	359	317	676	6	77	0.29	2	2	0	0	3.68

Surprise jump to the majors showed STL's confidence in Sierra and he fared surprisingly well. Athletic left-handed hitter with plus speed and elite CF defense, but not much power. Solid bat on ball skills and an acceptable BB% make him a potential top-of-the-order hitter. Traded to MIA in Ozuna deal.

Sierra,Miguelangel | 46 | Houston

EXP MLB DEBUT: 2020 | H/W: 5-11 165 | FUT: Starting SS | 7D

Bats R Age 20	Year	Lev	Team	AB	R	H	HR	RBI	Avg	OB	Slg	OPS	bb%	ct%	Eye	SB	CS	x/h%	Iso	RC/G
2014 FA (VZ)																				
Pwr ++																				
BAvg ++	2016	Rk	Greeneville	121	23	35	11	19	289	353	620	973	9	67	0.30	6	6	46	331	8.04
Spd +++	2016	A-	Tri City	93	6	13	0	5	140	200	183	383	7	63	0.21	0	3	23	43	-0.46
Def +++	2017	A-	Tri City	185	15	33	4	13	178	248	297	545	8	66	0.27	6	1	39	119	1.99

Young SS's second go-around in short-season ball was ugly, hitting sub-.200. Likes to swing and be aggressive, but often falls behind in counts and is caught out in front of off-speed. Should develop at least average power, but lack of ct% could hinder his progress. Good enough athlete with instincts and arm for SS and should stick there long-term.

Simcox,A.J. | 6 | Detroit

EXP MLB DEBUT: 2018 | H/W: 6-3 185 | FUT: Utility player | 6B

Bats R Age 23	Year	Lev	Team	AB	R	H	HR	RBI	Avg	OB	Slg	OPS	bb%	ct%	Eye	SB	CS	x/h%	Iso	RC/G
2015 (14) Tennessee	2015	Rk	GCL Tigers	15	4	5	0	1	333	375	333	708	6	80	0.33	2	0	0	0	4.10
Pwr ++	2015	A-	Connecticut	100	14	27	0	12	270	305	340	645	5	86	0.36	5	2	22	70	3.48
BAvg ++	2015	A	West Michigan	85	11	34	1	8	400	433	471	904	6	87	0.45	4	2	12	71	6.36
Spd +++	2016	A+	Lakeland	527	76	138	5	51	262	299	345	644	5	80	0.26	7	5	21	83	3.32
Def +++	2017	AA	Erie	436	55	109	8	36	250	294	378	672	6	83	0.38	12	5	32	128	3.76

Fundamentally sound INF who has advanced one level per year. Doesn't amaze with offensive talent, but is efficient with glove. Makes routine plays at SS with average hands and strong, accurate arm. Quickness and speed are solid. BA ability in question due to lack of batting eye. Hit highs in doubles and HR and has the frame to develop average pop.

Siri,Jose | 89 | Cincinnati

EXP MLB DEBUT: 2020 | H/W: 6-2 175 | FUT: Starting OF | 8E

Bats R Age 22	Year	Lev	Team	AB	R	H	HR	RBI	Avg	OB	Slg	OPS	bb%	ct%	Eye	SB	CS	x/h%	Iso	RC/G
2012 FA (DR)	2015	Rk	Billings	5	1	1	0	0	200	333	200	533	17	80	1.00	2	0	0	0	2.48
Pwr +++	2015	Rk	AZL Reds	171	34	42	3	19	246	259	444	703	2	63	0.05	9	2	45	199	4.57
BAvg +++	2016	Rk	Billings	241	52	77	10	35	320	341	560	902	3	73	0.12	17	4	39	241	6.66
Spd ++++	2016	A	Dayton	83	5	12	0	3	145	165	181	345	2	59	0.06	3	2	25	36	-1.22
Def +++	2017	A	Dayton	498	92	146	24	76	293	337	530	867	6	74	0.25	46	12	40	237	6.24

Wiry, toolsy OF had breakout season at Single-A. Aggressive power bat, but struggles getting trigger started and getting it quickly through zone. Improved selectivity somewhat. Plus power in frame despite wiriness. Plus runner, uses run tool well on bases and in CF. Has struggled with maturity.

Sisco,Chance | 2 | Baltimore

EXP MLB DEBUT: 2017 | H/W: 6-2 195 | FUT: Starting C | 8C

Bats L Age 23	Year	Lev	Team	AB	R	H	HR	RBI	Avg	OB	Slg	OPS	bb%	ct%	Eye	SB	CS	x/h%	Iso	RC/G
2013 (2) HS (CA)	2015	AA	Bowie	74	9	19	2	8	257	337	392	729	11	81	0.64	0	1	32	135	4.64
Pwr +++	2016	AA	Bowie	408	52	130	4	44	319	405	422	826	13	80	0.72	2	2	25	103	6.07
BAvg ++++	2016	AAA	Norfolk	16	4	4	2	7	250	333	625	958	11	69	0.40	0	0	50	375	7.47
Spd ++	2017	AAA	Norfolk	344	47	92	7	47	267	330	395	725	9	71	0.32	2	2	33	128	4.57
Def ++	2017	MLB	Baltimore	18	3	6	2	4	333	429	778	1206	14	61	0.43	0	0	67	444	12.67

Consistent hitting CA who took step back in BA, but set high in HR. Very athletic; has improved footwork and blocking but may only be fringe-average at best. Career .311 BA due to hand-eye coordination and natural feel. Uses level swing path to smash hard line drives and should get to average pop in time. Can be pull happy at times.

Skoug,Evan | 2 | Chicago (A)

EXP MLB DEBUT: 2020 | H/W: 5-11 200 | FUT: Starting C | 7C

Bats L Age 22	Year	Lev	Team	AB	R	H	HR	RBI	Avg	OB	Slg	OPS	bb%	ct%	Eye	SB	CS	x/h%	Iso	RC/G
2017 (7) Texas Christian																				
Pwr +++																				
BAvg ++	2017	NCAA	Texas Christian	261	59	71	20	71	272	369	544	913	13	62	0.41	3	0	44	272	7.71
Spd +	2017	Rk	AZL White Sox	17	6	9	1	3	529	600	882	1482	15	59	0.43	0	0	33	353	18.44
Def ++	2017	A	Kannapolis	65	6	10	2	7	154	247	308	554	11	55	0.28	0	0	40	154	2.35

Former top prep power prospect who regressed offensively in college. Sold out for power in 2017 and nearly set NCAA strikeout record. Needs to let strength in frame and short stroke propel power. Struggled in full-season debut. A bat-first catcher, will need to hit to be an MLB player.

Slater,Austin | 79 | San Francisco

EXP MLB DEBUT: 2017 | H/W: 6-2 215 | FUT: Starting OF | 7C

Bats R Age 25	Year	Lev	Team	AB	R	H	HR	RBI	Avg	OB	Slg	OPS	bb%	ct%	Eye	SB	CS	x/h%	Iso	RC/G
2014 (8) Stanford	2015	AA	Richmond	199	21	59	0	13	296	343	362	705	7	76	0.29	1	1	20	65	4.21
Pwr +++	2016	AA	Richmond	145	20	46	5	25	317	414	490	904	14	75	0.67	6	1	30	172	7.14
BAvg +++	2016	AAA	Sacramento	245	36	73	13	42	298	381	506	887	12	78	0.62	2	6	34	208	6.58
Spd ++	2017	AAA	Sacramento	184	28	59	5	27	321	372	467	839	8	79	0.38	4	3	29	147	5.84
Def ++	2017	MLB	SF Giants	117	15	33	3	16	282	328	402	730	6	75	0.28	0	0	21	120	4.39

Versatile, instinctual OF who had solid big league debut. Suffered sports hernia late. Kills LHP in simple approach and lines doubles to gaps. Uses whole field and covers plate with clean swing. Has average pop at present, though mostly to pull side. Fringy speed hampers defense, though average arm playable in corners.

Smith,Canaan | 79 | New York (A)

EXP MLB DEBUT: 2021 | H/W: 6-0 215 | FUT: Starting OF | 8E

Bats L Age 18	Year	Lev	Team	AB	R	H	HR	RBI	Avg	OB	Slg	OPS	bb%	ct%	Eye	SB	CS	x/h%	Iso	RC/G
2017 (4) HS (TX)																				
Pwr +++																				
BAvg +++																				
Spd ++																				
Def ++	2017	Rk	GCL Yankees	187	29	54	5	28	289	429	422	852	20	76	1.05	5	3	28	134	6.71

Young, strong OF who has very advanced eye for age. Drew more walks than Ks in pro debut and rarely chases pitches out of zone. Has some holes in swing and will generate lot of Ks. Exhibits good power potential to all fields and has the bat speed to produce BA. Can steal bases with good instincts, though a sub-par defender.

Smith,Dwight | 7 | Toronto

EXP MLB DEBUT: 2017 | H/W: 5-11 195 | FUT: Starting OF | 7D

Bats L Age 25	Year	Lev	Team	AB	R	H	HR	RBI	Avg	OB	Slg	OPS	bb%	ct%	Eye	SB	CS	x/h%	Iso	RC/G
2011 (S-1) HS (GA)	2014	A+	Dunedin	472	83	134	12	60	284	362	453	816	11	85	0.84	15	4	36	169	5.79
Pwr ++	2015	AA	New Hampshire	460	74	122	7	44	265	333	376	709	9	86	0.73	4	3	29	111	4.45
BAvg +++	2016	AA	New Hampshire	471	56	125	15	74	265	329	433	763	9	81	0.49	12	7	35	168	4.94
Spd +++	2017	AAA	Buffalo	395	56	108	8	46	273	351	392	743	11	82	0.66	8	8	28	119	4.84
Def +++	2017	MLB	Toronto	27	2	10	0	1	370	393	444	837	4	63	0.10	1	0	20	74	6.53

Natural-hitting OF who reached TOR for first time. Can be tough out with bat-to-ball skills and disciplined eye. Recognizes pitches and has hand-eye coordination to hit for BA. Good baserunner with average speed and can play OF corners despite fringy arm. Hasn't experienced power spike yet and that may ultimately decide starter or reserve role.

Smith,Kevin — 6 — Toronto

EXP MLB DEBUT: 2019 | H/W: 6-1 188 | FUT: Starting SS | 7C

Bats R Age 21 — 2017 (4) Maryland

Pwr +++ · BAvg ++ · Spd +++ · Def +++

Year	Lev	Team	AB	R	H	HR	RBI	Avg	OB	Slg	OPS	bb%	ct%	Eye	SB	CS	x/h%	Iso	RC/G
2017	NCAA	Maryland	194	38	52	13	48	268	317	552	869	7	75	0.29	4	0	50	284	6.14
2017	Rk	Bluefield	262	43	71	8	43	271	313	466	779	6	73	0.23	9	0	48	195	5.15

Fundamentally-sound SS who impressed in pro debut with natural power and strong defensive skills. Doesn't project well with hit tool due to choppy stroke, but swings aggressively and can put charge into ball. Too many Ks in profile and could use more disciplined eye. Positions himself well and has good hands and arm.

Smith,Pavin — 3 — Arizona

EXP MLB DEBUT: 2020 | H/W: 6-2 210 | FUT: Starting 1B | 8B

Bats L Age 22 — 2017 (1) Virginia

Pwr +++ · BAvg ++++ · Spd ++ · Def +++

Year	Lev	Team	AB	R	H	HR	RBI	Avg	OB	Slg	OPS	bb%	ct%	Eye	SB	CS	x/h%	Iso	RC/G
2017	NCAA	Virginia	228	53	78	13	77	342	436	570	1006	14	95	3.17	2	0	32	228	8.05
2017	A-	Hillsboro	195	34	62	0	27	318	401	415	816	12	88	1.13	2	1	27	97	6.01

Advanced approach and feel for hitting, many believed he held the 2nd best hit tool in draft. Works counts (more BB than K in pro debut) and peppers all fields with line drives. Power took step forward in college, and could see another boost in coming years. Limited athleticism keeps him to 1B only.

Smith,Will — 245 — Los Angeles (N)

EXP MLB DEBUT: 2019 | H/W: 6-0 192 | FUT: Utility player | 7C

Bats R Age 23 — 2016 (1) Louisville

Pwr ++ · BAvg +++ · Spd +++ · Def ++++

Year	Lev	Team	AB	R	H	HR	RBI	Avg	OB	Slg	OPS	bb%	ct%	Eye	SB	CS	x/h%	Iso	RC/G
2016	Rk	Ogden	28	4	9	1	5	321	406	429	835	13	96	4.00	0	0	11	107	6.13
2016	A	Great Lakes	81	12	21	1	7	259	348	309	656	12	78	0.61	2	1	10	49	3.73
2016	A+	Rancho Cuca	97	13	21	2	12	216	315	320	635	13	68	0.45	1	0	29	103	3.43
2017	A+	Rancho Cuca	250	38	58	11	43	232	331	448	779	13	72	0.52	6	2	50	216	5.42
2017	AA	Tulsa	1	0	0	0	0	0	0	0	0	0	0	0.00	1	0		0	

32nd overall pick in 2016 moved from SS in high school to C as a pro and is a plus defender with a strong arm. Short, flat swing plane results in plenty of contact, but only average to below power. Broken hand limited him to 251 AB and will need to hit for average to have value. Saw action at C, 2B, and 3B.

Solak,Nick — 4 — New York (A)

EXP MLB DEBUT: 2018 | H/W: 5-11 175 | FUT: Starting 2B | 7B

Bats R Age 23 — 2016 (2) Louisville

Pwr ++ · BAvg ++++ · Spd +++ · Def ++

Year	Lev	Team	AB	R	H	HR	RBI	Avg	OB	Slg	OPS	bb%	ct%	Eye	SB	CS	x/h%	Iso	RC/G
2016	NCAA	Louisville	165	49	62	5	29	376	466	564	1030	15	87	1.27	9	0	32	188	8.54
2016	A-	Staten Island	240	48	77	3	25	321	396	421	817	11	84	0.77	8	0	22	100	5.82
2017	A+	Tampa	346	56	104	10	44	301	393	460	853	13	78	0.70	13	4	30	159	6.38
2017	AA	Trenton	119	16	34	2	9	286	341	429	770	8	80	0.42	1	1	35	143	5.07

Natural-hitting 2B who led FSL in OBP and 2nd in BA. Easy contact and BA producer thanks to balanced swing and hand-eye coordination. Has strength to hit gaps and enough pull power to jerk out HR. Shows polish with stick and good batting eye. Average defender at best, though will commit errors with limited range. Runs well, but not a burner.

Sosa,Edmundo — 46 — St. Louis

EXP MLB DEBUT: 2020 | H/W: 5-11 170 | FUT: Starting SS | 7D

Bats R Age 22 — 2012 FA (PN)

Pwr + · BAvg +++ · Spd +++ · Def +++

Year	Lev	Team	AB	R	H	HR	RBI	Avg	OB	Slg	OPS	bb%	ct%	Eye	SB	CS	x/h%	Iso	RC/G
2016	A	Peoria	351	42	94	3	30	268	305	336	642	5	80	0.27	5	4	18	68	3.27
2016	A+	Palm Beach	34	3	10	0	4	294	314	412	726	3	76	0.13	0	0	20	118	4.37
2017	Rk	GCL Cardinals	22	7	8	1	2	364	391	545	937	4	91	0.50	0	0	25	182	6.53
2017	A+	Palm Beach	193	25	55	0	14	285	327	347	674	6	82	0.35	3	0	20	62	3.80
2017	AA	Springfield	4	0	0	0	0	0	200	0	200	20	100		0	0		0	0.30

Slick-fielding SS missed two months of action with a broken hamate bone. Quick bat and good contact skills but an aggressive approach and below average power limit his offensive upside as shown by his career .361 SLG%. Moves well at short, but average arm saw him splitting time at 2B when he returned to action.

Soto,Isael — 789 — Miami

EXP MLB DEBUT: 2021 | H/W: 6-0 190 | FUT: Starting OF | 8E

Bats L Age 21 — 2013 FA (DR)

Pwr +++ · BAvg ++ · Spd ++ · Def +++

Year	Lev	Team	AB	R	H	HR	RBI	Avg	OB	Slg	OPS	bb%	ct%	Eye	SB	CS	x/h%	Iso	RC/G
2015	Rk	GCL Marlins	26	3	9	1	5	346	452	615	1067	16	77	0.83	0	1	44	269	9.48
2015	A-	Batavia	21	1	2	0	0	95	136	95	232	5	52	0.10	0	0	0	0	-3.48
2015	A	Greensboro	64	2	8	0	1	125	164	141	305	4	58	0.11	0	0	13	16	-1.96
2016	A	Greensboro	401	51	99	9	38	247	320	399	719	10	71	0.37	3	0	38	152	4.56
2017	A	Greensboro	*(did not play - injured)*																

Physical Dominican OF missed all of 2017 with broken foot that required surgery and has been injury-prone, logging just 192 games since 2014. When healthy shows plus raw power, but also lots of swing and miss. Above-average runner with a plus arm for RF. Needs to stay healthy.

Soto,Juan — 9 — Washington

EXP MLB DEBUT: 2019 | H/W: 6-1 185 | FUT: Starting OF | 9C

Bats L Age 19 — 2015 FA (DR)

Pwr ++++ · BAvg ++++ · Spd ++ · Def +++

Year	Lev	Team	AB	R	H	HR	RBI	Avg	OB	Slg	OPS	bb%	ct%	Eye	SB	CS	x/h%	Iso	RC/G
2016	Rk	GCL Nationals	169	25	61	5	31	361	410	550	960	8	85	0.56	5	2	31	189	7.24
2016	A-	Auburn	21	3	9	0	1	429	500	571	1071	13	81	0.75	0	0	33	143	9.27
2017	Rk	GCL Nationals	25	3	8	0	4	320	370	440	810	7	96	2.00	0	0	25	120	5.77
2017	A	Hagerstown	86	15	31	3	14	360	427	523	950	10	91	1.25	1	2	26	163	7.21

Well-proportioned with some additional room for muscle, he plays with energy but under control. Has an innate feel to hit, and an approach to put himself into favorable counts. All-fields power that will only improve as he gets stronger. Strong arm but fringy range, but enough for RF. Still a teenager but the tools to move quickly.

Spanberger,Chad — 3 — Colorado

EXP MLB DEBUT: 2020 | H/W: 6-3 235 | FUT: Starting 1B | 8D

Bats L Age 22 — 2017 (6) Arkansas

Pwr ++++ · BAvg ++ · Spd + · Def ++

Year	Lev	Team	AB	R	H	HR	RBI	Avg	OB	Slg	OPS	bb%	ct%	Eye	SB	CS	x/h%	Iso	RC/G
2017	NCAA	Arkansas	239	54	73	20	67	305	374	619	993	10	73	0.40	2	0	47	314	7.97
2017	Rk	Grand Junction	235	49	69	19	51	294	366	617	983	10	70	0.38	2	0	52	323	8.11

Had a monster pro debut, blasting 19 HR in 235 AB in the Pioneer League. Left-handed power bat has bat speed and plus raw strength, but lots of swing and miss due to all-or-nothing approach. Below-average speed and defense limit him to 1B or future DH duties.

Sparks,Lamar — 8 — Baltimore

EXP MLB DEBUT: 2021 | H/W: 6-2 170 | FUT: Starting OF | 8E

Bats R Age 19 — 2017 (5) HS (TX)

Pwr ++ · BAvg +++ · Spd ++++ · Def +++

Year	Lev	Team	AB	R	H	HR	RBI	Avg	OB	Slg	OPS	bb%	ct%	Eye	SB	CS	x/h%	Iso	RC/G
2017	Rk	GCL Orioles	145	31	35	0	9	241	382	317	699	19	73	0.85	11	3	26	76	4.74

Projectable, athletic OF with advanced feel for game. Needs to add strength to tall, thin frame. Patrols CF with range and plus speed and gets good jumps. Draws ton of walks in professional approach and should hit for BA with cleaner swing. Not much power at present, but has chance for average pop as he grows into body.

Stephen,Josh — 7 — Philadelphia

EXP MLB DEBUT: 2021 | H/W: 6-0 185 | FUT: Starting OF | 7C

Bats L Age 20 — 2016 (11) HS (CA)

Pwr ++ · BAvg +++ · Spd +++ · Def ++

Year	Lev	Team	AB	R	H	HR	RBI	Avg	OB	Slg	OPS	bb%	ct%	Eye	SB	CS	x/h%	Iso	RC/G
2016	Rk	GCL Phillies	162	21	41	2	26	253	328	370	698	10	76	0.46	6	6	29	117	4.28
2017	A-	Williamsport	239	23	59	2	28	247	283	364	647	5	79	0.24	4	3	32	117	3.41

Owns a simple, balanced swing that peppers line drives into the gaps when it's on. Does have some contact issues, and could stand to be more patient at the plate. He'll need to hit, as OF defense is not good; route-running, arm and lack of speed are all currently subpar, so LF is his destination. Working on pull-side power will be one key.

Stephenson,Tyler — 2 — Cincinnati

EXP MLB DEBUT: 2020 | H/W: 6-4 225 | FUT: Starting C | 8E

Bats R Age 21 — 2015 (1) HS (GA)

Pwr +++ · BAvg +++ · Spd ++ · Def +++

Year	Lev	Team	AB	R	H	HR	RBI	Avg	OB	Slg	OPS	bb%	ct%	Eye	SB	CS	x/h%	Iso	RC/G
2015	Rk	Billings	194	28	52	1	16	268	343	361	703	10	78	0.52	0	2	31	93	4.39
2016	Rk	AZL Reds	20	4	5	1	2	250	318	450	768	9	65	0.29	0	0	40	200	5.27
2016	A	Dayton	139	17	30	3	16	216	278	324	602	8	68	0.27	0	0	27	108	2.79
2017	A	Dayton	295	39	82	6	50	278	372	414	785	13	80	0.76	2	1	34	136	5.52

Big-bodied, Injury-ridden RHH catcher broke out before thumb injury ended 2017 season. Another advanced approach in CIN system, shortened up swing mechanics, improving hard-contact rate. Raw power started materializing in swing. 18-25 HRs at projection. A strong defender despite size, best known for quick release and plus arm behind plate.

Stevenson,Andrew — 789 — Washington

EXP MLB DEBUT: 2017 | H/W: 6-0 185 | FUT: Starting OF | 7C

Bats L Age 23 — 2015 (2) Louisiana St

- Pwr ++
- BAvg +++
- Spd ++++
- Def +++

Year	Lev	Team	AB	R	H	HR	RBI	Avg	OB	Slg	OPS	bb%	ct%	Eye	SB	CS	x/h%	Iso	RC/G
2016	A+	Potomac	273	37	83	1	18	304	360	418	778	8	84	0.55	27	9	25	114	5.25
2016	AA	Harrisburg	256	38	63	2	16	246	301	328	629	7	80	0.39	12	5	24	82	3.27
2017	AA	Harrisburg	80	14	28	0	12	350	429	438	866	12	76	0.58	1	3	21	88	6.68
2017	AAA	Syracuse	309	38	78	2	26	252	296	320	616	6	77	0.26	10	1	17	68	2.97
2017	MLB	Washington	57	5	9	0	1	158	250	193	443	11	65	0.35	1	0	22	35	0.55

Speedy OF who rose quickly through system, but has found upper levels a challenge. Lack of punch in bat is a lot to overcome, and swing and miss becoming more prevalent. Keeps the ball on ground, which plays to his strengths, and would have SB value if he could find playing time. A standout defender; can handle CF despite weak arm.

Stewart,Christin — 7 — Detroit

EXP MLB DEBUT: 2018 | H/W: 6-0 205 | FUT: Starting OF | 8C

Bats L Age 24 — 2015 (1) Tennessee

- Pwr ++++
- BAvg ++
- Spd ++
- Def +

Year	Lev	Team	AB	R	H	HR	RBI	Avg	OB	Slg	OPS	bb%	ct%	Eye	SB	CS	x/h%	Iso	RC/G
2015	A-	Connecticut	49	7	12	2	11	245	315	490	805	9	63	0.28	0	0	50	245	6.16
2015	A	West Michigan	185	29	53	7	31	286	350	492	842	9	76	0.40	3	2	38	205	6.03
2016	A+	Lakeland	355	59	93	23	67	262	389	524	913	17	70	0.70	3	1	49	262	7.42
2016	AA	Erie	87	17	19	6	19	218	313	448	761	12	70	0.46	0	0	42	230	4.93
2017	AA	Erie	485	67	124	28	86	256	333	501	834	10	72	0.41	3	0	48	245	5.99

Massively-strong OF who led EL in both HR and K, which sums up profile well as he lacks secondary skills. Produces consistent pop with pure strength and selectivity. Reads pitches well and works deep counts, but has ton of swing and miss in game. Relegated to LF and is poor defender with below average arm and speed. Could be ideal DH.

Stewart,D.J. — 7 — Baltimore

EXP MLB DEBUT: 2018 | H/W: 6-0 230 | FUT: Starting OF | 7B

Bats L Age 24 — 2015 (1) Florida St

- Pwr +++
- BAvg +++
- Spd ++
- Def ++

Year	Lev	Team	AB	R	H	HR	RBI	Avg	OB	Slg	OPS	bb%	ct%	Eye	SB	CS	x/h%	Iso	RC/G
2015	NCAA	Florida State	214	62	68	15	59	318	484	593	1078	24	78	1.47	12	3	40	276	9.74
2015	A-	Aberdeen	238	25	52	6	24	218	287	345	632	9	78	0.44	4	1	31	126	3.28
2016	A	Delmarva	213	27	49	4	25	230	357	352	709	16	73	0.72	16	6	35	122	4.67
2016	A+	Frederick	201	41	56	6	30	279	388	448	836	15	77	0.78	10	3	36	169	6.28
2017	AA	Bowie	457	80	127	21	79	278	368	481	849	12	81	0.75	20	4	39	204	6.15

Short, stocky OF who had 20/20 season with easy high in HR. Becoming more diverse hitter who can hit LHP with good bat speed and pitch recognition. Draws lots of walks with mature approach and innate feel for strike zone. Steals bases despite fringy speed and has LF profile as below average defender. Works hard at deficiencies.

Stobbe,Cole — 5 — Philadelphia

EXP MLB DEBUT: 2022 | H/W: 6-1 200 | FUT: Starting 3B | 7D

Bats R Age 20 — 2016 (3) HS (NE)

- Pwr +++
- BAvg ++
- 4.45 Spd ++
- Def ++

Year	Lev	Team	AB	R	H	HR	RBI	Avg	OB	Slg	OPS	bb%	ct%	Eye	SB	CS	x/h%	Iso	RC/G
2016	Rk	GCL Phillies	148	23	40	4	13	270	333	405	739	9	80	0.47	3	6	30	135	4.62
2017	A-	Williamsport	197	28	40	8	22	203	266	376	642	8	66	0.25	2	3	43	173	3.34

Power-over-hit INF with some loft to swing and projection left in body, but who currently struggles wildly with breaking balls. Box approach is noisy, often sells out for power, doesn't engage lower half as much as he could. Hit tool may make it tough for pop to show up in games. Some arm strength, but not a fluid defender at 3B.

Straw,Myles — 789 — Houston

EXP MLB DEBUT: 2019 | H/W: 5-10 180 | FUT: Starting OF | 7C

Bats R Age 23 — 2015 (12) St. John's River JC

- Pwr +
- BAvg +++
- Spd ++++
- Def +++

Year	Lev	Team	AB	R	H	HR	RBI	Avg	OB	Slg	OPS	bb%	ct%	Eye	SB	CS	x/h%	Iso	RC/G
2016	A	Quad Cities	270	40	101	0	22	374	435	470	905	10	79	0.50	17	10	20	96	6.99
2016	A+	Lancaster	76	21	23	1	5	303	391	395	786	13	78	0.65	4	2	22	92	5.51
2017	A+	Buies Creek	437	81	129	1	41	295	412	373	785	17	84	1.24	36	9	19	78	5.84
2017	AA	Corpus Christi	46	9	11	0	3	239	340	239	579	13	80	0.78	2	0	0	0	2.91

Speedster OF with slash-and-dash offensive qualities. Works counts and draws walks exceptionally well for future OBP value; should have impact SB totals. Not much raw power to speak of, though he'll leg out plenty of doubles and put bat on ball as an effective lead-off type hitter. Plus range, instincts and arm for any OF position.

Stubbs,Garrett — 2 — Houston

EXP MLB DEBUT: 2018 | H/W: 5-10 175 | FUT: Starting C | 7B

Bats L Age 24 — 2015 (8) USC

- Pwr +
- BAvg +++
- Spd +++
- Def +++

Year	Lev	Team	AB	R	H	HR	RBI	Avg	OB	Slg	OPS	bb%	ct%	Eye	SB	CS	x/h%	Iso	RC/G
2015	A	Quad Cities	84	15	23	0	5	274	378	333	711	14	98	7.00	1	0	22	60	5.23
2016	A+	Lancaster	206	35	60	6	38	291	379	442	820	12	82	0.78	10	3	32	150	5.86
2016	AA	Corpus Christi	120	23	39	4	16	325	396	517	912	10	91	1.27	5	0	36	192	6.85
2017	AA	Corpus Christi	263	36	62	4	25	236	319	331	649	11	83	0.73	8	0	27	95	3.74
2017	AAA	Fresno	77	11	17	0	12	221	318	286	604	13	81	0.73	3	0	29	65	3.29

Short, athletic CA with quality defensive tools and chance for an average bat. Framing skills, plus arm and blocking ability will allow him to get regular PT behind plate. Makes consistent contact and draws BBs; can run a bit and picks spots well for SB. Not much pop, but could run into 10-12 HR. Think glove before bat, but still a decent stick.

Tatis,Fernando — 6 — San Diego

EXP MLB DEBUT: 2019 | H/W: 6-3 185 | FUT: Starting SS | 9C

Bats R Age 19 — 2015 FA (DR)

- Pwr ++++
- BAvg +++
- Spd +++
- Def ++++

Year	Lev	Team	AB	R	H	HR	RBI	Avg	OB	Slg	OPS	bb%	ct%	Eye	SB	CS	x/h%	Iso	RC/G
2016	Rk	AZL Padres	176	35	48	4	20	273	312	426	738	5	75	0.23	14	2	38	153	4.54
2016	A-	Tri-City	44	4	12	0	5	273	319	455	774	6	70	0.23	1	1	50	182	5.50
2017	A	Fort Wayne	431	78	121	21	69	281	387	520	907	15	71	0.60	29	15	45	239	7.33
2017	AA	San Antonio	55	6	14	1	6	255	281	327	608	4	69	0.12	3	0	14	73	2.64

Former glove-first Dominican SS whose offensive tools blossomed in MWL. Lean, wiry frame produces plus bat speed for solid ct% and future plus power. Patience improved in 2017 and has acclimated himself to quickly to offspeed. Likes to run; bigger frame suggests he won't yield impact SB. Has range and plus arm to stay SS, but could be 3B candidate.

Taveras,Leody — 8 — Texas

EXP MLB DEBUT: 2020 | H/W: 6-1 170 | FUT: Starting CF | 9C

Bats B Age 19 — 2015 FA (DR)

- Pwr +++
- BAvg +++
- Spd ++++
- Def ++++

Year	Lev	Team	AB	R	H	HR	RBI	Avg	OB	Slg	OPS	bb%	ct%	Eye	SB	CS	x/h%	Iso	RC/G
2016	Rk	AZL Rangers	144	22	40	1	15	278	329	382	711	7	83	0.46	11	4	25	104	4.35
2016	A-	Spokane	123	14	28	0	9	228	275	293	567	6	79	0.31	3	1	25	65	2.47
2017	A	Hickory	522	73	130	8	50	249	311	360	671	8	82	0.51	20	6	27	111	3.87

Athletic, thin OF with as much upside as any in minors. Had successful 1st year in full season ball and was among youngest players in SAL. Has all tools in arsenal including bat speed, barrel control, and leveraged swing to hit for BA and power. Can be aggressive with swing and needs to read spin better. True CF with plus arm and plentiful range.

Taylor,Chuck — 789 — Seattle

EXP MLB DEBUT: 2018 | H/W: 5-9 190 | FUT: Reserve OF | 6B

Bats B Age 24 — 2012 (4) HS (TX)

- Pwr ++
- BAvg ++
- Spd +++
- Def ++

Year	Lev	Team	AB	R	H	HR	RBI	Avg	OB	Slg	OPS	bb%	ct%	Eye	SB	CS	x/h%	Iso	RC/G
2015	A	Kane County	289	39	81	0	24	280	344	318	662	9	83	0.58	8	3	11	38	3.82
2015	A+	Visalia	179	22	42	2	9	235	318	341	659	11	75	0.49	4	7	29	106	3.80
2016	A+	Visalia	154	27	42	3	19	273	378	416	793	14	75	0.67	1	3	29	143	5.76
2016	AA	Mobile	84	11	20	1	11	238	289	345	634	7	82	0.40	1	0	35	107	3.35
2017	AA	Arkansas	471	74	129	9	58	274	363	397	760	12	81	0.73	10	2	29	123	5.16

Short, grinding OF who had career year and finished 3rd in TL in walks. Set easy high in HR and has advanced feel for hitting. Knows strike zone and rarely chases pitches. Can be beaten with good velocity and lacks bat speed to catch up. Below average HR pop, but focuses on gap power. Mostly LF due to below average arm. Has average speed for range.

Taylor,Samad — 4 — Toronto

EXP MLB DEBUT: 2021 | H/W: 5-10 160 | FUT: Starting 2B | 8E

Bats R Age 19 — 2016 (10) HS (CA)

- Pwr ++
- BAvg +++
- Spd +++
- Def +++

Year	Lev	Team	AB	R	H	HR	RBI	Avg	OB	Slg	OPS	bb%	ct%	Eye	SB	CS	x/h%	Iso	RC/G
2016	Rk	AZL Indians	116	25	34	1	14	293	354	397	751	9	79	0.46	6	2	24	103	4.89
2017	Rk	Bluefield	16	1	4	0	3	250	368	250	618	16	63	0.50	1	0	0	0	3.38
2017	A-	Vancouver	68	7	20	2	8	294	342	426	769	7	74	0.28	2	2	25	132	4.94
2017	A-	Mahoning Val	120	18	36	4	19	300	328	467	795	4	80	0.21	4	2	31	167	5.03

Nimble, quick athlete who is deep sleeper. Knows how to play game with professional approach and actions. Could develop into stud defender due to smooth actions and soft hands. Swings a fast bat and uses average speed effectively. Could grow into at least average power if he fills out lithe frame.

Tejeda,Anderson — 46 — Texas

EXP MLB DEBUT: 2020 | H/W: 5-11 185 | FUT: Starting SS | 7C

Bats L Age 19 — 2014 FA (DR)

- Pwr +++
- BAvg ++
- Spd +++
- Def ++

Year	Lev	Team	AB	R	H	HR	RBI	Avg	OB	Slg	OPS	bb%	ct%	Eye	SB	CS	x/h%	Iso	RC/G
2016	Rk	AZL Rangers	133	22	39	1	21	293	333	496	830	6	73	0.22	1	0	49	203	6.09
2016	A-	Spokane	94	15	26	8	19	277	313	553	866	5	65	0.15	1	0	35	277	6.39
2017	A	Hickory	401	68	99	8	53	247	309	411	720	8	67	0.27	10	7	41	165	4.70

Offense-first INF who started slow, but finished well in first year in full season. Played mostly SS, but also saw action at 2B. Owns gun for arm, yet makes careless errors with poor footwork. Lots of movement in swing and needs to hone aggressive nature. Swings fast bat and has 20+ HR potential. Solid hand-eye coordination and pitch recognition.

Tellez,Rowdy

3 | **Toronto** | EXP MLB DEBUT: 2018 | H/W: 6-4 220 | FUT: Starting 1B | **7B**

Bats L Age 23
2013 (30) HS (CA)

- Pwr + + +
- BAvg + + +
- Spd +
- Def + +

Year	Lev	Team	AB	R	H	HR	RBI	Avg	OB	Slg	OPS	bb%	ct%	Eye	SB	CS	x/h%	Iso	RC/G
2015	A	Lansing	270	36	80	7	49	296	354	444	798	8	79	0.43	2	2	33	148	5.37
2015	A+	Dunedin	131	17	36	7	28	275	345	473	818	10	79	0.50	3	0	33	198	5.54
2016	AA	New Hampshire	438	71	130	23	81	297	385	530	915	13	79	0.68	4	3	42	233	7.01
2017	AAA	Buffalo	445	45	99	6	56	222	297	333	629	10	79	0.50	6	1	36	110	3.38

Strong 1B who had big drop off at AAA. Power declined dramatically while BA fell off table. Struggled with LHP (.145 BA). Still possesses potential as run producer. Exhibits plus natural power with loft and leverage in stroke. Draws walks with pro approach, though can chase. Not a great defender, but has sufficient footwork and arm strength.

Thaiss,Matt

3 | **Los Angeles (A)** | EXP MLB DEBUT: 2018 | H/W: 6-0 195 | FUT: Starting 1B | **8C**

Bats L Age 22
2016 (1) Virginia

- Pwr + +
- BAvg + + + +
- Spd + +
- Def + +

Year	Lev	Team	AB	R	H	HR	RBI	Avg	OB	Slg	OPS	bb%	ct%	Eye	SB	CS	x/h%	Iso	RC/G
2016	NCAA	Virginia	232	55	87	10	59	375	465	578	1043	14	93	2.44	0	1	29	203	8.53
2016	Rk	Orem	65	16	22	2	12	338	377	569	946	6	94	1.00	2	4	45	231	6.96
2016	A	Burlington	199	24	55	4	31	276	348	427	776	10	86	0.79	1	0	35	151	5.28
2017	A+	Inland Empire	336	46	89	8	48	265	343	399	742	11	82	0.68	4	3	28	134	4.82
2017	AA	Mobile	178	29	52	1	25	292	414	388	802	17	72	0.74	4	3	29	96	6.14

Natural-hitting 1B with advanced bat-to-ball ability. Despite above average raw power, focuses on hard contact and going gap to gap with level swing path. Draws ton of walks with disciplined eye as he rarely chases bad pitches. Secondary skills are below average to fringe average. Defense is sub-par at present, but could get better with more reps.

Thompson,Bubba

8 | **Texas** | EXP MLB DEBUT: 2022 | H/W: 6-2 180 | FUT: Starting CF | **9D**

Bats R Age 19
2017 (1) HS (AL)

- Pwr + + +
- BAvg + + +
- Spd + + + +
- Def + +

Year	Lev	Team	AB	R	H	HR	RBI	Avg	OB	Slg	OPS	bb%	ct%	Eye	SB	CS	x/h%	Iso	RC/G
2017	Rk	AZL Rangers	113	23	29	3	12	257	294	434	728	5	75	0.21	5	5	41	177	4.40

Premium athlete with exemplary tools and showed improvement in debut. Owns elite speed and should steal bases. Exhibits above average bat speed and solid pitch recognition to hit for raw power. Room to add strength to projectable frame. Defense in CF needs work, but ranges well and gets good reads. Has all tools to be star. Just needs time.

Thompson,David

5 | **New York (N)** | EXP MLB DEBUT: 2018 | H/W: 6-0 210 | FUT: Starting 3B | **7C**

Bats R Age 24
2015 (4) Miami

- Pwr + +
- BAvg + + + +
- Spd + +
- Def + +

Year	Lev	Team	AB	R	H	HR	RBI	Avg	OB	Slg	OPS	bb%	ct%	Eye	SB	CS	x/h%	Iso	RC/G
2015	NCAA	Miami	253	59	83	19	90	328	426	640	1066	15	89	1.48	1	3	47	312	8.71
2015	A-	Brooklyn	206	22	45	3	22	218	258	320	578	5	79	0.25	3	0	31	102	2.48
2016	A	Columbia	228	45	67	5	58	294	335	474	808	6	79	0.29	3	0	43	180	5.47
2016	A+	St. Lucie	204	29	54	6	37	265	315	412	727	7	80	0.37	3	0	33	147	4.37
2017	AA	Binghamton	476	62	125	16	68	263	320	429	748	8	81	0.43	8	6	37	166	4.69

Stocky RH slugger turned in best season as professional. Has improved hit tool immensely since pro debut. Reworked swing, now quicker and more compact, and more patient in 2017. Raw power always there, appearing in games. Continues to make strides but likely below average defender in MLB. Poor runner.

Tilson,Charlie

789 | **Chicago (A)** | EXP MLB DEBUT: 2018 | H/W: 5-11 195 | FUT: Starting CF | **7B**

Bats L Age 25
2011 (2) HS (IL)

- Pwr + +
- BAvg + + + +
- Spd + + + +
- Def + + +

Year	Lev	Team	AB	R	H	HR	RBI	Avg	OB	Slg	OPS	bb%	ct%	Eye	SB	CS	x/h%	Iso	RC/G
2014	AA	Springfield	139	19	33	2	17	237	269	324	593	4	80	0.21	2	3	21	86	2.60
2015	AA	Springfield	539	85	159	4	32	295	350	388	738	8	87	0.64	46	19	21	93	4.73
2016	AAA	Memphis	351	53	99	4	34	282	344	407	751	9	85	0.65	15	3	28	125	4.94
2016	MLB	Chi White Sox	2	0	1	0	0	500	500	500	1000	0	100		0	0	0	0	6.83
2017	MLB	Chi White Sox	*(did not play - injured)*												0	0			

Speedy CF missed all of 2017 with a stress fracture in right ankle. Old school prototypical leadoff hitter approach works pitches to get on base. A line drive hitter, uses all fields, but lack power. Uses speed to be nuisance on bases and track down fly balls. Arm is limited to CF or LF.

Tobias,Josh

4 | **Boston** | EXP MLB DEBUT: 2018 | H/W: 5-9 195 | FUT: Utility player | **6B**

Bats R Age 25
2015 (10) Florida

- Pwr + +
- BAvg + +
- Spd + + +
- Def + +

Year	Lev	Team	AB	R	H	HR	RBI	Avg	OB	Slg	OPS	bb%	ct%	Eye	SB	CS	x/h%	Iso	RC/G
2015	A-	Williamsport	240	31	77	4	37	321	358	475	833	6	83	0.33	12	10	34	154	5.70
2016	A	Lakewood	365	49	111	7	55	304	359	444	802	8	84	0.53	6	4	31	140	5.43
2016	A+	Clearwater	126	21	32	2	14	254	319	357	676	9	76	0.40	4	1	28	103	3.87
2017	A+	Salem	87	16	30	2	11	345	400	494	894	8	82	0.50	4	2	30	149	6.57
2017	AA	Portland	332	32	89	3	34	268	308	352	660	5	78	0.26	4	3	25	84	3.53

Short INF who relies on instincts and fundamentals to offer value. Possesses some semblance of gap power with consistent, level swing path. Comfortable going to opposite field and shortens stroke with two strikes. Low OBP due to aggressive approach. Not blessed with quickness, though has decent foot speed. Can play 2B with OK range and arm.

Tocci,Carlos

8 | **Texas** | EXP MLB DEBUT: 2018 | H/W: 6-2 160 | FUT: Starting CF | **7C**

Bats R Age 22
2011 FA (VZ)

- Pwr + +
- BAvg + + +
- 4.50 Spd + + +
- Def + + + +

Year	Lev	Team	AB	R	H	HR	RBI	Avg	OB	Slg	OPS	bb%	ct%	Eye	SB	CS	x/h%	Iso	RC/G
2015	A	Lakewood	234	35	75	2	25	321	374	423	797	8	87	0.65	14	2	24	103	5.41
2015	A+	Clearwater	275	31	71	2	18	258	289	313	602	4	81	0.23	3	9	15	55	2.74
2016	A+	Clearwater	500	66	142	3	50	284	330	362	692	6	85	0.45	13	6	22	78	4.06
2017	AA	Reading	430	59	132	2	48	307	351	398	748	6	85	0.44	4	5	21	91	4.74
2017	AAA	Lehigh Valley	53	2	10	1	4	189	204	245	449	2	79	0.09	0	0	10	57	0.61

Slow-moving prospect took well to first taste of AA. A fluid athlete with long limbs, has bat-to-ball skills that give hit tool some promise. But still lacks strength; swing path is level and upper body-centric, so power unlikely to materialize. Also can be too passive, and/or misses drivable pitches. Excellent defender gives him an MLB floor.

Toffey,Will

5 | **Oakland** | EXP MLB DEBUT: 2020 | H/W: 6-2 205 | FUT: Starting 3B | **7D**

Bats L Age 23
2017 (4) Vanderbilt

- Pwr + +
- BAvg + +
- Spd + +
- Def + +

Year	Lev	Team	AB	R	H	HR	RBI	Avg	OB	Slg	OPS	bb%	ct%	Eye	SB	CS	x/h%	Iso	RC/G
2017	NCAA	Vanderbilt	206	55	73	12	64	354	476	602	1078	19	85	1.60	5	4	36	248	9.28
2017	A-	Vermont	209	38	55	1	22	263	377	349	726	15	78	0.84	2	2	25	86	4.95

Instinctual, grinding INF who makes most of limited tools. Stands out for extreme knowledge of strike zone. Takes a lot of pitches and puts bat to ball with solid two-strike approach. Not much power despite size and limited bat speed limits upside. Possesses strong arm at 3B, but lacks lateral quickness and doesn't have much range.

Toro,Abraham

25 | **Houston** | EXP MLB DEBUT: 2020 | H/W: 6-1 190 | FUT: Starting 3B | **7D**

Bats B Age 21
2016 (5) Seminole St JC

- Pwr + + +
- BAvg + + +
- Spd + +
- Def + +

Year	Lev	Team	AB	R	H	HR	RBI	Avg	OB	Slg	OPS	bb%	ct%	Eye	SB	CS	x/h%	Iso	RC/G
2016	Rk	Greeneville	177	20	45	0	19	254	294	322	616	5	82	0.32	2	1	20	68	3.10
2017	A-	Tri City	104	20	30	6	16	288	398	529	927	15	80	0.90	1	3	43	240	7.27
2017	A	Quad Cities	134	25	28	9	17	209	316	463	779	14	78	0.70	2	0	50	254	5.20

Switch-hitter who hit for big-time raw power in full-season debut. Makes solid contact from both sides and has natural loft in swing for HR. Future source of OBP given keen eye and ability to recognize pitches. Split time at CA/3B as pro, but sub-par arm strength likely lands him at the hot-corner long term; value will increase if he can remain CA.

Torres,Christopher

6 | **Miami** | EXP MLB DEBUT: 2021 | H/W: 5-11 170 | FUT: Starting SS | **8D**

Bats B Age 20
2014 FA (DR)

- Pwr + +
- BAvg + +
- Spd + + + +
- Def + + + +

Year	Lev	Team	AB	R	H	HR	RBI	Avg	OB	Slg	OPS	bb%	ct%	Eye	SB	CS	x/h%	Iso	RC/G
2016	Rk	AZL Mariners	167	31	43	0	17	257	333	359	693	10	74	0.43	12	4	30	102	4.33
2017	Rk	AZL Mariners	9	1	2	0	1	222	417	667	1083	25	44	0.60	1	0	100	444	16.15
2017	A-	Everett	193	44	46	6	22	238	326	435	761	11	67	0.39	13	3	43	197	5.37

Well-rounded, he exhibits good bat potential, but more defense-oriented at present. Range and arm good enough for any INF spot, but owns ideal quickness and nimble feet to stick at SS. Focuses on using whole field with hard liners and exhibits good pop for size, but won't be HR hitter at peak. Has plus speed and will steal bases consistently.

Torres,Gleyber

456 | **New York (A)** | EXP MLB DEBUT: 2018 | H/W: 6-1 175 | FUT: Starting SS | **9B**

Bats R Age 21
2013 FA (VZ)

- Pwr + + +
- BAvg + + + +
- Spd + + +
- Def + + +

Year	Lev	Team	AB	R	H	HR	RBI	Avg	OB	Slg	OPS	bb%	ct%	Eye	SB	CS	x/h%	Iso	RC/G
2015	A+	Myrtle Beach	23	1	4	0	2	174	208	174	382	4	70	0.14	0	1	0	0	-0.46
2016	A+	Tampa	122	19	31	2	19	254	341	385	726	12	81	0.70	2	3	32	131	4.73
2016	A+	Myrtle Beach	356	62	98	9	47	275	352	433	784	11	76	0.48	19	10	36	157	5.40
2017	AA	Trenton	121	22	33	5	18	273	362	496	858	12	83	0.81	5	4	48	223	6.32
2017	AAA	Scranton/WB	81	9	25	2	16	309	404	457	861	14	68	0.50	2	2	28	148	6.89

Exciting young INF who underwent Tommy John surgery in June, but will be ready for ST. Very advanced skills with bat and glove; profiles to hit for high BA due to bat speed, pitch recognition, and pretty swing. Should evolve into at least above average pull-side power. Plays all INF spots and has arm, hands, and range to be asset.

Trahan,Blake — 456 — Cincinnati

EXP MLB DEBUT: 2019 | H/W: 5-9 180 | FUT: Starting SS | 7D

Bats R Age 24
2015 (3) LA-Lafayette
Pwr +
BAvg ++
Spd ++++
Def ++++

Year	Lev	Team	AB	R	H	HR	RBI	Avg	OB	Slg	OPS	bb%	ct%	Eye	SB	CS	x/h%	Iso	RC/G
2015	NCAA	LA-Lafayette	254	51	80	2	29	315	404	406	810	13	87	1.19	17	0	23	91	5.91
2015	Rk	Billings	186	32	58	1	15	312	393	403	797	12	90	1.32	10	3	21	91	5.74
2015	A+	Daytona	35	1	4	0	0	114	114	114	229	0	86	0.00	0	0	0	0	-1.61
2016	A+	Daytona	521	90	137	4	47	263	326	361	687	9	86	0.67	25	8	25	98	4.19
2017	AA	Pensacola	455	55	101	2	27	222	302	275	577	10	82	0.63	12	7	20	53	2.82

Short-statured, athletic glove-first SS struggled producing solid contact in 2017. High contact rate due to solid bat-to-ball and patient approach. Hit less line drives and more pop ups. Little power in compact frame. Borderline plus-plus runner. Very accomplished defender. Rangy and has strong arm. Can stick at SS.

Trammell,Taylor — 78 — Cincinnati

EXP MLB DEBUT: 2020 | H/W: 6-2 195 | FUT: Starting OF | 9E

Bats L Age 20
2016 (S-1) HS (GA)
Pwr ++++
BAvg +++
Spd ++++
Def +++

Year	Lev	Team	AB	R	H	HR	RBI	Avg	OB	Slg	OPS	bb%	ct%	Eye	SB	CS	x/h%	Iso	RC/G
2016	Rk	Billings	228	39	69	2	34	303	367	421	788	9	75	0.40	24	7	25	118	5.47
2017	A	Dayton	491	80	138	13	77	281	372	450	822	13	75	0.58	41	12	34	169	6.03

Athletic, former 2-sport prep star made successful transition to full-season ball due to surprisingly advanced approach. Quick wrists and hands, though needs to cut down swing and trigger to fare well against velocity. Significant power throughout frame; 25-30 HR potential. Uses plus-plus speed to accumulate SBs. Potential 30/30 performer. Raw in CF.

Travis,Sam — 3 — Boston

EXP MLB DEBUT: 2017 | H/W: 6-0 205 | FUT: Starting 1B | 7A

Bats R Age 24
2014 (2) Indiana
Pwr +++
BAvg ++++
Spd ++
Def ++

Year	Lev	Team	AB	R	H	HR	RBI	Avg	OB	Slg	OPS	bb%	ct%	Eye	SB	CS	x/h%	Iso	RC/G
2015	A+	Salem	246	35	77	5	40	313	379	467	846	10	83	0.60	10	6	31	154	6.09
2015	AA	Portland	243	35	73	4	38	300	384	436	820	12	86	0.97	9	6	32	136	5.94
2016	AAA	Pawtucket	173	26	47	6	29	272	330	434	763	8	77	0.38	1	0	34	162	4.88
2017	AAA	Pawtucket	304	40	82	6	24	270	349	375	724	11	81	0.65	6	2	24	105	4.59
2017	MLB	Boston	76	13	20	0	1	263	317	342	659	7	70	0.26	1	0	30	79	3.73

Strong 1B who is natural hitter with advanced approach and ability to drive ball hard to gaps. Makes easy contact with simple swing and does not sell out for power. Raw pop is there; could sacrifice some BA for in-game power down line. Does not run well and is inconsistent defender at 1B.

Trevino,Jose — 2 — Texas

EXP MLB DEBUT: 2018 | H/W: 5-11 211 | FUT: Starting C | 7D

Bats R Age 25
2014 (6) Oral Roberts
Pwr ++
BAvg ++
Spd +
Def ++++

Year	Lev	Team	AB	R	H	HR	RBI	Avg	OB	Slg	OPS	bb%	ct%	Eye	SB	CS	x/h%	Iso	RC/G
2014	NCAA	Oral Roberts	230	37	70	10	43	304	360	491	851	8	89	0.80	4	0	31	187	5.90
2014	A-	Spokane	288	58	74	9	49	257	312	448	760	7	83	0.46	2	0	46	191	4.88
2015	A	Hickory	424	62	111	14	63	262	292	415	707	4	86	0.30	1	4	32	153	4.00
2016	A+	High Desert	433	67	131	9	68	303	342	434	776	6	89	0.53	2	1	30	132	4.99
2017	AA	Frisco	402	39	97	7	42	241	276	323	599	5	89	0.43	1	2	20	82	2.92

Short, stout C who has evolved into elite defender with plus receiving and blocking abilities. Strong, accurate arm is highlight with quick release. Makes very easy contact, but swings at everything in aggressive nature. Saw drop in power and only has moderate BA potential. Defense should get to majors, but offense may not become good enough.

Tucker,Cole — 6 — Pittsburgh

EXP MLB DEBUT: 2019 | H/W: 6-3 185 | FUT: Starting SS | 8C

Bats B Age 21
2014 (1) HS (AZ)
Pwr ++
BAvg +++
Spd ++++
Def +++

Year	Lev	Team	AB	R	H	HR	RBI	Avg	OB	Slg	OPS	bb%	ct%	Eye	SB	CS	x/h%	Iso	RC/G
2015	A	West Virginia	300	46	88	2	25	293	329	377	706	5	84	0.33	25	6	20	83	4.12
2016	A	West Virginia	61	9	16	1	2	262	308	443	750	6	85	0.44	1	1	44	180	4.82
2016	A+	Bradenton	269	36	64	1	25	238	312	301	613	10	77	0.47	5	6	22	63	3.16
2017	A+	Bradenton	277	46	79	4	32	285	363	426	789	11	75	0.49	36	12	32	141	5.58
2017	AA	Altoona	167	25	43	2	18	257	340	377	718	11	81	0.68	11	3	26	120	4.63

Former 1st rounder had his best season as a pro, hitting .275 with 47 SB between A+/AA. Plus runner has good range, a strong arm, and should stick at short. Could grow into average power once he fills out his frame, but 12-15 HR is his likely upside. Improve pitch recognition and OB ability allows speed to play up.

Tucker,Kyle — 789 — Houston

EXP MLB DEBUT: 2018 | H/W: 6-4 190 | FUT: Starting OF | 9B

Bats L Age 21
2015 (1) HS (FL)
Pwr ++++
BAvg ++++
Spd +++
Def +++

Year	Lev	Team	AB	R	H	HR	RBI	Avg	OB	Slg	OPS	bb%	ct%	Eye	SB	CS	x/h%	Iso	RC/G
2015	Rk	GCL Astros	119	18	25	2	13	210	260	319	579	6	88	0.57	4	2	28	109	2.84
2016	A	Quad Cities	373	43	103	6	56	276	346	402	748	10	80	0.53	31	9	29	126	4.89
2016	A+	Lancaster	59	13	20	3	13	339	435	661	1096	14	90	1.67	1	3	55	322	9.25
2017	A+	Buies Creek	177	31	51	9	43	288	373	554	927	12	75	0.53	13	5	49	266	7.34
2017	AA	Corpus Christi	287	39	76	16	47	265	317	512	829	7	78	0.34	8	4	50	247	5.63

Tall, lean OF with a chance to impact multiple categories. Started tapping into power with aggressive approach in AA, but swing remains fluid and compact for quality bat-to-ball skills/BA value. A good athlete who can run with enough arm for any OF position. Good makeup and feel for the game. He's coming quickly.

Urena,Jhoan — 35 — New York (N)

EXP MLB DEBUT: 2018 | H/W: 6-1 220 | FUT: Starting 3B | 7D

Bats B Age 23
2011 FA (DR)
Pwr +++
BAvg ++
Spd ++
Def +++

Year	Lev	Team	AB	R	H	HR	RBI	Avg	OB	Slg	OPS	bb%	ct%	Eye	SB	CS	x/h%	Iso	RC/G
2015	Rk	GCL Mets	15	4	5	2	2	333	474	800	1274	21	100		1	0	60	467	11.09
2015	A+	St. Lucie	210	15	45	0	18	214	253	267	520	5	81	0.28	2	0	18	52	1.86
2016	A+	St. Lucie	383	52	86	9	53	225	301	350	651	10	80	0.56	0	1	33	125	3.62
2017	A+	St. Lucie	458	72	129	11	62	282	365	437	802	12	75	0.53	17	3	36	155	5.70
2017	AAA	Las Vegas	44	5	10	3	8	227	292	477	769	8	64	0.25	1	0	40	250	5.24

Switch-hitting 3B stayed healthy and got to Triple-A. An advanced, contact bat, hard-hit rate improved substantially in 2017; raw power began materializing too. Hit career high HRs in pitcher's league. Could be 20+ w/ solid MLB playing time. Defense continues to improve. Should stick at 3B. Slow runner.

Urena,Richard — 46 — Toronto

EXP MLB DEBUT: 2017 | H/W: 6-0 185 | FUT: Starting SS | 8D

Bats B Age 22
2012 FA (DR)
Pwr +++
BAvg +++
Spd ++
Def +++

Year	Lev	Team	AB	R	H	HR	RBI	Avg	OB	Slg	OPS	bb%	ct%	Eye	SB	CS	x/h%	Iso	RC/G
2015	A+	Dunedin	124	9	31	1	8	250	268	315	582	2	79	0.12	3	1	16	65	2.37
2016	A+	Dunedin	394	52	120	8	41	305	346	447	793	6	84	0.39	9	6	28	142	5.19
2016	AA	New Hampshire	124	14	33	0	18	266	289	395	684	3	85	0.21	0	2	33	129	3.91
2017	AA	New Hampshire	510	44	126	5	60	247	289	359	648	6	80	0.30	0	1	35	112	3.45
2017	MLB	Toronto	68	6	14	1	4	206	270	309	579	8	59	0.21	1	0	36	103	2.71

Toolsy SS who led EL in doubles, but HR pop has declined last 3 years. Has feel for hitting despite erratic approach and offers power potential from left side. Tantalizes with natural skills, but haven't translated much to games yet. Has all tools to be standout defender, but hindered by sloppy actions. Still young and will need to step up game.

Urias,Luis — 46 — San Diego

EXP MLB DEBUT: 2018 | H/W: 5-9 160 | FUT: Starting 2B | 8B

Bats R Age 20
2013 FA (MX)
Pwr ++
BAvg ++++
Spd +++
Def +++

Year	Lev	Team	AB	R	H	HR	RBI	Avg	OB	Slg	OPS	bb%	ct%	Eye	SB	CS	x/h%	Iso	RC/G
2015	A-	Tri-City	31	6	11	0	1	355	444	387	832	14	97	5.00	3	3	9	32	6.40
2015	A	Fort Wayne	193	28	56	0	16	290	344	326	671	8	91	0.89	5	10	11	36	4.03
2016	A+	Lake Elsinore	466	71	154	5	52	330	383	440	823	8	92	1.11	7	13	23	109	5.77
2016	AAA	El Paso	9	6	4	1	3	444	643	778	1421	36	89	5.00	1	0	25	333	14.29
2017	AA	San Antonio	442	77	131	3	38	296	390	380	770	13	85	1.05	7	5	21	84	5.44

Young SS/2B with some of the best contact and plate skills in the minors. Exemplary feel for the barrel and ability to spray line drive to all parts of the field. Recognizes spin well and works deep into counts, and the Eye is legit. Smaller frame not conducive to much power and has only average speed. Solid defender with just enough arm for SS.

Uselton,Conner — 789 — Pittsburgh

EXP MLB DEBUT: 2021 | H/W: 6-3 185 | FUT: Starting OF | 8D

Bats R Age 19
2017 (S-2) HS (OK)
Pwr +++
BAvg ++
Spd ++++
Def +++

Year	Lev	Team	AB	R	H	HR	RBI	Avg	OB	Slg	OPS	bb%	ct%	Eye	SB	CS	x/h%	Iso	RC/G
2017	Rk	GCL Pirates	7	0	3	0	1	429	429	571	1000	0	86	0.00	0	0	33	143	7.25

Has solid across-the-board tools, including plus bat speed and solid raw power give him the potential to develop into a corner OF. Shows good range and a plus arm. Length in swing raises concerns about his ability to hit for average but he showed a more patient all-fields approach as a HS senior.

Valera,Breyvic — 479 — St. Louis

EXP MLB DEBUT: 2017 | H/W: 5-11 160 | FUT: Utility player | 6B

Bats B Age 26
2010 FA (PN)
Pwr +
BAvg ++++
Spd +++
Def +++

Year	Lev	Team	AB	R	H	HR	RBI	Avg	OB	Slg	OPS	bb%	ct%	Eye	SB	CS	x/h%	Iso	RC/G
2015	AA	Springfield	360	37	85	3	31	236	302	297	599	9	93	1.26	2	4	16	61	3.37
2016	AA	Springfield	178	16	46	0	12	258	294	298	592	5	90	0.50	3	1	13	39	2.96
2016	AAA	Memphis	217	32	74	0	31	341	423	415	838	13	90	1.41	8	4	20	74	6.28
2017	AAA	Memphis	424	68	133	8	41	314	370	450	821	8	92	1.12	11	11	27	137	5.74
2017	MLB	St. Louis	10	0	1	0	0	100	182	100	282	9	100		0	0	0	0	0.58

Switch-hitting 2B has plus bat-on-ball skills and more BB than K in his career. Professional hitter, but only average speed and very little power. Can play almost any position and profiles as a super utility-type and finally made his MLB debut. Career .303 hitter in the minors.

Valerio,Adrian

6 | Pittsburgh | EXP MLB DEBUT: 2020 | H/W: 5-11 150 | FUT: Starting SS | 7D

Bats B Age 21
2013 FA (DR)
Pwr ++
BAvg +++
Spd ++++
Def ++++

Year	Lev	Team	AB	R	H	HR	RBI	Avg	OB	Slg	OPS	bb%	ct%	Eye	SB	CS	x/h%	Iso	RC/G
2015	Rk	GCL Pirates	188	19	41	1	17	218	269	319	588	6	81	0.36	7	0	37	101	2.80
2016	Rk	Bristol	251	21	62	2	29	247	267	323	590	3	82	0.15	7	4	23	76	2.56
2017	A	West Virginia	326	55	89	11	34	273	297	442	738	3	81	0.17	8	7	35	169	4.30

Slick fielding SS had an impressive full-season debut. Above-average speed, soft hands, and a strong arm will allow him to stick at short. Needs to be more selective at the plate and drew just 11 BB in 326 AB. Surprising pop for his size, but power is average to below.

Vallot,Chase

2 | Kansas City | EXP MLB DEBUT: 2019 | H/W: 6-0 215 | FUT: Starting C | 8D

Bats R Age 21
2014 (S-1) HS (LA)
Pwr ++++
BAvg ++
Spd ++
Def ++

Year	Lev	Team	AB	R	H	HR	RBI	Avg	OB	Slg	OPS	bb%	ct%	Eye	SB	CS	x/h%	Iso	RC/G
2014	Rk	Burlington	186	29	40	7	27	215	311	403	715	12	56	0.32	0	1	53	188	5.16
2015	A	Lexington	279	46	61	13	40	219	319	427	745	13	62	0.39	1	0	48	208	5.21
2016	Rk	AZL Royals	30	5	4	2	2	133	212	367	579	9	53	0.21	0	0	75	233	2.62
2016	A	Lexington	272	37	67	13	44	246	341	463	804	13	57	0.33	0	0	49	217	6.67
2017	A+	Wilmington	281	34	65	12	37	231	374	438	812	19	55	0.50	0	0	52	206	7.10

Very strong C whose year ended in July due to injury. Provided consistent, plus pop to all fields and drastically increased walk rate. Continues to swing and miss frequently; will not hit for much BA. Outstanding arm strength, but needs polish to finer points of catching.

Vargas,Carlos

56 | Tampa Bay | EXP MLB DEBUT: 2022 | H/W: 6-3 170 | FUT: Starting 3B | 8E

Bats R Age 19
2015 FA (DR)
Pwr +++
BAvg ++
Spd ++
Def +++

Year	Lev	Team	AB	R	H	HR	RBI	Avg	OB	Slg	OPS	bb%	ct%	Eye	SB	CS	x/h%	Iso	RC/G
2017	Rk	GCL Rays	188	21	46	5	27	245	314	394	708	9	80	0.51	2	2	39	149	4.30

Lean, wiry strong INF with significant raw power at young age. Knows strike zone and brings picky eye to plate. BA in question as swing path not conducive to consistent contact and can be jammed inside. Not much of a threat to steal bases. Split time between SS and 3B and likely to end up in corner where arm is strong enough.

Varsho,Daulton

2 | Arizona | EXP MLB DEBUT: 2020 | H/W: 5-10 190 | FUT: Starting C | 8E

Bats L Age 21
2017 (S-2) UW-Milwaukee
Pwr +++
BAvg +++
Spd ++++
Def +++

Year	Lev	Team	AB	R	H	HR	RBI	Avg	OB	Slg	OPS	bb%	ct%	Eye	SB	CS	x/h%	Iso	RC/G
2017	NCAA	UW Milwaukee	199	47	72	11	39	362	482	643	1125	19	80	1.18	10	0	39	281	10.09
2017	A-	Hillsboro	193	36	60	7	39	311	367	534	900	8	84	0.57	7	2	43	223	6.59

Athletic LH hitting backstop got off to fast pro start. Swing is compact and easy, can catch up to velocity and spray the ball around. Power profiles above-average, especially for a catcher. Leverages strength in lower half to drive ball out of park. A plus runner and a SB threat. Advanced receiver, but weak throwing arm.

Ventura,Randy

789 | Cincinnati | EXP MLB DEBUT: 2019 | H/W: 5-9 165 | FUT: Reserve OF | 6B

Bats B Age 20
2015 FA (DR)
Pwr +
BAvg +++
Spd ++++
Def +++

Year	Lev	Team	AB	R	H	HR	RBI	Avg	OB	Slg	OPS	bb%	ct%	Eye	SB	CS	x/h%	Iso	RC/G
2016	Rk	GCL Braves	194	34	55	1	32	284	365	351	716	11	84	0.81	15	6	13	67	4.64
2017	A	Rome	381	46	112	1	16	294	336	325	661	6	78	0.29	29	12	8	31	3.52
2017	A	Dayton	105	22	29	1	10	276	345	400	745	9	81	0.55	9	2	34	124	4.90

Speedy slap-hitting switch-hitter acquired in trade with ATL mid-season. Short, compact swing will expand against better breaking balls. Uses all fields and plus speed to get on base. Surprising power despite stature, but doesn't project for much HR power. Gets quick jumps, utilizing run tool on bases. A solid defender.

Verdugo,Alex

789 | Los Angeles (N) | EXP MLB DEBUT: 2017 | H/W: 6-0 205 | FUT: Starting OF | 8B

Bats L Age 21
2014 (2) HS (AZ)
Pwr +++
BAvg ++++
Spd ++
Def ++++

Year	Lev	Team	AB	R	H	HR	RBI	Avg	OB	Slg	OPS	bb%	ct%	Eye	SB	CS	x/h%	Iso	RC/G
2015	A	Great Lakes	421	50	124	5	42	295	322	394	716	4	87	0.32	13	5	24	100	4.20
2015	A+	Rancho Cuca	91	20	35	4	19	385	411	659	1070	4	87	0.33	1	0	43	275	8.22
2016	AA	Tulsa	477	58	130	13	63	273	334	407	741	8	86	0.66	2	6	28	134	4.69
2017	AAA	Oklahoma City	433	67	136	6	62	314	388	436	824	11	88	1.04	9	3	27	122	5.93
2017	MLB	LA Dodgers	23	1	4	1	1	174	240	304	544	8	83	0.50	0	1	25	130	2.11

Uses a short compact stroke and some of the best strike zone judgement in the minors to barrel balls consistently. Flat swing keeps bat in the zone but results in lots of line drives. Should develop average to above power in time. Covers ground well in the OF with a plus arm.

Vientos,Mark

56 | New York (N) | EXP MLB DEBUT: 2021 | H/W: 6-4 185 | FUT: Starting 3B | 8D

Bats R Age 18
2017 (2) HS (FL)
Pwr +++
BAvg +++
Spd ++
Def +++

Year	Lev	Team	AB	R	H	HR	RBI	Avg	OB	Slg	OPS	bb%	ct%	Eye	SB	CS	x/h%	Iso	RC/G
2017	Rk	GCL Mets	174	22	45	4	24	259	314	397	710	7	76	0.33	0	2	36	138	4.25
2017	Rk	Kingsport	17	1	5	0	2	294	333	412	745	6	76	0.25	0	0	40	118	4.77

Potential first rounder dropped to 2nd due to uneven prep season, but was solid in pro debut. Hit tool is raw, but quick hands and strong wrists produce good bat speed. His swing is long, there's power in frame, but he doesn't have idea how to use it. Not athletic enough for SS; likely a solid 3B long term. Not a runner.

Vilade,Ryan

6 | Colorado | EXP MLB DEBUT: 2021 | H/W: 6-2 194 | FUT: Starting 3B | 8D

Bats R Age 19
2017 (2) HS (OK)
Pwr ++++
BAvg +++
Spd ++
Def +++

Year	Lev	Team	AB	R	H	HR	RBI	Avg	OB	Slg	OPS	bb%	ct%	Eye	SB	CS	x/h%	Iso	RC/G
2017	Rk	Grand Junction	117	23	36	5	21	308	438	496	933	19	74	0.87	5	5	28	188	7.78

Strong, physically mature prepster has quick bat and raw power give him 20+ HR potential. Has an advanced approach at the plate, but struggles with high-end velocity. Plus arm and soft hands, but below-average range make a move from SS to 3B likely. Raw power and ability to make hard contact will be his ticket to the show.

Viloria,Meibrys

2 | Kansas City | EXP MLB DEBUT: 2020 | H/W: 5-11 175 | FUT: Starting C | 7D

Bats L Age 21
2013 FA (CB)
Pwr +++
BAvg ++
Spd ++
Def ++

Year	Lev	Team	AB	R	H	HR	RBI	Avg	OB	Slg	OPS	bb%	ct%	Eye	SB	CS	x/h%	Iso	RC/G
2014	Rk	Burlington	40	4	8	1	5	200	360	325	685	20	75	1.00	0	0	38	125	4.41
2015	Rk	Burlington	150	20	39	0	16	260	335	260	595	10	85	0.74	0	0	0	0	3.08
2016	Rk	Idaho Falls	226	54	85	6	55	376	427	606	1033	8	84	0.56	1	1	44	230	8.26
2017	A	Lexington	363	42	94	8	52	259	307	394	701	6	78	0.32	4	3	35	135	4.07

Short, stocky backstop who got off to slow start, but ended well and showed intriguing skills. Very aggressive hitter who lacks pitch selectivity. Should settle on at least average power and has strength to drive gaps. Much better with bat than glove at present. Arm strength is valued, but needs to improve receiving and release.

Vogelbach,Dan

3 | Seattle | EXP MLB DEBUT: 2016 | H/W: 6-0 250 | FUT: Starting 1B | 7B

Bats L Age 25
2011 (2) HS (FL)
Pwr ++++
BAvg ++
Spd +
Def +

Year	Lev	Team	AB	R	H	HR	RBI	Avg	OB	Slg	OPS	bb%	ct%	Eye	SB	CS	x/h%	Iso	RC/G
2016	AAA	Tacoma	154	26	37	7	32	240	403	422	825	21	78	1.24	0	0	38	182	6.29
2016	AAA	Iowa	305	53	97	16	64	318	422	548	970	15	78	0.82	0	0	37	230	7.90
2016	MLB	Seattle	12	0	1	0	0	83	154	83	237	8	50	0.17	0	0	0	0	-3.55
2017	AAA	Tacoma	459	65	133	17	83	290	391	455	846	14	79	0.78	3	1	32	166	6.26
2017	MLB	Seattle	28	0	6	0	2	214	290	250	540	10	68	0.33	0	0	17	36	2.03

Big, burly 1B who led PCL in walks. Has always been slugger with very patient approach, but hasn't yet translated to big league success. Needs to hit as he has limited skills outside of power. Can be too patient at plate and let hittable pitches go by. Hefty frame limits agility at 1B and has little to no speed. Makes decent contact for profile.

Wade,LaMonte

789 | Minnesota | EXP MLB DEBUT: 2018 | H/W: 6-1 189 | FUT: Starting OF | 7D

Bats L Age 24
2015 (9) Maryland
Pwr ++
BAvg +++
Spd +++
Def ++

Year	Lev	Team	AB	R	H	HR	RBI	Avg	OB	Slg	OPS	bb%	ct%	Eye	SB	CS	x/h%	Iso	RC/G
2015	Rk	Elizabethton	231	36	72	9	44	312	426	506	932	17	85	1.35	12	1	31	195	7.46
2015	A	Cedar Rapids	14	1	2	0	1	143	200	143	343	7	86	0.50	0	0	0	0	0.01
2016	A	Cedar Rapids	207	32	58	4	27	280	406	396	803	18	87	1.63	5	3	22	116	6.05
2016	A+	Fort Myers	110	17	35	4	24	318	375	518	893	8	85	0.59	1	1	37	200	6.48
2017	AA	Chattanooga	424	74	124	7	67	292	400	408	808	15	83	1.07	9	2	26	116	5.95

Well-rounded OF who finished 3rd in SL in walks and OBP. Has been high BA/OBP guy due to plus bat speed and knowledge of strike zone. Has shown keen ability to hit LHP. Very patient approach, but has yet to hit double-digit HR in season. Speed is average and can play any OF spot. Best in LF with fringe-average arm.

Wade,Tyler — 4679 — New York (A)

EXP MLB DEBUT: 2017 | H/W: 6-1 185 | FUT: Starting MIF | 7B

Bats L Age 23
2013 (4) HS (CA)
Pwr ++
BAvg +++
Spd ++++
Def +++

Year	Lev	Team	AB	R	H	HR	RBI	Avg	OB	Slg	OPS	bb%	ct%	Eye	SB	CS	x/h%	Iso	RC/G
2015	A+	Tampa	368	51	103	2	28	280	349	353	702	10	82	0.60	31	15	17	73	4.34
2015	AA	Trenton	113	6	23	1	3	204	217	265	483	2	79	0.08	2	1	22	62	1.11
2016	AA	Trenton	505	90	131	5	27	259	345	349	694	12	80	0.64	27	8	21	89	4.30
2017	AAA	Scranton/WB	339	68	105	7	31	310	379	460	839	10	78	0.51	26	5	31	150	6.08
2017	MLB	NY Yankees	58	7	9	0	2	155	222	224	446	8	67	0.26	1	1	44	69	0.66

Versatile prospect who finished 2nd in IL in BA and 3rd in SB. Set high in HR, but succeeds more with speed and all-fields approach. Can expand strike zone and won't have impact power bat. Has wheels to leg out doubles and is getting on base more. Plays all over diamond with ample range and arm for any spot. Has chance to be super utility player.

Wakamatsu,Luke — 6 — Cleveland

EXP MLB DEBUT: 2020 | H/W: 6-3 185 | FUT: Starting SS | 7D

Bats B Age 21
2015 (20) HS (TX)
Pwr +++
BAvg ++
Spd +++
Def +++

Year	Lev	Team	AB	R	H	HR	RBI	Avg	OB	Slg	OPS	bb%	ct%	Eye	SB	CS	x/h%	Iso	RC/G
2015	Rk	AZL Indians	105	8	28	1	12	267	336	400	736	9	62	0.28	4	2	32	133	5.30
2016	A-	Mahoning Val	69	4	16	0	9	232	293	304	598	8	83	0.50	1	1	31	72	3.05
2017	A	Lake County	377	49	90	12	53	239	298	395	694	8	73	0.32	8	5	36	156	4.01

Tall, rangy SS who had power breakout in first full season. Has been more contact-oriented in past, but has now added strength and leverage to swing. Drives ball to pull side and possesses good speed. Poor pitch recognition brings BA potential into doubt. Very good defender with clean footwork and strong, accurate arm.

Wall,Forrest — 8 — Colorado

EXP MLB DEBUT: 2019 | H/W: 6-0 176 | FUT: Starting CF | 7C

Bats L Age 22
2014 (S-1) HS (FL)
Pwr ++
BAvg +++
Spd ++++
Def +++

Year	Lev	Team	AB	R	H	HR	RBI	Avg	OB	Slg	OPS	bb%	ct%	Eye	SB	CS	x/h%	Iso	RC/G
2014	Rk	Grand Junction	157	48	50	3	24	318	418	490	909	15	80	0.84	18	5	30	172	7.27
2015	A-	Boise	10	4	5	0	1	500	688	500	1188	38	80	3.00	2	2	0	0	12.68
2015	A	Asheville	361	57	101	7	46	280	353	438	791	10	80	0.57	23	9	33	158	5.48
2016	A+	Modesto	459	57	121	6	56	264	324	355	679	8	79	0.42	22	11	21	92	3.90
2017	A+	Lancaster	87	17	26	3	16	299	365	471	836	9	82	0.56	5	3	31	172	5.86

35th overall pick in 2014 draft has been slow to develop and missed all but 22 G with shoulder injury. When healthy owns a quick left-handed bat and a good all-fields approach. Above-average speed, but not an efficient base-stealer. Move from 2B to CF seems permanent.

Walls,Taylor — 6 — Tampa Bay

EXP MLB DEBUT: 2020 | H/W: 5-10 180 | FUT: Starting SS | 7D

Bats B Age 21
2017 (3) Florida St
Pwr +
BAvg ++
Spd +++
Def +++

Year	Lev	Team	AB	R	H	HR	RBI	Avg	OB	Slg	OPS	bb%	ct%	Eye	SB	CS	x/h%	Iso	RC/G
2017	NCAA	Florida State	260	82	71	8	47	273	422	423	845	20	83	1.49	10	2	28	150	6.63
2017	A-	Hudson Valley	164	22	35	1	21	213	332	287	618	15	68	0.55	5	4	29	73	3.36

Instinctual INF with limited upside but polished tools. Lacks pop in bat and won't hit many HR, but has value in consistent glovework and pitch recognition. Sprays balls to gaps and uses average speed to leg out xbh. Some BA potential, but swing can lengthen. Not a supreme athlete, though offers solid hands and ample range at SS.

Walton,Donnie — 46 — Seattle

EXP MLB DEBUT: 2019 | H/W: 5-10 184 | FUT: Starting 2B | 7D

Bats B Age 23
2016 (5) Oklahoma St
Pwr ++
BAvg ++
Spd +++
Def +++

Year	Lev	Team	AB	R	H	HR	RBI	Avg	OB	Slg	OPS	bb%	ct%	Eye	SB	CS	x/h%	Iso	RC/G
2016	NCAA	Oklahoma St.	246	45	83	3	44	337	414	447	861	12	85	0.89	14	0	24	110	6.38
2016	A-	Everett	178	43	50	5	23	281	360	421	781	11	87	0.92	6	0	28	140	5.33
2017	Rk	AZL Mariners	16	2	5	2	5	313	353	688	1040	6	100		2	0	40	375	7.46
2017	A+	Modesto	242	37	65	2	24	269	342	368	710	10	80	0.55	6	6	29	99	4.45

Short, consistent INF who bypassed Low-A in first full season. Missed two months with broken hand. Better hitter from left side, but rarely hits HR. Owns fast bat and puts bat to ball easily. Has enough strength to hit gappers. Split time between 2B and SS and arm likely to land him at 2B. Lacks quickness, but footwork is sound.

Ward,Drew — 5 — Washington

EXP MLB DEBUT: 2019 | H/W: 6-3 215 | FUT: Reserve 3B | 7D

Bats L Age 23
2013 (3) HS (OK)
Pwr +++
BAvg ++
4.52 Spd ++
Def ++

Year	Lev	Team	AB	R	H	HR	RBI	Avg	OB	Slg	OPS	bb%	ct%	Eye	SB	CS	x/h%	Iso	RC/G
2015	Rk	GCL Nationals	13	2	2	1	2	154	313	385	697	19	38	0.38	0	0	50	231	6.64
2015	A+	Potomac	377	47	94	6	47	249	320	358	678	9	71	0.35	2	1	29	109	3.96
2016	A+	Potomac	230	36	64	11	32	278	371	491	863	13	70	0.49	0	1	42	213	6.65
2016	AA	Harrisburg	178	19	39	3	24	219	305	309	614	11	71	0.43	0	1	26	90	3.08
2017	AA	Harrisburg	413	47	97	10	53	235	325	356	681	12	68	0.42	0	0	31	121	4.07

Good pull power and some loft to his swing, but is not able to drive the ball to the opposite field, and LHP give him fits (.526 OPS in 2017). Shows plate patience, but hit tool unable to make up for alarming strikeout rate. Average defender at 3B with good arm strength but questionable accuracy. Likely a backup COR IF.

Ward,Taylor — 2 — Los Angeles (A)

EXP MLB DEBUT: 2018 | H/W: 6-1 200 | FUT: Starting C | 7C

Bats R Age 24
2015 (1) Fresno St
Pwr ++
BAvg ++
Spd ++
Def +++

Year	Lev	Team	AB	R	H	HR	RBI	Avg	OB	Slg	OPS	bb%	ct%	Eye	SB	CS	x/h%	Iso	RC/G
2015	Rk	Orem	109	20	38	2	19	349	486	459	944	21	93	3.63	5	2	18	110	8.03
2015	A	Burlington	92	10	32	1	12	348	412	413	825	10	84	0.67	1	1	13	65	5.78
2016	A+	Inland Empire	466	61	116	10	56	249	319	337	656	9	83	0.59	0	0	18	88	3.65
2017	A+	Inland Empire	207	32	50	6	30	242	351	391	743	14	79	0.81	0	0	36	150	4.99
2017	AA	Mobile	119	14	34	3	19	286	397	387	784	16	86	1.29	0	0	18	101	5.61

Defensive-oriented backstop was promoted to AA in July and handled himself with aplomb. Has strong catch-and-throw skills that pair well with receiving ability. Calls good game and should be above average defender. Bat lags behind; has advanced approach/OBP skills, but lacks bat speed and can be pull happy. Makes acceptable contact.

Warmoth,Logan — 6 — Toronto

EXP MLB DEBUT: 2019 | H/W: 6-0 190 | FUT: Starting SS | 7B

Bats R Age 22
2017 (1) North Carolina
Pwr ++
BAvg ++++
Spd +++
Def +++

Year	Lev	Team	AB	R	H	HR	RBI	Avg	OB	Slg	OPS	bb%	ct%	Eye	SB	CS	x/h%	Iso	RC/G
2017	NCAA	North Carolina	271	60	91	10	49	336	398	554	951	9	83	0.60	18	3	37	218	7.30
2017	Rk	GCL Blue Jays	21	2	5	1	3	238	273	381	654	5	90	0.50	1	0	20	143	3.42
2017	A-	Vancouver	160	18	49	1	20	306	335	419	754	4	79	0.21	5	2	29	113	4.70

Savvy INF who has chance to be solid player with both bat and glove. Fundamentally-sound SS with sufficient range and accurate, plus arm. Hands work well and could play 2B down the line. Not a big power guy, but can pull balls out of park. Swings quick bat with simple approach and has barrel control for solid, hard contact. No major weaknesses.

Waters,Drew — 789 — Atlanta

EXP MLB DEBUT: 2021 | H/W: 6-2 185 | FUT: Starting OF | 8E

Bats B Age 19
2017 (2) HS (GA)
Pwr +++
BAvg +++
Spd ++++
Def ++++

Year	Lev	Team	AB	R	H	HR	RBI	Avg	OB	Slg	OPS	bb%	ct%	Eye	SB	CS	x/h%	Iso	RC/G
2017	Rk	Danville	149	20	38	2	14	255	327	383	710	10	60	0.27	4	2	37	128	4.92
2017	Rk	GCL Braves	49	13	17	2	10	347	429	571	1000	13	78	0.64	2	1	35	224	8.25

Toolsy, athletic switch-hitting OF with raw hit tool from both sides of plate, but susceptible to velocity, especially from LH box. Room to grow in power. Currently generates power through swing trajectory. A plus runner, has yet to translate to SBs. Run tool and arm play anywhere; has advanced feel for CF.

Wawoe,Gianfranco — 4579 — Seattle

EXP MLB DEBUT: 2019 | H/W: 5-11 170 | FUT: Utility player | 7D

Bats B Age 23
2011 FA (CC)
Pwr ++
BAvg +++
Spd +++
Def +++

Year	Lev	Team	AB	R	H	HR	RBI	Avg	OB	Slg	OPS	bb%	ct%	Eye	SB	CS	x/h%	Iso	RC/G
2015	AA	Jackson	12	1	4	0	0	333	333	500	833	0	92	0.00	0	1	50	167	5.45
2016	A+	Bakersfield	396	72	114	8	55	288	341	391	733	7	85	0.52	12	5	22	104	4.52
2017	A+	Modesto	374	36	101	2	62	270	312	364	676	6	84	0.39	15	8	25	94	3.86
2017	AA	Arkansas	58	8	14	0	7	241	267	328	594	3	86	0.25	2	0	36	86	2.86
2017	AAA	Tacoma	6	0	0	0	0	0	0	0	0	0	83	0.00	0	0		0	-4.39

Versatile prospect who is making strides with bat. Plays multiple positions, though master of none. Has range at all spots and enough arm to be asset. Hands are soft and quick for middle INF. Offers clean stroke from both sides for line drives to gaps. Has strength to reach seats, but HR output has declined in each of last two seasons.

Welker,Colton — 5 — Colorado

EXP MLB DEBUT: 2021 | H/W: 6-2 195 | FUT: Starting 3B | 8C

Bats R Age 20
2016 (4) HS (FL)
Pwr +++
BAvg ++++
Spd ++
Def +++

Year	Lev	Team	AB	R	H	HR	RBI	Avg	OB	Slg	OPS	bb%	ct%	Eye	SB	CS	x/h%	Iso	RC/G
2016	Rk	Grand Junction	210	38	69	5	36	329	368	490	858	6	87	0.46	6	4	32	162	5.93
2017	A	Asheville	254	32	89	6	33	350	393	500	893	7	83	0.43	5	7	28	150	6.40

Professional hitter has an advanced approach at the plate. Good pitch recognition and bat speed allows him to barrel balls consistently to all fields. Above-average defender at 3B with soft hands, good lateral movement and a strong arm. After two seasons owns a slash line of .341/.385/.496.

Wendle,Joey — 45 — Tampa Bay

EXP MLB DEBUT: 2016 | H/W: 6-1 190 | FUT: Starting 2B | 7D

Bats L Age 27
2012 (6) West Chester
Pwr ++
BAvg +++
Spd ++
Def +++

Year	Lev	Team	AB	R	H	HR	RBI	Avg	OB	Slg	OPS	bb%	ct%	Eye	SB	CS	x/h%	Iso	RC/G
2015	AAA	Nashville	577	80	167	10	57	289	316	442	757	4	80	0.19	12	2	36	153	4.68
2016	AAA	Nashville	491	81	137	12	61	279	315	452	767	5	77	0.23	14	4	38	173	4.89
2016	MLB	Oakland	96	11	25	1	11	260	304	302	606	6	83	0.38	2	0	8	42	2.89
2017	AAA	Nashville	478	67	136	8	54	285	312	429	741	4	83	0.23	13	4	33	144	4.47
2017	MLB	Oakland	13	3	4	1	5	308	357	615	973	7	77	0.33	0	0	50	308	7.39

Steady, consistent INF who continues to produce, but lacks plus tools. Offers moderate power to pull side and uses short stroke to make acceptable contact. Feel for bat control has led to moderately high BA, though rarely draws walks. Only owns average speed, but runs bases with savvy and instincts. Mostly 2B in minors and makes routine plays.

Westbrook,Jamie — 47 — Arizona

EXP MLB DEBUT: 2018 | H/W: 5-9 170 | FUT: Reserve 2B | 6C

Bats R Age 22
2013 (5) HS (AZ)
Pwr ++
BAvg ++
Spd +++
Def +++

Year	Lev	Team	AB	R	H	HR	RBI	Avg	OB	Slg	OPS	bb%	ct%	Eye	SB	CS	x/h%	Iso	RC/G
2014	A	South Bend	509	69	132	8	49	259	311	375	686	7	81	0.39	6	3	30	116	3.95
2015	A+	Visalia	480	75	153	17	72	319	351	510	862	5	86	0.35	14	4	35	192	5.85
2016	AA	Mobile	435	50	114	5	36	262	304	349	653	6	86	0.43	10	5	24	87	3.57
2017	Rk	AZL Dbacks	7	1	2	1	1	286	286	714	1000	0	100		0	0	50	429	6.56
2017	AA	Jackson	377	38	100	8	55	265	295	395	690	4	89	0.37	2	2	30	130	3.93

Smallish RH MIF repeated Double-A with similar results. Solid hand-eye coordination but chases pitches out of zone. Doesn't seem to read spin well. Surprising power that comes from leverage and lower body strength. An average runner and defender, profiles best at 2B. Saw time in LF in 2017.

Whatley,Matt — 2 — Texas

EXP MLB DEBUT: 2020 | H/W: 5-10 200 | FUT: Starting C | 7C

Bats R Age 22
2017 (3) Oral Roberts
Pwr +++
BAvg +++
Spd ++
Def +++

Year	Lev	Team	AB	R	H	HR	RBI	Avg	OB	Slg	OPS	bb%	ct%	Eye	SB	CS	x/h%	Iso	RC/G
2017	NCAA	Oral Roberts	212	45	64	11	49	302	435	509	945	19	81	1.22	10	1	34	208	7.70
2017	Rk	AZL Rangers	17	5	6	0	3	353	421	471	892	11	82	0.67	0	1	17	118	6.83
2017	A-	Spokane	149	23	43	6	25	289	358	450	807	10	81	0.57	3	4	28	161	5.45

Strong-armed backstop with quick release who has skill set to move quickly through minors. Receiving needs polish, but footwork and agility are sound. No plus offensive tool, though brings disciplined eye to plate and can exhibit pull power. Consistent, hard contact is focus and will smash line drives to gaps.

White,Evan — 3 — Seattle

EXP MLB DEBUT: 2019 | H/W: 6-3 205 | FUT: Starting 1B | 8C

Bats R Age 21
2017 (1) Kentucky
Pwr +++
BAvg +++
Spd ++
Def ++++

Year	Lev	Team	AB	R	H	HR	RBI	Avg	OB	Slg	OPS	bb%	ct%	Eye	SB	CS	x/h%	Iso	RC/G
2017	NCAA	Kentucky	212	48	79	10	41	373	439	637	1076	11	85	0.81	5	2	44	264	8.77
2017	A-	Everett	47	6	13	3	12	277	358	532	890	11	87	1.00	1	1	38	255	6.49

Talented prospect on both sides of ball who missed time upon signing due to quad injury. Possesses innate bat control for easy contact and plate coverage. Could hit for plus BA, but will need to add loft to level swing path to realize pop potential. Quite athletic for size and can play OF with plus arm. Has agility and quality footwork at 1B.

Whitefield,Aaron — 8 — Minnesota

EXP MLB DEBUT: 2020 | H/W: 6-4 200 | FUT: Starting CF | 7D

Bats R Age 21
2015 FA (AU)
Pwr ++
BAvg ++
Spd ++++
Def +++

Year	Lev	Team	AB	R	H	HR	RBI	Avg	OB	Slg	OPS	bb%	ct%	Eye	SB	CS	x/h%	Iso	RC/G
2016	Rk	GCL Twins	191	30	57	2	17	298	362	366	728	9	75	0.40	31	9	16	68	4.56
2017	A	Cedar Rapids	413	66	108	11	57	262	313	414	727	7	71	0.26	33	9	32	153	4.51

Tall, raw CF who started strong but faded at midseason. Brings athletic approach to game with plus speed and strong defense in CF, including range and an average arm. Approach needs work along with pitch recognition; makes lots of outs lunging at balls. Exhibits all five tools and has projectable frame to grow into plus power.

Whitley,Garrett — 789 — Tampa Bay

EXP MLB DEBUT: 2020 | H/W: 6-1 195 | FUT: Starting OF | 8D

Bats R Age 21
2015 (1) HS (NY)
Pwr +++
BAvg ++
Spd ++++
Def +++

Year	Lev	Team	AB	R	H	HR	RBI	Avg	OB	Slg	OPS	bb%	ct%	Eye	SB	CS	x/h%	Iso	RC/G
2015	Rk	GCL Rays	96	12	18	3	13	188	304	365	668	14	74	0.64	5	4	50	177	3.97
2015	A-	Hudson Valley	42	3	6	0	4	143	234	190	425	11	71	0.42	3	1	17	48	0.51
2016	A-	Hudson Valley	256	38	68	1	31	266	343	379	722	10	71	0.40	21	5	29	113	4.77
2017	A	Bowling Green	358	65	89	13	61	249	352	430	782	14	66	0.47	21	4	39	182	5.71

Very athletic OF who got off to slow start in first full-season experience. Developing well with bat with premium bat speed. Runs extremely well and steals lots of bases due to getting on base via walk. Pitch recognition is OK, but fans often by expanding strike zone. Improving arm strength and exhibits above avg range.

Wilkerson,Steve — 45 — Baltimore

EXP MLB DEBUT: 2018 | H/W: 6-1 195 | FUT: Utility player | 6B

Bats B Age 26
2014 (8) Clemson
Pwr ++
BAvg +++
Spd +++
Def ++

Year	Lev	Team	AB	R	H	HR	RBI	Avg	OB	Slg	OPS	bb%	ct%	Eye	SB	CS	x/h%	Iso	RC/G
2015	A	Delmarva	342	61	98	2	30	287	370	371	741	12	75	0.54	10	5	21	85	4.94
2016	A+	Frederick	402	49	101	4	36	251	327	343	670	10	76	0.46	18	6	25	92	3.89
2016	AA	Bowie	9	1	2	0	0	222	222	222	444	0	89	0.00	0	0	0	0	0.93
2017	A+	Frederick	155	29	50	2	15	323	397	426	822	11	74	0.48	2	3	24	103	5.98
2017	AA	Bowie	245	34	72	6	30	294	347	420	768	8	78	0.38	5	2	26	127	4.93

Had breakout season with stick—set highs in BA, HR, and doubles and is good hitter from both sides. More pop from right and better BA from left. Swings under control, but can be beaten by good velocity. SB declined, but has average speed. Has the versatility and quickness to play 2B or 3B. Suspended for first 50 games of 2018 due to amphetamines.

Williams,Justin — 9 — Tampa Bay

EXP MLB DEBUT: 2018 | H/W: 6-2 215 | FUT: Starting OF | 8C

Bats L Age 22
2013 (2) HS (LA)
Pwr +++
BAvg ++++
Spd ++
Def +++

Year	Lev	Team	AB	R	H	HR	RBI	Avg	OB	Slg	OPS	bb%	ct%	Eye	SB	CS	x/h%	Iso	RC/G
2015	A	Bowling Green	387	43	110	7	42	284	308	413	721	3	80	0.17	3	1	31	129	4.16
2015	A+	Charlotte	83	8	20	0	6	241	250	301	551	1	83	0.07	3	1	25	60	2.09
2016	A+	Charlotte	194	23	64	4	31	330	350	448	798	3	87	0.23	0	1	23	119	5.00
2016	AA	Montgomery	148	20	37	6	28	250	275	446	720	3	80	0.17	0	1	41	196	4.08
2017	AA	Montgomery	366	53	110	14	72	301	365	489	854	9	81	0.54	6	2	35	189	6.06

Emerging prospect who set high in HR; finished 3rd in SL in SLG. Adding polish in all facets of game, including feel for hitting. Uses short stroke and whole field and has gotten better against LHP. Still puts ball on ground too often and can be beaten on outer half. Below average speed, though gets good jumps in OF. Finished strong.

Williams,Nonie — 6 — Los Angeles (A)

EXP MLB DEBUT: 2021 | H/W: 6-2 200 | FUT: Starting SS | 8E

Bats B Age 19
2016 (3) HS (KS)
Pwr ++
BAvg ++
Spd +++
Def ++

Year	Lev	Team	AB	R	H	HR	RBI	Avg	OB	Slg	OPS	bb%	ct%	Eye	SB	CS	x/h%	Iso	RC/G
2016	Rk	AZL Angels	156	23	38	0	11	244	280	282	563	5	74	0.20	8	3	13	38	2.21
2017	Rk	AZL Angels	168	22	37	1	15	220	280	280	560	8	68	0.26	11	3	16	60	2.24

Athletic INF who repeated Rookie ball and struggled all year. Good upside predicated on solid tools. Mostly gap power now and should evolve into potential plus pop. Exhibits average speed and will steal bags. Needs to make more consistent contact to have chance and may eventually move to 3B long-term. Has strong arm suitable for any INF spot.

Wilson,D.J. — 8 — Chicago (N)

EXP MLB DEBUT: 2020 | H/W: 5-8 177 | FUT: Reserve OF | 7D

Bats L Age 21
2015 (4) HS (OH)
Pwr +++
BAvg ++
Spd ++++
Def ++++

Year	Lev	Team	AB	R	H	HR	RBI	Avg	OB	Slg	OPS	bb%	ct%	Eye	SB	CS	x/h%	Iso	RC/G
2015	Rk	AZL Cubs	79	12	21	0	6	266	318	354	672	7	81	0.40	5	1	24	89	3.89
2016	A-	Eugene	245	37	63	3	29	257	313	371	685	8	77	0.36	21	8	32	114	3.98
2017	Rk	AZL Cubs	8	5	4	3	5	500	600	1750	2350	20	88	2.00	1	0	100	1250	22.87
2017	A	South Bend	310	56	71	9	45	229	303	419	723	10	71	0.37	15	7	46	190	4.61

Short, athletic OF scuffled in his full-season debut. Does possess plus speed and should stick in CF, but impact is limited by inability to make consistent contact and get on base. Has a short, compact stroke with at least average power, but needs a better understanding of strike zone. Needs to show some improvement.

Wilson,Marcus — 78 — Arizona

EXP MLB DEBUT: 2019 | H/W: 6-3 175 | FUT: Starting CF | 8C

Bats R Age 21
2014 (S-2) HS (CA)
Pwr +++
BAvg +++
Spd ++++
Def ++++

Year	Lev	Team	AB	R	H	HR	RBI	Avg	OB	Slg	OPS	bb%	ct%	Eye	SB	CS	x/h%	Iso	RC/G
2014	Rk	AZL Dbacks	131	15	27	1	22	206	293	275	567	11	69	0.40	4	2	19	69	2.46
2015	Rk	Missoula	213	42	55	1	22	258	358	338	696	13	71	0.54	7	4	25	80	4.45
2016	A-	Hillsboro	136	24	34	0	15	250	414	316	730	22	71	0.95	18	3	21	66	5.31
2016	A	Kane County	99	11	25	1	5	253	339	384	723	12	68	0.41	7	2	40	131	4.88
2017	A	Kane County	383	56	113	9	54	295	384	446	830	13	77	0.61	15	7	31	151	6.10

Super-athletic OF has added strength and overall refinement to game. After three relatively quiet seasons, exploded on scene. Pitch recognition skills took step forward, swing became more compact and raw power began peeking through. A fast runner, very efficient on base path. True CF defensively.

Winker,Jesse | 7 | Cincinnati | EXP MLB DEBUT: 2017 | H/W: 6-3 215 | FUT: Starting OF | 8B

Bats L Age 24	Year	Lev	Team	AB	R	H	HR	RBI	Avg	OB	Slg	OPS	bb%	ct%	Eye	SB	CS	x/h%	Iso	RC/G
2012 (S-1) HS (FL)	2015	AA	Pensacola	443	69	125	13	55	282	385	433	818	14	81	0.89	8	4	31	151	5.95
Pwr +++	2016	Rk	AZL Reds	13	6	6	2	6	462	533	923	1456	13	69	0.50	0	0	33	462	14.68
BAvg ++++	2016	AAA	Louisville	380	39	115	3	45	303	396	384	781	13	84	1.00	0	0	22	82	5.55
Spd ++	2017	AAA	Louisville	299	33	94	2	41	314	392	408	800	11	85	0.83	2	4	26	94	5.67
Def ++	2017	MLB	Cincinnati	121	21	36	7	15	298	375	529	904	11	80	0.63	1	1	39	231	6.70

Advanced LH hitter who has struggled w/ hitting identity and injuries as professional. Made MLB debut in '17, hitting well in several stints. Bat-to-ball skills and approach both plus. Promising power potential disappeared for 2 years, came back 2nd half of '17. Smart base runner, will sneak SBs. Limited to LF due to arm.

Wiseman,Rhett | 9 | Washington | EXP MLB DEBUT: 2019 | H/W: 6-0 200 | FUT: Starting OF | 7C

Bats L Age 23	Year	Lev	Team	AB	R	H	HR	RBI	Avg	OB	Slg	OPS	bb%	ct%	Eye	SB	CS	x/h%	Iso	RC/G
2015 (3) Vanderbilt																				
Pwr +++	2015	NCAA	Vanderbilt	290	70	92	15	49	317	400	566	966	12	75	0.55	12	2	41	248	7.82
BAvg ++	2015	A-	Auburn	210	25	52	5	35	248	307	376	683	8	75	0.35	6	2	33	129	3.89
4.27 Spd +++	2016	A	Hagerstown	478	71	122	13	75	255	315	410	725	8	78	0.40	19	10	35	155	4.46
Def ++	2017	A+	Potomac	432	55	99	13	55	229	285	391	677	7	78	0.35	2	4	39	162	3.78

Steady line-drive hitter who makes good contact with a bit of power and improved going opposite field in 2017. Won't have huge HR numbers, but works counts and takes walks. Good speed, but inefficient baserunner. Solid COR outfielder who moves well and has the arm to play RF. Would benefit from more loft to his swing.

Wong,Connor | 2 | Los Angeles (N) | EXP MLB DEBUT: 2020 | H/W: 6-1 181 | FUT: Utility player | 7D

Bats R Age 21	Year	Lev	Team	AB	R	H	HR	RBI	Avg	OB	Slg	OPS	bb%	ct%	Eye	SB	CS	x/h%	Iso	RC/G
2017 (3) Houston																				
Pwr +++																				
BAvg ++	2017	NCAA	Houston	265	61	76	12	36	287	361	494	856	10	82	0.63	26	4	37	208	6.13
Spd +++	2017	Rk	AZL Dodgers	1	0	0	0	0	0	0	0	0	0	0	0.00	0	0		0	
Def +++	2017	A	Great Lakes	97	19	27	5	18	278	327	495	822	7	73	0.27	1	1	41	216	5.61

3rd round pick played multiple positions in college but was used exclusively at catcher in his debut. Shows average to above hit and power tools and moves well behind the plate with a strong arm and above-average speed. Future could be as a backup catcher and/or utility player.

Woodman,J.B. | 89 | St. Louis | EXP MLB DEBUT: 2019 | H/W: 6-2 195 | FUT: Starting OF | 7D

Bats L Age 23	Year	Lev	Team	AB	R	H	HR	RBI	Avg	OB	Slg	OPS	bb%	ct%	Eye	SB	CS	x/h%	Iso	RC/G
2016 (2) Mississippi																				
Pwr +++	2016	NCAA	Mississippi	232	53	75	14	55	323	408	578	985	12	79	0.69	12	7	40	254	7.85
BAvg ++	2016	A-	Vancouver	195	28	53	3	24	272	369	421	789	13	63	0.42	10	2	42	149	6.16
Spd +++	2016	A	Lansing	34	5	15	1	5	441	500	588	1088	11	62	0.31	0	1	20	147	10.84
Def +++	2017	A	Lansing	362	44	87	7	45	240	316	378	694	10	57	0.25	8	4	36	138	4.89

Toolsy OF who looks part of solid prospect, but detracts from skills by poor hand-eye coordination and erratic swing. Could evolve into power-hitting OF who gets on base consistently. Piles up strikeouts by viciously swinging at balls. Owns above average speed and solid defensive ability. Can play CF, though likely better in RF with strong arm.

Yerzy,Andy | 2 | Arizona | EXP MLB DEBUT: 2021 | H/W: 6-3 215 | FUT: Starting C | 8E

Bats L Age 19	Year	Lev	Team	AB	R	H	HR	RBI	Avg	OB	Slg	OPS	bb%	ct%	Eye	SB	CS	x/h%	Iso	RC/G
2016 (2) HS (ON)																				
Pwr ++++																				
BAvg ++	2016	Rk	Missoula	60	2	15	0	1	250	250	283	533	0	73	0.00	0	1	13	33	1.56
Spd ++	2016	Rk	AZL Dbacks	102	5	20	1	15	196	226	255	481	4	78	0.18	0	0	20	59	1.16
Def +	2017	Rk	Missoula	225	36	67	13	45	298	365	524	890	10	80	0.53	0	0	37	227	6.43

Powerful Canadian bat-first catcher who enjoyed explosive rookie ball season. Power is immense, though long-lumbering swing took advantage of inferior pitching. Will need to shorten up to be effective hitter in upper minors. Poor defensive catcher; very clunky behind home plate. Will need time to develop.

Ynfante,Wadye | 789 | St. Louis | EXP MLB DEBUT: 2020 | H/W: 6-0 160 | FUT: Starting CF | 8D

Bats R Age 20	Year	Lev	Team	AB	R	H	HR	RBI	Avg	OB	Slg	OPS	bb%	ct%	Eye	SB	CS	x/h%	Iso	RC/G
2014 FA (DR)																				
Pwr +++																				
BAvg +++																				
Spd +++	2016	Rk	GCL Cardinals	17	1	1	0	0	59	111	59	170	6	76	0.25	0	1	0	0	-2.82
Def +++	2017	Rk	Johnson City	167	27	50	7	23	299	364	491	855	9	69	0.33	11	3	36	192	6.40

Wiry, athletic OF moves well defensively with good range and a decent arm. Has a good all-fields approach at the plate with plus bat speed and impressive raw power, though strikes out a ton. Runs well, but isn't a true burner. Interesting upside.

Young,Chesny | 456 | Chicago (N) | EXP MLB DEBUT: 2018 | H/W: 6-0 170 | FUT: Utility player | 7D

Bats R Age 25	Year	Lev	Team	AB	R	H	HR	RBI	Avg	OB	Slg	OPS	bb%	ct%	Eye	SB	CS	x/h%	Iso	RC/G
2014 (14) Mercer	2014	A	Kane County	105	14	34	0	9	324	355	419	774	5	79	0.23	2	1	24	95	4.99
Pwr +	2015	A	South Bend	108	23	34	0	14	315	383	380	763	10	94	1.71	9	3	18	65	5.33
BAvg ++++	2015	A+	Myrtle Beach	402	65	129	1	30	321	389	388	777	10	89	1.02	12	5	17	67	5.37
Spd ++	2016	AA	Tennessee	491	60	149	4	37	303	376	387	763	10	87	0.89	16	14	21	84	5.17
Def +++	2017	AAA	Iowa	425	56	109	1	33	256	310	311	621	7	84	0.47	7	6	19	54	3.24

Uses a compact stroke to shoot line drives to all fields with plus bat-to-ball skills. Struggled for first time as a pro in 2017, but career slash line remains .298/.365/.368. Continues to play multiple positions, but fantasy impact is limited by barely-existent power.

Zagunis,Mark | 79 | Chicago (N) | EXP MLB DEBUT: 2017 | H/W: 6-0 205 | FUT: Reserve OF | 7C

Bats R Age 25	Year	Lev	Team	AB	R	H	HR	RBI	Avg	OB	Slg	OPS	bb%	ct%	Eye	SB	CS	x/h%	Iso	RC/G
2014 (3) Virginia Tech	2015	A+	Myrtle Beach	413	78	112	8	54	271	389	412	801	16	79	0.93	12	10	33	140	5.92
Pwr ++	2016	AA	Tennessee	179	30	54	4	24	302	402	453	854	14	80	0.83	1	2	33	151	6.48
BAvg +++	2016	AAA	Iowa	179	31	49	6	25	274	353	486	839	11	77	0.52	4	0	45	212	6.14
Spd +++	2017	AAA	Iowa	330	59	88	13	55	267	395	455	850	18	72	0.75	4	3	40	188	6.62
Def +++	2017	MLB	Chi Cubs	14	0	0	0	1	0	222	0	222	22	57	0.67	2	0		0	-3.82

Converted backstop has stalled as he's moved up and will have to work hard to establish himself as an everyday player. Has solid across the board tools, but none that are plus. Broken foot in 2016 slowed his development and speed is now average. Has a good approach at the plate with career best in walks and HR in 2017.

Zavala,Seby | 2 | Chicago (A) | EXP MLB DEBUT: 2019 | H/W: 5-11 205 | FUT: Starting C | 7D

Bats R Age 24	Year	Lev	Team	AB	R	H	HR	RBI	Avg	OB	Slg	OPS	bb%	ct%	Eye	SB	CS	x/h%	Iso	RC/G
2015 (12) San Diego St	2015	NCAA	San Diego St	231	42	67	14	67	290	372	537	908	11	77	0.58	4	2	42	247	6.84
Pwr +++	2015	Rk	AZL White Sox	129	33	42	4	35	326	396	628	1024	10	79	0.56	2	0	62	302	8.58
BAvg ++	2016	A	Kannapolis	360	40	91	7	49	253	319	381	700	9	70	0.32	1	1	32	128	4.26
Spd +	2017	A	Kannapolis	185	32	48	13	34	259	308	514	822	7	72	0.25	0	0	44	254	5.53
Def +++	2017	A+	Winston-Salem	202	31	61	8	38	302	376	485	861	11	74	0.46	1	0	34	183	6.36

Bat-first catcher who broke out both at plate and behind dish. Advanced approach, works pitcher. Swing path quick and compact, but can get beat by velocity. Power in frame; 21 HR between 2 levels, but sells out to pull side. Defensively, pitchers prefer throwing to him. Solid catch-throw ability, but struggles with blocking.

Ziegler,Malique | 8 | San Francisco | EXP MLB DEBUT: 2020 | H/W: 6-2 170 | FUT: Starting CF | 7E

Bats R Age 21	Year	Lev	Team	AB	R	H	HR	RBI	Avg	OB	Slg	OPS	bb%	ct%	Eye	SB	CS	x/h%	Iso	RC/G
2016 (22) North Iowa Area JC																				
Pwr ++																				
BAvg ++																				
Spd ++++	2016	Rk	AZL Giants	62	11	18	0	5	290	389	419	808	14	76	0.67	4	1	33	129	6.09
Def ++	2017	A-	Salem-Keizer	254	46	61	5	24	240	316	374	690	10	74	0.42	26	9	31	134	4.13

Extremely athletic OF with lean frame and plenty of projection. Has double-plus wheels which allow him to steal loads of bases and track down balls in CF. Needs to work counts more to get on base. Swing geared more towards line drives than power, but could add hint more pop with added strength. CF routes need polish and could build arm strength.

Zimmerman,Jordan | 4 | Los Angeles (A) | EXP MLB DEBUT: 2019 | H/W: 6-1 195 | FUT: Starting 2B | 7D

Bats R Age 23	Year	Lev	Team	AB	R	H	HR	RBI	Avg	OB	Slg	OPS	bb%	ct%	Eye	SB	CS	x/h%	Iso	RC/G
2016 (7) Michigan St	2016	NCAA	Michigan State	219	50	82	9	37	374	454	594	1048	13	85	0.97	10	6	34	219	8.60
Pwr ++	2016	Rk	Orem	83	22	35	4	22	422	461	639	1099	7	86	0.50	4	1	26	217	8.65
BAvg +++	2016	A	Burlington	130	15	20	0	13	154	231	208	438	9	74	0.38	0	3	30	54	0.76
Spd ++	2017	A	Burlington	326	43	88	5	43	270	326	393	718	8	76	0.34	8	4	27	123	4.41
Def +++	2017	A+	Inland Empire	184	30	54	4	28	293	330	457	786	5	78	0.24	1	0	39	163	5.13

Improving prospect with both the bat and glove. Performed on two levels in 2017 and better in A+. Decent hitter with average strength and raw power resulting in lots of doubles, but can overswing and lead to Ks. Doesn't have good speed, but owns clean hands and fundamental footwork. Could be utility guy.

Pitchers are classified as Starters (SP) or Relievers (RP).

THROWS: Handedness — right (RH) or left (LH).

AGE: Pitcher's age, as of April 1, 2018.

DRAFTED: The year, round, and school that the pitcher performed at as an amateur if drafted, or the year and country where the player was signed from, if a free agent.

EXP MLB DEBUT: The year a player is expected to debut in the major leagues.

H/W: The player's height and weight.

FUT: The role that the pitcher is expected to have for the majority of his major league career, not necessarily his greatest upside.

PITCHES: Each pitch that a pitcher throws is graded and designated with a "+", indicating the quality of the pitch, taking into context the pitcher's age and level pitched. Pitches are graded for their velocity, movement, and command. An average pitch will receive three "+" marks. If known, a pitcher's velocity for each pitch is indicated.

FB	fastball
CB	curveball
SP	split-fingered fastball
SL	slider
CU	change-up
CT	cut-fastball
KC	knuckle-curve
KB	knuckle-ball
SC	screwball
SU	slurve

PLAYER STAT LINES: Pitchers receive statistics for the last five teams that they played for (if applicable), including college and the major leagues.

TEAM DESIGNATIONS: Each team that the pitcher performed for during a given year is included.

LEVEL DESIGNATIONS: The level for each team a player performed is included. "AAA" means Triple-A, "AA" means Double-A, "A+" means high Class-A, "A-" means low Class-A and "Rk" means rookie level.

SABERMETRIC CATEGORIES: Descriptions of all the sabermetric categories appear in the glossary.

CAPSULE COMMENTARIES: For each pitcher, a brief analysis of their skills/statistics, and their future potential is provided.

ELIGIBILITY: Eligibility for inclusion is the standard for which Major League Baseball adheres to; 50 innings pitched or 45 days on the 25-man roster, not including the month of September.

POTENTIAL RATINGS: The Potential Ratings are a two-part system in which a player is assigned a number rating based on his upside potential (1-10) and a letter rating based on the probability of reaching that potential (A-E).

Potential

10:	Hall of Famer	5:	MLB reserve
9:	Elite player	4:	Top minor leaguer
8:	Solid regular	3:	Average minor leaguer
7:	Average regular	2:	Minor league reserve
6:	Platoon player	1:	Minor league roster filler

Probability Rating

A:	90% probability of reaching potential
B:	70% probability of reaching potential
C:	50% probability of reaching potential
D:	30% probability of reaching potential
E:	10% probability of reaching potential

FASTBALL: Scouts grade a fastball in terms of both velocity and movement. Movement of a pitch is purely subjective, but one can always watch the hitter to see how he reacts to a pitch or if he swings and misses. Pitchers throw four types of fastballs with varying movement. A two-seam fastball is often referred to as a sinker. A four-seam fastball appears to maintain its plane at high velocities. A cutter can move in different directions and is caused by the pitcher both cutting-off his extension out front and by varying the grip. A split-fingered fastball (forkball) is thrown with the fingers spread apart against the seams and demonstrates violent downward movement. Velocity is often graded on the 20-80 scale and is indicated by the chart below.

Scout Grade	Velocity (mph)
80	96+
70	94-95
60	92-93
50 (avg)	89-91
40	87-88
30	85-86
20	82-84

PITCHER RELEASE TIMES: The speed (in seconds) that a pitcher releases a pitch from the stretch is extremely important in terms of halting the running game and establishing good pitching mechanics. Pitchers are timed from the movement of the front leg until the baseball reaches the catcher's mitt. The phrases "slow to the plate" or "quick to the plate" may appear in the capsule commentary box.

1.0-1.2	+
1.3-1.4	MLB average
1.5+	–

Abbott, Cory

SP | **Chicago (N)** | EXP MLB DEBUT: 2020 | H/W: 6-2 210 | FUT: #4 starter | **7D**

Thrws R Age 22
2017 (2) Loyola Marymount

91-93	FB	++
85-88	CT	+++
75-78	CB	++
	CU	++

Year	Lev	Team	W	L	Sv	IP	K	ERA	WHIP	BF/G	OBA	H%	S%	xERA	Ctl	Dom	Cmd	hr/9	BPV
2017	NCAA	Loyola Marym't	11	2	0	98	130	1.74	0.91	24.4	181	28	81	1.31	2.6	11.9	4.6	0.3	163
2017	A-	Eugene	0	0	0	14	18	3.86	1.21	11.3	262	38	69	3.43	1.9	11.6	6.0	0.6	174

2nd round pick out of Loyola had a solid if brief pro debut. Lacks a true plus offering with fastball sitting at 91-93 mph, backed up by a cutter, curveball, and change-up. Throws all four offerings for strikes and hides the ball well. Stocky frame profiles as a back end starter.

Abreu,Albert

SP | **New York (A)** | EXP MLB DEBUT: 2019 | H/W: 6-2 175 | FUT: #3 starter | **8C**

Thrws R Age 22
2013 FA (DR)

92-96	FB	++++
79-81	CB	+++
82-85	SL	++
84-88	CU	++

Year	Lev	Team	W	L	Sv	IP	K	ERA	WHIP	BF/G	OBA	H%	S%	xERA	Ctl	Dom	Cmd	hr/9	BPV
2016	A	Quad Cities	2	8	4	90	104	3.50	1.23	17.4	196	28	72	2.53	4.9	10.4	2.1	0.5	73
2016	A+	Lancaster	1	0	0	11	11	5.63	1.88	17.5	275	33	74	6.22	7.2	8.8	1.2	1.6	-18
2017	Rk	GCL Yankees	0	0	0	4	8	2.20	0.73	7.3	206	46	67	0.84	0.0	17.6		0.0	334
2017	A	Charleston (Sc)	1	0	0	14	22	1.90	0.85	17.3	184	31	82	1.50	1.9	13.9	7.3	0.6	218
2017	A+	Tampa	1	3	0	34	31	4.22	1.41	16.0	255	32	70	3.76	4.0	8.2	2.1	0.5	58

Raw, talented SP who missed parts of season with elbow flare-ups. Pure stuff is among best in organization, but needs to mix better. Plus FB can overwhelm hitters with extreme velocity and movement. Varies speeds on breaking balls and hard CB is better of two. CU is distant 4th pitch but shows potential to be weapon against LHH. Needs to watch control.

Acevedo,Domingo

SP | **New York (A)** | EXP MLB DEBUT: 2018 | H/W: 6-7 250 | FUT: #2 starter | **9D**

Thrws R Age 23
2012 FA (DR)

93-99	FB	+++++
80-84	SL	++
85-87	CU	+++

Year	Lev	Team	W	L	Sv	IP	K	ERA	WHIP	BF/G	OBA	H%	S%	xERA	Ctl	Dom	Cmd	hr/9	BPV
2016	A	Charleston (Sc)	3	1	0	42		1.92	0.97	20.0	222	32	80	1.92	1.5	10.2	6.9	0.2	162
2016	A+	Tampa	2	3	0	50	54	3.23	1.28	20.5	258	35	75	3.46	2.7	9.7	3.6	0.5	120
2017	A+	Tampa	0	4	0	41	52	4.60	1.41	24.8	297	41	70	4.87	2.0	11.4	5.8	1.1	170
2017	AA	Trenton	5	1	0	79	82	2.39	1.04	21.8	226	29	82	2.79	1.9	9.3	4.8	0.9	134
2017	AAA	Scranton/WB	1	1	0	12	8	4.46	1.65	27.1	260	31	70	3.97	6.0	6.0	1.0	0.0	-36

Imposing SP with elite FB and very high K potential. All three pitches thrown with exceptional arm speed. SL needs polish, but throws with conviction; its development will determine future role. CU flashes plus and has consistent fading action. Exhibits nimble control for power stuff and doesn't beat himself. Some concern about injury history.

Adams,Chance

SP | **New York (A)** | EXP MLB DEBUT: 2018 | H/W: 6-1 210 | FUT: #3 starter | **8A**

Thrws R Age 23
2015 (5) Dallas Baptist

91-95	FB	++++
83-86	SL	++++
78-80	CB	++
82-85	CU	+++

Year	Lev	Team	W	L	Sv	IP	K	ERA	WHIP	BF/G	OBA	H%	S%	xERA	Ctl	Dom	Cmd	hr/9	BPV
2015	A+	Tampa	1	0	0	14	16	1.29	1.00	10.7	233	34	86	1.92	1.3	10.3	8.0	0.0	168
2016	A+	Tampa	5	0	0	57	73	2.67	0.98	18.1	203	30	75	2.08	2.4	11.5	4.9	0.6	161
2016	AA	Trenton	8	1	0	69	71	2.08	0.85	19.5	152	19	80	1.24	3.1	9.2	3.0	0.7	100
2017	AA	Trenton	4	0	0	35	32	1.03	1.09	22.8	189	24	94	2.11	3.9	8.2	2.1	0.5	62
2017	AAA	Scranton/WB	11	5	0	115	103	2.89	1.08	21.4	200	25	76	2.39	3.4	8.1	2.4	0.7	72

Strong, stocky SP who was good each month of season and on verge of majors. Tough to hit and has multiple K offerings in lively FB and hard, nasty SL. Pitches with ideal command and spots pitches to all quadrants. CU thrown with same arm speed and slot which adds to deception. CB lags behind, but gives him slow breaker for different look.

Adams,Spencer

SP | **Chicago (A)** | EXP MLB DEBUT: 2018 | H/W: 6-3 171 | FUT: Middle reliever | **6B**

Thrws R Age 21
2014 (2) HS (GA)

88-90	FB	++
81-83	SL	+++
82-84	CU	+++

Year	Lev	Team	W	L	Sv	IP	K	ERA	WHIP	BF/G	OBA	H%	S%	xERA	Ctl	Dom	Cmd	hr/9	BPV
2015	A	Kannapolis	9	5	0	100	73	3.24	1.22	21.3	282	33	75	3.78	1.0	6.6	6.6	0.6	110
2015	A+	Winston-Salem	3	0	0	29	23	2.16	1.31	24.0	274	34	84	3.57	2.2	7.1	3.3	0.3	88
2016	A+	Winston-Salem	8	7	0	107	74	4.03	1.32	24.6	284	33	69	4.01	1.8	6.2	3.5	0.6	82
2016	AA	Birmingham	2	5	0	55	26	3.92	1.25	24.9	275	31	67	3.49	1.6	4.2	2.6	0.3	50
2017	AA	Birmingham	7	15	0	152	113	4.43	1.39	24.6	285	32	71	4.70	2.4	6.7	2.8	1.1	74

Tall, thin RH who has struggled with poor K rates and overall lack of development. As a starter, the profile is fringy, lacking an out pitch. FB is low octane as a SP. Could add some velocity pitching out of pen. Around the zone with all three pitches. Secondary pitches are average offerings. SL could become plus if thrown harder in relief.

Adbullah, Imani

SP | **Los Angeles (N)** | EXP MLB DEBUT: 2020 | H/W: 6-4 205 | FUT: #4 starter | **7D**

Thrws R Age 20
2015 (11) HS (CA)

92-94	FB	++++
	CB	++
	CU	+++

Year	Lev	Team	W	L	Sv	IP	K	ERA	WHIP	BF/G	OBA	H%	S%	xERA	Ctl	Dom	Cmd	hr/9	BPV
2015	Rk	AZL Dodgers	0	1	0	13	13	4.85	1.08	8.4	197	28	50	1.69	3.5	9.0	2.6	0.0	87
2016	A	Great Lakes	4	4	0	72	59	3.62	1.14	17.8	256	29	74	3.77	1.5	7.4	4.9	1.2	110
2017	A	Great Lakes	0	2	0	12	13	5.21	1.57	8.9	260	34	67	4.42	5.2	9.7	1.9	0.7	51

Long, lean right-hander missed most of the season due to injury and has gotten into just 28 games since being drafted in 2015. When healthy, features an above-average low-90s fastball, curve, and change-up that flashes plus. Solid control gives this 11th rounder a chance to stick as a starter.

Adcock,Brett

SP | **Houston** | EXP MLB DEBUT: 2020 | H/W: 6-1 225 | FUT: Middle reliever | **7D**

Thrws L Age 22
2016 (4) Michigan

88-90	FB	++
73-80	CB	+++
81-85	CU	++

Year	Lev	Team	W	L	Sv	IP	K	ERA	WHIP	BF/G	OBA	H%	S%	xERA	Ctl	Dom	Cmd	hr/9	BPV
2016	NCAA	Michigan	7	5	0	78	100	3.23	1.46	22.3	191	29	77	2.89	7.1	11.5	1.6	0.3	33
2016	A-	Tri City	0	0	0	4	6	6.59	1.22	5.5	206	35	40	2.11	4.4	13.2	3.0	0.0	137
2017	A	Quad Cities	1	0	0	23	37	1.16	0.95	17.5	187	35	86	1.19	2.7	14.4	5.3	0.0	203
2017	A+	Buies Creek	4	4	1	84	80	4.71	1.31	17.3	248	31	65	3.82	3.4	8.6	2.5	1.0	80

Michigan product who lacks velocity but has racked up strikeouts as a pro. Survives off feel for and command of CB, which has the makings of a future out-pitch. FB is pedestrian 88-90 mph, but locates it well enough to set up hitters. CU remains work in progress. Strong, sturdy build; maxed out physically. Potential LOOGY if CU doesn't pan out.

Adon,Melvin

SP | **San Francisco** | EXP MLB DEBUT: 2020 | H/W: 6-3 195 | FUT: #3 starter | **8E**

Thrws R Age 23
2015 FA (DR)

94-99	FB	++++
85-88	SL	++
87-89	CU	++

Year	Lev	Team	W	L	Sv	IP	K	ERA	WHIP	BF/G	OBA	H%	S%	xERA	Ctl	Dom	Cmd	hr/9	BPV
2016	A-	Salem-Keizer	5	5	0	67	55	5.50	1.77	22.0	310	38	67	5.37	4.6	7.4	1.6	0.4	28
2017	A	Augusta	3	11	0	99	89	4.36	1.46	18.5	282	36	69	4.21	3.2	8.1	2.5	0.5	78

Live-armed SP who impressed in first full season. Uses very fast arm to generate velocity with all pitches. Needs greater separation from FB and CU, but keeps arm speed. FB features some life, but blows it by hitters up in zone. Can be hittable when pitches flatten, particularly SL. Has stuff and arm to be special, but needs lot of polish.

Agrazal, Dario

SP | **Pittsburgh** | EXP MLB DEBUT: 2020 | H/W: 6-3 216 | FUT: #3 starter | **8D**

Thrws R Age 23
2012 FA (PN)

92-95	FB	++++
	CB	+
	CU	+

Year	Lev	Team	W	L	Sv	IP	K	ERA	WHIP	BF/G	OBA	H%	S%	xERA	Ctl	Dom	Cmd	hr/9	BPV
2014	Rk	GCL Pirates	3	4	0	55	34	4.24	1.27	18.8	295	34	66	3.96	0.8	5.5	6.8	0.5	96
2015	A-	West Virginia	6	5	0	76	45	2.72	1.08	21.2	249	29	75	2.71	1.3	5.3	4.1	0.4	79
2016	A	West Virginia	8	12	0	150	88	4.20	1.27	22.7	290	32	70	4.46	1.1	5.3	4.9	1.1	84
2017	A+	Bradenton	5	3	0	80	63	2.92	1.04	22.1	244	30	72	2.61	1.1	7.1	6.3	0.4	115
2017	AA	Altoona	0	1	0	4	2	4.50	1.25	16.3	210	24	60	2.33	4.5	4.5	1.0	0.0	-23

Physically strong right-hander from Panama works off a plus 92-95 mph sinking fastball and gave up just 4 HR in 84.1 IP. Pounds the strike zone inducing weak groundballs instead of seeking strikeouts. Curve and change-up are average to below, but work to keep hitters of the heater. Should get a good test at Double-A in 2018.

Aiken,Brady

SP | **Cleveland** | EXP MLB DEBUT: 2020 | H/W: 6-4 205 | FUT: #3 starter | **8E**

Thrws L Age 21
2015 (1) HS (FL)

86-92	FB	+++
75-80	CB	+++
82-83	CU	+++

Year	Lev	Team	W	L	Sv	IP	K	ERA	WHIP	BF/G	OBA	H%	S%	xERA	Ctl	Dom	Cmd	hr/9	BPV
2015		*Did not play - injured*																	
2016	Rk	AZL Indians	0	4	0	24	35	7.13	1.88	12.5	321	49	59	5.72	4.9	13.1	2.7	0.4	123
2016	A-	Mahoning Val	2	1	0	22	22	4.48	1.27	18.1	243	30	68	3.88	3.3	9.0	2.8	1.2	91
2017	A	Lake County	5	13	0	132	89	4.77	1.78	22.5	265	30	74	5.12	6.9	6.1	0.9	0.8	-59

Tall, athletic SP who has regressed with arsenal and command. Underwent Tommy John surgery in 2015; velocity has declined from mid-90s. CB used to be much crisper, but still shows promise. Has feel for changing speeds. Led SAL in walks by a ton and needs to fine-tune release point. Tough on LHH and hitters bury ball into ground.

Akin,Keegan

SP | **Baltimore** | EXP MLB DEBUT: 2019 | H/W: 6-0 225 | FUT: #3 starter | **8D**

Thrws L Age 23
2016 (2) Western Michigan

91-94	FB	+++
81-84	SL	+++
	CU	++

Year	Lev	Team	W	L	Sv	IP	K	ERA	WHIP	BF/G	OBA	H%	S%	xERA	Ctl	Dom	Cmd	hr/9	BPV
2016	NCAA	Western Michigan	7	4	0	109	133	1.82	0.94	24.1	190	29	79	1.31	2.5	11.0	4.4	0.1	149
2016	A-	Aberdeen	0	1	0	26	29	1.04	0.85	10.6	170	25	86	0.79	2.4	10.0	4.1	0.0	133
2017	A+	Frederick	7	8	0	100	111	4.14	1.35	19.9	240	31	72	3.91	4.1	10.0	2.4	1.1	86

Compact SP who could be fast mover after skipping Low-A. Got off to slow start, but found consistency with deceptive delivery and velocity. Doesn't have plus pitch in arsenal, but FB and SL are both solid-average. FB is sneaky quick with fast arm while SL is tough on LHH. Pitches up in zone and can be hit and will need to add polish to fringy CU.

Albertos, Jose — SP — Chicago (N)

EXP MLB DEBUT: 2021 | H/W: 6-1 185 | FUT: #2 starter | **9D**

Thrws R Age 19 — 2015 FA (MX)

Velo	Pitch	Grade
94-96	FB	++++
80-83	CB	++
75-78	CU	++++

Year	Lev	Team	W	L	Sv	IP	K	ERA	WHIP	BF/G	OBA	H%	S%	xERA	Ctl	Dom	Cmd	hr/9	BPV
2016	Rk	AZL Cubs	0	0	0	4	7	0.00	0.50	13.3	81	19	100		2.3	15.8	7.0	0.0	241
2017	Rk	AZL Cubs	0	0	0	8	6	4.44	1.11	15.9	208	26	56	1.93	3.3	6.7	2.0	0.0	48
2017	A-	Eugene	2	1	0	34	42	2.89	1.11	16.8	199	31	71	1.78	3.7	11.1	3.0	0.0	117

Stock has soared since he was signed out of Mexico. Fastball sits at 93-95 topping out at 97 mph with good late sink. Slurvy breaking ball is below average, but change-up is already plus. Fringy command and lack of projection limit him to a #2 starter, but fantasy owners should follow closely.

Alcala,Jorge — SP — Houston

EXP MLB DEBUT: 2020 | H/W: 6-3 180 | FUT: #4 starter | **8E**

Thrws R Age 22 — 2014 FA (DR)

Velo	Pitch	Grade
93-96	FB	++++
84-87	SL	+++
	CU	++

Year	Lev	Team	W	L	Sv	IP	K	ERA	WHIP	BF/G	OBA	H%	S%	xERA	Ctl	Dom	Cmd	hr/9	BPV
2016	Rk	Greeneville	2	1	0	20	20	1.80	1.00	12.7	175	25	80	1.25	3.6	9.0	2.5	0.0	83
2016	Rk	GCL Astros	1	1	1	20	32	1.34	0.95	15.1	187	34	84	1.19	2.7	14.3	5.3	0.0	203
2016	A-	Tri City	0	1	0	13	15	5.45	1.82	20.4	350	46	70	6.37	2.7	10.2	3.8	0.7	128
2017	A	Quad Cities	2	0	0	31	35	2.03	0.90	19.2	155	20	84	1.59	3.5	10.2	2.9	0.9	107
2017	A+	Buies Creek	5	6	0	78	60	3.46	1.13	19.3	200	23	72	2.63	3.8	6.9	1.8	0.8	40

Dominican RH with quality velocity and a chance for two average-or-better off-speed pitches. Can run FB up to 98 mph and will show a plus SL when he's on. CU remains work in progress but has incorporated it more as he's moved up. Stays around the zone but command needs to improve. If it does, he could blossom into #4 SP with some Dom upside.

Alcantara, Sandy — SP — Miami

EXP MLB DEBUT: 2017 | H/W: 6-4 170 | FUT: #2 starter | **9E**

Thrws R Age 22 — 2013 FA (DR)

Velo	Pitch	Grade
95-97	FB	++++
83-85	CB	++
85-88	SL	++
88-91	CU	++

Year	Lev	Team	W	L	Sv	IP	K	ERA	WHIP	BF/G	OBA	H%	S%	xERA	Ctl	Dom	Cmd	hr/9	BPV
2015	Rk	GCL Cardinals	4	4	0	64		3.23	1.23	21.6	246	30	74	3.10	2.8	7.2	2.6	0.4	71
2016	A	Peoria	5	7	0	90	119	4.10	1.37	22.2	235	35	69	3.23	4.5	11.9	2.6	0.4	111
2016	A+	Palm Beach	0	4	0	32	34	3.64	1.21	21.6	216	31	67	2.26	3.9	9.5	2.4	0.0	84
2017	AA	Springfield	7	5	0	125	106	4.32	1.43	21.3	262	31	72	4.29	3.9	7.6	2.0	0.9	50
2017	MLB	St. Louis	0	0	0	8	10	4.44	1.85	4.7	283	35	85	6.82	6.7	11.1	1.7	2.2	38

Tall, lean right-hander has a big fastball that sits 95-97, topping at 102 mph. Holds velocity late into starts and backs up heater with a curve and slider that need work, and a fringe change-up. Secondary offerings and command are below average. Big time arm, but needs work to reach his full potential.

Alexander,Tyler — SP — Detroit

EXP MLB DEBUT: 2018 | H/W: 6-2 200 | FUT: #4 starter | **7C**

Thrws L Age 23 — 2015 (2) Texas Christian

Velo	Pitch	Grade
87-92	FB	+++
74-78	CB	++
77-80	SL	+++
81-83	CU	++

Year	Lev	Team	W	L	Sv	IP	K	ERA	WHIP	BF/G	OBA	H%	S%	xERA	Ctl	Dom	Cmd	hr/9	BPV
2015	NCAA	Texas Christian	6	3	0	93	72	3.09	1.09	21.5	259	31	74	3.17	1.0	7.0	7.2	0.7	117
2015	A-	Connecticut	0	2	0	37	33	0.97	0.59	10.5	140	16	95	0.55	1.2	8.0	6.6	0.7	130
2016	A+	Lakeland	6	7	0	101	82	2.14	1.00	21.5	232	28	81	2.44	1.3	7.3	5.5	0.5	113
2016	AA	Erie	2	1	0	34	23	3.17	1.17	22.7	272	30	78	3.92	1.1	6.1	5.8	1.1	99
2017	AA	Erie	8	9	0	138	120	5.08	1.46	21.9	314	37	68	5.47	1.5	7.8	5.2	1.3	118

Durable SP who fell on hard times in AA. Was very hittable by being around fat part of plate and RHH had field day. K rate rose, but likely to be below average in majors. Has excellent control and deft sequencing in profile. Changes speeds well and gets ton of groundballs from sinker. All pitches thrown for strikes.

Alexy,A.J. — SP — Texas

EXP MLB DEBUT: 2020 | H/W: 6-4 195 | FUT: #3 starter | **8D**

Thrws R Age 19 — 2016 (11) HS (PA)

Velo	Pitch	Grade
88-93	FB	+++
75-79	CB	++++
82-83	CU	++

Year	Lev	Team	W	L	Sv	IP	K	ERA	WHIP	BF/G	OBA	H%	S%	xERA	Ctl	Dom	Cmd	hr/9	BPV
2016	Rk	AZL Dodgers	1	0	0	13	12	4.77	1.52	8.2	314	37	72	5.67	2.0	8.2	4.0	1.4	110
2017	A	Hickory	1	1	0	20	27	3.12	1.39	17.0	186	25	84	3.57	6.7	12.0	1.8	1.3	54
2017	A	Great Lakes	2	6	0	73	86	3.69	1.13	15.2	182	26	66	2.00	4.5	10.6	2.3	0.4	86

Long, lean SP with ton of projection and quick arm. Plus CB exhibits nasty break and is legitimate out pitch, particularly to RHH. FB is merely average at present, but likely to add few ticks as he gains strength. Control comes and goes and has tendency to elevate ball in zone. Posted very low oppBA and has mid rotation upside.

Allard,Kolby — SP — Atlanta

EXP MLB DEBUT: 2018 | H/W: 6-1 190 | FUT: #2 starter | **9C**

Thrws L Age 20 — 2015 (1) HS (CA)

Velo	Pitch	Grade
89-94	FB	++++
74-77	CB	++++
82-84	CU	++++

Year	Lev	Team	W	L	Sv	IP	K	ERA	WHIP	BF/G	OBA	H%	S%	xERA	Ctl	Dom	Cmd	hr/9	BPV
2015	Rk	GCL Braves	0	0	0	6	12	0.00	0.17	6.0	56	17	100		0.0	18.0		0.0	342
2016	Rk	Danville	3	0	0	27	33	1.33	0.85	19.9	191	29	83	1.02	1.7	11.0	6.6	0.0	170
2016	A	Rome	5	3	0	60	62	3.74	1.23	22.1	242	31	71	3.33	3.0	9.3	3.1	0.7	104
2017	AA	Mississippi	8	11	0	150	129	3.18	1.27	22.7	257	31	77	3.57	2.7	7.7	2.9	0.7	84

Projectable LH spent 19-year-old season in Double-A. Was solid throughout, dominating late. Some funk in delivery creates deception. Everything works off 2-seam FB with solid arm-side run and plus sink. Deep and dropping off at the plate, 12-6 CB is best pitch. CU took step forward in 2nd half; profiles as a plus pitch with significant late tumble.

Allen,Logan — SP — San Diego

EXP MLB DEBUT: 2019 | H/W: 6-3 200 | FUT: #4 starter | **8D**

Thrws L Age 20 — 2015 (8) HS (FL)

Velo	Pitch	Grade
90-94	FB	+++
	CB	+++
	CU	+++

Year	Lev	Team	W	L	Sv	IP	K	ERA	WHIP	BF/G	OBA	H%	S%	xERA	Ctl	Dom	Cmd	hr/9	BPV
2016	Rk	Azl Padres	0	0	0	6	8	3.00	1.00	7.6	228	36	67	1.84	1.5	12.0	8.0	0.0	194
2016	A-	Tri-City	0	1	0	2	4	8.57	2.38	10.9	403	68	60	8.12	4.3	17.1	4.0	0.0	211
2016	A	Fort Wayne	3	4	0	54	47	3.33	1.30	14.8	240	30	74	3.09	3.7	7.8	2.1	0.3	60
2017	A	Fort Wayne	5	4	0	68	85	2.11	1.10	20.5	203	31	80	1.93	3.4	11.2	3.3	0.1	127
2017	A+	Lake Elsinore	2	5	0	56	57	4.00	1.39	21.5	275	36	70	3.77	2.9	9.1	3.2	0.3	104

Strong LH who was one of the youngest pitchers to reach High-A in 2017. Uses short, quick arm action to produce life on low-90s FB that can reach 94 mph. Shows ability to locate CB with 1/7 shape for swings and misses, but will need to incorporate CU more often. Good overall feel for pitching and has some Dom potential despite lack of plus pitch.

Almonte, Yency — SP — Colorado

EXP MLB DEBUT: 2018 | H/W: 6-3 205 | FUT: Setup reliever | **7C**

Thrws R Age 23 — 2012 (17) HS (FL)

Velo	Pitch	Grade
93-96	FB	++++
83-85	SL	+++
	CU	++

Year	Lev	Team	W	L	Sv	IP	K	ERA	WHIP	BF/G	OBA	H%	S%	xERA	Ctl	Dom	Cmd	hr/9	BPV
2015	A+	Winston-Salem	3	3	0	44	39	2.44	0.90	23.5	183	24	72	1.30	2.4	7.9	3.3	0.2	95
2016	A+	Modesto	8	9	0	138	134	3.71	1.18	25.1	242	30	71	3.36	2.5	8.7	3.4	0.9	107
2016	AA	Hartford	3	1	0	30	22	3.00	1.27	24.5	206	22	82	3.43	4.8	6.6	1.4	1.2	7
2017	AA	Hartford	5	3	0	76	71	2.01	1.17	21.7	213	27	85	2.56	3.7	8.4	2.3	0.5	70
2017	AAA	Albuquerque	3	1	0	35	22	4.89	1.77	20.1	293	31	78	6.44	5.4	5.7	1.0	1.8	-26

Strong-armed right-hander has had back-to-back productive seasons and should make his MLB debut in 2018. Plus mid-90s heater tops out at 98 mph along with a hard SL and improved CU. Two stints on the DL with arm fatigue raise concerns about durability and a move to relief would not be a surprise.

Almonte,Jose — SP — Arizona

EXP MLB DEBUT: 2019 | H/W: 6-2 185 | FUT: #3 starter | **8D**

Thrws R Age 22 — 2012 FA (DR)

Velo	Pitch	Grade
93-95	FB	++++
81-83	CB	+++
84-87	CU	+++

Year	Lev	Team	W	L	Sv	IP	K	ERA	WHIP	BF/G	OBA	H%	S%	xERA	Ctl	Dom	Cmd	hr/9	BPV
2014	Rk	GCL Red Sox	2	3	0	47	33	3.05	1.33	17.8	257	30	78	3.66	3.2	6.3	1.9	0.6	44
2015	A-	Lowell	3	3	0	65	64	3.45	1.17	18.6	171	24	68	1.76	5.2	8.8	1.7	0.1	35
2016	A	Kane County	2	4	0	55	59	3.26	1.27	20.5	236	31	76	3.25	3.6	9.6	2.7	0.7	94
2016	A	Greenville	2	2	0	53	45	3.91	1.19	21.2	251	31	68	3.29	2.2	7.6	3.5	0.7	96
2017	A+	Visalia	11	8	0	139	162	3.56	1.40	21.8	247	34	76	3.73	4.3	10.5	2.5	0.6	91

A proven strikeout machine, he's a bit underrated as has loads of ceiling left. Has three average-or-better pitches. FB is mid-90s with late movement; hard CB has potential to be an out pitch, but he struggles to get on top of 11-5 bender consistently. Has a good feel for CU, which flashes plus. Biggest issue is command and control.

Almonte,Miguel — SP — Kansas City

EXP MLB DEBUT: 2015 | H/W: 6-2 210 | FUT: #3 starter | **8D**

Thrws R Age 25 — 2010 FA (DR)

Velo	Pitch	Grade
92-95	FB	++++
76-79	CB	++
82-86	SL	++
83-87	CU	++++

Year	Lev	Team	W	L	Sv	IP	K	ERA	WHIP	BF/G	OBA	H%	S%	xERA	Ctl	Dom	Cmd	hr/9	BPV
2016	AA	NW Arkansas	2	1	0	16	15	7.31	1.75	6.6	347	40	63	7.65	2.3	8.4	3.8	2.3	109
2016	AAA	Omaha	3	7	0	60	57	5.55	1.75	13.1	271	34	68	5.05	6.3	8.6	1.4	0.8	2
2017	AA	NW Arkansas	1	0	0	29	35	1.86	0.97	15.7	212	30	85	2.15	1.9	10.9	5.8	0.6	163
2017	AAA	Omaha	0	1	0	18	17	1.50	1.50	8.6	283	36	92	4.35	3.5	8.5	2.4	0.5	77
2017	MLB	KC Royals	0	0	0	2	0	13.50	3.50	6.3	470	47	57	12.69	9.0	0.0	0.0	0.0	-225

Long-time prospect who hasn't been able to find consistency. Wows with natural stuff and improved command, but ended season in July due to shoulder strain. FB and plus CU are best offerings, but hasn't found breaking ball that works. Throws from lower slot which enhances look and action of CU. Still working on repeating delivery with moving parts.

Alvarez, Yadier — SP — Los Angeles (N)

EXP MLB DEBUT: 2019 | H/W: 6-3 175 | FUT: Closer | **9D**

Thrws R Age 22 — 2015 FA (CU)

Velo	Pitch	Grade
95-98	FB	+++++
86-88	SL	++++
87-90	CU	++

Year	Lev	Team	W	L	Sv	IP	K	ERA	WHIP	BF/G	OBA	H%	S%	xERA	Ctl	Dom	Cmd	hr/9	BPV
2016	Rk	AZL Dodgers	1	1	0	20	26	1.80	0.95	15.1	138	23	79	0.70	4.5	11.7	2.6	0.0	107
2016	A	Great Lakes	3	2	0	39	55	2.30	1.07	16.9	219	35	78	2.13	2.5	12.7	5.0	0.2	178
2017	A+	Rancho Cuca	2	4	1	59	61	5.33	1.46	18.0	268	35	61	3.97	3.8	9.3	2.4	0.5	82
2017	AA	Tulsa	2	2	0	33	36	3.55	1.64	21.0	238	33	77	3.85	6.8	9.8	1.4	0.3	11

Tall, athletic Cuban hurler has some of the easiest gas in the minors and impressed at the 2017 Futures Game. FB now sits at 95-98 topping at 100 mph. Mixes in a plus power SL in the upper-80s and CU remains below average. Struggles to find the strike zone seems likely to result in a move to relief where he has the stuff to close.

Alzolay, Adbert

SP | Chicago (N) | EXP MLB DEBUT: 2019 | H/W: 6-0 179 | FUT: #3 starter | 9D

Thrws R Age 23
2012 FA (VZ)

Velo	Pitch	Grade
93-96	FB	++++
80-83	CB	++++
85-88	CU	++

Year	Lev	Team	W	L	Sv	IP	K	ERA	WHIP	BF/G	OBA	H%	S%	xERA	Ctl	Dom	Cmd	hr/9	BPV
2014	A-	Boise	0	0	0	3	2	3.00	1.00	11.5	191	24	67	1.46	3.0	6.0	2.0	0.0	45
2015	A-	Eugene	6	2	0	53	49	2.04	0.83	16.1	163	19	82	1.49	2.5	8.3	3.3	0.8	99
2016	A	South Bend	9	4	0	120	81	4.35	1.22	22.1	260	30	64	3.52	2.1	6.1	2.9	0.7	71
2017	A+	Myrtle Beach	7	1	0	81	78	2.99	1.07	21.1	221	27	76	2.80	2.4	8.6	3.5	0.9	108
2017	AA	Tennessee	0	3	0	32	30	3.07	1.21	18.5	229	31	72	2.42	3.4	8.4	2.5	0.0	78

Late developing hurler had a breakout season, going 2.99 ERA between High-A and Double-A. Fastball sits at 93-96 mph with a plus low-80s curveball and a below-average change-up. Works quickly with a live arm and aggressive approach. Needs to improve command in the strike zone, but has #2 upside.

Anderson, Drew

SP | Philadelphia | EXP MLB DEBUT: 2017 | H/W: 6-3 185 | FUT: #4 starter | 7C

Thrws R Age 24
2012 (21) HS (NV)

Velo	Pitch	Grade
92-94	FB	+++
74-75	CB	+++
83-85	CU	++
82-84	SL	+

Year	Lev	Team	W	L	Sv	IP	K	ERA	WHIP	BF/G	OBA	H%	S%	xERA	Ctl	Dom	Cmd	hr/9	BPV
2016	A	Lakewood	1	3	0	37	41	3.40	1.11	20.8	217	29	71	2.67	2.9	9.9	3.4	0.7	118
2016	A+	Clearwater	2	1	0	32	37	1.96	1.12	15.9	223	33	81	2.09	2.8	10.3	3.7	0.0	129
2017	AA	Reading	9	4	0	107	86	3.61	1.13	20.2	211	24	72	3.03	3.4	7.2	2.2	1.1	57
2017	AAA	Lehigh Valley	0	0	0	6	7	1.45	1.13	24.5	222	28	100	3.48	2.9	10.2	3.5	1.5	123
2017	MLB	Philadelphia	0	0	0	2	2	25.71	3.33	6.5	503	60	14	13.13	4.3	8.6	2.0	0.0	57

Simple mechanics from a high 3/4 slot, stays tall in delivery; gets good plane to the plate and weak contact. Fastball has some life; slow CB is second-best pitch, which garners some swings and misses. CU is below average, and throws occasional SL. Needs a reliable third pitch to stick as a starter. Durability, injury history also a concern.

Anderson,Ian

SP | Atlanta | EXP MLB DEBUT: 2020 | H/W: 6-3 170 | FUT: #2 starter | 9E

Thrws R Age 19
2016 (1) HS (NY)

Velo	Pitch	Grade
93-96	FB	++++
81-83	SL	+++
84-86	CU	++++

Year	Lev	Team	W	L	Sv	IP	K	ERA	WHIP	BF/G	OBA	H%	S%	xERA	Ctl	Dom	Cmd	hr/9	BPV
2016	Rk	GCL Braves	1	0	0	18	18	0.00	1.00	13.8	216	30	100	1.73	2.0	9.0	4.5	0.0	126
2016	Rk	Danville	0	2	0	21	18	3.82	1.27	17.4	241	30	69	3.14	3.4	7.6	2.3	0.4	64
2017	A	Rome	4	5	0	83	101	3.14	1.35	17.3	228	34	74	2.73	4.7	11.0	2.3	0.0	89

Athletic RH had a solid full-season debut. Tons of projectability in profile. Struggled with control off and on all season. 2-seam FB has solid arm-side bore, maintaining velocity throughout. SL is a bit slurvy. Needs to tighten up and throw harder. CU is best secondary; has an advanced feel and is a swing-and-miss offering against LHH.

Anderson,Shaun

SP | San Francisco | EXP MLB DEBUT: 2019 | H/W: 6-4 225 | FUT: #4 starter | 7C

Thrws R Age 23
2016 (3) Florida

Velo	Pitch	Grade
91-95	FB	+++
84-88	SL	+++
77-79	CB	++
	CU	++

Year	Lev	Team	W	L	Sv	IP	K	ERA	WHIP	BF/G	OBA	H%	S%	xERA	Ctl	Dom	Cmd	hr/9	BPV
2016	NCAA	Florida	3	0	13	46	60	0.98	0.82	4.7	193	30	89	1.16	1.4	11.7	8.6	0.2	192
2016	A-	Lowell	0	0	0	2	4	36.82	5.45	9.1	659	83	27	29.14	0.0	16.4		4.1	313
2017	A	Greenville	3	0	0	38	37	2.59	1.07	21.2	218	28	77	2.38	2.6	8.7	3.4	0.5	105
2017	A+	San Jose	3	3	0	25	22	3.57	0.91	15.7	211	27	59	1.79	1.4	7.9	5.5	0.4	121
2017	A+	Salem	3	3	0	58	48	4.02	1.22	21.4	244	29	69	3.52	2.8	7.4	2.7	0.9	76

Tall, loose-armed SP who is putting himself on map as SP after relieving in college. Possesses good control with all pitches, though none profile as plus. Gets ahead of hitters with solid average FB and can knock out hitters with hard SL that flashes above average. Uses height to throw downhill and spot FB down. CB and CU show some promise.

Appel,Mark

SP | Philadelphia | EXP MLB DEBUT: 2018 | H/W: 6-5 220 | FUT: #5 SP/swingman | 7D

Thrws R Age 26
2013 (1) Stanford

Velo	Pitch	Grade
90-93	FB	+++
82-84	SL	+++
81-83	CU	++

Year	Lev	Team	W	L	Sv	IP	K	ERA	WHIP	BF/G	OBA	H%	S%	xERA	Ctl	Dom	Cmd	hr/9	BPV
2015	AA	Corpus Christi	5	1	0	63	49	4.28	1.44	20.7	276	32	73	4.59	3.3	7.0	2.1	1.0	55
2015	AAA	Fresno	5	2	0	68	61	4.49	1.40	23.9	259	32	69	4.02	3.7	8.1	2.2	0.8	63
2016	AAA	Lehigh Valley	3	3	0	38	34	4.49	1.57	20.9	271	34	72	4.57	4.7	8.0	1.7	0.7	35
2017	Rk	GCL Phillies	0	0	0	2	0	0.00	1.00	3.8	151	15	100	1.08	4.5	0.0	0.0	0.0	-104
2017	AAA	Lehigh Valley	5	4	0	82	60	5.27	1.76	22.1	282	32	71	5.46	5.8	6.6	1.1	1.0	-21

Unceremonious fall for former 1-1 pick. Shoulder injury ended his season after 17 starts; was DFA'd in November. FB flat and hittable, once-plus SL has backed up and overall lack of swings and misses in the high minors a concern. Will likely transition to relief role in hopes that shorter stints breathe new life into his stuff.

Arano,Victor

SP | Philadelphia | EXP MLB DEBUT: 2017 | H/W: 6-2 200 | FUT: Setup reliever | 8C

Thrws R Age 23
2013 FA (MX)

Velo	Pitch	Grade
93-95	FB	++++
82-84	SL	+++

Year	Lev	Team	W	L	Sv	IP	K	ERA	WHIP	BF/G	OBA	H%	S%	xERA	Ctl	Dom	Cmd	hr/9	BPV
2015	A+	Clearwater	4	12	0	124	69	4.72	1.27	21.1	273	31	61	3.65	1.9	5.0	2.7	0.5	57
2016	A+	Clearwater	4	1	4	63	71	2.29	1.06	7.0	226	31	81	2.54	2.1	10.1	4.7	0.6	143
2016	AA	Reading	1	1	1	16	24	2.22	0.93	5.5	194	29	85	2.28	2.2	13.3	6.0	1.1	198
2017	AA	Reading	1	2	9	38	38	4.24	1.31	4.9	266	31	74	4.70	2.6	9.0	3.5	1.6	109
2017	MLB	Philadelphia	1	0	0	10	13	1.76	0.98	3.9	173	28	80	1.15	3.5	11.5	3.3	0.0	129

Picked up velocity with move to the pen in 2016; early-2017 elbow injury delayed his promotion to PHI. When healthy, he has a mid-90s FB with life and a short, hard SL that both get swings and misses. Compact delivery, ball comes out easy. A chance to develop into high-K reliever, but must prove durability.

Araujo, Pedro

RP | Baltimore | EXP MLB DEBUT: 2018 | H/W: 6-3 214 | FUT: Middle reliever | 6B

Thrws R Age 24
2011 FA (DR)

Velo	Pitch	Grade
90-93	FB	+++
	CB	++++
	CU	++

Year	Lev	Team	W	L	Sv	IP	K	ERA	WHIP	BF/G	OBA	H%	S%	xERA	Ctl	Dom	Cmd	hr/9	BPV
2015	A-	Eugene	0	2	1	50	70	2.69	1.04	9.2	233	37	73	2.17	1.6	12.6	7.8	0.2	201
2016	A	South Bend	3	0	3	34	45	1.59	0.88	7.9	165	26	83	1.07	2.9	11.9	4.1	0.3	154
2016	A+	Myrtle Beach	0	2	1	19	22	5.21	1.63	6.5	251	34	69	4.64	6.2	10.4	1.7	0.9	39
2017	A+	Myrtle Beach	6	1	10	64	83	1.82	0.92	5.5	188	28	82	1.56	2.4	11.6	4.9	0.4	163
2017	AA	Tennessee	0	0	0	2	4	0.00	1.00	7.6	151	38	100	0.90	4.5	18.0	4.0	0.0	221

Physical RH RP has been slow to develop. Fastball is not overpowering but with good arm-side run and sink. Mixes in a plus power curveball that allows him to dominate vs. RHB (0.65 ERA in 41.1 IP). At 24 he's old for High-A, but has a career line of 2.63 ERA and 3.8 Cmd. Selected from CHC in Rule 5 draft

Armenteros,Rogelio

SP | Houston | EXP MLB DEBUT: 2018 | H/W: 6-1 215 | FUT: #5 SP/swingman | 7B

Thrws R Age 23
2014 FA (CU)

Velo	Pitch	Grade
88-92	FB	+++
73-77	CB	+++
80-82	CU	+++

Year	Lev	Team	W	L	Sv	IP	K	ERA	WHIP	BF/G	OBA	H%	S%	xERA	Ctl	Dom	Cmd	hr/9	BPV
2016	A	Quad Cities	0	2	0	18	20	1.98	0.82	16.6	190	28	73	0.96	1.5	9.9	6.7	0.0	156
2016	A+	Lancaster	6	4	1	90	107	4.20	1.38	19.9	255	33	74	4.38	3.7	10.7	2.9	1.3	111
2016	AA	Corpus Christi	2	0	0	18	13	1.99	1.16	24.0	250	30	85	3.05	2.0	6.5	3.3	0.5	81
2017	AA	Corpus Christi	2	3	1	65	74	1.94	1.04	18.0	211	30	83	2.15	2.6	10.2	3.9	0.4	131
2017	AAA	Fresno	8	1	0	58	72	2.17	1.05	22.5	204	29	84	2.41	2.9	11.2	3.8	0.8	139

Cuban SP with steady Dom/SwK track record despite lack of put-away pitch. Sinks FB anywhere from 89-92 mph and maintains arm speed well on CU for ground balls. CB and SL both average secondary pitches. Owns thick, sturdy frame required to rack up innings. Impressed in his AAA debut, and is knocking on big-league door.

Assad,Javier

SP | Chicago (N) | EXP MLB DEBUT: 2021 | H/W: 6-1 200 | FUT: #3 starter | 8D

Thrws R Age 20
2015 FA (MX)

Velo	Pitch	Grade
90-94	FB	+++
	SL	+++
	CB	++
	CU	+++

Year	Lev	Team	W	L	Sv	IP	K	ERA	WHIP	BF/G	OBA	H%	S%	xERA	Ctl	Dom	Cmd	hr/9	BPV
2016	Rk	AZL Cubs	2	2	1	37	42	2.90	1.40	15.7	271	38	78	3.66	3.1	10.2	3.2	0.2	116
2017	A-	Eugene	5	6	0	66	72	4.23	1.36	21.2	270	37	67	3.60	2.9	9.8	3.4	0.3	117

Short, physically mature RHP from Mexico impressed in short-season ball. Features four-pitch mix highlighted by a 90-94 fastball, curve, change-up, and an above-average slider. Shows good command of FB, but struggles with control of off-speed stuff. Will get a good test at A+.

Avila,Pedro

SP | San Diego | EXP MLB DEBUT: 2020 | H/W: 5-11 170 | FUT: #4 starter | 8C

Thrws R Age 21
2014 FA (VZ)

Velo	Pitch	Grade
92-94	FB	+++
82-84	CU	+++
74-76	CB	+++
82-83	SL	++

Year	Lev	Team	W	L	Sv	IP	K	ERA	WHIP	BF/G	OBA	H%	S%	xERA	Ctl	Dom	Cmd	hr/9	BPV
2016	A	Hagerstown	7	7	0	93	92	3.48	1.33	19.3	247	31	77	3.87	3.7	8.9	2.4	1.0	79
2017	A	Fort Wayne	7	1	0	85	117	3.06	1.04	23.5	235	37	70	2.34	1.6	12.4	7.8	0.3	198
2017	A+	Lake Elsinore	1	4	0	43	53	5.01	1.58	19.0	291	41	67	4.57	3.8	11.1	2.9	0.4	116

Shorter, muscular RH who owns 11.2 Dom as pro largely against advanced bats. Can spot 92-94 FB horizontally and maintain arm speed well for whiffs on future plus CU. Decent feel for mid-70s CB and will mix in so-so SL at times. Chance for three legitimate average-or-better pitches as dependable back-end starter at full maturity.

Baez,Joan

SP | Washington | EXP MLB DEBUT: 2020 | H/W: 6-3 190 | FUT: #5 SP/swingman | 7D

Thrws R Age 23
2014 FA (DR)

Velo	Pitch	Grade
92-95	FB	+++
77-79	CB	++
85-87	CU	++

Year	Lev	Team	W	L	Sv	IP	K	ERA	WHIP	BF/G	OBA	H%	S%	xERA	Ctl	Dom	Cmd	hr/9	BPV
2015	A-	Auburn	2	2	0	17	17	7.33	2.03	16.7	302	40	60	5.51	7.3	8.9	1.2	0.0	-20
2015	A	Hagerstown	0	1	0	10	6	11.58	1.88	15.8	313	35	33	6.17	5.3	5.3	1.0	0.9	-30
2016	A	Hagerstown	9	7	0	125	119	3.95	1.47	19.9	254	33	72	3.73	4.6	8.6	1.9	0.4	48
2017	Rk	GCL Nationals	2	0	0	18	23	1.49	0.77	16.3	150	24	79	0.38	2.5	11.4	4.6	0.0	157
2017	A+	Potomac	4	8	0	79	65	3.87	1.65	20.8	223	28	76	3.77	7.5	7.4	1.0	0.3	-52

Well-proportioned with a big fastball (up to 96) to match, but has never been able to harness his stuff into usable results. A stiff release point and inability to repeat his delivery hinders control of all his pitches. Will be tested at the higher levels.

Baez,Michel — SP — San Diego

EXP MLB DEBUT: 2020 | H/W: 6-8 220 | FUT: #3 starter | 9D

Thrws R Age 22
2016 FA (CU)

92-97	FB	++++
77-80	CB	+++
83-86	CU	+++

Year	Lev	Team	W	L	Sv	IP	K	ERA	WHIP	BF/G	OBA	H%	S%	xERA	Ctl	Dom	Cmd	hr/9	BPV
2017	Rk	AZL Padres	1	0	0	5	7	3.60	0.80	18.1	124	12	67	1.87	3.6	12.6	3.5	1.8	148
2017	A	Fort Wayne	6	2	0	58	82	2.47	0.84	21.3	200	29	80	2.26	1.2	12.7	10.3	1.2	213

Cuban RHP who defected and signed for $3 million in 2016. Towering build, high waist, long levers create imposing figure on mound. Has plane on mid-90s FB that will touch 98 mph and miss bats up in zone. Good feel for CU and flashes plus grade at next level; CB a work in progress. May struggle with Ctl given his size, but is a future source of Dom.

Baez,Sandy — SP — Detroit

EXP MLB DEBUT: 2018 | H/W: 6-2 180 | FUT: #4 starter | 7C

Thrws R Age 24
2011 FA (DR)

93-97	FB	+++
81-85	SL	+++
	CU	++

Year	Lev	Team	W	L	Sv	IP	K	ERA	WHIP	BF/G	OBA	H%	S%	xERA	Ctl	Dom	Cmd	hr/9	BPV
2014	Rk	GCL Tigers	1	2	0	61	48	3.09	1.27	20.9	264	32	76	3.48	2.4	7.1	3.0	0.4	82
2015	A-	Connecticut	3	4	0	65	52	4.15	1.46	19.9	285	34	71	4.33	3.0	7.2	2.4	0.6	65
2016	A	West Michigan	7	9	0	113	88	3.82	1.35	22.5	282	34	72	4.03	2.2	7.0	3.1	0.6	84
2017	A+	Lakeland	6	7	0	88	92	3.88	1.27	21.2	261	34	70	3.66	2.4	9.4	3.8	0.7	121
2017	AA	Erie	0	1	0	10	13	4.50	1.40	21.1	242	28	82	5.57	4.5	11.7	2.6	2.7	107

Powerful SP who got off to very slow start, but ended hot. Increased velocity with cleaner mechanics and saw K rate increase significantly. SL also turning into above average offering with tight action. Doesn't yet have pitch for LHH and must increase stamina as he loses velocity late. Possesses good control for arm action.

Bailey,Brandon — SP — Houston

EXP MLB DEBUT: 2019 | H/W: 5-10 175 | FUT: Setup reliever | 6B

Thrws R Age 23
2016 (6) Gonzaga

90-94	FB	+++
80-82	SL	++
	CU	+++

Year	Lev	Team	W	L	Sv	IP	K	ERA	WHIP	BF/G	OBA	H%	S%	xERA	Ctl	Dom	Cmd	hr/9	BPV
2016	NCAA	Gonzaga	10	3	0	100		2.43	1.11	24.6	221	33	79	2.37	2.8	11.2	4.0	0.4	145
2016	Rk	AZL Athletics	0	0	0	5	4	1.80	1.60	11.1	332	41	88	4.91	1.8	7.2	4.0	0.0	99
2016	A-	Vermont	3	1	0	38	42	3.08	0.92	14.2	195	28	65	1.49	2.1	9.9	4.7	0.2	140
2017	A	Beloit	1	1	0	57	73	2.68	1.07	14.8	199	29	77	2.27	3.3	11.5	3.5	0.6	136
2017	A+	Stockton	2	1	1	34	47	4.24	1.12	14.9	226	33	65	3.10	2.6	12.4	4.7	1.1	170

Small, deceptive SP with very good pitchability. Posts high K rate despite lack of plus stuff. Likes to throw hard with max effort delivery, but arm slot could be concern. Allows ton of flyballs when batters make contact. Establishes plate with commandable FB and keeps hitters off-balance with solid CU. SL may not be good enough for higher levels.

Ball,Trey — SP — Boston

EXP MLB DEBUT: 2019 | H/W: 6-6 185 | FUT: Setup reliever | 7E

Thrws L Age 23
2013 (1) HS (IN)

89-93	FB	+++
74-78	CB	++
82-85	SL	++
78-82	CU	++

Year	Lev	Team	W	L	Sv	IP	K	ERA	WHIP	BF/G	OBA	H%	S%	xERA	Ctl	Dom	Cmd	hr/9	BPV
2013	Rk	GCL Red Sox	0	1	0	7	5	6.43	2.29	7.1	336	38	73	7.93	7.7	6.4	0.8	1.3	-75
2014	A	Greenville	5	10	0	100	68	4.68	1.50	19.6	282	32	70	4.66	3.5	6.1	1.7	0.8	33
2015	A+	Salem	9	13	0	129	77	4.74	1.46	22.1	262	28	70	4.57	4.2	5.4	1.3	1.1	2
2016	A+	Salem	8	6	0	117	86	3.84	1.61	22.6	268	32	77	4.55	5.2	6.6	1.3	0.6	-4
2017	AA	Portland	7	12	0	124	103	5.29	1.76	22.7	315	37	72	6.18	4.1	7.5	1.8	1.2	41

Tall SP who was 3rd in EL in walks in first season at AA. Has impressive, natural stuff, but can't find consistency with command. Struggles with release point and hasn't been able to maintain velocity. Uses slow CB and hard SL in tandem, but can both be flat. Has struggled with RHH and victimized by HR. All hope not lost, but time running out.

Banda,Anthony — SP — Arizona

EXP MLB DEBUT: 2017 | H/W: 6-2 190 | FUT: #4 starter | 7B

Thrws L Age 24
2012 (10) San Jacinto JC

92-95	FB	+++
79-82	CB	++++
84-87	CU	++

Year	Lev	Team	W	L	Sv	IP	K	ERA	WHIP	BF/G	OBA	H%	S%	xERA	Ctl	Dom	Cmd	hr/9	BPV
2015	A+	Visalia	8	8	0	151	152	3.33	1.25	22.0	260	34	73	3.37	2.3	9.0	3.9	0.5	118
2016	AA	Mobile	6	2	0	76	84	2.13	1.29	24.0	246	34	85	3.26	3.3	9.9	3.0	0.5	107
2016	AAA	Reno	4	4	0	73	68	3.69	1.37	23.6	261	33	74	3.93	3.3	8.4	2.5	0.7	79
2017	AAA	Reno	8	7	0	122	116	5.39	1.44	23.6	267	33	64	4.54	3.8	8.6	2.3	1.1	70
2017	MLB	Arizona	2	3	0	25	25	6.07	1.43	13.4	268	35	54	3.82	3.6	8.9	2.5	0.4	82

LH pitcher made MLB debut in 2017. Added velocity to FB and maintained solid arm-side run. Did struggle commanding higher octane FB. CB is best pitch with great depth and solid break; a true swing-and-miss offering. CU is still wildly inconsistent. Shows a little more improvement each season.

Barlow, Scott — SP — Kansas City

EXP MLB DEBUT: 2018 | H/W: 6-3 215 | FUT: #5 SP/swingman | 7D

Thrws R Age 25
2011 (6) HS (CA)

92-94	FB	+++
78-81	SL	+++
80-83	CU	++

Year	Lev	Team	W	L	Sv	IP	K	ERA	WHIP	BF/G	OBA	H%	S%	xERA	Ctl	Dom	Cmd	hr/9	BPV
2015	A+	Rancho Cuca	8	3	0	71	64	2.53	1.31	21.0	233	29	82	3.20	4.1	8.1	2.0	0.5	54
2015	AAA	Oklahoma City	0	1	0	3	3	16.88	3.13	19.0	437	54	40	10.83	8.4	8.4	1.0	0.0	-58
2016	AA	Tulsa	4	7	0	124	102	3.99	1.43	22.0	263	32	73	4.04	3.8	7.4	2.0	0.7	49
2017	AA	Tulsa	6	3	0	107	124	2.10	0.91	21.0	166	22	82	1.61	3.1	10.4	3.4	0.8	122
2017	AAA	Oklahoma City	1	3	0	32	36	7.29	1.87	21.5	290	36	63	6.48	6.4	10.1	1.6	1.7	26

Tall, lanky RHP struggled when moved up to Triple-A, but regained his form when demoted. Comes after hitters with from a high 3/4 slot and has a decent low-90s FB with arm-side run. Mixes in a quality SL that is a true swing-and-miss offering. CB and CU have chance to play average. Struggles with control continue and now has a career 3.8 Ctl rate.

Barnes,Charlie — SP — Minnesota

EXP MLB DEBUT: 2019 | H/W: 6-2 160 | FUT: #4 starter | 7C

Thrws L Age 22
2017 (4) Clemson

87-91	FB	+++
77-79	CB	++
81-82	SL	+++
80-83	CU	+++

Year	Lev	Team	W	L	Sv	IP	K	ERA	WHIP	BF/G	OBA	H%	S%	xERA	Ctl	Dom	Cmd	hr/9	BPV
2017	NCAA	Clemson	5	5	0	101	113	3.20	1.19	25.3	256	35	74	3.28	2.0	10.1	5.1	0.6	146
2017	Rk	Elizabethton	2	1	0	22	23	1.22	1.08	14.4	183	25	91	1.92	4.1	9.3	2.3	0.4	76
2017	A	Cedar Rapids	2	1	0	25	23	3.93	1.23	17.0	245	28	74	4.01	2.9	8.2	2.9	1.4	89

Very lean SP who is all about command and control. Very stingy against LHH with variety of offerings, including tight SL that he can throw for strikes. Hits spots with sinking FB and keeps ball on ground. Doesn't throw hard, but pitches with control and precision. Has deep arsenal and has CU to keep RHH honest. Profiles as back-end starter.

Barria,Jaime — SP — Los Angeles (A)

EXP MLB DEBUT: 2018 | H/W: 6-1 210 | FUT: #4 starter | 7B

Thrws R Age 21
2013 FA (PN)

89-94	FB	+++
79-82	CB	+++
82-85	SL	++
	CU	+++

Year	Lev	Team	W	L	Sv	IP	K	ERA	WHIP	BF/G	OBA	H%	S%	xERA	Ctl	Dom	Cmd	hr/9	BPV
2015	Rk	AZL Angels	3	0	0	36	31	2.00	1.19	20.6	283	36	81	3.11	0.8	7.8	10.3	0.0	137
2016	A	Burlington	8	6	0	117	78	3.85	1.32	19.4	287	34	70	3.94	1.6	6.0	3.7	0.5	82
2017	A+	Inland Empire	4	3	0	65	57	2.49	0.94	22.2	207	25	78	2.25	1.8	7.9	4.4	0.8	111
2017	AA	Mobile	1	6	0	61	47	3.24	1.26	20.8	264	30	80	4.13	2.2	6.9	3.1	1.2	83
2017	AAA	Salt Lake	2	0	0	14	13	2.54	0.99	18.0	216	29	71	1.69	1.9	8.2	4.3	0.0	115

Strong, durable SP who emerged with improvement across the board. Has polished repertoire and ability to pound zone with four effective offerings. Slight uptick in velocity and continued solid command resulted in success. Uses clean delivery and arm speed to enhance CU, and also uses two breaking balls, but not much strikeout upside.

Bashlor,Tyler — RP — New York (N)

EXP MLB DEBUT: 2018 | H/W: 6-0 197 | FUT: Setup reliever | 7C

Thrws R Age 24
2013 (11) South Georgia JC

95-97	FB	++++
82-85	SL	+++
89-92	CU	+

Year	Lev	Team	W	L	Sv	IP	K	ERA	WHIP	BF/G	OBA	H%	S%	xERA	Ctl	Dom	Cmd	hr/9	BPV
2016	A	Columbia	4	2	3	50	68	2.51	1.26	6.0	199	31	80	2.47	5.0	12.2	2.4	0.4	102
2016	A+	St. Lucie	0	1	0	5	5	5.29	1.18	5.1	218	30	50	2.19	3.5	8.8	2.5	0.0	82
2017	A+	St. Lucie	2	2	10	35	61	4.89	1.54	4.5	251	46	66	3.71	5.4	15.7	2.9	0.3	155
2017	AA	Binghamton	1	0	3	14	23	0.00	0.77	4.3	149	29	100	0.35	2.5	14.6	5.8	0.0	212

Hard-throwing RH has progressed quickly through system after returning from TJ surgery. Dom increased significantly in 2017. High-octane FB has phenomenal late giddy-up with significant arm-side bore. Borderline plus-plus action. SL continues to make strides. More slurve than slide; could throw pitch harder. CU is non-factor.

Baumann, Michael — SP — Baltimore

EXP MLB DEBUT: 2020 | H/W: 6-4 225 | FUT: #3 starter | 8D

Thrws R Age 22
2017 (3) Jacksonville

91-95	FB	++++
82-85	SL	+++
77-78	CB	++
	CU	++

Year	Lev	Team	W	L	Sv	IP	K	ERA	WHIP	BF/G	OBA	H%	S%	xERA	Ctl	Dom	Cmd	hr/9	BPV
2017	NCAA	Jacksonville	5	3	0	87	97	3.10	1.21	25.0	222	29	77	3.08	3.6	10.0	2.8	0.8	101
2017	Rk	GCL Orioles	0	0	0	1	2	0.00	2.00	4.8	415	71	100	7.40	0.0	18.0		0.0	342
2017	A-	Aberdeen	4	2	0	41	41	1.31	1.07	16.0	177	23	90	1.86	4.2	9.0	2.2	0.4	67

Tall, powerful SP with some projection remaining and gets ample pitch movement to offerings. Can cut FB and has natural life at high velocity. Likes to use power SL often, though can be inconsistent at throwing it for strikes. Very tough on RHH and posts low oppBA with minimal contact. Has CB for different look and rarely uses ineffective CU.

Bautista,Gerson — RP — New York (N)

EXP MLB DEBUT: 2020 | H/W: 6-2 170 | FUT: Closer | 8E

Thrws R Age 22
2013 FA (DR)

95-97	FB	++++
86-88	SL	+++
	CU	+

Year	Lev	Team	W	L	Sv	IP	K	ERA	WHIP	BF/G	OBA	H%	S%	xERA	Ctl	Dom	Cmd	hr/9	BPV
2015	Rk	GCL Red Sox	3	3	0	52	41	2.77	1.21	17.5	197	25	76	2.21	4.7	7.1	1.5	0.2	20
2016	A-	Lowell	0	0	5	10	13	0.89	0.69	4.4	149	24	86	0.18	1.8	11.6	6.5	0.0	178
2016	A	Greenville	1	4	1	25	23	3.24	1.24	6.8	221	26	79	3.41	4.0	8.3	2.1	1.1	60
2017	A+	St. Lucie	0	1	5	14	20	1.28	0.92	5.3	201	34	85	1.31	1.9	12.8	6.7	0.0	196
2017	A+	Salem	3	2	4	45	53	5.19	1.82	7.7	298	41	70	5.26	5.6	10.6	1.9	0.4	58

Slow-developing, hard-throwing RH peaked in 2017. Acquired from BOS in Addison Reed deal, has excelled since moving to pen in 2016. Stuff has ticked up. 2-seam FB has solid bore, although it flattens out at higher velocities. SL is tight, with sharp downward break. Potential to become plus offering. No CU feel. Shaky control.

Baz, Shane

SP | Pittsburgh | EXP MLB DEBUT: 2021 | H/W: 6-3 190 | FUT: #1 starter | 9D

Thrws R Age 18
2017 (1) HS (TX)

Velo	Pitch	Grade
92-96	FB	+++++
84-88	CT	++++
	SL	+++
	CB	++

Year	Lev	Team	W	L	Sv	IP	K	ERA	WHIP	BF/G	OBA	H%	S%	xERA	Ctl	Dom	Cmd	hr/9	BPV
2017	Rk	GCL Pirates	0	3	0	23	19	3.88	1.72	10.5	284	34	79	5.21	5.4	7.4	1.4	0.8	4

12th overall pick in 2017 draft is a the rare physically mature high school hurler. Fastball already sits at 92-96 with good sink and tops at 98 mph. Backs the heater with a plus 84-88 mph cutter, a plus slider, curve, and a change-up that shows potential. Simple repeatable mechanics and bulldog mentality round out an impressive package of tools.

Bednar,David

RP | San Diego | EXP MLB DEBUT: 2019 | H/W: 6-1 205 | FUT: Middle reliever | 8C

Thrws R Age 23
2016 (35) Lafayette

Velo	Pitch	Grade
93-97	FB	++++
87-88	SP	++++
73-77	CB	++

Year	Lev	Team	W	L	Sv	IP	K	ERA	WHIP	BF/G	OBA	H%	S%	xERA	Ctl	Dom	Cmd	hr/9	BPV
2016	A-	Tri-City	1	0	2	10	15	0.00	0.70	4.4	199	35	100	0.72	0.0	13.5		0.0	261
2016	A	Fort Wayne	3	4	2	21	25	3.43	1.14	5.5	252	37	67	2.53	1.7	10.7	6.3	0.0	165
2017	A	Fort Wayne	1	1	9	33	50	1.90	0.87	5.1	161	28	79	0.99	3.0	13.6	4.5	0.3	181
2017	A+	Lake Elsinore	0	3	2	27	31	3.64	1.32	5.4	260	36	71	3.41	3.0	10.3	3.4	0.3	122

Stocky, strong RH with good Dom/Ctl credentials. Short, violent arm action produces mid-90s heat; will touch 98. FB has elite spin rate and is effective swing-and-miss pitch up in zone. Working on splitter that flashes nasty tumbling action; CB is fringy and can get slurvy. Great makeup with desire to succeed. Potential for Dom as 7th-inning type.

Beede,Tyler

SP | San Francisco | EXP MLB DEBUT: 2017 | H/W: 6-3 210 | FUT: #3 starter | 8B

Thrws R Age 24
2014 (1) Vanderbilt

Velo	Pitch	Grade
91-95	FB	+++
87-90	CT	+++
77-78	CB	+++
83-86	CU	+++

Year	Lev	Team	W	L	Sv	IP	K	ERA	WHIP	BF/G	OBA	H%	S%	xERA	Ctl	Dom	Cmd	hr/9	BPV
2014	A-	Salem-Kaizer	0	0	0	6		2.90	1.77	14.2	314	43	82	5.03	4.4	10.2	2.3	0.0	83
2015	A+	San Jose	2	2	0	52	37	2.25	1.15	23.0	258	31	81	2.99	1.6	6.4	4.1	0.3	91
2015	AA	Richmond	3	8	0	72	49	5.24	1.35	23.1	234	27	59	3.31	4.4	6.1	1.4	0.5	10
2016	AA	Richmond	8	7	0	147	135	2.81	1.28	25.2	247	31	79	3.36	3.2	8.3	2.5	0.6	79
2017	AAA	Sacramento	6	7	0	109	83	4.79	1.47	24.6	282	32	70	4.89	3.2	6.9	2.1	1.2	54

Tall, strong SP who struggled in first AA taste, then season ended in July due to groin injury. Owns deep arsenal, including very good FB that induces ton of GBs. K rate declined, but sequences like wily veteran. Holds velocity deep into games. CB may be best pitch with big breaking action. Needs to combat LHH better. Very good arm speed on CU.

Beeks,Jalen

SP | Boston | EXP MLB DEBUT: 2018 | H/W: 5-11 195 | FUT: #4 starter | 7C

Thrws L Age 24
2014 (12) Arkansas

Velo	Pitch	Grade
90-94	FB	+++
74-78	CB	++
	CT	++
	CU	+++

Year	Lev	Team	W	L	Sv	IP	K	ERA	WHIP	BF/G	OBA	H%	S%	xERA	Ctl	Dom	Cmd	hr/9	BPV
2015	A	Greenville	9	7	0	145	100	4.34	1.27	22.8	276	31	68	4.20	1.7	6.2	3.6	1.1	83
2016	A+	Salem	4	4	0	67	55	3.08	1.36	21.6	261	30	83	4.36	3.2	7.4	2.3	1.2	64
2016	AA	Portland	5	4	0	65	56	4.70	1.54	21.8	282	34	70	4.74	3.9	7.7	2.0	0.8	53
2017	AA	Portland	5	1	0	49	58	2.20	1.16	21.7	202	28	83	2.46	4.0	10.6	2.6	0.5	100
2017	AAA	Pawtucket	6	7	0	95	97	3.88	1.25	22.8	243	31	72	3.58	3.1	9.2	2.9	0.9	99

Emerging prospect who increased K rate while changing repertoire. Lacks plus pitch, but added CB and regained CU. Can rear back and add ticks to FB. Exhibits effort in delivery and may be better in pen due to small size. Likes to use CT to keep hitters off balance. Despite high K rate, doesn't have the stuff or durability to project well in majors.

Bernardino,Brennan

RP | Cincinnati | EXP MLB DEBUT: 2019 | H/W: 6-4 180 | FUT: Middle reliever | 7C

Thrws L Age 26
2014 (26) Cal St Dom Hills

Velo	Pitch	Grade
90-93	FB	+++
74-78	CB	++++
85-86	CU	+

Year	Lev	Team	W	L	Sv	IP	K	ERA	WHIP	BF/G	OBA	H%	S%	xERA	Ctl	Dom	Cmd	hr/9	BPV
2014	Rk	Billings	1	1	9	26	31	1.03	0.99	4.5	187	28	88	1.35	3.1	10.6	3.4	0.0	126
2015	A	Dayton	2	3	3	54	49	3.66	1.57	6.4	296	38	74	4.25	3.5	8.2	2.3	0.0	70
2015	AAA	Louisville	0	0	0	1	0	8.18	2.73	3.1	492	49	67	11.34	0.0	0.0		0.0	18
2016	A+	Daytona	5	3	1	60	61	3.74	1.45	5.1	268	34	76	4.22	3.7	9.1	2.4	0.7	81
2017	AA	Pensacola	2	4	0	40	42	4.49	1.52	4.6	271	34	73	4.80	4.3	9.4	2.2	1.1	73

Older LH prospect blossomed in AFL after sideways Double-A season. Has struggled repeating mechanics, affecting control. 2-seam FB is workhorse pitch. Has solid arm-side run but lacking command. Best pitch is 12-6, tightly wound CB with advanced spin rate. An out-pitch when around the zone. CU is primarily for show.

Bickford,Phil

SP | Milwaukee | EXP MLB DEBUT: 2019 | H/W: 6-4 200 | FUT: #4 starter | 7C

Thrws R Age 22
2015 (1) JC of So Nevada

Velo	Pitch	Grade
89-92	FB	+++
78-81	SL	+++
84-86	CU	+++

Year	Lev	Team	W	L	Sv	IP	K	ERA	WHIP	BF/G	OBA	H%	S%	xERA	Ctl	Dom	Cmd	hr/9	BPV
2015	Rk	AZL Giants	0	1	0	22	32	2.04	0.86	8.1	173	30	74	0.83	2.4	13.0	5.3	0.0	187
2016	A	Augusta	3	4	0	60	69	2.70	1.07	21.2	225	32	74	2.26	2.3	10.4	4.6	0.3	144
2016	A+	San Jose	2	2	0	33	36	2.73	1.00	21.0	184	24	77	2.11	3.3	9.8	3.0	0.8	106
2016	A+	Brevard County	2	1	0	27	30	3.67	1.52	19.5	255	35	75	3.83	5.0	10.0	2.0	0.3	63
2017	Rk	AZL Brewers	1	0	0	17	16	2.12	1.41	12.0	226	30	83	2.89	5.3	8.5	1.6	0.0	28

Former 1st rd pick missed significant time due to drug suspension and broken hand. FB velocity has dipped as professional. Solid 2-seam arm-side run but poor command. SL has tightened up, still a bit slurvy. CU may be best pitch. Stuff will play up in pen, especially FB.

Bieber,Shane

SP | Cleveland | EXP MLB DEBUT: 2018 | H/W: 6-3 195 | FUT: #4 starter | 7C

Thrws R Age 22
2016 (4) UC-Santa Barbara

Velo	Pitch	Grade
88-91	FB	+++
82-84	SL	+++
	CU	+++

Year	Lev	Team	W	L	Sv	IP	K	ERA	WHIP	BF/G	OBA	H%	S%	xERA	Ctl	Dom	Cmd	hr/9	BPV
2016	NCAA	UC Santa Barbara	12	4	0	134	109	2.75	1.06	28.9	250	31	74	2.63	1.1	7.3	6.8	0.3	121
2016	A-	Mahoning Val	0	0	0	24	21	0.38	0.50	8.9	129	18	92		0.8	7.9	10.5	0.0	140
2017	A	Lake County	2	3	0	29	31	3.10	1.21	23.4	294	39	74	3.58	0.3	9.6	31.0	0.3	183
2017	A+	Lynchburg	6	1	0	90	82	3.10	1.10	25.2	272	34	72	3.19	0.4	8.2	20.5	0.5	155
2017	AA	Akron	2	1	0	54	49	2.33	1.13	23.7	269	34	80	3.05	0.8	8.2	9.8	0.3	142

Command-oriented SP who was terrific on three levels in first full year as pro. Only allowed 10 BB in 173 IP and works both sides of plate with ease. Locates average FB with precision. Mixes in SL and CU, both of which grade as solid-average. Keeps ball in lower half. Works with clean, loose arm, but not a high K guy.

Bishop,Cameron

SP | Baltimore | EXP MLB DEBUT: 2020 | H/W: 6-4 215 | FUT: #4 starter | 7C

Thrws L Age 22
2017 (26) UC-Irvine

Velo	Pitch	Grade
90-94	FB	+++
80-82	SL	+++
77-79	CB	++
80-83	CU	++

Year	Lev	Team	W	L	Sv	IP	K	ERA	WHIP	BF/G	OBA	H%	S%	xERA	Ctl	Dom	Cmd	hr/9	BPV
2017	Rk	GCL Orioles	0	0	0	3	1	0.00	0.33	9.5	106	12	100		0.0	3.0		0.0	72
2017	A-	Aberdeen	1	1	0	34	38	0.79	1.05	16.6	172	25	94	1.58	4.2	10.0	2.4	0.3	84

Big-framed SP who missed all college season, but had impressive pro debut. Uses height and arm angle to keep ball in bottom half of zone and has velocity to pitch up. Needs better command and control and could get better with more IP. Power SL is go-to pitch and fringy CB and CU could use upgrade. Should become durable SP with deep pitch mix.

Blackburn,Clayton

SP | Texas | EXP MLB DEBUT: 2018 | H/W: 6-3 230 | FUT: #5 SP/swingman | 6B

Thrws R Age 25
2011 (16) HS (OK)

Velo	Pitch	Grade
89-93	FB	+++
82-84	SL	+++
77-78	CB	++
	CU	+++

Year	Lev	Team	W	L	Sv	IP	K	ERA	WHIP	BF/G	OBA	H%	S%	xERA	Ctl	Dom	Cmd	hr/9	BPV
2014	Rk	Azl Giants	0	1	0	5	9	3.60	0.80	9.1	221	44	50	1.21	0.0	16.2		0.0	310
2014	AA	Richmond	5	6	0	93	85	3.29	1.23	20.9	264	34	71	3.01	1.9	8.2	4.3	0.1	114
2016	AAA	Sacramento	7	10	0	136	101	4.36	1.30	22.4	270	30	70	4.33	2.3	6.7	2.9	1.2	76
2017	AAA	Sacramento	0	0	0	3	1	15.00	2.33	15.5	415	40	33	11.21	3.0	3.0	1.0	3.0	-9
2017	AAA	Round Rock	6	2	0	93	78	4.65	1.33	20.3	274	34	63	3.70	2.4	7.5	3.1	0.4	89

Big, durable SP who spent 3rd year in AAA and regressed. Repeats clean delivery and uses loose arm to generate OK velocity and pitch movement. Lacks plus offering and doesn't profile well for Ks. Sinking FB gets groundballs and doesn't harm himself with walks. Could be ideal middle RP who can get grounder.

Blewett,Scott

SP | Kansas City | EXP MLB DEBUT: 2019 | H/W: 6-6 210 | FUT: #3 starter | 8D

Thrws R Age 21
2014 (2) HS (NY)

Velo	Pitch	Grade
90-95	FB	+++
77-80	CB	+++
83-85	CU	++

Year	Lev	Team	W	L	Sv	IP	K	ERA	WHIP	BF/G	OBA	H%	S%	xERA	Ctl	Dom	Cmd	hr/9	BPV
2014	Rk	Burlington	1	2	0	28	29	4.82	1.50	15.1	255	32	69	4.38	4.8	9.3	1.9	1.0	56
2015	A	Lexington	3	5	0	81	60	5.22	1.38	18.9	278	33	61	4.15	2.7	6.7	2.5	0.7	66
2016	A	Lexington	8	11	0	129	121	4.32	1.46	22.1	275	34	71	4.33	3.6	8.4	2.4	0.7	74
2017	A+	Wilmington	7	10	0	152	129	4.08	1.35	23.5	263	31	72	4.11	3.1	7.6	2.5	0.9	72

Athletic sinkerballer who had decent debut in A+ after two years in Single-A. Generates velocity with easy, quick arm. FB exhibits heavy, tumbling action and can mix in improved CB that serves as go to pitch. Delivery has gotten more consistent, but pitches to fat part of plate. Has to enhance CU to be big league starter.

Borucki,Ryan

SP | Toronto | EXP MLB DEBUT: 2018 | H/W: 6-4 175 | FUT: #3 starter | 8D

Thrws L Age 24
2012 (15) HS (IL)

Velo	Pitch	Grade
91-95	FB	+++
80-83	SL	++
80-83	CU	++++

Year	Lev	Team	W	L	Sv	IP	K	ERA	WHIP	BF/G	OBA	H%	S%	xERA	Ctl	Dom	Cmd	hr/9	BPV
2016	A	Lansing	10	4	0	115	107	2.42	1.14	22.8	244	32	77	2.51	2.0	8.4	4.1	0.1	114
2016	A+	Dunedin	1	4	0	20	10	14.40	2.60	18.1	415	39	48	13.28	5.4	4.5	0.8	4.5	-47
2017	A+	Dunedin	6	5	0	98	109	3.58	1.24	21.0	256	35	71	3.27	2.5	10.0	4.0	0.5	131
2017	AA	New Hampshire	2	3	0	46	42	1.95	0.85	24.1	193	25	78	1.43	1.6	8.2	5.3	0.4	123
2017	AAA	Buffalo	0	0	0	6	6	0.00	1.17	23.9	262	35	100	2.74	1.5	9.0	6.0	0.0	140

Long, lean SP who set high in IP and is staying healthy. Maintained high K rate while showing excellent control. Very tough on LHH and plus CU is best offering. Keeps same arm speed as FB on CU and features tumbling action. Must command FB to succeed and SL could be tighter. Very intriguing profile.

Bowden, Ben — RP — Colorado

EXP MLB DEBUT: 2019 | H/W: 6-4 235 | FUT: Setup reliever | 7C

Thrws L Age 23
2016 (2) Vanderbilt

Velo	Pitch	Grade
92-95	FB	++++
80-83	SL	++
	CU	+++

Year	Lev	Team	W	L	Sv	IP	K	ERA	WHIP	BF/G	OBA	H%	S%	xERA	Ctl	Dom	Cmd	hr/9	BPV
2016	NCAA	Vanderbilt	2	1	10	48	65	3.55	1.29	8.2	261	39	73	3.52	2.6	12.1	4.6	0.6	166
2016	A	Asheville	0	1	0	23	29	3.10	1.64	4.0	260	38	81	4.24	5.8	11.3	1.9	0.4	63
2017	*Did not pitch - injured*																		

Physical lefty reliever missed all of 2017 with neck surgery. Works from 3B side of mound and runs 92-95 mph fastball away from RHB. Slider is average while change-up flashes plus at times. Inconsistent mechanics and release led to control issues in debut and need to be addressed.

Brigham, Jeff — SP — Miami

EXP MLB DEBUT: 2020 | H/W: 6-0 200 | FUT: Setup reliever | 8D

Thrws R Age 26
2014 (4) Washington

Velo	Pitch	Grade
95-98	FB	+++++
80-83	SL	+++
	CU	+

Year	Lev	Team	W	L	Sv	IP	K	ERA	WHIP	BF/G	OBA	H%	S%	xERA	Ctl	Dom	Cmd	hr/9	BPV
2015	A	Great Lakes	2	0	0	7	11	1.29	0.71	12.4	132	26	80	0.03	2.6	14.1	5.5	0.0	203
2015	A+	Rancho Cuca	4	5	0	68	64	5.96	1.68	18.0	289	35	65	5.41	4.8	8.5	1.8	1.1	42
2015	A+	Jupiter	2	2	0	33	22	1.90	1.30	22.8	266	32	84	3.15	2.4	6.0	2.4	0.0	59
2016	A+	Jupiter	7	8	1	122	112	4.05	1.33	18.8	250	32	69	3.40	3.5	8.2	2.4	0.4	73
2017	A+	Jupiter	4	2	0	59	53	2.90	1.17	21.4	228	29	75	2.59	3.1	8.1	2.7	0.3	81

Short, strong-armed hurler has some of the best velocity in the system. Fastball sits at 95-98 mph, topping at 100. Average slider and below-average change-up give him potential, but injury concerns and control issues could result in a move to relief. The Marlins view him as a starter for now, but was limited to 59 IP in 2017.

Buehler, Walker — SP — Los Angeles (N)

EXP MLB DEBUT: 2017 | H/W: 6-2 175 | FUT: #1 starter | 9B

Thrws R Age 23
2015 (1) Vanderbilt

Velo	Pitch	Grade
95-98	FB	+++++
80-85	SL	++++
76-80	CB	++++
	CU	++

Year	Lev	Team	W	L	Sv	IP	K	ERA	WHIP	BF/G	OBA	H%	S%	xERA	Ctl	Dom	Cmd	hr/9	BPV
2016	A	Great Lakes	0	0	0	3		0.00	1.00	5.7	0	0	100		9.0	9.0	1.0	0.0	-63
2017	A+	Rancho Cuca	0	0	0	16	27	1.12	0.81	11.7	150	30	85	0.43	2.8	15.1	5.4	0.0	214
2017	AA	Tulsa	2	2	0	49	64	3.49	1.12	17.6	224	32	72	2.97	2.8	11.8	4.3	0.9	155
2017	AAA	Oklahoma City	1	1	1	23	34	4.68	1.30	7.9	226	37	62	2.92	4.3	13.2	3.1	0.4	141
2017	MLB	LA Dodgers	1	0	0	9	12	7.91	2.09	5.6	300	40	65	7.44	7.9	11.9	1.5	2.0	18

24th overall pick in 2015 logged just 93.2 minor league IP before making his MLB debut. Fastball velocity up a tick from college and now sits at 95-98 topping at 100 mph. Backs heater with plus curveball and plus wipe-out slider. Shows some feel for change-up and raw stuff is as good as any prospect in baseball.

Bukauskas,J.B. — SP — Houston

EXP MLB DEBUT: 2019 | H/W: 6-0 196 | FUT: Closer | 8B

Thrws R Age 21
2017 (1) North Carolina

Velo	Pitch	Grade
92-96	FB	++++
81-87	SL	++++
86-88	CU	++

Year	Lev	Team	W	L	Sv	IP	K	ERA	WHIP	BF/G	OBA	H%	S%	xERA	Ctl	Dom	Cmd	hr/9	BPV
2017	NCAA	North Carolina	9	1	0	92	116	2.54	1.07	23.9	193	28	79	2.25	3.6	11.3	3.1	0.7	124
2017	Rk	GCL Astros	0	0	0	4	3	0.00	1.00	15.3	210	27	100	1.67	2.3	6.8	3.0	0.0	79
2017	A-	Tri City	0	0	0	6	6	4.50	1.33	12.5	191	27	63	2.27	6.0	9.0	1.5	0.0	18

Top collegian who pitched sparingly in his debut. Short, muscular build and quick arm speed produces lively mid-90s FB, but often struggles to maintain velo. SL can miss bats, though command is spotty and will require significant CU work to stick as SP. Arm action and frame suggest future late-inning RP who can provide some Ks.

Bummer,Aaron — RP — Chicago (A)

EXP MLB DEBUT: 2017 | H/W: 6-3 200 | FUT: Setup reliever | 7C

Thrws L Age 24
2014 (19) Nebraska

Velo	Pitch	Grade
91-94	FB	++++
81-84	SL	+++

Year	Lev	Team	W	L	Sv	IP	K	ERA	WHIP	BF/G	OBA	H%	S%	xERA	Ctl	Dom	Cmd	hr/9	BPV
2017	A+	Winston-Salem	0	2	2	11	15	4.91	1.18	5.5	244	33	64	4.04	2.5	12.3	5.0	1.6	173
2017	AA	Birmingham	1	3	3	33	34	3.00	1.36	8.1	238	31	79	3.42	4.4	9.3	2.1	0.5	67
2017	AAA	Charlotte	0	0	0	5	5	1.80	1.20	6.7	262	35	83	2.82	1.8	9.0	5.0	0.0	131
2017	MLB	Chi White Sox	1	3	0	22	17	4.50	1.27	3.0	173	17	71	3.47	6.1	7.0	1.1	1.6	-23

Solid, projectable pen arm made MLB debut in 2017. Struggled with FB command in MLB debut but was virtually unhittable, especially against LHH. Outside of the walk rate, fared well against RHH too. FB sits low 90s with solid arm-side bore. The development of SL will be key in developing into setup man.

Burdi,Nick — RP — Pittsburgh

EXP MLB DEBUT: 2018 | H/W: 6-5 220 | FUT: Closer | 7C

Thrws R Age 25
2014 (2) Louisville

Velo	Pitch	Grade
93-98	FB	++++
85-88	SL	+++
84-87	CU	+

Year	Lev	Team	W	L	Sv	IP	K	ERA	WHIP	BF/G	OBA	H%	S%	xERA	Ctl	Dom	Cmd	hr/9	BPV
2014	A+	Fort Myers	2	0	1	7	12	0.00	0.99	3.9	200	38	100	1.43	2.5	15.2	6.0	0.0	223
2015	A+	Fort Myers	2	2	2	20	29	2.25	0.75	5.5	175	29	71	1.01	1.4	13.1	9.7	0.5	216
2015	AA	Chattanooga	3	4	2	43	54	4.58	1.67	6.5	247	35	72	4.36	6.7	11.3	1.7	0.6	41
2016	AA	Chattanooga	1	0	0	3	1	9.00	1.67	4.5	321	35	40	4.94	3.0	3.0	1.0	0.0	-9
2017	AA	Chattanooga	2	0	1	17	20	0.53	0.76	4.4	158	22	100	0.95	2.1	10.6	5.0	0.5	151

Electric-armed RP who ended season in May after Tommy John surgery. Very tough to hit based upon power arsenal and arm slot. Throws downhill due to height and gets nasty sinking action on FB. SL can be downright filthy, but has trouble keeping in strike zone. Not much feel for CU. If control improves, he has closer upside. Rule 5 pick from MIN.

Burdi,Zack — RP — Chicago (A)

EXP MLB DEBUT: 2019 | H/W: 6-3 205 | FUT: Closer | 9E

Thrws R Age 23
2016 (1) Louisville

Velo	Pitch	Grade
97-99	FB	+++++
88-91	SL	++++
87-88	CU	+++

Year	Lev	Team	W	L	Sv	IP	K	ERA	WHIP	BF/G	OBA	H%	S%	xERA	Ctl	Dom	Cmd	hr/9	BPV
2016	Rk	AZL White Sox	0	0	0	1	1	0.00	1.00	3.8	262	35	100	2.32	0.0	9.0		0.0	180
2016	A+	Winston-Salem	0	0	0	5	4	5.40	1.20	5.0	299	33	60	5.06	0.0	7.2		1.8	148
2016	AA	Birmingham	0	0	0	16	24	3.94	1.00	5.1	134	19	64	1.83	5.1	13.5	2.7	1.1	124
2016	AAA	Charlotte	1	0	1	16	22	2.25	1.25	7.2	166	28	80	1.75	6.2	12.4	2.0	0.0	74
2017	AAA	Charlotte	0	4	7	33	51	4.08	1.42	4.8	243	40	71	3.59	4.6	13.9	3.0	0.5	143

Hard-throwing RH likely will miss 2018 after Tommy John surgery in July. FB is high octane but flattens out and can be hit. SL is a plus offering with solid tight 2-plane break. Uses deception to trick hitters into swinging through average CU. Struggles overthrowing FB and bouts of poor command. Violent delivery could be toned back.

Burke,Brock — SP — Tampa Bay

EXP MLB DEBUT: 2020 | H/W: 6-4 200 | FUT: #4 starter | 7C

Thrws L Age 21
2014 (3) HS (CO)

Velo	Pitch	Grade
90-94	FB	+++
80-83	SL	+++
	CU	++

Year	Lev	Team	W	L	Sv	IP	K	ERA	WHIP	BF/G	OBA	H%	S%	xERA	Ctl	Dom	Cmd	hr/9	BPV
2014	Rk	GCL Rays	0	3	0	13	12	10.99	2.14	8.1	302	38	44	6.42	8.2	8.2	1.0	0.7	-56
2015	Rk	Princeton	4	2	0	52	35	3.45	1.25	19.3	268	31	73	3.54	1.9	6.0	3.2	0.5	75
2016	A-	Hudson Valley	3	3	0	61	61	3.39	1.34	19.5	236	32	73	2.97	4.3	9.0	2.1	0.1	64
2017	A	Bowling Green	6	0	0	57	59	1.10	1.00	21.8	187	27	88	1.37	3.2	9.3	3.0	0.0	100
2017	A+	Charlotte	5	6	0	66	49	4.64	1.38	21.3	287	33	67	4.42	2.2	6.7	3.1	0.8	79

Strong, thick SP who was awesome in A-ball after three years in Rookie ball. Didn't fare as well upon promotion to A+, but has upped velocity while showing feel for secondaries. More of a flyball pitcher and needs consistency with release point. Throws good strikes, but may not have a swing-and-miss offering in repertoire.

Burnes,Corbin — SP — Milwaukee

EXP MLB DEBUT: 2018 | H/W: 6-3 205 | FUT: #2 starter | 9E

Thrws R Age 23
2016 (4) St. Mary's

Velo	Pitch	Grade
92-95	FB	++++
82-83	SL	++++
75-77	CB	+++
86-88	CU	+++

Year	Lev	Team	W	L	Sv	IP	K	ERA	WHIP	BF/G	OBA	H%	S%	xERA	Ctl	Dom	Cmd	hr/9	BPV
2016	Rk	AZL Brewers	0	0	0	7	10	1.29	0.71	8.2	132	24	80	0.04	2.6	12.9	5.0	0.0	180
2016	A	Wisconsin	3	0	0	28	31	2.23	1.28	12.8	201	28	83	2.53	5.1	9.9	1.9	0.3	58
2017	A+	Carolina	5	0	0	60	56	1.05	0.88	22.2	179	24	88	1.15	2.4	8.4	3.5	0.2	104
2017	AA	Biloxi	3	3	0	85	84	2.11	1.01	20.4	216	29	79	1.94	2.1	8.9	4.2	0.2	121

Fast-moving RH continues to excel at every level. Big FB and plus SL provide solid 1-2 strikeout punch. Made mechanical change to line arm up better with target. FB has solid, late run. SL has plus two-plane break. Can sweep SL too. CB solid eye-level changer. Has solid feel for CU. Gaining confidence in pitch.

Burrows,Beau — SP — Detroit

EXP MLB DEBUT: 2019 | H/W: 6-2 200 | FUT: #3 starter | 8C

Thrws R Age 21
2015 (1) HS (TX)

Velo	Pitch	Grade
92-96	FB	++++
76-79	CB	++
84-86	SL	++
	CU	++

Year	Lev	Team	W	L	Sv	IP	K	ERA	WHIP	BF/G	OBA	H%	S%	xERA	Ctl	Dom	Cmd	hr/9	BPV
2015	Rk	GCL Tigers	1	0	0	28	33	1.61	1.04	10.8	186	28	83	1.44	3.5	10.6	3.0	0.0	113
2016	A	West Michigan	6	4	0	97	67	3.15	1.21	18.6	241	29	72	2.76	2.8	6.2	2.2	0.2	55
2017	A+	Lakeland	4	3	0	58	62	1.24	0.96	20.0	215	29	91	2.05	1.7	9.6	5.6	0.5	145
2017	AA	Erie	6	4	0	76	75	4.73	1.47	21.8	269	35	67	4.16	3.9	8.9	2.3	0.6	72

Strong, durable SP who was dominant in A+ before promotion to AA in June. Exhibited consistently high velocity with FB which can be true out pitch. Needs to upgrade command, but has four pitches in arsenal. Has two breaking balls and may focus on hard CB that could be plus with consistent break. Uses same arm slot and speed on improving CU.

Buttrey,Ty — RP — Boston

EXP MLB DEBUT: 2018 | H/W: 6-6 230 | FUT: Setup reliever | 7D

Thrws R Age 25
2012 (4) HS (NC)

Velo	Pitch	Grade
93-96	FB	++++
83-86	SL	++
	CU	+

Year	Lev	Team	W	L	Sv	IP	K	ERA	WHIP	BF/G	OBA	H%	S%	xERA	Ctl	Dom	Cmd	hr/9	BPV
2015	A	Greenville	1	0	0	22	22	2.45	0.91	20.5	215	27	78	2.25	1.2	9.0	7.3	0.8	147
2015	A+	Salem	8	10	0	115	81	4.22	1.41	23.2	265	31	69	3.77	3.5	6.3	1.8	0.4	37
2016	AA	Portland	1	9	0	79	52	4.44	1.59	10.6	264	30	73	4.52	5.2	5.9	1.1	0.7	-17
2017	AA	Portland	1	4	4	46	56	3.72	1.35	6.4	231	34	70	2.95	4.5	11.0	2.4	0.2	94
2017	AAA	Pawtucket	1	1	0	17	18	7.85	1.80	8.0	302	38	55	5.90	5.2	9.4	1.8	1.0	46

Imposing RP who moved to bullpen in mid-2016 and has found niche. Misses ton more bats as RP and can let loose with plus FB. Lot of effort in delivery makes for difficulty in repeating and struggles with pitch location. Needs to find pitch to retire LHH. Introduced SL with good break, though will need consistency.

Cabrera, Edward — SP — Miami

EXP MLB DEBUT: 2022 | H/W: 6-4 175 | FUT: #2 SP/closer | 9E

Thrws R Age 19
2015 FA (DR)

Velo	Pitch	Grade
94-97	FB	+++++
	SL	++++
	CU	++

Year	Lev	Team	W	L	Sv	IP	K	ERA	WHIP	BF/G	OBA	H%	S%	xERA	Ctl	Dom	Cmd	hr/9	BPV
2016	Rk	GCL Marlins	2	6	0	47	28	4.21	1.36	17.9	289	34	67	3.84	1.9	5.4	2.8	0.2	63
2017	A-	Batavia	1	3	0	35	32	5.37	1.42	11.5	297	38	59	4.14	2.0	8.2	4.0	0.3	110

Tall, skinny Dominican hurler has a huge arm, but lots of work to do. Fastball sits at 94-97 mph and tops out at 101. Also has a plus hard slider, but his change-up needs refinement. Still has some projection left. Very raw, but tremendous long-term potential.

Cabrera,Genesis — SP — Tampa Bay

EXP MLB DEBUT: 2019 | H/W: 6-1 170 | FUT: #3 starter | 8E

Thrws L Age 21
2013 FA (DR)

Velo	Pitch	Grade
90-95	FB	++++
84-87	SL	+++
	CU	++

Year	Lev	Team	W	L	Sv	IP	K	ERA	WHIP	BF/G	OBA	H%	S%	xERA	Ctl	Dom	Cmd	hr/9	BPV
2015	Rk	Princeton	0	0	0	17	19	3.18	1.18	13.6	250	36	70	2.59	2.1	10.1	4.8	0.0	142
2016	A	Bowling Green	11	5	0	116	96	3.88	1.36	21.1	252	30	72	3.76	3.7	7.4	2.0	0.7	52
2017	A+	Charlotte	4	5	0	69	60	2.86	1.01	20.4	187	24	72	1.79	3.3	7.8	2.4	0.4	71
2017	AA	Montgomery	5	4	0	64	51	3.64	1.59	23.6	293	35	79	5.05	3.8	7.1	1.9	0.8	44

Unheralded SP who had success in first half at A+ before struggles at AA. Very adept at establishing plate early in count with lively FB and mixes in impressive SL. Delivery adds deception and allows stuff to play up. Lacks true dominant offering and may not have the durability or stamina to last as SP. Keys are strength and development of CU.

Callahan,Jamie — RP — New York (N)

EXP MLB DEBUT: 2017 | H/W: 6-2 230 | FUT: Setup reliever | 7C

Thrws R Age 23
2012 (2) HS (SC)

Velo	Pitch	Grade
94-97	FB	++++
88-90	CT	+++
87-90	SP	++

Year	Lev	Team	W	L	Sv	IP	K	ERA	WHIP	BF/G	OBA	H%	S%	xERA	Ctl	Dom	Cmd	hr/9	BPV
2016	A+	Salem	5	3	7	65		3.31	1.40	7.6	224	30	74	2.95	5.2	8.7	1.7	0.1	33
2017	AA	Portland	4	1	2	13	20	1.38	0.62	4.5	179	32	75	0.28	0.0	13.8		0.0	267
2017	AAA	Pawtucket	1	1	4	29	36	4.03	1.41	5.6	255	36	72	3.83	4.0	11.2	2.8	0.6	110
2017	AAA	Las Vegas	1	1	1	10	10	1.80	1.60	4.9	299	35	100	6.05	3.6	9.0	2.5	1.8	83
2017	MLB	NY Mets	0	0	0	6	5	4.35	1.29	2.8	286	36	63	3.41	1.5	7.3	5.0	0.0	109

Acquired in Addison Reed trade, RH power reliever made MLB debut in Sept. Former SP, is now primarily two-pitch RP. Started using split again with varying results during season. Best pitch is 2-seam high-octane FB with some arm-side run and sink. SL has developed more CT action as RP. No longer struggles with control.

Canning,Griffin — SP — Los Angeles (A)

EXP MLB DEBUT: 2019 | H/W: 6-1 170 | FUT: #3 starter | 8D

Thrws R Age 21
2017 (2) UCLA

Velo	Pitch	Grade
90-95	FB	+++
80-83	SL	++
78-81	CB	+++
	CU	+++

Year	Lev	Team	W	L	Sv	IP	K	ERA	WHIP	BF/G	OBA	H%	S%	xERA	Ctl	Dom	Cmd	hr/9	BPV
2017	NCAA	UCLA	7	4	0	119	140	2.34	1.05	27.1	217	31	79	2.27	2.4	10.6	4.4	0.5	143

Slightly-built SP who did not pitch upon signing due to heavy workload in college. Could move quickly with four-pitch arsenal. Velocity sufficient and commands plate well. CU is best pitch and uses same arm speed with good velocity separation. Very clean delivery assuages durability concerns. Has some K ability with two breaking balls.

Carlson,Sam — SP — Seattle

EXP MLB DEBUT: 2021 | H/W: 6-4 195 | FUT: #3 starter | 8D

Thrws R Age 19
2017 (2) HS (MN)

Velo	Pitch	Grade
90-94	FB	+++
77-80	SL	++
82-84	CU	+++

Year	Lev	Team	W	L	Sv	IP	K	ERA	WHIP	BF/G	OBA	H%	S%	xERA	Ctl	Dom	Cmd	hr/9	BPV
2017	Rk	AZL Mariners	0	0	0	3	3	3.00	1.33	6.2	321	42	75	4.04	0.0	9.0		0.0	180

Very projectable SP with ingredients to become legitimate mid-rotation option. Possesses terrific FB and CU at present and pitches play up due to deception and ability to hide ball. Inconsistent velocity should get better with pro instruction and will need to upgrade slower SL. Has good feel, yet will take time to develop.

Carroll,Cody — RP — New York (A)

EXP MLB DEBUT: 2018 | H/W: 6-5 210 | FUT: Setup reliever | 7C

Thrws R Age 25
2015 (22) Southern Miss

Velo	Pitch	Grade
92-97	FB	+++
84-88	SL	+++
	SP	++

Year	Lev	Team	W	L	Sv	IP	K	ERA	WHIP	BF/G	OBA	H%	S%	xERA	Ctl	Dom	Cmd	hr/9	BPV
2015	Rk	Pulaski	1	1	3	25	26	1.79	1.19	7.2	184	26	83	1.82	5.0	9.3	1.9	0.0	50
2016	A	Charleston (Sc)	4	4	3	91	90	3.16	1.43	14.9	257	34	77	3.61	4.1	8.9	2.2	0.3	69
2017	A+	Tampa	1	0	2	20	30	2.25	0.90	5.7	151	25	76	1.11	3.6	13.5	3.8	0.5	164
2017	AA	Trenton	2	5	5	47	59	2.68	1.23	7.3	213	30	81	2.97	4.2	11.3	2.7	0.8	107

Quick-armed, unheralded RP who flies under radar with large frame and FB that touches triple digits. Is inconsistent with pitch location and needs to harness arm action. Can wipe out hitters with FB and nasty, hard SL. Will mix in occasional SP, but is more of show-me pitch. Improved stuff in 2017 and could grow into setup guy in near future.

Castellani, Ryan — SP — Colorado

EXP MLB DEBUT: 2018 | H/W: 6-4 220 | FUT: #3 starter | 8C

Thrws R Age 22
2014 (2) HS (AZ)

Velo	Pitch	Grade
92-95	FB	++++
73-75	CB	+++
79-83	CU	+++
	SL	+++

Year	Lev	Team	W	L	Sv	IP	K	ERA	WHIP	BF/G	OBA	H%	S%	xERA	Ctl	Dom	Cmd	hr/9	BPV
2014	A-	Tri-City	1	2	0	37	25	3.65	1.19	14.8	251	29	69	3.13	2.2	6.1	2.8	0.5	68
2015	A	Asheville	2	7	0	113	94	4.46	1.44	17.8	296	36	68	4.31	2.3	7.5	3.2	0.4	90
2016	A+	Modesto	7	8	0	167	142	3.82	1.23	26.1	249	31	68	3.14	2.7	7.6	2.8	0.4	83
2017	AA	Hartford	9	12	0	157	132	4.81	1.34	24.2	269	32	65	4.14	2.7	7.6	2.8	0.9	81

Hard-throwing righty took a step back at Double-A, but remains an impact prospect. FB now sits at 92-95, topping at 97 mph with good, late sink. Left too many balls up in the zone, resulting in 16 HR allowed. SL and CU are both above-average and give him the tools to be a solid #3 starter.

Castillo,Jesus — SP — Los Angeles (A)

EXP MLB DEBUT: 2019 | H/W: 6-2 165 | FUT: #4 starter | 7C

Thrws R Age 22
2011 FA (VZ)

Velo	Pitch	Grade
89-93	FB	+++
77-79	CB	++
81-82	CU	+++

Year	Lev	Team	W	L	Sv	IP	K	ERA	WHIP	BF/G	OBA	H%	S%	xERA	Ctl	Dom	Cmd	hr/9	BPV
2016	A-	Eugene	2	3	0	33	38	3.27	1.18	18.9	231	31	75	3.13	3.0	10.4	3.5	0.8	124
2016	A	Burlington	3	2	0	29	23	2.47	1.37	20.4	286	35	82	3.90	2.2	7.1	3.3	0.3	87
2017	A	Burlington	1	1	0	19	22	2.37	0.79	17.1	195	28	71	1.38	0.9	10.4	11.0	0.5	180
2017	A+	Inland Empire	8	3	0	82	74	3.62	1.27	21.0	271	32	78	4.47	2.0	8.1	4.1	1.4	111
2017	AA	Mobile	0	2	0	23	22	3.10	1.42	19.7	292	37	81	4.55	2.3	8.5	3.7	0.8	109

Tall, lean SP with decent Dom despite no plus pitch in arsenal. Induces ton of groundballs with efficient, repeatable delivery. Relies more on pitch movement than power and has hint of deception. Throws strikes with CU which may be best current offering. Needs to upgrade CB for strikeout rate to continue. Now in third organization.

Cave,Garrett — RP — San Francisco

EXP MLB DEBUT: 2019 | H/W: 6-4 200 | FUT: Setup reliever | 7D

Thrws R Age 21
2017 (4) Tampa

Velo	Pitch	Grade
92-96	FB	++++
78-81	CB	+++
85-88	SL	++
	CU	+

Year	Lev	Team	W	L	Sv	IP	K	ERA	WHIP	BF/G	OBA	H%	S%	xERA	Ctl	Dom	Cmd	hr/9	BPV
2017	NCAA	Tampa	5	2	4	61	84	4.26	1.26	13.9	207	32	66	2.78	4.7	12.4	2.6	0.6	113
2017	A-	Salem-Keizer	1	1	3	20	29	5.85	1.55	6.2	252	41	58	3.53	5.4	13.1	2.4	0.0	107

Live-armed RP with deep repertoire for late innings work. FB command is current hindrance, but has both velocity and pitch movement. Electric FB can be thrown by hitters up in zone and has two hard breaking balls as chase pitches. Mixes in occasional CU. Can be high K guy, but needs to combat LHH better. Keep an eye on walk rate.

Cease,Dylan — SP — Chicago (A)

EXP MLB DEBUT: 2019 | H/W: 6-2 190 | FUT: #2 starter | 9E

Thrws R Age 22
2014 (6) HS (GA)

Velo	Pitch	Grade
94-98	FB	++++
79-82	CB	++++
82-85	CU	++

Year	Lev	Team	W	L	Sv	IP	K	ERA	WHIP	BF/G	OBA	H%	S%	xERA	Ctl	Dom	Cmd	hr/9	BPV
2015	Rk	AZL Cubs	1	2	0	24	25	2.63	1.17	8.7	151	22	75	1.40	6.0	9.4	1.6	0.0	25
2016	A-	Eugene	2	0	0	44	66	2.24	1.18	14.7	178	31	80	1.87	5.1	13.4	2.6	0.2	122
2017	A	South Bend	1	2	0	51	74	2.81	1.27	16.1	213	34	78	2.65	4.6	13.0	2.8	0.4	129
2017	A	Kannapolis	0	8	0	41	52	3.93	1.29	18.8	232	35	67	2.82	3.9	11.4	2.9	0.2	116

Hard throwing RHP acquired in Jose Quintana deal. Has grown tremendously mechanically in past two seasons. Big FB, can get up to triple digits with late, plus movement. Changes eye levels w/ 12-6 hammer CB, also plus. Profile dependent on development of CU—was better in 2017, but still lacks confidence in pitch.

Chalmers,Dakota — SP — Oakland

EXP MLB DEBUT: 2020 | H/W: 6-3 175 | FUT: #3 starter | 8D

Thrws R Age 21
2015 (3) HS (GA)

Velo	Pitch	Grade
92-95	FB	+++
75-78	CB	+++
80-84	SL	++
	CU	++

Year	Lev	Team	W	L	Sv	IP	K	ERA	WHIP	BF/G	OBA	H%	S%	xERA	Ctl	Dom	Cmd	hr/9	BPV
2015	Rk	AZL Athletics	0	1	0	20	18	2.69	1.59	8.1	209	28	81	3.14	7.6	8.1	1.1	0.0	-42
2016	A-	Vermont	5	4	0	67	62	4.70	1.37	18.7	225	27	68	3.80	5.0	8.3	1.7	1.1	34
2017	A	Beloit	2	2	0	29	47	4.34	1.52	12.6	155	29	70	2.57	9.0	14.6	1.6	0.3	38

Projectable SP who ended season in May due to personal issues. Has ideal athleticism, but hasn't found consistent mechanics or release point. Control is well below average at present. When on, shows four very good pitches highlighted by knockout CB and quick FB. Has good arm speed and action on CU, but needs significant development time.

Chargois,J.T.

RP | Minnesota | EXP MLB DEBUT: 2016 | H/W: 6-3 200 | FUT: Closer | 7C

Thrws R Age 27
2012 (2) Rice

- 94-97 FB +++
- 84-88 SL +++
- 84-86 CU +

Year	Lev	Team	W	L	Sv	IP	K	ERA	WHIP	BF/G	OBA	H%	S%	xERA	Ctl	Dom	Cmd	hr/9	BPV
2015	AA	Chattanooga	1	1	11	33	34	2.73	1.39	4.3	218	30	80	3.00	5.5	9.3	1.7	0.3	38
2016	AA	Chattanooga	0	0	7	11	14	1.61	1.16	4.1	202	28	92	2.69	4.0	11.3	2.8	0.8	112
2016	AAA	Rochester	2	1	9	35	41	1.29	1.00	4.8	215	31	88	1.93	2.1	10.5	5.1	0.3	152
2016	MLB	Minnesota	1	1	0	23	17	4.70	1.61	4.1	278	34	68	4.10	4.7	6.7	1.4	0.0	11
2017	AAA	Rochester	0	0	1	2	2	0.00	0.91	4.1	139	19	100	0.65	4.1	8.2	2.0	0.0	55

Hard-throwing RP who ended season early due to stress reaction in elbow. Injury history is big concern as he did not pitch in 2013 or 2014. Hindered by inconsistent command predicated from max-effort delivery. All pitches are hard and has stints of dominance. Electric sinking FB is highlight while induces weak contact with hard SL and CU.

Charles,Wandisson

RP | Oakland | EXP MLB DEBUT: 2021 | H/W: 6-6 220 | FUT: Closer | 8E

Thrws R Age 21
2015 FA (DR)

- 93-98 FB ++++
- 82-85 SL ++

Year	Lev	Team	W	L	Sv	IP	K	ERA	WHIP	BF/G	OBA	H%	S%	xERA	Ctl	Dom	Cmd	hr/9	BPV
2016	Rk	AZL Athletics	5	1	2	36	48	7.21	1.99	12.4	276	42	60	4.98	8.2	11.9	1.5	0.0	11
2017	A-	Vermont	2	0	5	21	29	3.43	1.57	6.1	202	32	78	3.37	7.7	12.4	1.6	0.4	33

Power-armed RP who saw little mound time due to injuries. Has big frame and blessed with plus, pure arm strength. Has trouble finding plate with erratic mechanics. Has ability to miss ton of bats with both FB and SL. Pitches aggressively up in zone and uses SL as chase pitch. Mature hitters have laid off SL and will need to throw for strikes.

Chirinos,Yonny

SP | Tampa Bay | EXP MLB DEBUT: 2018 | H/W: 6-2 170 | FUT: #4 starter | 7C

Thrws R Age 24
2012 FA (VZ)

- 90-94 FB +++
- 82-84 SL +++
- 83-84 SP +++
- CU ++

Year	Lev	Team	W	L	Sv	IP	K	ERA	WHIP	BF/G	OBA	H%	S%	xERA	Ctl	Dom	Cmd	hr/9	BPV
2016	A	Bowling Green	1	0	0	11		2.41	0.80	10.1	202	26	67	1.08	0.8	7.2	9.0	0.0	126
2016	A+	Charlotte	6	1	0	50	31	2.16	1.00	17.4	250	28	84	3.02	0.5	5.6	10.3	0.9	104
2016	AA	Montgomery	5	3	0	66	43	4.49	1.30	19.5	284	32	65	4.05	1.6	5.8	3.6	0.7	79
2017	AA	Montgomery	1	0	0	27	21	2.66	0.96	25.6	224	23	86	3.29	1.3	7.0	5.3	1.7	108
2017	AAA	Durham	12	5	0	141	120	2.74	0.98	23.3	226	28	74	2.40	1.4	7.7	5.5	0.6	118

Athletic SP who thrives with outstanding control. Locates FB with precision to corners and can cut and sink at will. All pitches thrown for strikes, though none grade as plus or are true out pitches. At best when sequencing and keeping hitters off balance. Has interesting SP in repertoire.

Civale,Aaron

SP | Cleveland | EXP MLB DEBUT: 2019 | H/W: 6-2 215 | FUT: #4 starter | 7C

Thrws R Age 22
2016 (3) Northeastern

- 89-93 FB +++
- 82-85 SL +++
- 78-82 CB +++
- CU ++

Year	Lev	Team	W	L	Sv	IP	K	ERA	WHIP	BF/G	OBA	H%	S%	xERA	Ctl	Dom	Cmd	hr/9	BPV
2016	NCAA	Northeastern	9	3	0	114	121	1.74	0.93	28.5	220	29	85	2.11	1.2	9.5	8.1	0.6	158
2016	A-	Mahoning Val	0	2	0	37	28	1.69	0.83	10.5	180	23	77	0.90	1.9	6.8	3.5	0.0	88
2017	A	Lake County	2	4	0	57	53	4.58	1.21	23.0	285	37	60	3.47	0.8	8.4	10.6	0.3	147
2017	A+	Lynchburg	11	2	0	107	88	2.60	0.98	24.0	241	28	79	2.87	0.8	7.4	9.8	0.9	131

Durable SP who was much better in A+ than A. Got better along the way due to incredible control and improving, hard SL. Mixes pitches well, though may lack true knockout offering. Repeats delivery which positively impacts command. CB and CU aren't go-to pitches, but gives hitters different look. Has to throw strikes to be successful.

Clarke,Taylor

SP | Arizona | EXP MLB DEBUT: 2018 | H/W: 6-4 200 | FUT: #4 starter | 7C

Thrws R Age 24
2015 (3) Towson

- 91-94 FB ++++
- 79-83 SL +++
- 76-77 CB +
- 82-85 CU +++

Year	Lev	Team	W	L	Sv	IP	K	ERA	WHIP	BF/G	OBA	H%	S%	xERA	Ctl	Dom	Cmd	hr/9	BPV
2016	A	Kane County	3	2	0	28	24	2.87	1.03	18.1	232	29	71	2.30	1.6	7.7	4.8	0.3	113
2016	A+	Visalia	1	1	0	23	22	2.74	1.13	22.7	227	27	83	3.29	2.7	8.6	3.1	1.2	99
2016	AA	Mobile	8	6	0	97	72	3.61	1.23	23.2	265	31	73	3.76	1.9	6.7	3.4	0.8	86
2017	AA	Jackson	9	7	0	111	107	2.92	1.20	21.3	231	30	77	2.94	3.2	8.7	2.7	0.6	89
2017	AAA	Reno	3	2	0	33	31	4.88	1.27	22.6	236	25	71	4.69	3.5	8.4	2.4	2.2	74

Tall-and-fall RH is knocking on the door of the big leagues. Does a lot of things well; nothing spectacular. Uses size very well, especially with boring 2-seam fastball. SL is sweepy at times, overall an average offering. CU took another step forward, but consistency is key to effectiveness. Added CB, but in infancy stages.

Clarkin,Ian

SP | Chicago (A) | EXP MLB DEBUT: 2019 | H/W: 6-2 215 | FUT: Setup reliever | 7B

Thrws L Age 23
2013 (1) HS (CA)

- 91-94 FB ++++
- 74-76 CB +++
- SL ++
- 84-86 CU ++

Year	Lev	Team	W	L	Sv	IP	K	ERA	WHIP	BF/G	OBA	H%	S%	xERA	Ctl	Dom	Cmd	hr/9	BPV
2014	A	Charleston (Sc)	3	3	0	70	71	3.21	1.23	17.7	245	31	76	3.39	2.8	9.1	3.2	0.8	106
2014	A+	Tampa	1	0	0	5	4	1.80	1.60	22.1	332	41	88	4.91	1.8	7.2	4.0	0.0	99
2016	A+	Tampa	6	9	0	98	72	3.31	1.33	22.6	266	32	75	3.56	2.8	6.6	2.4	0.4	63
2017	A+	Winston-Salem	0	0	0	11	5	2.45	1.36	15.3	184	19	86	3.08	6.5	4.1	0.6	0.8	-85
2017	A+	Tampa	4	5	0	75	58	2.63	1.28	20.5	251	30	80	3.33	3.0	6.9	2.3	0.5	62

Tall, projectable LHP has yet to throw 100 IP in 5-year career due to injury. Creates good deception due to a high leg kick that hides the ball in his frame. From a 3/4s delivery, best pitch is heavy FB with some arm-side run. 12-6 CB is successful at changing eye levels and getting swings out of zone. CU is a smidge below average.

Clifton, Trevor

SP | Chicago (N) | EXP MLB DEBUT: 2018 | H/W: 6-1 170 | FUT: #4 starter | 7C

Thrws R Age 22
2013 (12) HS (TN)

- 91-94 FB +++
- 80-83 CB ++
- CU ++

Year	Lev	Team	W	L	Sv	IP	K	ERA	WHIP	BF/G	OBA	H%	S%	xERA	Ctl	Dom	Cmd	hr/9	BPV
2013	Rk	AZL Cubs	0	0	0	10	15	7.13	2.08	6.2	313	49	62	5.75	7.1	13.4	1.9	0.0	66
2014	A-	Boise	4	2	0	61	54	3.69	1.46	20.1	255	32	74	3.81	4.4	8.0	1.8	0.4	42
2015	A	South Bend	8	10	0	108	103	3.99	1.28	19.3	230	29	69	3.14	3.9	8.6	2.2	0.6	67
2016	A+	Myrtle Beach	7	7	0	119	129	2.72	1.16	20.6	224	31	76	2.50	3.1	9.8	3.1	0.3	110
2017	AA	Tennessee	5	8	0	100	86	5.21	1.57	20.9	284	35	66	4.75	4.0	7.7	1.9	0.7	48

Tall, strong-bodied right-hander took a step back after breakout in 2016. Fastball sits at 91-94 mph and is backed by a slider, curve, and change-up all of which are average offerings. Lacks the arm speed and physicality to be more than a back-end starter and a move to relief seems likely.

Cody,Kyle

SP | Texas | EXP MLB DEBUT: 2019 | H/W: 6-7 245 | FUT: #3 starter | 8D

Thrws R Age 23
2016 (6) Kentucky

- 92-96 FB ++++
- 80-82 CB ++
- 82-83 SL ++
- 83-85 CU ++

Year	Lev	Team	W	L	Sv	IP	K	ERA	WHIP	BF/G	OBA	H%	S%	xERA	Ctl	Dom	Cmd	hr/9	BPV
2016	NCAA	Kentucky	6	2	0	83	75	3.36	1.30	24.5	250	32	73	3.22	3.2	8.1	2.5	0.3	76
2016	A-	Spokane	2	5	0	47	53	5.16	1.46	16.8	297	39	65	4.70	2.5	10.1	4.1	0.8	133
2017	A	Hickory	6	6	0	95	101	2.84	1.16	21.0	223	30	75	2.55	3.1	9.6	3.1	0.4	106
2017	A+	Down East	3	0	0	30	35	2.09	1.16	24.0	227	33	80	2.24	3.0	10.4	3.5	0.0	125

Large-framed SP who has shown progress in all elements of pitching. Exhibits control while missing bats consistently. Tough to make hard contact against, particularly RHH. Power arsenal highlighted by plus, sinking FB. CU in infancy stage and has tendency to slow arm. Uses both CB and SL with CB being better of two.

Conlon,PJ

SP | New York (N) | EXP MLB DEBUT: 2018 | H/W: 5-11 192 | FUT: #5 SP/swingman | 6C

Thrws L Age 24
2015 (13) San Diego

- 87-89 FB ++
- 85-87 CT ++
- 75-77 CB +++
- 81-83 CU +++

Year	Lev	Team	W	L	Sv	IP	K	ERA	WHIP	BF/G	OBA	H%	S%	xERA	Ctl	Dom	Cmd	hr/9	BPV
2015	NCAA	San Diego	6	4	1	91	82	2.17	0.98	23.1	199	26	76	1.57	2.5	8.1	3.3	0.1	97
2015	A-	Brooklyn	0	1	0	17	25	0.00	0.59	3.4	143	26	100		1.1	13.2	12.5	0.0	228
2016	A	Columbia	8	1	0	78	61	1.84	1.00	24.9	236	29	84	2.42	1.2	7.0	6.1	0.5	113
2016	A+	St. Lucie	4	1	1	63	51	1.42	0.97	19.9	209	27	85	1.70	2.0	7.3	3.6	0.1	95
2017	AA	Binghamton	8	9	1	136	108	3.38	1.24	19.7	253	30	76	3.68	2.5	7.1	2.8	0.9	79

Command and control LH had solid season in Double-A. Though far from dominating, he mixes 4 pitches that all hover around average with some funk in delivery. Has confidence locating any pitch in any count. Best pitch is CU, which has solid deception and tumble. Lots of success against LHH. Could fill LOOGY role.

Cooney,Tim

SP | Cleveland | EXP MLB DEBUT: 2015 | H/W: 6-3 195 | FUT: #4 starter | 7D

Thrws L Age 27
2012 (3) Wake Forest

- 88-92 FB +++
- 77-79 CB ++
- 80-82 SL ++
- CU +++

Year	Lev	Team	W	L	Sv	IP	K	ERA	WHIP	BF/G	OBA	H%	S%	xERA	Ctl	Dom	Cmd	hr/9	BPV
2014	AAA	Memphis	14	6	0	158	119	3.47	1.30	25.0	262	30	78	4.21	2.7	6.8	2.5	1.2	68
2015	AAA	Memphis	6	4	0	88	63	2.76	0.87	23.3	197	22	74	2.07	1.6	6.4	3.9	0.9	90
2015	MLB	St. Louis	1	0	0	31	29	3.18	1.22	21.0	242	30	77	3.43	2.9	8.4	2.9	0.9	91
2016	*Did no*																		
2017	Rk	AZL Indians	0	0	0	3	4	6.00	2.00	3.6	262	40	67	4.81	9.0	12.0	1.3	0.0	-9

Injury-riddled SP who did not pitch in 2016 and missed vast majority of 2017 due to shoulder surgery and forearm strain. Has good stuff when healthy with pitch movement and deep pitch mix. Locates quality FB to both sides of plate while CU is most effective pitch. Gets lazy swings with CU, though fringy breaking balls are hittable.

Coonrod,Sam

SP | San Francisco | EXP MLB DEBUT: 2019 | H/W: 6-2 225 | FUT: #4 starter | 7C

Thrws R Age 25
2014 (5) Southern Illinois

- 90-94 FB +++
- 82-85 SL ++
- 84-86 CU ++

Year	Lev	Team	W	L	Sv	IP	K	ERA	WHIP	BF/G	OBA	H%	S%	xERA	Ctl	Dom	Cmd	hr/9	BPV
2014	Rk	AZL Giants	1	0	0	27	25	3.97	1.40	7.6	294	38	68	3.79	2.0	8.3	4.2	0.0	113
2015	A	Augusta	7	5	0	111	114	3.16	1.23	19.6	247	33	73	2.93	2.8	9.2	3.4	0.2	110
2016	A+	San Jose	5	3	0	63	42	1.99	1.08	22.4	205	24	83	2.22	3.1	6.0	1.9	0.4	41
2016	AA	Richmond	4	3	0	77	52	3.04	1.26	24.2	213	24	79	3.14	4.4	6.1	1.4	0.8	7
2017	AA	Richmond	4	11	0	103	94	4.71	1.34	17.9	248	31	64	3.56	3.7	8.2	2.2	0.6	67

Intense SP who took step back then moved to pen late. Will miss all 2018 due to Tommy John surgery. Relies on heavy pitch movement from two-seam FB and potential average CU. Throws with deception in high effort delivery. Can rear back for more velocity and hard SL can miss bats. Could stay in pen full-time and use big frame and delivery to dominate.

Cooper, Morgan — SP — Los Angeles (N)

EXP MLB DEBUT: 2020 | H/W: 6-5 210 | FUT: #3 starter | 8D

Thrws R Age 23
2017 (2) Texas

Velo	Pitch	Grade
92-95	FB	+++
	CT	+++
	CB	+++
	CU	+++

Year	Lev	Team	W	L	Sv	IP	K	ERA	WHIP	BF/G	OBA	H%	S%	xERA	Ctl	Dom	Cmd	hr/9	BPV
2017	*Did not pitch*																		

2nd round right-hander from Texas has good size and projection. Had Tommy John surgery in 2015, but fastball velocity is back in the 92-95 mph range, topping at 96 with good, late life. Over the top delivery gets good downhill tilt and keeps the ball on the ground. Curve, cutter, and change-up are all average to a tick above. Will make his pro debut in 2018.

Corry,Seth — SP — San Francisco

EXP MLB DEBUT: 2022 | H/W: 6-2 195 | FUT: #3 starter | 8E

Thrws L Age 19
2017 (3) HS (UT)

Velo	Pitch	Grade
90-93	FB	+++
78-82	CB	+++
	CU	+

Year	Lev	Team	W	L	Sv	IP	K	ERA	WHIP	BF/G	OBA	H%	S%	xERA	Ctl	Dom	Cmd	hr/9	BPV
2017	Rk	AZL Giants	0	2	0	24	21	5.60	1.49	8.0	171	22	60	2.81	8.2	7.8	1.0	0.4	-63

Projectable, athletic SP who may need significant development time. Delivery needs major overhaul and has trouble commanding three pitches. FB flashes plus with some movement while CB could become elite offering. Not much feel for CU yet. Arm strength is impressive and could develop into something special.

Cosart,Jake — RP — Boston

EXP MLB DEBUT: 2018 | H/W: 6-2 175 | FUT: Closer | 8E

Thrws R Age 24
2014 (3) Seminole St JC

Velo	Pitch	Grade
93-98	FB	++++
85-88	SP	++
74-78	CB	++

Year	Lev	Team	W	L	Sv	IP	K	ERA	WHIP	BF/G	OBA	H%	S%	xERA	Ctl	Dom	Cmd	hr/9	BPV
2014	Rk	GCL Red Sox	0	1	0	16		2.25	1.13	9.0	134	19	78	1.14	6.2	9.0	1.5	0.0	13
2015	A-	Lowell	2	2	0	33	27	5.45	1.39	15.5	218	26	60	3.53	5.5	7.4	1.4	0.8	3
2016	A	Greenville	4	1	2	52	76	2.07	1.17	7.2	197	32	83	2.20	4.3	13.1	3.0	0.3	137
2016	A+	Salem	0	0	0	18	28	1.00	1.00	8.6	121	24	89	0.64	5.5	14.0	2.5	0.0	122
2017	AA	Portland	5	2	2	49	52	3.12	1.41	5.5	168	21	81	3.05	7.5	9.5	1.3	0.9	-13

Max-effort RP with incredible arm speed and menace to RHH (.119 oppBA). Has potential to be lights-out closer thanks to nasty FB w/ natural cutting action. Horrendous control is problem and can be victimized by flyballs. Inconsistent CB can be effective, but FB is true bread and butter.

Crawford, Leo — SP — Los Angeles (N)

EXP MLB DEBUT: 2021 | H/W: 6-0 180 | FUT: #5 SP/swingman | 6C

Thrws L Age 21
2014 FA (NI)

Velo	Pitch	Grade
90-92	FB	+++
	CB	+
	CU	+

Year	Lev	Team	W	L	Sv	IP	K	ERA	WHIP	BF/G	OBA	H%	S%	xERA	Ctl	Dom	Cmd	hr/9	BPV
2016	Rk	AZL Dodgers	2	1	0	38	39	2.60	1.00	18.2	224	30	73	2.03	1.7	9.2	5.6	0.2	139
2016	A	Great Lakes	4	1	0	28	24	2.23	1.10	18.4	217	25	86	2.89	2.9	7.7	2.7	1.0	78
2017	A	Great Lakes	7	10	0	135	97	4.60	1.34	22.5	260	30	66	3.93	3.1	6.5	2.1	0.8	50

Short LH from Nicaragua took a step back. Uses a high leg kick to drive home a good low-90s fastball and has the arm strength for more velocity. Also mixes in a CB and a rudimentary CU. Drop in Dom and Ctl heading the wrong direction.

Crichton,Stefan — RP — Baltimore

EXP MLB DEBUT: 2017 | H/W: 6-3 200 | FUT: Setup reliever | 6A

Thrws R Age 26
2013 (23) Texas Christian

Velo	Pitch	Grade
91-95	FB	++++
82-85	SL	+++
	CU	+

Year	Lev	Team	W	L	Sv	IP	K	ERA	WHIP	BF/G	OBA	H%	S%	xERA	Ctl	Dom	Cmd	hr/9	BPV
2015	A+	Frederick	0	0	2	13	18	4.12	1.15	7.4	275	42	60	2.83	0.7	12.4	18.0	0.0	222
2016	AA	Bowie	2	6	1	72	61	3.74	1.37	6.3	264	33	73	3.77	3.2	7.6	2.3	0.5	67
2017	Rk	GCL Orioles	0	1	0	3	2	2.81	1.56	4.7	0	0	80	1.11	14.1	5.6	0.4	0.0	-260
2017	AAA	Norfolk	7	2	2	47	50	3.05	1.23	6.6	261	35	75	3.23	2.1	9.5	4.5	0.4	133
2017	MLB	Baltimore	0	0	0	12	8	8.18	2.48	8.0	432	48	68	10.52	3.0	6.0	2.0	1.5	45

Tall, physical RP with dynamic, plus FB. Gets lot of sinking action with heavy FB and keeps ball low. Has strength and stamina to pitch more than 1 inning on back-to-back days. Can get hitters to chase SL that shows positive glimpses. Has tendency to aim secondary pitches, but throws with above average command.

Crismatt,Nabil — SP — New York (N)

EXP MLB DEBUT: 2019 | H/W: 6-1 222 | FUT: #5 SP/swingman | 6B

Thrws R Age 23
2011 FA (CB)

Velo	Pitch	Grade
88-90	FB	++
68-72	CB	++
80-84	CU	+++

Year	Lev	Team	W	L	Sv	IP	K	ERA	WHIP	BF/G	OBA	H%	S%	xERA	Ctl	Dom	Cmd	hr/9	BPV
2015	Rk	Kingsport	6	1	0	62	63	2.90	1.03	19.9	229	29	76	2.79	1.7	9.1	5.3	0.9	136
2016	A-	Brooklyn	0	1	1	31	35	3.19	0.97	14.7	229	30	73	2.89	1.2	10.2	8.8	1.2	170
2016	A	Columbia	1	2	0	28	32	1.91	0.78	25.4	201	29	76	1.28	0.6	10.2	16.0	0.3	185
2016	AA	Binghamton	0	1	0	6	7	1.50	1.00	22.9	228	29	100	3.27	1.5	10.5	7.0	1.5	167
2017	A+	St. Lucie	6	13	0	145	142	3.97	1.36	23.3	282	35	74	4.50	2.2	8.8	3.9	1.1	116

Soft-tossing, command-heavy RH who is at physical projection. Feautres 2-seam FB with solid arm-side run and drop. Has been up to 93 mph in shorter outings. Loopy CB. Slow, will very velocity Somtimes an eephus CB. Has solid feel for above-average CU. Overall projection is limited.

Crouse,Hans — SP — Texas

EXP MLB DEBUT: 2022 | H/W: 6-4 180 | FUT: #2 starter | 9D

Thrws R Age 19
2017 (2) HS (CA)

Velo	Pitch	Grade
94-98	FB	++++
78-82	CB	+++
83-85	SL	+++
88-91	CU	+

Year	Lev	Team	W	L	Sv	IP	K	ERA	WHIP	BF/G	OBA	H%	S%	xERA	Ctl	Dom	Cmd	hr/9	BPV
2017	Rk	AZL Rangers	0	0	0	20	30	0.45	0.70	7.0	110	19	100	0.21	3.2	13.5	4.3	0.5	176

Tall, lean SP with power arm and electric stuff. Throws with plus velocity now and more could be in tank. Could develop one of top FB in baseball at peak and already commands plate. Owns two solid-average breaking balls, but needs to add CU to mix. Has effort in delivery, but has deceptive arm action and speed.

Crowe, Wil — SP — Washington

EXP MLB DEBUT: 2020 | H/W: 6-2 240 | FUT: #3 starter | 7C

Thrws R Age 23
2017 (2) South Carolina

Velo	Pitch	Grade
91-94	FB	+++
77-79	CB	+++
79-82	SL	++
83-85	CU	++

Year	Lev	Team	W	L	Sv	IP	K	ERA	WHIP	BF/G	OBA	H%	S%	xERA	Ctl	Dom	Cmd	hr/9	BPV
2017	NCAA	South Carolina	6	5	0	92	90	3.42	1.30	25.3	255	33	74	3.45	3.0	8.8	2.9	0.5	95
2017	Rk	GCL Nationals	0	0	0	3	2	5.63	1.25	6.5	250	30	50	2.81	2.8	5.6	2.0	0.0	43
2017	A-	Auburn	0	0	0	20	15	2.67	1.04	11.1	240	26	83	3.41	1.3	6.7	5.0	1.3	102

Has big-college pedigree and a four-pitch arsenal that intrigues: FB that can touch 97; potential plus sharp CB; and a SL and CU that both project to average. He's thick-framed and there have been some injury concerns in his past, but he's shown good control and adequate polish.

Curtiss,John — RP — Minnesota

EXP MLB DEBUT: 2017 | H/W: 6-4 200 | FUT: Setup reliever | 7B

Thrws R Age 25
2014 (6) Texas

Velo	Pitch	Grade
93-97	FB	+++
81-85	SL	+++
	CU	+

Year	Lev	Team	W	L	Sv	IP	K	ERA	WHIP	BF/G	OBA	H%	S%	xERA	Ctl	Dom	Cmd	hr/9	BPV
2016	A	Cedar Rapids	0	0	2	8	17	0.00	0.50	4.4	81	26	100		2.3	19.1	8.5	0.0	302
2016	A+	Fort Myers	0	2	3	53	68	3.06	1.23	5.6	219	34	72	2.31	3.9	11.5	3.0	0.0	120
2017	AA	Chattanooga	2	0	13	25	35	0.72	0.96	4.5	145	25	92	0.80	4.3	12.6	2.9	0.0	128
2017	AAA	Rochester	0	0	6	24	33	1.87	0.87	4.9	139	24	76	0.51	3.7	12.3	3.3	0.0	139
2017	MLB	Minnesota	0	0	0	8	10	8.78	1.34	3.8	280	35	33	5.48	2.2	11.0	5.0	2.2	156

Burgeoning RP who reached majors after being nearly unhittable in AA/AAA. Uses tough angle to plate because of height and is able to miss bats with strong FB and improving SL. FB has tendency to flatten at higher velocities and will need more pinpoint location. Strikeout rate has been consistent at higher levels and took big step forward in 2017.

Davidson,Tucker — SP — Atlanta

EXP MLB DEBUT: 2020 | H/W: 6-2 215 | FUT: #3 starter | 8D

Thrws L Age 22
2016 (19) Midland JC

Velo	Pitch	Grade
93-97	FB	++++
79-81	CB	+++
83-85	CU	+++

Year	Lev	Team	W	L	Sv	IP	K	ERA	WHIP	BF/G	OBA	H%	S%	xERA	Ctl	Dom	Cmd	hr/9	BPV
2016	Rk	GCL Braves	0	3	0	29	32	1.54	1.23	10.8	280	38	89	3.44	1.2	9.9	8.0	0.3	162
2017	A	Rome	5	4	2	103	101	2.62	1.22	13.5	248	33	79	3.02	2.6	8.8	3.4	0.3	106

Hard-throwing reliever converted to starter mid-season. Sturdy build, cross-fire delivery. Uses lower half and quick arm for power. Solid arm-side run from 2-seam FB, living in lower half. Power CB has depth, lack consistency. Took huge step forward with CU late in season, looking plus at times.

Davila,Garrett — SP — Kansas City

EXP MLB DEBUT: 2020 | H/W: 6-2 180 | FUT: #4 starter | 7D

Thrws L Age 21
2015 (4) HS (NC)

Velo	Pitch	Grade
97-92	FB	+++
75-77	CB	++
81-84	CU	+++

Year	Lev	Team	W	L	Sv	IP	K	ERA	WHIP	BF/G	OBA	H%	S%	xERA	Ctl	Dom	Cmd	hr/9	BPV
2016	Rk	Burlington	7	0	0	65	55	2.77	1.28	22.2	234	30	78	2.92	3.7	7.6	2.0	0.3	54
2017	A	Lexington	8	8	3	125	92	5.10	1.43	19.7	265	31	63	4.00	3.7	6.6	1.8	0.6	36

Efficient SP who works quickly and offers advanced pitchability. Stuff may be a bit short to register Ks, but mixes well and keeps consistent arm speed on all pitches. Has solid CU, but has struggled with LHH. FB only has average velocity, though has late sinking action for groundballs. An uptick in velocity would help profile as well as better CB.

Davis,Rookie — SP — Cincinnati

EXP MLB DEBUT: 2017 | H/W: 6-5 255 | FUT: #4 starter | **7C**

Thrws R Age 24
2011 (14) HS (NC)

Velo	Pitch	Grade
91-93	FB	+++
85-87	SL	+++
81-83	CB	++
85-88	CU	++

Year	Lev	Team	W	L	Sv	IP	K	ERA	WHIP	BF/G	OBA	H%	S%	xERA	Ctl	Dom	Cmd	hr/9	BPV
2016	AAA	Louisville	0	2	0	24	15	7.50	1.88	22.5	360	40	60	7.16	2.6	5.6	2.1	1.1	48
2017	Rk	AZL Reds	0	1	0	9	10	1.98	0.77	16.3	163	20	83	1.46	2.0	9.9	5.0	1.0	143
2017	AA	Pensacola	0	0	0	13	11	4.77	1.36	18.4	244	28	69	4.29	4.1	7.5	1.8	1.4	43
2017	AAA	Louisville	4	4	0	60	54	4.79	1.35	22.8	286	33	69	4.96	1.9	8.1	4.2	1.5	111
2017	MLB	Cincinnati	1	3	0	24	20	8.63	2.17	17.1	360	39	64	9.29	5.3	7.5	1.4	2.6	11

Began 2017 season in big league rotation, struggling in limited action. Battled through various injuries past two seasons. 2-seam FB has solid arm-side bore around the zone. Hard SL is best secondary with solid depth and good command. Uses power CB to primarily change eye-levels. CU is ordinary. Needs to tighten up command to succeed.

De Jong, Chase — SP — Seattle

EXP MLB DEBUT: 2017 | H/W: 6-4 205 | FUT: #4 starter | **7D**

Thrws R Age 24
2012 (2) HS (CA)

Velo	Pitch	Grade
88-92	FB	+++
77-79	CB	+++
80-82	SL	++
	CU	++

Year	Lev	Team	W	L	Sv	IP	K	ERA	WHIP	BF/G	OBA	H%	S%	xERA	Ctl	Dom	Cmd	hr/9	BPV
2016	AA	Tulsa	14	5	0	141	125	2.87	1.03	21.7	210	25	77	2.63	2.5	8.0	3.2	1.0	94
2016	AAA	Oklahoma City	1	0	0	5	8	1.76	1.37	21.4	294	48	86	3.67	1.8	14.1	8.0	0.0	224
2017	AA	Arkansas	1	3	0	28	18	6.06	1.49	24.3	287	32	59	4.84	3.2	5.7	1.8	1.0	35
2017	AAA	Tacoma	3	6	0	84	61	6.00	1.50	24.2	295	32	65	5.89	2.9	6.5	2.3	1.9	58
2017	MLB	Seattle	0	3	0	28	13	6.41	1.57	17.6	281	28	62	5.57	4.2	4.2	1.0	1.6	-19

Tall, durable SP who got to big leagues for first time. Control usually good, but regressed in 2017. No pitch is plus nor projects as such, but changes speeds well and moves ball around strike zone. Needs pitch for LHH and may need to upgrade CU and SL. CB is go to pitch.

De La Cruz, Oscar — SP — Chicago (N)

EXP MLB DEBUT: 2020 | H/W: 6-4 200 | FUT: #3 starter | **8C**

Thrws R Age 23
2012 FA (DR)

Velo	Pitch	Grade
92-95	FB	++++
80-82	CB	++++
	CU	+++

Year	Lev	Team	W	L	Sv	IP	K	ERA	WHIP	BF/G	OBA	H%	S%	xERA	Ctl	Dom	Cmd	hr/9	BPV
2016	Rk	AZL Cubs	0	1	0	3		6.00	1.33	12.5	262	24	67	6.01	3.0	6.0	2.0	3.0	45
2016	A-	Eugene	0	0	0	8	14	1.11	0.86	14.9	180	31	100	1.94	2.2	15.6	7.0	1.1	238
2016	A	South Bend	1	2	0	27	35	3.31	1.10	17.8	223	35	67	2.04	2.6	11.6	4.4	0.0	155
2017	Rk	AZL Cubs	0	0	0	2	1	0.00	0.00	5.6	0	0			0.0	4.5		0.0	99
2017	A+	Myrtle Beach	4	3	0	54	47	3.49	1.25	18.4	265	32	76	3.94	2.2	7.8	3.6	1.0	100

Tall, athletic hurler has a plus fastball that sits in the mid-90s and tops out at 97 mph with good late life. Plus power curveball, improved change-up, and sturdy, athletic frame size give him the tools to be an impact starter. Room for more growth and is a breakout candidate for 2018.

De Leon,Jose — SP — Tampa Bay

EXP MLB DEBUT: 2016 | H/W: 6-1 220 | FUT: #3 starter | **8C**

Thrws R Age 25
2013 (24) Southern

Velo	Pitch	Grade
90-95	FB	++++
82-84	SL	+++
80-84	CU	++++

Year	Lev	Team	W	L	Sv	IP	K	ERA	WHIP	BF/G	OBA	H%	S%	xERA	Ctl	Dom	Cmd	hr/9	BPV
2016	MLB	LA Dodgers	2	0	0	17	15	6.35	1.53	18.5	284	30	67	6.46	3.7	7.9	2.1	2.6	61
2017	Rk	GCL Rays	1	0	0	12	12	0.75	0.42	12.9	106	12	100		0.8	9.0	12.0	0.8	160
2017	A+	Charlotte	1	0	0	14	18	1.91	1.42	14.9	217	34	85	2.76	5.7	11.5	2.0	0.0	70
2017	AAA	Durham	0	2	0	12	14	6.75	1.67	17.9	293	40	58	5.13	4.5	10.5	2.3	0.8	86
2017	MLB	Tampa Bay	1	0	0	2	2	12.27	3.18	13.2	392	42	67	13.84	12.3	8.2	0.7	4.1	-166

Promising SP who missed most of season due to variety of ailments. Durability is serious issue, but can be filthy dominant when on mound. Stuff plays up due to deceptive delivery and slot. Can succeed with two pitches in heavy, plus FB and dynamic CU that features late tumble. Uses average SL as chase pitch and may need to use more often.

De Los Santos,Enyel — SP — Philadelphia

EXP MLB DEBUT: 2018 | H/W: 6-3 170 | FUT: #4 starter | **7B**

Thrws R Age 22
2014 FA (DR)

Velo	Pitch	Grade
92-94	FB	+++
75-78	CB	+++
	CU	+++

Year	Lev	Team	W	L	Sv	IP	K	ERA	WHIP	BF/G	OBA	H%	S%	xERA	Ctl	Dom	Cmd	hr/9	BPV
2015	A-	Tri-City	3	0	0	37	42	4.11	1.34	19.4	261	36	69	3.61	3.1	10.2	3.2	0.5	116
2015	Rk	AZL Padres	3	0	0	24	29	2.60	1.20	19.4	260	37	79	3.12	1.9	10.8	5.8	0.4	162
2016	A	Fort Wayne	3	2	0	52	45	2.93	1.00	18.1	205	26	70	1.92	2.4	7.8	3.2	0.3	92
2016	A+	Lake Elsinore	5	3	0	68	52	4.36	1.38	19.1	267	30	73	4.74	3.2	6.9	2.2	1.5	56
2017	AA	San Antonio	10	6	0	150	138	3.78	1.19	23.2	236	29	69	3.15	2.9	8.3	2.9	0.7	89

Came over in the Galvis trade. Skinny and high-waisted, he has solid #4, innings-eating potential. Produces 92-94 FB with little effort; can hit 97. CU will flash above-average with fade and slow-bending CB projects as usable third pitch. Hits his spots and will not be a Ctl liability. Keeps ball on the ground and succeeds despite lack of Dom.

Dease,Ryan — SP — Texas

EXP MLB DEBUT: 2023 | H/W: 6-3 175 | FUT: #3 starter | **8E**

Thrws R Age 18
2017 (4) HS (FL)

Velo	Pitch	Grade
88-92	FB	+++
80-82	SL	++
	CU	+

Year	Lev	Team	W	L	Sv	IP	K	ERA	WHIP	BF/G	OBA	H%	S%	xERA	Ctl	Dom	Cmd	hr/9	BPV
2017	Rk	AZL Rangers	3	1	0	22	19	2.05	0.91	7.5	225	27	83	2.38	0.8	7.8	9.5	0.8	136

Quick-armed SP who is all about projection, but harnesses arm action to pepper zone with consistent strikes. Spots sinking FB low in zone with precision. Should be able to throw harder as he adds strength to slender frame. SL and CU need work. Slows arm on CU and lacks deception. SL thrown with speed, but needs to be more than FB guy to succeed.

Deetz,Dean — SP — Houston

EXP MLB DEBUT: 2018 | H/W: 6-1 195 | FUT: Middle reliever | **7D**

Thrws R Age 24
2014 (11) NE Oklahoma A&M

Velo	Pitch	Grade
91-94	FB	+++
80-83	SL	+++
	CU	++

Year	Lev	Team	W	L	Sv	IP	K	ERA	WHIP	BF/G	OBA	H%	S%	xERA	Ctl	Dom	Cmd	hr/9	BPV
2015	A	Quad Cities	5	1	0	35	29	0.77	0.85	18.4	147	20	90	0.60	3.3	7.4	2.2	0.0	62
2016	A+	Lancaster	6	5	1	93	86	4.25	1.41	17.1	247	30	71	3.96	4.4	8.3	1.9	0.9	50
2016	AA	Corpus Christi	2	0	0	12	17	0.00	0.75	21.4	171	29	100	0.54	1.5	12.8	8.5	0.0	207
2017	AA	Corpus Christi	4	2	0	39	42	1.84	0.92	18.3	196	26	85	1.92	2.1	9.6	4.7	0.7	136
2017	AAA	Fresno	3	4	0	45	55	6.40	1.93	12.6	266	36	67	5.65	8.2	11.0	1.3	1.0	-5

Strong RHP who has split time as SP/RP as pro. Can muscle FB to mid-90s from bullpen and flash plus SL for modest SwK/Dom production. Struggled mightily to throw strikes in AAA and needs more than just a fringe CU to remain SP. Viable middle-relief option if control isn't effectively honed.

DePaula,Juan — SP — New York (A)

EXP MLB DEBUT: 2021 | H/W: 6-3 165 | FUT: #4 starter | **7D**

Thrws R Age 20
2014 FA (DR)

Velo	Pitch	Grade
90-93	FB	+++
78-79	CB	++
80-84	CU	+++

Year	Lev	Team	W	L	Sv	IP	K	ERA	WHIP	BF/G	OBA	H%	S%	xERA	Ctl	Dom	Cmd	hr/9	BPV
2016	Rk	AZL Mariners	1	2	0	41	53	3.07	1.27	15.2	262	38	76	3.38	2.4	11.6	4.8	0.4	162
2017	A-	Staten Island	5	5	0	62	53	2.90	1.08	20.2	194	26	70	1.67	3.6	7.7	2.1	0.0	59

Lean SP with advanced pitchability and knack for changing speeds and eye levels. Hasn't pitched in full season yet. Needs to add major strength for durability and stamina. Loses velocity late in games. Controls strike zone with three offerings. FB can be flat at times and is more of flyball pitcher. Has back-end profile despite very low oppBA.

Diaz, Jairo — RP — Colorado

EXP MLB DEBUT: 2015 | H/W: 6-0 200 | FUT: Setup reliever | **8D**

Thrws R Age 26
2007 FA (VZ)

Velo	Pitch	Grade
96-98	FB	+++++
89-92	SL	+++

Year	Lev	Team	W	L	Sv	IP	K	ERA	WHIP	BF/G	OBA	H%	S%	xERA	Ctl	Dom	Cmd	hr/9	BPV
2015	MLB	Colorado	0	1	0	19	18	2.37	1.16	3.6	230	28	85	3.19	2.8	8.5	3.0	0.9	95
2016	*Did no*																		
2017	A+	Lancaster	0	0	0	2	3	9.00	1.50	4.3	347	43	50	9.09	0.0	13.5		4.5	261
2017	AAA	Albuquerque	0	1	3	18	17	5.00	1.28	3.7	240	31	59	3.20	3.5	8.5	2.4	0.5	77
2017	MLB	Colorado	0	0	0	5	2	9.00	3.40	7.8	460	50	71	12.13	9.0	3.6	0.4	0.0	-160

Older reliever missed all of 2016 with TJS and was finally rewarded with a brief stint in the majors. Double-plus fastball sits at 96-98, topping at 100 mph and is backed up by an above-average slider. Control comes and goes, but has the raw stuff to stick in the show.

Diaz,Yennsy — SP — Toronto

EXP MLB DEBUT: 2020 | H/W: 6-1 160 | FUT: #3 starter | **8E**

Thrws R Age 21
2014 FA (DR)

Velo	Pitch	Grade
89-95	FB	+++
78-80	CB	++
83-86	CU	++

Year	Lev	Team	W	L	Sv	IP	K	ERA	WHIP	BF/G	OBA	H%	S%	xERA	Ctl	Dom	Cmd	hr/9	BPV
2016	Rk	Bluefield	4	6	0	56	48	5.79	1.54	20.3	272	31	65	5.18	4.3	7.7	1.8	1.4	40
2017	A	Lansing	5	2	0	77	82	4.79	1.45	20.6	246	31	70	4.35	4.8	9.6	2.0	1.2	61

Raw, athletic SP who started season in June and pushed K rate upward. Starting to become more pitcher than thrower, but lot of work left to do. Has very fast arm that needs to be harnessed. FB can be very good, but tends to overthrow. Two-seamer can be effective. Struggles with HR and LHH. CB and CU have glimpses of becoming above average.

Dietz,Matthias — SP — Baltimore

EXP MLB DEBUT: 2020 | H/W: 6-5 220 | FUT: #3 starter | **8E**

Thrws R Age 22
2016 (2) Logan CC

Velo	Pitch	Grade
91-96	FB	+++
82-85	SL	+++
78-82	CB	++
	CU	++

Year	Lev	Team	W	L	Sv	IP	K	ERA	WHIP	BF/G	OBA	H%	S%	xERA	Ctl	Dom	Cmd	hr/9	BPV
2016	A-	Aberdeen	0	3	0	18	8	4.95	1.76	11.9	300	34	69	4.83	4.9	4.0	0.8	0.0	-44
2017	A	Delmarva	3	10	0	129	92	4.95	1.50	21.5	283	34	65	4.30	3.5	6.4	1.8	0.4	39

Physical SP who got off to slow start, but rebounded well late. Throws downhill and induces high amount of groundballs. Can throw hard, but loses natural sink at higher velocity. Lot of effort in delivery, yet repeats well. Added more power to SL and can mix in fringy CB and CU. Very durable frame and could become innings eater. Key is FB command.

Diplan,Marcos

SP | Milwaukee | EXP MLB DEBUT: 2019 | H/W: 6-0 160 | FUT: Setup reliever | 8E

Thrws R Age 21 — 2013 FA (DR)

Velo	Pitch	Grade
92-95	FB	++++
79-82	SL	++++
83-86	CU	++

Year	Lev	Team	W	L	Sv	IP	K	ERA	WHIP	BF/G	OBA	H%	S%	xERA	Ctl	Dom	Cmd	hr/9	BPV
2015	Rk	Helena	2	2	2	50	54	3.77	1.36	16.1	250	33	73	3.72	3.8	9.7	2.6	0.7	91
2016	A	Wisconsin	6	2	1	70	89	1.80	1.16	16.4	199	30	86	2.25	4.1	11.4	2.8	0.4	113
2016	A+	Brevard County	1	2	0	43	40	5.01	1.51	18.7	279	35	67	4.63	3.8	8.4	2.2	0.8	67
2017	A+	Carolina	7	8	0	125	119	5.25	1.57	21.2	263	33	67	4.52	5.1	8.6	1.7	0.8	34

Hard-throwing RH with slight frame struggled with control in 2017. Sits mid-90s with FB with late running action. SL is true out pitch with extremely late bite. CU is a below-average offering. FB/SL will play up in pen while masking command and control issues.

Dominguez,Seranthony

SP | Philadelphia | EXP MLB DEBUT: 2019 | H/W: 6-1 185 | FUT: #3 starter | 8C

Thrws R Age 23 — 2011 FA (DR)

Velo	Pitch	Grade
95-97	FB	+++++
80-83	CB	+++
85-86	CU	++

Year	Lev	Team	W	L	Sv	IP	K	ERA	WHIP	BF/G	OBA	H%	S%	xERA	Ctl	Dom	Cmd	hr/9	BPV
2015	Rk	GCL Phillies	1	1	0	7	9	2.50	1.81	16.7	228	31	92	5.06	8.8	11.3	1.3	1.3	-16
2016	A-	Williamsport	1	1	0	17	15	2.12	0.71	20.0	143	20	67	0.18	2.1	7.9	3.8	0.0	104
2016	A	Lakewood	5	2	0	48	50	2.43	1.12	19.0	200	27	79	2.19	3.7	9.4	2.5	0.4	85
2017	Rk	GCL Phillies	0	0	0	5	7	5.29	1.76	11.7	258	40	67	4.16	7.1	12.4	1.8	0.0	50
2017	A+	Clearwater	4	4	0	62	75	3.62	1.30	17.1	226	31	75	3.41	4.3	10.9	2.5	0.9	96

Bumped velocity up to mid-90s, and continued to get swings and misses on his lively FB. Breaking ball also has plus potential and CU flashes average. It's a strong package of stuff, and his repeatable delivery points to future command. But health woes have limited his innings, and will likely determine future role. Injury-free, he's an upside play.

Duensing,Cole

SP | Los Angeles (A) | EXP MLB DEBUT: 2022 | H/W: 6-4 175 | FUT: #3 starter | 8E

Thrws R Age 19 — 2016 (6) HS (KS)

Velo	Pitch	Grade
88-93	FB	+++
75-79	CB	++
81-83	CU	++

Year	Lev	Team	W	L	Sv	IP	K	ERA	WHIP	BF/G	OBA	H%	S%	xERA	Ctl	Dom	Cmd	hr/9	BPV
2016	Rk	AZL Angels	2	0	0	13	11	1.38	1.38	6.8	262	34	89	3.30	3.5	7.6	2.2	0.0	62
2017	Rk	Orem	3	5	0	32	22	10.90	1.83	16.6	316	32	40	7.61	4.8	6.1	1.3	2.5	0
2017	Rk	AZL Angels	0	1	0	8	3	3.29	1.95	9.8	257	26	87	5.74	8.8	3.3	0.4	1.1	-160

Very tall, projectable SP who has yet to pitch full season, but has high upside. Needs significant polish, but has the pitches to be mid-rotation guy. FB works at lower velocity with lively action, but can flatten out when overthrowing. Has tendency to allow HR and needs to repeat delivery. Lacks touch for CU. CB has chance to be knockout offering.

Dunn,Justin

SP | New York (N) | EXP MLB DEBUT: 2019 | H/W: 6-2 195 | FUT: #3 starter | 8C

Thrws R Age 22 — 2016 (1) Boston College

Velo	Pitch	Grade
92-95	FB	++++
84-87	SL	++++
77-79	CB	++
83-85	CU	++

Year	Lev	Team	W	L	Sv	IP	K	ERA	WHIP	BF/G	OBA	H%	S%	xERA	Ctl	Dom	Cmd	hr/9	BPV
2016	NCAA	Boston College	4	2	2	65	72	2.07	1.07	14.1	220	30	82	2.34	2.5	9.9	4.0	0.4	130
2016	A-	Brooklyn	1	1	0	30	35	1.50	1.17	10.9	228	33	88	2.56	3.0	10.5	3.5	0.3	126
2017	A+	St. Lucie	5	6	0	95	75	5.02	1.57	20.9	274	33	67	4.37	4.5	7.1	1.6	0.5	23

Athletic RH struggled mightily in High-A especially with corralling plus arm-side bore of 2-seam FB. Best secondary is a hard SL with tremendous tilt and 2-plane movement. CB has average potential with improved depth. Feel for CU still work-in-progress. Relatively new to starting.

Dunning,Dane

SP | Chicago (A) | EXP MLB DEBUT: 2019 | H/W: 6-4 200 | FUT: #3 starter | 8C

Thrws R Age 23 — 2016 (1) Florida

Velo	Pitch	Grade
89-92	FB	+++
77-78	CB	+++
82-84	CU	+++

Year	Lev	Team	W	L	Sv	IP	K	ERA	WHIP	BF/G	OBA	H%	S%	xERA	Ctl	Dom	Cmd	hr/9	BPV
2016	NCAA	Florida	6	3	2	78	88	2.30	1.02	9.1	236	33	78	2.34	1.4	10.1	7.3	0.3	163
2016	Rk	GCL Nationals	0	0	0	2	3	0.00	0.00	5.6	0	0			0.0	13.5		0.0	261
2016	A-	Auburn	3	2	0	33	29	2.17	0.99	18.1	217	28	78	1.99	1.9	7.9	4.1	0.3	108
2017	A	Kannapolis	2	0	0	26	33	0.35	0.58	22.1	151	24	93		0.7	11.4	16.5	0.0	205
2017	A+	Winston-Salem	6	8	0	118	135	3.51	1.27	21.9	255	33	77	3.97	2.7	10.3	3.8	1.1	129

Polished pitcher with 3 average or better offerings. Works down with everything and rarely changes eye levels. Some effort in delivery. Heavy FB is true workhorse pitch with solid arm-side run and significant drop. 11-5 CB isn't likely to develop into out pitch. Could transition to SL instead. CU much improved; mimics FB arm slot and movement.

Duplantier,Jon

SP | Arizona | EXP MLB DEBUT: 2019 | H/W: 6-4 225 | FUT: #2 starter | 9E

Thrws R Age 23 — 2016 (3) Rice

Velo	Pitch	Grade
91-94	FB	++++
76-78	SL	+++
82-85	CB	++
81-84	CU	+++

Year	Lev	Team	W	L	Sv	IP	K	ERA	WHIP	BF/G	OBA	H%	S%	xERA	Ctl	Dom	Cmd	hr/9	BPV
2016	NCAA	Rice	7	7	0	111	148	3.24	1.12	25.7	197	30	71	2.15	3.8	12.0	3.1	0.4	131
2016	A-	Hillsboro	0	0	0	1	3	0.00	2.00	4.8	0	0	100	2.00	18.0	27.0	1.5	0.0	18
2017	A	Kane County	6	1	0	72	78	1.25	0.83	20.3	181	25	89	1.35	1.9	9.7	5.2	0.5	143
2017	A+	Visalia	6	2	0	63	87	1.57	1.16	20.9	205	33	87	2.22	3.9	12.4	3.2	0.3	137

Tall and physically strong, he has makings of mid-rotation starter, maybe more. Peppers lower half of zone with a heavy 2-seam FB, but can lose command of it easily. Best two off-speed pitches are CB and CU. Added a SL, improving his overall bag of toys. Physically gifted, the ball comes out easy with a little deception.

Duran,Jhoan

SP | Arizona | EXP MLB DEBUT: 2020 | H/W: 6-5 175 | FUT: #3 starter | 8E

Thrws R Age 20 — 2014 FA (DR)

Velo	Pitch	Grade
94-96	FB	++++
77-79	CB	++
	CU	+

Year	Lev	Team	W	L	Sv	IP	K	ERA	WHIP	BF/G	OBA	H%	S%	xERA	Ctl	Dom	Cmd	hr/9	BPV
2016	Rk	Missoula	0	1	0	12	9	3.69	1.56	17.8	289	34	78	4.83	3.7	6.6	1.8	0.7	38
2016	Rk	AZL Dbacks	1	2	0	20	13	5.85	1.45	21.4	299	35	57	4.43	2.3	5.9	2.6	0.5	63
2017	Rk	AZL Dbacks	0	2	0	11	13	7.30	2.07	18.1	378	51	61	6.89	3.2	10.5	3.3	0.0	120
2017	A-	Hillsboro	6	3	0	51	36	4.24	1.20	18.6	234	27	66	3.30	3.0	6.4	2.1	0.9	51

Quick-armed starter with height and electric FB. Heavy fastball comes easy out of hand and is ground ball machine. Can spin a breaking ball, but lacks consistency. CB not a swing-and-miss pitch, and doesn't have great feel for CU Will need to add mass and improve secondaries significantly to project as MLB starter.

Ecker,Mark

RP | Detroit | EXP MLB DEBUT: 2018 | H/W: 6-0 180 | FUT: Setup reliever | 6B

Thrws R Age 22 — 2016 (5) Texas A&M

Velo	Pitch	Grade
92-97	FB	++++
84-86	SL	++
	CU	+++

Year	Lev	Team	W	L	Sv	IP	K	ERA	WHIP	BF/G	OBA	H%	S%	xERA	Ctl	Dom	Cmd	hr/9	BPV
2016	NCAA	Texas A&M	4	2	8	46	56	0.39	0.67	6.5	156	24	97	0.37	1.4	10.9	8.0	0.2	178
2016	A-	Connecticut	2	0	4	18	21	0.50	0.56	5.5	121	19	90		1.5	10.5	7.0	0.0	167
2016	A	West Michigan	0	0	5	9	10	1.96	1.20	4.1	258	33	90	3.66	2.0	9.8	5.0	1.0	141
2017	A+	Lakeland	2	4	7	43	63	3.54	1.25	4.9	233	37	73	3.11	3.5	13.1	3.7	0.6	159
2017	AA	Erie	0	0	3	18	18	2.00	1.28	4.9	228	28	90	3.51	4.0	9.0	2.3	1.0	72

Short, power-armed RP who is advancing quickly and is on verge of major league debut. Throws with fast arm and adds a touch of sink to plus FB. Gets grounders and Ks with FB while CU is best secondary offering. Good separation between FB and CU while SL is far from average. Has smallish frame, but has been durable since turning pro.

Elledge,Seth

RP | Seattle | EXP MLB DEBUT: 2019 | H/W: 6-3 230 | FUT: Setup reliever | 7C

Thrws R Age 21 — 2017 (4) Dallas Baptist

Velo	Pitch	Grade
92-96	FB	++++
80-83	SL	++
	CU	+

Year	Lev	Team	W	L	Sv	IP	K	ERA	WHIP	BF/G	OBA	H%	S%	xERA	Ctl	Dom	Cmd	hr/9	BPV
2017	NCAA	Dallas Baptist	2	1	13	31	42	2.60	1.22	5.7	222	33	81	2.87	3.8	12.2	3.2	0.6	135
2017	A-	Everett	0	0	0	4	7	4.50	1.00	3.8	151	32	50	0.92	4.5	15.8	3.5	0.0	180
2017	A	Clinton	3	0	5	21	35	3.00	0.95	5.3	191	35	68	1.65	2.6	15.0	5.8	0.4	219

Large-framed RP who could move quickly due to average FB command and potent sink. Heater exhibits heavy, late life and is tough to elevate. Gets ahead of hitters consistently and has hard SL that serves as put-away pitch. Needs crisper SL at higher levels. Can rely too much on FB, but it is plus offering.

Enlow,Blayne

SP | Minnesota | EXP MLB DEBUT: 2021 | H/W: 6-3 170 | FUT: #3 starter | 8D

Thrws R Age 19 — 2017 (3) HS (LA)

Velo	Pitch	Grade
88-94	FB	+++
77-81	CB	+++
81-82	CU	+

Year	Lev	Team	W	L	Sv	IP	K	ERA	WHIP	BF/G	OBA	H%	S%	xERA	Ctl	Dom	Cmd	hr/9	BPV
2017	Rk	GCL Twins	2	0	0	20	19	1.34	0.70	11.8	150	19	85	0.64	1.8	8.5	4.8	0.4	123

Projectable, athletic SP with significant potential. Needs to fill out lean frame, but already generates easy velocity with loose, fast arm. CB has potential to be elite offering and currently misses bats. Impressive arm speed on CU, but doesn't get enough depth on it. Keeps ball low in zone and is groundball guy. Delivery could be smoother.

Escobar, Luis

SP | Pittsburgh | EXP MLB DEBUT: 2020 | H/W: 6-1 155 | FUT: #3 starter | 8C

Thrws R Age 21 — 2013 FA (CB)

Velo	Pitch	Grade
93-95	FB	++++
79-83	CB	++
84-86	CU	++

Year	Lev	Team	W	L	Sv	IP	K	ERA	WHIP	BF/G	OBA	H%	S%	xERA	Ctl	Dom	Cmd	hr/9	BPV
2015	Rk	GCL Pirates	2	1	0	40	37	3.58	1.04	14.1	204	27	63	1.91	2.9	8.3	2.8	0.2	89
2015	A-	West Virginia	0	0	0	6	5	5.90	1.80	14.1	289	36	64	4.75	5.9	7.4	1.3	0.0	-9
2016	A-	West Virginia	6	5	0	67	61	2.95	1.16	17.8	209	26	76	2.55	3.8	8.2	2.2	0.5	64
2017	A	West Virginia	10	7	0	131	168	3.84	1.20	20.3	208	30	68	2.67	4.1	11.5	2.8	0.6	114

Has a power arm despite thin frame; fastball sits at 93-95, topping at 97 mph. Quick arm gives him some deception. Curveball and change-up project as average to a tick above. Posted impressive numbers in first crack at full-season ball with a great oppBA. On the rise.

Eshelman,Thomas — SP — Philadelphia

EXP MLB DEBUT: 2018 | H/W: 6-3 210 | FUT: #4 starter | 7A

Thrws R Age 23 — 2015 (2) Cal St Fullerton

Velo	Pitch	Grade
88-90	FB	+++
73-76	CB	++
80-84	CU	+++
82-84	SL	

Year	Lev	Team	W	L	Sv	IP	K	ERA	WHIP	BF/G	OBA	H%	S%	xERA	Ctl	Dom	Cmd	hr/9	BPV
2015	A	Quad Cities	0	0	0	6	5	4.43	1.97	14.6	343	42	75	6.03	4.4	7.4	1.7	0.0	31
2016	A+	Clearwater	4	2	0	59	64	3.35	1.17	21.4	258	33	76	3.68	1.7	9.7	5.8	1.1	148
2016	AA	Reading	5	5	0	61	55	5.16	1.57	20.6	314	39	66	5.10	2.5	8.1	3.2	0.6	96
2017	AA	Reading	3	0	0	29	22	3.10	1.10	22.8	248	26	85	4.16	1.6	6.8	4.4	1.9	99
2017	AAA	Lehigh Valley	10	3	0	121	80	2.23	0.94	25.3	228	26	79	2.32	1.0	6.0	6.2	0.6	99

Strike-thrower extraordinaire, he manipulates his fastball and commands all pitches within the strike zone, keeping hitters off balance. Changes speeds and has confidence in all pitches in all counts. Works quickly, but slim margin of error; gets hit hard when a pitch bleeds out over the plate. Advanced pitchability.

Espinoza,Anderson — SP — San Diego

EXP MLB DEBUT: 2020 | H/W: 6-0 160 | FUT: #3 starter | 9D

Thrws R Age 20 — 2014 FA (VZ)

Velo	Pitch	Grade
93-96	FB	++++
74-77	CB	++++
80-82	CU	++++

Year	Lev	Team	W	L	Sv	IP	K	ERA	WHIP	BF/G	OBA	H%	S%	xERA	Ctl	Dom	Cmd	hr/9	BPV
2015	A	Greenville	0	1	0	3	4	11.61	1.94	14.7	314	46	33	5.42	5.8	11.6	2.0	0.0	70
2015	Rk	GCL Red Sox	0	1	0	40	40	0.68	0.83	14.6	175	25	91	0.81	2.0	9.0	4.4	0.0	125
2016	A	Greenville	5	8	0	76	72	4.38	1.37	18.7	264	35	66	3.51	3.2	8.5	2.7	0.2	85
2016	A	Fort Wayne	1	3	0	32	28	4.77	1.43	17.1	296	37	64	4.17	2.2	7.9	3.5	0.3	99
2017	Did no																		

Missed all of 2017 on DL and underwent Tommy John surgery in August. Most recent version has showed plus mid-90s FB with wicked late life. Replicates fast arm speed on plus fading CU for whiffs and throws in quality hammer CB. Smaller frame but has room to get stronger. Good athlete and Ctl will improve. Big risk, but potentially a big reward.

Estrada, Jeremy — SP — Chicago (N)

EXP MLB DEBUT: 2021 | H/W: 6-1 185 | FUT: #3 starter | 8E

Thrws R Age 19 — 2017 (6) HS (CA)

Velo	Pitch	Grade
89-93	FB	+++
73-76	CB	++
83-85	SL	++
81-83	CU	+++

Year	Lev	Team	W	L	Sv	IP	K	ERA	WHIP	BF/G	OBA	H%	S%	xERA	Ctl	Dom	Cmd	hr/9	BPV
2017	Rk	AZL Cubs	0	0	0	6	6	1.48	1.80	7.1	225	31	91	3.86	8.9	8.9	1.0	0.0	-62

Athletic right-hander has a quick arm and a plus low-90s sinking fastball but velocity was down as a HS senior. Slider, change, and curve flash average to above potential, but need refinement. High risk/high reward prospect.

Eusebio, Breiling — SP — Colorado

EXP MLB DEBUT: 2021 | H/W: 6-1 175 | FUT: #4 starter | 7D

Thrws L Age 21 — 2013 FA (DR)

Velo	Pitch	Grade
91-95	FB	+++
	CB	+++
	CU	+

Year	Lev	Team	W	L	Sv	IP	K	ERA	WHIP	BF/G	OBA	H%	S%	xERA	Ctl	Dom	Cmd	hr/9	BPV
2016	A-	Boise	2	5	0	63	42	5.28	1.71	22.0	305	35	70	5.57	4.3	6.0	1.4	0.9	10
2017	A-	Boise	3	0	0	17	22	1.59	0.82	20.6	173	28	79	0.75	2.1	11.6	5.5	0.0	170
2017	A	Asheville	3	3	0	40	31	4.49	1.50	21.6	280	33	70	4.48	3.6	7.0	1.9	0.7	46

Continues to make strides; fastball now sits at 91-95 with good late sink. Mixes in an above-average curve and a change-up that needs work, but shows potential. Repeating mechanics and throwing strikes remain key areas of need.

Evans, Jacob — RP — St. Louis

EXP MLB DEBUT: 2018 | H/W: 6-2 215 | FUT: Middle reliever | 6B

Thrws L Age 24 — 2015 (6) Oklahoma

Velo	Pitch	Grade
88-91	FB	+++
	CB	++++
	CU	++

Year	Lev	Team	W	L	Sv	IP	K	ERA	WHIP	BF/G	OBA	H%	S%	xERA	Ctl	Dom	Cmd	hr/9	BPV
2015	A-	State College	4	3	1	49	42	3.11	0.98	11.7	228	29	66	2.00	1.3	7.7	6.0	0.2	122
2016	Rk	GCL Cardinals	0	0	0	5	5	1.80	1.00	9.6	262	35	80	2.32	0.0	9.0		0.0	180
2016	A+	Palm Beach	4	7	0	89	48	3.74	1.36	23.3	293	31	77	4.84	1.7	4.8	2.8	1.2	59
2017	A+	Palm Beach	3	3	3	24	27	1.88	0.71	5.3	140	21	71	0.13	2.3	10.1	4.5	0.0	140
2017	AA	Springfield	1	3	0	17	21	2.62	1.63	5.5	292	40	88	5.29	4.2	11.0	2.6	1.0	103

Strong bodied lefty reliever has a nice three pitch mix that includes an average FB in 88-91 mph range, a plus curveball, and a change-up that needs work. Strike thrower comes after hitters and posted good numbers out of bullpen. Move to relief seems permanent and could land him in the majors in 2018.

Faedo,Alex — SP — Detroit

EXP MLB DEBUT: 2019 | H/W: 6-5 225 | FUT: #3 starter | 8C

Thrws R Age 22 — 2017 (1) Florida

Velo	Pitch	Grade
90-95	FB	++++
81-84	SL	++++
	CU	++

Year	Lev	Team	W	L	Sv	IP	K	ERA	WHIP	BF/G	OBA	H%	S%	xERA	Ctl	Dom	Cmd	hr/9	BPV
2017	NCAA	Florida	9	2	1	123	157	2.26	1.11	24.2	215	32	80	2.24	3.1	11.5	3.7	0.3	142

Did not pitch upon signing due to college workload. Has two present plus offerings in sinking FB with excellent life, and SL which has chance to be elite pitch. Cuts FB at will and can locate all pitches for strikes. Needs to upgrade CU, but has potential to be solid-average. Throws strikes despite long arm action and consistent pitch movement.

Fanti,Nick — SP — Philadelphia

EXP MLB DEBUT: 2021 | H/W: 6-2 185 | FUT: #5 SP/swingman | 7D

Thrws L Age 21 — 2015 (31) HS (NY)

Velo	Pitch	Grade
86-89	FB	+++
78-79	CB	++
81-83	CU	++

Year	Lev	Team	W	L	Sv	IP	K	ERA	WHIP	BF/G	OBA	H%	S%	xERA	Ctl	Dom	Cmd	hr/9	BPV
2015	Rk	GCL Phillies	1	1	0	17	20	2.62	1.16	7.6	224	33	75	2.22	3.1	10.5	3.3	0.0	122
2016	Rk	GCL Phillies	7	0	0	51	65	1.58	0.88	17.2	200	31	82	1.36	1.6	11.4	7.2	0.2	181
2017	A	Lakewood	9	2	0	120	121	2.55	0.96	21.6	204	27	74	1.83	2.1	9.1	4.3	0.4	125

Fine numbers in first full season, including pitching in two no-hit games. Pure arsenal a bit short as FB barely touches 90 mph but is deceptive. Nothing special about his secondaries, but CB/CU both could get to average. But he changes speeds, commands, and generally keeps hitters off balance. A tick or two more velo would raise his projection.

Farris, James — RP — Colorado

EXP MLB DEBUT: 2018 | H/W: 6-2 210 | FUT: Middle reliever | 6B

Thrws R Age 26 — 2014 (9) Arizona

Velo	Pitch	Grade
92-95	FB	++++
	SL	+++
	CU	+

Year	Lev	Team	W	L	Sv	IP	K	ERA	WHIP	BF/G	OBA	H%	S%	xERA	Ctl	Dom	Cmd	hr/9	BPV
2015	A+	Myrtle Beach	0	4	0	17	17	4.71	1.69	4.6	292	39	69	4.48	4.7	8.9	1.9	0.0	51
2016	A+	Myrtle Beach	1	2	8	30	36	2.40	0.93	6.6	199	30	71	1.33	2.1	10.8	5.1	0.0	156
2016	AA	Tennessee	1	3	5	36	38	2.75	1.03	5.3	210	28	74	2.19	2.5	9.5	3.8	0.5	122
2017	AA	Hartford	0	0	9	18	28	1.48	0.88	4.0	214	36	87	1.81	1.0	13.8	14.0	0.5	241
2017	AAA	Albuquerque	1	3	2	39	41	4.62	1.33	5.2	252	30	73	4.75	3.5	9.5	2.7	1.8	95

Right-handed reliever came over from the Cubs in the Eddie Butler deal. Best offering is a plus 92-95 2-seam fastball that has good late life. Slider gives him 2nd above-average offering, but change-up needs work. Pounds the strike zone and FB/SL combo is enough to get hitters out.

Fedde,Erick — SP — Washington

EXP MLB DEBUT: 2017 | H/W: 6-4 180 | FUT: #3 starter | 8B

Thrws R Age 25 — 2014 (1) UNLV

Velo	Pitch	Grade
94-95	FB	++++
80-83	SL	+++
85-88	CU	+++
75-83	CB	++

Year	Lev	Team	W	L	Sv	IP	K	ERA	WHIP	BF/G	OBA	H%	S%	xERA	Ctl	Dom	Cmd	hr/9	BPV
2016	A+	Potomac	6	4	0	91	95	2.86	1.14	20.1	248	32	77	3.13	1.9	9.4	5.0	0.7	136
2016	AA	Harrisburg	2	1	0	29	28	4.02	1.48	25.0	287	37	71	4.17	3.1	8.7	2.8	0.3	90
2017	AA	Harrisburg	3	3	0	56	54	3.05	1.12	13.0	221	28	75	2.71	2.9	8.7	3.0	0.6	96
2017	AAA	Syracuse	1	2	0	34	25	4.76	1.24	11.5	278	32	62	3.91	1.3	6.6	5.0	0.8	101
2017	MLB	Washington	0	1	0	15	15	9.54	2.19	25.2	370	42	61	9.84	4.8	8.9	1.9	3.0	50

Loose and fluid delivery; stays tall and direct to the plate. FB plays up due to command and ability to run in on RHH. SL best secondary with sharp break; CU is average and new CB gives added dimension. Plus athleticism means MLB Ctl a bit fluky; still needs to refine offspeed to be able to show in any count.

Ferguson, Caleb — SP — Los Angeles (N)

EXP MLB DEBUT: 2019 | H/W: 6-3 215 | FUT: #4 starter | 7D

Thrws L Age 21 — 2014 (38) HS (OH)

Velo	Pitch	Grade
92-94	FB	+++
	CB	+++
	CU	+++

Year	Lev	Team	W	L	Sv	IP	K	ERA	WHIP	BF/G	OBA	H%	S%	xERA	Ctl	Dom	Cmd	hr/9	BPV
2016	Rk	Ogden	1	0	0	10	11	0.90	0.60	17.1	124	19	83		1.8	9.9	5.5	0.0	148
2016	Rk	AZL Dodgers	1	0	0	6	11	1.50	0.67	10.5	191	40	75	0.52	0.0	16.5		0.0	315
2016	A	Great Lakes	1	4	0	50	41	2.69	1.04	19.3	258	31	76	2.88	0.5	7.4	13.7	0.5	136
2017	A+	Rancho Cuca	9	4	0	122	140	2.87	1.38	20.5	247	34	80	3.47	4.1	10.3	2.5	0.4	94

38th round pick had Tommy John surgery in high school but had breakout in 2017. Lefty has power stuff including 92-94 mph sinking fastball. Curve and change-up are a tick above-average. Gave up just 6 HR in first full-season year.

Fernandez, Junior — SP — St. Louis

EXP MLB DEBUT: 2019 | H/W: 6-1 180 | FUT: #2 SP/closer | 8E

Thrws R Age 21 — 2014 FA (DR)

Velo	Pitch	Grade
94-98	FB	++++
85-88	SL	++
78-81	CU	++++

Year	Lev	Team	W	L	Sv	IP	K	ERA	WHIP	BF/G	OBA	H%	S%	xERA	Ctl	Dom	Cmd	hr/9	BPV
2015	Rk	GCL Cardinals	3	2	0	51	58	3.88	1.35	19.3	273	39	68	3.35	2.6	10.2	3.9	0.0	131
2015	A+	Palm Beach	0	0	0	6	5	1.45	1.61	13.7	314	39	90	4.65	2.9	7.3	2.5	0.0	70
2016	A	Peoria	6	5	0	78	63	3.34	1.34	23.2	244	30	75	3.28	3.9	7.3	1.9	0.3	43
2016	A+	Palm Beach	2	2	0	43	25	5.42	1.57	19.0	283	31	66	4.88	4.2	5.2	1.3	0.8	-1
2017	A+	Palm Beach	5	3	0	90	58	3.70	1.34	23.4	244	28	72	3.44	3.9	5.8	1.5	0.5	17

Athletic Dominican hurler has seen his Dom drop since his pro debut despite having a plus 94-98 mph fastball. Missed the second half of the season with a sore biceps. Good hard slider and improved change-up give him a chance to stick as a starter, but below-average control and plus heater suggest a move to relief.

Festa,Matt — RP — Seattle

EXP MLB DEBUT: 2018 | H/W: 6-2 195 | FUT: Setup reliever | 6B

Thrws R Age 25
2016 (7) East Stroudsburg

90-94	FB	+++
86-88	SL	+++
80-81	CB	++

Year	Lev	Team	W	L	Sv	IP	K	ERA	WHIP	BF/G	OBA	H%	S%	xERA	Ctl	Dom	Cmd	hr/9	BPV
2016	NCAA	East Stroudsburg	11	2	0	88	105	2.35	1.06	26.2	225	33	78	2.25	2.1	10.7	5.0	0.3	153
2016	A-	Everett	6	2	0	60	58	3.74	1.23	17.4	261	34	69	3.32	2.1	8.7	4.1	0.4	118
2017	A+	Modesto	4	2	6	69	99	3.25	1.16	6.6	238	36	75	3.21	2.5	12.9	5.2	0.9	183

Unheralded RP who started season slowly, but was great the rest of the year. Big and strong frame allows him to feature quality FB with plenty of late life. Keeps ball down in zone and induces high number of groundballs. Counters FB with very hard SL and able to mix in CB. Stuff isn't great, but good enough to profile as setup guy.

Fillmyer,Heath — SP — Oakland

EXP MLB DEBUT: 2018 | H/W: 6-1 180 | FUT: #4 starter | 7C

Thrws R Age 23
2014 (5) Mercer County CC

90-96	FB	+++
79-80	CB	++
84-88	CU	+++

Year	Lev	Team	W	L	Sv	IP	K	ERA	WHIP	BF/G	OBA	H%	S%	xERA	Ctl	Dom	Cmd	hr/9	BPV
2014	Rk	AZL Athletics	1	0	0	9	10	2.93	1.09	6.0	162	24	70	1.31	4.9	9.8	2.0	0.0	62
2015	A	Beloit	3	13	0	99	77	4.99	1.70	19.5	286	34	72	5.29	5.1	7.0	1.4	0.9	7
2016	A+	Stockton	5	6	0	95	89	3.60	1.39	22.2	274	35	73	3.83	2.9	8.4	2.9	0.4	90
2016	AA	Midland	2	0	0	39	29	2.54	1.00	18.6	220	26	78	2.44	1.8	6.7	3.6	0.7	89
2017	AA	Midland	11	5	0	149	115	3.50	1.40	21.7	273	31	79	4.58	3.1	6.9	2.3	1.1	60

Strong, athletic SP with average pitch mix. Has improved command over past few seasons and gets hitters to bury sinking FB into ground. Cleaned up delivery to take advantage of quick arm action. No pitch grades or projects as plus, but can mix well. CB can be tight, but not a swing-and-miss pitch. Will need to maintain control and command.

Flaherty, Jack — SP — St. Louis

EXP MLB DEBUT: 2017 | H/W: 6-4 205 | FUT: #2 starter | 9D

Thrws R Age 22
2014 (1) HS (CA)

92-95	FB	++++
83-86	SL	+++
73-75	CB	++
77-80	CU	+++

Year	Lev	Team	W	L	Sv	IP	K	ERA	WHIP	BF/G	OBA	H%	S%	xERA	Ctl	Dom	Cmd	hr/9	BPV
2015	A	Peoria	9	3	0	95	97	2.84	1.29	21.7	256	34	77	3.15	2.9	9.2	3.1	0.2	104
2016	A+	Palm Beach	5	9	0	134	126	3.56	1.30	23.0	254	32	73	3.48	3.0	8.5	2.8	0.5	89
2017	AA	Springfield	7	2	0	63	62	1.43	0.92	23.6	209	28	86	1.70	1.6	8.8	5.6	0.3	135
2017	AAA	Memphis	7	2	0	85	85	2.75	1.14	22.5	233	29	82	3.28	2.5	9.0	3.5	1.1	111
2017	MLB	St. Louis	0	2	0	21	20	6.40	1.56	15.4	279	32	62	5.58	4.3	8.5	2.0	1.7	56

Uptick in fastball velocity fueled an impressive breakout, going 14-4 with a 2.18 ERA across two levels, earning him five big-league starts. Fastball now sits at 92-95 mph with a good hard slider, and improved change-up. Threw more strike ones in 2017 giving him a chance to be a solid #2 starter.

Flexen,Chris — SP — New York (N)

EXP MLB DEBUT: 2017 | H/W: 6-3 250 | FUT: #4 starter | 7C

Thrws R Age 23
2012 (14) HS (CA)

91-93	FB	++++
85-87	SL	+++
75-77	CB	+++
81-84	CU	++

Year	Lev	Team	W	L	Sv	IP	K	ERA	WHIP	BF/G	OBA	H%	S%	xERA	Ctl	Dom	Cmd	hr/9	BPV
2015	A	Savannah	4	0	0	33	33	1.90	1.05	21.4	230	32	80	2.04	1.9	8.9	4.7	0.0	128
2016	A+	St. Lucie	10	9	0	134	95	3.56	1.31	22.2	249	30	72	3.33	3.4	6.4	1.9	0.4	40
2017	A+	St. Lucie	0	0	0	12	13	2.21	1.23	16.5	259	34	86	3.54	2.2	9.6	4.3	0.7	131
2017	AA	Binghamton	6	1	0	48	50	1.68	0.73	24.4	171	22	84	1.21	1.3	9.3	7.1	0.7	151
2017	MLB	NY Mets	3	6	0	48	36	7.88	2.02	16.6	314	34	64	7.62	6.6	6.8	1.0	2.1	-38

Oft-injured RH made MLB debut after phenomenal MiLB season. Struggled mightily against MLB competition; no true out pitch. Controls average 2-seam FB for strikes. Took to SL in 2017 and became primary secondary pitch. CB has moderate depth and sink. CU lags behind other three offerings; it's around zone but he lacks command of it.

Flores,Bernardo — SP — Chicago (A)

EXP MLB DEBUT: 2019 | H/W: 6-3 170 | FUT: #4 starter | 7E

Thrws L Age 22
2016 (7) USC

89-93	FB	+++
85-87	CB	++
77-79	CT	++
83-85	CU	+++

Year	Lev	Team	W	L	Sv	IP	K	ERA	WHIP	BF/G	OBA	H%	S%	xERA	Ctl	Dom	Cmd	hr/9	BPV
2016	NCAA	USC	1	0	0	41	36	6.77	1.60	11.4	301	37	56	5.03	3.5	7.9	2.3	0.7	65
2016	Rk	Great Falls	6	1	0	59	45	3.66	1.27	21.9	275	33	72	3.77	1.8	6.9	3.8	0.6	92
2016	Rk	AZL White Sox	0	1	0	6	7	1.50	0.67	7.0	191	29	75	0.58	0.0	10.5		0.0	207
2017	A	Kannapolis	8	4	0	78	70	3.00	1.10	21.9	249	31	74	2.95	1.5	8.1	5.4	0.6	123
2017	A+	Winston-Salem	2	3	0	40	33	4.26	1.55	19.5	275	32	75	4.95	4.3	7.4	1.7	1.1	36

Quick-armed, former collegiate reliever now working as starting pitcher. 2-seam FB lost velocity and some effectiveness, proving to be easier to lift than in college. CU is his best offering, mimicking FB delivery with greater sink. CB and CT are marginal pitches at present. Always around the zone.

Foley,Jason — RP — Detroit

EXP MLB DEBUT: 2020 | H/W: 6-4 215 | FUT: Closer | 7D

Thrws R Age 22
2016 (FA) Sacred Heart

94-98	FB	++++
84-88	SL	+
	CU	++

Year	Lev	Team	W	L	Sv	IP	K	ERA	WHIP	BF/G	OBA	H%	S%	xERA	Ctl	Dom	Cmd	hr/9	BPV
2016	NCAA	Sacred Heart	4	4	0	58	47	5.72	1.67	15.4	296	36	64	4.94	4.3	7.3	1.7	0.5	32
2016	Rk	GCL Tigers	0	0	1	1	1	0.00	1.00	3.8	262	35	100	2.32	0.0	9.0		0.0	180
2016	A-	Connecticut	0	0	0	6	6	4.43	2.13	6.0	259	35	77	5.12	10.3	8.9	0.9	0.0	-102
2017	A	West Michigan	3	1	5	29	36	1.55	0.86	5.9	197	30	80	1.12	1.6	11.2	7.2	0.0	177
2017	A+	Lakeland	0	2	1	7	5	6.34	1.41	5.0	285	32	56	4.90	2.5	6.3	2.5	1.3	64

Sleeper RP who was dominating A-ball before July Tommy John surgery. Owns power arsenal with all pitches thrown for strikes. Can retire hitters with just FB that exhibits late movement at significant velocity. CU is next best pitch, but not enough separation from FB. SL shows flashes of becoming average, but loses break at times.

Franklin,Austin — SP — Tampa Bay

EXP MLB DEBUT: 2021 | H/W: 6-3 215 | FUT: #3 starter | 8D

Thrws R Age 20
2016 (3) HS (FL)

90-94	FB	+++
77-80	CB	+++
	CU	++

Year	Lev	Team	W	L	Sv	IP	K	ERA	WHIP	BF/G	OBA	H%	S%	xERA	Ctl	Dom	Cmd	hr/9	BPV
2016	Rk	GCL Rays	1	2	1	43	40	2.71	1.07	15.2	198	27	72	1.68	3.3	8.4	2.5	0.0	78
2017	A-	Hudson Valley	4	2	0	69	71	2.21	1.19	21.3	207	28	83	2.58	4.0	9.2	2.3	0.5	75

Tall, durable SP who has yet to appear at full season affiliate, yet has advanced feel. Works with short arm action and downhill delivery to spot ball low in zone. Heavy sink on FB is tough to elevate and could add more velocity. Inconsistent mechanics hinder strike-throwing. Owns CB that flashes plus and CU that could grow into average offering.

Fried,Max — SP — Atlanta

EXP MLB DEBUT: 2017 | H/W: 6-4 200 | FUT: #3 starter | 8D

Thrws L Age 24
2012 (1) HS (CA)

90-93	FB	+++
72-79	CB	++++
82-85	CU	+++

Year	Lev	Team	W	L	Sv	IP	K	ERA	WHIP	BF/G	OBA	H%	S%	xERA	Ctl	Dom	Cmd	hr/9	BPV
2014	A	Fort Wayne	0	1	0	5	2	5.19	1.73	11.8	323	32	75	6.76	3.5	3.5	1.0	1.7	-13
2016	A	Rome	8	7	0	103	112	3.93	1.30	20.2	230	30	72	3.47	4.1	9.8	2.4	0.9	83
2017	AA	Mississippi	2	11	0	86	85	5.95	1.52	19.7	266	34	60	4.47	4.5	8.9	2.0	0.8	57
2017	AAA	Gwinnett	0	0	0	6	6	0.00	0.50	10.0	56	8	100		3.0	9.0	3.0	0.0	99
2017	MLB	Atlanta	1	1	0	26	22	3.81	1.62	12.8	290	34	79	5.26	4.2	7.6	1.8	1.0	43

Tall-and-fall LH made MLB debut after battling control issues throughout development. A 3-pitch pitcher with mid-rotation stuff, pitches off 90-93 mph 2-seam FB w/ solid arm-side run and spotty command. CB is a true out pitch and will change speed and look of pitch. Slow CB is 12-6 variety while harder CB is more slurvy. CU has solid tumble.

Fulmer,Carson — SP — Chicago (A)

EXP MLB DEBUT: 2016 | H/W: 6-0 195 | FUT: Closer | 8B

Thrws R Age 24
2015 (1) Vanderbilt

92-94	FB	++++
79-81	CB	+++
87-91	CT	++++
80-82	CU	++

Year	Lev	Team	W	L	Sv	IP	K	ERA	WHIP	BF/G	OBA	H%	S%	xERA	Ctl	Dom	Cmd	hr/9	BPV
2016	AA	Birmingham	4	9	0	87	90	4.76	1.53	22.3	251	33	69	4.17	5.3	9.3	1.8	0.7	43
2016	AAA	Charlotte	2	1	0	16	14	3.94	1.19	16.0	237	29	67	3.00	2.8	7.9	2.8	0.6	84
2016	MLB	Chi White Sox	0	2	0	11	10	8.84	1.70	6.3	275	32	47	5.78	5.6	8.0	1.4	1.6	11
2017	AAA	Charlotte	7	9	0	126	96	5.79	1.56	22.1	271	31	65	5.09	4.6	6.9	1.5	1.3	16
2017	MLB	Chi White Sox	3	1	0	23	19	3.90	1.26	13.4	197	21	76	3.62	5.1	7.4	1.5	1.6	14

Short, max-effort RH has struggled with command since pro debut. FB and spike CB project as plus pitches. Added CT lin 2017, turning the pitch into an effective weapon against LHH. CU still lags behind. Size, delivery and command point towards reliever profile long term.

Funkhouser,Kyle — SP — Detroit

EXP MLB DEBUT: 2018 | H/W: 6-2 220 | FUT: #3 starter | 8D

Thrws R Age 24
2016 (4) Louisville

89-95	FB	++++
82-86	SL	+++
79-83	CB	++
82-84	CU	++

Year	Lev	Team	W	L	Sv	IP	K	ERA	WHIP	BF/G	OBA	H%	S%	xERA	Ctl	Dom	Cmd	hr/9	BPV
2016	NCAA	Louisville	9	3	0	93	95	3.87	1.26	23.7	210	27	71	3.03	4.5	9.2	2.0	0.8	61
2016	A-	Connecticut	0	2	0	37	34	2.67	1.13	11.3	245	32	74	2.43	1.9	8.2	4.3	0.0	114
2017	A	West Michigan	4	1	0	31	49	3.18	1.38	18.7	255	41	80	3.95	3.8	14.2	3.8	0.9	172
2017	A+	Lakeland	1	1	0	31	34	1.74	0.93	23.3	208	29	82	1.72	1.7	9.8	5.7	0.3	148

Tall, strong SP who was dominating lower minors before elbow strain ended season in June. Has very solid arsenal, highlighted by plus FB that he spots in lower half of strike zone. Best secondary is hard SL that he can throw for strikes or use as chase pitch. Mixes in CB and occasional CU. The CU lacks polish and may need to change grip.

Gaddis, Will — SP — Colorado

EXP MLB DEBUT: 2021 | H/W: 6-1 185 | FUT: #4 starter | 7D

Thrws R Age 22
2017 (3) Furman

88-93	FB	+++
85-87	CT	++
71-73	CB	++
76-78	CU	++

Year	Lev	Team	W	L	Sv	IP	K	ERA	WHIP	BF/G	OBA	H%	S%	xERA	Ctl	Dom	Cmd	hr/9	BPV
2017	NCAA	Furman	9	3	1	105	89	1.89	0.92	23.1	215	27	82	1.93	1.4	7.6	5.6	0.4	118
2017	Rk	Grand Junction	3	1	0	44	26	5.71	1.66	17.9	347	38	67	6.47	1.4	5.3	3.7	1.2	75

Struggled in his rookie ball pro debut. Works off heavy 88-93 mph sinking fastball and mixes in a cutter, change-up, and curve all of which flash as average. Back-end starter potential.

Gallegos,Giovanny — RP — New York (A)

EXP MLB DEBUT: 2017 | H/W: 6-2 210 | FUT: Setup reliever | 6A

Thrws R Age 26 — 2011 FA (MX)

Velo	Pitch	Grade
92-95	FB	+++
80-82	CB	+++
	CU	+

Year	Lev	Team	W	L	Sv	IP	K	ERA	WHIP	BF/G	OBA	H%	S%	xERA	Ctl	Dom	Cmd	hr/9	BPV
2015	AA	Scranton/WB	0	0	0	3	3	0.00	0.67	5.2	191	27	100	0.59	0.0	9.0		0.0	180
2016	AA	Trenton	2	1	2	33	53	1.09	0.82	7.1	177	32	88	1.01	1.9	14.5	7.6	0.3	227
2016	AAA	Scranton/WB	5	1	2	45	53	1.40	0.84	6.6	181	25	91	1.66	2.0	10.6	5.3	0.8	155
2017	AAA	Scranton/WB	4	2	5	43	69	2.09	0.90	5.7	187	31	83	1.88	2.3	14.4	6.3	0.8	215
2017	MLB	NY Yankees	0	1	0	20	22	4.93	1.29	5.2	270	34	65	4.43	2.2	9.9	4.4	1.3	135

Strong RP who was on shuttle between AAA and NYY all season. Can dominate with two dynamic offerings, though none grade as plus. Gets electric, late life on FB and mixes in hard CB for swings and misses. FB features tailing action and is tough to hit hard. Generally can drop in CB for strikes, but lacks any semblance of CU.

Garabito,Gerson — SP — Kansas City

EXP MLB DEBUT: 2020 | H/W: 6-0 160 | FUT: #4 starter | 7C

Thrws R Age 22 — 2012 FA (DR)

Velo	Pitch	Grade
90-95	FB	+++
78-83	CB	+++
80-85	CU	++

Year	Lev	Team	W	L	Sv	IP	K	ERA	WHIP	BF/G	OBA	H%	S%	xERA	Ctl	Dom	Cmd	hr/9	BPV
2016	A	Lexington	2	11	0	80	61	4.83	1.41	18.8	256	29	67	4.24	3.9	6.8	1.7	1.0	35
2017	Rk	AZL Royals	0	0	0	3	2	6.00	1.67	6.7	321	32	75	7.73	3.0	6.0	2.0	3.0	45
2017	A	Lexington	4	5	0	77	72	2.81	0.92	19.2	193	23	75	2.14	2.2	8.4	3.8	0.9	110

Short, lean SP who missed almost two months with shoulder tendinitis. Repeated Low-A and impressed with low oppBA and increased K rate. Pitches off solid FB/CB combination while CU has good depth and fade. Has pitch mix to remain SP, but stamina is concern. Hasn't pitched deep into games. Doesn't use CU much and has little projection.

Garcia,Bryan — RP — Detroit

EXP MLB DEBUT: 2018 | H/W: 6-1 203 | FUT: Closer | 8D

Thrws R Age 22 — 2016 (6) Miami

Velo	Pitch	Grade
92-96	FB	++++
84-88	SL	+++
	CU	++

Year	Lev	Team	W	L	Sv	IP	K	ERA	WHIP	BF/G	OBA	H%	S%	xERA	Ctl	Dom	Cmd	hr/9	BPV
2016	A	West Michigan	0	1	0	0			15.00	3.6	842	117	0	74.41	0.0	45.0		0.0	828
2017	A	West Michigan	1	2	9	14	27	3.19	1.13	4.0	232	48	69	2.18	2.6	17.2	6.8	0.0	259
2017	A+	Lakeland	2	0	0	8	15	0.00	1.10	4.6	232	46	100	2.10	2.2	16.5	7.5	0.0	255
2017	AA	Erie	1	1	8	18	24	0.99	0.82	3.9	120	18	93	0.67	4.0	11.9	3.0	0.5	125
2017	AAA	Toledo	1	0	0	13	12	4.12	1.37	3.9	213	27	71	3.28	5.5	8.2	1.5	0.7	18

Rapidly progressing RP who pitched on four levels and had incredible season. Was college closer and has aggressive and competitive mentality to close in majors. Challenges hitters with plus, sinking FB and has power SL that is tough to hit. Ability to throw strikes is valuable in late-innings work. Lack of height hinders plane to plate.

Garcia,Deivi — SP — New York (A)

EXP MLB DEBUT: 2022 | H/W: 5-10 163 | FUT: #4 starter | 7C

Thrws R Age 18 — 2015 FA (DR)

Velo	Pitch	Grade
90-94	FB	+++
77-79	CB	+++
82-84	CU	++

Year	Lev	Team	W	L	Sv	IP	K	ERA	WHIP	BF/G	OBA	H%	S%	xERA	Ctl	Dom	Cmd	hr/9	BPV
2017	Rk	GCL Yankees	3	0	0	16	24	3.33	0.80	14.7	165	22	70	2.16	2.2	13.3	6.0	1.7	198
2017	Rk	Pulaski	2	1	0	28	43	4.50	1.29	19.2	226	36	67	3.42	4.2	13.8	3.3	1.0	154

Short, slender SP who may not look part, but can fire pure heat. Not much command at present and lacks current feel for changing speeds. Has chance to develop two plus offerings in FB and CB. Can register high K rate with CB that hitters chase. FB can be straight and flat and has high flyball rate. Quick arm action to dream on.

Garcia,Elniery — SP — Philadelphia

EXP MLB DEBUT: 2019 | H/W: 6-0 155 | FUT: #5 SP/swingman | 7D

Thrws L Age 23 — 2011 FA (DR)

Velo	Pitch	Grade
89-92	FB	++
74-77	CB	+++
83-86	CU	+++

Year	Lev	Team	W	L	Sv	IP	K	ERA	WHIP	BF/G	OBA	H%	S%	xERA	Ctl	Dom	Cmd	hr/9	BPV
2014	A-	Williamsport	0	0	0	4	5	6.43	1.90	5.0	336	42	71	7.73	4.3	10.7	2.5	2.1	95
2015	A	Lakewood	8	9	0	120	66	3.23	1.34	23.8	270	30	77	3.82	2.7	5.0	1.8	0.5	34
2016	A+	Clearwater	12	4	0	117	91	2.69	1.11	23.0	221	26	78	2.66	2.8	7.0	2.5	0.6	69
2017	Rk	GCL Phillies	0	0	0	5	3	0.00	1.00	9.6	175	21	100	1.29	3.6	5.4	1.5	0.0	18
2017	AA	Reading	2	1	0	25	10	1.79	1.35	21.0	193	22	85	2.39	6.1	3.6	0.6	0.0	-82

80-game PED suspension put a kink in his development, as the pitchability lefty needed reps at the higher levels. Stuff is only average across the board, and uncharacteristically struggled with control with upon his return. Went to AFL to make up innings; tested out a SP with mixed results. Was taken off 40-man roster in November; needs a reset.

Gardewine,Nick — RP — Texas

EXP MLB DEBUT: 2017 | H/W: 6-1 179 | FUT: Setup reliever | 6A

Thrws R Age 24 — 2013 (7) Kaskaskia JC

Velo	Pitch	Grade
90-95	FB	+++
85-87	SL	+++
	CU	+

Year	Lev	Team	W	L	Sv	IP	K	ERA	WHIP	BF/G	OBA	H%	S%	xERA	Ctl	Dom	Cmd	hr/9	BPV
2014	A-	Spokane	6	3	0	71	60	4.56	1.20	19.0	236	28	62	3.20	2.9	7.6	2.6	0.8	76
2015	A	Hickory	6	8	1	96	80	4.31	1.40	18.4	291	34	72	4.71	2.2	7.5	3.5	1.0	95
2016	A+	High Desert	5	1	7	54	60	2.49	0.98	7.1	203	27	79	2.29	2.3	10.0	4.3	0.8	135
2017	AA	Frisco	1	2	6	36	53	2.24	1.30	4.5	255	40	84	3.40	3.0	13.2	4.4	0.5	175
2017	MLB	Texas	0	0	0	8	3	5.63	2.13	3.3	307	32	75	6.93	7.9	3.4	0.4	1.1	-134

Power-armed RP who came out of nowhere to reach majors. Moved to pen in 2016 and has been wonder with ability to miss bats. Everything coming out of hand is hard. Keeps ball down with quick FB and complements with very hard, late-breaking SL. Doesn't have imposing figure and will need to keep walks in check. Setup potential.

Garrett, Braxton — SP — Miami

EXP MLB DEBUT: 2020 | H/W: 6-3 190 | FUT: #2 starter | 9D

Thrws L Age 20 — 2016 (1) HS (AL)

Velo	Pitch	Grade
91-94	FB	+++
76-80	CB	++++
80-83	CU	+++

Year	Lev	Team	W	L	Sv	IP	K	ERA	WHIP	BF/G	OBA	H%	S%	xERA	Ctl	Dom	Cmd	hr/9	BPV
2016		*Did not pitch*																	
2017	A	Greensboro	1	0	0	15	16	2.98	1.26	15.4	234	27	88	4.27	3.6	9.5	2.7	1.8	93

Had Tommy John surgery in June; will likely miss all of 2018. When healthy has a good low-90s FB, a plus 12-6 CB, and above average CU with good fade and sink. Uses a high leg kick to generate momentum and commands all three offerings. Raw ingredients to be one of the top LH pitchers in the minors, but future hinges on TJS recovery.

Gatto,Joe — SP — Los Angeles (A)

EXP MLB DEBUT: 2019 | H/W: 6-3 220 | FUT: #4 starter | 7C

Thrws R Age 22 — 2014 (2) HS (NJ)

Velo	Pitch	Grade
90-95	FB	+++
77-80	CB	+++
81-85	CU	++

Year	Lev	Team	W	L	Sv	IP	K	ERA	WHIP	BF/G	OBA	H%	S%	xERA	Ctl	Dom	Cmd	hr/9	BPV
2014	Rk	AZL Angels	2	1	0	25	15	5.40	1.68	11.3	319	37	66	5.25	3.2	5.4	1.7	0.4	28
2015	Rk	Orem	2	3	0	54	38	4.33	1.66	20.2	324	38	74	5.57	2.8	6.3	2.2	0.7	55
2016	A	Burlington	3	8	0	64	54	7.03	1.89	20.1	328	40	61	6.23	4.6	7.6	1.6	0.7	29
2017	A	Burlington	5	7	0	96	78	3.47	1.40	19.3	249	31	74	3.36	4.2	7.3	1.7	0.2	36
2017	A+	Inland Empire	3	2	0	32	23	3.36	1.40	22.6	255	31	75	3.53	3.9	6.4	1.6	0.3	28

Strong SP who has shown cleaner delivery and better command as he climbs ladder. Ended year very strong; starting to gain consistency with FB and CB combo. Rarely allows HR as he pitches downhill, though CU still needs work. Hammer CB can miss bats and needs to get ahead in count more frequently. Could become durable groundball guy at peak.

German,Domingo — SP — New York (A)

EXP MLB DEBUT: 2017 | H/W: 6-2 175 | FUT: #4 starter | 7C

Thrws R Age 25 — 2009 FA (DR)

Velo	Pitch	Grade
90-96	FB	+++
79-82	CB	++
80-83	CU	+++

Year	Lev	Team	W	L	Sv	IP	K	ERA	WHIP	BF/G	OBA	H%	S%	xERA	Ctl	Dom	Cmd	hr/9	BPV
2016	A	Charleston (Sc)	1	1	0	26	18	3.12	0.65	18.1	170	19	53	1.00	0.7	6.2	9.0	0.7	111
2016	A+	Tampa	0	2	0	23	20	3.10	1.51	20.1	284	35	79	4.29	3.5	7.8	2.2	0.4	63
2017	AA	Trenton	1	4	0	33	38	3.00	1.27	22.5	256	34	82	3.93	2.7	10.4	3.8	1.1	131
2017	AAA	Scranton/WB	7	2	0	76	81	2.84	1.06	21.1	216	29	75	2.43	2.6	9.6	3.7	0.6	120
2017	MLB	NY Yankees	0	1	0	14	18	3.19	1.42	8.5	217	31	79	3.36	5.7	11.5	2.0	0.6	70

Fast-rising SP despite missing all 2015 and half of 2016 due to arm ailments. Has potent FB/CU combination with solid separation and arm speed. Throws good strikes and FB can be sneaky quick. Command comes and goes and will need to improve fringe-average CB to maintain K rate in majors. Could be effective as either SP or RP.

Gohara,Luiz — SP — Atlanta

EXP MLB DEBUT: 2017 | H/W: 6-3 210 | FUT: #1 starter | 9C

Thrws L Age 21 — 2012 FA (BR)

Velo	Pitch	Grade
95-97	FB	++++
83-86	SL	++++
87-89	CU	+++

Year	Lev	Team	W	L	Sv	IP	K	ERA	WHIP	BF/G	OBA	H%	S%	xERA	Ctl	Dom	Cmd	hr/9	BPV
2016	A	Clinton	5	2	0	54	60	1.83	1.18	21.7	224	32	84	2.43	3.3	10.0	3.0	0.2	108
2017	A+	Florida	3	1	0	36	39	1.99	1.19	20.7	245	34	81	2.56	2.5	9.7	3.9	0.0	126
2017	AA	Mississippi	2	1	0	52	60	2.60	1.15	17.2	223	32	78	2.50	3.1	10.4	3.3	0.3	121
2017	AAA	Gwinnett	2	2	0	35	48	3.33	1.34	20.9	238	35	79	3.79	4.1	12.3	3.0	1.0	129
2017	MLB	Atlanta	1	3	0	29	31	4.95	1.37	24.4	281	37	63	4.10	2.5	9.6	3.9	0.6	124

Husky LH has best pure stuff in organization. Made MLB debut in 2017 after starting season in High-A. Size and 3/4s arm angle hides ball in body, creating deception. FB explodes out of hand, has late movement and reaches triple digits at times. SL is tight with significant two-plane movement. CU feel and pitchability in profile.

Gomber, Austin — SP — St. Louis

EXP MLB DEBUT: 2018 | H/W: 6-5 235 | FUT: #4 starter | 7C

Thrws L Age 24 — 2014 (4) Florida Atlantic

Velo	Pitch	Grade
90-92	FB	++
	CB	++++
	CU	++

Year	Lev	Team	W	L	Sv	IP	K	ERA	WHIP	BF/G	OBA	H%	S%	xERA	Ctl	Dom	Cmd	hr/9	BPV
2014	A-	State College	2	2	0	47	36	2.30	1.55	18.7	293	35	87	4.72	3.4	6.9	2.0	0.6	49
2015	A	Peoria	15	3	0	135	140	2.67	0.97	23.3	203	27	75	2.12	2.3	9.3	4.1	0.7	125
2016	A+	Palm Beach	6	8	0	107	101	2.94	1.07	24.5	231	30	73	2.50	2.0	8.5	4.2	0.4	116
2016	AA	Springfield	1	0	0	19	15	1.41	1.05	18.5	170	22	85	1.33	4.2	7.1	1.7	0.0	31
2017	AA	Springfield	10	7	0	143	140	3.34	1.17	21.9	223	27	76	3.24	3.2	8.8	2.7	1.1	90

Pitchability lefty started slowly, but was lights-out in the 2nd half, going 8-1 with a 2.41 ERA. Low-90s fastball lacks plus velocity, but is located well and has good downhill action. Change-up is average, but improved curveball is now plus and has the size to be a workhorse, back-end starter.

Gonsalves,Stephen — SP — Minnesota

EXP MLB DEBUT: 2018 | H/W: 6-5 215 | FUT: #4 starter | 7A

Thrws L Age 23 — 2013 (4) HS (CA)

Velo	Pitch	Grade
88-93	FB	+++
77-80	CB	++
81-83	SL	+++
81-83	CU	++++

Year	Lev	Team	W	L	Sv	IP	K	ERA	WHIP	BF/G	OBA	H%	S%	xERA	Ctl	Dom	Cmd	hr/9	BPV
2015	A+	Fort Myers	7	2	0	79	55	2.62	1.31	21.8	228	28	79	2.91	4.3	6.3	1.4	0.2	14
2016	A+	Fort Myers	5	4	0	65	66	2.35	0.97	22.4	190	26	75	1.58	2.8	9.1	3.3	0.3	107
2016	AA	Chattanooga	8	1	0	74	89	1.82	1.08	22.2	171	26	82	1.50	4.5	10.8	2.4	0.1	91
2017	AA	Chattanooga	8	3	0	87	96	2.69	1.03	22.4	214	29	77	2.46	2.4	9.9	4.2	0.7	132
2017	AAA	Rochester	1	2	0	22	22	5.68	1.58	19.5	301	36	68	5.87	3.2	8.9	2.8	1.6	91

Tall, loose-armed SP who has been great at all levels of minors. Has deep repertoire with variety of pitches. Velocity is stable, but adds deceptive life due to arm action. Plus CU features depth and sink and is weapon against RHH. Mixes in SL with cutting action and average CB. Has flyball tendencies and could use better command.

Gonzalez, Merandy — SP — Miami

EXP MLB DEBUT: 2019 | H/W: 6-0 216 | FUT: #3 starter | 8C

Thrws R Age 22 — 2013 FA (DR)

Velo	Pitch	Grade
92-95	FB	++++
77-81	CB	+++
82-85	CU	++

Year	Lev	Team	W	L	Sv	IP	K	ERA	WHIP	BF/G	OBA	H%	S%	xERA	Ctl	Dom	Cmd	hr/9	BPV
2015	Rk	GCL Mets	2	1	0	22	25	2.05	0.55	18.5	127	18	64		1.2	10.2	8.3	0.4	169
2016	A-	Brooklyn	6	3	0	69	71	2.87	1.33	20.5	250	34	78	3.24	3.5	9.3	2.6	0.3	90
2017	A	Columbia	8	1	0	69	65	1.56	0.91	23.5	204	27	85	1.72	1.7	8.5	5.0	0.4	125
2017	A+	St. Lucie	4	2	0	36	24	2.24	1.14	23.8	245	29	80	2.69	2.0	6.0	3.0	0.2	72
2017	A+	Jupiter	1	0	1	24	14	1.12	0.95	18.2	209	25	87	1.57	1.9	5.2	2.8	0.0	62

Dominican hurler came over in the A.J. Ramos trade in July. Short, solidly built frame generates a plus 93-95 mph fastball that tops at 97. Mixes in an above-average 11-5 power curve and a fringe change-up. Improved control fueled a breakout and resulted in a 13-3 season w/1.66 ERA at three levels.

Gore,MacKenzie — SP — San Diego

EXP MLB DEBUT: 2021 | H/W: 6-3 180 | FUT: #2 starter | 9B

Thrws L Age 19 — 2017 (1) HS (NC)

Velo	Pitch	Grade
91-94	FB	++++
74-77	CB	++++
83-85	SL	+++
80-83	CU	+++

Year	Lev	Team	W	L	Sv	IP	K	ERA	WHIP	BF/G	OBA	H%	S%	xERA	Ctl	Dom	Cmd	hr/9	BPV
2017	Rk	AZL Padres	0	1	0	21	34	1.28	1.00	11.5	190	35	86	1.35	3.0	14.5	4.9	0.0	198

Tall, lean LHP with an exciting combination of advanced stuff, feel and projectability. Fills zone and will flash plus command of low-90s FB that should add a few ticks of velo as he matures. CB is plus and is trusted pitch for Ks; SL and CU both have a chance to be at least average. Quality athlete with big-time upside. Invest while you still can.

Gowdy,Kevin — SP — Philadelphia

EXP MLB DEBUT: 2022 | H/W: 6-4 170 | FUT: #3 starter | 8E

Thrws R Age 20 — 2016 (2) HS (CA)

Velo	Pitch	Grade
91-94	FB	+++
86-88	SL	+++
83-84	CU	++

Year	Lev	Team	W	L	Sv	IP	K	ERA	WHIP	BF/G	OBA	H%	S%	xERA	Ctl	Dom	Cmd	hr/9	BPV
2016	Rk	GCL Phillies	0	1	0	9	9	4.00	1.22	9.1	262	35	64	2.88	2.0	9.0	4.5	0.0	126
2017		*Did not pitch - injured*																	

Never could get on the field in 2017 with arm injuries; mid-August Tommy John surgery should wipe out all of 2018. Still owns projectable frame, and the simple delivery, FB/SL combination and ability to adjust are characteristics that should still be present once he gets back on the mound. Still young, but quite a long shot now.

Graterol,Brusdar — SP — Minnesota

EXP MLB DEBUT: 2021 | H/W: 6-1 180 | FUT: #2 starter | 9E

Thrws R Age 19 — 2014 FA (VZ)

Velo	Pitch	Grade
92-97	FB	++++
84-85	SL	++
80-83	CB	++
	CU	++

Year	Lev	Team	W	L	Sv	IP	K	ERA	WHIP	BF/G	OBA	H%	S%	xERA	Ctl	Dom	Cmd	hr/9	BPV
2017	Rk	GCL Twins	2	0	0	19	21	1.41	0.73	13.6	157	21	85	0.81	1.9	9.9	5.3	0.5	145
2017	Rk	Elizabethton	2	1	0	20	24	4.01	1.24	16.4	219	31	67	2.76	4.0	10.7	2.7	0.4	102

High-upside SP who hasn't been in full-season yet and likely to be treated cautiously due to Tommy John surgery in past. Has loads of potential due to elite FB and potential for two plus breaking balls. Needs time to maintain delivery, release point, and arm speed on all pitches. CU not reliable yet, but hard SL and big-bending CB getting better.

Greene,Conner — SP — Toronto

EXP MLB DEBUT: 2018 | H/W: 6-3 185 | FUT: #3 starter | 8C

Thrws R Age 23 — 2013 (7) HS (CA)

Velo	Pitch	Grade
89-96	FB	++++
74-77	CB	+++
83-86	SL	++
81-85	CU	+++

Year	Lev	Team	W	L	Sv	IP	K	ERA	WHIP	BF/G	OBA	H%	S%	xERA	Ctl	Dom	Cmd	hr/9	BPV
2015	A+	Dunedin	2	3	0	40	35	2.25	1.10	22.4	242	31	79	2.52	1.8	7.9	4.4	0.2	111
2015	AA	New Hampshire	3	1	0	25	15	4.68	1.48	21.5	262	30	67	3.90	4.3	5.4	1.3	0.4	-1
2016	A+	Dunedin	4	4	0	77	51	2.91	1.45	22.0	254	29	81	3.92	4.4	5.9	1.3	0.6	5
2016	AA	New Hampshire	6	5	0	68	48	4.22	1.32	23.5	229	26	68	3.33	4.4	6.3	1.5	0.7	14
2017	AA	New Hampshire	5	10	0	132	92	5.31	1.69	23.0	274	32	67	4.72	5.7	6.3	1.1	0.5	-22

Lean SP who has explosive stuff, yet led EL in walks. Natural offerings are tantalizing, but sequences poorly and is inconsistent. Has potential to miss bats with multiple pitches. Gets groundballs from heavy two-seamer while can blow four-seamer past hitters. Both SL and CU show glimpses of becoming above average. K rate stuck in neutral.

Greene,Hunter — SP — Cincinnati

EXP MLB DEBUT: 2021 | H/W: 6-4 197 | FUT: #1 starter | 9E

Thrws R Age 18 — 2017 (1) HS (CA)

Velo	Pitch	Grade
97-101	FB	+++++
81-82	CB	++
87-88	SL	+++
90-92	CU	++++

Year	Lev	Team	W	L	Sv	IP	K	ERA	WHIP	BF/G	OBA	H%	S%	xERA	Ctl	Dom	Cmd	hr/9	BPV
2017	Rk	Billings	0	1	0	4	6	13.17	2.20	6.9	409	59	33	7.81	2.2	13.2	6.0	0.0	196

Athletic RH with big velocity. Regularly up to 101 in many appearances. Despite velocity, pitch is flat and very hittable. Divisive opinions from scouts on breaking pitches. Some see fringe stuff, others like one over other. Has a feel for CU. Plus athleticism should help development into plus pitch at projection.

Gregorio,Joan — SP — San Francisco

EXP MLB DEBUT: 2018 | H/W: 6-7 180 | FUT: #4 starter | 7D

Thrws R Age 26 — 2010 FA (DR)

Velo	Pitch	Grade
90-95	FB	+++
82-85	SL	+++
84-86	CU	++

Year	Lev	Team	W	L	Sv	IP	K	ERA	WHIP	BF/G	OBA	H%	S%	xERA	Ctl	Dom	Cmd	hr/9	BPV
2014	A+	San Jose	2	2	0	22	27	6.89	1.80	17.1	301	41	61	5.65	5.3	10.9	2.1	0.8	73
2015	AA	Richmond	3	2	1	78	72	3.11	1.23	8.6	225	28	77	3.06	3.7	8.3	2.3	0.7	68
2016	AA	Richmond	0	2	0	27	30	2.33	0.78	19.4	165	23	70	0.88	2.0	10.0	5.0	0.3	144
2016	AAA	Sacramento	6	8	0	107	122	5.29	1.45	21.8	271	35	65	4.58	3.6	10.3	2.8	1.1	105
2017	AAA	Sacramento	4	4	0	74	61	3.04	1.32	23.6	232	27	82	3.78	4.3	7.4	1.7	1.1	37

Long, lean SP who has come on strong last few years, but ended season in June due to PED suspension. Pitches with tough angle to plate, but can telegraph pitches by slowing arm speed, particularly with CU. Has been stingy against RHH with FB/SL combination. Curious, big drop in K rate despite size and stuff. Can be victimized by flyballs and HR.

Griffin,Foster — SP — Kansas City

EXP MLB DEBUT: 2018 | H/W: 6-3 200 | FUT: #4 starter | 7B

Thrws L Age 22 — 2014 (1) HS (FL)

Velo	Pitch	Grade
88-93	FB	+++
75-79	CB	+++
79-82	CU	+++

Year	Lev	Team	W	L	Sv	IP	K	ERA	WHIP	BF/G	OBA	H%	S%	xERA	Ctl	Dom	Cmd	hr/9	BPV
2015	A	Lexington	4	6	0	102	71	5.46	1.55	20.3	299	35	64	4.92	3.1	6.3	2.0	0.7	47
2016	A	Lexington	1	4	0	37	29	3.40	1.19	21.2	251	30	73	3.34	2.2	7.0	3.2	0.7	86
2016	A+	Wilmington	5	10	0	95	76	6.25	1.82	22.1	326	39	65	6.17	4.1	7.2	1.8	0.9	38
2017	A+	Wilmington	4	2	0	56	60	2.88	1.12	22.1	213	29	74	2.29	3.2	9.6	3.0	0.3	104
2017	AA	NW Arkansas	11	5	0	104	81	3.63	1.36	24.2	269	31	76	4.24	2.9	7.0	2.4	1.0	65

Durable SP who improved after disastrous 2016 and pitched in Futures Game. Lacks a premium pitch in arsenal, but all are effective in stints. Keeps hitters off balance with solid-average CU and locates FB to bottom half of zone. Exhibits above average control despite pitch movement. Could add more velocity, but would need cleaner arm action.

Groome,Jason — SP — Boston

EXP MLB DEBUT: 2021 | H/W: 6-6 220 | FUT: #1 starter | 9D

Thrws L Age 19 — 2016 (1) HS (NJ)

Velo	Pitch	Grade
91-95	FB	+++
79-82	CB	++++
82-85	CU	+

Year	Lev	Team	W	L	Sv	IP	K	ERA	WHIP	BF/G	OBA	H%	S%	xERA	Ctl	Dom	Cmd	hr/9	BPV
2016	Rk	GCL Red Sox	0	0	0	4	8	2.25	0.75	7.1	210	48	67	0.93	0.0	18.0		0.0	342
2016	A-	Lowell	0	0	0	2	2	4.09	1.82	10.2	0	0	75	1.73	16.4	8.2	0.5	0.0	-277
2017	A-	Lowell	0	2	0	11	14	1.64	0.91	13.7	139	23	80	0.61	4.1	11.5	2.8	0.0	114
2017	A	Greenville	3	7	0	44	58	6.73	1.56	17.6	261	36	57	4.85	5.1	11.8	2.3	1.2	93

Tall, powerful SP who got off to slow start and suffered thru minor injures. When healthy, has filthy, dominant stuff led by plus hammer CB that exhibits depth and power. Repeats delivery, but hasn't mastered control and command. FB is solid now and should grow to plus pitch. Good, downhill plane to plate and can be intimidating. Very raw CU.

Guerrero,Jordan — SP — Chicago (A)

EXP MLB DEBUT: 2018 | H/W: 6-3 195 | FUT: Middle reliever | 6C

Thrws L Age 23 — 2012 (15) HS (CA)

Velo	Pitch	Grade
89-92	FB	+++
80-82	CB	++
80-83	CU	+++

Year	Lev	Team	W	L	Sv	IP	K	ERA	WHIP	BF/G	OBA	H%	S%	xERA	Ctl	Dom	Cmd	hr/9	BPV
2014	A	Kannapolis	6	2	0	78	80	3.46	1.38	12.1	269	35	76	3.93	3.1	9.2	3.0	0.6	100
2015	A	Kannapolis	6	1	0	55	60	2.29	0.94	23.0	213	30	75	1.69	1.6	9.8	6.0	0.2	150
2015	A+	Winston-Salem	7	3	0	93	88	3.57	1.11	22.9	238	30	68	2.81	2.0	8.5	4.2	0.6	116
2016	AA	Birmingham	7	8	0	136	108	4.83	1.51	23.6	257	30	69	4.38	4.8	7.1	1.5	0.9	16
2017	AA	Birmingham	7	12	0	146	136	4.19	1.32	24.2	267	34	68	3.66	2.6	8.4	3.2	0.5	97

Lean, deceptive LH who could benefit from move to bullpen. Has struggled getting over the Double-A hump. Low 90s 2-seam FB is an average offering and is hittable against advanced competition. Will cut his FB on occasion too. CU is best pitch, showcasing wonderful deception. SL is not a fit for arsenal.

Guerrieri,Taylor

SP | **Toronto** | EXP MLB DEBUT: 2018 | H/W: 6-2 210 | FUT: #3 starter | **8E**

Thrws R Age 25
2011 (1) HS (SC)

Velo	Pitch	Grade
89-94	FB	+++
77-81	CB	+++
80-83	SL	+++
80-83	CU	+++

Year	Lev	Team	W	L	Sv	IP	K	ERA	WHIP	BF/G	OBA	H%	S%	xERA	Ctl	Dom	Cmd	hr/9	BPV
2014	Rk	GCL Devil Rays	0	0	0	9	10	0.00	0.99	6.9	214	31	100	1.67	2.0	9.9	5.0	0.0	143
2015	A+	Charlotte	2	2	0	42	44	2.14	1.14	13.9	238	33	79	2.35	2.4	9.4	4.0	0.0	124
2015	AA	Montgomery	3	1	0	36	28	1.50	1.00	17.2	216	26	88	2.22	2.0	7.0	3.5	0.5	90
2016	AA	Montgomery	12	6	1	146	89	3.76	1.21	21.0	240	27	70	3.21	2.8	5.5	1.9	0.7	40
2017	AAA	Durham	1	0	0	9	12	2.97	0.99	17.3	214	34	67	1.65	2.0	11.9	6.0	0.0	178

Tall, athletic SP who missed most of season due to elbow ailment, but it did not require surgery. Has missed time in past with drug suspension and other injuries. Pitches to contact with average pitch mix. Increase in velocity never materialized and works more with movement. Spots FB low in zone while CB is tough to make hard contact against.

Gustave,Jandel

RP | **Houston** | EXP MLB DEBUT: 2016 | H/W: 6-2 210 | FUT: Setup reliever | **8E**

Thrws R Age 25
2010 FA (DR)

Velo	Pitch	Grade
96-99	FB	++++
86-89	SL	++++

Year	Lev	Team	W	L	Sv	IP	K	ERA	WHIP	BF/G	OBA	H%	S%	xERA	Ctl	Dom	Cmd	hr/9	BPV
2014	A	Quad Cities	5	5	2	79	82	5.01	1.56	15.0	297	39	66	4.54	3.3	9.3	2.8	0.3	97
2015	AA	Corpus Christi	5	2	20	58	49	2.16	1.31	5.2	237	30	84	3.06	3.9	7.6	2.0	0.3	50
2016	AAA	Fresno	3	3	3	57	55	3.79	1.21	4.9	223	30	66	2.48	3.6	8.7	2.4	0.2	76
2016	MLB	Houston	1	0	0	15	16	3.58	1.13	4.3	234	29	73	3.38	2.4	9.5	4.0	1.2	125
2017	MLB	Houston	0	0	0	5	2	5.40	2.40	4.4	262	29	75	5.90	12.6	3.6	0.3	0.0	-257

Strong-armed RP blew out elbow in April, underwent Tommy John surgery in July. FB sits in upper-90s and will touch 100, but often lacks movement to miss many bats. SL produces empty swings in upper-80s and will be legit weapon. Considerable risk involved post-TJS, but could be effective setup/closer type if he returns to full health.

Gutierrez,Vladimir

SP | **Cincinnati** | EXP MLB DEBUT: 2019 | H/W: 6-0 190 | FUT: Closer | **7A**

Thrws R Age 22
2016 FA (CU)

Velo	Pitch	Grade
91-95	FB	++++
81-83	CB	++++
81-84	CU	+

Year	Lev	Team	W	L	Sv	IP	K	ERA	WHIP	BF/G	OBA	H%	S%	xERA	Ctl	Dom	Cmd	hr/9	BPV
2017	A+	Daytona	7	8	0	103	94	4.46	1.23	22.0	271	33	65	3.86	1.7	8.2	4.9	0.9	121

Converted RH starter made US debut after defecting from Cuba. Throws two variants of FB, a 91-93 mph two-seam FB with solid arm-side run and drop and a 94-95 mph 4-seam FB with tailing action. Features power 11-5 power CB with solid depth and violent break. CU very much a project. Gives pitch away by slowing delivery. Solid build.

Guzman,Jorge

SP | **Miami** | EXP MLB DEBUT: 2020 | H/W: 6-2 182 | FUT: #3 starter | **8E**

Thrws R Age 22
2014 FA (DR)

Velo	Pitch	Grade
95-99	FB	++++
80-84	CB	++
85-87	CU	+

Year	Lev	Team	W	L	Sv	IP	K	ERA	WHIP	BF/G	OBA	H%	S%	xERA	Ctl	Dom	Cmd	hr/9	BPV
2016	Rk	Greeneville	2	3	0	22	29	4.86	1.44	15.8	285	42	65	4.12	2.8	11.8	4.1	0.4	153
2016	Rk	GCL Astros	1	1	0	17	25	3.16	0.82	8.9	77	15	57		5.3	13.2	2.5	0.0	113
2017	A-	Staten Island	5	3	0	66	88	2.31	1.04	19.7	215	32	80	2.29	2.4	12.0	4.9	0.5	167

Quick-armed SP who still hasn't seen any action in full season, but has upside. FB can be electric at premium velocity and commands to bottom of zone. Secondary offerings show flashes, but need significant work. CU not used often and can telegraph by slowing arm. CB has chance to miss bats in time. Need to see how he fares against advanced hitters.

Hall,D.L.

SP | **Baltimore** | EXP MLB DEBUT: 2022 | H/W: 6-0 180 | FUT: #2 starter | **9E**

Thrws L Age 19
2017 (1) HS (GA)

Velo	Pitch	Grade
90-95	FB	+++
79-83	CB	++++
80-83	CU	+++

Year	Lev	Team	W	L	Sv	IP	K	ERA	WHIP	BF/G	OBA	H%	S%	xERA	Ctl	Dom	Cmd	hr/9	BPV
2017	Rk	GCL Orioles	0	0	0	10	12	7.13	1.98	9.7	260	35	63	5.58	8.9	10.7	1.2	0.9	-30

High-powered, projectable SP with potential for three plus to double-plus offerings. Doesn't have imposing size, but owns electric arm that can dominate. CB is best present pitch with extreme break and velocity. Has feel for CU while FB has chance to add more ticks and movement. Command is below average at present and has tendency to overthrow.

Hall,Matt

SP | **Detroit** | EXP MLB DEBUT: 2018 | H/W: 6-0 200 | FUT: #4 starter | **7E**

Thrws L Age 24
2015 (6) Missouri St

Velo	Pitch	Grade
85-89	FB	++
70-74	CB	++++
81-84	CU	++

Year	Lev	Team	W	L	Sv	IP	K	ERA	WHIP	BF/G	OBA	H%	S%	xERA	Ctl	Dom	Cmd	hr/9	BPV
2015	A-	Connecticut	0	1	0	31	30	2.90	1.16	12.3	249	31	79	3.37	2.0	8.7	4.3	0.9	120
2016	A	West Michigan	8	0	0	66	72	1.09	1.06	21.4	208	30	89	1.77	2.9	9.8	3.4	0.0	117
2016	A+	Lakeland	3	2	0	60	54	4.19	1.48	21.6	264	32	73	4.41	4.2	8.1	1.9	0.9	50
2017	A+	Lakeland	7	6	0	103	110	2.44	1.32	22.5	252	34	82	3.31	3.3	9.6	2.9	0.3	101
2017	AA	Erie	1	0	0	35	39	3.09	1.46	25.0	233	32	80	3.56	5.4	10.0	1.9	0.5	53

Stout LHP with below average FB and velocity, but one of better CB in organization. FB rarely touches 90 mph, but exhibits sinking action late. Keeps ball low, but mostly due to arm angle. Slow CB has ridiculous bend and is true weapon against LHH. CU also needs polish, but throws it for strikes. Walk rate rose and margin for error is slim.

Hamilton,Ian

RP | **Chicago (A)** | EXP MLB DEBUT: 2019 | H/W: 6-0 200 | FUT: Middle reliever | **6C**

Thrws R Age 22
2016 (11) Washington St

Velo	Pitch	Grade
94-96	FB	++++
84-87	SL	+++

Year	Lev	Team	W	L	Sv	IP	K	ERA	WHIP	BF/G	OBA	H%	S%	xERA	Ctl	Dom	Cmd	hr/9	BPV
2016	NCAA	Washington St.	2	10	0	87	62	4.86	1.46	24.8	281	32	67	4.55	3.2	6.4	2.0	0.8	47
2016	Rk	AZL White Sox	0	0	0	1	2	0.00	1.00	3.8	0	0	100		9.0	18.0	2.0	0.0	99
2016	A	Kannapolis	1	1	8	31	27	3.75	1.15	5.9	200	24	70	2.75	4.0	7.8	1.9	0.9	49
2017	A+	Winston-Salem	3	3	6	52	52	1.72	0.79	6.3	183	25	78	0.96	1.4	9.0	6.5	0.2	142
2017	AA	Birmingham	1	3	1	19	22	5.21	1.79	6.3	327	45	68	5.27	3.8	10.4	2.8	0.0	103

Max-effort, short stature RH moving quickly through the CHW system. 2-seam FB is overpowering due to late arm-side fade. Can work it up or down. Tight SL has makings of potential out pitch. However, currently lacks the swing-and-miss offering set-up men need. Injury risk due to violence in delivery.

Hanifee,Brenan

SP | **Baltimore** | EXP MLB DEBUT: 2021 | H/W: 6-5 180 | FUT: #3 starter | **8E**

Thrws R Age 19
2016 (4) HS (VA)

Velo	Pitch	Grade
88-92	FB	+++
81-83	SL	+++
	CU	+

Year	Lev	Team	W	L	Sv	IP	K	ERA	WHIP	BF/G	OBA	H%	S%	xERA	Ctl	Dom	Cmd	hr/9	BPV
2017	A-	Aberdeen	7	3	0	68	44	2.77	1.13	22.4	253	30	75	2.80	1.6	5.8	3.7	0.3	80

Tall and very lean SP who flashes intriguing stuff with projectable arm. FB is fringe-average now, but could evolve into dynamite offering. Has advanced ability to command plate with all offerings. Doesn't miss many bats, but is extreme groundball guy due to natural FB sink and downhill angle to plate. Lacks touch for CU and needs to throw more.

Hansen,Alec

SP | **Chicago (A)** | EXP MLB DEBUT: 2019 | H/W: 6-7 235 | FUT: #2 starter | **8C**

Thrws R Age 23
2016 (2) Oklahoma

Velo	Pitch	Grade
92-95	FB	++++
76-78	CB	+++
87-88	SL	+++
84-86	CU	++

Year	Lev	Team	W	L	Sv	IP	K	ERA	WHIP	BF/G	OBA	H%	S%	xERA	Ctl	Dom	Cmd	hr/9	BPV
2016	Rk	AZL White Sox	0	0	0	7	11	0.00	0.71	8.2	48	10	100		5.1	14.1	2.8	0.0	134
2016	A	Kannapolis	0	1	0	11	11	2.45	1.36	23.0	262	35	80	3.23	3.3	9.0	2.8	0.0	92
2017	A	Kannapolis	7	3	0	72	92	2.49	1.11	21.8	219	33	78	2.36	2.9	11.5	4.0	0.4	147
2017	A+	Winston-Salem	4	5	0	58	82	2.94	1.15	21.0	204	31	77	2.66	3.9	12.7	3.3	0.8	142
2017	AA	Birmingham	0	0	0	10	17	4.46	1.78	23.2	345	57	72	5.51	2.7	15.1	5.7	0.0	218

Big bodied, hard throwing RH with history of control problems broke out in 2017. Did a better job keeping his body in sync during delivery. Uses height in delivery to create downward plane with FB. Best secondary is a two-plane tight SL; 11-5 CB not too far behind development. CU is fringe average.

Harrington,Drew

SP | **Atlanta** | EXP MLB DEBUT: 2019 | H/W: 6-2 225 | FUT: #4 starter | **7D**

Thrws L Age 23
2016 (3) Louisville

Velo	Pitch	Grade
87-90	FB	+++
75-79	CB	+++
82-84	CU	++

Year	Lev	Team	W	L	Sv	IP	K	ERA	WHIP	BF/G	OBA	H%	S%	xERA	Ctl	Dom	Cmd	hr/9	BPV
2016	NCAA	Louisville	12	2	0	110	92	1.96	1.06	25.2	228	29	82	2.28	2.0	7.5	3.7	0.2	98
2016	Rk	Danville	1	0	0	14	15	2.54	1.34	6.6	259	34	83	3.72	3.2	9.5	3.0	0.6	104
2017	A+	Florida	4	8	0	70	55	4.50	1.51	20.2	299	37	68	4.28	2.8	7.1	2.5	0.1	69

Big-bodied command and control LHP made full season debut in High-A. 3 pitch pitcher, all fringe-to-average offerings. Locates 2-seam FB to each lower quadrant of zone with some arm-side run. CB is a bit slurvy, struggling to get on top of pitch. Has a feel for CU. Stuff would play up in pen.

Harris,Greg

SP | **Tampa Bay** | EXP MLB DEBUT: 2018 | H/W: 6-2 170 | FUT: #4 starter | **7D**

Thrws R Age 23
2013 (17) HS (CA)

Velo	Pitch	Grade
89-94	FB	+++
77-79	CB	++
85-88	CT	++
	CU	+++

Year	Lev	Team	W	L	Sv	IP	K	ERA	WHIP	BF/G	OBA	H%	S%	xERA	Ctl	Dom	Cmd	hr/9	BPV
2015	A	Bowling Green	7	5	0	83	84	2.17	1.23	21.0	240	33	81	2.70	3.0	9.1	3.0	0.1	100
2015	A+	Charlotte	1	4	0	39	24	3.44	1.38	18.3	266	31	74	3.57	3.2	5.5	1.7	0.2	30
2016	A+	Charlotte	10	6	0	147	134	3.12	1.20	22.8	223	28	75	2.91	3.6	8.2	2.3	0.6	70
2016	AAA	Durham	0	0	0	3	6	9.00	2.67	16.5	371	67	63	8.20	9.0	18.0	2.0	0.0	99
2017	AA	Montgomery	3	8	0	97	93	4.91	1.39	14.1	254	30	68	4.50	3.9	8.6	2.2	1.4	68

Loose-armed, projectable pitcher who was moved to bullpen at midseason. Extreme flyball profile with sub-par FB command. Stuff shows flashes of being solid-average, but may not be good enough. Gets ample movement with CU and FB often features late sink and run. Also uses hard CT and CB. Velocity could tick up as RP.

Harris,Jon — SP — Toronto

EXP MLB DEBUT: 2018 | H/W: 6-4 175 | FUT: #4 starter | 7C

Thrws R Age 24 — 2015 (1) Missouri St

Velo	Pitch	Grade
90-95	FB	+++
84-88	SL	+++
77-79	CB	+++
82-87	CU	+++

Year	Lev	Team	W	L	Sv	IP	K	ERA	WHIP	BF/G	OBA	H%	S%	xERA	Ctl	Dom	Cmd	hr/9	BPV
2015	NCAA	Missouri State	8	2	0	103	116	2.45	1.08	26.8	205	29	76	1.94	3.1	10.1	3.2	0.2	116
2015	A-	Vancouver	0	5	0	36	32	6.75	1.92	14.2	321	40	62	5.76	5.3	8.0	1.5	0.3	20
2016	A	Lansing	8	2	0	84	73	2.24	1.16	21.0	238	31	79	2.52	2.6	7.8	3.0	0.1	89
2016	A+	Dunedin	3	2	0	45	26	3.60	1.13	22.2	226	26	67	2.59	2.8	5.2	1.9	0.4	36
2017	AA	New Hampshire	7	11	0	143	113	5.41	1.51	23.8	295	34	66	5.29	3.0	7.1	2.4	1.3	66

Tall, lanky SP who saw big jump in HR while being hittable in AA. May not have plus pitch, but has four quality offerings in arsenal. Throws with average control and has solid plane to plate. SL with cutting action is go to pitch for K. Can throw harder FB at times with quick arm action, but more successful at lower velocity.

Harvey,Hunter — SP — Baltimore

EXP MLB DEBUT: 2018 | H/W: 6-3 175 | FUT: #3 starter | 8C

Thrws R Age 23 — 2013 (1) HS (NC)

Velo	Pitch	Grade
92-95	FB	++++
72-78	CB	++++
81-85	CU	++

Year	Lev	Team	W	L	Sv	IP	K	ERA	WHIP	BF/G	OBA	H%	S%	xERA	Ctl	Dom	Cmd	hr/9	BPV
2016	Rk	GCL Orioles	0	0	0	5	11	0.00	0.60	8.6	175	49	100	0.14	0.0	19.8		0.0	374
2016	A-	Aberdeen	0	1	0	7	7	3.75	2.08	11.8	307	40	80	5.71	7.5	8.8	1.2	0.0	-27
2017	Rk	GCL Orioles	0	0	0	5	6	0.00	1.20	6.7	299	43	100	3.33	0.0	10.8		0.0	212
2017	A-	Aberdeen	0	0	0	5	10	0.00	0.80	9.1	66	20	100		5.4	18.0	3.3	0.0	196
2017	A	Delmarva	0	1	0	8	14	2.20	0.85	10.0	147	30	71	0.52	3.3	15.4	4.7	0.0	206

Exciting SP, but can't stay on mound. Only 32 IP last 3 years and has never pitched more than 87 IP in season. Could advance quickly when healthy due to advanced repertoire and command. Has top-of-rotation stuff with potential double-plus CB and commandable FB. Uses clean, quick arm to generate velocity. CU shows signs of improvement.

Hatch, Thomas — SP — Chicago (N)

EXP MLB DEBUT: 2019 | H/W: 6-1 190 | FUT: #3 starter | 7C

Thrws R Age 23 — 2016 (3) Oklahoma St

Velo	Pitch	Grade
89-94	FB	+++
84-87	CT	+++
78-83	SL	++
78-82	CU	++

Year	Lev	Team	W	L	Sv	IP	K	ERA	WHIP	BF/G	OBA	H%	S%	xERA	Ctl	Dom	Cmd	hr/9	BPV
2017	A+	Myrtle Beach	5	11	0	124	126	4.06	1.42	20.2	265	36	69	3.54	3.6	9.1	2.5	0.1	85

3rd round pick out of Oklahoma in 2016 had a solid pro debut. FB sits at 91-94 topping at 96 mph with good late sink. 3/4 arm slot gives SL above-average action with fringe CU. Had Tommy John surgery in 2015 so Cubs have been cautious with his workload. Deliberate worker needs to improve command within the zone to reach his potential

Hearn, Taylor — SP — Pittsburgh

EXP MLB DEBUT: 2019 | H/W: 6-5 210 | FUT: #2 SP/closer | 9E

Thrws L Age 23 — 2015 (5) Oklahoma Baptist

Velo	Pitch	Grade
95-98	FB	+++++
84-87	SL	++
	CU	+

Year	Lev	Team	W	L	Sv	IP	K	ERA	WHIP	BF/G	OBA	H%	S%	xERA	Ctl	Dom	Cmd	hr/9	BPV
2016	Rk	GCL Nationals	0	0	0	6	8	1.48	1.31	12.6	104	10	100	2.67	8.9	11.8	1.3	1.5	-9
2016	A	West Virginia	1	1	0	22	36	2.03	1.13	11.0	193	33	87	2.48	4.1	14.6	3.6	0.8	171
2016	A	Hagerstown	1	0	0	22	31	3.24	1.44	11.8	285	41	83	4.87	2.8	12.6	4.4	1.2	168
2017	Rk	GCL Pirates	0	0	0	2	3	0.00	0.00	5.6	0	0			0.0	13.5		0.0	261
2017	A+	Bradenton	4	6	0	87	106	4.13	1.17	19.3	209	29	66	2.83	3.8	11.0	2.9	0.8	112

Strong-armed lefty was drafted 4 times before signing with PIT in 2015. Double-plus fastball sits at 95-98 topping at 99 mph. Slider and change-up remain below-average and will need to improve from him to remain a starter. Logged a career high in IP; tons of potential.

Heatherly,Jacob — SP — Cincinnati

EXP MLB DEBUT: 2021 | H/W: 6-2 208 | FUT: #3 starter | 8E

Thrws L Age 19 — 2017 (3) HS (AL)

Velo	Pitch	Grade
89-93	FB	+++
73-75	CB	+++
	SL	++
	CU	++

Year	Lev	Team	W	L	Sv	IP	K	ERA	WHIP	BF/G	OBA	H%	S%	xERA	Ctl	Dom	Cmd	hr/9	BPV
2017	Rk	AZL Reds	2	1	0	30	26	2.98	1.39	14.1	234	28	82	3.78	4.8	7.7	1.6	0.9	29
2017	Rk	Billings	0	1	0	9	5	12.00	2.33	15.5	401	45	43	8.08	4.0	5.0	1.3	0.0	0

Big-bodied LH close to physical projection fell in the draft due to underwhelming prep season. Primarily two-pitch pitcher. Commands 2-seam FB well, working up and down and left to right. 12-6 CB is a solid secondary with promising depth. Didn't feature SL or CU much as a pro. Has feel for CU. Struggles repeating delivery.

Heller,Ben — RP — New York (A)

EXP MLB DEBUT: 2016 | H/W: 6-3 205 | FUT: Setup reliever | 6B

Thrws R Age 26 — 2013 (22) Olivet Nazarene

Velo	Pitch	Grade
93-98	FB	+++
81-85	SL	+++

Year	Lev	Team	W	L	Sv	IP	K	ERA	WHIP	BF/G	OBA	H%	S%	xERA	Ctl	Dom	Cmd	hr/9	BPV
2016	AA	Akron	1	0	7	16	23	0.56	0.50	3.6	62	8	100		2.8	12.9	4.6	0.6	174
2016	AAA	Columbus	2	2	5	25	25	2.51	1.08	3.5	220	29	77	2.30	2.5	9.0	3.6	0.4	112
2016	MLB	NY Yankees	1	0	0	7	6	6.43	2.14	3.5	358	37	83	10.35	5.1	7.7	1.5	3.9	18
2017	AAA	Scranton/WB	5	4	6	56	82	2.89	0.98	5.2	177	27	76	2.08	3.4	13.2	3.9	1.0	164
2017	MLB	NY Yankees	1	0	0	11	9	0.82	1.00	4.7	139	19	91	0.88	4.9	7.4	1.5	0.0	18

Tall, durable RP who has been in majors each of last two seasons. Has enjoyed significant K rate on basis of two quality pitches. Everything comes out of hand hard and never uses change of pace. Control has gotten incrementally better, but still not a strength. Needs to stay on top of SL and can overthrow at times. FB has vicious, late action.

Helsley, Ryan — SP — St. Louis

EXP MLB DEBUT: 2018 | H/W: 6-1 195 | FUT: #3 starter | 8D

Thrws R Age 23 — 2015 (5) Northeastern St

Velo	Pitch	Grade
93-96	FB	++++
79-81	CB	++++
85-88	CT	++
	CU	++

Year	Lev	Team	W	L	Sv	IP	K	ERA	WHIP	BF/G	OBA	H%	S%	xERA	Ctl	Dom	Cmd	hr/9	BPV
2015	Rk	Johnson City	1	1	0	40	35	2.02	1.30	15.0	226	29	84	2.82	4.3	7.9	1.8	0.2	44
2016	A	Peoria	10	2	0	95	109	1.61	1.01	21.4	223	32	85	2.09	1.8	10.3	5.7	0.3	155
2017	A+	Palm Beach	8	2	0	93	91	2.70	1.09	21.5	215	29	75	2.22	2.9	8.8	3.0	0.3	98
2017	AA	Springfield	3	1	0	33	41	2.71	1.20	22.3	211	29	83	3.17	4.1	11.1	2.7	1.1	108
2017	AAA	Memphis	0	0	0	5	5	3.60	2.00	24.1	332	43	80	5.90	5.4	9.0	1.7	0.0	34

Pop-up prospect has a plus fastball that sits at 93-96 topping at 98 mph. Plus power curve has good late bite and is swing-and-miss. Change-up and cutter also flash plus, but need refinement. Uptick in velocity fueled breakout; pitched to a 2.72 ERA across three levels.

Heredia, Luis — RP — Pittsburgh

EXP MLB DEBUT: 2018 | H/W: 6-5 251 | FUT: Setup reliever | 7C

Thrws R Age 23 — 2010 FA (MX)

Velo	Pitch	Grade
90-93	FB	+++
	CB	+
	SP	+
83-85	CU	++

Year	Lev	Team	W	L	Sv	IP	K	ERA	WHIP	BF/G	OBA	H%	S%	xERA	Ctl	Dom	Cmd	hr/9	BPV
2013	A	West Virginia	7	3	0	65	55	3.05	1.37	19.5	221	27	80	3.38	5.1	7.6	1.5	0.7	17
2014	A	West Virginia	2	4	0	89	43	4.15	1.35	20.6	257	27	71	4.04	3.3	4.3	1.3	0.9	6
2015	A+	Bradenton	5	6	0	86	54	5.44	1.73	18.6	302	35	66	5.08	4.6	5.7	1.2	0.3	-5
2016	A+	Bradenton	4	6	12	54	42	3.66	1.59	5.3	265	33	75	4.02	5.2	7.0	1.4	0.2	5
2017	AA	Altoona	3	3	2	52	43	3.11	1.38	6.1	218	27	78	3.21	5.4	7.4	1.4	0.5	7

Former top prospect has established himself as a viable relief prospect. Tall, strong-armed hurler continues to struggle with control, walking 31 in 52.1 IP. Still has a good 90-93 mph fastball, but it lacks the zip it once had. Curve, slider, and change remain average or below-average offerings.

Herget,Jimmy — RP — Cincinnati

EXP MLB DEBUT: 2018 | H/W: 6-3 170 | FUT: Middle reliever | 7B

Thrws R Age 24 — 2015 (6) South Florida

Velo	Pitch	Grade
94-96	FB	++++
80-83	SL	+++
		+

Year	Lev	Team	W	L	Sv	IP	K	ERA	WHIP	BF/G	OBA	H%	S%	xERA	Ctl	Dom	Cmd	hr/9	BPV
2015	NCAA	South Florida	10	3	0	101	113	2.93	1.23	24.1	236	32	78	3.19	3.2	10.0	3.1	0.7	112
2015	Rk	Billings	3	0	15	25	26	3.23	1.08	4.1	184	25	69	1.88	3.9	9.3	2.4	0.4	79
2016	A+	Daytona	4	4	24	60	83	1.79	1.15	4.8	217	34	86	2.49	3.3	12.4	3.8	0.4	153
2017	AA	Pensacola	1	3	16	29	44	2.77	1.16	4.8	211	35	76	2.32	3.7	13.6	3.7	0.3	162
2017	AAA	Louisville	3	1	9	32	28	3.08	1.21	4.6	249	29	80	3.75	2.5	7.9	3.1	1.1	91

Hard throwing, arm-slot varying RH relief prospect. Primarily throws from side-arm delivery, varying arm-slot up to low 3/4s. Mostly pitches off mid-90s 2-seam FB with solid arm-side run. Around strike zone but varying arm angles prevent solid command. Will throw SL out of any arm slot. The movement is more sweepy out of side arm slot.

Hernandez,Ariel — RP — Cincinnati

EXP MLB DEBUT: 2017 | H/W: 6-4 230 | FUT: Closer | 9E

Thrws R Age 26 — 2008 FA (DR)

Velo	Pitch	Grade
96-100	FB	+++++
86-88	CB	++++
90-91	CU	++

Year	Lev	Team	W	L	Sv	IP	K	ERA	WHIP	BF/G	OBA	H%	S%	xERA	Ctl	Dom	Cmd	hr/9	BPV
2016	A	Dayton	0	1	2	31	40	2.60	1.00	6.6	111	19	71	0.57	5.8	11.6	2.0	0.0	70
2016	A+	Daytona	3	1	3	30	34	1.79	1.23	4.9	174	25	86	2.08	5.7	10.1	1.8	0.3	48
2017	AA	Pensacola	2	0	1	33	39	2.18	1.15	5.5	162	25	79	1.47	5.5	10.6	2.0	0.0	62
2017	AAA	Louisville	1	2	0	17	19	5.29	1.94	5.4	226	31	72	4.71	10.1	10.1	1.0	0.5	-73
2017	MLB	Cincinnati	0	0	0	24	29	5.23	1.49	5.5	171	17	73	4.53	8.2	10.8	1.3	2.2	-9

Hard-throwing, quick-arm RH made MLB debut despite control issues that continue to plague career. 2-seam FB is an elite pitch because of velocity and late-life explosion. Power CB mixes SL velocity with unforgiving CB depth to projects as plus, maybe more. CU more a show-me offering.

Hernandez,Darwinzon — SP — Boston

EXP MLB DEBUT: 2020 | H/W: 6-2 185 | FUT: #3 starter | 8D

Thrws L Age 21 — 2013 FA (VZ)

Velo	Pitch	Grade
91-96	FB	++++
82-84	SL	++
80-81	CB	++
	CU	++

Year	Lev	Team	W	L	Sv	IP	K	ERA	WHIP	BF/G	OBA	H%	S%	xERA	Ctl	Dom	Cmd	hr/9	BPV
2016	A-	Lowell	3	5	0	48	58	4.12	1.56	15.0	223	33	72	3.38	6.7	10.9	1.6	0.2	31
2017	A	Greenville	4	5	0	103	116	4.02	1.30	18.5	226	31	70	3.25	4.3	10.1	2.4	0.7	85

Vastly improving prospect who upgraded control in first full year. Posts very high K rate and stingy against LHH (.140 oppBA). Keeps ball down with dynamic FB and two breaking pitches. Both SL and CB are raw, but have high K potential. Should add strength over time to better durability and stamina; currently loses velocity late.

Hernandez,Jonathan

SP | Texas | EXP MLB DEBUT: 2019 | H/W: 6-2 175 | FUT: #4 starter | 7C

Thrws R Age 21
2013 FA (DR)

Velo	Pitch	Grade
91-96	FB	+++
78-82	SL	++
82-85	CU	++

Year	Lev	Team	W	L	Sv	IP	K	ERA	WHIP	BF/G	OBA	H%	S%	xERA	Ctl	Dom	Cmd	hr/9	BPV
2015	Rk	AZL Rangers	1	1	0	45	33	3.00	1.27	16.7	262	32	74	3.01	2.4	6.6	2.8	0.0	72
2016	A	Hickory	10	9	0	116	85	4.57	1.37	20.3	251	28	69	4.15	3.8	6.6	1.7	1.1	34
2017	A	Hickory	2	5	0	46	46	4.88	1.48	22.0	297	37	68	4.94	2.5	9.0	3.5	1.0	111
2017	A+	Down East	3	6	0	65	64	3.46	1.49	20.0	264	35	76	3.85	4.3	8.8	2.1	0.3	62

Lean SP who still needs to add strength, but was spectacular late in season. Upped velocity and maintained explosive late action. Delivery can be difficult to repeat, but has some deception. K rate increased as he mixed better, but still needs enhancement to both SL and CU. Pitches off FB and will need both secondaries to remain SP.

Hernandez,Wilkel

SP | Detroit | EXP MLB DEBUT: 2023 | H/W: 6-3 160 | FUT: #3 starter | 8E

Thrws R Age 18
2015 FA (VZ)

Velo	Pitch	Grade
90-95	FB	+++
78-82	CB	++
	CU	++

Year	Lev	Team	W	L	Sv	IP	K	ERA	WHIP	BF/G	OBA	H%	S%	xERA	Ctl	Dom	Cmd	hr/9	BPV
2017	Rk	Orem	1	0	0	3	2	3.00	1.33	12.5	191	24	75	2.30	6.0	6.0	1.0	0.0	-36
2017	Rk	AZL Angels	3	1	0	41	42	2.63	1.05	14.4	166	23	74	1.47	4.4	9.2	2.1	0.2	65

Long, lanky SP with extreme projection. Will need to focus on delivery and maintaining consistent arm slot and angle. Hindered by inconsistent control, but quick arm gets ample movement to FB and CB. Has confidence to use CU and should get better with improved mechanics. A sleeper to keep an eye on.

Herrera,Carlos

SP | Milwaukee | EXP MLB DEBUT: 2020 | H/W: 6-2 150 | FUT: #3 starter | 7E

Thrws R Age 20
2014 FA (DR)

Velo	Pitch	Grade
88-92	FB	+++
73-77	CB	+++
	CU	++

Year	Lev	Team	W	L	Sv	IP	K	ERA	WHIP	BF/G	OBA	H%	S%	xERA	Ctl	Dom	Cmd	hr/9	BPV
2016	Rk	AZL Brewers	3	6	0	50	49	4.50	1.28	14.6	269	34	65	3.81	2.2	8.8	4.1	0.7	118
2017	Rk	Helena	2	0	0	21	26	4.29	1.00	20.1	213	25	69	3.68	2.1	11.1	5.2	2.1	161
2017	A	Wisconsin	3	2	0	38	26	3.79	1.08	16.5	183	20	68	2.45	4.0	6.2	1.5	0.9	20

Projectable RH with slim build made it to Low-A. Has struggled putting weight on frame. FB sits 88-92, up to 95 at times, with solid 2-seam movement. Flattens out at higher velocities. CB has good shape and solid break. Has a below-average feel for breaking pitch. Delivery may make it hard to get anything more than that.

Hess,David

SP | Baltimore | EXP MLB DEBUT: 2018 | H/W: 6-2 180 | FUT: #4 starter | 7D

Thrws R Age 24
2014 (5) Tennessee Tech

Velo	Pitch	Grade
90-93	FB	+++
80-81	CB	++
82-84	SL	++
	CU	++

Year	Lev	Team	W	L	Sv	IP	K	ERA	WHIP	BF/G	OBA	H%	S%	xERA	Ctl	Dom	Cmd	hr/9	BPV
2014	A	Delmarva	0	0	0	8	12	3.38	0.88	14.8	237	40	57	1.62	0.0	13.5		0.0	261
2015	A+	Frederick	9	4	0	133	110	3.58	1.24	21.6	230	28	71	3.02	3.6	7.4	2.1	0.5	55
2015	AA	Bowie	1	1	0	10	12	4.50	1.40	21.1	262	38	64	3.31	3.6	10.8	3.0	0.0	115
2016	AA	Bowie	5	13	0	127	85	5.38	1.58	22.4	311	34	69	5.80	2.8	6.0	2.2	1.3	52
2017	AA	Bowie	11	9	0	154	123	3.85	1.23	23.1	240	28	71	3.50	3.1	7.2	2.3	0.9	64

Extreme flyball SP who repeated AA to better success and finished 3rd in EL in K. Posted much lower opopBA and found consistency with delivery and arm angle. Needs pitch to counter LHH and max-effort delivery could be better in pen where FB could be harder. CU may be best secondary, but far from out pitch.

Hicks, Jordan

SP | St. Louis | EXP MLB DEBUT: 2019 | H/W: 6-2 185 | FUT: #2 starter | 9D

Thrws R Age 21
2015 (S-3) HS (TX)

Velo	Pitch	Grade
93-96	FB	++++
78-82	CB	++++
83-85	CU	++

Year	Lev	Team	W	L	Sv	IP	K	ERA	WHIP	BF/G	OBA	H%	S%	xERA	Ctl	Dom	Cmd	hr/9	BPV
2016	Rk	Johnson City	2	1	0	30	20	4.20	1.53	21.8	281	33	71	4.24	3.9	6.0	1.5	0.3	21
2016	A-	State College	4	1	0	30	22	1.79	1.36	21.0	227	28	85	2.78	4.8	6.6	1.4	0.0	7
2017	A	Peoria	8	2	0	78	63	3.35	1.46	23.9	254	31	77	3.72	4.5	7.3	1.6	0.3	27
2017	A+	Palm Beach	0	1	1	27	32	1.00	1.00	12.9	216	32	89	1.71	2.0	10.7	5.3	0.0	156

Athletic right-hander was 3rd round compensation pick in 2015 and has some of the best raw stuff in the system. Fastball sits at 93-96, topping at 100 mph with good late sink. Power curve grades as plus an mid-80s change-up is fringe-average. Fared well in full-season debut, with 2.74 ERA in two A-ball levels.

Hill,Brigham

SP | Washington | EXP MLB DEBUT: 2020 | H/W: 6-0 185 | FUT: #4 starter | 7C

Thrws R Age 22
2017 (5) Texas A&M

Velo	Pitch	Grade
90-91	FB	+++
79-82	CU	+++
	CB	++

Year	Lev	Team	W	L	Sv	IP	K	ERA	WHIP	BF/G	OBA	H%	S%	xERA	Ctl	Dom	Cmd	hr/9	BPV
2017	NCAA	Texas A&M	8	3	0	100	111	3.15	1.19	23.6	238	33	74	2.89	2.8	10.0	3.6	0.5	122
2017	A-	Auburn	0	1	0	13	9	2.73	1.14	13.1	244	30	73	2.45	2.0	6.1	3.0	0.0	73
2017	A	Hagerstown	0	1	0	29	30	6.16	1.58	21.4	332	41	62	5.99	1.5	9.2	6.0	1.2	143

Undersized RH that relies heavily on a FB/CU combination to keep hitters off balance. Sports good control of the 90-91 heater, but best pitch is CU with wicked drop that gets soft GB contact when it's on. Breaking stuff a work in progress. Throws strikes and a decent athlete.

Hillman,Juan

SP | Cleveland | EXP MLB DEBUT: 2021 | H/W: 6-2 185 | FUT: #4 starter | 7D

Thrws L Age 20
2015 (2) HS (FL)

Velo	Pitch	Grade
88-93	FB	+++
79-81	CB	++
	CU	+++

Year	Lev	Team	W	L	Sv	IP	K	ERA	WHIP	BF/G	OBA	H%	S%	xERA	Ctl	Dom	Cmd	hr/9	BPV
2015	Rk	AZL Indians	0	2	0	24	20	4.13	1.29	12.3	278	35	65	3.29	1.9	7.5	4.0	0.0	102
2016	A-	Mahoning Val	3	4	0	63	47	4.43	1.43	17.8	271	32	69	4.22	3.4	6.7	2.0	0.7	46
2017	A	Lake County	7	10	0	137	101	6.10	1.50	22.8	290	32	61	5.36	3.1	6.6	2.1	1.4	52

Athletic, loose-armed SP who was lit up all year long. Has good, natural stuff, but has trouble hitting spots with FB. Doesn't have poor walk rate, but lives in middle of plate and can be hit hard. Offers hint of projection in lean frame and will need more muscle to maintain velocity. Allowed lot of HR in 2017 and needs to upgrade CB.

Hinsz, Gage

SP | Pittsburgh | EXP MLB DEBUT: 2019 | H/W: 6-4 210 | FUT: #4 starter | 8E

Thrws R Age 21
2014 (11) HS (MT)

Velo	Pitch	Grade
91-94	FB	+++
74-77	CB	++
	CU	++

Year	Lev	Team	W	L	Sv	IP	K	ERA	WHIP	BF/G	OBA	H%	S%	xERA	Ctl	Dom	Cmd	hr/9	BPV
2014	Rk	GCL Pirates	0	0	0	8	7	3.38	1.50	11.5	262	34	75	3.59	4.5	7.9	1.8	0.0	38
2015	Rk	Bristol	3	4	0	38	24	3.79	1.58	16.7	257	30	75	3.96	5.4	5.7	1.0	0.2	-27
2016	A	West Virginia	6	8	0	93	67	3.67	1.27	22.4	262	30	73	3.74	2.4	6.5	2.7	0.8	69
2017	A+	Bradenton	5	5	0	94	52	5.64	1.52	20.4	297	33	63	4.97	3.0	5.0	1.7	0.9	27

Big bodied, hard-throwing right-hander took a step back. Solid 92-94 mph fastball with a mid-70s curve that flashes as plus but needs more consistency and a fringe change. Has an easy high 3/4 arm slot and throws downhill, but struggled to find the strike zone or miss bats. Showed signs of life in the second half (3.89 ERA), but needs a reboot.

Holmes, Clay

SP | Pittsburgh | EXP MLB DEBUT: 2018 | H/W: 6-5 230 | FUT: #3 starter | 7D

Thrws R Age 25
2011 (9) HS (AL)

Velo	Pitch	Grade
92-96	FB	++++
80-83	CB	++
	CU	++

Year	Lev	Team	W	L	Sv	IP	K	ERA	WHIP	BF/G	OBA	H%	S%	xERA	Ctl	Dom	Cmd	hr/9	BPV
2015	Rk	GCL Pirates	1	0	0	13	10	2.06	1.07	17.0	260	33	79	2.49	0.7	6.9	10.0	0.0	123
2015	A+	Bradenton	0	2	0	23	16	2.74	1.09	15.0	217	27	72	1.98	2.7	6.3	2.3	0.0	57
2016	AA	Altoona	10	9	0	136	101	4.23	1.48	22.5	264	31	72	4.22	4.2	6.7	1.6	0.7	24
2017	AAA	Indianapolis	10	5	0	112	99	3.37	1.38	18.9	233	30	75	3.21	4.7	7.9	1.7	0.3	33

Mixed results in 2017. Plus sinking fastball was a tick better than in the past, sitting in the mid-90s and topping at 99 mph. A ton of ground ball outs at AAA, but control remained inconsistent and now owns a career 4.5 Ctl rate. Curveball and change-up are fringe-average and a move to relief seems likely.

Holmes,Grant

SP | Oakland | EXP MLB DEBUT: 2018 | H/W: 6-1 215 | FUT: #3 starter | 8B

Thrws R Age 22
2014 (1) HS (SC)

Velo	Pitch	Grade
91-95	FB	++++
87-90	CT	+++
80-83	CB	+++
	CU	++

Year	Lev	Team	W	L	Sv	IP	K	ERA	WHIP	BF/G	OBA	H%	S%	xERA	Ctl	Dom	Cmd	hr/9	BPV
2014	Rk	AZL Dodgers	1	2	0	30	33	3.00	0.90	15.9	191	26	68	1.73	2.1	9.9	4.7	0.6	140
2015	A	Great Lakes	6	4	0	103	117	3.14	1.36	17.9	228	32	78	3.26	4.7	10.2	2.2	0.5	75
2016	A+	Stockton	3	3	0	28	24	7.02	1.91	22.3	356	42	64	7.32	3.2	7.7	2.4	1.3	70
2016	A+	Rancho Cuca	8	4	1	105	100	4.02	1.39	22.1	258	33	71	3.73	3.7	8.6	2.3	0.5	73
2017	AA	Midland	11	12	0	148	150	4.50	1.42	21.6	263	33	70	4.24	3.7	9.1	2.5	0.9	82

Power-armed SP who led Texas League in K and BB. Inconsistent mechanics lead to command issues, but set high in IP with a deep arsenal. Keeps ball low in zone w/ velocity and has power CB that serves as out pitch. Cutter added to repertoire and has shown advanced feel for it. Has to improve CU and clean up delivery in order to throw more strikes.

Honeywell,Brent

SP | Tampa Bay | EXP MLB DEBUT: 2018 | H/W: 6-2 180 | FUT: #2 starter | 8A

Thrws R Age 23
2014 (S-2) Walters St CC

Velo	Pitch	Grade
90-95	FB	+++
81-84	SL	+++
75-79	CB	+++
81-85	CU	+++

Year	Lev	Team	W	L	Sv	IP	K	ERA	WHIP	BF/G	OBA	H%	S%	xERA	Ctl	Dom	Cmd	hr/9	BPV
2015	A+	Charlotte	5	2	0	65	53	3.46	1.11	21.3	237	30	67	2.53	2.1	7.3	3.5	0.3	94
2016	A+	Charlotte	4	1	0	56	64	2.41	0.96	21.2	214	29	80	2.35	1.8	10.3	5.8	0.8	155
2016	AA	Montgomery	3	2	0	59	53	2.28	1.10	23.2	234	29	82	2.78	2.1	8.1	3.8	0.6	106
2017	AA	Montgomery	1	1	0	13	20	2.08	0.62	22.3	98	15	71	0.11	2.8	13.8	5.0	0.7	192
2017	AAA	Durham	12	8	0	123	152	3.65	1.31	21.2	272	38	74	3.97	2.3	11.1	4.9	0.8	157

Consistent SP who was 2nd in IL in strikeouts. Owns very deep arsenal of solid average offerings, including screwball. Locates lively FB to all quadrants of zone and best secondary is excellent CU. Pitching with more consistent velocity and release point. Has two breaking balls, though may not have just one out pitch.

Houck,Tanner

SP | Boston | EXP MLB DEBUT: 2020 | H/W: 6-5 220 | FUT: #3 starter | 8C

Thrws R Age 21
2017 (1) Missouri

90-95	FB	++++
83-86	SL	+++
	CU	++

Year	Lev	Team	W	L	Sv	IP	K	ERA	WHIP	BF/G	OBA	H%	S%	xERA	Ctl	Dom	Cmd	hr/9	BPV
2017	NCAA	Missouri	4	7	0	94	95	3.34	1.08	26.3	227	30	69	2.52	2.3	9.1	4.0	0.5	119
2017	A-	Lowell	0	3	0	22	25	3.67	1.31	9.1	252	36	69	2.96	3.3	10.2	3.1	0.0	113

Tall SP who succeeds with plus FB deception and keen pitch movement. Throws across body, but fools hitters with delivery. Very tough on RHH with combo of plus FB and average SL. Can retire hitters with both pitches, though will need to add polish to rudimentary CU. Potential average CU thrown with good arm speed.

Houser,Adrian

SP | Milwaukee | EXP MLB DEBUT: 2015 | H/W: 6-4 235 | FUT: Middle reliever | 7B

Thrws R Age 25
2011 (2) HS (OK)

93-96	FB	++++
78-81	CB	++++
85-87	CU	++

Year	Lev	Team	W	L	Sv	IP	K	ERA	WHIP	BF/G	OBA	H%	S%	xERA	Ctl	Dom	Cmd	hr/9	BPV
2015	AA	Corpus Christi	1	2	0	33	23	6.25	1.63	21.0	295	32	65	5.94	4.1	6.3	1.5	1.6	20
2015	MLB	Milwaukee	0	0	0	2	0	0.00	1.50	4.3	151	15	100	2.34	9.0	0.0	0.0	0.0	-225
2016	AA	Biloxi	3	7	0	70	56	5.26	1.40	22.7	278	33	61	4.16	2.8	7.2	2.5	0.6	71
2017	Rk	AZL Brewers	0	1	0	8	16	1.10	0.98	5.2	147	30	100	1.84	4.4	17.6	4.0	1.1	216
2017	A	Wisconsin	1	0	0	9	11	1.00	0.56	10.1	165	26	80		0.0	11.0		0.0	216

Hard throwing RH missed parts of last two seasons with Tommy John surgery. Heavy FB, sits mid-90s with RP plane. Power 12-6 CB is best pitch, a swing-and-miss offering. Has had a feel for CU for several years but it hasn't progressed into solid third pitch. Likely RP in MLB.

Houston,Zac

RP | Detroit | EXP MLB DEBUT: 2019 | H/W: 6-5 250 | FUT: Setup reliever | 7D

Thrws R Age 23
2016 (11) Mississippi St

92-96	FB	+++
82-84	SL	+++
80-81	CB	++
	CU	++

Year	Lev	Team	W	L	Sv	IP	K	ERA	WHIP	BF/G	OBA	H%	S%	xERA	Ctl	Dom	Cmd	hr/9	BPV
2016	NCAA	Mississippi St	6	0	0	38		1.65	1.26	8.7	212	29	89	2.76	4.5	9.9	2.2	0.5	75
2016	A-	Connecticut	1	0	0	10	19	0.00	1.00	5.5	199	43	100	1.44	2.7	17.1	6.3	0.0	253
2016	A	West Michigan	1	0	4	19	30	0.47	0.89	5.5	85	17	94	0.01	5.6	14.1	2.5	0.0	119
2017	A	West Michigan	0	0	2	46	71	2.54	1.00	7.3	156	28	73	1.17	4.3	13.9	3.2	0.2	152
2017	A+	Lakeland	0	1	4	11	20	0.80	0.98	5.3	87	21	91	0.26	6.4	16.1	2.5	0.0	134

Aggressive, large-framed RP who has spent entire career in pen. Uses herky jerky delivery to provide deception and has vicious, late sinking action on FB. Command comes and goes and could use better CU. Has significantly high K rate thanks to deception and power stuff. May shelve CB in favor of better SL.

Howard, Sam

SP | Colorado | EXP MLB DEBUT: 2018 | H/W: 6-3 170 | FUT: #4 starter | 7C

Thrws L Age 25
2014 (3) Georgia Southern

91-94	FB	++++
80-83	SL	+++
	CU	+++

Year	Lev	Team	W	L	Sv	IP	K	ERA	WHIP	BF/G	OBA	H%	S%	xERA	Ctl	Dom	Cmd	hr/9	BPV
2015	A	Asheville	11	9	0	134	122	3.43	1.22	21.6	257	32	72	3.31	2.1	8.2	3.8	0.5	107
2016	A+	Modesto	4	3	0	65	73	2.48	1.03	22.8	190	27	77	1.86	3.3	10.1	3.0	0.4	110
2016	AA	Hartford	5	6	0	90	67	4.00	1.56	24.7	308	35	78	5.47	2.8	6.7	2.4	1.1	63
2017	AA	Hartford	1	4	0	46	40	2.34	0.89	19.0	193	22	81	2.10	2.0	7.8	4.0	1.0	106
2017	AAA	Albuquerque	4	4	0	81	64	3.89	1.42	22.9	264	32	73	4.05	3.7	7.1	1.9	0.7	47

Projectable lefty is starting to tap into his potential. Fastball now sits at 91-94 topping at 96 mph with heavy late sink. Slider is average and change-up is deadly vs LHB (0.82 ERA vs. LHB at AA). Not overpowering, but a consistent strike thrower with good deception and plenty of ground ball outs.

Howard,Spencer

SP | Philadelphia | EXP MLB DEBUT: 2020 | H/W: 6-3 205 | FUT: #3 starter | 7C

Thrws R Age 21
2017 (2) Cal Poly

91-94	FB	+++
84-86	CU	++
79-80	SL	++
74-76	CB	++

Year	Lev	Team	W	L	Sv	IP	K	ERA	WHIP	BF/G	OBA	H%	S%	xERA	Ctl	Dom	Cmd	hr/9	BPV
2017	NCAA	Cal Poly	8	1	1	87	97	1.96	1.09	20.1	226	31	85	2.65	2.4	10.0	4.2	0.6	134
2017	A-	Williamsport	1	1	0	28	40	4.48	1.42	13.2	217	36	65	2.77	5.8	12.8	2.2	0.0	93

Four-pitch collegian who improved as the season went on. Sturdily built, he pitches off a lively FB/deceptive CU combination that produces swings and misses. Breaking stuff still needs work, and though delivery is clean, he can lose his release point at times. Solid foundation, just needs reps.

Hu,Chih-Wei

RP | Tampa Bay | EXP MLB DEBUT: 2017 | H/W: 6-0 220 | FUT: Setup reliever | 7B

Thrws R Age 24
2012 FA (TW)

91-96	FB	+++
82-84	SL	++
75-78	CB	++
82-85	CU	+++

Year	Lev	Team	W	L	Sv	IP	K	ERA	WHIP	BF/G	OBA	H%	S%	xERA	Ctl	Dom	Cmd	hr/9	BPV
2015	AAA	Rochester	1	0	0	6	6	1.50	1.00	22.9	106	15	83	0.55	6.0	9.0	1.5	0.0	18
2016	AA	Montgomery	7	8	0	142	107	2.59	1.15	23.5	242	29	78	2.87	2.3	6.8	3.0	0.4	78
2016	AAA	Durham	0	1	0	4	7	8.57	2.14	20.8	371	55	63	8.92	4.3	15.0	3.5	2.1	172
2017	AAA	Durham	4	1	2	61	57	3.09	1.16	7.9	255	30	81	3.87	1.8	8.4	4.8	1.3	121
2017	MLB	Tampa Bay	1	1	0	10	9	2.70	0.90	6.2	151	14	86	2.44	3.6	8.1	2.3	1.8	67

Short, burly pitcher who was moved to bullpen in 2017. Has very solid FB/CU combo and is able to maintain arm speed while creating separation. Very stingy against RHH as result of pitch movement. Keeps ball low in zone with all offerings. Has two below average breaking balls and may shelve one.

Hudson, Bryan

SP | Chicago (N) | EXP MLB DEBUT: 2020 | H/W: 6-8 220 | FUT: #5 SP/swingman | 7D

Thrws L Age 20
2015 (3) HS (IL)

89-92	FB	++
75-78	CB	+++
78-80	CU	++

Year	Lev	Team	W	L	Sv	IP	K	ERA	WHIP	BF/G	OBA	H%	S%	xERA	Ctl	Dom	Cmd	hr/9	BPV
2015	Rk	AZL Cubs	0	0	0	6	5	2.90	1.29	5.1	255	32	75	2.98	2.9	7.3	2.5	0.0	70
2016	A-	Eugene	5	4	0	58	41	5.10	1.67	20.1	254	30	69	4.50	6.3	6.3	1.0	0.6	-39
2017	A	South Bend	9	3	0	124	81	3.92	1.45	22.1	268	30	74	4.25	3.8	5.9	1.6	0.7	22

Tall, projectable lefty has a huge 6-8 frame. FB currently sits at 89-92 with sink, up a tick from when drafted. CB is potentially plus if he can figure out a consistent release point. CU has movement but lacks deception. Fared well in full-season debut, but his 5.9 Dom raises concerns about his ability to remain a starter.

Hudson, Dakota

SP | St. Louis | EXP MLB DEBUT: 2018 | H/W: 6-5 215 | FUT: #4 starter | 7C

Thrws R Age 23
2016 (1) Mississippi St

93-95	FB	+++
87-91	CB	+++
75-78	CT	++
	CU	++

Year	Lev	Team	W	L	Sv	IP	K	ERA	WHIP	BF/G	OBA	H%	S%	xERA	Ctl	Dom	Cmd	hr/9	BPV
2016	NCAA	Mississippi St	9	5	0	113	115	2.55	1.25	27.0	250	34	78	2.92	2.8	9.2	3.3	0.2	108
2016	Rk	GCL Cardinals	1	0	0	4	9	0.00	1.00	3.8	262	64	100	2.20	0.0	20.3		0.0	383
2016	A+	Palm Beach	1	1	3	9	10	0.99	1.43	4.8	190	28	92	2.48	6.9	9.9	1.4	0.0	9
2017	AA	Springfield	9	4	0	114	77	2.53	1.27	25.9	257	30	81	3.33	2.7	6.1	2.3	0.4	55
2017	AAA	Memphis	1	1	0	38	19	4.48	1.34	22.7	250	28	65	3.49	3.5	4.5	1.3	0.5	3

Tall, strong-armed 1st rounder had a solid season, but doesn't dominate despite a plus 93-95 fastball that hits 97 mph. Secondary offerings include a cutter, power curve, and seldom used change-up. Throws plenty of strikes and keeps the ball on the ground, but below average command results in too much hard contact.

Humphreys,Jordan

SP | New York (N) | EXP MLB DEBUT: 2020 | H/W: 6-2 223 | FUT: #4 starter | 8E

Thrws R Age 21
2015 (18) HS (FL)

91-94	FB	+++
76-78	CB	+++
83-85	SL	++
82-85	CU	+++

Year	Lev	Team	W	L	Sv	IP	K	ERA	WHIP	BF/G	OBA	H%	S%	xERA	Ctl	Dom	Cmd	hr/9	BPV
2015	Rk	GCL Mets	0	0	2	11	7	1.61	1.16	6.4	275	33	85	2.94	0.8	5.6	7.0	0.0	98
2016	Rk	Kingsport	3	5	0	69	76	3.78	1.16	22.9	250	34	66	2.91	2.0	9.9	5.1	0.4	143
2016	A-	Brooklyn	0	1	0	6	9	1.50	1.33	24.9	293	47	88	3.55	1.5	13.5	9.0	0.0	221
2017	A	Columbia	10	1	0	69	80	1.43	0.72	22.3	174	25	81	0.76	1.2	10.4	8.9	0.3	174
2017	A+	St. Lucie	0	0	0	11	3	4.09	1.82	25.5	354	36	79	6.66	2.5	2.5	1.0	0.8	-4

Big-bodied SP opened eyes before Tommy John surgery ended season. Command/control type, lives in lower half of zone. FB is solid workhorse with average action. Can spin CB but lacks consistent depth. CU flashes plus with tumble out of zone. Needs to tighten up SL. At physical projection, needs to refine secondaries to succeed.

Irvin,Cole

SP | Philadelphia | EXP MLB DEBUT: 2018 | H/W: 6-4 180 | FUT: #4 starter | 7B

Thrws L Age 24
2016 (5) Oregon

89-92	FB	+++
82-86	SL	+++
75-77	CB	++
82-84	CU	++

Year	Lev	Team	W	L	Sv	IP	K	ERA	WHIP	BF/G	OBA	H%	S%	xERA	Ctl	Dom	Cmd	hr/9	BPV
2016	NCAA	Oregon	6	4	0	105	93	3.17	1.11	24.3	254	31	74	3.24	1.4	8.0	5.8	0.8	124
2016	A-	Williamsport	5	1	0	45	37	1.99	0.97	17.1	220	27	81	2.10	1.6	7.4	4.6	0.4	108
2017	A+	Clearwater	4	6	0	67	52	2.55	1.22	22.6	265	33	79	3.19	1.9	7.0	3.7	0.3	93
2017	AA	Reading	5	3	0	84	66	4.07	1.14	25.6	233	26	69	3.52	2.6	7.1	2.8	1.3	76

Four-pitch lefty with no knockout offering, but whose good control, command and sequencing help all his pitches play up. Moves low-90s FB in and out, including busting it in on RHH. Throws curve for strikes, and sells CU with good arm speed. Fills up the strike zone and has a durable, solid frame.

Ivey,Tyler

SP | Houston | EXP MLB DEBUT: 2020 | H/W: 6-4 195 | FUT: #5 SP/swingman | 7C

Thrws R Age 21
2017 (3) Grayson CC

89-93	FB	+++
75-78	CB	+++
	SL	++
	CU	++

Year	Lev	Team	W	L	Sv	IP	K	ERA	WHIP	BF/G	OBA	H%	S%	xERA	Ctl	Dom	Cmd	hr/9	BPV
2017	NCAA	Grayson CC	9	0	0	78	122	2.08	1.13	25.7	214	38	80	2.08	3.2	14.1	4.4	0.1	184
2017	Rk	GCL Astros	0	0	0	2	3	0.00	1.50	8.6	151	27	100	2.20	9.0	13.5	1.5	0.0	18
2017	A-	Tri City	0	3	0	36	41	5.98	1.47	14.1	287	39	57	4.31	3.0	10.2	3.4	0.5	121

Lean, athletic RH who was highly-ranked JUCO arm in 2017 draft class. FB sits low-90s and lacks sufficient movement to overpower hitters; often barreled up. Will throw in flashes of above-average CB to miss majority of bats; short SL and developing CU round out his arsenal. Chance to add muscle to lower half for more velocity. Back-end SP profile.

Jackson,Zach

RP | Toronto | EXP MLB DEBUT: 2018 | H/W: 6-4 215 | FUT: Closer | 7C

Thrws R Age 23
2016 (3) Arkansas

93-96	FB	+++
84-87	CB	++++
83-89	CU	++

Year	Lev	Team	W	L	Sv	IP	K	ERA	WHIP	BF/G	OBA	H%	S%	xERA	Ctl	Dom	Cmd	hr/9	BPV
2016	NCAA	Arkansas	3	4	4	53	66	5.09	1.64	13.1	239	35	68	4.09	6.8	11.2	1.7	0.5	36
2016	Rk	GCL Blue Jays	0	0	0	1	0	0.00	1.00	3.8	262	26	100	2.41	0.0	0.0		0.0	18
2016	A-	Vancouver	1	1	0	17	23	3.66	1.45	5.7	211	34	72	2.78	6.3	12.0	1.9	0.0	65
2017	A	Lansing	1	0	1	20	25	3.15	1.05	5.2	187	26	74	2.34	3.6	11.3	3.1	0.9	123
2017	A+	Dunedin	1	2	4	31	43	2.03	1.19	4.6	179	30	81	1.74	5.2	12.5	2.4	0.0	102

Career RP with pedigree and demeanor for late innings work. Posts low oppBA on basis of power arsenal. Command is still work in progress, but gets hitters to chase multiple offerings. FB can be straight, but tough to hit. Plus CB may be best breaking ball in organization with hard, late break. Sprinkles in occasional CU, but not dependable.

Jaskie,Oliver

SP | Seattle | EXP MLB DEBUT: 2020 | H/W: 6-3 210 | FUT: #5 SP/swingman | 7E

Thrws L Age 22
2017 (6) Michigan

87-90	FB	+++
78-82	SL	++
81-82	CB	++

Year	Lev	Team	W	L	Sv	IP	K	ERA	WHIP	BF/G	OBA	H%	S%	xERA	Ctl	Dom	Cmd	hr/9	BPV
2017	NCAA	Michigan	8	3	0	93	119	3.77	1.23	23.5	240	34	71	3.39	3.0	11.5	3.8	0.9	144
2017	A-	Everett	0	1	0	30	33	6.88	1.86	10.8	336	42	65	7.02	3.9	9.9	2.5	1.5	91

Tall, durable SP who looks more menacing than pitches suggest. Lacks premium velocity, but has deception in unorthodox delivery. Throws with effort, but adds to effectiveness. Induces groundballs with solid sinker and counters with fringy SL and CU with late action. Works inside and is tough on LHH.

Javier,Cristian

SP | Houston | EXP MLB DEBUT: 2020 | H/W: 6-1 170 | FUT: #5 SP/swingman | 8E

Thrws R Age 21
2015 FA (DR)

88-91	FB	++
	SL	+++
	CB	+++
	CU	++

Year	Lev	Team	W	L	Sv	IP	K	ERA	WHIP	BF/G	OBA	H%	S%	xERA	Ctl	Dom	Cmd	hr/9	BPV
2016	Rk	Greeneville	1	1	0	25		1.79	0.99	13.7	174	25	83	1.54	3.6	10.4	2.9	0.4	108
2016	Rk	GCL Astros	3	1	1	25	37	2.87	1.08	16.3	212	35	73	2.15	2.9	13.3	4.6	0.4	179
2017	A-	Tri City	0	0	0	16	24	2.78	1.23	16.4	194	34	75	2.01	5.0	13.3	2.7	0.0	123
2017	A	Quad Cities	2	0	1	37	47	2.42	1.08	18.1	192	28	81	2.29	3.6	11.4	3.1	0.7	125
2017	A+	Buies Creek	1	0	0	5	9	0.00	0.96	9.8	120	26	100	0.52	5.2	15.6	3.0	0.0	158

Spin-savvy SP who scooted up three levels in 2017. Thrives off SL/CB tandem to get outs and miss bats and keeps RHH at bay effectively. FB sits high-80s/low-90s and often gets left up in the zone for fly-ball contact. Still young for his age and level, which makes his Dom production intriguing. Biggest obstacle is toning down that Ctl.

Jay,Tyler

RP | Minnesota | EXP MLB DEBUT: 2018 | H/W: 6-1 185 | FUT: Closer | 8D

Thrws L Age 23
2015 (1) Illinois

91-96	FB	++++
87-90	SL	+++
77-79	CB	+++
83-87	CU	++

Year	Lev	Team	W	L	Sv	IP	K	ERA	WHIP	BF/G	OBA	H%	S%	xERA	Ctl	Dom	Cmd	hr/9	BPV
2016	A+	Fort Myers	5	5	0	69	68	2.86	1.23	21.5	247	32	79	3.30	2.7	8.8	3.2	0.7	103
2016	AA	Chattanooga	0	0	0	14	9	5.79	1.29	11.5	248	27	56	4.09	3.2	5.8	1.8	1.3	35
2017	Rk	GCL Twins	0	0	0	3	7	5.63	2.19	5.3	399	71	83	10.17	2.8	19.7	7.0	2.8	296
2017	A+	Fort Myers	3	0	0	6	10	1.50	0.67	7.0	191	37	75	0.53	0.0	15.0		0.0	288
2017	AA	Chattanooga	0	0	0	2	2	4.50	2.00	4.8	151	0	100	7.74	13.5	9.0	0.7	4.5	-185

Quick-armed pitcher who missed significant time due to shoulder impingement. Looked good in AFL as RP and could be future role. Has two very good offerings in hard FB and late-breaking SL. Pitches aggressively and loves to challenge. Would have deep arsenal for RP with multiple breaking balls. Injury history is only concern.

Jefferies,Daulton

SP | Oakland | EXP MLB DEBUT: 2020 | H/W: 6-0 180 | FUT: #4 starter | 7B

Thrws R Age 22
2016 (S-1) California

89-94	FB	+++
81-84	SL	++
83-85	CU	+++

Year	Lev	Team	W	L	Sv	IP	K	ERA	WHIP	BF/G	OBA	H%	S%	xERA	Ctl	Dom	Cmd	hr/9	BPV
2016	NCAA	California	7	0	0	50	53	1.08	0.84	22.9	194	25	95	1.73	1.4	9.5	6.6	0.7	151
2016	Rk	AZL Athletics	0	0	0	11	17	2.43	1.17	8.9	260	43	77	2.67	1.6	13.8	8.5	0.0	222
2017	A+	Stockton	0	0	0	7	6	2.57	1.14	13.9	262	34	75	2.69	1.3	7.7	6.0	0.0	122

Athletic SP who ended season in April due to Tommy John surgery. When healthy, uses fast arm action to generate lively FB that hitters have difficulty elevating. Likes to use above average CU early in count and will mix in fringy SL. Should add more Ks with more time, but durability is in question.

Jennings, Steven

SP | Pittsburgh | EXP MLB DEBUT: 2021 | H/W: 6-2 175 | FUT: #3 starter | 8D

Thrws R Age 19
2017 (2) HS (TN)

90-94	FB	+++
85-87	SL	+++
75-78	CB	+++
	CU	++

Year	Lev	Team	W	L	Sv	IP	K	ERA	WHIP	BF/G	OBA	H%	S%	xERA	Ctl	Dom	Cmd	hr/9	BPV
2017	Rk	GCL Pirates	0	2	0	26	13	4.14	1.57	11.5	296	32	74	4.95	3.4	4.5	1.3	0.7	6

With a lean, projectable frame, his fastball currently sits at 88-92, but has been as high at 96 mph and has room for more velocity. Slider shows plus potential to go along with an average curve and seldom used change-up. Struggled with control in brief pro debut, but showed some ability in HS.

Jerez,Williams

RP | Boston | EXP MLB DEBUT: 2018 | H/W: 6-4 200 | FUT: Setup reliever | 7D

Thrws L Age 25
2011 (2) HS (NY)

91-95	FB	+++
80-82	SL	+++
	CU	+

Year	Lev	Team	W	L	Sv	IP	K	ERA	WHIP	BF/G	OBA	H%	S%	xERA	Ctl	Dom	Cmd	hr/9	BPV
2014	A+	Salem						0.74	1.24	#####	244	33	93	2.68	3.0	8.9	3.0	0.0	98
2015	AA	Portland	1	2	1	37	31	3.65	1.38	7.1	246	30	73	3.53	4.1	7.5	1.8	0.5	42
2016	AA	Portland	1	6	0	65	65	4.71	1.54	7.1	276	35	70	4.66	4.2	9.0	2.2	0.8	68
2017	AA	Portland	2	0	4	51	47	3.17	1.31	7.3	258	33	77	3.55	3.0	8.3	2.8	0.5	86
2017	AAA	Pawtucket	0	2	0	12	10	3.75	1.25	5.4	210	20	83	4.41	4.5	7.5	1.7	2.3	32

Career RP who was promoted to AAA in August and is on cusp of majors. Mostly successful against LHH with nasty, sinking FB and improving SL. Spent most of last 3 years in AA after converting to pitcher in '14. Velocity has been more consistent and has enough ability to miss bats. Doesn't profile as closer, but has good stuff.

Jewell,Jake

SP | Los Angeles (A) | EXP MLB DEBUT: 2018 | H/W: 6-3 200 | FUT: #4 starter | 7D

Thrws R Age 24
2014 (5) NE Oklahoma A&M

90-95	FB	+++
84-86	SL	+++
77-80	CB	++
75-78	CU	++

Year	Lev	Team	W	L	Sv	IP	K	ERA	WHIP	BF/G	OBA	H%	S%	xERA	Ctl	Dom	Cmd	hr/9	BPV
2014	Rk	AZL Angels	1	0	0	30	26	1.50	1.16	13.3	213	28	86	2.11	3.6	7.8	2.2	0.0	61
2015	A	Burlington	6	8	2	111	110	4.78	1.27	14.7	260	33	62	3.58	2.5	8.9	3.5	0.6	111
2016	A+	Inland Empire	2	15	0	137	104	6.31	1.87	22.9	331	39	65	6.19	4.3	6.8	1.6	0.7	26
2017	A+	Inland Empire	0	1	0	16	15	2.25	0.88	19.7	196	25	77	1.70	1.7	8.4	5.0	0.6	124
2017	AA	Mobile	7	8	0	124	81	4.86	1.43	22.0	280	31	67	4.62	3.0	5.9	2.0	1.0	43

Tall, durable SP who has deep pitch mix and increasing velocity, but can't find success. Has never had solid season, yet still has potential. Owns lively FB and mixes in two-seamer for late movement. SL can be decent offering while CU and CB lack polish. CU used to be go-to pitch. K rate falling and LHH have had their way with him.

Jimenez,Joe

RP | Detroit | EXP MLB DEBUT: 2017 | H/W: 6-3 220 | FUT: Closer | 7C

Thrws R Age 23
2013 FA (PR)

92-95	FB	+++
84-88	SL	+++
85-87	CU	+

Year	Lev	Team	W	L	Sv	IP	K	ERA	WHIP	BF/G	OBA	H%	S%	xERA	Ctl	Dom	Cmd	hr/9	BPV
2016	AA	Erie	3	2	12	20	34	2.23	0.99	3.7	174	34	75	1.15	3.6	15.1	4.3	0.0	194
2016	AAA	Toledo	0	1	8	15	16	2.37	0.86	3.3	174	23	75	1.42	2.4	9.5	4.0	0.6	125
2017	A+	Lakeland	0	0	0	1	1	0.00	1.00	3.8	262	35	100	2.32	0.0	9.0		0.0	180
2017	AAA	Toledo	1	1	4	25	36	1.44	1.24	3.9	212	34	90	2.58	4.3	13.0	3.0	0.4	135
2017	MLB	Detroit	0	2	0	19	17	12.32	2.11	3.9	367	42	39	8.57	4.3	8.1	1.9	1.9	48

Career RP who continued dominance in minors, but was hammered in majors. Velocity drop is slight concern, but also working to firm up secondary offerings. Both FB and SL can be out pitches, especially SL that features great break at times. Absolutely needs to fine-tune command as he works behind in count often due to inconsistent mechanics.

Johnson,Brian

SP | Boston | EXP MLB DEBUT: 2015 | H/W: 6-4 235 | FUT: #4 starter | 7D

Thrws L Age 27
2012 (1) Florida

85-90	FB	++
80-83	CT	++
73-78	CB	+++
81-83	CU	++

Year	Lev	Team	W	L	Sv	IP	K	ERA	WHIP	BF/G	OBA	H%	S%	xERA	Ctl	Dom	Cmd	hr/9	BPV
2015	AAA	Pawtucket	9	6	0	96	90	2.53	1.10	20.9	215	27	79	2.50	3.0	8.4	2.8	0.6	89
2016	AAA	Pawtucket	5	6	0	77	54	4.09	1.43	21.8	254	28	74	4.31	4.2	6.3	1.5	1.1	18
2017	A-	Lowell	0	0	0	2	4	4.09	1.82	10.2	244	48	75	4.06	8.2	16.4	2.0	0.0	92
2017	AAA	Pawtucket	3	4	0	90	70	3.10	1.22	21.4	244	28	79	3.59	2.8	7.0	2.5	1.0	68
2017	MLB	Boston	2	0	0	27	21	4.33	1.48	23.2	296	33	77	5.61	2.7	7.0	2.6	1.7	72

Long-time prospect with medical history. Mixes deep repertoire, though control and command have regressed. Lacks frontline velocity and wipeout pitch, but has feel for changing speeds and keeps hitters off balance. Can cut FB at will, but has tendency to pitch up which won't work at low velocity. Very tough on LHH and could end up as RP.

Johnson,Jordan

SP | San Francisco | EXP MLB DEBUT: 2018 | H/W: 6-3 200 | FUT: #4 starter | 7C

Thrws R Age 24
2014 (23) Cal St Northridge

90-94	FB	+++
78-82	CB	+++
82-84	CU	+++

Year	Lev	Team	W	L	Sv	IP	K	ERA	WHIP	BF/G	OBA	H%	S%	xERA	Ctl	Dom	Cmd	hr/9	BPV
2015	Rk	AZL Giants	0	1	0	23	32	1.56	0.87	12.2	226	36	80	1.47	0.4	12.5	32.0	0.0	232
2015	A-	Salem-Kaizer	0	1	0	4	6	4.29	1.19	16.8	297	46	60	3.26	0.0	12.9		0.0	249
2015	A+	San Jose	2	3	0	31	33	4.34	1.41	22.0	279	36	71	4.42	2.9	9.5	3.3	0.9	112
2016	A+	San Jose	8	9	0	120	111	5.33	1.43	23.2	282	32	68	5.39	2.9	8.3	2.8	1.8	89
2017	AA	Richmond	4	6	0	92	65	4.50	1.37	18.4	255	28	70	4.28	3.6	6.4	1.8	1.2	35

Tall, durable SP who didn't pitch much after June. Saw big drop in K rate while control regressed. More of flyball pitcher, but has three good pitches in repertoire. Inconsistent velocity, though throws with deceptive arm speed. Shelved SL in favor of CB and CU and CB may be best pitch with late drop. Has been hit hard by LHH.

Jones, Connor

SP	St. Louis	EXP MLB DEBUT: 2019	H/W: 6-3 200	FUT: #4 starter	7C

Thrws R Age 23
2016 (2) Virginia

90-93	FB	+++
80-83	SL	+++
	CB	+
	CU	++

Year	Lev	Team	W	L	Sv	IP	K	ERA	WHIP	BF/G	OBA	H%	S%	xERA	Ctl	Dom	Cmd	hr/9	BPV
2016	NCAA	Virginia	11	1	0	103	72	2.35	1.19	27.6	226	27	80	2.60	3.3	6.3	1.9	0.3	42
2016	Rk	GCL Cardinals	0	0	0	4	3	2.25	1.00	3.8	210	27	75	1.67	2.3	6.8	3.0	0.0	79
2016	A-	State College	0	0	1	10	8	4.41	1.67	6.5	343	42	71	5.26	1.8	7.1	4.0	0.0	97
2017	A+	Palm Beach	8	5	1	113	76	3.98	1.49	20.3	273	33	72	3.98	3.9	6.0	1.6	0.2	22
2017	AA	Springfield	1	0	0	6	2	2.90	1.45	26.5	255	24	88	4.79	4.4	2.9	0.7	1.5	-47

Strong-armed hurler has a good low-90s sinking fastball, a four-seamer that can hit 96 mph, above-avg slider, curve, and change-up. Simple, repeatable mechanics allow him to pound the strike zone and sinker keeps the ball on the ground, but low Dom points to a back-end starter.

Jorge,Felix

SP	Minnesota	EXP MLB DEBUT: 2017	H/W: 6-2 170	FUT: #4 starter	7C

Thrws R Age 24
2011 FA (DR)

88-94	FB	+++
78-82	SL	+++
81-84	CU	+++

Year	Lev	Team	W	L	Sv	IP	K	ERA	WHIP	BF/G	OBA	H%	S%	xERA	Ctl	Dom	Cmd	hr/9	BPV
2016	A+	Fort Myers	9	3	0	93	77	1.55	0.94	24.9	225	28	85	1.96	1.1	7.5	7.0	0.3	123
2016	AA	Chattanooga	3	5	0	74	32	4.13	1.28	27.6	284	30	69	4.19	1.5	3.9	2.7	0.9	49
2017	AA	Chattanooga	10	3	0	134	99	3.55	1.33	25.3	273	32	75	4.03	2.5	6.6	2.7	0.7	71
2017	AAA	Rochester	0	1	0	14	9	5.11	1.56	20.6	323	34	74	6.48	1.9	5.7	3.0	1.9	70
2017	MLB	Minnesota	1	0	0	7	4	11.25	2.22	18.2	408	38	58	12.64	2.5	5.0	2.0	5.0	41

Durable, stable SP who excels with control-oriented approach. Has pitched over 100 IP in each full season as pro. Gets ton of groundballs with heavy FB and is able to locate pitches due to clean, loose delivery. Doesn't project as a bat-misser as he is efficient and pitches to contact. Power stuff not evident, but sequences well.

Jurado,Ariel

SP	Texas	EXP MLB DEBUT: 2018	H/W: 6-1 180	FUT: #4 starter	7C

Thrws R Age 22
2012 FA (PN)

88-94	FB	+++
79-83	SL	++
81-82	CU	+++

Year	Lev	Team	W	L	Sv	IP	K	ERA	WHIP	BF/G	OBA	H%	S%	xERA	Ctl	Dom	Cmd	hr/9	BPV
2014	Rk	AZL Rangers	2	1	0	38		1.65	1.13	10.8	245	32	86	2.64	1.9	8.2	4.4	0.2	116
2015	A	Hickory	12	1	0	99	95	2.45	1.05	17.4	248	32	78	2.69	1.1	8.6	7.9	0.5	144
2016	A+	High Desert	7	2	0	79	71	3.87	1.35	20.6	271	34	71	3.77	2.7	8.1	3.0	0.5	90
2016	AA	Frisco	1	4	0	43	35	3.33	1.25	22.0	265	32	75	3.60	2.1	7.3	3.5	0.6	93
2017	AA	Frisco	9	11	0	157	95	4.59	1.43	24.7	298	33	69	4.83	2.1	5.4	2.6	0.9	59

Durable sinkerballer who suffered through inconsistent season. Had only one good month and needs to find some semblance of out pitch. Thrives on pitch movement low in zone and very good control. Very hittable—LHH hit .342 against him despite solid-average CU. FB and SL only have average potential, but he sequences well.

Justo, Salvador

RP	Colorado	EXP MLB DEBUT: 2021	H/W: 6-5 210	FUT: Setup reliever	7D

Thrws R Age 23
2013 FA (DR)

95-97	FB	++++
	SL	+
	CU	++

Year	Lev	Team	W	L	Sv	IP	K	ERA	WHIP	BF/G	OBA	H%	S%	xERA	Ctl	Dom	Cmd	hr/9	BPV
2015	A-	Boise	2	0	0	22	13	3.26	1.63	3.9	252	29	80	4.19	6.1	5.3	0.9	0.4	-52
2016	A	Asheville	3	1	2	46	34	2.15	1.24	4.9	217	26	85	2.90	4.1	6.6	1.6	0.6	27
2017	A-	Boise	2	0	0	8	7	1.11	1.11	6.4	208	27	89	1.92	3.3	7.8	2.3	0.0	68
2017	A	Asheville	1	1	0	16	18	2.25	1.63	4.4	285	40	85	4.21	4.5	10.1	2.3	0.0	79
2017	A+	Lancaster	2	4	3	23	14	10.09	2.07	4.5	300	30	52	7.78	7.8	5.4	0.7	2.3	-94

Long, lean reliever started the season well, but faltered when moved up to the hitter-friendly CAL. Comes after hitters with a plus 95-97 heater to bumps 100 mph with good late sinking action. Mixes in a hard slider and a change-up that shows some potential. Has the frame to pitch in the majors, but needs refinement.

Kaprielian,James

SP	Oakland	EXP MLB DEBUT: 2019	H/W: 6-4 200	FUT: #2 starter	9D

Thrws R Age 24
2015 (1) UCLA

90-96	FB	++++
75-78	CB	+++
81-85	SL	+++
84-86	CU	+++

Year	Lev	Team	W	L	Sv	IP	K	ERA	WHIP	BF/G	OBA	H%	S%	xERA	Ctl	Dom	Cmd	hr/9	BPV
2015	NCAA	UCLA	10	4	0	106	114	2.03	1.12	24.6	223	30	85	2.66	2.8	9.7	3.5	0.6	116
2015	Rk	GCL Yankees 2	0	0	0	2	2	12.86	1.90	5.0	252	34	25	4.47	8.6	8.6	1.0	0.0	-59
2015	A-	Staten Island	0	1	0	9	12	2.00	1.11	11.8	240	37	80	2.27	2.0	12.0	6.0	0.0	180
2016	A+	Tampa	2	1	0	18	22	1.50	0.61	20.6	136	20	80	0.31	1.5	11.0	7.3	0.5	176
2017		*Did not pitch; injured*																	

Injury-prone SP who missed entire season after Tommy John surgery in April. Likely to return in May and will be treated cautiously. Has ace stuff when healthy with four pitches in impressive repertoire. FB can be elite, and two breaking balls flash plus. Effort in delivery, but throws strikes. Decent CU should get better.

Karinchak,James

SP	Cleveland	EXP MLB DEBUT: 2020	H/W: 6-3 230	FUT: #3 starter	8E

Thrws R Age 22
2017 (9) Bryant

90-94	FB	+++
80-83	CB	+++
	CU	++

Year	Lev	Team	W	L	Sv	IP	K	ERA	WHIP	BF/G	OBA	H%	S%	xERA	Ctl	Dom	Cmd	hr/9	BPV
2017	NCAA	Bryant	6	3	0	56	86	3.68	1.25	17.6	185	29	73	2.83	5.4	13.8	2.5	1.0	119
2017	A-	Mahoning Val	2	2	0	23	31	5.84	1.69	10.4	315	46	63	5.18	3.5	12.1	3.4	0.4	141

Large-framed SP who could find himself in bullpen due to potential power repertoire. Posted high K rate despite hittable stuff. Establishes plate with solid FB that could go higher in shorter stints. Command has been inconsistent at best. Hard CB gets swings and misses while CU shows nifty, late action. Delivery has moving parts, but OK.

Kay,Anthony

SP	New York (N)	EXP MLB DEBUT: 2020	H/W: 6-0 190	FUT: #3 starter	8C

Thrws L Age 23
2016 (1) Connecticut

91-93	FB	+++
	SL	+++
	CU	+++

Year	Lev	Team	W	L	Sv	IP	K	ERA	WHIP	BF/G	OBA	H%	S%	xERA	Ctl	Dom	Cmd	hr/9	BPV
2017		*Did not pitch; signed late*																	

Has yet to make his pro debut due to Tommy John surgery. When healthy, has advanced command of three average or better offerings. High pitchability, relies on keeping hitters off balance by changing speeds and eye levels. CU is only pitch in arsenal that could eventually grade out as plus, with solid fade and excellent deception off FB.

Keating,Sam

SP	San Diego	EXP MLB DEBUT: 2021	H/W: 6-3 190	FUT: #4 starter	8D

Thrws R Age 19
2017 (4) HS (FL)

90-93	FB	+++
78-82	SL	+++
	CU	++

Year	Lev	Team	W	L	Sv	IP	K	ERA	WHIP	BF/G	OBA	H%	S%	xERA	Ctl	Dom	Cmd	hr/9	BPV
2017	Rk	AZL Padres	0	3	0	18	16	6.96	2.04	12.6	385	48	62	7.00	2.5	8.0	3.2	0.0	94

Lean RH who signed for above-slot value in 4th round last summer. Sits 90-93 mph with fastball and has chance to add more as he fills out. Feel for SL can be spotty at times, but shows potential to be quality second pitch. Did not throw CU much as amateur and will need to develop it to stick in the rotation.

Keller, Mitch

SP	Pittsburgh	EXP MLB DEBUT: 2018	H/W: 6-3 195	FUT: #2 starter	9D

Thrws R Age 22
2014 (2) HS (IA)

93-96	FB	++++
75-77	CB	+++
	CU	+++

Year	Lev	Team	W	L	Sv	IP	K	ERA	WHIP	BF/G	OBA	H%	S%	xERA	Ctl	Dom	Cmd	hr/9	BPV
2016	A	West Virginia	8	5	0	124	131	2.47	0.92	20.2	215	30	73	1.78	1.3	9.5	7.3	0.3	154
2016	A+	Bradenton	1	0	0	6	7	0.00	1.00	22.9	228	34	100	1.86	1.5	10.5	7.0	0.0	167
2017	A-	West Virginia	0	0	0	4	7	0.00	0.75	7.1	151	32	100	0.29	2.3	15.8	7.0	0.0	241
2017	A+	Bradenton	6	3	0	77	64	3.15	1.00	19.6	208	25	69	2.18	2.3	7.5	3.2	0.6	89
2017	AA	Altoona	2	2	0	34	45	3.16	1.05	22.1	206	31	71	2.20	2.9	11.8	4.1	0.5	153

Strong, physically mature right-hander has the best stuff in the system, but continues to battle injuries. Mid-90s fastball tops out at 98 mph with good late sink. Improved change-up, above-average curveball, and solid command give him the tools to be a front-line starter. Career Dom of 9.5 and Cmd of 3.9 highlight the upside.

Keller,Brad

SP	Kansas City	EXP MLB DEBUT: 2018	H/W: 6-5 230	FUT: #4 starter	7D

Thrws R Age 22
2013 (8) HS (GA)

89-92	FB	+++
82-84	SL	++
82-84	CU	+++

Year	Lev	Team	W	L	Sv	IP	K	ERA	WHIP	BF/G	OBA	H%	S%	xERA	Ctl	Dom	Cmd	hr/9	BPV
2014	Rk	AZL Dbacks	4	0	0	31	20	2.32	1.25	21.1	255	29	84	3.44	2.6	5.8	2.2	0.6	52
2014	A-	Hillsboro	1	0	0	6	8	0.00	0.33	18.9	56	10	100		1.5	12.0	8.0	0.0	194
2015	A	Kane County	8	9	0	142	109	2.60	1.16	21.7	242	30	77	2.66	1.5	6.9	2.9	0.2	79
2016	A+	Visalia	9	7	0	135	99	4.47	1.28	23.1	279	32	66	4.10	1.7	6.6	3.8	0.9	90
2017	AA	Jackson	10	9	0	130	111	4.70	1.53	21.8	279	35	68	4.36	3.9	7.7	1.9	0.5	50

Big-bodied, formerly strike-throwing RH stuff took a step back in Double-A. Tall-and-fall guy, Lost velocity on heavy FB, resulting in harder contact. Compensated by nitpicking around the zone. SL is a below-average offering that hitters lay off of. CU may be best pitch and will flash plus at times. Workhorse body. Rule 5 pick from ARI.

Kilome,Franklyn

SP	Philadelphia	EXP MLB DEBUT: 2019	H/W: 6-6 175	FUT: #3 starter	8C

Thrws R Age 22
2013 FA (DR)

93-95	FB	+++
79-82	CB	++++
83-85	CU	++
82-84	SL	++

Year	Lev	Team	W	L	Sv	IP	K	ERA	WHIP	BF/G	OBA	H%	S%	xERA	Ctl	Dom	Cmd	hr/9	BPV
2014	Rk	GCL Phillies	3	1	0	40	25	3.14	1.17	14.6	241	28	73	2.93	2.5	5.6	2.3	0.4	52
2015	A-	Williamsport	3	2	0	49	36	3.30	1.26	18.2	228	28	72	2.74	3.8	6.6	1.7	0.2	33
2016	A	Lakewood	5	8	0	114	130	3.86	1.43	21.1	260	36	73	3.80	3.9	10.2	2.6	0.5	96
2017	A+	Clearwater	6	4	0	97	83	2.60	1.37	21.4	260	32	82	3.67	3.4	7.7	2.2	0.5	64
2017	AA	Reading	1	3	0	29	20	3.70	1.37	24.5	233	27	74	3.47	4.6	6.2	1.3	0.6	4

Though got to Double-A, was stagnant overall as Dom dipped; FB command didn't materialize. Despite tall frame, can struggle to get downhill plane. FB 93-95, but can get flat. CB a sharp 12-6 out pitch; CU has improved; new SL gives him fourth offering. Still projectable, but lack of quality strikes, swing/miss questions has lowered his ceiling.

Kingham, Nick — SP — Pittsburgh

EXP MLB DEBUT: 2018 | H/W: 6-5 225 | FUT: #4 starter | 7C

Thrws R Age 26 — 2010 (4) HS (NV)

Velo	Pitch	Grade
90-94	FB	+++
85-87	CB	++
75-78	CU	++++

Year	Lev	Team	W	L	Sv	IP	K	ERA	WHIP	BF/G	OBA	H%	S%	xERA	Ctl	Dom	Cmd	hr/9	BPV
2016	Rk	GCL Pirates	0	4	0	24	16	3.00	1.00	15.3	254	31	67	2.23	0.4	6.0	16.0	0.0	116
2016	A+	Bradenton	2	0	0	11	10	0.00	0.82	20.0	205	28	100	1.14	0.8	8.2	10.0	0.0	143
2016	AA	Altoona	1	1	0	11	10	5.73	0.91	20.5	162	19	33	1.66	3.3	8.2	2.5	0.8	77
2017	A+	Bradenton	1	0	0	5	0	0.00	0.20	15.1	66	7	100		0.0	0.0		0.0	18
2017	AAA	Indianapolis	9	6	0	113	93	4.14	1.31	23.3	272	33	69	3.85	2.3	7.4	3.2	0.6	89

Ankle injury caused him to miss two months, but he was sharp in July and August. Gets downward tilt on low-90s heater and keeps hitters off-balance with plus change-up and solid curve. Not overpowering, but pounds the strike zone and should settle in as a solid back-end starter.

Kolek, Tyler — SP — Miami

EXP MLB DEBUT: 2020 | H/W: 6-5 260 | FUT: Setup reliever | 8E

Thrws R Age 22 — 2014 (1) HS (TX)

Velo	Pitch	Grade
92-95	FB	++++
85-87	SL	++
	CU	++

Year	Lev	Team	W	L	Sv	IP	K	ERA	WHIP	BF/G	OBA	H%	S%	xERA	Ctl	Dom	Cmd	hr/9	BPV
2014	Rk	GCL Marlins	0	3	0	22	18	4.50	1.59	10.8	262	33	69	3.82	5.3	7.4	1.4	0.0	7
2015	A	Greensboro	4	10	0	108	81	4.57	1.56	19.0	261	31	70	4.30	5.1	6.7	1.3	0.6	2
2016		Did not pitch; injured																	
2017	Rk	GCL Marlins	0	0	0	3	1	33.75	5.63	5.4	307	33	33	14.70	39.4	2.8	0.1	0.0	-995

2nd pick of 2014 draft has been a bust so far. Tommy John surgery cost all of 2016 and most of 2017. Should be ready to go in 2018, but will be 22 and has just 134.1 IP. When healthy pitches off a mid-90s fastball. Slider and change both and need work. Big frame gives him potential, but needs to show something soon.

Kopech, Michael — SP — Chicago (A)

EXP MLB DEBUT: 2018 | H/W: 6-3 205 | FUT: #1 starter | 9C

Thrws R Age 21 — 2014 (1) HS (TX)

Velo	Pitch	Grade
95-98	FB	+++++
87-90	SL	++++
89-93	CU	+++

Year	Lev	Team	W	L	Sv	IP	K	ERA	WHIP	BF/G	OBA	H%	S%	xERA	Ctl	Dom	Cmd	hr/9	BPV
2015	A	Greenville	4	5	0	65	70	2.63	1.23	16.5	224	31	78	2.66	3.7	9.7	2.6	0.3	92
2016	A-	Lowell	0	0	0	4		0.00	1.95	19.6	257	35	100	4.65	8.8	8.8	1.0	0.0	-61
2016	A+	Salem	4	1	0	52	82	2.25	1.04	18.2	146	27	77	1.14	5.0	14.2	2.8	0.2	138
2017	AA	Birmingham	8	7	0	119	155	2.87	1.15	21.5	187	28	76	2.15	4.5	11.7	2.6	0.5	106
2017	AAA	Charlotte	1	1	0	15	17	3.00	1.33	20.8	262	37	75	3.14	3.0	10.2	3.4	0.0	121

Tall, power pitcher with three-pitch arsenal of filth. High velocity FB with plus arm-side run makes it difficult to catch up to or square up. Tightly-wound SL has sharp, two plane break and best when working FB up and down. CU is a solid third pitch with some tumble and late fade. Aggressive on the mound; has transformed into a pitcher.

Kranick, Max — SP — Pittsburgh

EXP MLB DEBUT: 2021 | H/W: 6-3 175 | FUT: #4 starter | 7D

Thrws R Age 20 — 2016 (11) HS (PA)

Velo	Pitch	Grade
87-93	FB	+++
	CB	++
	CU	++

Year	Lev	Team	W	L	Sv	IP	K	ERA	WHIP	BF/G	OBA	H%	S%	xERA	Ctl	Dom	Cmd	hr/9	BPV
2016	Rk	GCL Pirates	1	2	0	33	21	2.45	1.06	14.3	249	29	76	2.58	1.1	5.7	5.3	0.3	91
2017	Rk	Bristol	1	0	0	11	9	2.41	1.07	21.8	240	28	82	2.98	1.6	7.2	4.5	0.8	105
2017	Rk	GCL Pirates	0	0	0	12	9	0.00	1.31	16.8	259	32	100	3.08	3.0	6.6	2.3	0.0	58

11th round pick in 2016 competes well despite a pedestrian low-90s heater. Shows some feel for curve and change-up, but both need to be more consistent. Above-average command of fastball allows him to keep hitters off-balance, but lack of velocity will provide a challenge as he moves up.

Krook, Matt — SP — Tampa Bay

EXP MLB DEBUT: 2019 | H/W: 6-4 225 | FUT: #3 starter | 8E

Thrws L Age 23 — 2016 (4) Oregon

Velo	Pitch	Grade
91-95	FB	+++
81-85	SL	+++
80-82	CB	++++
	CU	++

Year	Lev	Team	W	L	Sv	IP	K	ERA	WHIP	BF/G	OBA	H%	S%	xERA	Ctl	Dom	Cmd	hr/9	BPV
2016	NCAA	Oregon	4	3	0	53	68	5.08	1.60	15.7	194	31	65	2.94	8.3	11.5	1.4	0.0	1
2016	Rk	AZL Giants	0	1	0	5	2	1.73	1.54	11.3	290	32	88	4.14	3.5	3.5	1.0	0.0	-13
2016	A-	Salem-Keizer	1	3	0	35	39	6.17	1.94	15.2	262	36	67	5.16	8.5	10.0	1.2	0.5	-31
2017	A+	San Jose	4	9	0	91	105	5.14	1.55	15.9	226	32	65	3.58	6.5	10.4	1.6	0.4	29

Tall, durable SP who is extreme sinkerballer and has plus stuff when on, which isn't often. Has been stingy against LHH with incredible CB. Finished 2nd in CAL in walks and has struggled in career with very poor command. Has tendency to overthrow and fails to repeat delivery and arm slot. Rarely allows HR.

Labourt, Jairo — RP — Detroit

EXP MLB DEBUT: 2017 | H/W: 6-4 205 | FUT: Setup reliever | 8D

Thrws L Age 24 — 2011 FA (DR)

Velo	Pitch	Grade
91-95	FB	+++
83-86	SL	+++
81-83	CU	+

Year	Lev	Team	W	L	Sv	IP	K	ERA	WHIP	BF/G	OBA	H%	S%	xERA	Ctl	Dom	Cmd	hr/9	BPV
2016	A+	Lakeland	7	9	1	87	81	5.27	1.55	12.7	209	27	64	3.32	7.2	8.4	1.2	0.3	-27
2017	A+	Lakeland	0	0	0	13	22	0.68	0.83	6.0	177	34	91	0.79	2.0	15.0	7.3	0.0	233
2017	AA	Erie	1	1	4	30	36	2.68	0.99	5.5	213	29	78	2.49	2.1	10.7	5.1	0.9	155
2017	AAA	Toledo	0	0	0	22	21	2.45	1.59	6.1	162	21	85	2.99	9.4	8.6	0.9	0.4	-81
2017	MLB	Detroit	0	0	0	6	4	4.50	1.83	4.7	191	24	73	3.56	10.5	6.0	0.6	0.0	-158

Tall, large RP who pitched on 4 levels, including majors. Converted to RP in 2016 and upped K rate while improving control. Starting to repeat delivery and slot more frequently which impacts command. SL has progressed to near plus status and FB shows continual sink. Needs polish to be dependable, but can dominate hitters.

Lakins, Travis — SP — Boston

EXP MLB DEBUT: 2018 | H/W: 6-1 180 | FUT: #4 starter | 7C

Thrws R Age 23 — 2015 (6) The Ohio State

Velo	Pitch	Grade
91-95	FB	+++
81-84	SL	+++
75-78	CB	+++
81-86	CU	++

Year	Lev	Team	W	L	Sv	IP	K	ERA	WHIP	BF/G	OBA	H%	S%	xERA	Ctl	Dom	Cmd	hr/9	BPV
2015	NCAA	Ohio State	4	4	0	96	84	3.75	1.34	26.6	264	33	73	3.84	3.0	7.9	2.6	0.7	79
2015	A-	Lowell	0	0	0	2	3	0.00	0.50	6.6	0	0	100		4.5	13.5	3.0	0.0	140
2016	A+	Salem	6	3	0	91	79	5.93	1.62	21.2	302	37	63	5.20	3.6	7.8	2.2	0.8	63
2017	A+	Salem	5	0	0	38	43	2.61	1.18	21.7	230	32	79	2.79	3.1	10.2	3.3	0.5	118
2017	AA	Portland	0	4	0	30	19	6.28	1.83	17.5	286	33	64	5.34	6.3	5.7	0.9	0.6	-49

Athletic SP who has been hindered by minor injuries. Ended season in July and saw erratic velocity and drop in K rate. Has nice arsenal with four pitches that work together. Generally commands FB to lower half and sprinkles in slow CB and CU that flashes plus. Has ingredients to be mid-rotation guy, but needs durability.

Lambert, Peter — SP — Colorado

EXP MLB DEBUT: 2019 | H/W: 6-2 185 | FUT: #3 starter | 8C

Thrws R Age 20 — 2015 (2) HS (CA)

Velo	Pitch	Grade
92-95	FB	++++
73-75	CB	+++
82-84	CU	+++

Year	Lev	Team	W	L	Sv	IP	K	ERA	WHIP	BF/G	OBA	H%	S%	xERA	Ctl	Dom	Cmd	hr/9	BPV
2015	Rk	Grand Junction	0	4	0	31	26	3.47	1.29	16.0	248	30	76	3.69	3.2	7.5	2.4	0.9	67
2016	A	Asheville	5	8	0	126	108	3.93	1.25	19.7	260	32	68	3.42	2.4	7.7	3.3	0.5	93
2017	A+	Lancaster	9	8	0	142	131	4.18	1.25	22.2	268	32	70	4.10	1.9	8.3	4.4	1.1	116

Survived a full season at hitter-friendly Lancaster, where he served up 18 HR, but posted a great 30 BB/131 K ratio. Velocity up a tick from when he was drafted and FB now sits at 92-95, topping at 97 mph. CB and CU both play well and he locates all three well, keeping the ball down in the zone.

Lange, Alex — SP — Chicago (N)

EXP MLB DEBUT: 2020 | H/W: 6-3 197 | FUT: #3 starter | 8C

Thrws R Age 22 — 2017 (1) Louisiana St

Velo	Pitch	Grade
92-95	FB	+++
80-83	CB	++++
84-87	CU	++

Year	Lev	Team	W	L	Sv	IP	K	ERA	WHIP	BF/G	OBA	H%	S%	xERA	Ctl	Dom	Cmd	hr/9	BPV
2017	NCAA	LSU	10	5	0	124	150	2.97	1.24	26.5	232	32	78	3.20	3.5	10.9	3.1	0.7	120
2017	A-	Eugene	0	1	0	9	13	4.95	1.32	9.4	260	42	58	3.05	3.0	12.9	4.3	0.0	169

3-year starter at LSU was key to two CWS runs. Uses height to pitch downhill and keep the ball down in the zone where his above-average 92-94 mph fastball plays well. Plus curve and inconsistent change-up round out his arsenal. Can be max effort at times, which leads to inconsistent mechanics and loss of command. Professional hurler.

Lara, Janser — SP — Kansas City

EXP MLB DEBUT: 2021 | H/W: 6-0 170 | FUT: #3 starter | 8E

Thrws R Age 21 — 2015 FA (DR)

Velo	Pitch	Grade
92-97	FB	++++
76-84	CB	++
81-87	CU	++

Year	Lev	Team	W	L	Sv	IP	K	ERA	WHIP	BF/G	OBA	H%	S%	xERA	Ctl	Dom	Cmd	hr/9	BPV
2017	Rk	Idaho Falls	4	2	0	52	57	4.15	1.54	18.9	258	32	78	4.90	5.0	9.8	2.0	1.4	60

Lean, fast-armed SP who features an elite FB thrown with minimal effort. Lack of height means ball delivered on flat plane and allows lot of flyballs. Can mix in erratic CB with big bend and CU that features depth and fade. Control comes and goes and needs better command. Polishing secondary pitches will be in the offing.

Lauer, Eric — SP — San Diego

EXP MLB DEBUT: 2018 | H/W: 6-3 205 | FUT: #4 starter | 8C

Thrws L Age 22 — 2016 (1) Kent St

Velo	Pitch	Grade
91-94	FB	+++
83-85	SL	+++
81-84	CU	+++

Year	Lev	Team	W	L	Sv	IP	K	ERA	WHIP	BF/G	OBA	H%	S%	xERA	Ctl	Dom	Cmd	hr/9	BPV
2016	Rk	AZL Padres	0	1	0	4	7	6.75	2.00	9.6	383	58	71	8.87	2.3	15.8	7.0	2.3	241
2016	A-	Tri-City	1	0	0	25	28	1.44	0.96	13.5	194	29	83	1.35	2.5	10.1	4.0	0.0	131
2016	A	Fort Wayne	0	0	0	2	2	0.00	0.50	6.6	0	0	100		4.5	9.0	2.0	0.0	59
2017	A+	Lake Elsinore	2	5	0	67	84	2.81	1.25	22.8	255	37	79	3.34	2.5	11.3	4.4	0.5	152
2017	AA	San Antonio	4	3	0	55	48	3.93	1.25	22.4	251	30	71	3.75	2.8	7.9	2.8	1.0	84

Athletic LH with mid-rotation profile and potential for three solid-average offerings. Spots low-90s FB effectively with minimal effort. Will miss some bats with quality vertical SL and blends in average CU that separates well from FB. Build and ease of delivery suggest he'll rack up innings long term. High-floor type of arm who should move quick.

Lawrence, Justin | RP | Colorado

EXP MLB DEBUT: 2020 | H/W: 6-3 220 | FUT: Setup reliever | 7B

Thrws R Age 23
2015 (12) Daytona State JC

Velo	Pitch	Grade
92-94	FB	++++
	SL	+++

Year	Lev	Team	W	L	Sv	IP	K	ERA	WHIP	BF/G	OBA	H%	S%	xERA	Ctl	Dom	Cmd	hr/9	BPV
2015	Rk	Grand Junction	0	0	0	5	3	10.38	2.12	4.3	405	44	50	9.24	1.7	5.2	3.0	1.7	65
2015	A-	Boise	0	3	0	19	15	8.05	1.89	5.6	282	32	58	6.20	7.1	7.1	1.0	1.4	-46
2016	A-	Boise	2	1	8	28	40	2.23	1.17	4.9	253	41	79	2.59	1.9	12.8	6.7	0.0	196
2016	A	Asheville	2	5	0	36	23	7.23	1.72	6.3	320	36	57	5.97	3.5	5.7	1.6	1.0	27
2017	A	Asheville	0	2	6	16	20	1.68	0.87	3.7	180	26	85	1.48	2.2	11.2	5.0	0.6	159

Right-handed reliever from Daytona State was in the midst of a nice breakout when a tear in his trapezius muscle ended his season. Low 3/4 fastball sits at 92-94 with good late sink and is tough on RHB. Above-average slider gives him a quality 2nd offering.

Lawson,Reggie | SP | San Diego

EXP MLB DEBUT: 2021 | H/W: 6-4 205 | FUT: #5 SP/swingman | 8D

Thrws R Age 20
2016 (S-2) HS (CA)

Velo	Pitch	Grade
91-93	FB	+++
75-78	CB	+++
86-88	CU	++

Year	Lev	Team	W	L	Sv	IP	K	ERA	WHIP	BF/G	OBA	H%	S%	xERA	Ctl	Dom	Cmd	hr/9	BPV
2016	Rk	AZL Padres	0	0	0	8	7	8.78	1.83	7.6	342	43	47	5.65	3.3	7.7	2.3	0.0	67
2017	A	Fort Wayne	4	6	0	73	89	5.30	1.37	18.0	240	33	62	3.86	4.3	11.0	2.5	1.0	99

Lanky, athletic RH who posted big K rate as a starter in his full-season debut. Operates in low-90s with FB and can reach back for 94; potential for more as he fills out. Depth of CB produces swings and misses, but will need to incorporate CU more to keep hitters honest. Delivery can get out of whack, and Ctl could be an issue, but he's young.

Leach,Landon | SP | Minnesota

EXP MLB DEBUT: 2022 | H/W: 6-4 220 | FUT: #3 starter | 8E

Thrws R Age 18
2017 (2) HS (ON)

Velo	Pitch	Grade
90-94	FB	+++
77-80	CB	++
78-82	CU	++

Year	Lev	Team	W	L	Sv	IP	K	ERA	WHIP	BF/G	OBA	H%	S%	xERA	Ctl	Dom	Cmd	hr/9	BPV
2017	Rk	GCL Twins	2	0	0	13	10	3.44	1.30	10.8	229	29	71	2.66	4.1	6.9	1.7	0.0	30

Tall, durable SP who has intriguing potential with raw arm strength. May take time to develop, but pay-off could be big. Shows current velocity and heavy action with FB that is tough to elevate. Locates FB down in zone. Repeats delivery and should improve control. CB and CU both show moments, but need more polish.

Lee,Chris | SP | Baltimore

EXP MLB DEBUT: 2018 | H/W: 6-3 180 | FUT: #4 starter | 7C

Thrws L Age 25
2011 (4) Santa Fe CC

Velo	Pitch	Grade
89-94	FB	+++
81-84	SL	+++
	CU	+++

Year	Lev	Team	W	L	Sv	IP	K	ERA	WHIP	BF/G	OBA	H%	S%	xERA	Ctl	Dom	Cmd	hr/9	BPV
2015	A+	Frederick	3	6	0	76	48	3.07	1.38	22.8	262	31	76	3.41	3.4	5.7	1.7	0.1	28
2015	AA	Bowie	4	2	0	38	26	3.08	1.37	22.7	230	28	75	2.85	4.7	6.2	1.3	0.0	1
2016	AA	Bowie	5	0	0	51	19	2.99	1.06	24.8	221	23	74	2.65	2.3	3.3	1.5	0.7	16
2017	AAA	Norfolk	5	6	0	116	83	5.12	1.71	19.5	305	35	71	5.56	4.2	6.4	1.5	0.9	21

Tall, lean SP who hasn't exhibited much durability, but impresses with natural pitch mix. Despite good stuff, doesn't put away hitters and RHH have hit him hard. Doesn't repeat delivery, which impacts command. Induces groundballs with above average, sinking FB. SL can be very good and has feel for changing speeds.

Lemieux,Mack | SP | Arizona

EXP MLB DEBUT: 2020 | H/W: 6-3 205 | FUT: #4 starter | 7D

Thrws L Age 21
2016 (6) Palm Beach St

Velo	Pitch	Grade
90-92	FB	+++
76-78	CB	+++
82-83	CU	++

Year	Lev	Team	W	L	Sv	IP	K	ERA	WHIP	BF/G	OBA	H%	S%	xERA	Ctl	Dom	Cmd	hr/9	BPV
2016	Rk	AZL Dbacks	1	0	0	12	17	1.48	0.90	6.5	189	29	90	1.81	2.2	12.5	5.7	0.7	184
2016	A-	Hillsboro	1	2	0	23	26	3.91	1.57	14.4	270	37	74	4.21	4.7	10.2	2.2	0.4	74
2017	A	Kane County	7	5	0	101	80	4.71	1.43	22.7	280	34	65	4.02	3.0	7.1	2.4	0.4	64

Tall, projectable lefty with 2-seam FB that has solid arm-side bore. It's complemented nicely by a 11-5 CB with depth and consistent drop. Is not afraid to work on CU during outings. Calling card is command/control. Lives in the lower half of zone. May never overpower but can pitch.

Lemons,Caden | SP | Milwaukee

EXP MLB DEBUT: 2021 | H/W: 6-6 175 | FUT: #2 starter | 9E

Thrws R Age 19
2017 (2) HS (AL)

Velo	Pitch	Grade
87-92	FB	+++
80-81	SL	+++
72-75	CB	++
	CU	++

Year	Lev	Team	W	L	Sv	IP	K	ERA	WHIP	BF/G	OBA	H%	S%	xERA	Ctl	Dom	Cmd	hr/9	BPV
2017	Rk	AZL Brewers	0	1	0	2	1	8.18	0.91	2.7	244	16	0	5.74	0.0	4.1		4.1	92

Tall, lanky LH popped up in spring to become 2nd rd pick. Lots of projection in frame, should add velocity with strength. FB sat 90-94 as amateur. Was 86-90 late in pro ball. SL best secondary, creating solid plane and drop. CB & CU developing. Tons of projection overall.

Lillie, Ryan | SP | Miami

EXP MLB DEBUT: 2020 | H/W: 6-0 210 | FUT: Middle reliever | 6C

Thrws R Age 21
2017 (5) UC-Riverside

Velo	Pitch	Grade
91-95	FB	+++
	CB	+++
	CU	+++

Year	Lev	Team	W	L	Sv	IP	K	ERA	WHIP	BF/G	OBA	H%	S%	xERA	Ctl	Dom	Cmd	hr/9	BPV
2017	NCAA	UC Riverside	2	7	4	71	80	4.69	1.34	14.8	273	35	67	4.38	2.5	10.1	4.0	1.1	132
2017	Rk	GCL Marlins	0	0	0	2	3	0.00	0.45	3.6	0	0	100		4.1	12.3	3.0	0.0	128
2017	A-	Batavia	0	5	0	31	27	4.35	1.26	14.0	280	35	63	3.51	1.5	7.8	5.4	0.3	120
2017	A	Greensboro	0	0	0	2	4	0.00	0.50	6.6	151	38	100		0.0	18.0		0.0	342

Undersized right-hander has a good 91-95 mph fastball. Curve and change-up are both above-average and he finds the strike zone frequently. Throws at max-effort and is likely headed to a relief role as he moves up.

Linares,Resly | SP | Tampa Bay

EXP MLB DEBUT: 2021 | H/W: 6-2 170 | FUT: #3 starter | 8E

Thrws L Age 20
2014 FA (DR)

Velo	Pitch	Grade
89-93	FB	+++
77-78	CB	+++
79-83	CU	+

Year	Lev	Team	W	L	Sv	IP	K	ERA	WHIP	BF/G	OBA	H%	S%	xERA	Ctl	Dom	Cmd	hr/9	BPV
2016	Rk	Princeton	2	3	0	32	30	5.34	1.50	17.3	307	36	69	5.83	2.3	8.4	3.8	1.7	109
2017	A-	Hudson Valley	3	3	0	61	60	2.36	0.97	17.8	173	23	75	1.42	3.4	8.8	2.6	0.3	86

Fast-armed SP who had easy success in short-season ball. Has very lean frame, yet should grow into move velocity in time. Has been tough to hit with repeatable delivery and good FB/CB combo. CU lags far behind, but has depth and fade. Could become third average or better offering. Gaining strength is paramount to pitching deep into games.

Lindow,Ethan | SP | Philadelphia

EXP MLB DEBUT: 2022 | H/W: 6-3 180 | FUT: #4 starter | 7C

Thrws L Age 19
2017 (5) HS (GA)

Velo	Pitch	Grade
86-88	FB	++
71-73	CB	+++
76-81	CU	++

Year	Lev	Team	W	L	Sv	IP	K	ERA	WHIP	BF/G	OBA	H%	S%	xERA	Ctl	Dom	Cmd	hr/9	BPV
2017	Rk	GCL Phillies	2	2	0	27	34	4.63	1.40	14.3	253	36	67	3.80	4.0	11.3	2.8	0.7	113

Tall three-pitch lefty with some feel for offspeed, though remains raw. Uneven senior season led to draft-stock drop, but some projection left in his frame. FB doesn't consistently break 90 mph yet, but gets good extension and show a repeatable delivery. Needs to add some strength in hopes of finding a bit more FB velocity.

Liranzo,Jesus | RP | Baltimore

EXP MLB DEBUT: 2019 | H/W: 6-2 175 | FUT: Setup reliever | 7D

Thrws R Age 23
2012 FA (DR)

Velo	Pitch	Grade
92-96	FB	++++
82-86	SL	+++
84-86	SP	++

Year	Lev	Team	W	L	Sv	IP	K	ERA	WHIP	BF/G	OBA	H%	S%	xERA	Ctl	Dom	Cmd	hr/9	BPV
2016	A	Delmarva	0	0	0	34	46	1.06	0.79	7.7	111	19	85	0.04	4.0	12.1	3.1	0.0	130
2016	AA	Bowie	1	1	0	18	20	3.46	1.10	6.5	135	14	76	2.46	5.9	9.9	1.7	1.5	36
2017	AA	Bowie	3	4	2	65	75	4.85	1.49	9.0	228	28	73	4.65	6.0	10.4	1.7	1.7	44

Emerging RP with incredibly fast arm and very good FB/SL combo. Has some experience as SP, though likely to work on secondary offerings. Can be lights out with explosive FB and late-breaking SL. Has lot of difficulty throwing strikes and walk rate is problematic. Extreme flyball pitcher who needs to find consistent slot.

Littell,Zack | SP | Minnesota

EXP MLB DEBUT: 2018 | H/W: 6-4 220 | FUT: #5 SP/swingman | 7D

Thrws R Age 22
2013 (11) HS (NC)

Velo	Pitch	Grade
88-93	FB	+++
80-85	SL	++
78-80	CB	+++
	CU	+++

Year	Lev	Team	W	L	Sv	IP	K	ERA	WHIP	BF/G	OBA	H%	S%	xERA	Ctl	Dom	Cmd	hr/9	BPV
2016	A	Clinton	5	5	0	97	95	2.78	1.18	24.3	255	33	77	3.13	1.9	8.8	4.5	0.5	124
2016	A+	Bakersfield	8	1	0	68	61	2.51	1.13	22.4	250	32	78	2.87	1.7	8.1	4.7	0.4	117
2017	A+	Tampa	9	1	0	71	57	1.77	1.13	21.6	245	30	87	2.90	1.9	7.2	3.8	0.5	97
2017	AA	Trenton	5	0	0	44	52	2.05	1.02	24.2	230	32	83	2.51	1.6	10.6	6.5	0.6	165
2017	AA	Chattanooga	5	0	0	41	33	2.84	1.24	23.9	221	28	76	2.61	3.9	7.2	1.8	0.2	42

Emerging SP who led minors in wins. Now in 3rd org and possesses plus control with excellent feel for four pitches. Groundball pitcher who establishes plate early in count with two-seamer and can mix in variety of offerings of varying velocities and shapes. Lacks premium pitch, but sequences well and induces weak contact. CB can be out pitch.

Little, Brendon — SP — Chicago (N)

EXP MLB DEBUT: 2020 | H/W: 6-1 195 | FUT: #3 starter | 8D

Thrws L Age 21
2017 (1) State JC of Florida

92-95	FB	+++
75-77	CB	+++
	CU	+

Year	Lev	Team	W	L	Sv	IP	K	ERA	WHIP	BF/G	OBA	H%	S%	xERA	Ctl	Dom	Cmd	hr/9	BPV
2017	A-	Eugene	0	2	0	16	12	9.50	1.86	12.6	316	36	46	6.37	5.0	6.7	1.3	1.1	3

27th overall pick in 2017 is a smallish lefty with a good 91-94 mph fastball that tops at 96 mph and a plus curve. Throws with effort and needs to refine his mechanics and develop a usable CU if he is to remain a starter. Struggled in his pro debut, but Cubs remain optimistic about his raw stuff.

Long,Grayson — SP — Detroit

EXP MLB DEBUT: 2018 | H/W: 6-5 230 | FUT: #4 starter | 7C

Thrws R Age 23
2015 (3) Texas A&M

90-92	FB	+++
80-83	SL	+++
	CU	++

Year	Lev	Team	W	L	Sv	IP	K	ERA	WHIP	BF/G	OBA	H%	S%	xERA	Ctl	Dom	Cmd	hr/9	BPV
2016	A	Burlington	3	3	0	40	45	1.58	1.08	19.5	193	27	88	2.05	3.6	10.1	2.8	0.5	103
2016	A+	Inland Empire	2	1	0	14	15	5.14	1.29	19.2	262	27	77	6.05	2.6	9.6	3.8	3.2	122
2017	A+	Inland Empire	0	2	0	12	14	4.50	1.50	17.3	293	41	67	4.00	3.0	10.5	3.5	0.0	126
2017	AA	Mobile	8	6	0	121	111	2.52	1.14	20.9	226	29	79	2.70	2.8	8.2	2.9	0.5	90
2017	AA	Erie	0	1	0	4	3	13.50	2.25	20.3	415	42	43	12.37	2.3	6.8	3.0	4.5	79

Physical SP who led SL in ERA. Throws with easy delivery and smooth arm action. Not a flamethrower, but can spot FB and reach back for more when needed. Arm slot conducive to solid SL and firm CU flashes average. Needs to improve against LHH and can be victim of flyballs and HR. Doesn't possess great stuff, but good enough.

Lopez, Pablo — SP — Miami

EXP MLB DEBUT: 2020 | H/W: 6-3 200 | FUT: #4 starter | 7B

Thrws R Age 22
2012 FA (VZ)

88-91	FB	++
	CB	+++
	CU	+++

Year	Lev	Team	W	L	Sv	IP	K	ERA	WHIP	BF/G	OBA	H%	S%	xERA	Ctl	Dom	Cmd	hr/9	BPV
2016	A	Clinton	7	1	0	84	56	2.14	0.92	18.5	223	26	78	2.03	1.0	6.0	6.2	0.4	100
2017	A+	Jupiter	0	3	0	45	32	2.20	1.09	22.0	248	31	78	2.38	1.4	6.4	4.6	0.0	95
2017	A+	Modesto	5	8	0	100	89	5.04	1.26	21.5	286	36	58	3.83	1.2	8.0	6.8	0.5	131

Venezuelan right-hander came over from the Marlins in the D. Phelps trade. Pounds the strike zone with a pedestrian 88-91 mph fastball that does have good sink. Curveball and change-up both play above-average due to ability to throw for strikes. Walked just 20 in 145.1 innings of work and profiles as a solid back-end starter.

Lopez,Jose — SP — Cincinnati

EXP MLB DEBUT: 2018 | H/W: 6-1 185 | FUT: #4 starter | 7D

Thrws R Age 24
2014 (6) Seton Hall

91-94	FB	+++
76-78	CB	+++
82-84	CU	++

Year	Lev	Team	W	L	Sv	IP	K	ERA	WHIP	BF/G	OBA	H%	S%	xERA	Ctl	Dom	Cmd	hr/9	BPV
2015	Rk	Billings	3	2	0	57	67	3.16	1.26	15.5	248	34	76	3.37	3.0	10.6	3.5	0.6	127
2016	A	Dayton	6	9	0	113	113	3.98	1.33	22.3	270	36	68	3.40	2.5	9.0	3.5	0.2	111
2016	A+	Daytona	0	3	0	34	34	4.47	1.14	22.6	231	29	61	3.01	2.6	8.9	3.4	0.8	108
2017	A+	Daytona	2	4	0	50	48	2.87	1.27	22.8	261	33	79	3.51	2.5	8.6	3.4	0.5	105
2017	AA	Pensacola	7	2	0	96	95	2.43	1.03	21.8	191	24	81	2.30	3.3	8.9	2.7	0.8	90

Command-and-control RH made strides cleaning up delivery and getting more swings and misses in 2017. Slowed down delivery, keeping better balance. 2-seam FB has solid arm-side run and a little sink. Inconsistent CB. Struggles staying on top of 11-5 CB. Has feel for CU with solid fade and tumble, though struggles in repeating FB delivery.

Lovelady,Richard — RP — Kansas City

EXP MLB DEBUT: 2018 | H/W: 6-0 175 | FUT: Setup reliever | 7C

Thrws L Age 22
2016 (10) Kennesaw St

91-96	FB	+++
79-84	SL	++
	CU	+

Year	Lev	Team	W	L	Sv	IP	K	ERA	WHIP	BF/G	OBA	H%	S%	xERA	Ctl	Dom	Cmd	hr/9	BPV
2016	NCAA	Kennesaw St	4	2	4	45	52	2.99	1.22	4.9	191	28	73	1.96	5.0	10.4	2.1	0.0	70
2016	Rk	Idaho Falls	0	1	6	14	16	1.90	1.20	4.4	200	29	82	2.02	4.4	10.1	2.3	0.0	81
2016	Rk	AZL Royals	2	0	3	10	14	1.78	0.59	4.3	123	22	67		1.8	12.5	7.0	0.0	194
2017	A+	Wilmington	1	0	7	33	41	1.09	0.66	5.5	162	26	82	0.24	1.1	11.1	10.3	0.0	189
2017	AA	NW Arkansas	3	2	3	33	36	2.18	1.24	6.4	231	32	83	2.76	3.5	9.8	2.8	0.3	99

Short RP who may not look part of big league pitcher, but thrives with lower arm slot, velocity, and plus control. Ball tough to pick up out of hand and hitters rarely elevate any pitch. Only allowed 1 HR in career. Very tough on LHH with sweeping SL and hard FB. Spots pitches well in zone, but has no change-of-pace pitch.

Lowther,Zac — SP — Baltimore

EXP MLB DEBUT: 2019 | H/W: 6-2 235 | FUT: #4 starter | 7D

Thrws L Age 21
2017 (S-2) Xavier

86-91	FB	+++
78-81	SL	++
	CU	++

Year	Lev	Team	W	L	Sv	IP	K	ERA	WHIP	BF/G	OBA	H%	S%	xERA	Ctl	Dom	Cmd	hr/9	BPV
2017	NCAA	Xavier	5	5	0	83	123	2.92	0.97	21.0	170	27	73	1.80	3.6	13.3	3.7	0.8	161
2017	A-	Aberdeen	2	2	0	54	75	1.66	0.85	16.5	187	30	80	1.12	1.8	12.5	6.8	0.2	193

Large-framed SP who is all about deception and difficult, low angle to plate. Stats suggest dominance, but he is more about hiding ball and fooling hitters. May not project to upper levels, but worth a shot. Gets late action on FB and mixes in slurvy SL and below average CU. All pitches play up due to delivery. Notches Ks and gets groundball outs.

Lucchesi,Joey — SP — San Diego

EXP MLB DEBUT: 2018 | H/W: 6-5 204 | FUT: #4 starter | 7B

Thrws L Age 24
2016 (4) SE Missouri St

90-93	FB	+++
77-80	CB	+++
78-81	CU	+++

Year	Lev	Team	W	L	Sv	IP	K	ERA	WHIP	BF/G	OBA	H%	S%	xERA	Ctl	Dom	Cmd	hr/9	BPV
2016	NCAA	SE Missouri St	10	5	1	111	149	2.19	1.20	26.2	235	36	83	2.81	3.0	12.1	4.0	0.4	154
2016	A-	Tri-City	0	2	1	40	53	1.35	0.73	10.1	193	31	79	0.73	0.5	11.9	26.5	0.0	221
2016	A	Fort Wayne	0	0	0	2	3	0.00	2.50	10.6	415	60	100	8.71	4.5	13.5	3.0	0.0	140
2017	A+	Lake Elsinore	6	4	0	78	95	2.53	0.96	21.1	203	27	80	2.41	2.2	10.9	5.0	1.0	156
2017	AA	San Antonio	5	3	1	60	53	1.80	1.00	22.9	213	27	84	2.12	2.1	7.9	3.8	0.4	104

Large-framed LH whose stuff translated well to AA. Can reach back for 95 mph and sit low-90s with heavy action on FB. Has feel for CB and will sink and cut CU depending on L/R; both should be average. Creates deception with funky delivery and misses bats despite lack of premium velocity. Throws plenty of quality strikes and keeps hitters guessing.

Luzardo,Jesus — SP — Oakland

EXP MLB DEBUT: 2021 | H/W: 6-1 205 | FUT: #2 starter | 9D

Thrws L Age 20
2016 (3) HS (FL)

91-96	FB	++++
78-80	CB	+++
82-85	SL	++
	CU	+++

Year	Lev	Team	W	L	Sv	IP	K	ERA	WHIP	BF/G	OBA	H%	S%	xERA	Ctl	Dom	Cmd	hr/9	BPV
2017	Rk	GCL Nationals	1	0	0	13	15	1.36	1.06	17.1	273	37	92	3.26	0.0	10.2		0.7	202
2017	Rk	AZL Athletics	0	1	0	11	13	1.61	0.89	10.4	222	33	80	1.51	0.8	10.4	13.0	0.0	184
2017	A-	Vermont	1	0	0	18	20	2.00	0.89	13.4	191	26	80	1.61	2.0	10.0	5.0	0.5	144

High-upside arm who missed all 2016 after Tommy John surgery but was dominant in pro debut. Throws from strong frame and has feel for throwing strikes. Has velocity and sink with plus FB and has ability to change speeds. With high K ability and premium control, could front rotation some day. Needs more innings to polish secondaries.

MacGregor, Travis — SP — Pittsburgh

EXP MLB DEBUT: 2020 | H/W: 6-3 180 | FUT: #4 starter | 7D

Thrws R Age 20
2016 (2) HS (FL)

88-92	FB	++++
	CB	+
	CU	++

Year	Lev	Team	W	L	Sv	IP	K	ERA	WHIP	BF/G	OBA	H%	S%	xERA	Ctl	Dom	Cmd	hr/9	BPV
2016	Rk	GCL Pirates	1	1	0	31	19	3.17	1.25	14.1	248	29	74	3.06	2.9	5.5	1.9	0.3	39
2017	Rk	Bristol	1	4	0	41	32	7.88	1.97	16.4	345	41	58	6.68	4.4	7.0	1.6	0.7	26

Lean projectable hurler struggled in rookie ball, walking 20 in 41.1 IP. Fastball sits at 88-92 mph, topping at 94 with room for more. Shows ability to spin a good 12-6 curve with good feel for his change-up. Good athlete with simple, repeatable mechanics.

Mark,Tyler — RP — Arizona

EXP MLB DEBUT: 2021 | H/W: 6-1 195 | FUT: Setup reliever | 7D

Thrws R Age 23
2015 (6) Concordia

93-96	FB	++++
83-84	SL	+++
	SP	++

Year	Lev	Team	W	L	Sv	IP	K	ERA	WHIP	BF/G	OBA	H%	S%	xERA	Ctl	Dom	Cmd	hr/9	BPV
2015	Rk	AZL Dbacks	1	0	0	4	5	4.50	1.75	6.1	307	44	71	4.85	4.5	11.3	2.5	0.0	99
2015	A-	Hillsboro	2	2	0	36	24	5.25	1.44	17.1	298	33	65	4.92	2.3	6.0	2.7	1.0	65
2016	A-	Hillsboro	5	5	0	78	75	3.92	1.31	21.5	264	33	72	3.99	2.7	8.6	3.3	0.9	102
2016	A	Kane County	0	5	0	24	25	8.18	1.94	16.5	333	43	56	6.46	4.8	9.3	1.9	0.7	55
2017	A	Kane County	5	3	3	64	54	3.79	1.23	6.7	233	28	70	3.19	3.4	7.6	2.3	0.7	63

Athletic RH with control of strike zone. FB is best pitch, living in the mid-90s with solid bore. Complementing the FB is a mid-80s SL, which has plus potential but is incredibly erratic. Has made strides learning split. Acting as his CU, the split generates grounders but not a swing-and-miss pitch at this time.

Maddox,Austin — RP — Boston

EXP MLB DEBUT: 2017 | H/W: 6-3 220 | FUT: Setup reliever | 6A

Thrws R Age 26
2012 (3) Florida

92-95	FB	+++
80-82	SL	+
83-86	CU	+++

Year	Lev	Team	W	L	Sv	IP	K	ERA	WHIP	BF/G	OBA	H%	S%	xERA	Ctl	Dom	Cmd	hr/9	BPV
2016	AA	Portland	2	3	0	38	38	4.01	1.18	6.6	212	27	67	2.79	3.8	9.0	2.4	0.7	77
2016	AAA	Pawtucket	1	0	0	4	2	2.14	1.19	5.6	252	23	100	4.73	2.1	4.3	2.0	2.1	37
2017	AA	Portland	0	1	2	13	8	1.37	1.07	5.1	196	24	86	1.69	3.4	5.5	1.6	0.0	24
2017	AAA	Pawtucket	2	2	6	36	38	3.50	1.19	5.4	178	24	71	2.24	5.3	9.5	1.8	0.5	47
2017	MLB	Boston	0	0	0	17	14	0.53	0.88	4.9	212	26	100	1.88	1.1	7.4	7.0	0.5	122

Big-framed RP who reached majors and surprised with vastly improved control and command. Has upped K rate in each of last two seasons and is tough to hit hard. FB has added a few ticks and now grades as solid-average. Not much ability with breaking ball while CU is best secondary by far. Features nasty, late action, but doesn't command well.

Mader,Michael — RP — Atlanta

EXP MLB DEBUT: 2018 | H/W: 6-2 205 | FUT: Middle reliever | 7C

Thrws L Age 24
2014 (S-3) Chipola JC

92-95	FB	++++
76-79	CB	++
84-85	CU	+++

Year	Lev	Team	W	L	Sv	IP	K	ERA	WHIP	BF/G	OBA	H%	S%	xERA	Ctl	Dom	Cmd	hr/9	BPV
2014	A-	Batavia	1	0	0	45	28	2.00	1.04	14.5	196	22	84	2.20	3.2	5.6	1.8	0.6	32
2015	A	Greensboro	6	12	0	140	86	4.75	1.41	22.0	263	30	65	3.89	3.7	5.5	1.5	0.5	19
2016	A+	Jupiter	7	6	0	103	81	3.50	1.27	19.2	250	31	72	3.28	3.0	7.1	2.4	0.4	65
2016	AA	Mississippi	0	3	0	30	26	2.40	1.10	23.5	242	32	76	2.31	1.8	7.8	4.3	0.0	110
2017	AA	Mississippi	5	5	4	64	57	4.21	1.53	8.0	239	30	73	4.01	5.7	8.0	1.4	0.7	7

Former starter converted to reliever in 2017 with mixed results. Touched 90 as starter, up to 96 mph with max effort out of pen. FB was uncontrollable, primary factor for increase in Ctl and decrease Cmd Relied on CB as main secondary out of pen. Tightened up some from 2016 but still lacked consistent depth. CU most effective pitch as starter.

Maese,Justin — SP — Toronto

EXP MLB DEBUT: 2020 | H/W: 6-3 190 | FUT: #4 starter | 7B

Thrws R Age 21
2015 (3) HS (TX)

90-94	FB	++++
83-87	SL	+++
81-82	CU	++

Year	Lev	Team	W	L	Sv	IP	K	ERA	WHIP	BF/G	OBA	H%	S%	xERA	Ctl	Dom	Cmd	hr/9	BPV
2015	Rk	GCL Blue Jays	5	0	0	35	19	1.02	1.08	17.2	244	29	89	2.32	1.5	4.9	3.2	0.0	64
2016	A-	Vancouver	2	2	0	26	20	2.07	0.80	18.9	214	26	75	1.55	0.3	6.9	20.0	0.3	133
2016	A	Lansing	2	4	0	56	44	3.37	1.30	23.1	272	33	73	3.53	2.2	7.1	3.1	0.3	84
2017	Rk	GCL Blue Jays	0	0	0	9	9	5.00	1.56	13.1	339	42	69	5.84	1.0	9.0	9.0	1.0	153
2017	A	Lansing	5	3	0	70	60	4.87	1.48	25.2	283	35	65	4.20	3.3	7.7	2.3	0.4	66

Efficient, athletic SP who repeated Low-A, though missed most of 2nd half due to shoulder. More command and control oriented, but can induce weak contact with sinking, lively FB. Very high groundball rate by keeping ball down and FB tough to elevate. Introduced hard SL and has plus potential. CU needs work, but not afraid to use it.

Mahle,Tyler — SP — Cincinnati

EXP MLB DEBUT: 2017 | H/W: 6-3 210 | FUT: #3 starter | 8B

Thrws R Age 23
2013 (7) HS (CA)

91-94	FB	++++
74-76	CB	+++
82-85	SL	+++
83-85	CU	+++

Year	Lev	Team	W	L	Sv	IP	K	ERA	WHIP	BF/G	OBA	H%	S%	xERA	Ctl	Dom	Cmd	hr/9	BPV
2016	A+	Daytona	8	3	0	79		2.50	0.95	22.9	206	26	77	2.12	1.9	8.6	4.5	0.7	121
2016	AA	Pensacola	6	3	0	71	65	4.94	1.38	21.3	280	33	69	4.96	2.5	8.2	3.3	1.5	98
2017	AA	Pensacola	7	3	0	85	87	1.59	0.87	22.4	192	25	86	1.61	1.8	9.2	5.1	0.5	135
2017	AAA	Louisville	3	4	0	59	51	2.74	1.10	23.2	238	29	77	2.83	2.0	7.8	3.9	0.6	104
2017	MLB	Cincinnati	1	2	0	20	14	2.70	1.50	21.6	252	31	80	3.47	5.0	6.3	1.3	0.0	-2

Command-and-control RH had breakout 2017 and made MLB debut. Mixes four pitches. Best pitch is 2-seam FB with solid arm-side run and sink. Works to all quadrants of zone. SL and CU primary secondary offerings, both project as above-average offerings. Lacks confidence in CB; still an average pitch; especially adept at changing eye levels.

Manning,Matt — SP — Detroit

EXP MLB DEBUT: 2020 | H/W: 6-6 190 | FUT: #1 starter | 9D

Thrws R Age 20
2016 (1) HS (CA)

88-95	FB	++++
79-83	CB	+++
83-85	CU	++

Year	Lev	Team	W	L	Sv	IP	K	ERA	WHIP	BF/G	OBA	H%	S%	xERA	Ctl	Dom	Cmd	hr/9	BPV
2016	Rk	GCL Tigers	0	2	0	29	46	4.02	1.17	11.6	248	41	66	3.08	2.2	14.2	6.6	0.6	216
2017	A-	Connecticut	2	2	0	33	36	1.90	1.24	14.9	224	32	83	2.42	3.8	9.8	2.6	0.0	91
2017	A	West Michigan	2	0	0	17	26	5.76	1.45	14.7	224	38	56	2.92	5.8	13.6	2.4	0.0	107

Long, athletic SP who began year in extended spring training. Very long arms, but has quality extension. Peppers zone with lively FB and mixes in CB as out pitch. Delivery can be inconsistent and has tendency to slow arm on CU. Has significant upside predicated on plus athleticism and easy velocity. Should have three plus pitches at maturity.

Maples, Dillon — RP — Chicago (N)

EXP MLB DEBUT: 2017 | H/W: 6-2 225 | FUT: Setup reliever | 8C

Thrws R Age 25
2011 (14) HS (NC)

95-100	FB	+++++
85-88	SL	++++
75-78	CB	+++

Year	Lev	Team	W	L	Sv	IP	K	ERA	WHIP	BF/G	OBA	H%	S%	xERA	Ctl	Dom	Cmd	hr/9	BPV
2016	A+	Myrtle Beach	0	1	0	7	6	7.71	2.29	4.0	313	40	63	6.33	9.0	7.7	0.9	0.0	-86
2017	A+	Myrtle Beach	4	0	3	31	44	2.03	1.16	5.9	193	30	85	2.36	4.3	12.7	2.9	0.6	130
2017	AA	Tennessee	1	1	6	13	28	3.41	1.67	4.2	228	54	77	3.45	7.5	19.1	2.5	0.0	159
2017	AAA	Iowa	1	2	4	18	28	1.99	1.27	4.4	190	32	86	2.52	5.5	13.9	2.5	0.5	121
2017	MLB	Chi Cubs	0	0	0	5	11	10.59	2.35	4.4	294	64	50	6.09	10.6	19.4	1.8	0.0	82

Reliever comes after hitters with a plus 95-98 mph FB that tops at 100 mph with good run and sink. Mixes in a plus high-80 SL and a usable 12-6 CB. Whiffed a career best 14.2/9 while posting a 2.27 ERA in 63.1 IP across three levels. Has the stuff to close if given the chance.

Marinan, James — SP — Los Angeles (N)

EXP MLB DEBUT: 2022 | H/W: 6-5 220 | FUT: #3 starter | 8D

Thrws R Age 19
2017 (4) HS (FL)

92-96	FB	++++
	CB	+++
	CU	++

Year	Lev	Team	W	L	Sv	IP	K	ERA	WHIP	BF/G	OBA	H%	S%	xERA	Ctl	Dom	Cmd	hr/9	BPV
2017	Rk	AZL Dodgers	2	0	0	17	14	1.59	1.65	8.4	226	29	89	3.49	7.4	7.4	1.0	0.0	-49

Tall, projectable two-way player signed for over-slot at $822,000. Plus mid-90s fastball tops at 96 mph with good tilt and sink. Mixes in a slurvy curveball and below-average change-up. Raw on the mound, but has clean and repeatable mechanics. Struggled with control in pro debut, but limited damage and induced weak contact.

Martin,Brett — SP — Texas

EXP MLB DEBUT: 2019 | H/W: 6-4 190 | FUT: #3 starter | 8E

Thrws L Age 22
2014 (4) Walters St CC

90-94	FB	+++
78-82	CB	+++
86-88	CT	++
84-87	CU	+

Year	Lev	Team	W	L	Sv	IP	K	ERA	WHIP	BF/G	OBA	H%	S%	xERA	Ctl	Dom	Cmd	hr/9	BPV
2015	A	Hickory	5	6	0	95	72	3.50	1.24	19.3	255	30	72	3.39	2.5	6.8	2.8	0.6	74
2016	Rk	AZL Rangers	0	0	0	2	6	4.29	1.43	4.5	336	103	67	4.37	0.0	25.7		0.0	481
2016	A	Hickory	2	3	0	43	48	4.58	1.67	21.5	323	43	72	5.48	2.9	10.0	3.4	0.6	119
2016	A+	High Desert	2	1	0	23	16	4.29	1.34	16.0	269	30	71	4.41	2.7	6.2	2.3	1.2	57
2017	A+	Down East	4	8	0	84	90	4.71	1.53	22.9	284	37	70	4.67	3.7	9.6	2.6	0.7	90

Physical SP who missed time early with back injury and was horrendous upon return. Upped K rate with improved CB leading way. Has controlled delivery, but walk rate regressed. Usually throws with good command with average velocity. Injury history a concern for durability. FB and CB are two solid offerings, but not much effectiveness from CT and CU.

Martin,Corbin — SP — Houston

EXP MLB DEBUT: 2019 | H/W: 6-2 200 | FUT: Closer | 8D

Thrws R Age 22
2017 (2) Texas A&M

92-95	FB	++++
79-82	CB	++++
84-86	SL	+++
	CU	++

Year	Lev	Team	W	L	Sv	IP	K	ERA	WHIP	BF/G	OBA	H%	S%	xERA	Ctl	Dom	Cmd	hr/9	BPV
2017	NCAA	Texas A&M	7	4	0	87	95	3.82	1.46	15.5	266	36	74	4.00	3.9	9.8	2.5	0.5	89
2017	Rk	GCL Astros	0	0	0	5	5	0.00	0.20	7.6	0	0	100		1.8	9.0	5.0	0.0	131
2017	A-	Tri City	0	1	1	27	38	2.65	1.03	13.1	207	33	74	1.96	2.6	12.6	4.8	0.3	173

2nd rd pick who was strikeout machine at Texas A&M and impressed in summer Cape Cod league. Good athlete with short, quick arm action that produces good run on FB. Quality feel for spin on power CB, which could evolve as a real weapon; CU remains raw. More control than command at this point. FB-CB combo makes him candidate for late-inning work.

Martinez,Luis — SP — Chicago (A)

EXP MLB DEBUT: 2020 | H/W: 6-6 190 | FUT: Middle reliever | 6C

Thrws R Age 23
2011 FA (VZ)

90-93	FB	+++
82-84	SL	++
84-87	CU	+++

Year	Lev	Team	W	L	Sv	IP	K	ERA	WHIP	BF/G	OBA	H%	S%	xERA	Ctl	Dom	Cmd	hr/9	BPV
2014	Rk	AZL White Sox	3	2	0	33	40	4.09	1.42	20.0	250	35	73	3.97	4.4	10.9	2.5	0.8	97
2015	A	Kannapolis	4	14	0	108	69	5.41	1.43	19.2	251	28	61	3.91	4.4	5.7	1.3	0.7	2
2016	A	Kannapolis	8	9	0	137	141	3.81	1.29	20.1	246	32	71	3.39	3.4	9.3	2.8	0.6	94
2017	A	Kannapolis	8	2	0	79	85	3.19	1.18	22.6	236	33	71	2.63	2.7	9.7	3.5	0.2	118
2017	A+	Winston-Salem	0	2	0	16	8	9.00	2.19	16.0	357	39	56	7.37	5.6	4.5	0.8	0.6	-53

Long, lean RH who spent his third season in Single-A. Uses size to create downward plane. Lives down in zone with 2-seam FB w/ natural bore. CU has taken step forward in development, increasing fade and lining up with FB delivery. SL is marginal, breaking on only horizontal axis.

Martinez,Nolan — SP — New York (A)

EXP MLB DEBUT: 2021 | H/W: 6-2 165 | FUT: #3 starter | 8E

Thrws R Age 19
2016 (3) HS (CA)

87-93	FB	+++
77-79	CB	+++
	CU	++

Year	Lev	Team	W	L	Sv	IP	K	ERA	WHIP	BF/G	OBA	H%	S%	xERA	Ctl	Dom	Cmd	hr/9	BPV
2017	Rk	Pulaski	0	0	0	4	2	0.00	0.50	13.3	151	18	100		0.0	4.5		0.0	99
2017	Rk	GCL Yankees	0	0	0	9	12	0.98	0.98	7.0	188	30	89	1.31	2.9	11.7	4.0	0.0	150

Young, lean SP who hasn't seen much action due to sore shoulder. Very projectable and athletic frame should lead to more velocity down road. Repeats clean delivery and enhances CB that should become plus. FB exhibits ton of movement, but needs more strength to sustain velocity deep into games. Very exciting road, but has to stay healthy.

Martinez,Rodolfo — RP — San Francisco

EXP MLB DEBUT: 2018 | H/W: 6-2 180 | FUT: Closer | 7C

Thrws R Age 24
2013 FA (DR)

95-99	FB	++++
85-87	SL	++
85-86	CU	+

Year	Lev	Team	W	L	Sv	IP	K	ERA	WHIP	BF/G	OBA	H%	S%	xERA	Ctl	Dom	Cmd	hr/9	BPV
2016	A+	San Jose	1	1	21	30	33	0.89	1.09	3.7	213	30	94	2.19	3.0	9.8	3.3	0.3	115
2016	AA	Richmond	0	3	3	23	17	6.65	1.91	4.4	309	37	63	5.70	5.9	6.7	1.1	0.4	-21
2017	Rk	AZL Giants	0	0	0	2	2	0.00	1.00	3.8	262	35	100	2.32	0.0	9.0		0.0	180
2017	A+	San Jose	2	0	0	13	12	4.12	1.15	5.2	275	32	69	4.16	0.7	8.2	12.0	1.4	148
2017	AA	Richmond	0	0	0	8	5	5.63	2.13	4.9	347	41	71	6.51	5.6	5.6	1.0	0.0	-33

Intimidating, aggressive RP who missed most of season due to oblique and shoulder maladies. Owns double-plus FB when healthy and generates plus velocity with ease. Can cut FB at times for different look, though has tendency to overthrow and rely on it too often. Both secondaries are below average and telegraphs SL.

Mata,Bryan

SP | **Boston** | **EXP MLB DEBUT:** 2020 | **H/W:** 6-3 160 | **FUT:** #3 starter | **8D**

Thrws R Age 18
2016 FA (VZ)

Velo	Pitch	Grade
89-93	FB	+++
78-80	CB	++
83-85	CU	++

Year	Lev	Team	W	L	Sv	IP	K	ERA	WHIP	BF/G	OBA	H%	S%	xERA	Ctl	Dom	Cmd	hr/9	BPV
2017	A	Greenville	5	6	0	77	74	3.74	1.31	18.7	257	33	70	3.36	3.0	8.6	2.8	0.4	92

Advanced, lean SP who is putting himself on map with quick arm and quality stuff. Nothing overpowering or plus at moment, but flashes three potential above average pitches. Induces ton of groundballs and rarely allows HR. Quick arm adds pitch movement to solid FB from downward angle. Has lot of work to do to stick as SP, but off to good start.

Matuella,Michael

SP | **Texas** | **EXP MLB DEBUT:** 2019 | **H/W:** 6-6 220 | **FUT:** #2 starter | **9E**

Thrws R Age 23
2015 (3) Duke

Velo	Pitch	Grade
93-97	FB	++++
80-82	CB	+++
84-85	SL	+++
83-86	CU	++

Year	Lev	Team	W	L	Sv	IP	K	ERA	WHIP	BF/G	OBA	H%	S%	xERA	Ctl	Dom	Cmd	hr/9	BPV
2015	*Did not pitch; injured*																		
2016	A-	Spokane	0	0	0	3	1	0.00	1.00	11.5	106	12	100	0.61	6.0	3.0	0.5	0.0	-90
2017	A	Hickory	4	6	0	75	60	4.20	1.48	15.4	294	35	72	4.68	2.8	7.2	2.6	0.7	73

Very tall SP with Tommy John injury history and little time on mound. Started to stretch outings out in August and exhibited electric stuff when on. Could be frontline SP with devastating pitch movement. Features plus FB with late life and uses two power breaking balls to keep hitters off guard. Durability is major concern.

May, Dustin

SP | **Los Angeles (N)** | **EXP MLB DEBUT:** 2020 | **H/W:** 6-6 180 | **FUT:** #2 starter | **9D**

Thrws R Age 20
2016 (3) HS (TX)

Velo	Pitch	Grade
91-94	FB	++++
80-82	SL	+++
	CU	++

Year	Lev	Team	W	L	Sv	IP	K	ERA	WHIP	BF/G	OBA	H%	S%	xERA	Ctl	Dom	Cmd	hr/9	BPV
2016	Rk	AZL Dodgers	0	1	1	30	34	3.89	1.36	12.6	304	42	68	3.82	1.2	10.2	8.5	0.0	169
2017	A	Great Lakes	9	6	0	123	113	3.88	1.20	21.5	259	33	68	3.32	1.9	8.3	4.3	0.6	115
2017	A+	Rancho Cuca	0	0	0	11	15	0.82	0.64	19.0	162	27	86	0.16	0.8	12.3	15.0	0.0	217

Tall, projectable high schooler with FB velocity at 91-94 mph with potentially more on the way. Low-80s SL projects as above-average, but he currently lacks third offering. Should add more bulk as he matures, and plus command gives him a chance of being a top-end starter.

Mazza,Domenic

SP | **San Francisco** | **EXP MLB DEBUT:** 2019 | **H/W:** 6-1 195 | **FUT:** #5 SP/swingman | **6B**

Thrws L Age 23
2015 (22) UC-Santa Barbara

Velo	Pitch	Grade
85-89	FB	++
74-77	CB	+++
80-81	SL	++
81-84	CU	+++

Year	Lev	Team	W	L	Sv	IP	K	ERA	WHIP	BF/G	OBA	H%	S%	xERA	Ctl	Dom	Cmd	hr/9	BPV
2015	A-	Salem-Kaizer	0	0	0	4	4	0.00	0.24	6.3	80	12	100		0.0	8.8		0.0	176
2016	A	Augusta	8	3	0	84	79	3.95	1.35	25.1	292	37	71	4.25	1.7	8.4	4.9	0.6	124
2017	A	Augusta	7	9	0	119	97	3.02	1.08	24.5	245	31	71	2.60	1.5	7.3	4.9	0.3	109
2017	A+	San Jose	0	2	0	11	4	8.04	1.88	26.3	363	38	55	6.95	2.4	3.2	1.3	0.8	11

Soft-tossing LHP who threw perfect game in April. Spent much of last 2 seasons in Low-A and relies on groundballs and pitch location. Rarely beats himself and keeps hitters off balance with variety of offerings. Keeps ball low in zone and doesn't allow many flyballs or HR. Command is essential for promotion as K rate likely to flounder.

McCreery,Adam

RP | **Atlanta** | **EXP MLB DEBUT:** 2019 | **H/W:** 6-8 195 | **FUT:** Middle reliever | **7C**

Thrws L Age 25
2014 (22) Azusa Pacific

Velo	Pitch	Grade
93-96	FB	++++
82-84	SL	+++

Year	Lev	Team	W	L	Sv	IP	K	ERA	WHIP	BF/G	OBA	H%	S%	xERA	Ctl	Dom	Cmd	hr/9	BPV
2015	Rk	AZL Angels	0	0	0	18	28	2.47	1.32	4.7	163	30	79	1.87	6.9	13.8	2.0	0.0	80
2016	Rk	Danville	2	0	0	18	19	3.96	1.15	6.6	226	32	62	2.23	3.0	9.4	3.2	0.0	107
2016	A	Rome	0	3	0	15	14	4.74	1.64	6.2	296	38	68	4.44	4.1	8.3	2.0	0.0	55
2017	A	Rome	2	0	2	31	47	2.88	1.31	6.4	228	39	76	2.62	4.3	13.6	3.1	0.0	145
2017	A+	Florida	1	1	5	30	43	2.68	1.46	7.2	198	32	81	2.90	6.9	12.8	1.9	0.3	64

Enormous lefthander who fills out a uniform. Struggles repeating mechanics and maintaining command. Uses size to create depth on pitches, but strictly FB/SL. FB is 2-seam variety w/ some arm-side run. SL is slurvy, sometimes acting like a hard CB. Will need to tighten up spin and find more break to be successful out of pen.

McKenzie,Triston

SP | **Cleveland** | **EXP MLB DEBUT:** 2019 | **H/W:** 6-5 165 | **FUT:** #3 starter | **8B**

Thrws R Age 20
2015 (S-1) HS (FL)

Velo	Pitch	Grade
91-94	FB	++++
78-82	CB	+++
	CU	++

Year	Lev	Team	W	L	Sv	IP	K	ERA	WHIP	BF/G	OBA	H%	S%	xERA	Ctl	Dom	Cmd	hr/9	BPV
2015	Rk	AZL Indians	1	1	0	12	17	0.75	0.58	10.2	106	19	86		2.3	12.8	5.7	0.0	187
2016	A-	Mahoning Val	4	3	0	49	55	0.55	0.96	20.6	183	26	98	1.56	2.9	10.1	3.4	0.4	120
2016	A	Lake County	2	2	0	34	49	3.18	0.97	21.5	220	35	68	2.15	1.6	13.0	8.2	0.5	209
2017	A+	Lynchburg	12	6	0	143	186	3.46	1.05	22.1	207	30	70	2.53	2.8	11.7	4.1	0.9	152

Lean SP who was young for level, yet finished 2nd in minors in K and 3rd in CAR in ERA. Very stingy to hit based upon pitch mix, touch, and angle to plate. Needs to add strength to pitch deeper into games. Shows above average control for age and misses bats with both FB and sharp CB. Emerging CU could improve to average status in near-term.

Means,John

SP | **Baltimore** | **EXP MLB DEBUT:** 2018 | **H/W:** 6-3 230 | **FUT:** #4 starter | **7D**

Thrws L Age 24
2014 (11) West Virginia

Velo	Pitch	Grade
88-92	FB	+++
77-79	CB	+++
79-84	CU	++

Year	Lev	Team	W	L	Sv	IP	K	ERA	WHIP	BF/G	OBA	H%	S%	xERA	Ctl	Dom	Cmd	hr/9	BPV
2015	A	Delmarva	9	8	0	118	89	3.51	1.37	21.5	290	34	76	4.39	2.0	6.8	3.4	0.8	87
2015	A+	Frederick	0	3	0	19	10	6.56	1.67	21.5	289	31	60	5.31	4.7	4.7	1.0	0.9	-24
2016	A+	Frederick	5	0	0	50	54	1.80	1.06	21.6	234	33	83	2.26	1.8	9.7	5.4	0.2	144
2016	AA	Bowie	4	8	0	96	51	4.69	1.44	22.7	294	33	67	4.55	2.3	4.8	2.0	0.7	41
2017	AA	Bowie	9	9	0	142	124	4.12	1.37	22.9	283	34	72	4.50	2.3	7.9	3.4	1.0	98

Durable, tall SP who essentially repeated AA and finished 2nd in EL in K. Can be around plate too much and get hit hard. K rate increased slightly and uses height to throw on downward plane. Gets lot of groundballs with all pitches, especially FB. Nice arm action on CB with fast arm and will mix in CU that flashes average.

Medeiros,Kodi

SP | **Milwaukee** | **EXP MLB DEBUT:** 2019 | **H/W:** 6-2 180 | **FUT:** Closer | **8D**

Thrws L Age 21
2014 (1) HS (HI)

Velo	Pitch	Grade
93-95	FB	++++
79-82	SL	++++
82-85	CU	++

Year	Lev	Team	W	L	Sv	IP	K	ERA	WHIP	BF/G	OBA	H%	S%	xERA	Ctl	Dom	Cmd	hr/9	BPV
2014	Rk	AZL Brewers	0	2	1	17	26	7.33	2.15	9.5	331	49	66	7.20	6.8	13.6	2.0	1.0	79
2015	A	Wisconsin	4	5	1	93	94	4.45	1.28	15.3	231	32	61	2.61	3.9	9.1	2.4	0.0	77
2016	A+	Brevard County	4	12	0	85	64	5.93	1.94	17.6	299	36	68	5.64	6.7	6.8	1.0	0.4	-40
2017	A+	Carolina	8	9	1	128	121	4.99	1.31	19.6	241	31	60	3.30	3.7	8.5	2.3	0.5	70

Hard-throwing LH continues to struggle with Ctl since modification in delivery. Dropped arm-angle to low 3/4s to make FB/SL combo more effective, now misses away from RHH a lot. FB is heavy with late break. SL has two-plane break, will sweep from time to time. Has feel for CU, but not consistently.

Medina,Adonis

SP | **Philadelphia** | **EXP MLB DEBUT:** 2020 | **H/W:** 6-1 185 | **FUT:** #3 starter | **9C**

Thrws R Age 21
2014 FA (DR)

Velo	Pitch	Grade
93-95	FB	++++
80-81	SL	++++
86-87	CU	++
75-77	CB	++

Year	Lev	Team	W	L	Sv	IP	K	ERA	WHIP	BF/G	OBA	H%	S%	xERA	Ctl	Dom	Cmd	hr/9	BPV
2015	Rk	GCL Phillies	3	2	0	45	35	2.99	1.20	18.1	248	31	74	2.84	2.4	7.0	2.9	0.2	79
2016	A-	Williamsport	5	3	0	64	34	2.94	1.11	19.4	206	22	76	2.57	3.4	4.8	1.4	0.7	13
2017	A	Lakewood	4	9	0	119	133	3.02	1.19	21.7	235	32	76	2.92	2.9	10.0	3.4	0.5	119

Strikeout rate rose, as did nearly all parts of his arsenal. FB now sits 93-95 with heavy arm-side run. Hard SL with big break became an out pitch, and showed great arm speed on his CU that got both swings and misses and weak contact. With excellent control and outstanding athleticism, he has a solid foundation.

Medina,Luis

SP | **New York (A)** | **EXP MLB DEBUT:** 2022 | **H/W:** 6-1 175 | **FUT:** #2 starter | **9E**

Thrws R Age 18
2015 FA (DR)

Velo	Pitch	Grade
95-99	FB	++++
81-83	CB	+++
	CU	+

Year	Lev	Team	W	L	Sv	IP	K	ERA	WHIP	BF/G	OBA	H%	S%	xERA	Ctl	Dom	Cmd	hr/9	BPV
2017	Rk	Pulaski	1	1	0	23	22	5.09	1.22	15.5	178	23	56	2.20	5.5	8.6	1.6	0.4	25

High-upside arm who is more thrower than pitcher. At peak, could have premium velocity with double-plus FB that exhibits cutting action. Can be straight and hittable and erratic mechanics hinder command. Pops with big-breaking CB, but has trouble throwing for strikes. High K guy who also keeps ball on ground. Lot to dream on with long road ahead.

Meisner,Casey

SP | **Oakland** | **EXP MLB DEBUT:** 2018 | **H/W:** 6-7 190 | **FUT:** #4 starter | **7E**

Thrws R Age 22
2013 (3) HS (TX)

Velo	Pitch	Grade
90-94	FB	+++
78-81	CB	++
83-85	CU	+++

Year	Lev	Team	W	L	Sv	IP	K	ERA	WHIP	BF/G	OBA	H%	S%	xERA	Ctl	Dom	Cmd	hr/9	BPV
2015	A+	Stockton	3	1	0	32	24	2.80	1.06	17.8	230	28	73	2.33	2.0	6.7	3.4	0.3	86
2015	A+	St. Lucie	3	2	0	35	23	2.83	1.40	24.6	262	29	84	4.32	3.6	5.9	1.6	1.0	27
2016	A+	Stockton	1	14	1	117	100	4.85	1.58	18.4	276	33	71	4.86	4.5	7.7	1.7	0.9	34
2017	A+	Stockton	6	5	0	74	80	4.00	1.25	18.9	259	33	71	3.93	2.4	9.7	4.0	1.1	127
2017	AA	Midland	4	4	0	59	37	4.12	1.39	20.7	248	28	71	3.72	4.1	5.6	1.4	0.6	8

Tall, lean SP who gets off to slow starts, but rebounds for overall decent performance. Despite height, throws from lower arm slot. Velocity becoming more consistent as he has firmed up delivery. Has tendency to keep balls up in zone. FB is best pitch, though CU can be very tough to hitters from both sides. Has to improve CB to have chance.

Mekkes, Dakota

RP | **Chicago (N)** | EXP MLB DEBUT: 2019 | H/W: 6-7 252 | FUT: Setup reliever | **7C**

Thrws R Age 23
2016 (10) Michigan St

Velo	Pitch	Grade
90-93	FB	++++
79-84	SL	++
78-80	CU	++

Year	Lev	Team	W	L	Sv	IP	K	ERA	WHIP	BF/G	OBA	H%	S%	xERA	Ctl	Dom	Cmd	hr/9	BPV
2016	NCAA	Michigan St	3	2	7	57	96	1.74	1.18	8.1	139	29	84	1.25	6.5	15.2	2.3	0.0	116
2016	Rk	AZL Cubs	0	0	0	3	6	0.00	0.33	4.7	106	29	100		0.0	18.0		0.0	342
2016	A-	Eugene	1	1	0	17	21	2.12	0.88	7.0	187	27	79	1.56	2.1	11.1	5.3	0.5	161
2017	A	South Bend	3	0	4	31	47	0.58	0.90	6.4	138	24	96	0.84	4.1	13.6	3.4	0.3	154
2017	A+	Myrtle Beach	5	2	3	42	45	1.28	1.07	6.8	174	25	87	1.40	4.3	9.6	2.3	0.0	76

Late blooming reliever continues to dominate. Uses his huge frame to pitch downhill. FB sits at 90-93 but he hides it well and it explodes on hitters from a low 3/4 arm slot. SL and CU are average offerings, but the FB is the main weapon. Career numbers: 1.16 ERA, 0.95 WHIP.

Mella,Keury

SP | **Cincinnati** | EXP MLB DEBUT: 2017 | H/W: 6-2 200 | FUT: #3 starter | **8E**

Thrws R Age 24
2011 FA (DR)

Velo	Pitch	Grade
93-97	FB	++++
81-83	SL	++++
84-86	CU	+++

Year	Lev	Team	W	L	Sv	IP	K	ERA	WHIP	BF/G	OBA	H%	S%	xERA	Ctl	Dom	Cmd	hr/9	BPV
2015	A+	Daytona	3	1	0	21	23	2.99	1.23	21.4	156	20	79	2.42	6.4	9.8	1.5	0.9	22
2016	A+	Daytona	8	9	0	131	95	3.91	1.57	23.0	288	34	75	4.61	3.8	6.5	1.7	0.5	32
2016	AAA	Louisville	1	0	0	7	6	1.29	0.57	23.7	132	13	100	0.94	1.3	7.7	6.0	1.3	122
2017	AA	Pensacola	4	10	1	134	109	4.30	1.33	20.6	263	31	70	4.06	2.9	7.3	2.5	0.9	72
2017	MLB	Cincinnati	0	0	0	4	1	6.75	1.75	9.1	307	28	67	7.05	4.5	2.3	0.5	2.3	-63

Strong, hard-throwing RH took step forward cleaning up delivery. Improved control a benefit of change. 2-seam FB sits mid-90s with solid, late arm-side bore. Change in mechanics altered his SL, which now has significant two-plane break. CU is a solid, underused pitch. Control may push him into the pen.

Mendez,Yohander

SP | **Texas** | EXP MLB DEBUT: 2016 | H/W: 6-5 200 | FUT: #3 starter | **8C**

Thrws L Age 23
2011 FA (VZ)

Velo	Pitch	Grade
88-94	FB	+++
80-82	SL	++
82-84	CB	++
82-84	CU	++++

Year	Lev	Team	W	L	Sv	IP	K	ERA	WHIP	BF/G	OBA	H%	S%	xERA	Ctl	Dom	Cmd	hr/9	BPV
2016	AA	Frisco	4	1	0	46		3.12	1.15	18.3	230	31	73	2.64	2.7	9.0	3.3	0.4	106
2016	AAA	Round Rock	4	1	0	31	22	0.58	0.90	16.5	120	15	93	0.46	4.6	6.4	1.4	0.0	8
2016	MLB	Texas	0	0	0	3	0	18.00	2.33	7.7	371	37	14	7.54	6.0	0.0	0.0	0.0	-144
2017	AA	Frisco	7	8	0	137	124	3.80	1.14	22.7	228	26	74	3.66	2.8	8.1	2.9	1.5	88
2017	MLB	Texas	0	1	0	12	7	5.21	1.32	7.2	276	27	69	5.46	2.2	5.2	2.3	2.2	51

Tall, loose-armed SP who returned to AA and posted career high in IP. Tough to hit due to quality stuff, highlighted by plus CU. Good separation between FB and CU which allows FB to play up. Improving SL has chance to be solid-average and may eventually shelve CB. Already sequences well.

Mercado,Michael

SP | **Tampa Bay** | EXP MLB DEBUT: 2022 | H/W: 6-4 160 | FUT: #2 starter | **9E**

Thrws R Age 18
2017 (2) HS (CA)

Velo	Pitch	Grade
89-92	FB	+++
75-79	CB	+++
84-85	CT	+++
	CU	++

Year	Lev	Team	W	L	Sv	IP	K	ERA	WHIP	BF/G	OBA	H%	S%	xERA	Ctl	Dom	Cmd	hr/9	BPV
2017	Rk	GCL Rays	0	0	0	21	14	1.71	1.18	10.6	261	31	88	3.20	1.7	6.0	3.5	0.4	79

Lean, projectable SP who needs time to add strength to frame. Has potential to add significant velocity to already-solid CB. Advanced feel for pitching enhanced by ability to throw strikes with four pitches. CB could become plus pitch while has ability to cut FB. Generates lot of pitch movement, including CU that is distant fourth pitch.

Merritt,Ryan

SP | **Cleveland** | EXP MLB DEBUT: 2016 | H/W: 6-0 180 | FUT: #5 SP/swingman | **6A**

Thrws L Age 26
2011 (16) McLennan CC

Velo	Pitch	Grade
85-88	FB	+++
74-75	CB	++
79-82	SL	+
81-84	CU	+++

Year	Lev	Team	W	L	Sv	IP	K	ERA	WHIP	BF/G	OBA	H%	S%	xERA	Ctl	Dom	Cmd	hr/9	BPV
2016	AAA	Columbus	11	8	0	143	92	3.71	1.25	24.3	279	31	73	4.11	1.4	5.8	4.0	0.9	83
2016	MLB	Cleveland	1	0	0	11	6	1.64	0.55	9.3	162	19	67	0.00	0.0	4.9		0.0	106
2017	A	Lake County	1	0	0	7	4	2.57	1.14	27.7	262	31	75	2.71	1.3	5.1	4.0	0.0	76
2017	AAA	Columbus	10	5	0	116	85	3.03	1.22	24.6	262	29	84	4.27	1.9	6.6	3.4	1.5	84
2017	MLB	Cleveland	2	0	0	20	7	1.78	1.49	17.4	313	34	87	4.36	1.8	3.1	1.8	0.0	26

Short, lean SP who relies more on command than natural stuff. Changes speeds adeptly and repeats delivery and arm action to provide semblance of deception. Far from K guy and isn't dominant. Plus-plus control is best attribute and knows how to set hitters up. Has very little margin for error, but has value in sinker and pitch sequencing.

Merryweather,Julian

SP | **Cleveland** | EXP MLB DEBUT: 2018 | H/W: 6-4 200 | FUT: #4 starter | **7C**

Thrws R Age 26
2014 (5) Oklahoma Baptist

Velo	Pitch	Grade
91-95	FB	+++
79-83	CB	++
	CU	++

Year	Lev	Team	W	L	Sv	IP	K	ERA	WHIP	BF/G	OBA	H%	S%	xERA	Ctl	Dom	Cmd	hr/9	BPV
2015	A	Lake County	2	3	1	70	69	4.10	1.44	14.2	310	39	73	4.86	1.5	8.8	5.8	0.8	136
2016	A+	Lynchburg	8	2	0	61	58	1.03	1.02	21.3	215	27	95	2.31	2.2	8.6	3.9	0.6	112
2016	AA	Akron	5	4	0	74	61	3.89	1.24	23.1	264	32	70	3.67	2.1	7.4	3.6	0.7	96
2017	AA	Akron	4	2	0	50	52	3.41	0.94	21.0	207	28	64	1.96	1.8	9.3	5.2	0.5	137
2017	AAA	Columbus	3	7	0	78	76	6.58	1.67	21.9	323	39	62	6.33	2.9	8.8	3.0	1.5	98

Emerging SP who works with strong delivery and solid-average velocity. Gets good extension to deliver quality FB to bottom of zone. Was very good in AA by dominating with electric FB before falling apart in AAA. Has tendency to overthrow and needs polish for CB and CU, both of which should evolve to average. Could be option for late innings work.

Mezquita,Jhordany

SP | **Philadelphia** | EXP MLB DEBUT: 2022 | H/W: 6-1 185 | FUT: #4 starter | **7D**

Thrws L Age 20
2017 (8) HS (PA)

Velo	Pitch	Grade
88-92	FB	++
	CB	++
	CU	++

Year	Lev	Team	W	L	Sv	IP	K	ERA	WHIP	BF/G	OBA	H%	S%	xERA	Ctl	Dom	Cmd	hr/9	BPV
2017	Rk	GCL Phillies	3	0	0	37	35	0.73	0.86	15.2	160	22	91	0.74	2.9	8.5	2.9	0.0	92

Originally an international signee from DR, MLB voided the deal and PHI took him in the 8th round. Some projection left in the southpaw who sits in the low-90s. Can spin a CB but it lacks true depth; CU is a bit further along. Posted good K/BB numbers in first pro exposure and knows how to pitch, but upside is still back end starter.

Miller, Brandon

SP | **Miami** | EXP MLB DEBUT: 2020 | H/W: 6-4 210 | FUT: #5 SP/swingman | **7D**

Thrws R Age 22
2016 (6) Millersville

Velo	Pitch	Grade
91-93	FB	+++
	SL	++++
	CB	++
	CU	+

Year	Lev	Team	W	L	Sv	IP	K	ERA	WHIP	BF/G	OBA	H%	S%	xERA	Ctl	Dom	Cmd	hr/9	BPV
2016	NCAA	Millersville	12	2	0	107	115	1.43	0.71	25.2	172	25	80	0.64	1.1	9.7	8.8	0.2	162
2016	A-	Everett	4	2	0	56	51	2.73	0.96	15.2	229	29	73	2.25	1.1	8.2	7.3	0.5	135
2017	A	Greensboro	0	3	0	21	12	8.96	1.80	19.5	343	33	57	8.83	3.0	5.1	1.7	3.4	30
2017	A	Clinton	9	4	0	101	94	3.65	1.18	22.4	252	31	72	3.56	2.0	8.4	4.1	1.0	113

Tall right-hander came over from Seattle in the D. Phelps deal. Pounds the strike zone with a 91-93 fastball that is a tick above average. Mixes in a plus hard slider, a below-average change-up, and a fringe curveball. Locates all four offerings well and walked just 30 in 122.1 innings. Back-end starter.

Miller,Jared

RP | **Arizona** | EXP MLB DEBUT: 2019 | H/W: 6-7 240 | FUT: Setup reliever | **7B**

Thrws L Age 24
2014 (11) Vanderbilt

Velo	Pitch	Grade
95-98	FB	++++
86-88	CT	+++
78-80	CB	++

Year	Lev	Team	W	L	Sv	IP	K	ERA	WHIP	BF/G	OBA	H%	S%	xERA	Ctl	Dom	Cmd	hr/9	BPV
2016	A+	Visalia	0	1	1	14	20	1.91	0.85	4.3	185	31	75	0.94	1.9	12.8	6.7	0.0	196
2016	AA	Mobile	0	1	2	26	36	3.78	1.18	5.5	196	31	67	2.23	4.5	12.4	2.8	0.3	120
2016	AAA	Reno	0	0	0	6	3	6.00	1.17	4.8	228	18	60	5.16	3.0	4.5	1.5	3.0	18
2017	AA	Jackson	0	3	2	39	51	3.91	1.30	5.2	230	34	69	3.07	4.1	11.7	2.8	0.5	117
2017	AAA	Reno	3	3	1	31	43	1.74	0.84	5.2	154	24	83	1.12	2.9	12.4	4.3	0.6	164

Pop-up guy from 2016 AFL, the behemoth LH struggled early with FB command, but dominated late. Continued strides with heavy sinking FB; a borderline plus-plus offering when at its best. CT is mistaken for SL, but mph increased and could be plus at maturity. Overthrows his CB, and uses it less and less. Will be primarily two-pitch pitcher in MLB.

Mills, Alec

SP | **Chicago (N)** | EXP MLB DEBUT: 2016 | H/W: 6-4 190 | FUT: #5 SP/swingman | **6C**

Thrws R Age 26
2012 (22) TN-Martin

Velo	Pitch	Grade
90-95	FB	+++
	CB	+++
	SL	+++
	CU	++

Year	Lev	Team	W	L	Sv	IP	K	ERA	WHIP	BF/G	OBA	H%	S%	xERA	Ctl	Dom	Cmd	hr/9	BPV
2016	AAA	Omaha	4	3	0	58	54	4.19	1.40	20.4	275	33	74	4.67	2.9	8.4	2.8	1.2	89
2016	MLB	KC Royals	0	0	0	3	4	14.52	2.58	5.6	255	39	38	6.19	14.5	11.6	0.8	0.0	-165
2017	Rk	AZL Cubs	0	0	0	5	6	0.00	0.60	8.6	124	20	100		1.8	10.8	6.0	0.0	164
2017	A+	Myrtle Beach	0	1	0	9	7	3.00	1.00	17.2	240	30	67	2.04	1.0	7.0	7.0	0.0	117
2017	AAA	Iowa	2	0	0	14	7	3.21	1.07	18.2	233	27	67	2.16	1.9	4.5	2.3	0.0	47

22nd round pick has developed into a viable back-end starter, but was limited by injury to just 28 IP. Fastball sits at 91-95 backed by a curve, slider, and change-up, but none profile as plus offerings. Does pound the strike zone and walked just 90 in 420.1 minor league IP.

Mills, McKenzie

SP | **Philadelphia** | EXP MLB DEBUT: 2020 | H/W: 6-4 205 | FUT: #5 SP/swingman | **7D**

Thrws L Age 22
2014 (18) HS (GA)

Velo	Pitch	Grade
90-93	FB	++
75-77	CU	++
70-73	CB	+

Year	Lev	Team	W	L	Sv	IP	K	ERA	WHIP	BF/G	OBA	H%	S%	xERA	Ctl	Dom	Cmd	hr/9	BPV
2016	A-	Auburn	4	5	0	53	46	3.73	1.34	18.4	223	28	72	3.15	4.7	7.8	1.6	0.5	30
2017	A	Hagerstown	12	2	0	104	118	3.02	0.95	21.8	208	27	74	2.46	1.9	10.2	5.4	1.0	150
2017	A+	Clearwater	0	1	0	15	16	4.74	1.38	21.3	329	43	65	4.84	0.0	9.5		0.6	189

Big-bodied lefty who came to PHI in Howie Kendrick trade. Had some success in first full season at Low-A due to throwing more strikes. Hides the ball well in his delivery, and gets some deception from large leg kick that allows stuff to play up a touch. But no current knockout secondary pitch, though CU shows more promise than his slow CB.

Mills,Wyatt — RP — Seattle

EXP MLB DEBUT: 2019 | H/W: 6-3 175 | FUT: Setup reliever | 6B

Thrws R Age 23
2017 (3) Gonzaga

Velo	Pitch	Grade
91-94	FB	+++
82-85	SL	+++

Year	Lev	Team	W	L	Sv	IP	K	ERA	WHIP	BF/G	OBA	H%	S%	xERA	Ctl	Dom	Cmd	hr/9	BPV
2017	NCAA	Gonzaga	2	2	12	40	58	1.80	1.10	7.1	261	41	84	2.72	0.9	13.0	14.5	0.2	228
2017	A-	Everett	0	1	2	7	11	2.57	0.86	3.7	132	26	67	0.39	3.9	14.1	3.7	0.0	168
2017	A	Clinton	0	1	4	13	18	1.37	0.84	4.4	119	21	82	0.24	4.1	12.4	3.0	0.0	129

Long, lean sidearmer who should elevate thru minors quickly. Has solid velocity for arm slot and mixes in tight SL that is tough on RHH. Not much upside due to profile, but is effective in short stints. Can spot FB in bottom half of zone and retire hitters with sweeping SL. Key to ascension will be better control.

Minter,AJ — RP — Atlanta

EXP MLB DEBUT: 2017 | H/W: 6-0 205 | FUT: Closer | 8B

Thrws L Age 24
2015 (S-2) Texas A&M

Velo	Pitch	Grade
94-97	FB	++++
89-91	CT	++++

Year	Lev	Team	W	L	Sv	IP	K	ERA	WHIP	BF/G	OBA	H%	S%	xERA	Ctl	Dom	Cmd	hr/9	BPV
2017	A	Rome	0	0	0	1	1	0.00	1.00	3.8	262	35	100	2.32	0.0	9.0		0.0	180
2017	A+	Florida	0	0	0	5	9	1.80	0.60	3.4	175	28	100	1.87	0.0	16.2		1.8	310
2017	AA	Mississippi	0	0	0	3	3	0.00	1.00	3.8	106	15	100	0.55	6.0	9.0	1.5	0.0	18
2017	AAA	Gwinnett	1	2	0	15	17	4.77	1.66	4.0	260	35	71	4.50	6.0	10.1	1.7	0.6	39
2017	MLB	Atlanta	0	1	0	15	26	3.00	1.00	3.6	235	42	71	2.46	1.2	15.6	13.0	0.6	266

Smallish power LHP who projects to back end of the pen. Made MLB debut in 2017. Two-pitch pitcher, using both at the same frequency. Hard 2-seam FB lives in lower half of zone with solid arm-side bore and plus sink. Dropped SL, throwing hard, late-cut CT instead. Both pitches grade as plus with plus-plus potential.

Molina,Marcos — SP — New York (N)

EXP MLB DEBUT: 2018 | H/W: 6-3 206 | FUT: #4 starter | 8D

Thrws R Age 23
2012 FA (DR)

Velo	Pitch	Grade
91-93	FB	+++
84-87	SL	++++
84-86	CU	+++

Year	Lev	Team	W	L	Sv	IP	K	ERA	WHIP	BF/G	OBA	H%	S%	xERA	Ctl	Dom	Cmd	hr/9	BPV
2015	Rk	GCL Mets	0	0	0	3		0.00	0.00	8.5	0	0			0.0	9.0		0.0	180
2015	A+	St. Lucie	1	5	0	41	36	4.60	1.46	22.0	297	38	66	4.20	2.4	7.9	3.3	0.2	95
2016		*Did not pitch - injured*																	
2017	A+	St. Lucie	2	3	0	28	23	1.28	0.78	20.3	176	22	86	1.02	1.6	7.3	4.6	0.3	107
2017	AA	Binghamton	3	7	0	78	63	3.92	1.26	24.5	259	31	69	3.49	2.4	7.3	3.0	0.6	83

Oft-injured RH struggled once again with various ailments, landing twice on DL. Stuff hasn't come back from 2015 Tommy John surgery. FB still with natural cut, but not as explosive. SL is best pitch, wound tight but doesn't throw as much. CU is an average third pitch. Struggled corralling pitches in 2017. Move to pen may be warranted.

Morales, Francisco — SP — Philadelphia

EXP MLB DEBUT: 2021 | H/W: 6-4 185 | FUT: #3 starter | 9E

Thrws R Age 18
2016 FA (VZ)

Velo	Pitch	Grade
91-94	FB	+++
83-86	SL	+++
81-85	CU	++

Year	Lev	Team	W	L	Sv	IP	K	ERA	WHIP	BF/G	OBA	H%	S%	xERA	Ctl	Dom	Cmd	hr/9	BPV
2017	Rk	GCL Phillies	3	2	0	41	44	3.07	1.31	17.0	227	31	75	2.85	4.4	9.6	2.2	0.2	73

Big fish in 2016 international market, he didn't disappoint in first stateside action, boasting a FB that touched 96 with a hard SL. Also has the beginnings of a good change-up. The body is lean and projectable, delivery is mostly clean, and he has a sense of sequencing. Oozes upside, but far away.

Moran,Jovani — RP — Minnesota

EXP MLB DEBUT: 2021 | H/W: 6-1 167 | FUT: Setup reliever | 7E

Thrws L Age 20
2015 (7) HS (PR)

Velo	Pitch	Grade
90-93	FB	++++
81-85	SL	++
81-84	CU	++

Year	Lev	Team	W	L	Sv	IP	K	ERA	WHIP	BF/G	OBA	H%	S%	xERA	Ctl	Dom	Cmd	hr/9	BPV
2015	Rk	GCL Twins	0	2	0	19	17	4.22	1.30	13.2	228	30	64	2.64	4.2	8.0	1.9	0.0	48
2016		*Did not pitch - injured*																	
2017	Rk	Elizabethton	3	1	0	24	45	0.37	0.74	7.8	150	32	100	0.60	2.2	16.7	7.5	0.4	259

Projectable, lean RP who dominated in short-season ball after missing all 2016. Only allowed 1 ER while posting very high K rate with smooth, deceptive delivery and release. Can thrive in lower minors with plus FB that features late action. Mixes in SL and occasional CU with feel and touch. Could return to SP due to clean arm.

Morejon,Adrian — SP — San Diego

EXP MLB DEBUT: 2021 | H/W: 6-0 165 | FUT: #4 starter | 8C

Thrws L Age 19
2016 FA (CU)

Velo	Pitch	Grade
90-93	FB	+++
77-80	CB	+++
81-84	CU	+++

Year	Lev	Team	W	L	Sv	IP	K	ERA	WHIP	BF/G	OBA	H%	S%	xERA	Ctl	Dom	Cmd	hr/9	BPV
2017	A-	Tri-City	2	2	0	35	35	3.59	1.14	19.9	272	35	68	3.29	0.8	9.0	11.7	0.5	159
2017	A	Fort Wayne	1	2	0	27	23	4.30	1.51	19.6	267	33	72	4.31	4.3	7.6	1.8	0.7	39

Young Cuban LH who made stateside debut in 2017. Features solid but not overwhelming three-pitch mix including low-90s FB that could get a bump with added strength. Has advanced feel for CB and CU and both have potential for above-average grade. Thick lower half; delivery doesn't require much effort. More control than command, but fills the zone.

Moreno, Erling — SP — Chicago (N)

EXP MLB DEBUT: 2021 | H/W: 6-3 200 | FUT: #4 starter | 7D

Thrws R Age 21
2013 FA (CB)

Velo	Pitch	Grade
92-95	FB	++++
	SL	++
	CU	+++

Year	Lev	Team	W	L	Sv	IP	K	ERA	WHIP	BF/G	OBA	H%	S%	xERA	Ctl	Dom	Cmd	hr/9	BPV
2015	Rk	AZL Cubs	1	1	0	4	2	2.14	1.19	5.6	202	23	80	2.08	4.3	4.3	1.0	0.0	-21
2016	Rk	AZL Cubs	2	2	0	32	33	2.80	1.09	20.9	255	34	74	2.71	1.1	9.3	8.3	0.3	154
2016	A-	Eugene	2	1	0	30	22	0.90	0.70	17.6	159	18	95	0.91	1.5	6.6	4.4	0.6	96
2017	A	South Bend	2	4	0	64	57	4.22	1.36	19.1	237	30	68	3.30	4.4	8.0	1.8	0.4	45

Moreno has been slow to develop after Tommy John surgery cost him most of '14 and '15. Finally made his full-season debut in 2017 with mixed results. Best offering is a plus 92-95 mph sinking fastball. Change-up gives him solid second offering and slider shows potential but needs refinement. Potential back-end starter.

Moreno,Gerson — RP — Detroit

EXP MLB DEBUT: 2019 | H/W: 6-0 175 | FUT: Setup reliever | 7D

Thrws R Age 22
2012 FA (DR)

Velo	Pitch	Grade
93-98	FB	+++
82-85	SL	++
	CU	+

Year	Lev	Team	W	L	Sv	IP	K	ERA	WHIP	BF/G	OBA	H%	S%	xERA	Ctl	Dom	Cmd	hr/9	BPV
2015	A	West Michigan	0	0	1	9	9	0.00	0.66	6.3	105	15	100		3.0	8.9	3.0	0.0	98
2016	A	West Michigan	1	1	11	25	27	1.08	1.08	4.2	212	30	89	1.87	2.9	9.7	3.4	0.0	115
2016	A+	Lakeland	0	3	3	24	27	7.07	1.74	5.2	244	30	61	5.32	7.4	10.0	1.4	1.5	-2
2017	A+	Lakeland	1	0	8	22	30	2.04	1.22	4.3	234	36	85	2.85	3.3	12.2	3.8	0.4	150
2017	AA	Erie	0	3	0	28	36	6.43	1.43	5.9	226	31	56	4.10	5.5	11.6	2.1	1.3	79

Quick-armed RP who was terrific in A+ before getting hit hard in AA. Had big spike in K rate thanks to increasing velocity and improved SL. Breaking ball is quite inconsistent, though, and needs 2nd pitch for prominent role. Lacks feel and touch for changing speeds. Has bouts of above average command and then follows up with sub-par control.

Morimando,Shawn — SP — Cleveland

EXP MLB DEBUT: 2016 | H/W: 6-0 200 | FUT: #5 SP/swingman | 6B

Thrws L Age 25
2011 (19) HS (VA)

Velo	Pitch	Grade
89-93	FB	+++
84-87	SL	+++
78-79	CB	++
	CU	++

Year	Lev	Team	W	L	Sv	IP	K	ERA	WHIP	BF/G	OBA	H%	S%	xERA	Ctl	Dom	Cmd	hr/9	BPV
2015	AA	Akron	10	12	0	158	128	3.19	1.29	23.2	238	29	76	3.22	3.7	7.3	2.0	0.5	49
2016	AA	Akron	10	3	0	93	73	3.09	1.21	23.5	227	28	75	2.87	3.5	7.1	2.0	0.5	51
2016	AAA	Columbus	5	2	0	59	46	3.51	1.44	22.9	278	33	78	4.39	3.2	7.0	2.2	0.8	58
2016	MLB	Cleveland	0	0	0	4	5	12.86	3.33	12.9	432	51	67	15.24	10.7	10.7	1.0	4.3	-78
2017	AAA	Columbus	10	9	0	159	128	4.41	1.47	26.3	283	33	74	4.99	3.2	7.2	2.2	1.2	61

Stocky SP who gets by without plus stuff. Has deep repertoire and has significantly improved mixing ability. Gets lot of life with average FB and effectively changes speeds. SL is best pitch and can miss bats. Has a lot of stamina and durability and could be back-end SP or multiple inning RP. K rate is minimal and exhibits fringy control.

Moronta,Reyes — RP — San Francisco

EXP MLB DEBUT: 2017 | H/W: 6-0 175 | FUT: Closer | 7B

Thrws R Age 25
2010 FA (DR)

Velo	Pitch	Grade
94-98	FB	++++
82-85	SL	+++
	CU	+

Year	Lev	Team	W	L	Sv	IP	K	ERA	WHIP	BF/G	OBA	H%	S%	xERA	Ctl	Dom	Cmd	hr/9	BPV
2016	A+	San Jose	0	3	14	59	93	2.59	1.07	3.8	205	33	82	2.72	3.1	14.2	4.7	1.1	191
2017	Rk	AZL Giants	0	0	0	2	4	0.00	0.00	2.8	0	0			0.0	18.0		0.0	342
2017	AA	Richmond	0	1	5	18	26	4.00	1.50	4.1	228	36	73	3.56	6.0	13.0	2.2	0.5	90
2017	AAA	Sacramento	3	0	0	17	17	2.12	1.24	5.3	213	28	85	2.78	4.2	9.0	2.1	0.5	66
2017	MLB	SF Giants	0	0	0	6	11	2.90	1.45	3.8	255	44	88	4.66	4.4	16.0	3.7	1.5	188

Short, strong RP with closing experience. Reached majors on basis of hard arsenal. Uses violent delivery to generate plus velocity and posts high K rate with plus FB and average SL combo. Erratic control could limit high leverage work in SF, but dominates when on. Very tough to hit when spotting FB in lower half.

Morris,Akeel — RP — Atlanta

EXP MLB DEBUT: 2015 | H/W: 6-1 195 | FUT: Middle reliever | 7B

Thrws R Age 25
2010 (10) HS (VG)

Velo	Pitch	Grade
92-94	FB	++++
81-84	SL	++
76-79	CU	++++

Year	Lev	Team	W	L	Sv	IP	K	ERA	WHIP	BF/G	OBA	H%	S%	xERA	Ctl	Dom	Cmd	hr/9	BPV
2015	AA	Binghamton	0	1	0	29	35	2.47	1.10	5.0	172	25	77	1.73	4.6	10.8	2.3	0.3	88
2016	AA	Binghamton	2	2	6	25	36	4.66	1.39	4.8	212	30	71	3.97	5.7	12.9	2.3	1.4	95
2017	AA	Mississippi	0	0	4	7	9	0.00	0.56	4.1	90	15	100		2.5	11.3	4.5	0.0	153
2017	AAA	Gwinnett	1	3	1	46	53	3.12	1.32	6.4	226	31	78	3.19	4.5	10.3	2.3	0.6	83
2017	MLB	Atlanta	0	0	0	7	9	1.27	1.41	3.8	231	35	90	2.91	5.1	11.4	2.3	0.0	86

Max-effort RH prospect re-emerged as a solid RP prospect. Three-pitch pitcher, struggling to refine breaking pitch. FB sits low-to-mid-90s with late life. SL is slurvy and a work-in-progress. Struggling from arm-slot to throw effective breaking-pitch. Best pitch is drop-off-the-table CU with tremendous deception. A plus pitch.

Moss,Scott

SP | Cincinnati | EXP MLB DEBUT: 2020 | H/W: 6-5 215 | FUT: #4 starter | 7C

Thrws L Age 23
2016 (4) Florida

Velo	Pitch	Grade
88-91	FB	+++
81-83	CB	++++
81-83	CU	++

Year	Lev	Team	W	L	Sv	IP	K	ERA	WHIP	BF/G	OBA	H%	S%	xERA	Ctl	Dom	Cmd	hr/9	BPV
2016	NCAA	Florida	3	0	0	23	31	1.57	1.04	6.3	188	31	83	1.47	3.5	12.1	3.4	0.0	141
2016	Rk	Billings	3	1	0	38	29	2.36	1.29	15.6	246	30	83	3.29	3.3	6.9	2.1	0.5	52
2017	A	Dayton	13	6	0	135	156	3.46	1.20	20.9	230	31	73	3.07	3.2	10.4	3.3	0.7	119

Big-bodied, LH converted starter had solid full-season debut. Didn't pitch much as amateur; missed 2 seasons after Tommy John surgery. Average FB with late, two-seam life. Should add velocity as he matures. Hard CB is best pitch with good spin and late 11-5 drop. Has a feel for CU, but lacks consistency.

Moya,Gabriel

RP | Minnesota | EXP MLB DEBUT: 2017 | H/W: 6-0 175 | FUT: Setup reliever | 6A

Thrws L Age 23
2012 FA (VZ)

Velo	Pitch	Grade
88-93	FB	+++
82-84	SL	++
78-79	CB	++
	CU	++++

Year	Lev	Team	W	L	Sv	IP	K	ERA	WHIP	BF/G	OBA	H%	S%	xERA	Ctl	Dom	Cmd	hr/9	BPV
2016	A	Kane County	1	0	0	19	20	0.47	0.84	5.8	183	26	94	0.93	1.9	9.5	5.0	0.0	137
2016	A+	Visalia	5	1	5	44	62	2.04	0.88	4.1	173	28	78	1.27	2.6	12.6	4.8	0.4	174
2017	AA	Jackson	4	1	17	43	68	0.83	0.79	4.6	153	28	91	0.62	2.5	14.2	5.7	0.2	206
2017	AA	Chattanooga	2	0	7	14	19	0.63	0.77	3.9	167	25	100	1.15	1.9	12.0	6.3	0.6	183
2017	MLB	Minnesota	0	0	1	6	5	4.43	1.15	3.5	225	20	80	5.00	3.0	7.4	2.5	3.0	71

Light-framed RP who finished 2nd in SL in saves and was rewarded with September callup. K rate increased and has maintained as he climbed minors. Velocity is only average, but plays up due to arm action. Rare ability to miss bats while mitigating walks. CU grades as plus to double-plus. Can get swings and misses and keep RHH at bay.

Muller,Kyle

SP | Atlanta | EXP MLB DEBUT: 2020 | H/W: 6-6 225 | FUT: #4 starter | 7E

Thrws L Age 20
2016 (2) HS (TX)

Velo	Pitch	Grade
88-91	FB	+++
74-76	CB	++
81-84	CU	++

Year	Lev	Team	W	L	Sv	IP	K	ERA	WHIP	BF/G	OBA	H%	S%	xERA	Ctl	Dom	Cmd	hr/9	BPV
2016	Rk	GCL Braves	1	0	0	27	38	0.66	0.96	10.3	154	27	92	0.88	4.0	12.6	3.2	0.0	137
2017	Rk	Danville	1	1	0	47	49	4.19	1.29	17.6	244	31	70	3.71	3.4	9.3	2.7	1.0	94

Tall, athletic LH who pounds the lower half of the zone with three fringe-to-average pitches. Uses height and repeatable delivery to create solid downward plane. 2-seam FB primary pitch with below-average arm-side run. Relies on location over stuff. CB is wildly inconsistent, struggling with wrapping wrist and getting on top of ball. Doesn't have CU feel.

Murphy,Brendan

SP | Milwaukee | EXP MLB DEBUT: 2021 | H/W: 6-4 200 | FUT: #3 starter | 8E

Thrws L Age 19
2017 (4) HS (IL)

Velo	Pitch	Grade
88-91	FB	+++
77-79	SL	++
81-83	CU	++++

Year	Lev	Team	W	L	Sv	IP	K	ERA	WHIP	BF/G	OBA	H%	S%	xERA	Ctl	Dom	Cmd	hr/9	BPV
2017	Rk	AZL Brewers	0	2	0	16	11	6.19	2.06	8.7	318	37	69	6.38	6.8	6.2	0.9	0.6	-53

Tall, projectable prep lefthander struggled with control in his pro debut. 2-seam FB has solid arm-side run. Velocity will come as he adds strength. Has advanced feel for CU with plus tumble action. SL has below average projection.

Murphy,Patrick

SP | Toronto | EXP MLB DEBUT: 2019 | H/W: 6-4 220 | FUT: #4 starter | 7D

Thrws R Age 22
2013 (3) HS (AZ)

Velo	Pitch	Grade
91-95	FB	+++
75-80	CB	+++
	CU	++

Year	Lev	Team	W	L	Sv	IP	K	ERA	WHIP	BF/G	OBA	H%	S%	xERA	Ctl	Dom	Cmd	hr/9	BPV
2016	A-	Vancouver	4	5	0	69	48	2.86	1.36	22.2	267	33	77	3.31	3.0	6.2	2.1	0.0	50
2016	A	Lansing	0	1	2	21	20	4.29	1.81	12.2	288	35	80	5.95	6.0	8.6	1.4	1.3	10
2017	Rk	GCL Blue Jays	1	0	0	9	15	0.00	0.89	11.1	216	40	100	1.39	1.0	15.0	15.0	0.0	261
2017	A	Lansing	4	3	0	88	57	2.96	1.36	24.6	259	30	79	3.70	3.4	5.8	1.7	0.5	32
2017	A+	Dunedin	0	1	0	9	5	7.00	1.89	21.2	356	41	59	6.07	3.0	5.0	1.7	0.0	27

Injury-prone SP who has potential to take big step forward due to impressive arsenal and big frame. Missed significant time from '13 thru '15 due to elbow and shoulder injuries. Generates plus velocity with quick arm and natural strength. Has chance for three solid offerings if he can polish CU. Power CB is out pitch, but has focused on FB command.

Myers,Tobias

SP | Tampa Bay | EXP MLB DEBUT: 2021 | H/W: 6-0 193 | FUT: #4 starter | 7C

Thrws R Age 19
2016 (6) HS (FL)

Velo	Pitch	Grade
91-95	FB	+++
79-83	CB	+++
83-86	CU	++

Year	Lev	Team	W	L	Sv	IP	K	ERA	WHIP	BF/G	OBA	H%	S%	xERA	Ctl	Dom	Cmd	hr/9	BPV
2016	Rk	GCL Orioles	0	0	0	7	4	5.00	1.67	10.8	330	36	73	6.24	2.5	5.0	2.0	1.3	41
2017	A-	Hudson Valley	2	0	0	26	38	3.10	0.80	18.9	188	31	60	1.18	1.4	13.1	9.5	0.3	217
2017	A-	Aberdeen	2	2	0	29	35	4.01	1.16	16.6	254	37	62	2.60	1.8	10.8	5.8	0.0	162

Young, promising SP who was acquired from BAL mid-season and shows exquisite control and command for age. Not blessed with great size, but has good enough stuff to start. Has to enhance CU to retire LHH. Gets groundballs and Ks with heavy, hard FB and big-bending CB. Able to repeat athletic, fast-armed delivery.

Neidert,Nick

SP | Miami | EXP MLB DEBUT: 2019 | H/W: 6-1 180 | FUT: #3 starter | 8B

Thrws R Age 21
2015 (2) HS (GA)

Velo	Pitch	Grade
90-95	FB	++++
81-84	SL	+++
77-79	CB	++
	CU	+++

Year	Lev	Team	W	L	Sv	IP	K	ERA	WHIP	BF/G	OBA	H%	S%	xERA	Ctl	Dom	Cmd	hr/9	BPV
2015	Rk	AZL Mariners	0	2	0	35	23	1.54	0.97	12.1	202	24	85	1.74	2.3	5.9	2.6	0.3	62
2016	A	Clinton	7	3	0	91	69	2.57	0.97	18.1	226	27	77	2.44	1.3	6.8	5.3	0.7	106
2017	A+	Modesto	10	3	0	104	109	2.77	1.08	21.3	244	32	76	2.84	1.5	9.4	6.4	0.6	148
2017	AA	Arkansas	1	3	0	23	13	6.62	1.65	17.2	336	36	62	6.58	1.9	5.1	2.6	1.6	57

Young, improving SP who won CAL pitcher of year after increasing K rate drastically. Has slight frame, but upped velocity while maintaining command. SL has evolved into true out pitch while CU used with same arm speed and shows late fade. Power arm with projection and just needs polish to put himself into upper echelon.

Neuweiler,Charlie

SP | Kansas City | EXP MLB DEBUT: 2021 | H/W: 6-1 205 | FUT: #3 starter | 8E

Thrws R Age 19
2017 (5) HS (NY)

Velo	Pitch	Grade
87-92	FB	++
79-82	CB	+++
80-82	CU	+++

Year	Lev	Team	W	L	Sv	IP	K	ERA	WHIP	BF/G	OBA	H%	S%	xERA	Ctl	Dom	Cmd	hr/9	BPV
2017	Rk	AZL Royals	3	3	0	41	34	1.76	0.98	13.0	195	23	86	2.05	2.6	7.5	2.8	0.7	81

Well-built SP who peppers strike zone with good pitches and won't beat himself. Induces ton of groundballs with FB that exhibits late drop and sink. Tough to elevate FB, but has tendency to hang CB. Needs to find consistency in CB to serve as out pitch at higher levels. Not much projection in frame.

Nikorak, Mike

SP | Colorado | EXP MLB DEBUT: 2021 | H/W: 6-5 205 | FUT: Setup reliever | 9E

Thrws R Age 21
2015 (1) HS (PA)

Velo	Pitch	Grade
92-95	FB	++++
80-83	CB	++
78-81	CU	++

Year	Lev	Team	W	L	Sv	IP	K	ERA	WHIP	BF/G	OBA	H%	S%	xERA	Ctl	Dom	Cmd	hr/9	BPV
2015	Rk	Grand Junction	0	4	0	17	14	12.03	3.37	13.3	349	42	61	10.16	16.7	7.3	0.4	0.5	-302
2016	Rk	Grand Junction	1	0	0	29	20	3.71	1.79	19.2	287	33	80	5.26	5.9	6.2	1.1	0.6	-29
2017		*Did not pitch - injured*																	

Former 1st rounder had Tommy John surgery and missed all of 2017. Prior to the injury, plus fastball velocity gave him potential. Fastball sits at 92-95 with late sink topping at 97 mph. Curve and a solid-avg change-up round out the arsenal. Inability to find the strike zone with consistency raises red flag.

Nix,Jacob

SP | San Diego | EXP MLB DEBUT: 2018 | H/W: 6-4 220 | FUT: #4 starter | 7B

Thrws R Age 22
2015 (3) HS (FL)

Velo	Pitch	Grade
92-95	FB	++++
79-81	CB	+++
84-86	CU	++

Year	Lev	Team	W	L	Sv	IP	K	ERA	WHIP	BF/G	OBA	H%	S%	xERA	Ctl	Dom	Cmd	hr/9	BPV
2015	Rk	AZL Padres	0	2	0	19	19	5.63	1.56	12.0	298	38	62	4.70	3.3	8.9	2.7	0.5	90
2016	A	Fort Wayne	3	7	0	105	90	3.94	1.28	17.3	280	35	68	3.70	1.7	7.7	4.5	0.4	110
2017	A+	Lake Elsinore	4	3	0	66	51	4.35	1.33	25.0	295	35	67	4.28	1.4	6.9	5.1	0.7	106
2017	AA	San Antonio	1	2	0	27	22	5.63	1.51	19.6	294	37	59	4.08	3.0	7.3	2.4	0.0	69

Strong RHP who has moved quickly through the system and could debut in 2018. Will touch 97 mph with plus FB and will sit mid-90s with some movement. Both CB and CU have improved markedly and knows how to throw strikes with both. Pitches deep into games and will be an innings eater at the next level. Has the look of a quality #3/4 SP.

Nogosek,Stephen

RP | New York (N) | EXP MLB DEBUT: 2019 | H/W: 6-2 205 | FUT: Setup reliever | 7C

Thrws R Age 23
2016 (6) Oregon

Velo	Pitch	Grade
92-97	FB	++++
83-85	SL	++
87-89	CT	+++
82-84	CU	+

Year	Lev	Team	W	L	Sv	IP	K	ERA	WHIP	BF/G	OBA	H%	S%	xERA	Ctl	Dom	Cmd	hr/9	BPV
2016	A-	Lowell	1	0	0	13	19	2.06	1.22	5.3	196	28	93	3.29	4.8	13.1	2.7	1.4	123
2016	A	Greenville	0	2	2	14	12	5.14	1.43	5.9	301	37	63	4.58	1.9	7.7	4.0	0.6	105
2017	A	Greenville	2	3	13	35	45	2.56	1.00	5.8	195	27	81	2.41	2.8	11.5	4.1	1.0	150
2017	A+	St. Lucie	1	1	0	16	15	5.06	1.50	7.7	262	35	63	3.58	4.5	8.4	1.9	0.0	48
2017	A+	Salem	2	1	6	17	18	4.19	1.45	5.7	236	28	77	4.59	5.2	9.4	1.8	1.6	46

Hard-throwing RH mixes 5 pitches out of pen. 2-seam FB is workhorse and best pitch. Sits 92-94 mph with significant arm-side bore. 4-seam FB sits 95-97 with late run. Also throws CT and SL; cutter more effective and projects as potential plus pitch. Has feel for CU, which shows FB movement but he slows down arm. Struggles with control overall.

Oaks, Trevor — SP — Kansas City

EXP MLB DEBUT: 2019 | H/W: 6-3 220 | FUT: #4 starter | 7C

Thrws R Age 25 — 2014 (7) California Baptist

- 92-95 FB +++
- 83-85 CT +++
- 85-87 SL +++
- CU +++

Year	Lev	Team	W	L	Sv	IP	K	ERA	WHIP	BF/G	OBA	H%	S%	xERA	Ctl	Dom	Cmd	hr/9	BPV
2016	AA	Tulsa	8	1	0	63	38	2.14	1.03	24.3	240	28	78	2.27	1.3	5.4	4.2	0.1	81
2016	AAA	Oklahoma City	5	1	0	63	48	3.00	1.16	25.1	265	31	79	3.72	1.3	6.9	5.3	1.0	107
2017	Rk	Ogden	0	0	0	5	6	8.65	2.50	13.8	450	56	67	11.18	1.7	10.4	6.0	1.7	158
2017	Rk	AZL Dodgers	0	0	0	2	3	0.00	0.00	5.6	0	0			0.0	13.5		0.0	261
2017	AAA	Oklahoma City	4	3	0	84	72	3.64	1.25	21.4	269	33	71	3.56	1.9	7.7	4.0	0.5	105

Tall, strong-bodied righty comes after hitters with a plus 92-95 mph sinking FB. Secondary offerings include a CT, SL, and CU all of which profile as average. CT and Cmd are his best weapons and has a career 1.6 BB/9. Solid back-end workhorse starter. Traded to Kansas City in the offseason.

Ogle, Braeden — SP — Pittsburgh

EXP MLB DEBUT: 2020 | H/W: 6-2 170 | FUT: #4 starter | 7D

Thrws L Age 20 — 2016 (4) HS (FL)

- 91-93 FB +++
- SL ++
- CU ++

Year	Lev	Team	W	L	Sv	IP	K	ERA	WHIP	BF/G	OBA	H%	S%	xERA	Ctl	Dom	Cmd	hr/9	BPV
2016	Rk	GCL Pirates	0	2	0	27	20	2.65	1.07	13.2	190	22	78	2.23	3.6	6.6	1.8	0.7	39
2017	Rk	Bristol	2	3	0	43	35	3.14	1.30	17.7	248	31	75	3.11	3.3	7.3	2.2	0.2	59

Projectable LHP had a solid rookie league debut. Already features a plus 91-93 mph fastball that tops at 96 mph. Scrapped his CB in favor of a hard SL and CU shows potential. Mechanics need refinement and he tends to rush his delivery and fly open on the front-side, resulting in below-average control.

Ortiz, Luis — SP — Milwaukee

EXP MLB DEBUT: 2018 | H/W: 6-3 230 | FUT: #3 starter | 8C

Thrws R Age 22 — 2014 (1) HS (CA)

- 93-96 FB ++++
- 82-84 SL ++++
- 83-86 CU +++

Year	Lev	Team	W	L	Sv	IP	K	ERA	WHIP	BF/G	OBA	H%	S%	xERA	Ctl	Dom	Cmd	hr/9	BPV
2015	A	Hickory	4	1	0	50		1.80	1.08	15.0	242	32	83	2.43	1.6	8.3	5.1	0.2	123
2016	A+	High Desert	3	2	0	27	28	2.65	1.07	15.1	231	28	84	3.31	2.0	9.3	4.7	1.3	131
2016	AA	Frisco	1	4	1	39	34	4.13	1.38	18.3	298	37	71	4.45	1.6	7.8	4.9	0.7	115
2016	AA	Biloxi	2	2	0	23	16	1.95	1.56	16.9	285	33	91	4.82	3.9	6.2	1.6	0.8	25
2017	AA	Biloxi	4	7	0	94	79	4.02	1.23	17.3	229	26	71	3.57	3.5	7.6	2.1	1.1	58

Stocky RH had better season than traditional stats indicated. Struggled with leg injury mid-season. OBA, Cmd and Dom took steps forward; Ctl stayed relatively the same. Relies on late run on FB to induce soft contact. Tight SL is true out pitch. Two-plane break, can adjust movement to achieve more break. CU deceptive, struggles staying down.

Oswalt, Corey — SP — New York (N)

EXP MLB DEBUT: 2018 | H/W: 6-5 250 | FUT: #4 starter | 7C

Thrws R Age 24 — 2012 (7) HS (CA)

- 91-94 FB +++
- 88-89 SL +++
- 82-84 CB ++
- 86-87 CU ++

Year	Lev	Team	W	L	Sv	IP	K	ERA	WHIP	BF/G	OBA	H%	S%	xERA	Ctl	Dom	Cmd	hr/9	BPV
2014	A-	Brooklyn	6	2	0	67	59	2.28	1.04	21.6	225	29	77	2.07	2.0	7.9	3.9	0.1	106
2015	A	Savannah	11	5	0	128	99	3.37	1.36	23.3	297	36	75	4.15	1.5	7.0	4.7	0.4	103
2016	Rk	GCL Mets	0	0	0	1	3	0.00	0.00	2.8	0	0			0.0	27.0		0.0	504
2016	A+	St. Lucie	4	2	0	67	68	4.15	1.35	20.0	278	36	69	3.94	2.4	9.1	3.8	0.5	117
2017	AA	Binghamton	12	5	0	134	119	2.28	1.18	22.3	238	30	83	3.02	2.7	8.0	3.0	0.6	89

Physically mature RH turned in best season as professional. Relies heavily on mixing and commanding 4-pitch arsenal. FB is an average offering with solid arm-side run. SL is best pitch that could become MLB out-pitch if tightened up. CB is slurvy and is similar to slider. Has a feel for CU but struggles repeating tumbling action.

Otto, Glenn — SP — New York (A)

EXP MLB DEBUT: 2020 | H/W: 6-5 240 | FUT: #4 starter | 7D

Thrws R Age 22 — 2017 (5) Rice

- 90-94 FB +++
- 78-79 CB +++
- CU +

Year	Lev	Team	W	L	Sv	IP	K	ERA	WHIP	BF/G	OBA	H%	S%	xERA	Ctl	Dom	Cmd	hr/9	BPV
2017	NCAA	Rice	7	4	8	59	81	3.80	1.33	9.5	230	35	71	3.14	4.4	12.3	2.8	0.5	121
2017	Rk	GCL Yankees	0	0	0	2	3	0.00	0.50	6.6	151	27	100		0.0	13.5		0.0	261
2017	A-	Staten Island	3	0	0	17	25	1.59	1.00	9.3	200	34	82	1.49	2.6	13.2	5.0	0.0	185

Sturdy, strong SP with big FB and power asrenal. Could eventually move to pen due to frame and lack of offspeed pitch. Has some effort in delivery, but generally repeats. Knocks out hitters with FB/CB combo. FB lacks movement at times and can be elevated. If he finds effective CU, then could stick as back-end guy.

Oviedo, Johan — SP — St. Louis

EXP MLB DEBUT: 2021 | H/W: 6-6 210 | FUT: #3 starter | 8D

Thrws R Age 20 — 2016 FA (CU)

- 92-95 FB ++++
- CB +++
- CU ++

Year	Lev	Team	W	L	Sv	IP	K	ERA	WHIP	BF/G	OBA	H%	S%	xERA	Ctl	Dom	Cmd	hr/9	BPV
2017	Rk	Johnson City	2	1	0	27	31	4.96	1.47	19.5	223	32	63	2.98	6.0	10.3	1.7	0.0	42
2017	A-	State College	2	2	0	47	39	4.59	1.51	25.5	285	35	69	4.48	3.4	7.5	2.2	0.6	59

Cuban hurler was signed for $1.9 million in 2016. Struggled with control in his state-side debut, walking 4.3/9 while posting a 4.68 ERA. Above-average fastball sits at 92-95 topping at 96 mph. Curveball flashes plus but needs to be more consistent and shows some feel for a change-up. Huge 6-6 frame leaves some projection, but lots of work to do.

Paddack, Chris — SP — San Diego

EXP MLB DEBUT: 2019 | H/W: 6-4 195 | FUT: #4 starter | 8D

Thrws R Age 22 — 2015 (8) HS (TX)

- 91-93 FB +++
- 83-85 CU ++++
- 74-76 CB +++

Year	Lev	Team	W	L	Sv	IP	K	ERA	WHIP	BF/G	OBA	H%	S%	xERA	Ctl	Dom	Cmd	hr/9	BPV
2015	Rk	GCL Marlins	4	3	0	45	39	2.20	0.98	15.6	225	29	77	1.98	1.4	7.8	5.6	0.2	120
2016	A	Greensboro	2	0	0	28	48	0.96	0.39	15.0	102	18	89		0.6	15.4	24.0	0.6	277
2016	A	Fort Wayne	0	0	0	14	23	0.64	1.00	17.8	218	40	93	1.69	1.9	14.8	7.7	0.0	232
2017		*Did not pitch - injured*																	

Breakout RH from 2016 missed all year after Tommy John surgery. Athletic, lean frame produces 91-93 FB with slight cutting action; could add velo as he fills out. Excellent feel for CU that separates well from FB and will be a good bat-misser. CB can get loopy but will be usable third pitch. Advanced command for age. Biggest question is how he'll look post-TJS.

Palumbo, Joe — SP — Texas

EXP MLB DEBUT: 2019 | H/W: 6-1 168 | FUT: #4 starter | 7C

Thrws L Age 23 — 2013 (30) HS (NY)

- 90-95 FB +++
- 75-79 CB ++++
- 82-85 CU ++

Year	Lev	Team	W	L	Sv	IP	K	ERA	WHIP	BF/G	OBA	H%	S%	xERA	Ctl	Dom	Cmd	hr/9	BPV
2014	Rk	AZL Rangers	4	4	0	42	49	2.35	1.04	11.6	196	29	75	1.58	3.2	10.5	3.3	0.0	120
2015	A-	Spokane	3	3	0	54	42	2.83	1.37	18.9	254	31	80	3.63	3.7	7.0	1.9	0.5	45
2015	A	Hickory	0	0	0	4	1	6.59	1.95	19.6	302	32	63	5.36	6.6	2.2	0.3	0.0	-120
2016	A	Hickory	7	5	8	96	122	2.25	1.11	11.5	208	31	81	2.32	3.4	11.4	3.4	0.5	133
2017	A+	Down East	1	0	0	13	22	0.68	0.61	15.1	97	21	88		2.7	15.0	5.5	0.0	214

Athletic SP who underwent Tommy John surgery in April and likely to return in mid '18. When healthy, has solid three-pitch mix. Commands plate well with late-breaking CB his best offering. CB misses bats consistently and can drop in zone for strikes. FB has gotten firmer and delivery provides hint of deception. CU flashes average, but not often enough.

Pannone, Thomas — SP — Toronto

EXP MLB DEBUT: 2018 | H/W: 6-0 195 | FUT: #5 SP/swingman | 6B

Thrws L Age 23 — 2013 (9) JC of So Nevada

- 89-93 FB +++
- 75-77 CB +++
- CU +++

Year	Lev	Team	W	L	Sv	IP	K	ERA	WHIP	BF/G	OBA	H%	S%	xERA	Ctl	Dom	Cmd	hr/9	BPV
2016	A	Lake County	5	5	0	89	84	3.03	1.10	20.5	225	28	75	2.76	2.5	8.5	3.4	0.7	103
2016	A+	Lynchburg	3	0	0	43	38	1.67	1.09	21.1	203	26	85	1.99	3.3	7.9	2.4	0.2	71
2017	A+	Lynchburg	2	0	0	27	39	0.00	0.63	18.7	115	21	100		2.3	12.9	5.6	0.0	188
2017	AA	New Hampshire	1	2	0	34	29	3.68	1.14	22.6	243	25	83	4.66	2.1	7.6	3.6	2.4	99
2017	AA	Akron	6	1	0	82	81	2.63	1.07	22.8	224	29	77	2.52	2.3	8.9	3.9	0.5	116

Efficient, deceptive SP who was acquired from CLE at deadline. Was 2nd in EL in ERA and posted high K rate by keeping hitters off balance. Throws strikes with all pitches and doesn't beat himself. Lacks prominent offering in repertoire, but sequences well while adding and subtracting velocity. Added a few ticks to FB in 2017.

Paredes, Eduardo — RP — Los Angeles (A)

EXP MLB DEBUT: 2017 | H/W: 6-1 170 | FUT: Setup reliever | 6A

Thrws R Age 23 — 2012 FA (VZ)

- 91-95 FB +++
- 82-85 SL +++

Year	Lev	Team	W	L	Sv	IP	K	ERA	WHIP	BF/G	OBA	H%	S%	xERA	Ctl	Dom	Cmd	hr/9	BPV
2016	A+	Inland Empire	1	2	4	22	32	3.27	1.09	4.5	225	35	73	2.79	2.5	13.1	5.3	0.8	187
2016	AA	Arkansas	0	3	8	48	43	3.37	1.25	5.6	253	30	78	3.89	2.6	8.0	3.1	1.1	92
2017	AA	Mobile	0	0	1	12	17	1.48	1.23	5.5	242	39	87	2.60	3.0	12.5	4.3	0.0	164
2017	AAA	Salt Lake	1	0	2	37	38	2.92	1.19	5.9	206	27	78	2.76	4.1	9.2	2.2	0.7	73
2017	MLB	LA Angels	0	1	1	22	17	4.48	1.22	5.0	252	30	64	3.53	2.4	6.9	2.8	0.8	77

Career RP who was on shuttle between AAA and majors. Had success with solid two-pitch repertoire. Exhibits good control with FB and SL despite amount of sink on heater. SL can be too easy to read at times, but also can drop in zone for strikes. Can drop arm angle for different looks. Stuff a bit short for closer profile, but enough for set-up role.

Paulino, Jose — SP — Chicago (N)

EXP MLB DEBUT: 2020 | H/W: 6-2 165 | FUT: #5 SP/swingman | 7D

Thrws L Age 22 — 2011 FA (DR)

- 90-94 FB +++
- SL ++
- CU ++

Year	Lev	Team	W	L	Sv	IP	K	ERA	WHIP	BF/G	OBA	H%	S%	xERA	Ctl	Dom	Cmd	hr/9	BPV
2014	Rk	AZL Cubs	3	4	0	46	42	6.04	1.62	17.1	297	37	61	4.95	3.9	8.2	2.1	0.6	60
2015	A-	Eugene	4	6	0	55	57	4.42	1.45	19.6	276	36	71	4.42	3.4	9.3	2.7	0.8	93
2016	A-	Eugene	4	0	0	35	37	0.51	0.63	20.1	161	24	91	0.16	0.8	9.5	12.3	0.0	168
2016	A	South Bend	3	1	0	40	32	3.15	1.15	22.7	242	29	74	3.08	2.3	7.2	3.2	0.7	87
2017	A	South Bend	7	6	0	123	94	4.53	1.36	19.1	265	32	65	3.68	3.1	6.9	2.2	0.4	59

Dominican lefty has a good low-90s fastball that tops at 96 mph with good late sink (career 1.6 GB/FB), a hard slider, a fringe-average change-up. Herky-jerky delivery and poor front-side mechanics result in below-average control and a move to relief seems likely, though he did have a strong 2nd half (3.45 ERA w/19BB/59K).

Paulino,David — SP — Houston

EXP MLB DEBUT: 2016 | H/W: 6-7 215 | FUT: #4 starter | 8C

Thrws R Age 24 — 2010 FA (DR)

Velo	Pitch	Grade
91-94	FB	+++
73-77	CB	+++
80-83	SL	++
81-84	CU	+++

Year	Lev	Team	W	L	Sv	IP	K	ERA	WHIP	BF/G	OBA	H%	S%	xERA	Ctl	Dom	Cmd	hr/9	BPV
2016	AA	Corpus Christi	5	2	1	64	72	1.83	0.91	17.0	207	29	82	1.76	1.5	10.1	6.5	0.4	158
2016	AAA	Fresno	0	2	0	14	20	3.86	1.57	20.5	288	44	76	4.70	3.9	12.9	3.3	0.6	145
2016	MLB	Houston	0	1	0	7	2	5.14	1.29	9.6	233	25	56	2.72	3.9	2.6	0.7	0.0	-40
2017	AAA	Fresno	0	1	0	14	13	4.50	1.43	19.8	218	23	76	4.65	5.8	8.4	1.4	1.9	12
2017	MLB	Houston	2	0	0	29	34	6.52	1.48	20.8	306	37	63	6.49	2.2	10.6	4.9	2.5	149

Tall, lean RH missed latter half of 2017 from PED-related suspension. Once touched 98 mph with FB, but now sits 91-94 with downhill plane. Wields big-bending CB as primary whiff pitch; CU has improved and will flash plus; SL is more of a complementary average offering. More control than command, but effectively fills zone and has good Dom history.

Payano,Pedro — SP — Texas

EXP MLB DEBUT: 2018 | H/W: 6-2 170 | FUT: #4 starter | 7D

Thrws R Age 23 — 2011 FA (DR)

Velo	Pitch	Grade
88-93	FB	+++
77-79	CB	++
79-83	SL	++
	CU	+++

Year	Lev	Team	W	L	Sv	IP	K	ERA	WHIP	BF/G	OBA	H%	S%	xERA	Ctl	Dom	Cmd	hr/9	BPV
2015	Rk	AZL Rangers	6	0	0	40	46	1.57	1.04	19.4	225	33	83	1.94	2.0	10.3	5.1	0.0	149
2015	A	Hickory	3	1	0	32	31	1.12	1.15	21.3	229	30	92	2.53	2.8	8.7	3.1	0.3	98
2016	A	Hickory	3	3	0	73	82	2.09	1.20	19.6	222	31	83	2.53	3.6	10.1	2.8	0.2	103
2017	A+	Down East	2	3	0	50	41	4.30	1.16	22.2	203	24	64	2.81	3.9	7.4	1.9	0.9	44
2017	AA	Frisco	4	5	0	84	77	3.64	1.40	20.9	243	31	74	3.49	4.5	8.2	1.8	0.4	45

Sturdy SP who is progressing nicely after two years in Low-A. Throws on extreme downhill plane and lives in lower half of zone. Has proven difficult to hit from slot as well as sequencing. Lacks frontline velocity and could be better in pen. Loves to use CU early in count with deceptive arm speed. Has to limit walks and find better breaker.

Pearson,Nate — SP — Toronto

EXP MLB DEBUT: 2019 | H/W: 6-6 245 | FUT: #3 starter | 8C

Thrws R Age 21 — 2017 (1) JC of Central FL

Velo	Pitch	Grade
92-97	FB	++++
82-84	SL	+++
77-80	CB	+++
83-87	CU	+++

Year	Lev	Team	W	L	Sv	IP	K	ERA	WHIP	BF/G	OBA	H%	S%	xERA	Ctl	Dom	Cmd	hr/9	BPV
2017	Rk	GCL Blue Jays	0	0	0	1	2	0.00	1.00	3.8	262	55	100	2.23	0.0	18.0		0.0	342
2017	A-	Vancouver	0	0	0	19	24	0.95	0.58	9.2	101	17	82		2.4	11.4	4.8	0.0	159

Hulking SP with imposing presence on mound. Impressed in pro debut with stuff that is hard to hit. Owns athletic delivery that he repeats and gets plus action on all offerings. FB can be electric and generally locates to both sides of plate. Uses SL as K pitch while CB also flashes plus. Fading CU can be good, but inconsistent. Could become closer.

Peguero,Joel — SP — Tampa Bay

EXP MLB DEBUT: 2021 | H/W: 5-11 160 | FUT: #3 starter | 8E

Thrws R Age 20 — 2015 FA (DR)

Velo	Pitch	Grade
95-98	FB	++++
85-89	SL	++
86-87	CU	+

Year	Lev	Team	W	L	Sv	IP	K	ERA	WHIP	BF/G	OBA	H%	S%	xERA	Ctl	Dom	Cmd	hr/9	BPV
2017	Rk	Princeton	3	5	0	44	31	8.16	1.77	15.6	350	40	52	6.62	2.2	6.3	2.8	1.0	71

Short SP with dazzling FB that can serve as out pitch. Hasn't spent time in full season and needs time to revise secondary offerings. Throws consistent strikes, but lives in middle of plate. Can be hit hard due to flat plane. Hard SL is more of control pitch than swing-and-miss offering. Could be intriguing in pen if starting doesn't work.

Pennington,Josh — SP — Milwaukee

EXP MLB DEBUT: 2019 | H/W: 6-0 175 | FUT: Setup reliever | 8E

Thrws R Age 22 — 2014 (29) HS (NJ)

Velo	Pitch	Grade
93-97	FB	++++
77-80	CB	+++
	CU	+

Year	Lev	Team	W	L	Sv	IP	K	ERA	WHIP	BF/G	OBA	H%	S%	xERA	Ctl	Dom	Cmd	hr/9	BPV
2015	Rk	GCL Red Sox	2	1	0	22	22	0.82	1.36	13.1	215	30	93	2.63	5.3	9.0	1.7	0.0	36
2016	A-	Lowell	5	3	0	56	49	2.88	1.17	17.3	197	25	75	2.25	4.3	7.8	1.8	0.3	43
2017	Rk	AZL Brewers	0	0	0	2	2	0.00	0.50	6.6	151	22	100		0.0	9.0		0.0	180
2017	A	Wisconsin	1	3	0	30	29	2.99	1.06	13.0	220	26	79	3.06	2.4	8.7	3.6	1.2	109

Hard-throwing RH missed first half of season after surgery to clean up elbow. High-velocity FB, sitting mid-90s mostly with little plane. Has average depth to 11-5 CB. Would work better with more power behind it. Lacks feel for CU. Will likely progress as starter but future is in pen where FB/CB will play up.

Peralta,Freddy — SP — Milwaukee

EXP MLB DEBUT: 2018 | H/W: 5-11 175 | FUT: #3 starter | 8C

Thrws R Age 21 — 2013 FA (DR)

Velo	Pitch	Grade
89-93	FB	++++
84-87	SL	++++
81-84	CU	+++

Year	Lev	Team	W	L	Sv	IP	K	ERA	WHIP	BF/G	OBA	H%	S%	xERA	Ctl	Dom	Cmd	hr/9	BPV
2015	Rk	AZL Mariners	2	3	0	57	67	4.11	1.05	20.1	244	35	58	2.35	1.3	10.6	8.4	0.2	174
2016	A	Wisconsin	4	1	2	60	77	2.85	1.15	14.9	210	31	76	2.43	3.6	11.6	3.2	0.5	129
2016	A+	Brevard County	0	3	0	22	20	5.73	1.77	12.6	303	35	71	6.41	4.9	8.2	1.7	1.6	33
2017	A+	Carolina	1	3	0	56	78	3.05	1.25	19.0	198	29	80	3.00	5.0	12.5	2.5	1.0	109
2017	AA	Biloxi	2	5	1	63	91	2.28	1.09	19.0	176	29	79	1.72	4.4	13.0	2.9	0.3	132

Shorter RH with advanced pitchability. Gets most out of average velocity FB with deception and by manipulating grips without sacrificing velocity and effectiveness. Can cut, sink and run in on batters at will. SL is true out pitch with sharp, biting movement. CU is solid offering, mimicking running FB with tumble.

Peralta,Ofelky — SP — Baltimore

EXP MLB DEBUT: 2020 | H/W: 6-5 195 | FUT: #3 starter | 8E

Thrws R Age 20 — 2013 FA (DR)

Velo	Pitch	Grade
91-95	FB	++++
84-85	SL	++
79-82	CB	++
	CU	+++

Year	Lev	Team	W	L	Sv	IP	K	ERA	WHIP	BF/G	OBA	H%	S%	xERA	Ctl	Dom	Cmd	hr/9	BPV
2015	Rk	GCL Orioles	0	2	0	25	31	5.71	1.55	10.0	220	33	59	3.13	6.8	11.1	1.6	0.0	34
2016	A	Delmarva	8	5	0	103	101	4.02	1.43	19.0	230	31	70	3.22	5.2	8.8	1.7	0.3	35
2017	A+	Frederick	2	10	0	104	95	5.44	1.87	18.8	271	34	71	5.29	7.4	8.2	1.1	0.7	-35

Live-armed SP with potential to dominate, but can't throw consistent strikes. More of flyball pitcher as he loses arm slot and wiry frame may not be able to withstand starting full-time. Has electric stuff with rising FB and solid-average CU. Uses same arm speed on all pitches, but needs to improve one of breaking balls. Command is major concern.

Perdomo,Angel — SP — Toronto

EXP MLB DEBUT: 2019 | H/W: 6-6 200 | FUT: #4 starter | 7C

Thrws L Age 23 — 2011 FA (DR)

Velo	Pitch	Grade
88-93	FB	++++
80-83	SL	++
80-82	CU	++

Year	Lev	Team	W	L	Sv	IP	K	ERA	WHIP	BF/G	OBA	H%	S%	xERA	Ctl	Dom	Cmd	hr/9	BPV
2014	Rk	GCL Blue Jays	3	2	1	46	57	2.54	1.24	14.4	217	32	79	2.50	4.1	11.2	2.7	0.2	108
2015	Rk	Bluefield	4	1	0	48	36	2.63	1.17	21.3	237	28	79	2.95	2.6	6.8	2.6	0.6	69
2015	A-	Vancouver	2	0	0	21	31	2.56	1.23	17.1	144	24	80	1.86	6.8	13.2	1.9	0.4	72
2016	A	Lansing	5	7	1	127	156	3.19	1.22	19.0	220	32	73	2.57	3.8	11.1	2.9	0.3	114
2017	A+	Dunedin	5	6	0	75	65	3.72	1.56	20.5	259	31	78	4.48	5.2	7.8	1.5	0.8	19

Angular, tall SP who took big step back and ended season in July. Can by filthy dominant at times with plus FB that is very sneaky due to release point and long arms. Command has been issue as he tends to rush delivery. Downhill angle helps with sharp SL, but has trouble throwing it for strikes. Could eventually move to pen.

Perez, Sam — SP — Miami

EXP MLB DEBUT: 2020 | H/W: 6-3 210 | FUT: #5 SP/swingman | 7D

Thrws R Age 23 — 2016 (5) Missouri St

Velo	Pitch	Grade
92-94	FB	+++
	CB	+++
	CU	++

Year	Lev	Team	W	L	Sv	IP	K	ERA	WHIP	BF/G	OBA	H%	S%	xERA	Ctl	Dom	Cmd	hr/9	BPV
2016	NCAA	Missouri State	8	0	1	91	112	2.86	1.10	9.9	202	30	73	2.06	3.5	11.1	3.2	0.3	124
2016	A-	Batavia	1	1	0	48	36	3.56	1.16	12.0	232	27	71	3.06	2.8	6.7	2.4	0.7	63
2017	A-	Batavia	4	2	0	77	53	2.22	1.06	21.4	241	29	80	2.55	1.5	6.2	4.1	0.4	88
2017	A	Greensboro	2	1	0	33	30	6.25	1.24	7.9	273	31	53	4.87	1.6	8.2	5.0	1.9	121

Tall righty struggled to start the year in the SAL, but got things back on track when moved to the NYPL and was put into the rotation. Fastball is best offering and sits at 92-94, topping at 96 mph. Curve and change-up are fringe-average and need to improve for him to remain a starter.

Perez,Cionel — SP — Houston

EXP MLB DEBUT: 2019 | H/W: 5-11 170 | FUT: #5 SP/swingman | 8E

Thrws L Age 21 — 2016 FA (CU)

Velo	Pitch	Grade
89-93	FB	+++
80-84	SL	+++
73-78	CB	+++
82-85	CU	++

Year	Lev	Team	W	L	Sv	IP	K	ERA	WHIP	BF/G	OBA	H%	S%	xERA	Ctl	Dom	Cmd	hr/9	BPV
2017	A	Quad Cities	4	3	2	55	55	4.41	1.25	18.7	251	33	63	3.11	2.8	9.0	3.2	0.3	105
2017	A+	Buies Creek	2	1	0	25	18	2.87	1.27	20.6	276	33	77	3.57	1.8	6.5	3.6	0.4	86
2017	AA	Corpus Christi	0	0	0	13	10	5.54	1.54	14.2	290	34	63	4.75	3.5	6.9	2.0	0.7	49

Young Cuban scooted up three levels in 2017. Requires pitchability and feel for spin and will miss bats with CB/SL. Lacks premium velocity, but should gain a few ticks as he adds mass to lean frame. Low-effort delivery and stays around the zone; size will be biggest obstacle in his quest to remain SP. High floor rather than high ceiling.

Perez,Franklin — SP — Detroit

EXP MLB DEBUT: 2019 | H/W: 6-3 197 | FUT: #2 starter | 9D

Thrws R Age 20 — 2014 FA (VZ)

Velo	Pitch	Grade
90-95	FB	++++
80-82	SL	++
75-79	CB	+++
82-84	CU	+++

Year	Lev	Team	W	L	Sv	IP	K	ERA	WHIP	BF/G	OBA	H%	S%	xERA	Ctl	Dom	Cmd	hr/9	BPV
2016	A	Quad Cities	3	3	1	66	75	2.85	1.24	17.9	252	36	75	2.90	2.6	10.2	3.9	0.1	132
2017	A+	Buies Creek	4	2	2	54	53	2.99	1.00	17.2	199	25	72	2.15	2.7	8.8	3.3	0.7	105
2017	AA	Corpus Christi	2	1	1	32	25	3.09	1.38	19.2	268	32	79	3.89	3.1	7.0	2.3	0.6	61

Steady, athletic SP with elite arm and potential for four above average offerings. Establishes plate with plus FB that he commands to both sides and has hard CB that is tough to hit. Keeps low oppBA by advanced sequencing and has frame to hold velocity deep into games. CU can flash plus. Has been treated cautiously and is ready to be let loose.

Perez,Freicer

SP | **New York (A)** | EXP MLB DEBUT: 2019 | H/W: 6-8 190 | FUT: #3 starter | **8D**

Thrws R Age 22
2014 FA (DR)

Velo	Pitch	Grade
93-97	FB	++++
76-80	CB	++
	CU	++

Year	Lev	Team	W	L	Sv	IP	K	ERA	WHIP	BF/G	OBA	H%	S%	xERA	Ctl	Dom	Cmd	hr/9	BPV
2016	A-	Staten Island	2	4	0	52	49	4.49	1.46	17.1	258	33	68	3.91	4.3	8.5	2.0	0.5	54
2017	A	Charleston (Sc)	10	3	0	123	117	2.85	1.14	20.4	216	28	75	2.44	3.3	8.5	2.6	0.4	83

Very tall, lanky SP who had tough April in first full season, but very tough after that. Has long arms and angle to plate is difficult for hitters. Added few ticks to plus FB, though will need to add strength in order to hold velocity deep into games. CB and CU progressing, but far from polished. Could be more dominant in time.

Perez,Hector

SP | **Houston** | EXP MLB DEBUT: 2019 | H/W: 6-3 190 | FUT: Closer | **8E**

Thrws R Age 21
2014 FA (DR)

Velo	Pitch	Grade
93-96	FB	++++
85-88	SL	+++
	CB	++
	SP	++

Year	Lev	Team	W	L	Sv	IP	K	ERA	WHIP	BF/G	OBA	H%	S%	xERA	Ctl	Dom	Cmd	hr/9	BPV
2016	A-	Tri City	2	0	0	28	36	1.60	1.10	15.8	193	30	84	1.67	3.8	11.5	3.0	0.0	121
2016	A	Quad Cities	2	1	0	31	44	4.63	1.61	19.7	242	38	69	3.82	6.4	12.7	2.0	0.3	75
2017	A	Quad Cities	1	1	0	18	24	2.50	1.11	17.7	151	21	83	2.18	5.5	12.0	2.2	1.0	86
2017	A+	Buies Creek	6	5	2	89	104	3.64	1.53	18.4	215	30	77	3.60	6.8	10.5	1.6	0.6	24

Hard-throwing RH with quality FB/SL tandem but also major control issues yet to hammer out. Track record for Dom is from explosive life to FB and hard slider that will miss bats. Splitter acts as CU substitute and is still raw. High-effort delivery makes Ctl, WHIP totals both concerning moving forward, but is still young with time to remain SP.

Peters, Dillon

SP | **Miami** | EXP MLB DEBUT: 2017 | H/W: 5-9 195 | FUT: #4 starter | **7A**

Thrws L Age 25
2014 (10) Texas

Velo	Pitch	Grade
91-94	FB	++++
76-80	CB	+++
81-84	CU	++

Year	Lev	Team	W	L	Sv	IP	K	ERA	WHIP	BF/G	OBA	H%	S%	xERA	Ctl	Dom	Cmd	hr/9	BPV
2016	AA	Jacksonville	3	0	0	22		2.03	0.95	20.9	214	24	84	2.34	1.6	6.5	4.0	0.8	91
2017	Rk	GCL Marlins	0	1	0	6	6	1.45	1.13	12.2	146	21	86	1.27	5.8	8.7	1.5	0.0	18
2017	A+	Jupiter	1	0	0	10	9	0.00	0.69	17.9	148	20	100	0.18	1.8	7.9	4.5	0.0	113
2017	AA	Jacksonville	6	2	0	45	40	1.99	0.97	19.1	206	27	79	1.73	2.2	8.0	3.6	0.2	102
2017	MLB	Miami	1	2	0	31	27	5.21	1.64	23.1	267	32	69	4.83	5.5	7.8	1.4	0.9	10

Short lefty has surprisingly good stuff. Fastball sits at 91-94 bumping 96 with good late sink. High-70s power curve has tight, late action and circle change is solid 3rd offering. Ability to spin the breaking ball and locate well should secure him a spot at the back-end of the Marlins rotation.

Peterson,David

SP | **New York (N)** | EXP MLB DEBUT: 2019 | H/W: 6-6 240 | FUT: #3 starter | **8C**

Thrws L Age 22
2017 (1) Oregon

Velo	Pitch	Grade
91-94	FB	+++
84-87	SL	+++
79-81	CB	+
82-83	CU	+++

Year	Lev	Team	W	L	Sv	IP	K	ERA	WHIP	BF/G	OBA	H%	S%	xERA	Ctl	Dom	Cmd	hr/9	BPV
2017	NCAA	Oregon	11	4	0	100	140	2.52	1.03	25.7	238	38	74	2.20	1.3	12.6	9.3	0.2	208
2017	A-	Brooklyn	0	0	0	3	6	2.81	1.56	4.7	307	57	80	4.32	2.8	16.9	6.0	0.0	246

Big-bodied LH was first round pick despite limited ceiling. Three of four pitches grade out average or better. Lives in lower right quadrant of zone w/ 2-seam FB that has solid sink and arm-side fade. Relies heavily on CU to keep RHH off balance, mimicking FB in location and look. SL is solid pitch vs LHH; struggles with CB. Low 3/4s arm angle.

Pfeifer,Philip

RP | **Atlanta** | EXP MLB DEBUT: 2018 | H/W: 6-0 200 | FUT: Middle reliever | **7C**

Thrws L Age 25
2015 (3) Vanderbilt

Velo	Pitch	Grade
95-98	FB	++++
78-81	CB	++++

Year	Lev	Team	W	L	Sv	IP	K	ERA	WHIP	BF/G	OBA	H%	S%	xERA	Ctl	Dom	Cmd	hr/9	BPV
2015	A	Rome	1	2	2	16	20	4.47	1.30	5.5	223	32	65	3.07	4.5	11.2	2.5	0.6	98
2016	A+	Carolina	0	0	2	7	10	2.57	1.00	4.5	132	24	71	0.76	5.1	12.9	2.5	0.0	111
2016	AA	Mississippi	1	0	0	10	8	4.46	1.49	4.0	240	31	67	3.27	5.3	7.1	1.3	0.0	2
2017	AA	Mississippi	1	3	3	44	68	3.47	1.59	6.5	229	38	78	3.70	6.7	13.9	2.1	0.4	86
2017	AAA	Gwinnett	0	2	1	15	9	3.60	1.27	5.6	191	23	68	2.14	5.4	5.4	1.0	0.0	-31

Hard-throwing, max-effort LH struggled with control in 2017. Wayward delivery, hard to repeat release point. High octane FB on flat plane. Needs to locate to be effective. Power CB untouchable at times with terrific depth and sink. True swing-and-miss package.

Phillips,Evan

RP | **Atlanta** | EXP MLB DEBUT: 2018 | H/W: 6-2 215 | FUT: Middle reliever | **6C**

Thrws R Age 23
2015 (17) UNC-Wilmington

Velo	Pitch	Grade
94-96	FB	++++
82-84	SL	+++

Year	Lev	Team	W	L	Sv	IP	K	ERA	WHIP	BF/G	OBA	H%	S%	xERA	Ctl	Dom	Cmd	hr/9	BPV
2016	A+	Carolina	2	1	8	28	19	1.28	0.93	5.0	185	23	85	1.20	2.6	6.1	2.4	0.0	58
2016	AA	Mississippi	6	3	2	34	43	4.49	1.44	6.6	255	37	68	3.80	4.2	11.3	2.7	0.5	108
2017	AA	Mississippi	1	1	1	21	24	8.14	1.57	6.1	271	33	50	5.88	4.7	10.3	2.2	2.1	76
2017	AAA	Gwinnett	2	3	2	30	29	4.78	1.76	5.5	261	34	71	4.51	6.9	8.7	1.3	0.3	-12

Hard-throwing RH reliever struggled with pitch location and control throughout season. FB can reach 98, sitting in mid-90s with solid movement within the zone. SL has solid 2-plane movement, not enough to get swings and misses against advanced hitters. Will need to refine control and SL to be successful in MLB.

Pike,Tyler

SP | **Atlanta** | EXP MLB DEBUT: 2019 | H/W: 6-0 180 | FUT: #4 starter | **7C**

Thrws L Age 24
2012 (S-3) HS (FL)

Velo	Pitch	Grade
89-93	FB	+++
82-84	CU	++++
	CU	++

Year	Lev	Team	W	L	Sv	IP	K	ERA	WHIP	BF/G	OBA	H%	S%	xERA	Ctl	Dom	Cmd	hr/9	BPV
2015	A+	Bakersfield	6	6	0	122	114	4.27	1.49	21.1	257	30	76	4.73	4.6	8.4	1.8	1.3	44
2015	AA	Jackson	0	2	0	11	7	4.91	2.09	18.0	262	31	74	5.10	9.8	5.7	0.6	0.0	-144
2016	A+	Bakersfield	6	5	0	125	134	4.03	1.33	20.8	219	29	71	3.34	4.9	9.6	2.0	0.8	59
2017	A+	Florida	5	2	0	69	68	2.21	1.20	23.2	223	30	81	2.56	3.5	8.8	2.5	0.3	82
2017	AA	Mississippi	0	9	0	74	86	4.61	1.68	22.3	229	32	71	3.93	7.6	10.4	1.4	0.4	-1

ATL revamped mechanics, creating better plane on FB. FB was harder, missing bats regularly. Struggled mightily with control. CU is best secondary pitch with plus, arm-side run and tumble. CB lags behind rest of profile.

Pint, Riley

SP | **Colorado** | EXP MLB DEBUT: 2020 | H/W: 6-4 195 | FUT: #1 starter | **9D**

Thrws R Age 20
2016 (1) HS (KS)

Velo	Pitch	Grade
95-99	FB	+++++
80-83	CB	+++
86-88	SL	+++
	CU	+++

Year	Lev	Team	W	L	Sv	IP	K	ERA	WHIP	BF/G	OBA	H%	S%	xERA	Ctl	Dom	Cmd	hr/9	BPV
2016	Rk	Grand Junction	1	5	0	37	36	5.35	1.78	15.5	292	37	69	5.18	5.6	8.8	1.6	0.5	25
2017	A	Asheville	2	11	0	93	79	5.42	1.67	19.0	268	34	65	4.37	5.7	7.6	1.3	0.3	1

Has top-of-the rotation stuff, but struggles repeating mechanics and finding the strike zone. Double-plus FB sits at 95-99, topping at 101 mph is backed up by plus CB, along with SL and CU that flashes plus with late fade. Throws with effort and needs work to reach his potential.

Plutko,Adam

SP | **Cleveland** | EXP MLB DEBUT: 2016 | H/W: 6-3 200 | FUT: #4 starter | **7D**

Thrws R Age 26
2013 (11) UCLA

Velo	Pitch	Grade
88-93	FB	+++
80-83	SL	+++
79-82	CB	++
	CU	+++

Year	Lev	Team	W	L	Sv	IP	K	ERA	WHIP	BF/G	OBA	H%	S%	xERA	Ctl	Dom	Cmd	hr/9	BPV
2015	AA	Akron	9	5	0	116	90	2.87	1.02	23.5	227	27	75	2.59	1.8	7.0	3.9	0.7	95
2016	AA	Akron	3	3	0	71	63	3.29	1.07	21.3	242	30	70	2.82	1.5	8.0	5.3	0.6	120
2016	AAA	Columbus	6	5	0	90	67	4.10	1.34	25.0	255	30	71	3.87	3.4	6.7	2.0	0.8	47
2016	MLB	Cleveland	0	0	0	3	3	8.44	2.19	8.0	357	40	67	9.45	5.6	8.4	1.5	2.8	18
2017	AAA	Columbus	7	12	0	135	103	5.92	1.52	24.5	286	32	64	5.51	3.5	6.9	1.9	1.6	46

Tall SP who had poor year and underwent hip surgery in October—likely to return in mid-2018. Was hittable as he was around plate too much. Lacks premium velocity and must rely on pitch sequencing. CU may be best pitch and repeats arm speed. Hasn't been good above AA and is extreme flyball pitcher. At best when locating FB to both sides.

Ponce,Cody

SP | **Milwaukee** | EXP MLB DEBUT: 2019 | H/W: 6-6 265 | FUT: #3 starter | **8C**

Thrws R Age 23
2015 (2) Cal Poly Pomona

Velo	Pitch	Grade
93-96	FB	++++
87-89	CT	+++
77-79	CB	++
83-85	CU	+++

Year	Lev	Team	W	L	Sv	IP	K	ERA	WHIP	BF/G	OBA	H%	S%	xERA	Ctl	Dom	Cmd	hr/9	BPV
2015	Rk	Helena	0	0	0	5	4	3.60	0.80	9.1	221	28	50	1.30	0.0	7.2		0.0	148
2015	A	Wisconsin	2	1	3	46	36	2.15	1.13	15.1	249	31	80	2.67	1.8	7.0	4.0	0.2	97
2016	A+	Brevard County	2	8	0	72	69	5.25	1.40	17.9	293	37	62	4.48	2.1	8.6	4.1	0.8	116
2017	A+	Carolina	8	8	0	120	94	3.45	1.30	22.5	279	32	77	4.32	1.9	7.1	3.8	1.1	94
2017	AA	Biloxi	2	1	0	17	9	1.57	0.87	21.2	171	20	80	0.92	2.6	4.7	1.8	0.0	32

Big-bodied, hard-throwing RH improved secondaries in solid 2017. Up to 97-98, sitting mid-90s with solid, late run. Added velocity to CT, adding to effectiveness. Added shape to CB but struggled finishing pitch and hooking wrist. CU has solid tumble and deception.

Poteet, Cody

SP | **Miami** | EXP MLB DEBUT: 2019 | H/W: 6-1 190 | FUT: #5 SP/swingman | **7D**

Thrws R Age 23
2015 (4) UCLA

Velo	Pitch	Grade
88-91	FB	++
75-77	CB	+++
84-86	SL	++
	CU	++

Year	Lev	Team	W	L	Sv	IP	K	ERA	WHIP	BF/G	OBA	H%	S%	xERA	Ctl	Dom	Cmd	hr/9	BPV
2015	NCAA	UCLA	7	1	0	73	68	2.46	1.26	11.0	231	30	81	2.92	3.7	8.4	2.3	0.4	69
2015	A-	Batavia	0	1	0	12	12	2.21	0.90	9.1	207	26	80	2.07	1.5	8.9	6.0	0.7	138
2016	A	Greensboro	4	9	0	117	106	2.92	1.30	20.1	246	31	78	3.23	3.4	8.1	2.4	0.4	73
2017	Rk	GCL Marlins	0	1	0	14	12	3.21	0.93	13.1	218	29	62	1.58	1.3	7.7	6.0	0.0	122
2017	A+	Jupiter	3	7	0	80	40	4.16	1.34	20.8	271	31	67	3.55	2.6	4.5	1.7	0.2	29

Soft-tossing rigthy competes well despite the lack of a true out pitch. Fastball sits at 88-91 mph with an average slider, curve, and improved change-up. Keeps the ball down in the zone and gave up just 2 HR in 94 IP. 4-pitch mix gives him a chance to stick as a back-end starter.

Povse,Max — SP — Seattle

EXP MLB DEBUT: 2017 | H/W: 6-8 185 | FUT: #4 starter | 7B

Thrws R Age 24
2014 (3) UNC-Greensboro

Velo	Pitch	Grade
89-95	FB	+++
80-84	CB	+++
84-85	CU	++

Year	Lev	Team	W	L	Sv	IP	K	ERA	WHIP	BF/G	OBA	H%	S%	xERA	Ctl	Dom	Cmd	hr/9	BPV
2016	A+	Carolina	5	5	0	87	91	3.72	1.22	23.4	266	35	69	3.40	1.8	9.4	5.4	0.5	140
2016	AA	Mississippi	4	1	0	70	48	2.95	1.04	24.6	236	28	72	2.58	1.5	6.2	4.0	0.5	87
2017	AA	Arkansas	3	2	0	39	32	3.46	1.23	17.6	236	30	70	2.79	3.2	7.4	2.3	0.2	64
2017	AAA	Tacoma	1	4	0	31	29	7.50	1.70	10.8	318	39	54	5.73	3.5	8.4	2.4	0.9	75
2017	MLB	Seattle	0	0	0	3	2	8.44	3.13	6.3	499	53	78	15.16	2.8	5.6	2.0	2.8	43

Very tall, lean SP who reached majors for first time. Repeats delivery and arm slot to pitch effectively downhill. Overhand CB could be best pitch and can throw for consistent strikes. Can start or relieve, but will need better CU to stick in rotation. Velocity has been consistent and could become innings-eater over time.

Puckett,AJ — SP — Chicago (A)

EXP MLB DEBUT: 2019 | H/W: 6-4 200 | FUT: #4 starter | 7C

Thrws R Age 22
2016 (2) Pepperdine

Velo	Pitch	Grade
90-94	FB	+++
77-79	CB	++
80-84	CU	++++

Year	Lev	Team	W	L	Sv	IP	K	ERA	WHIP	BF/G	OBA	H%	S%	xERA	Ctl	Dom	Cmd	hr/9	BPV
2016	NCAA	Pepperdine	9	3	0	99	95	1.27	0.92	26.5	189	25	87	1.37	2.4	8.6	3.7	0.2	110
2016	Rk	AZL Royals	0	1	0	7	8	3.86	1.14	13.9	288	37	71	4.25	0.0	10.3		1.3	203
2016	A	Lexington	2	3	0	51	37	3.69	1.11	18.3	225	26	68	2.81	2.6	6.5	2.5	0.7	64
2017	A+	Winston-Salem	1	0	0	27	21	4.32	1.48	23.3	314	37	71	4.93	1.7	7.0	4.2	0.7	99
2017	A+	Wilmington	9	7	0	108	98	3.91	1.42	22.9	260	33	73	3.89	3.8	8.2	2.1	0.6	61

Big, strong RHP acquired in Melky Cabrera deal. Pitchability through the roof. Uses frame to create deception. Sits low 90s with boring 2-seam FB. Best pitch is terrific CU, which tumbles effortlessly out of the zone. CB lacks depth. Doesn't get on top of pitch.

Puk,A.J. — SP — Oakland

EXP MLB DEBUT: 2018 | H/W: 6-7 220 | FUT: #2 starter | 9C

Thrws L Age 22
2016 (1) Florida

Velo	Pitch	Grade
93-97	FB	++++
78-81	CB	++
84-86	SL	++++
83-86	CU	++

Year	Lev	Team	W	L	Sv	IP	K	ERA	WHIP	BF/G	OBA	H%	S%	xERA	Ctl	Dom	Cmd	hr/9	BPV
2016	NCAA	Florida	2	3	0	73	101	3.07	1.20	17.3	198	30	77	2.68	4.5	12.4	2.7	0.7	119
2016	A-	Vermont	0	4	0	32	40	3.07	1.09	12.6	202	31	69	1.75	3.4	11.2	3.3	0.0	129
2017	A+	Stockton	4	5	0	61	98	3.69	1.10	17.1	204	37	64	1.91	3.4	14.5	4.3	0.1	187
2017	AA	Midland	2	5	0	64	86	4.36	1.39	20.7	262	40	67	3.53	3.5	12.1	3.4	0.3	141

Long, lanky SP who uses height well and finished 3rd in minors in K. Has filthy stuff when delivery is consistent, especially dynamite FB and SL. Doesn't repeat mechanics, but has thrown more strikes. Lots of bite and movement to secondary stuff and has the size and stuff to be very high K guy. Also needs to work on efficiency.

Quantrill,Cal — SP — San Diego

EXP MLB DEBUT: 2018 | H/W: 6-2 165 | FUT: #3 starter | 9C

Thrws R Age 23
2016 (1) Stanford

Velo	Pitch	Grade
92-97	FB	++++
80-83	CU	++++
77-82	CB	+++

Year	Lev	Team	W	L	Sv	IP	K	ERA	WHIP	BF/G	OBA	H%	S%	xERA	Ctl	Dom	Cmd	hr/9	BPV
2016	A-	Tri-City	0	2	0	18	28	1.98	0.93	13.7	226	39	76	1.63	1.0	13.8	14.0	0.0	241
2016	A	Fort Wayne	0	1	0	4	2	19.29	3.81	13.9	503	53	47	16.39	8.6	4.3	0.5	2.1	-136
2017	A+	Lake Elsinore	6	5	0	73	76	3.69	1.39	22.0	274	36	74	4.06	3.0	9.3	3.2	0.6	107
2017	AA	San Antonio	1	5	0	42	34	4.06	1.62	23.3	305	36	78	5.51	3.4	7.3	2.1	1.1	56

Former top-10 pick with ingredients for quality #3 SP. Sits mid-90s with four-seam FB and gets misses with it up in the zone. Circle CU is true plus pitch, though can over-rely on it at times. CB/SL are works in progress and will be sticking points moving forward, but should be average pitches. Good athlete with sound mechanics and easy delivery.

Ragans,Cole — SP — Texas

EXP MLB DEBUT: 2021 | H/W: 6-4 190 | FUT: #3 starter | 8C

Thrws L Age 20
2016 (1) HS (FL)

Velo	Pitch	Grade
90-95	FB	++++
75-77	CB	++
78-84	CU	+++

Year	Lev	Team	W	L	Sv	IP	K	ERA	WHIP	BF/G	OBA	H%	S%	xERA	Ctl	Dom	Cmd	hr/9	BPV
2016	Rk	AZL Rangers	0	0	0	7	9	5.00	2.36	9.3	351	49	76	7.12	7.5	11.3	1.5	0.0	18
2017	A-	Spokane	3	2	0	57	87	3.63	1.49	18.9	237	38	78	3.91	5.5	13.7	2.5	0.8	116

Athletic, advanced SP who has yet to see full season action, but posts very high K rate due to multiple out pitches. Lacks consistency with delivery and performance. Has chance to own three plus pitches. FB is quick and plays up due to angle to plate. CU is best secondary with depth and fade. CB shows flashes, but loses arm slot and can lack break.

Rainey,Tanner — RP — Cincinnati

EXP MLB DEBUT: 2018 | H/W: 6-2 235 | FUT: Setup reliever | 8E

Thrws R Age 25
2015 (S-2) West Alabama

Velo	Pitch	Grade
94-97	FB	++++
85-88	SL	++++

Year	Lev	Team	W	L	Sv	IP	K	ERA	WHIP	BF/G	OBA	H%	S%	xERA	Ctl	Dom	Cmd	hr/9	BPV
2015	NCAA	West Alabama	4	1	9	28	50	1.60	0.89	4.0	122	25	83	0.65	4.5	16.0	3.6	0.3	185
2015	Rk	Billings	2	2	0	59	57	4.27	1.46	16.8	258	34	69	3.71	4.3	8.7	2.0	0.3	59
2016	A+	Dayton	5	10	1	103	113	5.59	1.70	16.1	273	36	67	4.95	5.8	9.9	1.7	0.8	40
2017	A+	Dayton	2	2	9	45	77	3.80	0.96	4.4	142	25	62	1.48	4.4	15.4	3.5	0.8	176
2017	AA	Pensacola	1	1	4	17	27	1.59	1.12	4.8	143	22	94	2.15	5.8	14.3	2.5	1.1	118

Hard-throwing RH transitioned back to reliever full-time in 2017. Body fights staying balanced in delivery, control suffers. FB velocity played up in shorter stints. Explosive, late-breaking movement remained. SL became sharper and harder in relief role. Improvement in effectiveness of both pitches contributed in Dom improvement. Has scrapped CU.

Ramirez,Carlos — RP — Toronto

EXP MLB DEBUT: 2017 | H/W: 6-5 205 | FUT: Setup reliever | 6A

Thrws R Age 26
2009 FA (DR)

Velo	Pitch	Grade
93-96	FB	+++
85-86	SL	+++

Year	Lev	Team	W	L	Sv	IP	K	ERA	WHIP	BF/G	OBA	H%	S%	xERA	Ctl	Dom	Cmd	hr/9	BPV
2015	A+	Dunedin	0	2	0	7	7	6.34	2.82	6.7	333	43	75	7.98	12.7	8.9	0.7	0.0	-165
2016	A+	Dunedin	3	0	9	41	41	2.20	1.29	5.6	217	29	84	2.88	4.6	9.0	2.0	0.4	56
2017	AA	New Hampshire	0	0	3	23	29	0.78	0.73	4.6	133	22	88	0.11	2.7	11.3	4.1	0.0	147
2017	AAA	Buffalo	1	0	0	14	16	0.00	0.64	6.9	132	20	100		1.9	10.3	5.3	0.0	151
2017	MLB	Toronto	0	0	0	17	14	2.78	0.56	4.8	116	9	67	1.10	1.7	7.8	4.7	1.7	113

Tall RP who converted from OF to pitcher in 2014 and shows surprising polish. Did not allow an ER in minors in 2017 and reached TOR where he looked good. Succeeded with improved control and command while knocking out hitters with good FB/SL combo. Lot of moving parts in delivery keeps him in pen. Tends to elevate pitches, but that is nit-picking.

Ramirez,Nick — RP — Milwaukee

EXP MLB DEBUT: 2018 | H/W: 6-3 225 | FUT: Middle reliever | 7C

Thrws L Age 28
2011 (4) Cal St Fullerton

Velo	Pitch	Grade
89-92	FB	+++
77-80	CB	+++
81-82	CU	+++

Year	Lev	Team	W	L	Sv	IP	K	ERA	WHIP	BF/G	OBA	H%	S%	xERA	Ctl	Dom	Cmd	hr/9	BPV
2017	AA	Biloxi	7	4	3	79	56	1.37	1.01	6.3	201	24	89	2.03	2.7	6.4	2.3	0.5	59

Converted 1B was dynamic returning to the mound. Was Cal State Fullerton's closer in college. Dominated Double-A hitters with three solid pitches. FB has plus arm-side bore. Solid groundball tendencies. CB is effective eye-level changer while CU has makings of swing-and-miss offering against RHH. It has advanced deception and some tumble.

Ramirez,Yefry — SP — Baltimore

EXP MLB DEBUT: 2018 | H/W: 6-2 215 | FUT: #4 starter | 7C

Thrws R Age 24
2011 FA (DR)

Velo	Pitch	Grade
91-93	FB	+++
79-81	CB	+++
82-84	CU	+++

Year	Lev	Team	W	L	Sv	IP	K	ERA	WHIP	BF/G	OBA	H%	S%	xERA	Ctl	Dom	Cmd	hr/9	BPV
2015	Rk	Missoula	5	5	0	69	61	5.35	1.29	20.3	259	30	62	4.37	2.7	8.0	2.9	1.4	87
2016	A	Charleston (Sc)	4	2	0	61	66	2.80	1.02	21.3	218	29	74	2.34	2.1	9.7	4.7	0.6	138
2016	A+	Tampa	3	7	0	63	66	2.85	0.82	20.9	160	21	68	1.31	2.6	9.4	3.7	0.7	118
2017	AA	Trenton	10	3	0	92	91	3.42	1.26	20.9	231	29	76	3.39	3.7	8.9	2.4	0.9	78
2017	AA	Bowie	5	0	0	31	26	3.77	1.23	20.9	236	25	78	4.19	3.2	7.5	2.4	1.7	68

Rapidly developing SP who converted from OF in 2012. Possesses natural control due to athletic, repeatable delivery and slot. Lacks knockout pitch, but thrives with advanced sequencing. K rate has risen despite no out pitch and has three average offerings. Can allow too many flyballs and HR. Intriguing pitchability.

Raquet,Nick — SP — Washington

EXP MLB DEBUT: 2020 | H/W: 6-0 215 | FUT: #5 SP/swingman | 7D

Thrws L Age 22
2017 (3) William & Mary

Velo	Pitch	Grade
91-95	FB	+++
	CU	+++
	CB	++
	SL	

Year	Lev	Team	W	L	Sv	IP	K	ERA	WHIP	BF/G	OBA	H%	S%	xERA	Ctl	Dom	Cmd	hr/9	BPV
2017	NCAA	William & Mary	2	2	0	77	95	4.67	1.61	21.3	267	38	71	4.44	5.3	11.1	2.1	0.6	76
2017	Rk	GCL Nationals	0	0	0	2	2	0.00	1.00	7.6	262	35	100	2.32	0.0	9.0		0.0	180
2017	A-	Auburn	3	2	0	51	22	2.47	1.23	18.8	280	31	80	3.54	1.2	3.9	3.1	0.4	54

With some funk to his delivery and an over-the-top slot, he fooled hitters in college, but not so much in his first pro stop. Considerable arm strength gets the FB into the mid-90s, and CU shows some promise, but two breaking balls need work. Stuff is raw and will start for now; could move into relief at some point.

Raudes,Roniel — SP — Boston

EXP MLB DEBUT: 2019 | H/W: 6-1 160 | FUT: #4 starter | 7C

Thrws R Age 20
2014 FA (NI)

Velo	Pitch	Grade
88-92	FB	+++
78-80	CB	+++
81-82	CU	+++

Year	Lev	Team	W	L	Sv	IP	K	ERA	WHIP	BF/G	OBA	H%	S%	xERA	Ctl	Dom	Cmd	hr/9	BPV
2016	A	Greenville	11	6	0	113	104	3.66	1.19	18.9	260	33	70	3.38	1.8	8.3	4.5	0.6	118
2017	A+	Salem	4	7	0	116	95	4.50	1.53	22.0	291	34	73	5.11	3.4	7.4	2.2	1.1	59

Quick-armed, slender SP who saw walk rate increase with slight drop in K rate. Was too hittable and lacks plus offering. Still, has advanced mixing ability and offers deception with arm action. Has potential to add velocity and has keen ability to locate all offerings. Can pitch backwards effectively by starting with CU and wiping out with FB.

Ravenelle,Adam — RP — Detroit

EXP MLB DEBUT: 2018 | H/W: 6-3 185 | FUT: Setup reliever | 7C

Thrws R Age 25
2014 (4) Vanderbilt
92-97 FB ++++
83-87 SL +++
CU +

Year	Lev	Team	W	L	Sv	IP	K	ERA	WHIP	BF/G	OBA	H%	S%	xERA	Ctl	Dom	Cmd	hr/9	BPV
2015	Rk	GCL Tigers	0	0	0	4	1	0.00	0.75	7.1	0	0	100		6.8	2.3	0.3	0.0	-124
2015	A	West Michigan	2	0	0	34	40	3.96	1.47	7.7	244	34	73	3.73	5.0	10.6	2.1	0.5	73
2016	A+	Lakeland	2	1	3	28	34	2.88	1.21	4.9	177	24	81	2.68	5.4	10.9	2.0	1.0	67
2016	AA	Erie	1	1	1	29	23	4.93	1.58	4.8	267	30	71	5.02	4.9	7.1	1.4	1.2	12
2017	AA	Erie	0	5	1	52	49	5.18	1.54	5.4	287	34	69	5.32	3.6	8.5	2.3	1.4	72

Tall, athletic RP with ideal frame for velocity and durability. Has tendency to overthrow at times, which negatively impacts command. Improved walk rate in 2017 while spotting plus, sinking FB to bottom half of zone. Uses height and arm slot to use effective SL, but FB is out pitch. Not much feel or touch for limited CU.

Reed,Cody — SP — Arizona

EXP MLB DEBUT: 2019 | H/W: 6-3 245 | FUT: #3 starter | 8E

Thrws L Age 21
2014 (2) HS (AL)
90-92 FB +++
82-84 SL +++
81-83 CU ++++

Year	Lev	Team	W	L	Sv	IP	K	ERA	WHIP	BF/G	OBA	H%	S%	xERA	Ctl	Dom	Cmd	hr/9	BPV
2015	A-	Hillsboro	5	4	0	63	72	3.28	1.14	16.7	223	30	73	2.82	3.0	10.3	3.4	0.7	122
2016	A	Kane County	5	2	0	39	55	1.84	0.89	20.8	224	36	79	1.74	0.7	12.6	18.3	0.2	227
2016	A+	Visalia	0	5	0	35	29	6.14	1.62	19.5	287	34	62	5.21	4.3	7.4	1.7	1.0	34
2017	A	Kane County	3	2	0	46	49	1.75	0.87	21.3	182	26	79	1.17	2.1	9.5	4.5	0.2	132
2017	A+	Visalia	5	6	0	89	90	3.93	1.39	22.1	272	33	77	4.77	3.0	9.1	3.0	1.4	100

Big-bodied LH finally came into his own this season. Cmd has been there for a few years; Dom took a step forward with stuff. Commands FB up and down, in and out. SL is sharp breaker, an above average pitch. Feel for CU really improved: look and arm speed of FB with significant tumble; hard to lay off.

Reed,Jake — RP — Minnesota

EXP MLB DEBUT: 2018 | H/W: 6-2 190 | FUT: Setup reliever | 7C

Thrws R Age 25
2014 (5) Oregon
91-96 FB ++++
83-86 SL ++
CU ++

Year	Lev	Team	W	L	Sv	IP	K	ERA	WHIP	BF/G	OBA	H%	S%	xERA	Ctl	Dom	Cmd	hr/9	BPV
2015	AA	Chattanooga	4	4	1	47		6.32	1.62	6.0	293	36	59	4.88	4.0	7.5	1.9	0.6	44
2016	AA	Chattanooga	3	3	3	60	64	3.90	1.22	5.9	232	32	66	2.74	3.3	9.6	2.9	0.3	102
2016	AAA	Rochester	1	1	0	10	8	1.76	0.98	4.3	218	28	80	1.71	1.8	7.1	4.0	0.0	97
2017	AA	Chattanooga	1	0	1	7	8	2.54	1.41	6.0	167	25	80	2.17	7.6	10.1	1.3	0.0	-5
2017	AAA	Rochester	1	0	5	30	25	2.09	1.16	5.5	220	28	82	2.47	3.3	7.5	2.3	0.3	64

Power-armed RP who started season late due to back injury. Has spent entire career in pen and has power arsenal to be asset. K rate dropped in AAA and could benefit from better sequencing. Likes to go to heavy FB early in count and has commanded it better. SL has shown incremental improvement while he rarely changes speeds.

Reid-Foley,Sean — SP — Toronto

EXP MLB DEBUT: 2018 | H/W: 6-3 220 | FUT: #2 starter | 9D

Thrws R Age 22
2014 (2) HS (FL)
92-95 FB ++++
82-86 SL +++
77-79 CB +++
84-87 CU ++

Year	Lev	Team	W	L	Sv	IP	K	ERA	WHIP	BF/G	OBA	H%	S%	xERA	Ctl	Dom	Cmd	hr/9	BPV
2015	A	Lansing	3	5	0	63	90	3.71	1.58	16.3	243	38	76	3.90	6.1	12.8	2.1	0.4	83
2015	A+	Dunedin	1	5	0	32	35	5.31	1.52	17.5	216	30	63	3.29	6.7	9.8	1.5	0.3	13
2016	A	Lansing	4	3	0	58	59	2.95	1.12	20.8	208	28	73	2.22	3.4	9.2	2.7	0.3	91
2016	A+	Dunedin	6	2	0	57	71	2.68	0.89	21.2	179	27	69	1.29	2.5	11.2	4.4	0.3	151
2017	AA	New Hampshire	10	11	0	132	122	5.11	1.50	21.1	280	33	70	5.24	3.6	8.3	2.3	1.5	70

Tall, durable SP who struggled in AA, but was young for level and still shows above average stuff. Throws with steep angle to plate and gives hint of deception. Saw big increase in HR and will need consistency with secondary pitches. Throws hard stuff with plus FB with life, big SL, and improving CB. CU flashes average and could use against LHH.

Requena,Hildemaro — SP — Boston

EXP MLB DEBUT: 2020 | H/W: 6-2 170 | FUT: #4 starter | 7D

Thrws R Age 20
2013 FA (VZ)
86-92 FB +++
74-76 CB +++
79-82 CU ++

Year	Lev	Team	W	L	Sv	IP	K	ERA	WHIP	BF/G	OBA	H%	S%	xERA	Ctl	Dom	Cmd	hr/9	BPV
2016	Rk	GCL Red Sox	3	4	2	65	52	2.35	0.97	18.9	237	30	75	2.19	0.8	7.2	8.7	0.3	125
2017	A	Greenville	11	3	3	95	84	1.99	1.08	11.6	212	28	81	2.07	2.9	7.9	2.7	0.2	82

Extreme sinkerballer who pitched out of bullpen before move to SP in late July. Needs to add stamina and strength to stick as SP. Lacks ideal velocity now, but has projection in lean frame. Throws good strikes and spots sinker to bottom of zone. Slow CB exhibits good shape and thrown with clean arm action. CU has chance to be 3rd solid offering.

Reyes, Alex — SP — St. Louis

EXP MLB DEBUT: 2016 | H/W: 6-3 175 | FUT: #1 starter | 9B

Thrws R Age 23
2012 FA (DR)
95-97 FB +++++
75-78 CB ++++
88-90 CU +++

Year	Lev	Team	W	L	Sv	IP	K	ERA	WHIP	BF/G	OBA	H%	S%	xERA	Ctl	Dom	Cmd	hr/9	BPV
2015	A+	Palm Beach	2	5	0	63	96	2.28	1.27	19.9	216	37	80	2.34	4.4	13.7	3.1	0.0	145
2015	AA	Springfield	3	2	0	34	52	3.16	1.14	16.9	179	31	71	1.84	4.7	13.7	2.9	0.3	136
2016	AAA	Memphis	2	3	0	65	93	4.98	1.46	19.9	255	39	66	4.13	4.4	12.9	2.9	0.8	130
2016	MLB	St. Louis	4	1	1	46	52	1.57	1.22	15.5	203	29	87	2.28	4.5	10.2	2.3	0.2	80
2016	*Did not pitch - injured*																		

Dynamic hurler missed all of 2017 with Tommy Johns surgery, but should be ready to go by spring training. Double plus fastball sits in the mid-to-upper 90s topping out at 102 mph. Plus 12-6 power curve gives him the tools to dominate, but change-up needs to improve for him to reach his potential as a #1 starter. If not, can still dominate as a shut-down closer.

Reyes, Luis — SP — Washington

EXP MLB DEBUT: 2020 | H/W: 6-2 175 | FUT: #5 SP/swingman | 7C

Thrws R Age 23
2012 FA (DR)
91-93 FB +++
76-80 CB ++
83-86 CU ++

Year	Lev	Team	W	L	Sv	IP	K	ERA	WHIP	BF/G	OBA	H%	S%	xERA	Ctl	Dom	Cmd	hr/9	BPV
2015	A	Hagerstown	6	7	0	117	72	4.84	1.42	20.7	261	29	66	4.14	3.8	5.5	1.4	0.8	14
2016	A-	Auburn	0	1	0	8	3	1.13	0.88	9.9	210	23	86	1.39	1.1	3.4	3.0	0.0	48
2016	A	Hagerstown	0	2	0	16	7	2.81	1.50	23.0	274	28	86	4.85	3.9	3.9	1.0	1.1	-17
2016	A+	Potomac	4	8	0	70	46	5.64	1.64	22.4	258	29	66	4.75	5.9	5.9	1.0	0.9	-35
2017	A+	Potomac	8	13	0	143	133	4.34	1.43	23.4	270	32	73	4.64	3.5	8.4	2.4	1.2	73

Lanky but well-proportioned, has a loose arm that comes from a tall delivery. FB up to 94, can get on batter quick, and not afraid to use it inside, though at times has trouble commanding it. Secondaries still need work to get to average; CB more effective at higher velocity. Not a high ceiling, but some athleticism and a FB to work with.

Rhame,Jacob — RP — New York (N)

EXP MLB DEBUT: 2017 | H/W: 6-1 215 | FUT: Middle reliever | 7C

Thrws R Age 25
2013 (6) Grayson Cty CC
92-97 FB ++++
86-89 SL ++
82-84 SP ++

Year	Lev	Team	W	L	Sv	IP	K	ERA	WHIP	BF/G	OBA	H%	S%	xERA	Ctl	Dom	Cmd	hr/9	BPV
2015	AA	Tulsa	3	3	2	50	57	3.06	1.06	5.0	194	26	75	2.45	3.4	10.3	3.0	0.9	110
2016	AAA	Oklahoma City	1	7	7	63	70	3.29	1.29	4.8	230	31	76	3.28	4.0	10.0	2.5	0.7	90
2017	AAA	Oklahoma City	0	2	2	48	55	4.31	1.29	4.8	278	36	70	4.32	1.9	10.3	5.5	1.1	153
2017	AAA	Las Vegas	0	1	0	6	11	1.50	0.33	4.7	106	25	50		0.0	16.5		0.0	315
2017	MLB	NY Mets	1	1	0	9	7	9.00	2.11	4.9	321	35	59	7.90	7.0	7.0	1.0	2.0	-45

Hard-throwing RH made MLB debut after being return in Granderson deal. Extreme fly ball tendency; mixes 2-seam and 4- seam FBs to keep hitters off balance. Both pitches are plus; 4-seam FB has wicked movement late. Hasn't nailed down true secondary pitch. Power SL lacks tilt and splitter isn't sharp at all.

Richards, Trevor — SP — Miami

EXP MLB DEBUT: 2018 | H/W: 6-2 190 | FUT: #5 SP/swingman | 7D

Thrws R Age 24
2016 (NDFA) Drury
87-91 FB ++
CB ++
80-83 CU ++++

Year	Lev	Team	W	L	Sv	IP	K	ERA	WHIP	BF/G	OBA	H%	S%	xERA	Ctl	Dom	Cmd	hr/9	BPV
2016	A-	Batavia	0	0	0	10	15	1.76	1.08	13.3	238	37	90	2.99	1.8	13.2	7.5	0.9	209
2016	A	Greensboro	2	3	0	43	38	2.71	1.00	20.6	192	24	75	2.03	2.9	7.9	2.7	0.6	82
2017	A+	Jupiter	7	4	0	70	81	2.18	0.94	20.3	214	31	77	1.78	1.5	10.4	6.8	0.3	163
2017	AA	Jacksonville	5	7	0	75	77	2.88	1.13	21.2	240	32	75	2.81	2.2	9.2	4.3	0.5	126

Independent League find had a breakout season at two stops. Fringe-average fastball rarely breaks 90 mph and curveball lacks late bite, but his plus change-up is a weapon and keeps hitters off-balance. Hides the ball well and pounds the strike zone giving him a chance to stick as a back-end starter.

Rios,Francisco — SP — Toronto

EXP MLB DEBUT: 2019 | H/W: 6-1 180 | FUT: #4 starter | 7D

Thrws R Age 22
2012 FA (MX)
89-93 FB +++
80-82 SL ++
74-76 CB +++
CU +

Year	Lev	Team	W	L	Sv	IP	K	ERA	WHIP	BF/G	OBA	H%	S%	xERA	Ctl	Dom	Cmd	hr/9	BPV
2014	Rk	Bluefield	3	2	0	53	38	5.93	1.83	19.0	345	40	67	6.52	3.1	6.4	2.1	0.8	52
2015	A-	Vancouver	3	6	0	65	59	4.29	1.49	18.7	282	36	69	3.97	3.5	8.2	2.4	0.1	72
2016	A	Lansing	2	0	0	30	43	1.20	0.97	18.9	199	34	86	1.40	2.4	12.9	5.4	0.0	185
2016	A+	Dunedin	5	6	0	90	65	3.49	1.21	19.1	257	30	71	3.27	2.1	6.5	3.1	0.5	78
2017	AA	New Hampshire	3	9	0	86	63	4.29	1.50	16.2	271	31	74	4.71	4.1	6.6	1.6	1.0	26

Aggressive SP with clean, deceptive delivery. Control regressed and needs pitch to retire LHH. Has deep mix of pitches and all flash at least average except CU. FB exhibits natural movement and is tough to square up. Complements with slow CB and power SL. Has frail frame and stamina can be concern. Has chance to succeed if CU improves.

Robinson,Alex — RP — Minnesota

EXP MLB DEBUT: 2019 | H/W: 6-3 217 | FUT: Setup reliever | 7D

Thrws L Age 23
2015 (5) Maryland
92-96 FB ++++
80-83 SL ++
CU +

Year	Lev	Team	W	L	Sv	IP	K	ERA	WHIP	BF/G	OBA	H%	S%	xERA	Ctl	Dom	Cmd	hr/9	BPV
2015	NCAA	Maryland	1	1	3	27	32	1.65	1.18	4.3	135	20	87	1.57	6.6	10.6	1.6	0.3	30
2015	Rk	Elizabethton	0	3	0	12	15	9.00	2.17	6.0	228	35	54	4.79	12.0	11.3	0.9	0.0	-104
2016	Rk	Elizabethton	0	1	0	33	52	3.00	1.61	9.7	170	29	82	3.18	9.3	14.2	1.5	0.5	23
2017	A	Cedar Rapids	2	5	2	38	51	2.84	1.16	5.4	213	32	76	2.50	3.6	12.1	3.4	0.5	140
2017	A+	Fort Myers	4	0	0	17	27	4.74	1.58	5.8	225	38	69	3.74	6.8	14.2	2.1	0.5	89

Big-framed RP with electric arm that produces velocity and pitch movement from lower arm angle. Has been lethal to LHH and very tough to hit. Improved control while in Low-A, but regressed upon promotion to A+ in first full season. Has high K ability with sharp SL. Has dominant stretches, but comes back to earth with walks.

Robles, Domingo | SP | Pittsburgh | EXP MLB DEBUT: 2022 | H/W: 6-2 170 | FUT: #4 starter | 7D

Thrws L Age 19
2014 FA (DR)

Velo	Pitch	Grade
88-93	FB	+ + +
	CB	+ +
	CU	+

Year	Lev	Team	W	L	Sv	IP	K	ERA	WHIP	BF/G	OBA	H%	S%	xERA	Ctl	Dom	Cmd	hr/9	BPV
2016	Rk	GCL Pirates	1	2	1	36	18	4.25	1.22	16.2	283	31	66	3.92	1.0	4.5	4.5	0.8	72
2017	Rk	Bristol	4	8	0	69	51	4.83	1.32	20.4	278	33	63	3.99	2.1	6.7	3.2	0.7	81

Athletic, projectable lefty continues to make slow but steady progress. Pounds the strike zone with an average low-90s fastball. Shows some feel for spinning a breaking ball, but for now it lacks depth and deception and change-up is fringe-average. Should head to full-season ball in 2018.

Rodriguez,Chris | SP | Los Angeles (A) | EXP MLB DEBUT: 2021 | H/W: 6-2 185 | FUT: #3 starter | 8E

Thrws R Age 19
2016 (4) HS (FL)

Velo	Pitch	Grade
89-95	FB	+ + +
80-84	SL	+ +
79-83	CB	+ + +
82-85	CU	+ + +

Year	Lev	Team	W	L	Sv	IP	K	ERA	WHIP	BF/G	OBA	H%	S%	xERA	Ctl	Dom	Cmd	hr/9	BPV
2016	Rk	AZL Angels	0	0	0	11	17	1.62	0.81	5.8	161	30	78	0.57	2.4	13.8	5.7	0.0	200
2017	Rk	Orem	4	1	0	32	32	6.45	1.31	16.6	279	37	46	3.60	2.0	9.0	4.6	0.3	127
2017	A	Burlington	1	2	0	24	24	5.95	1.61	17.9	319	41	61	5.06	2.6	8.9	3.4	0.4	108

Lean, athletic SP with quick arm and plenty of projection remaining. Has deep pitch mix and all exhibit good movement. Has feel for changing speeds and CU could develop into true plus pitch. Establishes plate with two-seamer and can rear back for more velocity. Has been hittable despite strong stuff and could eventually move to pen.

Rodriguez,Elian | SP | Houston | EXP MLB DEBUT: 2021 | H/W: 6-4 205 | FUT: #4 starter | 8E

Thrws R Age 21
2017 FA (CU)

Velo	Pitch	Grade
92-95	FB	+ + + +
83-87	SL	+ + +
	CU	+

Year	Lev	Team	W	L	Sv	IP	K	ERA	WHIP	BF/G	OBA	H%	S%	xERA	Ctl	Dom	Cmd	hr/9	BPV
2017		*Did not pitch in U.S.*																	

Young, Cuban RH who has yet to make state-side debut. Quality athlete with lean, flexible frame. Can run FB up to 97 mph and mostly operates 92-95. SL features hard dive and flashes plus potential. CU very raw and control requires work. A long-term project worth monitoring in the coming years.

Rodriguez,Elvin | SP | Detroit | EXP MLB DEBUT: 2022 | H/W: 6-3 160 | FUT: #3 starter | 8E

Thrws R Age 20
2014 FA (DR)

Velo	Pitch	Grade
87-92	FB	+ + +
75-76	CB	+ +
	CU	+

Year	Lev	Team	W	L	Sv	IP	K	ERA	WHIP	BF/G	OBA	H%	S%	xERA	Ctl	Dom	Cmd	hr/9	BPV
2016	Rk	AZL Angels	2	2	2	28	23	1.60	0.85	14.8	185	23	83	1.30	1.9	7.3	3.8	0.3	98
2017	Rk	Orem	5	1	0	54	49	2.50	1.04	18.9	228	28	80	2.76	1.8	8.2	4.5	0.8	116
2017	A	Burlington	0	2	0	14	12	4.50	1.64	20.8	336	40	76	6.29	1.9	7.7	4.0	1.3	105

Tall, ultra-thin SP who is extremely raw with pitches, but has athletic delivery. Is able to control plate with three offerings, yet seems to aim more than pitch. FB has chance to become more prominent with greater velocity, but needs to revise arm action to do so. CB is best secondary at present, but CU is only in infancy stage. Moved to DET in Justin Upton trade.

Rogers, Trevor | SP | Miami | EXP MLB DEBUT: 2021 | H/W: 6-6 185 | FUT: #2 starter | 9D

Thrws L Age 20
2017 (1) HS (NM)

Velo	Pitch	Grade
93-95	FB	+ + + +
	SL	+ + +
75-78	CB	+
	CU	+ +

Year	Lev	Team	W	L	Sv	IP	K	ERA	WHIP	BF/G	OBA	H%	S%	xERA	Ctl	Dom	Cmd	hr/9	BPV
2017		*Did not pitch*																	

13th overall pick signed for $3.4 million. Plus size and stuff highlighted by a 93-95 fastball that tops at 97 mph from low 3/4 slot with good command. Showed both a slider and curveball in high school with slider being potentially plus. Shows some feel for change-up and hides the ball well.

Romano,Jordan | SP | Toronto | EXP MLB DEBUT: 2018 | H/W: 6-4 200 | FUT: Middle reliever | 6B

Thrws R Age 24
2014 (10) Oral Roberts

Velo	Pitch	Grade
91-94	FB	+ + +
84-87	SL	+ + +
	CU	+

Year	Lev	Team	W	L	Sv	IP	K	ERA	WHIP	BF/G	OBA	H%	S%	xERA	Ctl	Dom	Cmd	hr/9	BPV
2014	Rk	GCL Blue Jays	0	0	0	3	1	0.00	2.00	7.2	191	21	100	4.01	12.0	3.0	0.3	0.0	-252
2014	Rk	Bluefield	1	1	0	25	33	2.16	1.12	9.0	212	34	79	1.95	3.2	11.9	3.7	0.0	144
2016	A	Lansing	3	2	0	72	72	2.12	1.05	18.6	194	26	81	1.95	3.4	9.0	2.7	0.4	89
2017	A+	Dunedin	7	5	0	138	138	3.39	1.41	20.9	266	36	74	3.54	3.5	9.0	2.6	0.1	85

Tall SP who set career high in IP while finishing 2nd in FSL in K and 3rd in ERA. Has injury past and could end up in bullpen without better CU. FB and SL are all about power. Uses height to throw downhill and has max effort delivery. SL exhibits late breaking action and can flash plus. Upped K rate as he used SL more.

Romero,Fernando | SP | Minnesota | EXP MLB DEBUT: 2018 | H/W: 6-0 215 | FUT: #3 starter | 8C

Thrws R Age 23
2011 FA (DR)

Velo	Pitch	Grade
91-97	FB	+ + + +
84-88	SL	+ + +
84-87	CU	+ + +

Year	Lev	Team	W	L	Sv	IP	K	ERA	WHIP	BF/G	OBA	H%	S%	xERA	Ctl	Dom	Cmd	hr/9	BPV
2014	A	Cedar Rapids	0	0	0	12	9	3.00	1.50	17.3	278	33	82	4.52	3.8	6.8	1.8	0.8	38
2015		*Did not pitch - injured*																	
2016	A	Cedar Rapids	4	1	0	28	25	1.93	0.82	20.4	186	25	74	0.93	1.6	8.0	5.0	0.0	119
2016	A+	Fort Myers	5	2	0	62	65	1.88	0.93	21.2	215	30	79	1.68	1.4	9.4	6.5	0.1	148
2017	AA	Chattanooga	11	9	0	125	120	3.53	1.35	21.7	260	34	73	3.46	3.2	8.6	2.7	0.3	86

Strong SP who was dynamite in 2nd half of season. Has three average to plus pitches and succeeds with high groundball rate and K rate. FB can flash double-plus with vicious movement and very hard SL is out pitch. Walk rate rose, but still acceptable. Could use polish to command. Rarely allows HR (6 HR in career) and has chance to be special.

Romero,JoJo | SP | Philadelphia | EXP MLB DEBUT: 2019 | H/W: 6-0 190 | FUT: #3 starter | 7B

Thrws L Age 21
2016 (4) Yavapai JC

Velo	Pitch	Grade
91-94	FB	+ + +
80-82	CU	+ + +
80-85	SL	+ + +
75-78	CB	+ +

Year	Lev	Team	W	L	Sv	IP	K	ERA	WHIP	BF/G	OBA	H%	S%	xERA	Ctl	Dom	Cmd	hr/9	BPV
2016	A-	Williamsport	2	2	0	45	31	2.59	1.22	18.2	257	30	79	3.19	2.2	6.2	2.8	0.4	70
2017	A	Lakewood	5	1	0	76	79	2.13	1.08	22.8	221	30	80	2.20	2.5	9.3	3.8	0.2	119
2017	A+	Clearwater	5	2	0	52	49	2.25	1.11	20.5	226	30	80	2.47	2.6	8.5	3.3	0.3	100

Four-pitch lefty whose stuff doesn't wow, but polish and command does. FB sits low-90s, but cuts and sinks it at will. Keeps CU down, sells it well and gets swings/misses and soft contact. SL has similar plus potential, and also throws a get-me-over CB. Compact, repeatable delivery and advanced sequencing round out a potential mid-rotation package.

Romero,Seth | SP | Washington | EXP MLB DEBUT: 2019 | H/W: 6-3 240 | FUT: #2 starter | 9D

Thrws L Age 21
2017 (1) Houston

Velo	Pitch	Grade
94-97	FB	+ + + +
82-84	SL	+ + +
81-84	CU	+ + +

Year	Lev	Team	W	L	Sv	IP	K	ERA	WHIP	BF/G	OBA	H%	S%	xERA	Ctl	Dom	Cmd	hr/9	BPV
2017	NCAA	Houston	4	5	0	48	85	3.55	1.37	20.2	253	46	73	3.41	3.7	15.9	4.3	0.4	203
2017	A-	Auburn	0	1	0	20	32	5.40	1.25	13.6	252	44	52	2.76	2.7	14.4	5.3	0.0	204

With three potential plus pitches, he's a top-flight talent, but fell in 2018 draft due to off-the-field issues. Throwing from a low slot, FB sits in the mid-90s with life; sharp-breaking SL and deceptive CU are both advanced offerings that result big K numbers. Advanced arm who could move quickly, but high-risk.

Rucker, Michael | SP | Chicago (N) | EXP MLB DEBUT: 2020 | H/W: 6-1 185 | FUT: #4 starter | 7B

Thrws R Age 23
2016 (11) BYU

Velo	Pitch	Grade
91-94	FB	+ + +
73-75	CB	+ + +
80-83	CU	+

Year	Lev	Team	W	L	Sv	IP	K	ERA	WHIP	BF/G	OBA	H%	S%	xERA	Ctl	Dom	Cmd	hr/9	BPV
2016	NCAA	Brigham Young	11	1	0	102	94	2.73	1.09	24.9	217	28	75	2.38	2.7	8.3	3.0	0.4	93
2016	Rk	AZL Cubs	3	0	0	8	11	0.00	0.61	5.6	147	25	100		1.1	12.1	11.0	0.0	206
2016	A-	Eugene	0	0	0	4	7	0.00	1.25	8.1	307	54	100	3.54	0.0	15.8		0.0	302
2017	A	South Bend	0	0	1	12	22	1.48	0.57	5.9	169	33	83	0.73	0.0	16.2		0.7	310
2017	A+	Myrtle Beach	5	5	1	93	92	2.51	1.11	18.3	238	31	79	2.72	2.0	8.9	4.4	0.5	123

Strong, competitive who continues to exceed expectations. Pounds the strike zone with a 91-94 mph fastball that has good movement and tops at 96 mph. CB and CU give him the tools to start. Stuff plays up due to deceptive delivery and aggressive approach.

Ruiz,Norge | SP | Oakland | EXP MLB DEBUT: 2019 | H/W: 6-0 185 | FUT: #4 starter | 7C

Thrws R Age 24
2016 FA (CU)

Velo	Pitch	Grade
91-95	FB	+ + +
87-88	SP	+ + +
81-83	SL	+ + +
	CU	+ +

Year	Lev	Team	W	L	Sv	IP	K	ERA	WHIP	BF/G	OBA	H%	S%	xERA	Ctl	Dom	Cmd	hr/9	BPV
2017	Rk	AZL Athletics	0	1	0	4	4	11.25	1.75	18.3	307	41	29	4.87	4.5	9.0	2.0	0.0	59
2017	A+	Stockton	3	1	0	34	24	5.79	1.73	19.4	328	37	67	6.15	3.2	6.3	2.0	1.1	46

Advanced SP whose stuff is better than stats suggest. Varies arm angle to give hitters different looks and has feel for secondary stuff. Size isn't ideal, but rarely allows flyballs or HR. May not project to high K prospect, but exhibits above average control and mixes shape and speed of breaking balls. Should be dependable and durable in time.

Sadzeck,Connor — SP — Texas

EXP MLB DEBUT: 2018 | H/W: 6-7 240 | FUT: #4 starter | 7C

Thrws R Age 26
2011 (11) Howard College

93-96	FB	+++
83-85	SL	+++
84-88	CU	++

Year	Lev	Team	W	L	Sv	IP	K	ERA	WHIP	BF/G	OBA	H%	S%	xERA	Ctl	Dom	Cmd	hr/9	BPV
2015	A+	High Desert	2	1	0	40	48	4.03	1.39	15.4	220	30	73	3.59	5.4	10.7	2.0	0.9	66
2015	AA	Frisco	1	1	0	19	16	9.84	2.03	13.3	289	36	47	5.76	8.0	7.5	0.9	0.5	-62
2016	AA	Frisco	10	8	0	140	133	4.17	1.28	23.0	243	29	71	3.85	3.3	8.5	2.6	1.2	82
2017	AA	Frisco	4	8	0	93	111	6.28	1.53	10.7	284	37	60	5.13	3.8	10.7	2.8	1.3	109

Big-framed pitcher who struggled thru season before move to pen in June. Still has SP upside due to solid arsenal. Inconsistent delivery is root of issues and needs to use height to throw downhill. FB shows velocity and sink, but has trouble finding consistency with SL and CU. Keeps ball low in zone and control getting better.

Salinas,Jhonleider — SP — Tampa Bay

EXP MLB DEBUT: 2020 | H/W: 6-7 215 | FUT: #4 starter | 7E

Thrws R Age 22
2015 FA (VZ)

91-96	FB	+++
80-84	CB	++
	CU	+

Year	Lev	Team	W	L	Sv	IP	K	ERA	WHIP	BF/G	OBA	H%	S%	xERA	Ctl	Dom	Cmd	hr/9	BPV
2016	Rk	GCL Rays	1	0	0	23	14	1.95	1.08	18.0	187	23	80	1.63	3.9	5.5	1.4	0.0	11
2017	A-	Hudson Valley	3	1	0	56	63	3.52	1.35	18.0	229	32	74	3.21	4.6	10.1	2.2	0.5	74

Very long, interesting SP who throws with quality angle to plate. Hasn't pitched above short-season yet. Has height and arm slot to cause fright in hitters. Add in plus velocity and he can dominate in short stints. CB can be flat while CU is distant third pitch. More thrower than pitcher at this point.

Sanchez,Ricardo — SP — Atlanta

EXP MLB DEBUT: 2019 | H/W: 5-11 170 | FUT: #4 starter | 7C

Thrws L Age 20
2013 FA (VZ)

91-93	FB	+++
78-80	CB	+++
84-85	CU	+++

Year	Lev	Team	W	L	Sv	IP	K	ERA	WHIP	BF/G	OBA	H%	S%	xERA	Ctl	Dom	Cmd	hr/9	BPV
2014	Rk	AZL Angels	2	2	0	38	43	3.53	1.62	14.1	271	38	76	4.00	5.2	10.1	2.0	0.0	60
2015	A	Rome	1	6	0	39	31	5.51	1.48	16.9	251	30	62	4.04	4.8	7.1	1.5	0.7	16
2016	A	Rome	7	10	0	119	103	4.76	1.45	21.2	262	31	69	4.46	4.1	7.8	1.9	1.1	48
2017	A+	Florida	4	12	0	100	101	4.95	1.63	20.2	293	37	71	5.20	4.1	9.1	2.2	0.9	70

Short-statured, projectable LH continues to struggle repeating delivery. Easy low-90s velocity out of 3/4s slot. Natural sink and arm-side run, but hard to control. CB is harder and profiles better than before. Has a feel for a CU, but like FB, lacks consistent control of it thus mitigating its fading action.

Sanchez,Sixto — SP — Philadelphia

EXP MLB DEBUT: 2019 | H/W: 6-0 185 | FUT: #1 starter | 9C

Thrws R Age 19
2015 FA (DR)

96-99	FB	+++++
80-82	CB	+++
88-90	CU	+++

Year	Lev	Team	W	L	Sv	IP	K	ERA	WHIP	BF/G	OBA	H%	S%	xERA	Ctl	Dom	Cmd	hr/9	BPV
2016	Rk	GCL Phillies	5	0	0	54	44	0.50	0.76	17.6	178	23	93	0.69	1.3	7.3	5.5	0.0	114
2017	A	Lakewood	5	3	0	67	64	2.41	0.82	18.8	196	26	69	1.16	1.2	8.6	7.1	0.1	140
2017	A+	Clearwater	0	4	0	27	20	4.63	1.32	22.5	260	31	63	3.45	3.0	6.6	2.2	0.3	57

Passed the first-full-season test with aplomb. Package is uncanny for a teenager: ability to manipulate lively high-90s FB; understands sequencing; composed and works quickly; outstanding athleticism. Starts with premium arm speed; often ends with strikeout or weak contact. Secondaries still need consistency, but sky-high upside.

Sands, Carson — RP — Chicago (N)

EXP MLB DEBUT: 2020 | H/W: 6-3 205 | FUT: Middle reliever | 6C

Thrws L Age 23
2014 (4) HS (FL)

88-92	FB	++
73-75	CB	++
76-78	CU	++

Year	Lev	Team	W	L	Sv	IP	K	ERA	WHIP	BF/G	OBA	H%	S%	xERA	Ctl	Dom	Cmd	hr/9	BPV
2015	A-	Eugene	3	4	0	57	41	3.94	1.45	17.4	278	34	70	3.71	3.3	6.5	2.0	0.0	45
2016	A	South Bend	7	4	1	74	51	5.94	1.63	15.7	274	32	62	4.56	5.1	6.2	1.2	0.5	-8
2017	Rk	AZL Cubs	0	1	0	11	10	3.21	1.70	12.6	202	27	79	3.32	8.8	8.0	0.9	0.0	-76
2017	A-	Eugene	1	0	0	2	1	13.50	2.00	9.6	262	18	33	9.11	9.0	4.5	0.5	4.5	-144
2017	A	South Bend	0	3	0	6	5	25.08	4.26	14.4	411	47	36	14.51	20.7	7.4	0.4	1.5	-407

Fourth rounder from 2014 has been a complete bust as a pro. Big, strong lefty has fringe fastball that now sits at 88-92 and lacks deception or command. Injuries and ineffectiveness have taken their toll and he has logged just 171 innings and a 5.37 ERA since 2014. A move to relief seems like his last chance.

Santana, Dennis — SP — Los Angeles (N)

EXP MLB DEBUT: 2019 | H/W: 6-2 160 | FUT: Setup reliever | 8D

Thrws R Age 21
2013 FA (DR)

93-95	FB	++++
	SL	++++
	CU	+

Year	Lev	Team	W	L	Sv	IP	K	ERA	WHIP	BF/G	OBA	H%	S%	xERA	Ctl	Dom	Cmd	hr/9	BPV
2015	Rk	Ogden	0	4	0	21		11.46	2.64	16.5	369	43	55	9.39	8.9	7.6	0.9	1.3	-85
2015	Rk	AZL Dodgers	2	1	0	26	34	2.42	1.15	17.2	151	23	79	1.67	5.9	11.8	2.0	0.3	71
2016	A	Great Lakes	5	9	0	111	124	3.08	1.26	18.1	211	30	74	2.46	4.5	10.0	2.2	0.2	76
2017	A+	Rancho Cuca	5	6	0	85	92	3.59	1.28	20.5	266	36	72	3.56	2.3	9.7	4.2	0.5	130
2017	AA	Tulsa	3	1	0	32	37	5.59	1.71	20.8	261	36	66	4.59	6.4	10.3	1.6	0.6	31

Converted SS has an electric arm and comes after hitters with a heavy 93-95 mph fastball that has good late sink. Backs the FB up with a plus hard SL, and a below-average CU. Cross-fire motion leads to concerns about durability and below-average control—4.5 career bb/9.

Santillan,Tony — SP — Cincinnati

EXP MLB DEBUT: 2020 | H/W: 6-3 240 | FUT: #3 starter | 8C

Thrws R Age 20
2015 (2) HS (TX)

94-96	FB	++++
85-88	SL	++++
	CU	++

Year	Lev	Team	W	L	Sv	IP	K	ERA	WHIP	BF/G	OBA	H%	S%	xERA	Ctl	Dom	Cmd	hr/9	BPV
2015	Rk	AZL Reds	0	2	0	19	19	5.16	1.35	10.0	217	28	60	3.07	5.2	8.9	1.7	0.5	39
2016	Rk	Billings	1	0	0	39	46	3.92	1.23	19.7	225	30	70	3.27	3.7	10.6	2.9	0.9	109
2016	A	Dayton	2	3	0	30	38	6.88	1.69	19.4	241	34	58	4.61	7.2	11.4	1.6	0.9	29
2017	A	Dayton	9	8	0	128	128	3.38	1.25	20.8	224	29	74	3.04	3.9	9.0	2.3	0.6	74

Projectable RH with huge upside. Primarily a two-pitch pitcher. Throws mid-90s FB with late arm-side run and some sink. Can reach back for additional velocity. SL is combination of power and tilt. Explosive two-plane movement. Swing-and-miss offering. Lacks solid feel for CU. Physically strong and athletic.

Sauer,Matt — SP — New York (A)

EXP MLB DEBUT: 2022 | H/W: 6-4 195 | FUT: #3 starter | 8D

Thrws R Age 19
2017 (2) HS (CA)

91-94	FB	+++
81-84	SL	+++
75-78	CB	++
82-85	CU	++

Year	Lev	Team	W	L	Sv	IP	K	ERA	WHIP	BF/G	OBA	H%	S%	xERA	Ctl	Dom	Cmd	hr/9	BPV
2017	Rk	GCL Yankees	0	2	0	11	12	5.63	1.88	8.8	292	40	67	4.94	6.4	9.6	1.5	0.0	18

Tall, raw SP who may take time to develop. Natural stuff is quite good, but could get much better with smoother, cleaner mechanics. Throws across body which negatively impacts command. Lively FB is go-to pitch and SL could be potent with more time. Slower CB is fringy and he rarely uses CU. Adds to profile by hiding ball in delivery.

Sborz, Josh — SP — Los Angeles (N)

EXP MLB DEBUT: 2018 | H/W: 6-3 225 | FUT: #5 SP/swingman | 6C

Thrws R Age 24
2015 (S-2) Virginia

91-95	FB	++++
	SL	+++
	CU	+

Year	Lev	Team	W	L	Sv	IP	K	ERA	WHIP	BF/G	OBA	H%	S%	xERA	Ctl	Dom	Cmd	hr/9	BPV
2015	A	Great Lakes	0	1	0	6	9	2.95	1.15	12.1	225	27	100	4.94	3.0	13.3	4.5	3.0	177
2015	A+	Rancho Cuca	0	0	2	12	12	1.50	1.25	5.4	262	33	93	3.65	2.3	9.0	4.0	0.8	119
2016	A+	Rancho Cuca	8	4	0	108	108	2.66	1.04	20.8	212	27	77	2.39	2.5	9.0	3.6	0.7	112
2016	AA	Tulsa	0	1	1	16	17	3.89	1.42	6.9	271	34	76	4.54	3.3	9.4	2.8	1.1	98
2017	AA	Tulsa	8	8	0	116	81	3.87	1.39	20.4	244	28	73	3.68	4.3	6.3	1.4	0.6	14

Was used exclusively as a starter with mixed results. Plus 91-95 mph fastball that tops out at 98 mph with late life and backs it up with an above-average slider. Mixes in change-up to keep hitters off-balance. Has effort to delivery, but also some nice deception. Spike in Ctl and dip in Dom don't bode well despite the respectable ERA.

Scherff,Alex — SP — Boston

EXP MLB DEBUT: 2022 | H/W: 6-3 205 | FUT: #3 starter | 8D

Thrws R Age 20
2017 (5) HS (TX)

91-96	FB	++++
81-85	SL	++
75-78	CB	+
	CU	+++

Year	Lev	Team	W	L	Sv	IP	K	ERA	WHIP	BF/G	OBA	H%	S%	xERA	Ctl	Dom	Cmd	hr/9	BPV
2017		*Did not pitch*																	

Raw, live-armed SP who DNP upon signing. Has to rework delivery which features moving parts. Adds lively action to plus FB and hitters have difficulty making clean contact and elevating. Crude delivery leads to control issues, but shows feel for changing speeds. Uses same arm speed on CU for deception and exhibits quality depth and fade.

Schmidt,Clarke — SP — New York (A)

EXP MLB DEBUT: 2020 | H/W: 6-1 205 | FUT: #3 starter | 8C

Thrws R Age 22
2017 (1) South Carolina

91-95	FB	+++
83-86	SL	+++
78-81	CB	+++
82-86	CU	+++

Year	Lev	Team	W	L	Sv	IP	K	ERA	WHIP	BF/G	OBA	H%	S%	xERA	Ctl	Dom	Cmd	hr/9	BPV
2017	NCAA	South Carolina	4	2	0	60	70	1.35	0.98	25.4	195	28	89	1.83	2.7	10.5	3.9	0.4	134

16th overall pick in draft who underwent Tommy John surgery in May. Has deep, impressive pitch mix and has confidence to use any pitch in any count. Hits spots with heavy FB and can throw 4-seamer past hitters up in zone. Sinking CU is solid-average offering and good weapon against lefties. Hard SL is out pitch while CB is effective as well.

Schultz,Jaime — SP — Tampa Bay

EXP MLB DEBUT: 2018 | H/W: 5-10 200 | FUT: #4 starter | 7B

Thrws R Age 26
2013 (14) High Point

Velo	Pitch	Grade
94-97	FB	++++
80-84	CB	+++
83-87	CU	++

Year	Lev	Team	W	L	Sv	IP	K	ERA	WHIP	BF/G	OBA	H%	S%	xERA	Ctl	Dom	Cmd	hr/9	BPV
2015	AA	Montgomery	9	5	0	135	168	3.67	1.44	21.3	216	31	76	3.51	6.0	11.2	1.9	0.7	58
2016	AAA	Durham	5	7	0	130	163	3.59	1.39	20.3	235	33	76	3.70	4.7	11.3	2.4	0.8	94
2017	Rk	GCL Rays	0	0	0	3	4	0.00	0.94	4.0	250	37	100	1.97	0.0	11.3		0.0	221
2017	A+	Charlotte	0	1	1	4	7	6.59	1.46	5.9	257	40	60	5.42	4.4	15.4	3.5	2.2	176
2017	AAA	Durham	1	0	0	11	21	4.02	1.25	3.5	240	46	69	3.34	3.2	16.9	5.3	0.8	235

Short, strong pitcher who missed most of season due to groin injury. Pitched out of pen and continued extremely high K rate. Can blow plus FB by hitters with lightning quick arm speed. Maintains velocity, but may still end up as RP due to inability to repeat mechanics. Power arsenal could play up in short stints.

Scott,Tanner — RP — Baltimore

EXP MLB DEBUT: 2017 | H/W: 6-2 220 | FUT: Closer | 8C

Thrws L Age 23
2014 (6) Howard JC

Velo	Pitch	Grade
95-99	FB	++++
87-91	SL	++++
	CU	+

Year	Lev	Team	W	L	Sv	IP	K	ERA	WHIP	BF/G	OBA	H%	S%	xERA	Ctl	Dom	Cmd	hr/9	BPV
2015	A	Delmarva	0	3	2	21	29	4.29	1.38	9.8	243	39	66	2.99	4.3	12.4	2.9	0.0	126
2016	A+	Frederick	4	2	5	48	63	4.49	1.33	6.9	140	22	63	1.86	7.9	11.8	1.5	0.2	18
2016	AA	Bowie	1	2	0	16	18	5.63	2.06	5.6	285	40	70	5.31	8.4	10.1	1.2	0.0	-28
2017	AA	Bowie	0	2	0	69	87	2.22	1.32	11.9	188	29	83	2.42	6.0	11.3	1.9	0.3	60
2017	MLB	Baltimore	0	0	0	1	2	15.00	3.33	3.7	371	59	50	9.91	15.0	15.0	1.0	0.0	-117

Intimidating pitcher who was used as SP in 2017, but still profiles as hard-throwing RP. Only pitched about 3 IP per start. All about arm strength and velocity. Incredible FB is best pitch and wipes out hitters with plus, hard SL. Inability to throw strikes keeps from high-leverage role. Needs SL to show more consistency.

Seabold,Connor — SP — Philadelphia

EXP MLB DEBUT: 2022 | H/W: 6-3 190 | FUT: #4 starter | 7C

Thrws R Age 22
2017 (3) Cal St Fullerton

Velo	Pitch	Grade
90-92	FB	+++
83-85	CU	+++
	CB	++

Year	Lev	Team	W	L	Sv	IP	K	ERA	WHIP	BF/G	OBA	H%	S%	xERA	Ctl	Dom	Cmd	hr/9	BPV
2017	NCAA	CalSt Fullerton	11	5	0	127	122	2.97	1.16	28.1	257	33	74	3.04	1.6	8.6	5.3	0.4	129
2017	A-	Williamsport	2	0	0	10	13	0.90	0.70	7.0	151	25	86	0.20	1.8	11.7	6.5	0.0	180

After logging 127 collegiate innings, the Phillies limited him to only five outings after he signed. Control, command and pitchability are the hallmarks here, as stuff is relatively modest. Spots low-90s FB; has good arm action on CU with average potential; CB still improving. K rate could decline as he climbs the ladder.

Sears,J.P. — RP — New York (A)

EXP MLB DEBUT: 2019 | H/W: 5-11 180 | FUT: Middle reliever | 6B

Thrws L Age 22
2017 (11) The Citadel

Velo	Pitch	Grade
87-90	FB	+++
78-79	SL	++
75-80	CU	++

Year	Lev	Team	W	L	Sv	IP	K	ERA	WHIP	BF/G	OBA	H%	S%	xERA	Ctl	Dom	Cmd	hr/9	BPV
2017	NCAA	The Citadel	7	3	0	95	142	2.65	1.01	26.0	205	33	76	2.19	2.6	13.4	5.3	0.7	191
2017	A-	Everett	1	1	0	10	22	1.76	0.88	5.4	173	47	78	0.82	2.6	19.4	7.3	0.0	296
2017	A	Clinton	0	1	3	17	29	0.00	0.94	6.4	127	27	100	0.54	4.8	15.4	3.2	0.0	166

Short, aggressive RP who throws with lot of deception. Doesn't wow with velocity or pitch movement, but gets weak contact from ability to locate. Stats look amazing, but arsenal isn't that good. Low arm slot has proven difficult and can locate FB to both sides. Mixes in sharp SL and fringy CU.

Sedlock,Cody — SP — Baltimore

EXP MLB DEBUT: 2019 | H/W: 6-3 190 | FUT: #3 starter | 8D

Thrws R Age 22
2016 (1) Illinois

Velo	Pitch	Grade
91-94	FB	+++
80-84	SL	+++
78-80	CB	+++
	CU	++

Year	Lev	Team	W	L	Sv	IP	K	ERA	WHIP	BF/G	OBA	H%	S%	xERA	Ctl	Dom	Cmd	hr/9	BPV
2016	NCAA	Illinois	5	3	0	101	116	2.49	1.10	28.3	219	31	78	2.33	2.8	10.3	3.7	0.4	129
2016	A-	Aberdeen	0	1	0	27	25	3.00	1.07	11.7	174	23	71	1.74	4.3	8.3	1.9	0.3	51
2017	A+	Frederick	4	5	0	90	69	5.90	1.72	20.4	319	37	67	6.05	3.6	6.9	1.9	1.1	45

Very athletic SP who bypassed Low-A and struggled, but had minor injuries. Exhibits both power and touch with lively, sinking FB and two quality breaking balls. Repeats delivery and generally throws strikes despite mediocre walk rate. Disappointing K rate, but should improve with better sequencing. Can aim ball instead of letting pitch fly.

Seijas, Alvaro — SP — St. Louis

EXP MLB DEBUT: 2022 | H/W: 5-8 175 | FUT: #4 starter | 8D

Thrws R Age 19
2015 FA (VZ)

Velo	Pitch	Grade
91-94	FB	+++
	CB	+++
	CU	+++

Year	Lev	Team	W	L	Sv	IP	K	ERA	WHIP	BF/G	OBA	H%	S%	xERA	Ctl	Dom	Cmd	hr/9	BPV
2016	Rk	GCL Cardinals	3	2	0	50	33	3.06	1.22	20.2	254	29	77	3.47	2.3	5.9	2.5	0.7	62
2017	Rk	Johnson City	4	3	0	63	63	4.99	1.57	23.1	307	40	66	4.69	2.9	9.0	3.2	0.3	103

Short right-hander from Venezuela generates surprising velocity from his small frame. Fastball sits at 91-94 mph and backs it up with an above-average curveball and change-up that flashes as plus. Still learning how to pitch, but shows intriguing potential.

Shawaryn,Mike — SP — Boston

EXP MLB DEBUT: 2019 | H/W: 6-2 200 | FUT: #4 starter | 7C

Thrws R Age 23
2016 (5) Maryland

Velo	Pitch	Grade
89-94	FB	+++
80-82	CB	++
	CU	+++

Year	Lev	Team	W	L	Sv	IP	K	ERA	WHIP	BF/G	OBA	H%	S%	xERA	Ctl	Dom	Cmd	hr/9	BPV
2016	NCAA	Maryland	6	4	0	99	97	3.18	0.96	24.9	198	27	65	1.58	2.4	8.8	3.7	0.2	113
2016	A-	Lowell	0	1	0	15	22	2.96	1.45	10.8	259	42	77	3.37	4.1	13.0	3.1	0.0	141
2017	A	Greenville	3	2	0	53	78	3.90	1.07	20.7	227	35	65	2.80	2.2	13.2	6.0	0.8	196
2017	A+	Salem	5	5	0	81	91	3.77	1.31	20.9	237	31	75	3.79	3.9	10.1	2.6	1.1	95

Durable, consistent SP who was promoted to High-A in June in first full season. Throws strikes and uses deceptive delivery and mature sequencing to miss bats and induce weak contact. No plus pitch in arsenal, but all exhibit good life. Deceptive CU may be best secondary and repeats arm speed consistently.

Sheffield, Jordan — SP — Los Angeles (N)

EXP MLB DEBUT: 2019 | H/W: 5-10 190 | FUT: #3 starter | 9D

Thrws R Age 22
2016 (1) Vanderbilt

Velo	Pitch	Grade
94-97	FB	++++
80-83	SL	+++
87-89	CU	+++

Year	Lev	Team	W	L	Sv	IP	K	ERA	WHIP	BF/G	OBA	H%	S%	xERA	Ctl	Dom	Cmd	hr/9	BPV
2016	NCAA	Vanderbilt	8	6	0	101	113	3.02	1.21	25.5	223	31	74	2.57	3.6	10.0	2.8	0.3	103
2016	Rk	AZL Dodgers	0	0	0	1	0	0.00	0.00	2.8	0	0			0.0	0.0		0.0	18
2016	A	Great Lakes	0	1	0	11	13	4.09	1.55	6.9	262	33	80	5.21	4.9	10.6	2.2	1.6	77
2017	A	Great Lakes	3	7	0	89	91	4.04	1.44	19.0	255	32	74	4.18	4.2	9.2	2.2	0.9	69
2017	A+	Rancho Cuca	0	2	0	18	18	8.00	2.11	17.8	312	39	61	6.79	7.5	9.0	1.2	1.0	-23

Short starter has a plus 94-97 mph fastball. Change-up shows plus potential and slider is above-average. Below average command hurt him in 2017 and it was tough sledding when he moved up to High-A. Had Tommy John surgery in 2013, but has been healthy since.

Sheffield,Justus — SP — New York (A)

EXP MLB DEBUT: 2018 | H/W: 5-11 200 | FUT: #3 starter | 8C

Thrws L Age 21
2014 (1) HS (TN)

Velo	Pitch	Grade
91-95	FB	++++
82-85	SL	+++
84-88	CU	++

Year	Lev	Team	W	L	Sv	IP	K	ERA	WHIP	BF/G	OBA	H%	S%	xERA	Ctl	Dom	Cmd	hr/9	BPV
2016	A+	Tampa	3	1	0	26	27	1.73	0.92	19.5	160	23	79	0.89	3.5	9.3	2.7	0.0	93
2016	A+	Lynchburg	7	5	0	95	93	3.60	1.38	21.0	253	33	74	3.69	3.8	8.8	2.3	0.6	74
2016	AA	Trenton	0	0	0	4	9	0.00	1.25	16.3	151	47	100	1.51	6.8	20.3	3.0	0.0	200
2017	Rk	GCL Yankees	0	1	0	4	6	2.14	1.19	8.4	252	41	80	2.63	2.1	12.9	6.0	0.0	192
2017	AA	Trenton	7	6	0	93	82	3.19	1.36	22.9	264	31	83	4.54	3.2	7.9	2.5	1.4	75

Short, fast-armed SP who missed time with oblique. Owns average control with 3 potential plus offerings. FB exhibits sinking action, but can be flat when overthrown. Commands FB to both sides of plate. K rate dropped as he worked on sequencing and polishing SL. Has touch for CU, but needs to maintain arm speed. Could be candidate for bullpen.

Shepherd,Chandler — RP — Boston

EXP MLB DEBUT: 2018 | H/W: 6-3 185 | FUT: Setup reliever | 6B

Thrws R Age 25
2014 (13) Kentucky

Velo	Pitch	Grade
91-93	FB	+++
82-84	SL	++
78-81	CB	+++
	CU	++

Year	Lev	Team	W	L	Sv	IP	K	ERA	WHIP	BF/G	OBA	H%	S%	xERA	Ctl	Dom	Cmd	hr/9	BPV
2015	A	Greenville	3	0	1	14	16	1.27	1.34	8.4	285	38	94	4.09	1.9	10.1	5.3	0.6	149
2015	A+	Salem	0	2	6	52	46	3.63	1.06	7.2	246	31	65	2.74	1.2	7.9	6.6	0.5	128
2016	AA	Portland	1	1	6	30	39	1.80	0.80	4.9	142	19	86	1.21	3.0	11.7	3.9	0.9	148
2016	AAA	Pawtucket	1	2	1	34	23	3.71	1.06	7.3	226	26	67	2.77	2.1	6.1	2.9	0.8	70
2017	AAA	Pawtucket	1	5	2	59	68	4.10	1.30	7.2	261	35	69	3.76	2.7	10.3	3.8	0.8	130

Tall, lean RP who increased K rate while consistently pitching to lower half of zone. Has deep repertoire for RP and gets movement on all pitches thanks to quick arm action. Could benefit by shortening arsenal as his sequencing needs work. CB is out pitch and used as chase option. Command may be best attribute and could lead to setup opportunities.

Sherfy,Jimmie — RP — Arizona

EXP MLB DEBUT: 2017 | H/W: 6-0 175 | FUT: Setup reliever | 7A

Thrws R Age 26
2013 (10) Oregon

Velo	Pitch	Grade
93-96	FB	++++
77-79	CB	++++
88-89	CU	+

Year	Lev	Team	W	L	Sv	IP	K	ERA	WHIP	BF/G	OBA	H%	S%	xERA	Ctl	Dom	Cmd	hr/9	BPV
2016	A+	Visalia	0	0	8	12	21	0.00	0.91	3.8	128	28	100	0.46	4.5	15.6	3.5	0.0	179
2016	AA	Mobile	2	0	10	19	31	0.47	0.57	4.1	100	18	100		2.3	14.5	6.2	0.5	216
2016	AAA	Reno	1	4	12	23	27	6.23	1.43	4.1	235	28	61	4.85	5.1	10.5	2.1	1.9	71
2017	AAA	Reno	2	1	20	49	61	3.12	0.96	4.2	211	29	73	2.58	1.8	11.2	6.1	1.1	170
2017	MLB	Arizona	2	0	1	10	9	0.00	0.69	3.3	148	20	100	0.18	1.8	7.9	4.5	0.0	113

Max-effort RH made MLB debut in 2017. Continued improvement of FB command led to promotion. FB bores in on RHH hitters' hands, making it difficult to square up. CB complements FB nicely, though more drop than sweep, and is a true out pitch. Needs to improve CU to give LHH something else to look at. Has role in MLB pen regardless.

Shore,Logan — SP — Oakland

EXP MLB DEBUT: 2018 | H/W: 6-2 215 | FUT: #4 starter | 7B

Thrws R Age 23 — 2016 (2) Florida

Velo	Pitch	Grade
89-93	FB	+++
80-85	SL	++
81-82	CU	++++

Year	Lev	Team	W	L	Sv	IP	K	ERA	WHIP	BF/G	OBA	H%	S%	xERA	Ctl	Dom	Cmd	hr/9	BPV
2016	NCAA	Florida	12	1	0	105	96	2.31	0.96	22.1	217	28	76	1.96	1.6	8.2	5.1	0.3	122
2016	A-	Vermont	0	2	0	21	21	2.57	1.14	11.9	223	30	78	2.57	3.0	9.0	3.0	0.4	99
2017	Rk	AZL Athletics	0	0	0	8	13	0.00	0.25	8.2	81	17	100		0.0	14.6		0.0	281
2017	A+	Stockton	2	5	1	72	74	4.11	1.34	17.7	285	37	70	4.09	2.0	9.2	4.6	0.6	130

Strong SP who missed 2 months with lat strain, but exhibited plus command when on mound. FB is merely average, but he commands it despite heavy, late sink. Induces ton of groundballs and can cut ball at will. Velocity increased in 2017, but best pitch is plus CU. Has confidence to use in any count. Will need to upgrade SL to give third viable option.

Skoglund,Eric — SP — Kansas City

EXP MLB DEBUT: 2017 | H/W: 6-7 200 | FUT: #4 starter | 7B

Thrws L Age 25 — 2014 (3) Central Florida

Velo	Pitch	Grade
89-94	FB	+++
74-75	CB	+++
81-85	SL	++
83-85	CU	++

Year	Lev	Team	W	L	Sv	IP	K	ERA	WHIP	BF/G	OBA	H%	S%	xERA	Ctl	Dom	Cmd	hr/9	BPV
2015	A+	Wilmington	6	3	0	84	66	3.53	1.12	22.1	259	32	66	2.80	1.2	7.1	6.0	0.2	113
2016	AA	NW Arkansas	7	10	0	156	134	3.46	1.11	22.7	235	27	73	3.27	2.2	7.7	3.5	1.1	98
2017	AA	NW Arkansas	0	0	0	3	1	2.90	2.58	16.7	364	39	88	7.99	8.7	2.9	0.3	0.0	-165
2017	AAA	Omaha	4	5	0	100	102	4.13	1.39	22.2	280	35	74	4.73	2.6	9.2	3.5	1.3	113
2017	MLB	KC Royals	1	2	0	18	14	9.50	2.33	13.3	371	43	58	8.41	6.0	7.0	1.2	1.0	-18

Tall SP who uses height to throw downhill. Progressing nicely with more consistent sequencing and delivery. Pitches to all quadrants of strike zone with four pitches and exhibits above average command. Pitches quickly and keeps hitters off balance. Could use better CU and SL could be tighter. Lacks plus pitch, but effective.

Smith,Caleb — RP — Miami

EXP MLB DEBUT: 2017 | H/W: 6-2 205 | FUT: #5 SP/swingman | 6B

Thrws L Age 26 — 2013 (14) Sam Houston St

Velo	Pitch	Grade
91-94	FB	+++
83-85	SL	++
	CU	+++

Year	Lev	Team	W	L	Sv	IP	K	ERA	WHIP	BF/G	OBA	H%	S%	xERA	Ctl	Dom	Cmd	hr/9	BPV
2015	AAA	Scranton/WB	0	0	0	4		6.59	2.44	21.6	302	35	78	8.59	11.0	8.8	0.8	2.2	-120
2016	AA	Trenton	3	5	3	63	70	3.99	1.36	9.8	270	36	71	3.87	2.8	10.0	3.5	0.6	121
2017	AA	Trenton	0	0	0	2	5	4.09	1.82	10.2	139	0	100	6.66	12.3	20.5	1.7	4.1	55
2017	AAA	Scranton/WB	9	1	0	98	97	2.39	1.05	21.1	213	27	80	2.43	2.6	8.9	3.5	0.6	109
2017	MLB	NY Yankees	0	1	0	18	18	7.91	1.70	9.1	290	34	56	6.36	4.9	8.9	1.8	2.0	45

Tall, versatile pitcher who started in 2017, but is likely RP long-term. Can be tough to hit, particularly against LHH with solid FB/CU combo. Mixes in SL with cutter action, but fringe-average at best. No plus offering in arsenal and has flyball tendencies. Locates all pitches to corners of plate.

Smith,Nate — SP — Los Angeles (A)

EXP MLB DEBUT: 2019 | H/W: 6-3 210 | FUT: #4 starter | 7B

Thrws L Age 26 — 2013 (8) Furman

Velo	Pitch	Grade
87-91	FB	++
80-82	SL	++
74-77	CB	+++
75-78	CU	+++

Year	Lev	Team	W	L	Sv	IP	K	ERA	WHIP	BF/G	OBA	H%	S%	xERA	Ctl	Dom	Cmd	hr/9	BPV
2015	AA	Arkansas	8	4	0	101	81	2.49	1.09	23.3	223	26	82	2.88	2.5	7.2	2.9	0.9	80
2015	AAA	Salt Lake	2	4	0	36	23	7.75	1.75	23.5	321	34	57	6.77	3.8	5.8	1.5	1.8	20
2016	AAA	Salt Lake	8	9	0	150	122	4.62	1.40	24.4	282	33	69	4.63	2.6	7.3	2.8	1.1	78
2017	Rk	AZL Angels	0	0	0	9	10	0.00	0.55	10.2	105	16	100		2.0	9.9	5.0	0.0	143
2017	AAA	Salt Lake	1	0	0	5	4	0.00	0.19	15.7	64	9	100		0.0	6.9		0.0	143

Tall SP who missed most of year with ailments and will miss all of 2018 after shoulder surgery. Doesn't possess frontline stuff or velocity, but mixes well and has feel for changing speeds. Arm action is a bit unorthodox, but he throws strikes. Lacks dynamic out pitch, but can get hitters to chase slow CB. Has limited upside, but has solid chance.

Sodders,Austin — SP — Detroit

EXP MLB DEBUT: 2019 | H/W: 6-3 180 | FUT: #4 starter | 7C

Thrws L Age 22 — 2016 (7) UC-Riverside

Velo	Pitch	Grade
87-92	FB	+++
74-77	CB	++
79-82	SL	+++
81-83	CU	++

Year	Lev	Team	W	L	Sv	IP	K	ERA	WHIP	BF/G	OBA	H%	S%	xERA	Ctl	Dom	Cmd	hr/9	BPV
2016	NCAA	UC Riverside	7	4	0	80	69	2.58	1.31	22.1	231	30	80	2.91	4.2	7.7	1.9	0.2	45
2016	A-	Connecticut	0	3	0	39	33	2.30	1.02	11.6	241	30	79	2.54	1.2	7.6	6.6	0.5	124
2017	A	West Michigan	7	0	0	64	65	1.40	0.97	22.1	213	29	87	1.87	1.8	9.1	5.0	0.3	133
2017	A+	Lakeland	4	5	0	74	57	2.18	0.97	23.4	208	27	75	1.57	2.1	6.9	3.4	0.0	87

Breakout SP who thrives with deception, command, and pitchability. May not have eye-popping arsenal or velocity, but knows how to pitch and set hitters up. K rate fell upon promotion to A+, but his game is angle and movement. Commands all pitches and doesn't beat himself with walks. Lively FB is best offering and SL getting quite good.

Soriano,Jose — SP — Los Angeles (A)

EXP MLB DEBUT: 2022 | H/W: 6-3 168 | FUT: #3 starter | 8E

Thrws R Age 19 — 2016 FA (DR)

Velo	Pitch	Grade
91-94	FB	+++
83-85	SL	++
83-86	CU	++

Year	Lev	Team	W	L	Sv	IP	K	ERA	WHIP	BF/G	OBA	H%	S%	xERA	Ctl	Dom	Cmd	hr/9	BPV
2017	Rk	Orem	0	0	0	3	2	2.90	2.58	16.7	314	37	88	7.10	11.6	5.8	0.5	0.0	-191
2017	Rk	AZL Angels	2	2	0	49	37	2.94	1.16	16.3	237	29	75	2.77	2.6	6.8	2.6	0.4	71

Lean, loose-armed SP with decent stuff and lot of projection. Induces ton of groundballs with heavy sinking FB. SL shows flashes of plus action, far too inconsistent. CU is distant third pitch, but repeats arm speed and gets OK fade and depth. Very thin frame needs strength for durability and stamina.

Soroka,Mike — SP — Atlanta

EXP MLB DEBUT: 2018 | H/W: 6-5 225 | FUT: #2 starter | 8B

Thrws R Age 20 — 2015 (1) HS (AB)

Velo	Pitch	Grade
91-94	FB	++++
85-88	SL	+++
82-85	CU	++++

Year	Lev	Team	W	L	Sv	IP	K	ERA	WHIP	BF/G	OBA	H%	S%	xERA	Ctl	Dom	Cmd	hr/9	BPV
2015	Rk	GCL Braves	0	0	0	10	11	1.80	0.60	8.6	151	23	67		0.9	9.9	11.0	0.0	172
2015	Rk	Danville	0	2	0	24	26	3.75	1.33	16.6	293	40	69	3.59	1.5	9.8	6.5	0.0	153
2016	A	Rome	9	9	0	143	125	3.02	1.13	22.6	244	31	72	2.60	2.0	7.9	3.9	0.2	105
2017	AA	Mississippi	11	8	0	153	125	2.76	1.09	23.0	235	29	76	2.76	2.0	7.3	3.7	0.6	96

Big-bodied RH close to physical projection and was young for Double-A. Pitched well, cleaned up delivery and refined stuff. 2-seam FB profiles as plus with solid arm-side run and sink. Ditched CB for SL. SL is tightly woven and has average two-plane break. Athleticism plays up CU. Movement mimics FB with additional tumble and deception.

Soto,Gregory — SP — Detroit

EXP MLB DEBUT: 2019 | H/W: 6-1 180 | FUT: #4 starter | 7B

Thrws L Age 23 — 2012 FA (DR)

Velo	Pitch	Grade
90-95	FB	+++
74-80	CB	+++
	CU	++

Year	Lev	Team	W	L	Sv	IP	K	ERA	WHIP	BF/G	OBA	H%	S%	xERA	Ctl	Dom	Cmd	hr/9	BPV
2015	A-	Connecticut	0	1	0	2	5	22.50	3.50	6.3	151	61	29	7.15	27.0	22.5	0.8	0.0	-306
2016	A-	Connecticut	3	2	0	71	62	3.04	1.43	20.2	253	33	77	3.42	4.3	7.8	1.8	0.1	43
2017	A	West Michigan	10	1	0	96	116	2.25	1.29	21.9	205	30	83	2.58	5.1	10.9	2.1	0.3	77
2017	A+	Lakeland	2	1	0	28	28	2.25	1.36	23.4	255	34	84	3.42	3.5	9.0	2.5	0.3	85

Breakout SP who had success on two levels in first time in full season. Did not allow ER in April. Pitches off solid-average FB that has potential to go higher. Features heavy sink that hitters can't elevate. Varies size and shape of CB, though can telegraph by slowing arm. Has feel for changing speeds and CU could develop to above average.

Speas,Alex — SP — Texas

EXP MLB DEBUT: 2022 | H/W: 6-4 180 | FUT: #2 starter | 9E

Thrws R Age 20 — 2016 (2) HS (GA)

Velo	Pitch	Grade
92-96	FB	++++
83-86	SL	+++
	CU	++

Year	Lev	Team	W	L	Sv	IP	K	ERA	WHIP	BF/G	OBA	H%	S%	xERA	Ctl	Dom	Cmd	hr/9	BPV
2016	Rk	AZL Rangers	0	0	0	8	11	0.00	1.36	8.5	149	25	100	1.84	7.8	12.2	1.6	0.0	28
2017	A-	Spokane	1	6	1	33	45	6.23	1.63	9.2	236	33	63	4.80	6.8	12.2	1.8	1.4	55

Athletic, very raw SP who was filthy dominant in August after slow start. Has incredible upside predicated on quick arm and pitch movement. Very erratic control needs to be tamed and delivery can get out of sync. All arsenal shows potential. FB exhibits explosive action and power SL is ideal out pitch. Needs to upgrade CU to stay a SP.

Stanek,Ryne — RP — Tampa Bay

EXP MLB DEBUT: 2017 | H/W: 6-4 215 | FUT: Closer | 8D

Thrws R Age 26 — 2013 (1) Arkansas

Velo	Pitch	Grade
94-99	FB	++++
87-89	SL	+++
84-88	SP	++
	CU	++

Year	Lev	Team	W	L	Sv	IP	K	ERA	WHIP	BF/G	OBA	H%	S%	xERA	Ctl	Dom	Cmd	hr/9	BPV
2015	AA	Montgomery	4	3	1	61	41	4.12	1.36	16.0	232	25	72	3.81	4.6	6.0	1.3	1.0	3
2016	AA	Montgomery	2	6	2	78	91	3.80	1.27	17.7	225	31	71	3.15	4.0	10.5	2.6	0.7	98
2016	AAA	Durham	2	4	1	24	22	5.98	1.45	6.4	245	29	59	4.28	4.9	8.2	1.7	1.1	35
2017	AAA	Durham	3	0	8	44	60	1.22	0.95	4.5	173	29	86	1.06	3.3	12.2	3.8	0.0	150
2017	MLB	Tampa Bay	0	0	0	20	29	5.85	1.90	4.5	316	42	78	7.88	5.4	13.1	2.4	2.7	107

Tall, hard-throwing RP who transitioned to pen in 2016 and likely in role for long-term. Pitched with better command and control and has deep arsenal for RP. Delivery tough to repeat with long arm action, but velocity on rise. Knocks out hitters with SL and added new SPL. If he improves command, he could become closer in big leagues.

Staumont,Josh — SP — Kansas City

EXP MLB DEBUT: 2018 | H/W: 6-3 200 | FUT: #2 starter | 9E

Thrws R Age 24 — 2015 (2) Azusa Pacific

Velo	Pitch	Grade
92-98	FB	++++
82-84	CB	++++
	CU	+

Year	Lev	Team	W	L	Sv	IP	K	ERA	WHIP	BF/G	OBA	H%	S%	xERA	Ctl	Dom	Cmd	hr/9	BPV
2015	Rk	Idaho Falls	3	1	1	31	51	3.18	1.35	9.3	170	33	74	2.02	6.9	14.8	2.1	0.0	96
2016	A+	Wilmington	2	10	0	73	94	5.05	1.77	18.6	231	35	70	4.17	8.3	11.6	1.4	0.4	4
2016	AA	NW Arkansas	2	1	0	50	73	3.05	1.58	20.0	229	37	81	3.64	6.6	13.1	2.0	0.4	75
2017	AA	NW Arkansas	3	4	0	48	45	4.48	1.58	21.2	236	31	70	3.78	6.3	8.4	1.3	0.4	-2
2017	AAA	Omaha	3	8	0	76	93	6.28	1.67	21.3	230	29	65	5.13	7.5	11.0	1.5	1.7	15

Power-armed SP who began year in AAA before demotion to AA in July. Has significant trouble finding plate with any pitch, but intrigues with easy, effortless velocity. Mixes in two-seamer with devastating sink and plus CB. All pitches miss bats, but erratic release point hinders command. Very tough to hit when on.

Steele, Justin

SP | **Chicago (N)** | EXP MLB DEBUT: 2019 | H/W: 6-2 195 | FUT: #4 starter | **7C**

Thrws L Age 22
2014 (5) HS (MS)

Velo	Pitch	Grade
90-93	FB	+++
75-78	CB	+++
84-87	CU	++

Year	Lev	Team	W	L	Sv	IP	K	ERA	WHIP	BF/G	OBA	H%	S%	xERA	Ctl	Dom	Cmd	hr/9	BPV
2014	Rk	AZL Cubs	0	0	0	18	25	2.97	1.26	8.3	226	36	74	2.48	4.0	12.4	3.1	0.0	134
2015	A-	Eugene	3	1	0	40	38	2.69	1.32	16.6	251	34	77	2.98	3.4	8.5	2.5	0.0	80
2016	A	South Bend	5	7	0	77	76	5.02	1.71	18.4	300	39	69	4.99	4.6	8.9	1.9	0.4	55
2017	A+	Myrtle Beach	6	7	0	98	82	2.93	1.38	20.6	265	33	80	3.87	3.3	7.5	2.3	0.5	64

Athletic, projectable lefty continues to make steady progress. Works off a good 90-93 mph fastball that he hides well. Mixes in an above-average curveball and change-up that keeps hitters off balance. Aggressive, confident approach on the mound allows his stuff to play up and he's allowed just 9 HR in 235.1 IP.

Steele, Evan

SP | **Kansas City** | EXP MLB DEBUT: 2020 | H/W: 6-5 210 | FUT: #4 starter | **7C**

Thrws L Age 21
2017 (S-2) Chipola JC

Velo	Pitch	Grade
90-94	FB	+++
81-84	SL	+++
	CU	+++

Year	Lev	Team	W	L	Sv	IP	K	ERA	WHIP	BF/G	OBA	H%	S%	xERA	Ctl	Dom	Cmd	hr/9	BPV
2017	NCAA	Chipola JC	5	0	0	40	58	2.02	1.15	15.9	210	34	82	2.19	3.6	13.0	3.6	0.2	155
2017	Rk	AZL Royals	0	2	0	8	16	5.63	1.63	7.1	328	58	73	6.91	2.3	18.0	8.0	2.3	281

Tall, raw SP who could intrigue with potential for three average-to-plus offerings. Command and secondary pitches have way to go in order to be effective, but have potential. Deceptive delivery adds to pitches, particularly CU that could become plus. Offers average velocity and is stingy against LHH.

Stephan, Trevor

SP | **New York (A)** | EXP MLB DEBUT: 2019 | H/W: 6-4 210 | FUT: #4 starter | **7C**

Thrws R Age 22
2017 (3) Arkansas

Velo	Pitch	Grade
91-95	FB	+++
78-82	SL	+++
	CU	++

Year	Lev	Team	W	L	Sv	IP	K	ERA	WHIP	BF/G	OBA	H%	S%	xERA	Ctl	Dom	Cmd	hr/9	BPV
2017	NCAA	Arkansas	6	3	0	91	120	2.87	1.02	21.9	221	33	74	2.47	2.0	11.9	6.0	0.7	178
2017	Rk	GCL Yankees	0	0	0	2	1	0.00	0.00	5.6	0	0			0.0	4.5		0.0	99
2017	A-	Staten Island	1	1	0	32	43	1.40	0.81	11.7	181	30	81	0.80	1.7	12.1	7.2	0.0	190

Tall, strong SP who could be big-time sleeper. Some see move to pen, but has three quality offerings at disposal. Needs to enhance CU with consistent arm speed, but adds and subtracts from FB well. Gets hitters to chase strong SL and sets up hitters with commandable FB. Can throw harder in short stints and is tough to hit.

Stephens, Jordan

SP | **Chicago (A)** | EXP MLB DEBUT: 2018 | H/W: 6-1 190 | FUT: Setup reliever | **7B**

Thrws R Age 25
2015 (5) Rice

Velo	Pitch	Grade
92-95	FB	++++
77-79	CB	++++
87-89	CT	++
85-86	CU	++

Year	Lev	Team	W	L	Sv	IP	K	ERA	WHIP	BF/G	OBA	H%	S%	xERA	Ctl	Dom	Cmd	hr/9	BPV
2015	NCAA	Rice	6	5	1	59	75	3.19	1.15	13.8	234	35	70	2.44	2.6	11.4	4.4	0.2	153
2015	Rk	Great Falls	0	0	0	3	3	0.00	1.00	5.7	191	27	100	1.43	3.0	9.0	3.0	0.0	99
2015	Rk	AZL White Sox	0	0	0	14	18	0.63	0.63	5.4	149	24	89	0.02	1.3	11.4	9.0	0.0	189
2016	A+	Winston-Salem	7	10	0	141	155	3.45	1.26	21.3	245	33	75	3.44	3.1	9.9	3.2	0.8	113
2017	AA	Birmingham	3	7	0	91	83	3.16	1.30	23.5	246	31	76	3.25	3.5	8.2	2.4	0.4	72

Power pitcher with two plus offerings. FB is heavy and explosive down in zone. 12-6 CB has terrific depth and solid break. Both pitches project as swing-and-miss pitches. Doesn't have pitch to get lefties out. Both CT and CU fringe-average at best. Likely projects as high-leverage pen arm.

Stewart, Kohl

SP | **Minnesota** | EXP MLB DEBUT: 2018 | H/W: 6-3 195 | FUT: #4 starter | **7C**

Thrws R Age 23
2013 (1) HS (TX)

Velo	Pitch	Grade
90-94	FB	+++
85-87	SL	+++
75-79	CB	++
	CU	++

Year	Lev	Team	W	L	Sv	IP	K	ERA	WHIP	BF/G	OBA	H%	S%	xERA	Ctl	Dom	Cmd	hr/9	BPV
2015	A+	Fort Myers	7	8	0	129	71	3.21	1.39	24.7	269	31	75	3.56	3.1	4.9	1.6	0.1	22
2016	A+	Fort Myers	3	2	0	51	44	2.64	1.13	22.5	213	27	77	2.36	3.3	7.7	2.3	0.4	67
2016	AA	Chattanooga	9	6	0	92	47	3.03	1.47	24.7	260	29	79	3.88	4.3	4.6	1.1	0.4	-15
2017	AA	Chattanooga	5	6	0	77	52	4.09	1.52	20.9	249	29	73	3.92	5.3	6.1	1.2	0.5	-15
2017	AAA	Rochester	1	0	0	5	5	7.20	1.60	22.1	332	40	57	6.58	1.8	9.0	5.0	1.8	131

Tall, athletic SP who looks better than stats indicate. Suffered thru minor ailments in 2017 and took step back with poor control and disappointing K rate. Has stuff to excel with velocity and movement. Works efficiently and pitches to contact. Has velocity in tank, but uses two-seam FB early in count. Sequencing and command need work.

Strotman, Drew

SP | **Tampa Bay** | EXP MLB DEBUT: 2020 | H/W: 6-3 195 | FUT: #4 starter | **7C**

Thrws R Age 21
2017 (4) St. Mary's

Velo	Pitch	Grade
91-95	FB	+++
82-85	SL	+++
80-85	CU	++

Year	Lev	Team	W	L	Sv	IP	K	ERA	WHIP	BF/G	OBA	H%	S%	xERA	Ctl	Dom	Cmd	hr/9	BPV
2017	NCAA	St. Mary's (CA)	6	1	1	67	75	4.57	1.45	15.9	279	39	66	3.80	3.2	10.1	3.1	0.1	112
2017	A-	Hudson Valley	2	3	0	50	42	1.79	0.76	16.3	170	23	74	0.60	1.6	7.5	4.7	0.0	110

Slender SP who is likely to move to SP full-time after being college RP. Throws with clean, fast arm to generate both velocity and movement. Lives in lower half and induces high number of groundballs. Has made improvements to delivery and arm/body work in tandem. Showed better CU than advertised, but still has ways to go. SL serves as out pitch.

Suarez, Andrew

SP | **San Francisco** | EXP MLB DEBUT: 2018 | H/W: 6-2 205 | FUT: #4 starter | **7B**

Thrws L Age 25
2015 (2) Miami

Velo	Pitch	Grade
89-93	FB	+++
81-82	SL	+++
78-80	CB	++
81-84	CU	++

Year	Lev	Team	W	L	Sv	IP	K	ERA	WHIP	BF/G	OBA	H%	S%	xERA	Ctl	Dom	Cmd	hr/9	BPV
2015	A+	San Jose	1	0	0	15	16	1.80	1.00	19.1	235	29	92	3.08	1.2	9.6	8.0	1.2	158
2016	A+	San Jose	2	1	0	29	34	2.47	1.03	22.5	233	32	79	2.57	1.5	10.5	6.8	0.6	165
2016	AA	Richmond	7	7	0	114	90	3.95	1.34	25.0	286	34	73	4.36	1.9	7.1	3.8	0.9	95
2017	AA	Richmond	4	4	0	67	55	2.96	1.30	25.1	276	34	77	3.66	2.0	7.4	3.7	0.4	97
2017	AAA	Sacramento	6	6	0	88	80	3.57	1.37	24.6	274	34	75	4.11	2.8	8.2	3.0	0.7	91

Command-oriented SP who is advancing quickly. Pitches to all quadrants of strike zone and induces ton of groundballs with solid-average sinker. Can add tick or two to FB and has SL that serves as out pitch. CB and CU are a bit below average, but play up due to advanced sequencing. Not overpowering, but ability to locate pitches is admirable.

Suarez, Jose

SP | **Los Angeles (A)** | EXP MLB DEBUT: 2020 | H/W: 5-10 170 | FUT: #4 starter | **7E**

Thrws L Age 20
2014 FA (VZ)

Velo	Pitch	Grade
88-92	FB	+++
74-77	CB	++
77-79	CU	+++

Year	Lev	Team	W	L	Sv	IP	K	ERA	WHIP	BF/G	OBA	H%	S%	xERA	Ctl	Dom	Cmd	hr/9	BPV
2016	Rk	Orem	0	1	0	4	7	0.00	1.71	18.6	342	57	100	5.26	2.2	15.4	7.0	0.0	235
2016	Rk	AZL Angels	1	3	0	40	46	5.39	1.52	15.8	298	41	62	4.35	2.9	10.3	3.5	0.2	125
2017	Rk	AZL Angels	1	0	0	14	19	1.93	1.00	17.8	202	31	85	2.13	2.6	12.2	4.8	0.6	168
2017	A	Burlington	5	1	0	54	71	3.65	1.24	18.3	243	34	75	3.72	3.0	11.8	3.9	1.2	150

Short, advanced SP who thrives with lively FB and ability to repeat delivery. FB tough to elevate as it is spotted low in zone and he can also pitch to both sides of plate. Misses a lot of bats, but mostly due to delivery than stuff. CB a bit slow, though improving to average status. Not a ton of upside.

Suarez, Ranger

SP | **Philadelphia** | EXP MLB DEBUT: 2021 | H/W: 6-1 180 | FUT: #4 starter | **7C**

Thrws L Age 22
2012 FA (VZ)

Velo	Pitch	Grade
91-93	FB	++++
83-86	SL	+++
	CU	+++

Year	Lev	Team	W	L	Sv	IP	K	ERA	WHIP	BF/G	OBA	H%	S%	xERA	Ctl	Dom	Cmd	hr/9	BPV
2016	A-	Williamsport	6	4	0	73	53	2.83	1.16	22.4	228	27	77	2.77	3.0	6.5	2.2	0.5	56
2017	A	Lakewood	6	2	0	85	90	1.59	0.89	22.6	178	24	85	1.41	2.5	9.5	3.8	0.4	121
2017	A+	Clearwater	2	4	0	37	38	3.87	1.45	19.9	291	39	72	4.09	2.7	9.2	3.5	0.2	112

Velocity ticked up and so did prospect status. Projectable frame, athletic delivery and keeps ball down in the zone. Three pitches (FB, SL, CU) all play up due to outstanding command and pitchability more than pure stuff. Going forward, more likely to get soft contact than lots of strikeouts. Could improve stamina, as he faded late.

Supak, Trey

SP | **Milwaukee** | EXP MLB DEBUT: 2019 | H/W: 6-5 235 | FUT: #4 starter | **7C**

Thrws R Age 21
2014 (S-2) HS (TX)

Velo	Pitch	Grade
91-93	FB	+++
74-78	CB	+++
83-84	CU	++

Year	Lev	Team	W	L	Sv	IP	K	ERA	WHIP	BF/G	OBA	H%	S%	xERA	Ctl	Dom	Cmd	hr/9	BPV
2015	Rk	Bristol	1	2	0	28	23	6.73	1.42	14.9	306	37	50	4.65	1.6	7.4	4.6	0.6	107
2016	Rk	Helena	1	1	0	14	11	1.29	0.79	12.6	202	26	82	1.04	0.6	7.1	11.0	0.0	128
2016	A	Wisconsin	2	3	1	44	40	3.88	1.47	17.2	278	35	74	4.33	3.5	8.2	2.4	0.6	71
2017	A	Wisconsin	2	2	0	41	53	1.76	0.76	18.3	154	24	77	0.59	2.2	11.6	5.3	0.2	168
2017	A+	Carolina	3	4	1	72	57	4.62	1.29	19.8	242	27	69	4.21	3.5	7.1	2.0	1.5	52

Tall RH uses size to create downward plane on pitches. Three-pitch pitcher. 2-seam FB has solid arm-side run with natural sink. CB has good shape and depth, inconsistent getting on top of pitch. Flashes projectable CU. Low effort delivery works in rotation.

Swanda, John

SP | **Los Angeles (A)** | EXP MLB DEBUT: 2023 | H/W: 6-2 185 | FUT: #3 starter | **8E**

Thrws R Age 19
2017 (4) HS (IA)

Velo	Pitch	Grade
90-93	FB	+++
75-79	CB	+++
	CU	+

Year	Lev	Team	W	L	Sv	IP	K	ERA	WHIP	BF/G	OBA	H%	S%	xERA	Ctl	Dom	Cmd	hr/9	BPV
2017	Rk	AZL Angels	1	2	0	9	6	9.78	2.07	6.4	334	38	50	7.05	5.9	5.9	1.0	1.0	-35

Athletic, projectable SP with lot of development time ahead. Uses quick arm to generate both velocity and movement. Needs to revise mechanics to take advantage of natural arm action. Throws with average control and should develop two above average offerings in FB and tight CB. CU needs significant work, but repeats arm speed.

Szapucki,Thomas — SP — New York (N)

EXP MLB DEBUT: 2020 | H/W: 6-2 181 | FUT: #2 starter | 9E

Thrws L Age 21
2015 (5) HS (FL)

93-96	FB	++++
81-84	CB	++++
83-86	CU	+++

Year	Lev	Team	W	L	Sv	IP	K	ERA	WHIP	BF/G	OBA	H%	S%	xERA	Ctl	Dom	Cmd	hr/9	BPV
2015	Rk	GCL Mets	0	0	0	2	3	17.14	2.38	3.6	458	63	20	9.42	0.0	12.9		0.0	249
2016	Rk	Kingsport	2	1	0	29	47	0.62	0.86	21.4	164	29	100	1.30	2.8	14.6	5.2	0.6	205
2016	A-	Brooklyn	2	2	0	23	39	2.35	0.91	21.5	134	28	71	0.53	4.3	15.3	3.5	0.0	176
2017	A	Columbia	1	2	0	29	27	2.79	1.17	19.3	227	30	74	2.30	3.1	8.4	2.7	0.0	85

Oft-injured and currently rehabbing from July 2017 Tommy John surgery. Struggles repeating mechanics. A combo of deception, velocity and late movement define 4-seam FB effectiveness, complemented nicely with 12-6 spike CB. Also has a feel for CU, which could be above average at maturity. Has not pitched a full season yet.

Tabor,Matt — SP — Arizona

EXP MLB DEBUT: 2021 | H/W: 6-2 160 | FUT: #3 starter | 8D

Thrws R Age 19
2017 (3) HS (MA)

91-95	FB	++++
79-81	SL	++
82-83	CU	+++

Year	Lev	Team	W	L	Sv	IP	K	ERA	WHIP	BF/G	OBA	H%	S%	xERA	Ctl	Dom	Cmd	hr/9	BPV
2017	Rk	AZL Dbacks	0	1	0	4	9	2.14	1.90	5.0	403	74	88	6.89	0.0	19.3		0.0	365

Northeast prep pitcher who added strength in his senior year to advance up draft board. Was up to 95 early in 2017 spring and didn't let up into rookie ball. CB is very slurvy. Added some mph and it works as a SL. Solid feel for CU; very deceptive; could be plus at maturity. Big, physical, some projection left.

Tarnok,Freddy — SP — Atlanta

EXP MLB DEBUT: 2021 | H/W: 6-3 185 | FUT: #3 starter | 8E

Thrws R Age 19
2017 (3) HS (FL)

91-94	FB	++++
78-80	CB	++
	CU	++

Year	Lev	Team	W	L	Sv	IP	K	ERA	WHIP	BF/G	OBA	H%	S%	xERA	Ctl	Dom	Cmd	hr/9	BPV
2017	Rk	GCL Braves	0	3	0	14	10	2.57	1.00	6.7	218	27	71	1.77	1.9	6.4	3.3	0.0	82

Tall, projectable RH with plus arm speed. Needs to fill out physically. FB sits low 90s with inconsistent movement. Can reach back for additional velocity but loses velocity as game progresses. CB and CU are both in infancy stages of development. CB is loopy and doesn't sell CU.

Tate,Dillon — SP — New York (A)

EXP MLB DEBUT: 2018 | H/W: 6-2 185 | FUT: #3 starter | 8C

Thrws R Age 23
2015 (1) UC-Santa Barbara

92-96	FB	++++
83-86	SL	+++
81-84	CU	+++

Year	Lev	Team	W	L	Sv	IP	K	ERA	WHIP	BF/G	OBA	H%	S%	xERA	Ctl	Dom	Cmd	hr/9	BPV
2015	A	Hickory	0	0	0	7	5	1.29	0.43	5.7	132	12	100	0.59	0.0	6.4		1.3	134
2016	A	Hickory	3	3	0	65	55	5.12	1.62	17.0	299	36	68	5.06	3.7	7.6	2.0	0.7	54
2016	A	Charleston (Sc)	1	0	0	17	15	3.16	1.58	10.7	303	38	81	4.89	3.2	7.9	2.5	0.5	75
2017	A+	Tampa	6	0	0	58	46	2.63	1.08	25.2	227	27	78	2.67	2.3	7.1	3.1	0.6	84
2017	AA	Trenton	1	2	0	25	17	3.24	1.28	25.6	246	27	79	3.85	3.2	6.1	1.9	1.1	41

Live-armed SP who started year in June due to shoulder injury. Regained prospect status with return of plus FB with velocity and late action. Secondary pitches remain inconsistent, but show glimpses of dominance. Repeats lively delivery and throws strikes. Quick arm gets good break on SL while CU showing improvement. Needs to battle LHH better.

Taveras,Jose — SP — Philadelphia

EXP MLB DEBUT: 2018 | H/W: 6-4 210 | FUT: Middle reliever | 7C

Thrws R Age 24
2013 FA (DR)

90-92	FB	+++
	CU	++
	SL	++

Year	Lev	Team	W	L	Sv	IP	K	ERA	WHIP	BF/G	OBA	H%	S%	xERA	Ctl	Dom	Cmd	hr/9	BPV
2015	A-	Williamsport	7	4	0	62	59	3.91	1.35	20.0	264	34	70	3.65	3.0	8.5	2.8	0.4	90
2016	A	Lakewood	8	8	0	137	154	3.28	1.04	21.1	231	30	72	2.91	1.7	10.1	5.9	1.0	154
2017	A+	Clearwater	6	4	0	102	92	2.38	1.07	24.8	230	27	85	3.16	2.0	8.1	4.0	1.1	109
2017	AA	Reading	0	1	0	11	11	4.05	0.99	21.2	242	28	67	3.55	0.8	8.9	11.0	1.6	157
2017	AAA	Lehigh Valley	3	1	0	41	37	1.32	1.00	22.4	184	21	97	2.38	3.3	8.1	2.5	1.1	75

Has succeeded so far on exquisite control and changing speeds, keeping hitters off balance. Throws across his body and gets good extension, which makes his FB play up to average. CU ahead of fringy SL, but locates everything and strikeouts held up surprisingly well in seven Triple-A starts. Back-end starter at best.

Taylor,Ben — RP — Boston

EXP MLB DEBUT: 2017 | H/W: 6-3 225 | FUT: Setup reliever | 6B

Thrws R Age 25
2015 (7) South Alabama

91-94	FB	+++
83-86	SL	+++

Year	Lev	Team	W	L	Sv	IP	K	ERA	WHIP	BF/G	OBA	H%	S%	xERA	Ctl	Dom	Cmd	hr/9	BPV
2016	A+	Salem	0	2	3	45	56	2.60	1.00	11.5	216	33	71	1.70	2.0	11.2	5.6	0.0	166
2016	AA	Portland	1	0	5	34	42	3.44	1.18	6.5	226	31	75	3.27	3.2	11.1	3.5	1.1	132
2017	A-	Lowell	0	0	0	2	1	0.00	0.95	4.0	144	17	100	0.85	4.3	4.3	1.0	0.0	-21
2017	AAA	Pawtucket	0	0	2	13	12	2.75	0.92	4.1	159	17	80	2.17	3.4	8.2	2.4	1.4	74
2017	MLB	Boston	0	1	1	17	18	5.26	1.70	5.5	293	36	73	6.00	4.7	9.5	2.0	1.6	61

Big-bodied RP who moved to pen in 2016 and made BOS roster on Opening Day. Missed time due to oblique injury, but has nice future. Deceptive FB is sneaky quick and he can reach back for more velocity on occasion. FB operates as K pitch while SL can also be effective, especially against RHH. Two pitch reliever with little upside.

Taylor,Corey — RP — New York (N)

EXP MLB DEBUT: 2018 | H/W: 5-11 252 | FUT: Middle reliever | 7C

Thrws R Age 25
2015 (7) Texas Tech

94-96	FB	++++
85-87	SL	++

Year	Lev	Team	W	L	Sv	IP	K	ERA	WHIP	BF/G	OBA	H%	S%	xERA	Ctl	Dom	Cmd	hr/9	BPV
2015	NCAA	Texas Tech	4	0	2	57	32	0.32	0.86	11.1	183	22	96	1.02	2.0	5.0	2.5	0.0	53
2015	A-	Brooklyn	1	1	0	18	16	1.50	1.00	3.8	216	27	88	2.21	2.0	8.0	4.0	0.5	108
2016	A+	St. Lucie	4	5	20	53	45	1.87	1.25	4.8	262	33	85	3.11	2.2	7.6	3.5	0.2	96
2017	AA	Binghamton	5	5	3	62	47	3.62	1.34	6.1	283	34	73	3.89	2.0	6.8	3.4	0.4	86

Standout stocky RP from AFL in 2016, struggled with command in 2017. Strong, RH max-effort two-pitch RP. FB is solid workhorse with arm-side run and some sink. SL is wildly inconsistent but flashes plus when his grip is tight. Needs to turn SL in out pitch to meet projection.

Taylor,Cory — SP — San Francisco

EXP MLB DEBUT: 2018 | H/W: 6-2 255 | FUT: #4 starter | 7D

Thrws R Age 24
2015 (8) Dallas Baptist

90-95	FB	+++
80-83	SL	+++
84-85	CU	+

Year	Lev	Team	W	L	Sv	IP	K	ERA	WHIP	BF/G	OBA	H%	S%	xERA	Ctl	Dom	Cmd	hr/9	BPV
2015	A-	Salem-Kaizer	2	0	1	33	50	2.45	1.45	7.8	279	45	83	3.91	3.3	13.6	4.2	0.3	175
2016	A	Augusta	9	5	0	97	100	2.59	1.28	22.1	265	35	80	3.40	2.3	9.3	4.0	0.4	122
2016	A+	San Jose	1	1	0	9	11	6.92	1.76	13.9	319	45	56	5.05	4.0	10.9	2.8	0.0	107
2016	AA	Richmond	1	0	0	12	10	0.75	1.25	24.4	228	30	93	2.52	3.8	7.5	2.0	0.0	52
2017	AA	Richmond	4	11	0	127	100	4.32	1.44	21.7	258	31	70	3.99	4.1	7.1	1.7	0.6	35

Big-framed SP with heavy sinker who led EL in walks. Has frame and stuff to project more as RP, but SF insistent on keeping him as SP. Induces ton of groundballs with heavy sinker and hard SL has stingy late action. FB plays up due to arm slot and natural sink. Control has been issue and K rate has fallen. CU could use attention.

Taylor,Curtis — SP — Tampa Bay

EXP MLB DEBUT: 2020 | H/W: 6-6 215 | FUT: Closer | 8E

Thrws R Age 22
2016 (4) British Columbia

93-95	FB	++++
87-89	SL	+++
84-86	CU	++

Year	Lev	Team	W	L	Sv	IP	K	ERA	WHIP	BF/G	OBA	H%	S%	xERA	Ctl	Dom	Cmd	hr/9	BPV
2016	A-	Hillsboro	1	0	3	16	23	2.24	1.12	3.7	223	37	78	2.06	2.8	12.9	4.6	0.0	174
2017	A	Kane County	3	4	0	62	68	3.33	1.26	19.5	239	32	74	3.19	3.3	9.9	3.0	0.6	105

Tall, projectable SP with two above-average or better pitches. 2-seam FB is borderline plus-plus. Heavy sink and significant arm-side run in on RHH. SL is hard and tight. Would grade up with some consistency. Doesn't use CU much. Best suited for pen.

Thompson, Keegan — SP — Chicago (N)

EXP MLB DEBUT: 2020 | H/W: 6-0 193 | FUT: #4 starter | 7C

Thrws R Age 23
2017 (3) Auburn

90-93	FB	+++
	CB	+++
	CU	+++

Year	Lev	Team	W	L	Sv	IP	K	ERA	WHIP	BF/G	OBA	H%	S%	xERA	Ctl	Dom	Cmd	hr/9	BPV
2017	NCAA	Auburn	7	4	0	93	75	2.42	0.90	23.1	203	24	77	1.98	1.6	7.3	4.4	0.7	104
2017	A-	Eugene	1	2	0	19	23	2.37	1.00	10.4	219	31	78	2.18	1.9	10.9	5.8	0.5	163

3rd round pick out of Auburn had Tommy John surgery and missed all of 2016. Now fully recovered and features a low-90s fastball along with a plus curve and above-average change-up. Works from 1B side of mound and is tough on RHH (0.84 ERA in 10.2 IP). No projection left and lacks physicality but has potential as a back-end starter.

Thompson,Jake — SP — Boston

EXP MLB DEBUT: 2020 | H/W: 6-1 200 | FUT: #3 starter | 8E

Thrws R Age 23
2017 (4) Oregon St

91-95	FB	+++
82-85	SL	+++
82-84	CU	++

Year	Lev	Team	W	L	Sv	IP	K	ERA	WHIP	BF/G	OBA	H%	S%	xERA	Ctl	Dom	Cmd	hr/9	BPV
2017	NCAA	Oregon State	14	1	0	128	119	1.97	0.98	24.3	190	25	81	1.69	2.8	8.4	3.0	0.4	93
2017	A-	Lowell	0	3	0	11	11	3.24	1.44	6.8	242	33	75	3.17	4.9	8.9	1.8	0.0	47

Strongly-built SP who cleaned up mechanics and has two potential plus pitches in repertoire. Still has ways to go with command, as FB is electric and lively. Has experience in pen and could be eventual role. Hard SL flashes plus at times, but CU lags far behind. Not much feel for changing speeds.

Thompson,Mason
SP | **San Diego** | EXP MLB DEBUT: 2020 | H/W: 6-7 186 | FUT: #4 starter | **8C**

Thrws R Age 20
2016 (3) HS (TX)

Velo	Pitch	Grade
91-93	FB	+++
76-78	CB	+++
85-87	CU	+++

Year	Lev	Team	W	L	Sv	IP	K	ERA	WHIP	BF/G	OBA	H%	S%	xERA	Ctl	Dom	Cmd	hr/9	BPV
2016	Rk	AZL Padres	0	0	0	12	12	2.25	1.08	9.4	191	27	77	1.64	3.8	9.0	2.4	0.0	79
2017	A	Fort Wayne	2	4	0	27	28	4.67	1.30	15.9	232	30	64	3.29	4.0	9.3	2.3	0.7	78

Towering RHP with mid-rotation profile and chance for three average-or-better pitches. Large frame and long levers produce FB with ease; chance to add more as he matures. CU remains raw but shows feel for CB and has solid SwK profile already in place. Decent enough athlete and should develop average command. An arm with some upside.

Thorpe,Lewis
SP | **Minnesota** | EXP MLB DEBUT: 2019 | H/W: 6-1 160 | FUT: #3 starter | **8D**

Thrws L Age 22
2012 FA (AU)

Velo	Pitch	Grade
90-94	FB	+++
78-80	CB	++
81-83	SL	+++
80-83	CU	+++

Year	Lev	Team	W	L	Sv	IP	K	ERA	WHIP	BF/G	OBA	H%	S%	xERA	Ctl	Dom	Cmd	hr/9	BPV
2015	*Did not pitch - injured*																		
2016	*Did not pitch - injured*																		
2017	A+	Fort Myers	3	4	0	77	84	2.69	1.21	19.4	222	31	78	2.64	3.6	9.8	2.7	0.4	97
2017	AA	Chattanooga	1	0	0	6	7	6.00	1.17	23.9	228	23	60	5.10	3.0	10.5	3.5	3.0	126

Advanced SP who returned in May after missing all '2015-16 due to Tommy John surgery and knee issue. Treated cautiously upon return, but will be let loose in 2018. Has potential for four average to plus offerings, highlighted by CU that features great depth and fade. FB should add a few ticks with more strength. Uses two breaking balls that flash plus.

Tillo,Daniel
SP | **Kansas City** | EXP MLB DEBUT: 2020 | H/W: 6-5 215 | FUT: #3 starter | **8E**

Thrws L Age 21
2017 (3) Iowa Western JC

Velo	Pitch	Grade
90-95	FB	+++
81-85	SL	+++
	CU	+

Year	Lev	Team	W	L	Sv	IP	K	ERA	WHIP	BF/G	OBA	H%	S%	xERA	Ctl	Dom	Cmd	hr/9	BPV
2017	NCAA	Iowa Western	5	1	0	44	57	2.86	1.07	19.0	205	32	72	1.93	3.1	11.7	3.8	0.2	145
2017	Rk	Burlington	3	2	0	31	25	3.48	1.32	18.3	286	35	73	3.76	1.7	7.3	4.2	0.3	102
2017	Rk	AZL Royals	0	0	0	5	7	10.38	1.54	7.6	353	51	25	5.07	0.0	12.1		0.0	236

Raw SP who could grow into solid mid-rotation guy. Lacks experience, but has impressive pitch mix. Posts incredible groundball rate thanks to FB that features velocity and heavy, late action. Both FB and SL could grow to plus, but needs consistency with release point and mechanics. Hasn't shown durability yet and needs touch on CU.

Torrez, Daury
RP | **Chicago (N)** | EXP MLB DEBUT: 2018 | H/W: 6-3 170 | FUT: Middle reliever | **7C**

Thrws R Age 24
2010 FA (DR)

Velo	Pitch	Grade
90-94	FB	+++
83-85	SL	+++
	CU	+

Year	Lev	Team	W	L	Sv	IP	K	ERA	WHIP	BF/G	OBA	H%	S%	xERA	Ctl	Dom	Cmd	hr/9	BPV
2013	A	Kane County	0	1	0	5	2	5.40	1.20	20.1	262	25	60	4.57	1.8	3.6	2.0	1.8	34
2014	A	Kane County	11	7	0	131	81	2.75	1.00	21.8	229	26	74	2.44	1.4	5.6	3.9	0.5	79
2015	A+	Myrtle Beach	10	6	0	134	86	3.76	1.18	22.3	266	30	69	3.55	1.4	5.8	4.1	0.7	84
2016	A+	Myrtle Beach	2	2	2	68	69	3.57	1.37	6.8	278	36	76	4.21	2.5	9.1	3.6	0.8	114
2017	AA	Tennessee	6	4	1	77	56	1.40	0.92	6.7	211	24	91	2.14	1.5	6.5	4.3	0.7	95

Dominican reliever had his best season yet. Attacks hitters with a 90-94 mph fastball from a low 3/4 almost side-arm delivery that results in plus late action. Mixes in an above-average slider and fringe change-up. Doesn't get a ton of swings and misses, but does limit hard contact and posted a stellar .209 BAA and a 0.92 WHIP at AA.

Toussaint,Touki
SP | **Atlanta** | EXP MLB DEBUT: 2018 | H/W: 6-3 185 | FUT: #3 starter | **8C**

Thrws R Age 21
2014 (1) HS (FL)

Velo	Pitch	Grade
92-95	FB	++++
77-79	CB	++++
83-85	CU	++

Year	Lev	Team	W	L	Sv	IP	K	ERA	WHIP	BF/G	OBA	H%	S%	xERA	Ctl	Dom	Cmd	hr/9	BPV
2015	A	Rome	3	5	0	48	38	5.79	1.51	20.9	227	26	63	4.23	6.2	7.1	1.2	1.1	-21
2015	A	Kane County	2	2	0	39	29	3.69	1.18	22.3	220	25	71	3.11	3.5	6.7	1.9	0.9	45
2016	A	Rome	4	8	0	132	128	3.88	1.33	20.3	220	27	73	3.44	4.8	8.7	1.8	0.9	44
2017	A+	Florida	3	9	0	105	123	5.05	1.36	23.1	254	35	62	3.75	3.6	10.5	2.9	0.7	110
2017	AA	Mississippi	3	4	0	39	44	3.21	1.33	23.2	213	29	78	3.15	5.1	10.1	2.0	0.7	63

Athletic RH had up-and-down season in 2017. More mechanical tinkering left him with a choppy delivery. Added strength to frame, helping FB tick up. FB has solid 2-seam movement, flattening up at higher velocities. CB still plus-plus offering. Best breaking ball in organization. Feel for CU comes and go. Likely, destined for bullpen role.

Tovar,Oscar
SP | **Oakland** | EXP MLB DEBUT: 2021 | H/W: 6-1 160 | FUT: Setup reliever | **7D**

Thrws R Age 20
2014 FA (VZ)

Velo	Pitch	Grade
91-95	FB	+++
81-82	SL	++
	CU	++

Year	Lev	Team	W	L	Sv	IP	K	ERA	WHIP	BF/G	OBA	H%	S%	xERA	Ctl	Dom	Cmd	hr/9	BPV
2016	Rk	AZL Athletics	3	2	0	43	31	3.56	1.35	17.9	253	31	71	3.10	3.6	6.5	1.8	0.0	39
2017	A-	Vermont	3	2	2	65	45	3.46	1.29	17.8	240	28	74	3.31	3.6	6.2	1.7	0.6	33

Aggressive, efficient pitcher who delayed start of year after PED suspension. Very projectable arm and will need to fill out frame for stamina. Has quick arm to generate solid-average FB with late movement. Has improved SL and will need to stay on top of it. Throws CU with good arm speed, but not much separation from FB.

Tseng, Jen-Ho
SP | **Chicago (N)** | EXP MLB DEBUT: 2017 | H/W: 6-1 195 | FUT: #5 SP/swingman | **7D**

Thrws R Age 23
2013 FA (TW)

Velo	Pitch	Grade
89-93	FB	++
75-78	CB	+++
80-82	CU	++

Year	Lev	Team	W	L	Sv	IP	K	ERA	WHIP	BF/G	OBA	H%	S%	xERA	Ctl	Dom	Cmd	hr/9	BPV
2015	A+	Myrtle Beach	7	7	0	119	87	3.55	1.22	21.8	255	31	70	3.16	2.3	6.6	2.9	0.4	75
2016	AA	Tennessee	6	8	0	113	69	4.30	1.50	22.2	302	34	73	5.10	2.5	5.5	2.2	1.0	48
2017	AA	Tennessee	7	3	0	90	83	3.00	1.14	23.8	237	30	76	3.01	2.4	8.3	3.5	0.7	103
2017	AAA	Iowa	6	1	0	55	39	1.80	1.13	24.1	236	27	89	3.09	2.3	6.4	2.8	0.8	71
2017	MLB	Chi Cubs	1	0	0	6	8	7.50	1.17	12.0	228	25	40	5.08	3.0	12.0	4.0	3.0	153

Slender Taiwanese right-hander uses a deliberate approach on the mound with a slight hesitation before exploding towards the plate. Average FB sits at 90-93 with good location. CB and CU both show average to above potential and he pounds the strike zone. Simple repeatable mechanics allows his fringe stuff to play up.

Turnbull,Spencer
SP | **Detroit** | EXP MLB DEBUT: 2018 | H/W: 6-3 215 | FUT: #3 starter | **8D**

Thrws R Age 25
2014 (2) Alabama

Velo	Pitch	Grade
92-96	FB	++++
83-87	SL	+++
76-82	CB	++
85-88	CU	++

Year	Lev	Team	W	L	Sv	IP	K	ERA	WHIP	BF/G	OBA	H%	S%	xERA	Ctl	Dom	Cmd	hr/9	BPV
2015	A	West Michigan	11	3	0	116	106	3.02	1.36	22.1	244	32	75	3.00	4.0	8.2	2.0	0.0	57
2016	A+	Lakeland	1	1	0	30	27	3.00	1.13	19.8	221	29	73	2.41	3.0	8.1	2.7	0.3	83
2017	Rk	GCL Tigers	0	0	0	9	16	4.00	1.11	17.7	240	46	60	2.23	2.0	16.0	8.0	0.0	252
2017	A+	Lakeland	7	3	0	82	64	3.07	1.13	21.7	227	28	72	2.52	2.7	7.0	2.6	0.3	70
2017	AA	Erie	0	3	0	20	22	6.27	1.49	21.7	280	38	55	4.22	3.6	9.9	2.8	0.4	99

Big-bodied SP who overcame shoulder injury in 2016 and flashes plus stuff. Heavy sinking FB can be devastating to hitters from both sides. Exhibits unique movement when on his game. Uses two breaking balls in average, hard SL and knuckle CB. Improved control in 2017 and could be one to keep eye on. CU is below average, but repeats arm speed.

Tyler, Robert
SP | **Colorado** | EXP MLB DEBUT: 2020 | H/W: 6-4 226 | FUT: Setup reliever | **8E**

Thrws R Age 22
2016 (S-1) Georgia

Velo	Pitch	Grade
92-96	FB	+++++
	CB	+
	CU	++

Year	Lev	Team	W	L	Sv	IP	K	ERA	WHIP	BF/G	OBA	H%	S%	xERA	Ctl	Dom	Cmd	hr/9	BPV
2016	NCAA	Georgia	3	5	0	74	89	4.12	1.33	22.0	202	29	69	2.95	5.6	10.8	1.9	0.6	62
2016	A-	Boise	0	2	0	7	5	6.43	2.57	7.5	92	12	72	4.40	20.6	6.4	0.3	0.0	-422
2017	*Did not pitch - injured*																		

38th overall pick in 2016 draft has logged just seven professional innings. Shoulder fatigue caused him to miss all of 2017. In college, fastball sat at 92-96 topping out at 100 mph. Breaking ball well below average, but does show some feel for a change-up. Lottery ticket.

Underwood, Duane
SP | **Chicago (N)** | EXP MLB DEBUT: 2018 | H/W: 6-2 210 | FUT: #4 starter | **7D**

Thrws R Age 23
2012 (2) HS (GA)

Velo	Pitch	Grade
92-95	FB	+++
86-88	CT	+++
76-78	CB	++
82-84	CU	++

Year	Lev	Team	W	L	Sv	IP	K	ERA	WHIP	BF/G	OBA	H%	S%	xERA	Ctl	Dom	Cmd	hr/9	BPV
2016	Rk	AZL Cubs	0	0	0	1	2	0.00	1.00	3.8	262	55	100	2.23	0.0	18.0		0.0	342
2016	A	South Bend	0	1	0	8	12	2.20	1.10	10.7	178	31	78	1.48	4.4	13.2	3.0	0.0	137
2016	A+	Myrtle Beach	0	0	0	4	2	2.14	0.71	14.8	202	23	67	0.88	0.0	4.3		0.0	95
2016	AA	Tennessee	0	5	0	58	46	4.95	1.67	20.1	287	33	72	5.39	4.8	7.1	1.5	1.1	17
2017	AA	Tennessee	13	7	0	138	98	4.43	1.30	22.8	250	29	67	3.75	3.3	6.4	2.0	0.8	45

2nd round pick in 2012 has been slow to develop. Spent the entire year at Double-A with pedestrian results. Works off a plus 92-95 sinking fastball that tops at 98. Scrapped slider in favor of above-average cutter along with curve and below-average change-up. Below-average control and command within the zone results in lots of hard contact.

Unsworth,Dylan
SP | **Seattle** | EXP MLB DEBUT: 2018 | H/W: 6-1 175 | FUT: #5 SP/swingman | **7E**

Thrws R Age 25
2009 FA (SA)

Velo	Pitch	Grade
87-90	FB	++
74-78	CB	++
80-82	CU	+++

Year	Lev	Team	W	L	Sv	IP	K	ERA	WHIP	BF/G	OBA	H%	S%	xERA	Ctl	Dom	Cmd	hr/9	BPV
2015	A+	Bakersfield	1	3	0	40	44	3.36	1.09	14.3	261	34	73	3.37	0.9	9.9	11.0	0.9	171
2015	AA	Jackson	4	7	0	66	51	4.36	1.38	21.3	295	35	69	4.53	1.8	6.9	3.9	0.8	95
2016	AA	Jackson	3	1	0	46	35	1.17	1.06	19.9	244	30	91	2.61	1.4	6.8	5.0	0.4	104
2017	AA	Arkansas	9	8	0	119	86	3.32	1.11	23.4	250	29	72	3.09	1.5	6.5	4.3	0.7	94
2017	AAA	Tacoma	0	1	0	8	4	3.29	1.46	17.6	302	34	75	4.11	2.2	4.4	2.0	0.0	38

Command-oriented SP who finished 2nd in TL in ERA. Returned after missing most of 2016 due to hamstring injury. Far from overpowering, but effective by throwing consistent strikes to all parts of plate. Owns very good CU, but doesn't have true out pitch in repertoire. Gets groundballs and is tough on LHH.

Valdez,Framber

SP | Houston | EXP MLB DEBUT: 2019 | H/W: 5-11 170 | FUT: #5 SP/swingman | 7D

Thrws L Age 24
2015 FA (DR)

Velo	Pitch	Grade
89-94	FB	+ + +
77-80	CB	+ + +
84-87	CU	+ + +

Year	Lev	Team	W	L	Sv	IP	K	ERA	WHIP	BF/G	OBA	H%	S%	xERA	Ctl	Dom	Cmd	hr/9	BPV
2016	A-	Tri City	2	1	0	21	28	3.82	1.37	17.8	269	41	69	3.31	3.0	11.9	4.0	0.0	152
2016	A	Quad Cities	1	3	0	35	35	3.08	1.20	23.5	238	32	73	2.74	2.8	9.0	3.2	0.3	103
2016	A+	Lancaster	0	1	0	5	1	5.19	1.92	24.7	353	37	70	6.14	3.5	1.7	0.5	0.0	-44
2017	A+	Buies Creek	2	3	1	61	73	2.80	1.15	18.6	192	28	76	2.21	4.3	10.8	2.5	0.4	96
2017	AA	Corpus Christi	5	5	0	49	53	5.88	1.69	18.4	303	40	65	5.34	4.2	9.7	2.3	0.7	79

Dominican LH with track record of Dom, but lacking ingredients necessary for rotation. Shows aptitude for CB spin and will miss some bats, occasionally flashing plus. FB velo is inconsistent and often gets left up in zone. CU shows potential. Ctl has been an issue vs. advanced bats. Stuff better in shorter stints; likely a long-relief option.

Vieira,Thyago

RP | Chicago (A) | EXP MLB DEBUT: 2017 | H/W: 6-2 210 | FUT: Closer | 7B

Thrws R Age 25
2010 FA (BR)

Velo	Pitch	Grade
94-98	FB	+ + + +
89-92	SL	+ + +
82-84	CB	+ +

Year	Lev	Team	W	L	Sv	IP	K	ERA	WHIP	BF/G	OBA	H%	S%	xERA	Ctl	Dom	Cmd	hr/9	BPV
2015	A	Clinton	1	4	0	31	22	6.97	1.77	6.5	286	34	58	5.18	5.8	6.4	1.1	0.6	-24
2016	A+	Bakersfield	1	0	8	44	53	2.86	1.25	5.3	229	34	76	2.68	3.7	10.8	2.9	0.2	114
2017	AA	Arkansas	2	3	2	36	35	3.74	1.25	5.1	228	30	68	2.72	3.7	8.7	2.3	0.2	74
2017	AAA	Tacoma	0	1	2	17	11	4.71	1.45	6.1	271	31	67	4.11	3.7	5.8	1.6	0.5	23
2017	MLB	Seattle	0	0	0	1	1	0.00	0.00	2.8	0	0			0.0	9.0		0.0	180

Power-armed RP who can fire plus FB into zone and becoming more of pitcher than thrower. Reached majors with improved command, but still only average at best. Hard SL becoming more consistent with power and shape while slower CB has potential. Delivery can get out of whack. Much better K rate since moved to pen in 2014 and could go higher.

Voth,Austin

SP | Washington | EXP MLB DEBUT: 2018 | H/W: 6-2 215 | FUT: Middle reliever | 7D

Thrws R Age 25
2013 (5) Washington

Velo	Pitch	Grade
87-89	FB	+ +
76-79	CB	+ + +
82-84	CU	+ +

Year	Lev	Team	W	L	Sv	IP	K	ERA	WHIP	BF/G	OBA	H%	S%	xERA	Ctl	Dom	Cmd	hr/9	BPV
2015	AA	Harrisburg	6	7	0	157		2.92	1.11	22.0	232	30	75	2.74	2.3	8.5	3.7	0.6	109
2016	AAA	Syracuse	7	9	0	157	133	3.15	1.24	23.6	238	29	76	3.21	3.3	7.6	2.3	0.6	67
2017	A-	Auburn	0	1	0	2	2	13.50	2.50	10.6	415	52	40	8.75	4.5	9.0	2.0	0.0	59
2017	AA	Harrisburg	3	4	0	54	44	5.16	1.40	22.9	292	34	66	5.04	2.2	7.3	3.4	1.3	91
2017	AAA	Syracuse	1	7	0	66	42	6.40	1.80	23.5	313	34	67	6.66	4.6	5.7	1.2	1.6	-4

Thin-framed starter short on stuff who got hit hard in 2017. Struggles to get FB up to 90; a CB with depth is probably best pitch, but is inconsistent. CU below average due to lack of separation from FB. Tends to leave pitches up in zone, making them easily trackable. Might be time to try as RP.

Waddell, Brandon

SP | Pittsburgh | EXP MLB DEBUT: 2019 | H/W: 6-3 180 | FUT: #5 SP/swingman | 6C

Thrws L Age 23
2015 (5) Virginia

Velo	Pitch	Grade
89-93	FB	+ +
	CB	+ + +
	CU	+ +

Year	Lev	Team	W	L	Sv	IP	K	ERA	WHIP	BF/G	OBA	H%	S%	xERA	Ctl	Dom	Cmd	hr/9	BPV
2016	A+	Bradenton	4	0	0	29	26	0.93	0.52	19.4	137	18	86		0.6	8.1	13.0	0.3	146
2016	AA	Altoona	7	9	0	118	94	4.12	1.55	23.4	268	32	74	4.46	4.7	7.2	1.5	0.7	21
2017	Rk	GCL Pirates	1	0	0	3	4	0.00	0.33	9.5	106	18	100		0.0	12.0		0.0	234
2017	A-	West Virginia	1	0	0	9	11	1.00	0.89	16.7	165	22	100	1.78	3.0	11.0	3.7	1.0	135
2017	AA	Altoona	3	3	0	66	56	3.55	1.32	18.2	244	30	73	3.27	3.7	7.6	2.1	0.4	56

Workhorse back-end lefty starter. Fastball sits at 89-93 but lacks late life. Mixes in an average 11-5 curveball and change-up, but lacks a true swing-and-miss pitch. Mechanics need refinement and he tends to rush his delivery and fly open on the front-side, resulting in below-avg Cmd.

Wahl,Bobby

RP | Oakland | EXP MLB DEBUT: 2017 | H/W: 6-2 210 | FUT: Setup reliever | 7C

Thrws R Age 26
2013 (5) Mississippi

Velo	Pitch	Grade
94-98	FB	+ + + +
82-84	CB	+ +
80-82	CU	+ +

Year	Lev	Team	W	L	Sv	IP	K	ERA	WHIP	BF/G	OBA	H%	S%	xERA	Ctl	Dom	Cmd	hr/9	BPV
2016	AA	Midland	0	1	10	40	48	2.24	1.07	4.7	187	26	83	2.17	3.8	10.7	2.8	0.7	109
2016	AAA	Nashville	1	0	4	9	14	2.93	1.41	4.3	212	37	77	2.67	5.9	13.7	2.3	0.0	106
2017	A+	Stockton	0	0	0	2	6	0.00	1.50	4.3	0	0	100	0.74	13.5	27.0	2.0	0.0	140
2017	AAA	Nashville	1	1	3	13	22	4.15	1.38	5.0	262	41	80	5.17	3.5	15.2	4.4	2.1	199
2017	MLB	Oakland	0	0	0	7	8	5.00	1.67	4.6	283	39	67	4.28	5.0	10.0	2.0	0.0	63

Big RP who reached majors, but ended season in July and underwent thoracic outlet surgery. Should be healthy by spring training. Moved to RP in 2014 and has been dominant when he throws strikes. FB reaches triple digits, but hasn't mastered 2nd pitch. CB shows flashes, but more of a change of pace. Everything is hard, but FB can often be too straight.

Walker,Jeremy

SP | Atlanta | EXP MLB DEBUT: 2019 | H/W: 6-5 205 | FUT: #4 starter | 7C

Thrws R Age 22
2016 (5) Gardner-Webb

Velo	Pitch	Grade
92-95	FB	+ + + +
83-85	SL	+ + +
77-79	CB	+ +
82-84	CU	+ +

Year	Lev	Team	W	L	Sv	IP	K	ERA	WHIP	BF/G	OBA	H%	S%	xERA	Ctl	Dom	Cmd	hr/9	BPV
2016	NCAA	Gardner-Webb	9	5	0	100	99	3.78	1.29	27.4	265	34	72	3.77	2.4	8.9	3.7	0.7	113
2016	Rk	Danville	3	3	0	39	37	3.21	1.22	12.2	266	34	74	3.37	1.8	8.5	4.6	0.5	121
2017	A	Rome	7	11	0	138	100	3.98	1.37	21.4	290	34	70	4.10	2.0	6.5	3.3	0.5	83

Tall RHP had a solid full-season debut in Single-A. Relies heavily on locating FB with little movement. Stays tall and falls off the mound, creating downward plane on pitches. Best secondary is a tight SL, which ATL took away at times to work on other pitches. CB is loopy but can spin off true 12-6 CB at times. CU is work-in-progress.

Watson,Nolan

SP | Kansas City | EXP MLB DEBUT: 2020 | H/W: 6-2 195 | FUT: #4 starter | 7E

Thrws R Age 21
2015 (1) HS (IN)

Velo	Pitch	Grade
90-93	FB	+ + +
78-82	CB	+ +
81-84	SL	+ +
	CU	+ +

Year	Lev	Team	W	L	Sv	IP	K	ERA	WHIP	BF/G	OBA	H%	S%	xERA	Ctl	Dom	Cmd	hr/9	BPV
2015	Rk	Burlington	0	3	0	29	16	4.95	1.72	12.0	322	36	71	5.65	3.4	4.9	1.5	0.6	15
2016	A	Lexington	3	11	0	96	60	7.59	1.76	18.3	316	33	59	6.73	4.1	5.6	1.4	1.8	8
2017	Rk	Burlington	0	1	0	11	10	7.36	1.64	16.3	326	42	50	4.89	2.5	8.2	3.3	0.0	99
2017	Rk	AZL Royals	0	1	0	4	2	27.86	4.52	7.7	559	60	32	18.07	8.6	4.3	0.5	0.0	-136
2017	A	Lexington	1	10	1	69	41	6.78	1.94	21.9	342	38	65	6.94	4.3	5.3	1.2	1.0	-2

Strong SP who hasn't lived up to hype. Stuck in Low-A and was hit hard with iffy stuff. FB remains best pitch, but hasn't added velocity as hoped. SL has chance to be out pitch, though telegraphs it and lacks big break. Changing speeds has proven difficult and CB is too ordinary. The hope is that he adds ticks to FB and finds consistent breaking ball.

Watson,Tyler

SP | Minnesota | EXP MLB DEBUT: 2019 | H/W: 6-5 200 | FUT: #4 starter | 7C

Thrws L Age 20
2015 (34) HS (AZ)

Velo	Pitch	Grade
88-92	FB	+ + +
77-81	CB	+ + +
	CU	+ +

Year	Lev	Team	W	L	Sv	IP	K	ERA	WHIP	BF/G	OBA	H%	S%	xERA	Ctl	Dom	Cmd	hr/9	BPV
2015	Rk	GCL Nationals	1	1	0	13	16	0.00	0.84	9.6	159	25	100	0.65	2.7	11.0	4.0	0.0	142
2016	A-	Auburn	1	2	0	43	48	1.88	0.91	17.8	198	28	79	1.46	1.9	10.0	5.3	0.2	148
2016	A	Hagerstown	1	1	0	15	16	4.80	1.47	21.4	274	38	64	3.66	3.6	9.6	2.7	0.0	94
2017	A	Hagerstown	6	4	0	93	98	4.35	1.25	21.0	260	34	65	3.54	2.3	9.5	4.1	0.7	126
2017	A	Cedar Rapids	1	3	0	27	18	4.32	1.33	22.5	268	29	72	4.51	2.7	6.0	2.3	1.3	54

Big-framed SP who lost steam late in season, but was solid acquisition from WAS. Has advanced stuff and command with three solid offerings. May not project to high K rate at upper levels, but is tough to hit with downward angle and ability to locate FB. Throws CB and CU for strikes and uses athleticism to repeat delivery and slot.

Weigel,Patrick

SP | Atlanta | EXP MLB DEBUT: 2019 | H/W: 6-6 240 | FUT: #4 starter | 7B

Thrws R Age 23
2015 (7) Houston

Velo	Pitch	Grade
92-96	FB	+ + + +
83-86	SL	+ + +
75-77	CB	+ + +
82-85	CU	+ +

Year	Lev	Team	W	L	Sv	IP	K	ERA	WHIP	BF/G	OBA	H%	S%	xERA	Ctl	Dom	Cmd	hr/9	BPV
2016	A	Rome	10	4	0	129	135	2.51	1.08	22.9	202	27	78	2.20	3.3	9.4	2.9	0.5	99
2016	AA	Mississippi	1	2	0	20	17	2.23	0.84	24.7	136	15	80	1.30	3.6	7.6	2.1	0.9	58
2017	AA	Mississippi	3	0	0	37	38	2.91	1.16	21.1	234	31	76	2.80	2.7	9.2	3.5	0.5	112
2017	AAA	Gwinnett	3	2	0	41	30	5.27	1.44	21.8	266	30	65	4.54	3.7	6.6	1.8	1.1	36

Tall, big-bodied RH made strides early but succumbed to Tommy John surgery in June. 4-pitch pitcher who maxes out delivery. Best pitch is two-seam FB with solid arm-side run; can change speeds with it and reach back for added velocity. SL took step forward, now with above-average potential. CB has solid depth but lacks swing-and-miss potential. Has feel for CU.

Wells,Alex

SP | Baltimore | EXP MLB DEBUT: 2020 | H/W: 6-1 190 | FUT: #4 starter | 7D

Thrws L Age 21
2015 FA (AU)

Velo	Pitch	Grade
86-90	FB	+ +
74-77	CB	+ + +
80-83	CU	+ + +

Year	Lev	Team	W	L	Sv	IP	K	ERA	WHIP	BF/G	OBA	H%	S%	xERA	Ctl	Dom	Cmd	hr/9	BPV
2016	A-	Aberdeen	4	5	0	62	50	2.17	0.92	17.9	215	27	75	1.65	1.3	7.2	5.6	0.1	113
2017	A	Delmarva	11	5	0	140	113	2.38	0.91	20.9	230	27	81	2.67	0.6	7.3	11.3	1.0	131

Advanced SP who did not allow ER in July (31 IP) and led SAL in ERA. Works with exceptional control and spots below average FB anywhere he wants. Has shrewd ability to change speeds and can add and subtract from all offerings. Far from imposing or dominant. Uses slow CB for change-of-pace and has solid CU to keep RHH honest.

Wentz,Joey

SP | Atlanta | EXP MLB DEBUT: 2020 | H/W: 6-5 210 | FUT: #2 starter | 9D

Thrws L Age 20
2016 (S-1) HS (KS)

Velo	Pitch	Grade
89-93	FB	+ + + +
72-75	CB	+ + + +
82-84	CU	+ + +

Year	Lev	Team	W	L	Sv	IP	K	ERA	WHIP	BF/G	OBA	H%	S%	xERA	Ctl	Dom	Cmd	hr/9	BPV
2016	Rk	GCL Braves	0	0	0	12	18	0.00	0.67	10.5	81	16	100		3.8	13.5	3.6	0.0	160
2016	Rk	Danville	1	4	0	32	35	5.06	1.59	17.7	256	36	65	3.72	5.6	9.8	1.8	0.0	43
2017	A	Rome	8	3	0	131	152	2.61	1.11	19.8	211	30	76	2.17	3.2	10.4	3.3	0.3	120

Tall, athletic LH with plus stuff and pitchability off the charts. Stays tall and falls with deceptive delivery, creating downward plane on pitches. 2-seam FB gets job done with arm-side run and late sink. 12-6 CB is best pitch with incredible depth and late drop. Has feel for CU mimicking FB but struggles with release point. Needs to add strength.

Whalen,Rob — SP — Seattle

EXP MLB DEBUT: 2016 | H/W: 6-2 220 | FUT: #4 starter | 7C

Thrws R Age 24
2012 (12) HS (FL)

Velo	Pitch	Grade
90-93	FB	+++
82-84	CB	+++
75-80	SL	+++
	CU	++

Year	Lev	Team	W	L	Sv	IP	K	ERA	WHIP	BF/G	OBA	H%	S%	xERA	Ctl	Dom	Cmd	hr/9	BPV
2016	AA	Mississippi	7	5	0	101	94	2.49	1.23	22.7	234	30	80	2.86	3.3	8.4	2.5	0.4	80
2016	AAA	Gwinnett	0	1	0	18	18	1.98	1.04	23.4	190	26	79	1.52	3.5	8.9	2.6	0.0	85
2016	MLB	Atlanta	1	2	0	24	25	6.69	1.32	20.0	227	27	50	4.06	4.5	9.3	2.1	1.5	65
2017	AAA	Tacoma	0	7	0	53	43	6.61	1.53	23.1	289	33	58	5.49	3.4	7.3	2.2	1.5	58
2017	MLB	Seattle	0	1	0	7	2	6.34	1.27	14.5	259	25	50	4.21	2.5	2.5	1.0	1.3	-5

Strong, durable SP who missed lot of time due to an off-the-field matter. Impressive arsenal, but hasn't yet maximized production. Deceptive; no offering is straight, but has been victimized by HR. K rate has dropped at upper levels, but has CB that misses bats. Can vary shape on CB and generally commands all pitches for strikes.

White, Mitchell — SP — Los Angeles (N)

EXP MLB DEBUT: 2019 | H/W: 6-4 207 | FUT: #3 starter | 8C

Thrws R Age 23
2016 (2) Santa Clara

Velo	Pitch	Grade
94-97	FB	++++
86-88	SL	++++
75-78	CB	+++
	CU	+

Year	Lev	Team	W	L	Sv	IP	K	ERA	WHIP	BF/G	OBA	H%	S%	xERA	Ctl	Dom	Cmd	hr/9	BPV
2016	A	Great Lakes	0	0	0	16	20	0.00	0.56	6.8	62	11	100		3.4	11.3	3.3	0.0	129
2016	A+	Rancho Cuca	1	0	0	2	2	0.00	0.50	6.6	151	22	100		0.0	9.0		0.0	180
2017	Rk	AZL Dodgers	0	0	0	7	8	0.00	0.57	7.9	92	15	100		2.6	10.3	4.0	0.0	134
2017	A+	Rancho Cuca	2	1	0	38	49	3.77	1.10	16.6	194	31	62	1.69	3.8	11.5	3.1	0.0	124
2017	AA	Tulsa	1	1	0	28	31	2.57	1.07	15.6	177	24	79	2.05	4.2	10.0	2.4	0.6	85

Tall, athletic right-hander has seen his stuff improve since being drafted. Fastball now sits at 94-97 mph with plus late sink and run. Slider is also plus and has swing-and-miss action and curve is above-average. Had Tommy John surgery in high school and missed a month of action with a broken toe.

Whitley,Forrest — SP — Houston

EXP MLB DEBUT: 2019 | H/W: 6-7 240 | FUT: #3 starter | 9D

Thrws R Age 20
2016 (1) HS (TX)

Velo	Pitch	Grade
91-95	FB	++++
74-76	CB	++++
85-87	SL	+++
81-83	CU	+++

Year	Lev	Team	W	L	Sv	IP	K	ERA	WHIP	BF/G	OBA	H%	S%	xERA	Ctl	Dom	Cmd	hr/9	BPV
2016	Rk	Greeneville	0	1	0	11		3.24	1.26	11.3	260	38	71	2.93	2.4	10.5	4.3	0.0	142
2016	Rk	GCL Astros	0	1	0	4	6	10.98	1.71	6.2	302	47	29	4.64	4.4	13.2	3.0	0.0	137
2017	A	Quad Cities	2	3	0	46	67	2.93	1.37	16.1	244	39	79	3.33	4.1	13.1	3.2	0.4	143
2017	A+	Buies Creek	3	1	0	31	50	3.18	1.19	17.8	242	41	74	3.02	2.6	14.5	5.6	0.6	208
2017	AA	Corpus Christi	0	0	0	14	26	1.90	0.85	13.0	167	33	82	1.29	2.5	16.5	6.5	0.6	246

Towering SP who moved through 3 levels in 2017. Misses bats with hard-biting mid-70s CB and complements with good plane on FB. CU and SL are both raw; will need to develop to remain SP. Smooth delivery, repeats arm slot, but often struggles to hit his spots. Could find role as late-inning RP if command doesn't improve.

Widener,Taylor — SP — New York (A)

EXP MLB DEBUT: 2019 | H/W: 6-0 195 | FUT: #3 starter | 8D

Thrws R Age 23
2016 (12) South Carolina

Velo	Pitch	Grade
92-96	FB	+++
82-86	SL	++++
	CU	++

Year	Lev	Team	W	L	Sv	IP	K	ERA	WHIP	BF/G	OBA	H%	S%	xERA	Ctl	Dom	Cmd	hr/9	BPV
2015	NCAA	South Carolina	1	5	9	32	44	4.78	1.63	7.5	268	39	71	4.73	5.3	12.4	2.3	0.8	96
2016	NCAA	South Carolina	4	2	0	55	68	4.24	1.27	13.3	258	36	68	3.68	2.6	11.1	4.3	0.8	147
2016	A-	Staten Island	0	0	1	15	25	0.00	0.40	8.1	45	10	100		2.4	14.9	6.3	0.0	222
2016	A	Charleston	1	0	3	23	34	0.78	0.78	11.8	188	30	100	1.54	1.2	13.3	11.3	0.8	226
2017	A+	Tampa	7	8	0	119	129	3.40	1.15	17.5	206	28	70	2.33	3.8	9.7	2.6	0.4	91

Unheralded SP who posted nice results in first full season as pro. Very low oppBA thanks to electric stuff and repeatable delivery. FB has some giddyup while SL is true out pitch. Became more effective while velocity increased. Very athletic delivery should allow for better CU in time. Some concern about injury history.

Williams, Ronnie — RP — St. Louis

EXP MLB DEBUT: 2020 | H/W: 6-0 170 | FUT: Setup reliever | 8E

Thrws R Age 22
2014 (2) HS (FL)

Velo	Pitch	Grade
95-97	FB	++++
	SL	+++
	CU	++

Year	Lev	Team	W	L	Sv	IP	K	ERA	WHIP	BF/G	OBA	H%	S%	xERA	Ctl	Dom	Cmd	hr/9	BPV
2014	Rk	GCL Cardinals	0	5	1	36	30	4.74	1.33	15.0	277	35	62	3.61	2.2	7.5	3.3	0.2	92
2015	Rk	Johnson City	3	3	0	56	43	3.70	1.25	19.0	222	26	72	3.20	4.0	6.9	1.7	0.8	34
2016	A-	State College	4	2	0	46	33	2.73	0.95	24.9	222	27	70	1.89	1.4	6.4	4.7	0.2	97
2016	A	Peoria	1	3	0	35	36	4.35	1.36	24.5	238	28	76	4.59	4.3	9.2	2.1	1.8	66
2017	A	Peoria	4	6	1	83	95	6.94	1.65	10.3	280	36	58	5.42	5.0	10.3	2.1	1.3	69

Short, strong-armed pitcher has electric stuff, but had a disastrous statistical campaign. Plus fastball sits at 94-97 with a wipe-out slider and a change-up that shows potential. Plus raw stuff plays down due to poor control and command. 10.3 Dom undermined by 5.0 Ctl and a move to relief didn't help.

Williams,Garrett — SP — San Francisco

EXP MLB DEBUT: 2019 | H/W: 6-1 205 | FUT: #3 starter | 8D

Thrws L Age 23
2016 (7) Oklahoma St

Velo	Pitch	Grade
92-96	FB	++++
80-83	CB	+++
84-86	CU	++

Year	Lev	Team	W	L	Sv	IP	K	ERA	WHIP	BF/G	OBA	H%	S%	xERA	Ctl	Dom	Cmd	hr/9	BPV
2016	NCAA	Oklahoma St	2	0	0	13	20	6.18	1.76	4.3	245	39	64	4.59	7.6	13.7	1.8	0.7	61
2016	Rk	AZL Giants	1	0	0	7	5	2.57	1.00	8.9	168	21	71	1.20	3.9	6.4	1.7	0.0	30
2016	A-	Salem-Keizer	1	2	0	25	22	5.74	1.67	16.1	283	36	63	4.67	5.0	7.9	1.6	0.4	24
2017	A	Augusta	4	3	0	64	58	2.25	1.31	22.0	246	33	81	2.90	3.5	8.2	2.3	0.0	70
2017	A+	San Jose	2	2	0	33	38	2.45	1.15	21.8	231	31	83	3.05	2.7	10.4	3.8	0.8	131

Strong SP who thrives on groundballs and Ks. Can dominate hitters with combo of velocity and tight CB. Continues to improve control and lives in lower half of zone. Very tough on LHH with CB, but has to improve CU to remain SP. Very competitive and knows how to set up hitters.

Wilson,Bryse — SP — Atlanta

EXP MLB DEBUT: 2019 | H/W: 6-1 225 | FUT: #3 starter | 8C

Thrws R Age 20
2016 (4) HS (NC)

Velo	Pitch	Grade
91-94	FB	++++
83-85	SL	+++
82-85	CU	+++

Year	Lev	Team	W	L	Sv	IP	K	ERA	WHIP	BF/G	OBA	H%	S%	xERA	Ctl	Dom	Cmd	hr/9	BPV
2016	Rk	GCL Braves	1	1	0	26	29	0.69	0.92	10.9	178	26	92	1.06	2.7	10.0	3.6	0.0	123
2017	A	Rome	10	7	0	137	139	2.50	1.04	20.3	214	28	78	2.28	2.4	9.1	3.8	0.5	117

Physically-mature RH spent 19-year-old season succeeding at Single-A. Think Mike Soroka Lite. Relies heavily on command and control, just more than that because of pure stuff. FB is plus, 2-seam offering with solid arm-side run and sink. SL is sweepy with effective two-plane break. Has a feel for an average CU with solid tumble. Bulldog mentality.

Wood,Hunter — SP — Tampa Bay

EXP MLB DEBUT: 2017 | H/W: 6-1 165 | FUT: #4 starter | 7D

Thrws R Age 24
2013 (29) Howard College

Velo	Pitch	Grade
89-94	FB	+++
77-80	CB	+++
81-82	SL	++
	CU	++

Year	Lev	Team	W	L	Sv	IP	K	ERA	WHIP	BF/G	OBA	H%	S%	xERA	Ctl	Dom	Cmd	hr/9	BPV
2016	A+	Charlotte	3	3	0	63	56	1.71	0.92	21.5	160	21	82	1.16	3.4	8.0	2.3	0.3	69
2016	AA	Montgomery	6	2	0	49	49	3.30	1.14	19.4	206	26	75	2.82	3.7	9.0	2.5	0.9	81
2017	AA	Montgomery	4	4	0	70	68	4.76	1.31	24.1	256	32	65	3.88	3.1	8.7	2.8	0.9	92
2017	AAA	Durham	3	1	0	53	47	4.41	1.39	11.8	265	31	73	4.64	3.4	8.0	2.4	1.4	70
2017	MLB	Tampa Bay	0	0	0	0	0	0.00	0.00	0.3	0	0	0		0.0	0.0		0.0	18

Versatile pitcher who was moved to bullpen in 2nd half and may be future role. Has relatively polished arsenal with clean arm action. Can add few ticks to electric FB and can get outs with solid, late-breaking CB. Maintains arm speed on CU for deception and will mix in occasional SL. Will need better command to earn prominent role.

Woodford, Jake — SP — St. Louis

EXP MLB DEBUT: 2020 | H/W: 6-4 210 | FUT: #4 starter | 7D

Thrws R Age 21
2015 (S-1) HS (FL)

Velo	Pitch	Grade
90-93	FB	+++
	SL	+++
	CU	++

Year	Lev	Team	W	L	Sv	IP	K	ERA	WHIP	BF/G	OBA	H%	S%	xERA	Ctl	Dom	Cmd	hr/9	BPV
2015	Rk	GCL Cardinals	1	0	1	26	21	2.41	1.26	13.3	261	32	81	3.31	2.4	7.2	3.0	0.3	83
2016	A	Peoria	5	5	0	108	82	3.33	1.30	21.2	254	30	75	3.54	3.1	6.8	2.2	0.6	58
2017	A+	Palm Beach	7	6	0	119	72	3.10	1.40	21.9	276	31	79	4.07	2.9	5.4	1.8	0.5	36

39th pick of 2015 draft continues to make steady progress. Bread and butter is an effective 90-93 mph sinking fastball. Slider and change-up are usable but are not swing and miss pitches. Tall, lean frame gives him some projection and held his own at High-A.

Woodruff,Brandon — SP — Milwaukee

EXP MLB DEBUT: 2017 | H/W: 6-4 215 | FUT: #3 starter | 8C

Thrws R Age 25
2014 (11) Mississippi St

Velo	Pitch	Grade
93-95	FB	++++
85-87	SL	+++
85-86	CU	+++

Year	Lev	Team	W	L	Sv	IP	K	ERA	WHIP	BF/G	OBA	H%	S%	xERA	Ctl	Dom	Cmd	hr/9	BPV
2016	A+	Brevard County	4	1	0	44	49	1.84	0.98	20.9	210	29	83	1.96	2.0	10.0	4.9	0.4	143
2016	AA	Biloxi	10	8	0	113	124	3.02	1.04	21.9	216	30	70	2.12	2.4	9.9	4.1	0.3	131
2017	Rk	AZL Brewers	0	0	0	2	1	4.50	1.50	8.6	262	30	67	3.62	4.5	4.5	1.0	0.0	-23
2017	AAA	Col Springs	6	5	0	75	70	4.31	1.37	19.7	269	33	71	4.26	3.0	8.4	2.8	1.0	88
2017	MLB	Milwaukee	2	3	0	43	32	4.81	1.33	22.3	262	30	65	4.14	2.9	6.7	2.3	1.0	59

Tall, high-floor RH made MLB debut after sideways 2017. Stuggled corralling movement of heavy FB. FB has plus arm-side bore, diving out of the zone. Heavy groundball tendencies. SL is a solid offering. Could miss bats if tightened up. CU wildly inconsistent. Flashes plus w/ solid deception and plus tumble.

Woods,Stephen — SP — Tampa Bay

EXP MLB DEBUT: 2020 | H/W: 6-2 200 | FUT: #4 starter | 7D

Thrws R Age 22
2016 (8) at Albany

Velo	Pitch	Grade
91-95	FB	+++
79-82	CB	+++
84-87	SL	+++
	CU	++

Year	Lev	Team	W	L	Sv	IP	K	ERA	WHIP	BF/G	OBA	H%	S%	xERA	Ctl	Dom	Cmd	hr/9	BPV
2016	NCAA	SUNY - Albany	3	5	0	64	88	5.61	1.71	20.8	276	41	66	4.81	5.7	12.3	2.1	0.6	85
2016	Rk	AZL Giants	0	2	0	27	25	2.67	1.56	11.8	247	33	81	3.53	5.7	8.3	1.5	0.0	15
2016	A-	Salem-Keizer	1	0	0	8	12	5.63	1.50	17.3	237	36	64	4.26	5.6	13.5	2.4	1.1	109
2017	A	Augusta	6	7	0	110	113	2.95	1.43	20.3	231	31	79	3.21	5.2	9.2	1.8	0.2	43

Strong, durable SP who led SAL in walks in first full season as pro. Has very good pitch mix thrown with excellent arm speed. All pitches are hard, led by FB and power CB. Uses SL that can miss bats, but CB is far better of two. Inability to command plate could lead to bullpen. Could use better offspeed pitch for LHH.

Wright,Kyle

SP | Atlanta | EXP MLB DEBUT: 2019 | H/W: 6-4 200 | FUT: #2 starter | 9C

Thrws R Age 22
2017 (1) Vanderbilt

92-96	FB	++++
82-84	CB	+++
87-89	CT	+++
87-89	CU	++++

Year	Lev	Team	W	L	Sv	IP	K	ERA	WHIP	BF/G	OBA	H%	S%	xERA	Ctl	Dom	Cmd	hr/9	BPV
2015	NCAA	Vanderbilt	6	1	4	58	62	1.24	1.01	7.7	180	26	86	1.33	3.6	9.6	2.7	0.0	95
2016	NCAA	Vanderbilt	8	4	0	93	107	3.09	1.22	23.5	238	33	76	3.10	3.1	10.3	3.3	0.6	121
2017	NCAA	Vanderbilt	5	6	0	103	121	3.40	1.10	25.2	220	32	67	2.24	2.7	10.6	3.9	0.3	135
2017	Rk	GCL Braves	0	0	0	5	8	1.73	0.96	6.6	170	31	80	1.05	3.5	13.8	4.0	0.0	174
2017	A+	Florida	0	1	0	11	10	3.24	1.08	7.2	204	27	67	1.79	3.2	8.1	2.5	0.0	76

Tall, athletic RH has makings of solid top-of-the-rotation starter. College starter with projection left, tightened up mechanics last season. Struggled continually corralling two-seam FB with plus arm-side movement. Hard CB is best breaking pitch; the SL, which looks more like CT, lags behind. Athleticism plays up tumbling CU.

Yacabonis,Jimmy

RP | Baltimore | EXP MLB DEBUT: 2017 | H/W: 6-2 190 | FUT: Setup reliever | 6B

Thrws R Age 26
2013 (13) Saint Joseph's

91-95	FB	++++
84-88	SL	++

Year	Lev	Team	W	L	Sv	IP	K	ERA	WHIP	BF/G	OBA	H%	S%	xERA	Ctl	Dom	Cmd	hr/9	BPV
2015	A+	Frederick	3	3	2	62	66	4.05	1.72	6.6	297	39	76	5.04	4.8	9.5	2.0	0.4	61
2016	A+	Frederick	0	2	5	20	21	4.03	1.14	5.0	231	30	67	3.11	2.7	9.4	3.5	0.9	115
2016	AA	Bowie	2	2	6	44	46	2.04	1.09	5.1	215	29	83	2.31	2.9	9.4	3.3	0.4	110
2017	AAA	Norfolk	4	0	11	61	48	1.33	0.95	5.6	148	19	84	0.86	4.1	7.1	1.7	0.0	34
2017	MLB	Baltimore	2	0	0	20	8	4.46	1.58	6.4	240	25	73	4.39	6.2	3.6	0.6	0.9	-86

Large, power-armed RP who has spent entire career in pen and reached majors thanks to miniscule oppBA. Cleaned up delivery and ball appears quicker out of hand. Cuts and sinks plus FB, though can be erratic with location. Despite hard stuff, doesn't miss as many bats as hoped. Rarely changes speeds.

Yamamoto,Jordan

SP | Milwaukee | EXP MLB DEBUT: 2019 | H/W: 6-0 185 | FUT: #3 starter | 7C

Thrws R Age 21
2014 (12) HS (HI)

89-93	FB	+++
81-83	SL	+++
	CU	++

Year	Lev	Team	W	L	Sv	IP	K	ERA	WHIP	BF/G	OBA	H%	S%	xERA	Ctl	Dom	Cmd	hr/9	BPV
2014	Rk	AZL Brewers	0	1	0	21		4.67	1.65	9.5	269	33	75	5.25	5.5	9.3	1.7	1.3	37
2015	Rk	Helena	1	6	1	62	59	7.84	1.95	21.1	362	43	61	7.94	3.2	8.6	2.7	1.7	86
2016	A	Wisconsin	7	8	0	134	152	3.83	1.20	20.0	256	35	67	3.11	2.1	10.2	4.9	0.4	145
2017	A+	Carolina	9	4	1	111	113	2.51	1.09	19.7	225	29	80	2.67	2.4	9.2	3.8	0.6	117

Underrated RH with average stuff that plays up due to solid Cmd 2-seam FB features solid arm-side movement. SL has tighted up in FSL. Still lacking bite of plus pitch. CU lags behind development of other pitches. Scouts believe FB/SL combo would play up in relief role.

Yarbrough,Ryan

SP | Tampa Bay | EXP MLB DEBUT: 2018 | H/W: 6-5 205 | FUT: #4 starter | 7C

Thrws L Age 26
2014 (4) Old Dominion

90-94	FB	+++
81-83	SL	++
80-82	CU	+++

Year	Lev	Team	W	L	Sv	IP	K	ERA	WHIP	BF/G	OBA	H%	S%	xERA	Ctl	Dom	Cmd	hr/9	BPV
2015	Rk	AZL Mariners	0	0	0	10	13	1.80	1.20	10.1	281	42	83	3.06	0.9	11.7	13.0	0.0	204
2015	A	Clinton	0	1	0	5	1	14.12	3.14	15.2	455	47	50	11.37	7.1	1.8	0.3	0.0	-141
2015	A+	Bakersfield	4	7	0	81	74	3.77	1.28	20.8	273	34	72	3.93	2.0	8.2	4.1	0.8	112
2016	AA	Jackson	12	4	0	128	99	2.95	1.12	20.2	237	29	74	2.76	2.2	7.0	3.2	0.5	84
2017	AAA	Durham	13	6	0	157	159	3.44	1.16	24.1	245	30	75	3.58	2.2	9.1	4.1	1.1	122

Tall SP who surprisingly led IL in Ks. Dramatic increase in K rate, though doesn't own legitimate out pitch. Gets by with downward angle, advanced sequencing, and polished CU. Very tough on LHH and could be option for LOOGY work. Sinking FB is spotted low in zone, but doesn't have enough juice to blow ball by hitters.

Ynoa,Huascar

SP | Atlanta | EXP MLB DEBUT: 2021 | H/W: 6-3 175 | FUT: Middle reliever | 7E

Thrws R Age 19
2014 FA (DR)

93-95	FB	++++
	CB	++
	CU	++

Year	Lev	Team	W	L	Sv	IP	K	ERA	WHIP	BF/G	OBA	H%	S%	xERA	Ctl	Dom	Cmd	hr/9	BPV
2016	Rk	GCL Twins	3	5	0	51	51	3.18	1.10	18.2	234	32	69	2.36	2.1	9.0	4.3	0.2	123
2017	Rk	Danville	0	3	0	25	27	5.36	1.55	15.7	252	34	63	3.90	5.4	9.6	1.8	0.4	47
2017	Rk	Elizabethton	0	1	0	25	23	5.36	1.67	18.8	283	36	66	4.63	5.0	8.2	1.6	0.4	31

Tall power RH acquired in trade with MIN. Big FB sits 93-95, up to 97 mph. Doesn't have FB plane to keep advanced hitters off pitch. Struggles repeating delivery and controlling pitches. Features two secondary pitches, both seldom used. Hard CB is slurvy and lacks feel for CU. Will need a lot of work to reach projection.

Young,Alex

SP | Arizona | EXP MLB DEBUT: 2018 | H/W: 6-2 205 | FUT: #4 starter | 7C

Thrws L Age 24
2015 (2) Texas Christian

90-92	FB	+++
82-85	SL	++++
82-85	CU	++

Year	Lev	Team	W	L	Sv	IP	K	ERA	WHIP	BF/G	OBA	H%	S%	xERA	Ctl	Dom	Cmd	hr/9	BPV
2015	Rk	AZL Dbacks	0	0	0	1	1	0.00	0.00	2.8	0	0			0.0	9.0		0.0	180
2015	A-	Hillsboro	0	0	1	6	5	1.50	1.00	3.8	228	30	83	1.89	1.5	7.5	5.0	0.0	113
2016	A	Kane County	3	1	0	50	37	2.16	1.10	21.8	217	27	80	2.18	2.9	6.7	2.3	0.2	60
2016	A+	Visalia	2	7	0	68	56	4.62	1.47	24.4	291	34	72	5.17	2.8	7.4	2.7	1.3	76
2017	AA	Jackson	9	9	0	137	103	3.68	1.34	21.1	244	29	74	3.69	3.8	6.8	1.8	0.8	37

Former college RP hit stride as SP in '17. FB is ordinary but well placed. Doesn't get a ton of swings and misses with pitch. SL is best pitch. Hard, sweeping action. Most of his swing-and-misses resulted from SL. CU took a few steps forward. Has gained a feel but still very ordinary. Best bet is return to pen.

Young,Kyle

SP | Philadelphia | EXP MLB DEBUT: 2022 | H/W: 6-10 205 | FUT: #5 SP/swingman | 7D

Thrws L Age 20
2016 (22) HS (NY)

88-90	FB	+++
75-79	SL	++
	CU	++

Year	Lev	Team	W	L	Sv	IP	K	ERA	WHIP	BF/G	OBA	H%	S%	xERA	Ctl	Dom	Cmd	hr/9	BPV
2016	Rk	GCL Phillies	3	0	0	27	19	2.67	0.93	11.2	232	29	68	1.76	0.7	6.3	9.5	0.0	114
2017	A-	Williamsport	7	2	0	65	72	2.77	1.12	19.7	240	34	74	2.46	2.1	10.0	4.8	0.1	141

Tall is an understatement, but couples it with body control and repeatable delivery, leading to consistent strikes. Current FB velocity nothing special, but plays up due to extension/deception. Breaking ball is slurvy, and CU below average but each has average potential. A teenage project who could blossom with added strength.

Ysla,Luis

RP | Los Angeles (N) | EXP MLB DEBUT: 2018 | H/W: 6-1 185 | FUT: Middle reliever | 6B

Thrws L Age 25
2012 FA (VZ)

92-97	FB	+++
80-83	SL	+++
82-84	CU	++

Year	Lev	Team	W	L	Sv	IP	K	ERA	WHIP	BF/G	OBA	H%	S%	xERA	Ctl	Dom	Cmd	hr/9	BPV
2015	A+	San Jose	3	6	0	79	95	6.25	1.89	11.3	328	44	67	6.51	4.7	10.8	2.3	1.0	87
2016	AA	Portland	2	5	3	55	60	4.08	1.47	6.1	258	34	73	4.05	4.4	9.8	2.2	0.7	75
2016	AAA	Pawtucket	0	0	1	1	2	0.00	1.00	3.8	262	55	100	2.23	0.0	18.0		0.0	342
2017	AA	Portland	1	5	1	46	44	5.08	1.71	7.2	266	34	69	4.54	6.2	8.6	1.4	0.4	4
2017	AA	Tulsa	0	0	0	11	8	6.43	1.79	7.4	292	34	63	5.50	5.6	6.4	1.1	0.8	-18

Power RP who has the arm to succeed, but can't consistently find strike zone. FB is best pitch, but lacks requisite command to be dependable late-inning arm. When ahead in count, uses SL to wipe out hitters, particularly LHH. Not blessed with great size, but has very quick arm speed. Keeps ball low and induces high number of groundballs.

Zastryzny, Rob

RP | Chicago (N) | EXP MLB DEBUT: 2016 | H/W: 6-3 205 | FUT: Middle reliever | 6B

Thrws L Age 26
2013 (2) Missouri

90-93	FB	+++
80-83	CT	+++
	CB	++

Year	Lev	Team	W	L	Sv	IP	K	ERA	WHIP	BF/G	OBA	H%	S%	xERA	Ctl	Dom	Cmd	hr/9	BPV
2016	AAA	Iowa	7	3	0	81	77	4.33	1.21	21.8	227	28	65	3.12	3.4	8.6	2.5	0.8	79
2016	MLB	Chi Cubs	1	0	0	16	17	1.13	1.06	7.8	210	30	88	1.80	2.8	9.6	3.4	0.0	114
2017	Rk	AZL Cubs	0	1	0	8	4	1.10	1.22	11.0	280	32	90	3.17	1.1	4.4	4.0	0.0	67
2017	AAA	Iowa	2	3	1	47	40	5.94	1.36	14.0	274	32	58	4.67	2.7	7.7	2.9	1.3	83
2017	MLB	Chi Cubs	0	0	0	13	11	8.31	2.00	15.7	341	40	58	7.38	4.8	7.6	1.6	1.4	24

Lefty reliever struggled at AAA and in 4 outings with Cubs. Pounds the zone with 2 and 4 seam heater that works at 90-95 and at CT that shows some potential. Deception and movement make him tough on LHH (0.77 ERA at AAA). Fared well in 2016 with the Cubs and should get another shot at a LOOGY role in 2018.

Zeuch,T.J.

SP | Toronto | EXP MLB DEBUT: 2019 | H/W: 6-7 225 | FUT: #3 starter | 8C

Thrws R Age 22
2016 (1) Pittsburgh

92-95	FB	++++
78-80	CB	+++
81-84	SL	+++
84-88	CU	++

Year	Lev	Team	W	L	Sv	IP	K	ERA	WHIP	BF/G	OBA	H%	S%	xERA	Ctl	Dom	Cmd	hr/9	BPV
2016	Rk	GCL Blue Jays	0	0	0	3	2	0.00	0.00	8.5	0	0			0.0	6.0		0.0	126
2016	A-	Vancouver	0	1	0	23	22	3.52	1.13	15.1	245	32	68	2.78	2.0	8.6	4.4	0.4	120
2016	A	Lansing	0	1	0	8	14	9.00	1.50	17.3	307	51	36	5.23	2.3	15.8	7.0	1.1	241
2017	Rk	GCL Blue Jays	0	2	0	7	5	5.14	1.57	10.2	313	35	70	5.75	2.6	6.4	2.5	1.3	64
2017	A+	Dunedin	3	4	0	58	46	3.40	1.37	20.3	277	34	75	3.93	2.6	7.1	2.7	0.5	75

Angular SP who missed most of season, but was very good in AFL. Has knockout stuff which is enhanced by sound delivery that he repeats. Very hard FB shows heavy, late action and mixes in hard SL and slower, big-breaking CB. All about groundballs and Ks as he commands FB to lower half of plate. Needs to upgrade fringy CU.

Zimmer,Kyle

SP | Kansas City | EXP MLB DEBUT: 2018 | H/W: 6-3 225 | FUT: #3 starter | 8D

Thrws R Age 26
2012 (1) San Francisco

91-96	FB	++++
80-81	CB	++++
82-84	SL	++
83-85	CU	++

Year	Lev	Team	W	L	Sv	IP	K	ERA	WHIP	BF/G	OBA	H%	S%	xERA	Ctl	Dom	Cmd	hr/9	BPV
2016	A+	Wilmington	0	1	0	4	9	2.14	1.67	9.4	202	51	86	3.13	8.6	19.3	2.3	0.0	134
2016	AA	NW Arkansas	0	1	0	1	2	0.00	3.00	5.8	262	55	100	7.27	18.0	18.0	1.0	0.0	-144
2017	AA	NW Arkansas	0	0	0	4	6	2.25	1.50	17.3	347	53	83	4.86	0.0	13.5		0.0	261
2017	AAA	Omaha	0	0	3	32	34	5.87	1.58	7.1	278	35	64	5.06	4.5	9.5	2.1	1.1	68

High upside arm, but hasn't pitched much in 4 years and missed lot of 2017 due to arm fatigue. Shows plus arsenal when healthy—lively FB and CB that flashes double-plus. Could front rotation, but has only exceeded 100 IP once. Velocity is up and down, but byproduct of ailments. SL and CU have moments of brilliance and could become average.

MAJOR LEAGUE EQUIVALENTS

In his 1985 *Baseball Abstract,* Bill James introduced the concept of major league equivalencies. His assertion was that, with the proper adjustments, a minor leaguer's statistics could be converted to an equivalent major league level performance with a great deal of accuracy.

Because of wide variations in the level of play among different minor leagues, it is difficult to get a true reading on a player's potential. For instance, a .300 batting average achieved in the high-offense Pacific Coast League is not nearly as much of an accomplishment as a similar level in the Eastern League. MLEs normalize these types of variances, for all statistical categories.

The actual MLEs are not projections. They represent how a player's previous performance might look at the major league level. However, the MLE stat line can be used in forecasting future performance in just the same way as a major league stat line would.

The model we use contains a few variations to James' version and updates all of the minor league and ballpark factors. In addition, we designed a module to convert pitching statistics, which is something James did not originally do.

Do MLEs really work?

Used correctly, MLEs are excellent indicators of potential. But just like we cannot take traditional major league statistics at face value, the same goes for MLEs. The underlying measures of base skill—batting eye ratios, pitching command ratios, etc.—are far more accurate in evaluating future talent than raw home runs, batting averages or ERAs.

The charts we present here also provide the unique perspective of looking at up to five years' worth of data. Ironically, the longer the history, the less likely the player is a legitimate prospect—he should have made it to the majors before compiling a long history in AA and/or AAA ball. Of course, the shorter trends are more difficult to read despite them often belonging to players with higher ceilings. But even here we can find small indications of players improving their skills, or struggling, as they rise through more difficult levels of competition. Since players—especially those with any talent—are promoted rapidly through major league systems, a two or three-year scan is often all we get to spot any trends.

Here are some things to look for as you scan these charts:

Target players who...

- spent a full year in AA and then a full year in AAA
- had consistent playing time from one year to the next
- improved their base skills as they were promoted

Raise the warning flag for players who...

- were stuck at a level for multiple seasons, or regressed
- displayed marked changes in playing time from one year to the next
- showed large drops in BPIs from one year to the next

Players are listed on the charts if they spent at least part of 2013-2017 in Triple-A or Double-A and had at least 100 AB or 30 IP within those two levels. Each is listed with the organization with which they finished the season.

Only statistics accumulated in Triple-A and Double-A ball are included (players who split a season are indicated as a/a); Single-A stats are excluded.

Each player's actual AB and IP totals are used as the base for the conversion. However, it is more useful to compare performances using common levels, so rely on the ratios and sabermetric gauges. Complete explanations of these formulas appear in the Glossary.

BATTER	B	Yr	Age	Pos	Lvl	Tm	AB	R	H	D	T	HR	RBI	BB	K	SB	CS	BA	OB	Slg	OPS	bb%	ct%	Eye	PX	SX	RC/G	BPV
Abreu,Osvaldo	R	17	23	SS	aa	WAS	431	33	95	15	3	4	35	23	118	1	7	220	259	293	552	5%	73%	0.19	49	51	1.94	-43
Acuna,Ronald	R	17	20	CF	a/a	ATL	442	66	135	17	3	16	62	36	118	29	18	306	358	468	826	8%	73%	0.30	94	113	5.03	19
Adames,Willy	R	16	21	SS	aa	TAM	486	75	120	27	5	9	48	63	135	11	7	247	333	380	713	11%	72%	0.46	92	114	3.37	21
		17	22	SS	aaa	TAM	506	69	131	28	4	9	58	62	148	10	5	258	339	383	722	11%	71%	0.42	84	100	3.61	4
Alfaro,Jorge	R	15	22	C	aa	TEX	190	17	43	13	2	4	16	7	66	2	1	225	253	374	628	4%	65%	0.11	126	89	2.36	-2
		16	23	C	aa	PHI	404	55	102	20	1	14	54	18	122	2	2	253	285	410	696	4%	70%	0.15	106	75	3.40	-3
		17	24	C	aaa	PHI	324	29	69	11	2	6	37	14	132	1	1	212	244	316	561	4%	59%	0.10	79	65	2.13	-70
Alford,Anthony	R	17	23	CF	a/a	TOR	257	38	76	15	0	5	22	33	52	16	3	297	376	412	789	11%	80%	0.63	73	93	5.04	31
Allen,Greg	B	16	23	CF	aa	CLE	145	22	39	7	2	3	11	16	29	6	7	270	343	402	745	10%	80%	0.56	79	121	3.45	42
		17	24	CF	aa	CLE	258	30	62	16	1	2	19	18	55	17	2	241	291	327	617	7%	79%	0.33	60	117	2.78	13
Alonso,Peter	R	17	23	DH	aa	NYM	45	7	13	4	1	2	5	2	8	0	0	290	322	543	865	5%	82%	0.27	138	81	4.96	73
Anderson,Brian	R	16	23	3B	aa	MIA	301	34	67	9	1	6	35	32	63	0	0	222	297	318	615	10%	79%	0.51	57	43	2.75	-4
		17	24	3B	a/a	MIA	429	66	104	20	2	18	72	43	114	1	2	243	313	427	740	9%	73%	0.38	108	64	3.83	20
Andujar,Miguel	R	16	21	3B	aa	NYY	282	28	74	15	2	2	42	21	45	2	1	262	313	352	666	7%	84%	0.47	59	67	3.09	19
		17	22	3B	a/a	NYY	481	62	145	33	1	18	77	27	79	5	3	302	339	487	826	5%	84%	0.35	103	63	5.02	49
Aquino,Aristides	R	17	23	RF	aa	CIN	459	56	99	20	5	19	58	42	161	9	3	215	281	408	689	8%	65%	0.26	125	114	3.13	12
Arozarena,Randy	R	17	22	LF	aa	STL	163	30	38	10	1	3	8	24	35	7	3	236	332	352	684	13%	78%	0.67	73	115	3.14	34
Arroyo,Christian	R	16	21	SS	aa	SF	474	55	125	35	1	2	47	29	78	1	1	263	305	358	663	6%	84%	0.37	68	55	2.93	18
		17	22	SS	aaa	SF	91	15	33	7	0	3	14	5	13	2	0	362	397	528	925	5%	85%	0.39	94	63	7.40	48
Austin,Tyler	R	13	22	RF	aa	NYY	319	36	75	15	1	6	34	35	85	3	0	236	312	342	655	10%	73%	0.41	84	70	3.09	3
		14	23	RF	aa	NYY	396	44	97	17	3	8	37	29	89	2	2	244	296	366	662	7%	78%	0.33	89	78	3.01	20
		15	24	RF	a/a	NYY	341	35	74	11	1	6	30	30	110	10	3	218	281	310	591	8%	68%	0.27	72	99	2.48	-24
		16	25	1B	a/a	NYY	378	55	102	30	1	18	71	57	121	5	1	270	366	494	860	13%	68%	0.47	161	72	5.29	51
		17	26	1B	a/a	NYY	185	29	47	13	2	10	28	17	64	0	0	254	318	509	827	9%	65%	0.27	169	74	4.56	38
Avelino,Abiatal	R	16	21	2B	aa	NYY	127	15	30	11	0	0	14	10	20	1	2	239	295	322	617	7%	84%	0.49	67	57	2.22	23
		17	22	2B	a/a	NYY	291	38	71	12	4	3	32	18	47	7	1	245	288	345	634	6%	84%	0.38	55	121	2.79	29
Bader,Harrison	R	16	22	CF	a/a	STL	465	56	109	17	4	15	47	30	151	10	14	235	281	381	662	6%	68%	0.20	98	98	2.76	-8
		17	23	CF	aaa	STL	431	61	109	17	1	16	45	28	126	12	10	254	299	406	705	6%	71%	0.22	93	89	3.49	-2
Barreto,Franklin	R	16	20	SS	a/a	OAK	479	58	130	25	4	9	47	32	97	27	18	271	317	396	712	6%	80%	0.33	78	119	3.35	32
		17	21	SS	aaa	OAK	469	52	124	18	6	11	45	22	147	12	9	264	297	401	698	4%	69%	0.15	86	116	3.32	-11
Bauers,Jake	L	15	20	1B	aa	TAM	257	30	64	16	0	4	30	18	45	5	3	249	297	357	654	6%	83%	0.39	78	70	2.90	29
		16	21	RF	aa	TAM	493	67	121	25	1	12	66	62	99	8	7	246	330	371	701	11%	80%	0.62	78	69	3.45	27
		17	22	LF	aaa	TAM	486	74	119	29	1	12	59	74	126	19	3	245	345	379	725	13%	74%	0.59	87	102	3.85	25
Bautista,Rafael	R	16	23	CF	aa	WAS	543	67	143	12	2	3	34	40	101	49	11	263	313	310	623	7%	81%	0.40	29	129	3.27	3
		17	24	CF	aaa	WAS	176	19	39	8	1	0	9	7	29	6	5	220	251	273	524	4%	83%	0.25	37	101	1.70	3
Beaty,Matt	L	17	24	1B	aa	LA	438	50	126	29	1	13	57	27	63	2	3	288	328	444	772	6%	86%	0.42	87	45	4.30	39
Bishop,Braden	R	17	24	CF	aa	SEA	125	15	37	8	1	1	9	13	18	5	1	295	360	390	750	9%	86%	0.71	59	94	4.26	39
Blandino,Alex	R	15	23	SS	aa	CIN	115	13	25	6	0	3	15	16	24	2	2	214	307	349	656	12%	79%	0.64	92	50	2.78	30
		16	24	2B	aa	CIN	401	49	88	17	0	9	35	54	133	13	6	219	311	326	637	12%	67%	0.40	80	79	2.89	-19
		17	25	2B	a/a	CIN	393	53	94	32	1	12	45	58	102	4	8	239	337	415	752	13%	74%	0.57	116	53	3.48	33
Boyd,B.J.	L	16	23	RF	aaa	OAK	30	2	7	0	0	0	1	2	3	0	0	248	290	248	538	6%	89%	0.57	0	15	2.44	-25
		17	24	CF	aa	OAK	533	65	151	26	5	4	44	26	81	13	6	283	317	371	688	5%	85%	0.33	52	109	3.39	25
Bradley,Bobby	L	17	21	1B	aa	CLE	467	55	112	26	2	20	75	48	116	3	3	241	311	434	744	9%	75%	0.41	114	58	3.77	29
Brinson,Lewis	R	15	21	CF	a/a	TEX	140	19	41	8	1	6	22	11	37	4	1	295	345	489	834	7%	74%	0.29	133	95	5.25	46
		16	22	CF	a/a	MIL	393	50	98	21	5	13	50	16	92	12	6	249	278	423	701	4%	77%	0.17	106	131	3.16	40
		17	23	CF	aaa	MIL	299	47	85	19	3	11	34	23	72	8	6	284	335	472	807	7%	76%	0.32	112	107	4.47	41
Brito,Socrates	L	15	23	RF	aa	ARI	490	58	138	15	15	8	47	24	92	17	7	283	315	425	741	5%	81%	0.26	81	138	3.70	42
		16	24	RF	aaa	ARI	303	32	77	9	8	4	27	9	69	5	7	253	275	374	649	3%	77%	0.13	68	114	2.55	6
		17	25	RF	aaa	ARI	292	27	71	12	7	3	28	14	75	4	1	243	276	368	645	4%	74%	0.18	74	110	2.59	0
Burks,Charcer	R	17	22	LF	aa	CHC	456	62	116	20	3	9	37	66	117	15	13	255	349	372	721	13%	74%	0.56	73	93	3.57	11
Calhoun,Willie	L	16	22	2B	aa	LA	503	70	121	25	1	26	82	39	70	0	0	241	296	449	745	7%	86%	0.56	110	36	3.95	59
		17	23	2B	aaa	TEX	486	61	130	23	6	24	71	33	66	3	2	267	314	487	801	6%	86%	0.50	107	81	4.49	70
Caratini,Victor	B	16	23	C	aa	CHC	412	45	107	22	2	5	37	43	91	2	1	259	330	358	687	10%	78%	0.48	68	56	3.34	4
		17	24	C	aaa	CHC	292	38	86	23	2	8	47	21	57	1	0	293	341	467	808	7%	81%	0.38	105	72	4.59	44
Cave,Jake	L	15	23	CF	a/a	NYY	529	64	135	23	4	2	35	42	119	15	3	256	310	325	635	7%	78%	0.35	53	117	2.92	4
		16	24	LF	a/a	NYY	426	55	106	24	7	8	51	34	120	6	8	249	305	397	701	7%	72%	0.28	99	111	3.02	17
		17	25	CF	a/a	NYY	406	58	113	22	3	21	49	25	133	2	3	278	319	503	822	6%	67%	0.18	144	78	4.70	21
Cecchini,Gavin	R	15	22	SS	aa	NYM	439	55	125	23	3	6	44	36	62	3	4	286	340	395	735	8%	86%	0.58	72	65	3.87	38
		16	23	SS	aaa	NYM	446	49	118	23	1	6	38	33	65	3	1	264	316	359	674	7%	85%	0.51	59	61	3.30	23
		17	24	2B	aaa	NYM	453	48	96	21	2	4	27	31	75	4	5	211	262	295	556	6%	83%	0.41	51	70	1.97	10
Chang,Yu-Cheng	R	17	22	SS	aa	CLE	439	60	92	25	3	21	55	44	129	9	4	210	282	422	705	9%	71%	0.34	131	106	3.16	40
Chavis,Michael	R	17	22	3B	aa	BOS	248	32	59	20	0	11	32	16	58	1	0	239	287	450	737	6%	77%	0.28	128	46	3.58	37
Ciuffo,Nick	L	17	22	C	aa	TAM	371	37	82	26	1	6	37	38	107	2	0	221	293	343	636	9%	71%	0.35	89	56	2.61	-7
Collins,Zack	L	17	22	C	aa	CHW	34	7	8	2	0	2	5	11	12	0	0	229	421	465	887	25%	64%	0.93	159	25	5.67	44

BATTER	B	Yr	Age	Pos	Lvl	Tm	AB	R	H	D	T	HR	RBI	BB	K	SB	CS	BA	OB	Slg	OPS	bb%	ct%	Eye	PX	SX	RC/G	BPV
Cooper,Garrett	R	15	25	1B	aa	MIL	29	3	15	2	1	0	4	6	2	0	0	504	592	624	1	18%	92%	2.65	71	58	15.32	79
		16	26	1B	a/a	MIL	428	34	106	23	1	7	53	23	89	2	4	248	287	354	640	5%	79%	0.27	70	39	2.80	-3
		17	27	1B	a/a	NYY	306	58	96	25	0	18	71	30	67	0	0	314	376	570	946	9%	78%	0.46	148	37	6.83	62
Cordell,Ryan	R	15	23	CF	aa	TEX	221	20	42	4	2	4	14	9	80	8	1	191	223	285	508	4%	64%	0.12	69	134	1.79	-39
		16	24	CF	aa	TEX	405	57	95	19	4	16	58	28	107	10	5	234	283	419	703	6%	74%	0.26	114	123	3.26	37
		17	25	RF	aaa	MIL	261	33	61	15	3	8	30	17	78	6	5	232	279	402	681	6%	70%	0.22	108	116	2.84	16
Cordero,Franchy	L	16	22	CF	a/a	SD	258	25	68	7	6	5	15	16	81	9	7	262	305	391	696	6%	68%	0.20	81	121	3.18	-11
		17	23	CF	aaa	SD	390	47	106	18	11	11	44	15	133	10	5	273	300	460	760	4%	66%	0.12	119	129	3.72	7
Cozens,Dylan	L	15	21	RF	aa	PHI	40	5	13	2	0	3	7	2	8	2	1	318	358	564	922	6%	80%	0.31	146	54	6.45	67
		16	22	RF	aa	PHI	521	87	132	34	2	37	103	51	210	17	1	254	320	541	862	9%	60%	0.24	217	126	5.27	70
		17	23	RF	aaa	PHI	476	59	91	11	2	25	65	50	221	7	3	192	269	383	652	10%	54%	0.23	141	89	2.95	-25
Crawford,J.P.	L	15	20	SS	aa	PHI	351	43	84	19	5	4	27	40	50	6	2	241	319	364	683	10%	86%	0.81	78	110	3.00	61
		16	21	SS	a/a	PHI	472	57	111	18	1	7	39	66	89	11	7	235	329	322	650	12%	81%	0.74	55	70	3.01	16
		17	22	SS	aaa	PHI	474	67	106	18	5	14	56	70	109	4	4	224	324	373	698	13%	77%	0.65	83	88	3.29	29
Cuevas,Noel	R	14	23	CF	aa	LA	425	35	80	10	5	5	31	21	105	4	3	189	228	270	498	5%	75%	0.20	57	94	1.57	-13
		15	24	LF	aa	COL	406	37	100	19	2	4	40	13	93	24	13	245	269	330	599	3%	77%	0.14	64	117	2.34	3
		16	25	CF	a/a	COL	331	31	91	16	6	3	27	11	56	6	7	274	296	384	680	3%	83%	0.19	66	111	2.89	26
		17	26	RF	aaa	COL	493	53	136	15	11	11	53	17	109	11	3	275	299	416	715	3%	78%	0.15	74	124	3.61	16
Davis,J.D.	R	16	23	3B	aa	HOU	485	48	115	30	1	20	63	35	164	1	3	236	288	422	710	7%	66%	0.21	135	34	3.34	-2
		17	24	3B	a/a	HOU	412	43	97	19	0	19	57	29	131	4	2	234	284	422	706	7%	68%	0.22	119	46	3.50	-3
De La Guerra,Chad	L	17	25	SS	aa	BOS	196	26	48	15	0	3	18	18	53	2	1	246	308	369	677	8%	73%	0.34	90	57	2.99	0
De Leon,Michael	B	17	20	SS	aa	TEX	394	26	86	15	1	2	32	17	48	3	2	218	250	277	526	4%	88%	0.35	36	53	1.87	6
Dean,Austin	R	16	23	LF	aa	MIA	480	53	105	22	5	8	59	43	118	1	2	220	283	340	623	8%	75%	0.36	77	74	2.47	4
		17	24	LF	aa	MIA	234	28	60	14	3	4	29	13	53	3	1	257	298	388	686	5%	77%	0.25	80	103	3.10	17
Demeritte,Travis	R	17	23	2B	aa	ATL	458	60	93	12	5	13	44	50	156	5	8	203	281	341	623	10%	66%	0.32	86	96	2.48	-17
Dewees,Donnie	L	17	24	CF	aa	KC	464	58	117	24	6	7	45	39	87	17	9	252	310	375	685	8%	81%	0.44	71	124	3.09	36
Diaz,Yusniel	R	17	21	RF	aa	LA	108	13	33	8	0	3	11	8	32	2	5	309	357	456	813	7%	70%	0.25	104	49	4.19	-5
Dozier,Hunter	R	14	23	3B	aa	KC	234	26	43	11	0	3	17	25	74	2	2	186	263	270	533	9%	68%	0.33	79	60	1.80	-24
		15	24	3B	aa	KC	475	50	87	24	1	9	41	34	163	5	2	182	238	293	531	7%	66%	0.21	94	81	1.77	-22
		16	25	3B	a/a	KC	486	61	125	41	1	17	58	41	138	5	1	256	314	446	760	8%	72%	0.30	135	76	3.89	35
		17	26	3B	a/a	KC	100	12	20	7	1	3	9	10	51	1	1	200	272	369	641	9%	49%	0.20	160	98	2.38	-26
Dubon,Mauricio	R	16	22	SS	aa	BOS	251	40	82	21	5	5	34	9	39	5	3	327	351	510	861	4%	85%	0.24	109	130	4.97	74
		17	23	SS	a/a	MIL	492	61	121	26	0	8	47	32	86	31	17	247	293	346	639	6%	83%	0.37	61	100	2.78	23
Duenez,Samir	L	16	20	DH	aa	KC	54	4	15	5	0	0	8	4	12	2	0	273	329	369	698	8%	78%	0.37	83	52	3.36	10
		17	21	1B	aa	KC	523	59	127	24	2	14	68	33	119	9	3	243	288	378	666	6%	77%	0.28	79	86	3.14	12
Duggar,Steven	L	16	23	CF	aa	SF	243	33	74	15	5	1	22	27	57	8	8	306	374	420	794	10%	77%	0.47	77	120	4.06	26
		17	24	CF	aaa	SF	46	6	10	1	0	1	5	7	14	2	2	224	321	331	652	13%	70%	0.48	63	69	2.93	-22
Edman,Tommy	S	17	22	SS	aa	STL	219	18	51	11	2	2	23	14	35	4	2	232	278	323	600	6%	84%	0.40	55	84	2.34	19
Ervin,Phil	R	15	23	LF	aa	CIN	51	6	11	3	0	2	7	11	17	3	3	216	357	389	746	18%	66%	0.65	133	64	3.41	28
		16	24	LF	aa	CIN	419	67	95	21	2	14	42	63	103	34	11	227	328	387	715	13%	76%	0.62	100	130	3.61	49
		17	25	LF	aaa	CIN	363	37	80	17	1	6	32	30	99	18	7	221	281	326	607	8%	73%	0.30	70	103	2.52	-5
Evans,Phillip	R	16	24	SS	aa	NYM	361	41	104	27	0	7	32	16	71	1	1	289	319	418	737	4%	80%	0.22	88	39	3.89	14
		17	25	3B	aaa	NYM	466	40	101	20	2	8	39	32	100	1	4	217	267	319	586	6%	79%	0.32	62	46	2.27	-8
Farmer,Kyle	R	15	25	C	aa	LA	283	21	67	23	1	2	33	11	64	0	1	238	267	343	610	4%	77%	0.18	89	38	2.25	1
		16	26	C	aa	LA	266	27	59	16	1	4	27	20	52	2	0	221	275	342	617	7%	80%	0.38	79	72	2.47	23
		17	27	C	a/a	LA	347	40	90	20	1	8	42	20	61	1	5	259	300	387	687	6%	82%	0.33	75	40	3.18	15
Fletcher,David	R	16	22	SS	aa	LAA	80	9	23	6	0	0	6	3	14	1	0	285	309	356	666	3%	82%	0.20	58	60	3.21	1
		17	23	2B	a/a	LAA	448	48	103	17	1	2	32	21	64	16	7	230	265	290	555	5%	86%	0.34	37	102	2.16	14
Fowler,Dustin	L	16	22	CF	aa	NYY	541	66	149	29	12	13	87	22	93	25	12	275	303	447	750	4%	83%	0.24	96	145	3.62	61
		17	23	CF	aaa	NYY	297	44	81	17	6	14	38	13	70	12	5	273	304	505	810	4%	76%	0.19	129	143	4.24	62
Gallagher,Cam	R	16	24	C	aa	KC	301	20	71	15	1	3	20	31	56	2	2	236	307	325	632	9%	81%	0.55	60	42	2.68	6
		17	25	C	aaa	KC	260	20	66	12	0	4	29	14	37	0	1	254	291	341	632	5%	86%	0.37	52	21	2.86	3
Garcia,Aramis	R	17	24	C	aa	SF	78	10	20	11	0	0	7	8	24	0	0	257	328	398	726	10%	70%	0.35	128	34	2.89	12
Garcia,Jose Adolis	R	17	24	RF	a/a	STL	445	53	115	31	2	12	54	27	117	12	10	258	301	415	716	6%	74%	0.23	103	88	3.30	17
Garver,Mitch	R	16	25	C	a/a	MIN	434	41	103	27	0	9	60	40	118	1	3	237	301	365	666	8%	73%	0.34	92	25	2.95	-9
		17	26	C	aaa	MIN	320	50	84	27	0	15	41	44	93	2	0	263	352	489	841	12%	71%	0.47	148	51	4.97	44
Gassaway,Randolph	R	17	22	RF	aa	BAL	27	3	5	0	0	0	2	4	2	0	0	168	285	168	453	14%	92%	1.98	0	36	1.47	8
Gerber,Michael	L	16	24	CF	aa	DET	153	13	36	7	3	3	16	16	44	5	0	233	306	378	684	10%	71%	0.37	94	116	3.15	17
		17	25	CF	a/a	DET	367	56	96	21	2	12	41	34	101	8	7	262	325	428	753	9%	72%	0.34	104	99	3.86	21
Gillaspie,Casey	B	16	23	1B	a/a	TAM	472	66	120	30	2	15	54	68	134	4	2	253	347	418	765	13%	72%	0.51	114	70	4.11	25
		17	24	1B	aaa	CHW	458	49	88	18	2	12	49	42	117	1	1	192	260	319	579	8%	74%	0.36	76	53	2.22	-7
Gomez,Miguel	B	17	25	2B	aa	SF	308	38	84	17	2	6	33	11	42	0	0	273	298	401	699	3%	87%	0.26	70	60	3.45	29
Gordon,Nick	L	17	22	SS	aa	MIN	519	74	136	28	8	8	61	48	135	12	7	262	325	394	719	8%	74%	0.35	83	123	3.41	18

BATTER	B	Yr	Age	Pos	Lvl	Tm	AB	R	H	D	T	HR	RBI	BB	K	SB	CS	BA	OB	Slg	OPS	bb%	ct%	Eye	PX	SX	RC/G	BPV
Granite,Zach	L	16	24	CF	aa	MIN	525	68	138	16	6	3	41	32	46	44	16	263	306	336	642	6%	91%	0.71	39	149	3.00	55
		17	25	CF	aaa	MIN	284	42	90	15	4	5	27	21	36	14	7	315	363	443	806	7%	87%	0.59	68	122	4.79	56
Greiner,Grayson	R	16	24	C	a/a	DET	212	17	54	8	3	6	25	9	61	1	0	256	285	405	689	4%	71%	0.14	94	76	3.30	-7
		17	25	C	a/a	DET	342	29	71	18	1	12	37	34	83	0	0	207	279	370	649	9%	76%	0.41	97	28	2.79	9
Guillorme,Luis	L	17	23	2B	aa	NYM	481	69	126	18	0	1	42	78	64	4	3	262	365	307	671	14%	87%	1.22	31	52	3.35	17
Gurriel,Lourdes	R	17	24	2B	aa	TOR	170	17	37	10	0	4	23	8	34	2	0	220	257	340	596	5%	80%	0.25	74	56	2.42	8
Guzman,Ronald	L	16	22	1B	a/a	TEX	463	51	116	19	5	13	57	34	112	2	2	251	303	402	705	7%	76%	0.31	91	79	3.43	16
		17	23	1B	aaa	TEX	470	60	124	19	3	9	48	37	92	3	1	264	318	376	694	7%	80%	0.40	64	76	3.57	12
Hawkins,Courtney	R	15	22	LF	aa	CHW	300	34	68	18	2	9	36	19	110	1	4	227	273	383	656	6%	63%	0.17	130	68	2.65	-8
		16	23	LF	aa	CHW	418	28	73	21	0	10	48	24	157	0	3	175	220	299	519	5%	63%	0.15	100	18	1.62	-52
		17	24	LF	aa	CHW	295	30	52	8	1	10	25	21	121	0	0	176	230	307	538	7%	59%	0.17	92	51	1.96	-60
Hays,Austin	R	17	22	CF	aa	BAL	261	33	75	10	1	14	46	12	52	1	1	286	317	494	811	4%	80%	0.23	107	57	4.97	33
Heineman,Scott	R	17	25	LF	aa	TEX	468	68	120	23	7	8	37	42	134	10	10	257	318	384	703	8%	71%	0.32	81	117	3.15	4
Hermosillo,Michael	R	17	22	CF	a/a	LAA	393	50	90	17	2	7	35	38	115	25	12	229	297	337	634	9%	71%	0.33	71	117	2.73	-6
Hernandez,Yadiel	L	17	30	RF	aa	WAS	397	41	90	17	1	8	43	41	85	4	3	228	300	335	635	9%	79%	0.48	64	53	2.84	3
Hinojosa,C.J.	R	16	22	SS	aa	SF	226	26	54	7	3	2	18	19	47	1	0	238	298	323	621	8%	79%	0.42	51	83	2.71	1
		17	23	SS	aa	SF	373	43	92	15	0	3	32	29	46	5	4	247	301	312	613	7%	88%	0.62	39	58	2.69	15
Howard,Ryan	L	17	38	DH	aaa	COL	90	4	13	3	0	3	8	1	32	0	0	150	161	277	438	1%	64%	0.04	88	1	1.17	-69
Ibanez,Andy	R	16	23	2B	aa	TEX	307	33	72	16	2	5	26	22	51	4	2	235	286	348	635	7%	83%	0.43	69	83	2.70	29
		17	24	2B	aa	TEX	310	28	75	13	2	7	25	22	52	5	1	242	292	363	654	7%	83%	0.42	65	83	3.07	25
Jackson,Alex	R	17	22	C	aa	ATL	110	12	25	2	0	5	20	10	36	0	0	232	298	379	677	9%	67%	0.29	90	19	3.53	-36
Jackson,Drew	R	17	24	2B	aa	LA	111	18	23	5	1	1	8	8	32	6	2	203	258	277	536	7%	71%	0.26	53	137	1.89	-17
Jansen,Danny	R	17	22	C	a/a	TOR	246	29	73	20	2	5	28	30	28	1	0	295	373	451	823	11%	89%	1.09	88	60	4.80	67
Jimenez,Eloy	R	17	21	RF	aa	CHW	68	11	24	5	0	3	7	5	18	1	1	346	392	556	948	7%	74%	0.30	131	51	7.05	33
Kelly,Carson	R	16	22	C	a/a	STL	329	35	84	15	0	5	26	21	73	0	1	255	299	343	642	6%	78%	0.28	60	31	3.00	-18
		17	23	C	aaa	STL	244	30	62	12	0	8	34	27	43	0	2	254	328	400	728	10%	83%	0.63	81	28	3.78	25
Kemmer,Jon	L	15	25	RF	aa	HOU	364	50	100	23	3	14	48	34	108	7	1	275	336	473	809	8%	70%	0.31	144	109	4.68	48
		16	26	RF	aaa	HOU	407	36	87	19	3	13	47	26	157	6	12	215	262	377	639	6%	61%	0.17	123	81	2.36	-18
		17	27	LF	aaa	HOU	304	42	68	13	2	10	35	26	125	4	3	224	286	378	664	8%	59%	0.21	114	96	2.97	-27
Kiner-Falefa,Isiah	R	16	21	3B	aa	TEX	402	48	96	7	2	0	24	37	53	5	6	239	304	267	570	8%	87%	0.70	18	75	2.34	3
		17	22	3B	aa	TEX	513	52	141	29	3	5	43	37	75	15	6	275	324	370	694	7%	85%	0.50	58	92	3.43	31
Kingery,Scott	R	16	22	2B	aa	PHI	156	13	35	6	0	2	15	4	41	3	2	224	244	300	545	3%	74%	0.10	56	67	2.02	-32
		17	23	2B	a/a	PHI	543	89	149	25	6	24	56	35	126	25	6	275	319	478	797	6%	77%	0.28	112	142	4.65	54
Knizner,Andrew	R	17	22	C	aa	STL	182	24	56	13	0	3	20	12	28	0	1	305	349	430	780	6%	85%	0.44	76	35	4.52	24
Kramer,Kevin	L	17	24	2B	aa	PIT	202	27	55	16	3	5	24	15	54	6	2	273	323	452	775	7%	73%	0.28	116	124	3.92	40
Krieger,Tyler	B	17	23	2B	aa	CLE	418	45	88	25	1	5	35	35	105	10	7	210	271	313	584	8%	75%	0.33	71	89	2.10	1
Laureano,Ramon	R	16	22	CF	aa	HOU	124	16	37	8	2	4	10	16	37	8	3	294	375	496	872	11%	70%	0.43	136	129	5.34	52
		17	23	RF	aa	HOU	463	55	95	19	6	9	47	33	127	20	5	206	259	334	594	7%	73%	0.26	78	144	2.29	12
LaValley,Gavin	R	17	23	1B	aa	CIN	247	25	61	16	0	3	35	20	75	0	0	248	305	354	659	8%	70%	0.27	80	25	3.00	-32
Leyba,Domingo	B	16	21	SS	aa	ARI	156	19	46	7	1	4	18	15	23	4	2	295	359	429	788	9%	85%	0.67	75	84	4.67	46
		17	22	SS	aa	ARI	58	9	15	4	0	2	8	4	6	0	0	263	313	423	736	7%	89%	0.66	87	44	3.84	54
Lin,Tzu-Wei	L	15	21	SS	aa	BOS	173	17	33	5	2	0	12	13	28	7	3	193	251	251	502	7%	84%	0.47	38	131	1.54	21
		16	22	SS	aa	BOS	372	33	79	11	4	2	23	28	59	8	7	213	269	277	546	7%	84%	0.49	38	100	1.88	14
		17	23	SS	a/a	BOS	300	36	77	15	4	6	24	27	58	8	6	257	317	389	706	8%	81%	0.46	75	105	3.27	33
Long,Shed	L	17	22	2B	aa	CIN	141	14	32	6	2	4	15	21	34	4	1	230	329	372	701	13%	76%	0.61	82	97	3.39	26
Longhi,Nick	R	17	22	1B	aa	CIN	256	30	69	16	0	8	42	17	49	0	1	269	316	428	743	6%	81%	0.36	93	28	3.95	21
Lopez,Nicky	L	17	22	SS	aa	KC	232	23	58	6	1	0	10	14	30	6	4	248	291	284	576	6%	87%	0.47	23	85	2.39	6
Lowe,Brandon	L	17	23	2B	aa	TAM	95	7	21	4	1	2	10	2	30	1	1	225	239	339	578	2%	68%	0.06	78	76	2.08	-35
Lugo,Dawel	R	17	22	3B	aa	DET	516	50	132	24	6	11	56	29	76	3	1	256	295	390	685	5%	85%	0.38	71	79	3.25	34
Lund,Brennon	L	17	23	LF	aa	LAA	122	16	33	3	0	1	6	3	38	1	2	267	283	312	596	2%	69%	0.07	33	64	2.65	-71
Luplow,Jordan	R	17	24	LF	a/a	PIT	414	65	114	20	1	19	49	40	87	4	4	274	338	466	804	9%	79%	0.46	106	67	4.75	40
Marlette,Tyler	R	15	22	C	aa	SEA	178	13	41	12	1	2	10	8	35	0	0	232	266	348	614	4%	80%	0.23	85	33	2.42	10
		16	23	C	aa	SEA	50	4	14	2	0	1	6	3	13	1	0	281	319	375	693	5%	75%	0.22	63	39	3.93	-26
		17	24	C	aa	SEA	368	40	78	19	1	10	55	26	105	0	1	213	265	350	615	7%	72%	0.25	89	48	2.46	-13
Marmolejos,Jose	L	16	23	1B	aa	WAS	127	13	36	9	0	2	13	4	31	0	0	280	305	387	692	3%	76%	0.14	80	28	3.43	-17
		17	24	LF	aa	WAS	400	55	101	16	3	11	54	36	90	0	2	252	314	387	702	8%	78%	0.40	77	59	3.50	8
Martin,Jason	L	17	22	LF	aa	HOU	300	33	76	22	3	10	32	16	93	6	6	253	292	445	737	5%	69%	0.18	130	98	3.25	21
Martin,Richie	R	17	23	SS	aa	OAK	286	34	57	10	3	2	22	19	60	10	3	198	247	274	521	6%	79%	0.31	46	128	1.77	5
Mateo,Jorge	R	17	22	SS	aa	OAK	257	42	70	13	9	6	38	19	68	20	11	272	323	461	783	7%	74%	0.28	108	162	3.59	45
Mathias,Mark	R	17	23	3B	aa	CLE	104	14	20	5	1	1	11	11	33	3	0	196	273	282	554	9%	68%	0.33	64	112	2.06	-22
Mathisen,Wyatt	R	17	24	3B	aa	PIT	375	38	93	15	2	4	27	39	80	3	2	249	320	332	651	9%	79%	0.49	51	62	3.03	-5
Mazeika,Patrick	L	17	24	DH	aa	NYM	21	3	6	5	0	0	5	2	7	0	0	300	365	517	882	9%	66%	0.30	208	33	3.99	60
McCarthy,Joe	L	17	23	1B	aa	TAM	454	66	115	27	6	6	48	79	109	17	6	254	365	379	744	15%	76%	0.73	80	122	3.73	37

BATTER	B	Yr	Age	Pos	Lvl	Tm	AB	R	H	D	T	HR	RBI	BB	K	SB	CS	BA	OB	Slg	OPS	bb%	ct%	Eye	PX	SX	RC/G	BPV
McGuire,Reese	L	16	21	C	aa	TOR	319	30	78	19	2	1	37	32	37	5	6	243	312	322	635	9%	88%	0.86	53	73	2.53	38
		17	22	C	aa	TOR	115	17	31	5	1	6	17	14	21	2	1	266	345	470	815	11%	82%	0.68	105	82	4.83	61
McKinney,Billy	L	15	21	RF	aa	CHC	274	23	72	25	1	2	31	22	52	0	0	262	318	384	702	8%	81%	0.43	97	30	3.16	28
		16	22	RF	aa	NYY	426	51	103	18	3	4	43	59	105	4	6	241	333	330	663	12%	75%	0.56	61	70	2.92	-3
		17	23	RF	a/a	NYY	441	61	115	26	5	17	59	36	105	2	1	260	316	460	776	8%	76%	0.34	115	83	4.10	39
McMahon,Ryan	L	16	22	3B	aa	COL	466	42	113	27	6	11	65	47	154	9	6	243	312	399	711	9%	67%	0.30	112	101	3.25	8
		17	23	1B	a/a	COL	470	57	160	38	4	17	68	32	92	8	3	340	382	547	929	6%	80%	0.34	120	88	6.59	59
Meadows,Austin	L	15	20	CF	aa	PIT	25	4	9	2	2	0	1	2	5	1	0	340	380	596	976	6%	79%	0.32	151	131	5.27	92
		16	21	CF	a/a	PIT	293	45	74	22	9	10	43	28	68	15	5	252	317	489	806	9%	77%	0.41	143	155	3.82	88
		17	22	CF	aaa	PIT	284	43	67	18	0	3	33	22	51	10	3	236	291	336	627	7%	82%	0.43	66	101	2.69	27
Mejia,Francisco	B	17	22	C	aa	CLE	347	43	98	22	1	12	43	21	51	6	2	283	323	458	781	6%	85%	0.40	94	80	4.44	53
Mercado,Oscar	R	17	23	CF	aa	STL	477	66	126	19	3	11	40	27	118	33	21	265	305	386	691	5%	75%	0.23	72	127	3.19	9
Mercedes,Yermin	R	17	24	C	aa	BAL	44	4	11	2	0	1	6	2	10	1	0	242	271	335	606	4%	78%	0.18	57	52	2.81	-17
Michalczewski,Trey	B	16	21	3B	aa	CHW	487	51	98	21	4	10	49	50	171	3	0	202	276	320	595	9%	65%	0.29	88	90	2.33	-23
		17	22	3B	aa	CHW	368	39	83	14	2	9	37	40	138	8	1	226	302	349	651	10%	62%	0.29	87	93	3.06	-31
Mieses,Johan	R	17	22	CF	aa	LA	294	29	43	7	0	14	30	21	127	0	0	145	202	310	511	7%	57%	0.16	117	27	1.73	-55
Miller,Anderson	L	17	23	RF	aa	KC	213	15	46	8	0	2	17	8	59	3	2	215	243	276	519	4%	72%	0.13	45	51	1.83	-51
Miller,Ian	L	15	23	CF	aa	SEA	347	33	77	12	3	0	19	23	61	24	14	223	271	275	546	6%	83%	0.38	37	130	1.89	13
		16	24	CF	aa	SEA	430	60	100	7	5	0	26	41	63	46	3	232	299	274	572	9%	85%	0.65	23	169	2.78	30
		17	25	CF	a/a	SEA	512	69	133	18	3	3	28	27	124	35	6	261	297	329	626	5%	76%	0.21	45	143	3.09	-6
Montgomery,Troy	L	17	23	CF	aa	LAA	68	14	15	2	0	0	3	9	14	4	0	218	312	245	557	12%	80%	0.68	21	113	2.53	-3
Moran,Colin	L	14	22	3B	aa	HOU	112	9	30	5	0	2	17	7	26	0	1	268	312	359	671	6%	77%	0.27	75	25	3.25	-12
		15	23	3B	aa	HOU	366	36	97	22	2	7	52	34	92	1	0	266	328	395	723	8%	75%	0.37	95	53	3.73	10
		16	24	3B	aaa	HOU	459	36	99	15	1	8	50	34	146	2	2	216	270	304	574	7%	68%	0.23	63	46	2.32	-48
		17	25	3B	aaa	HOU	302	34	73	12	1	12	40	19	70	0	4	240	286	400	686	6%	77%	0.28	90	37	3.23	5
Mountcastle,Ryan	R	17	20	3B	aa	BAL	153	16	28	8	0	3	13	3	39	0	0	181	196	283	479	2%	74%	0.07	68	49	1.42	-28
Mundell,Brian	R	17	23	1B	aa	COL	172	25	51	12	0	3	16	21	26	1	1	297	373	415	788	11%	85%	0.81	73	44	4.60	36
Munoz,Yairo	R	16	21	SS	aa	OAK	387	36	84	15	3	7	32	19	79	5	8	217	253	322	576	5%	79%	0.24	64	80	2.06	4
		17	22	SS	a/a	OAK	446	54	121	24	4	10	56	17	85	18	5	272	298	407	705	4%	81%	0.20	78	118	3.54	31
Murphy,Sean	R	17	23	C	aa	OAK	191	20	35	6	0	3	18	16	36	0	0	183	248	261	509	8%	81%	0.46	47	34	1.76	-10
Murphy,Tom	R	15	24	C	a/a	COL	394	39	91	23	3	16	45	20	132	4	3	231	268	429	697	5%	66%	0.15	150	80	3.07	21
		16	25	C	aaa	COL	303	38	90	23	7	15	43	11	81	1	1	296	322	567	889	4%	73%	0.14	169	87	5.12	64
		17	26	C	aaa	COL	141	15	31	9	1	3	13	6	60	0	0	222	254	360	614	4%	57%	0.10	116	63	2.37	-49
Naylor,Josh	L	17	20	1B	aa	SD	156	17	39	9	0	2	18	15	37	2	1	247	312	341	653	9%	77%	0.41	65	53	2.97	-6
Neuse,Sheldon	R	17	23	3B	aa	OAK	67	7	22	4	0	0	5	5	23	0	0	335	379	390	769	7%	66%	0.21	53	24	4.86	-71
Newman,Kevin	R	16	23	SS	aa	PIT	233	35	60	10	2	2	24	21	26	5	3	258	321	333	654	8%	89%	0.84	45	98	3.00	40
		17	24	SS	a/a	PIT	509	57	124	27	4	3	36	26	66	10	3	245	281	331	612	5%	87%	0.39	52	105	2.52	33
Nido,Tomas	R	17	23	C	aa	NYM	367	40	79	17	1	8	59	32	73	0	0	215	278	334	612	8%	80%	0.44	70	39	2.55	6
Norwood,John	R	17	25	RF	aa	MIA	473	64	120	16	3	16	58	56	158	4	5	254	332	405	738	11%	67%	0.35	96	76	3.95	-11
Nottingham,Jacob	R	16	21	C	aa	MIL	415	43	95	14	0	11	35	28	145	9	2	228	277	337	614	6%	65%	0.19	79	77	2.82	-39
		17	22	C	aa	MIL	325	37	68	21	2	10	48	37	93	7	3	210	291	382	673	10%	71%	0.40	112	93	2.86	25
Nunez,Dom	L	17	22	C	aa	COL	297	31	60	10	1	10	24	45	80	6	1	203	308	350	658	13%	73%	0.56	86	75	3.10	12
Nunez,Renato	R	15	21	3B	aa	OAK	381	47	92	21	0	13	47	22	71	1	0	242	283	397	680	5%	81%	0.31	100	47	3.27	32
		16	22	3B	aaa	OAK	505	56	108	20	2	19	68	29	124	2	0	214	256	378	634	5%	76%	0.23	98	67	2.76	13
		17	23	LF	aaa	OAK	473	59	102	25	2	23	62	37	151	2	1	216	273	423	696	7%	68%	0.24	131	61	3.21	12
Ockimey,Josh	L	17	22	1B	aa	BOS	103	10	27	8	0	2	9	14	34	0	0	261	350	403	753	12%	67%	0.41	107	14	3.97	-17
O'Hearn,Ryan	L	16	23	1B	aa	KC	414	43	99	25	2	12	52	41	139	3	5	240	308	396	704	9%	66%	0.29	116	55	3.22	-5
		17	24	1B	a/a	KC	479	45	109	26	2	16	53	44	151	1	0	227	292	393	685	8%	68%	0.29	110	49	3.18	-5
O'Neill,Tyler	R	16	21	RF	aa	SEA	492	67	139	25	3	23	101	59	166	12	2	282	359	487	846	11%	66%	0.36	141	103	5.47	33
		17	22	LF	aaa	STL	495	64	111	24	2	25	79	45	157	12	2	224	288	434	722	8%	68%	0.28	131	101	3.61	27
Palka,Daniel	L	16	25	RF	a/a	MIN	503	60	112	22	3	27	73	44	205	7	6	223	286	439	725	8%	59%	0.22	161	87	3.48	10
		17	26	RF	aaa	MIN	332	42	83	12	3	10	38	24	87	1	2	250	299	391	690	7%	74%	0.27	82	72	3.35	-3
Papi,Mike	L	16	24	LF	aa	CLE	259	28	54	15	1	7	34	34	78	3	0	208	300	359	658	12%	70%	0.44	107	79	2.85	14
		17	25	RF	a/a	CLE	415	55	96	17	0	10	43	57	88	5	3	231	324	344	668	12%	79%	0.64	67	56	3.20	12
Patterson,Jordan	L	15	23	RF	aa	COL	185	21	50	18	0	6	26	9	44	7	4	271	304	473	777	5%	76%	0.20	149	81	3.79	60
		16	24	RF	aaa	COL	427	55	115	22	7	11	46	34	120	7	0	270	324	434	758	7%	72%	0.29	106	130	4.06	29
		17	25	1B	aaa	COL	484	53	122	29	6	20	63	25	134	2	6	253	289	460	750	5%	72%	0.18	126	80	3.52	25
Peter,Jake	L	16	23	2B	a/a	CHW	481	46	119	23	0	5	43	42	112	7	2	246	307	327	634	8%	77%	0.37	58	60	2.91	-11
		17	24	2B	a/a	CHW	463	54	116	17	3	12	42	37	145	9	7	250	306	375	680	7%	69%	0.26	80	89	3.28	-18
Peterson,Dustin	R	16	22	LF	aa	ATL	524	65	142	37	2	11	88	46	112	4	1	271	330	414	744	8%	79%	0.41	95	73	3.90	30
		17	23	LF	aaa	ATL	314	30	65	10	1	1	26	25	92	1	2	207	265	250	515	7%	71%	0.27	34	51	1.78	-59
Phillips,Brett	L	15	21	CF	aa	MIL	214	33	61	14	6	1	22	21	61	8	3	285	348	425	773	9%	72%	0.34	105	143	3.75	33
		16	22	CF	aa	MIL	441	56	98	13	5	15	58	64	164	11	7	222	320	380	700	13%	63%	0.39	109	111	3.32	-1
		17	23	RF	aaa	MIL	383	56	101	19	7	16	55	32	149	6	1	263	319	470	789	8%	61%	0.21	144	125	4.28	14

BATTER	B	Yr	Age	Pos	Lvl	Tm	AB	R	H	D	T	HR	RBI	BB	K	SB	CS	BA	OB	Slg	OPS	bb%	ct%	Eye	PX	SX	RC/G	BPV
Polo,Tito	R	17	23	CF	aa	CHW	127	23	39	8	3	1	23	11	26	13	4	308	364	440	803	8%	80%	0.43	78	166	4.54	48
Pullin,Andrew	L	16	23	LF	aa	PHI	188	26	58	9	0	9	26	11	42	0	0	311	348	505	852	5%	78%	0.25	114	26	5.88	22
		17	24	LF	a/a	PHI	504	52	120	37	2	18	58	29	109	4	1	238	280	429	709	6%	78%	0.27	114	75	3.26	40
Quinn,Roman	B	15	22	CF	aa	PHI	232	35	63	5	4	4	12	14	48	23	11	272	314	379	693	6%	79%	0.30	63	171	3.28	32
		16	23	CF	aa	PHI	286	47	73	12	4	5	20	25	79	25	9	255	314	386	700	8%	72%	0.31	85	168	3.37	26
		17	24	CF	aaa	PHI	175	21	42	7	2	2	11	15	58	9	5	242	304	340	644	8%	67%	0.27	67	129	2.75	-21
Ramirez,Harold	R	16	22	CF	aa	TOR	383	53	113	18	6	2	44	19	73	6	11	295	329	387	716	5%	81%	0.27	58	110	3.35	15
		17	23	RF	aa	TOR	444	39	110	19	2	5	45	27	72	4	3	247	291	335	626	6%	84%	0.38	51	63	2.76	9
Ramirez,Tyler	L	17	22	LF	aa	OAK	208	24	58	10	1	3	20	23	56	2	3	279	350	380	730	10%	73%	0.41	68	65	3.81	-12
Read,Raudy	R	17	24	C	aa	WAS	411	36	95	22	1	13	50	22	89	2	0	232	271	386	658	5%	78%	0.25	91	43	2.99	11
Reinheimer,Jack	R	15	23	SS	aa	ARI	485	53	121	23	3	4	35	42	102	17	7	249	309	337	646	8%	79%	0.41	64	111	2.93	18
		16	24	SS	aaa	ARI	500	44	123	25	7	1	33	33	107	14	13	246	293	330	623	6%	79%	0.31	57	107	2.37	7
		17	25	SS	aaa	ARI	482	55	109	16	2	3	35	29	101	8	9	225	270	282	552	6%	79%	0.29	37	82	2.02	-16
Reyes,Victor	B	17	23	RF	aa	ARI	479	49	132	28	6	3	43	22	87	15	10	276	309	382	690	4%	82%	0.26	65	109	3.12	23
Riley,Austin	R	17	20	3B	aa	ATL	178	29	53	6	1	8	28	22	56	2	0	296	372	467	839	11%	69%	0.39	103	81	5.81	5
Rios,Edwin	L	16	22	3B	aa	LA	122	13	29	7	0	5	16	7	34	0	0	240	281	416	697	5%	72%	0.20	116	23	3.39	2
		17	23	1B	a/a	LA	475	58	131	32	0	20	75	27	126	1	2	276	315	473	787	5%	73%	0.21	122	31	4.42	13
Robles,Victor	R	17	20	CF	aa	WAS	139	21	43	12	1	3	12	11	23	10	3	307	356	455	811	7%	83%	0.45	91	118	4.76	57
Rodgers,Brendan	R	17	21	SS	aa	COL	150	17	39	5	0	6	15	7	34	0	2	263	295	412	707	4%	77%	0.20	83	33	3.62	-5
Rondon,Jose	R	15	21	SS	aa	SD	100	5	17	2	1	0	7	3	17	1	3	168	196	203	398	3%	83%	0.20	22	74	0.84	-18
		16	22	SS	a/a	SD	456	42	114	22	1	5	42	13	89	10	6	250	270	338	608	3%	80%	0.14	59	88	2.55	3
		17	23	SS	a/a	SD	300	30	77	18	2	4	33	17	65	2	1	256	295	367	662	5%	78%	0.26	72	76	2.95	7
Santander,Anthony	B	17	23	RF	aa	BAL	50	11	16	3	0	4	12	6	11	0	0	320	398	636	1	11%	78%	0.59	168	37	8.63	83
Schrock,Max	L	16	22	2B	aa	OAK	23	2	8	1	0	0	2	0	0	0	1	357	357	399	756	0%	###	0.00	28	51	4.06	40
		17	23	2B	aa	OAK	417	45	119	17	1	5	37	27	45	3	2	286	329	369	698	6%	89%	0.60	46	57	3.75	25
Senzel,Nick	R	17	22	3B	aa	CIN	209	42	72	14	1	12	36	28	47	5	4	345	423	588	1	12%	78%	0.61	137	86	8.04	72
Shaw,Chris	L	16	23	1B	aa	SF	232	24	54	15	5	4	28	19	61	0	0	233	291	393	684	8%	74%	0.31	105	78	2.74	20
		17	24	LF	a/a	SF	469	50	120	32	1	17	68	33	151	0	0	257	306	438	744	7%	68%	0.22	124	30	3.84	-6
Sierra,Magneuris	L	17	21	RF	aa	STL	326	28	84	17	3	1	31	18	60	15	5	257	295	334	629	5%	82%	0.29	51	108	2.72	11
Simcox,A.J.	R	17	23	SS	aa	DET	436	46	99	19	6	7	30	23	77	10	6	226	265	342	607	5%	82%	0.30	64	117	2.34	28
Sisco,Chance	L	15	20	C	aa	BAL	74	8	18	4	0	2	7	8	14	0	1	248	322	379	702	10%	80%	0.56	88	33	3.38	24
		16	21	C	a/a	BAL	426	51	128	26	1	6	45	54	92	2	2	300	378	406	784	11%	78%	0.58	74	40	4.66	9
		17	22	C	aaa	BAL	344	43	80	13	0	6	43	31	114	2	2	232	296	327	623	8%	67%	0.28	68	49	2.77	-44
Slater,Austin	R	15	23	2B	aa	SF	199	20	55	10	1	0	12	14	53	1	1	278	324	342	666	6%	73%	0.26	57	62	3.14	-28
		16	24	LF	a/a	SF	390	48	103	18	1	13	58	50	103	7	8	265	349	417	766	11%	74%	0.48	98	65	4.18	17
		17	25	RF	aaa	SF	184	22	50	10	0	3	22	12	46	3	4	274	319	384	703	6%	75%	0.26	74	59	3.48	-9
Smith,Dwight	L	15	23	LF	aa	TOR	460	62	113	26	2	6	37	39	73	3	3	246	305	352	657	8%	84%	0.53	73	76	2.92	35
		16	24	LF	aa	TOR	471	47	115	24	4	14	63	38	104	10	8	243	300	399	699	7%	78%	0.36	95	90	3.22	31
		17	25	RF	aaa	TOR	395	52	101	21	1	8	42	43	80	7	9	257	330	374	704	10%	80%	0.54	72	69	3.36	19
Solak,Nick	R	17	22	2B	aa	NYY	119	15	33	8	1	2	9	10	26	1	1	275	330	416	746	8%	78%	0.37	89	75	3.77	23
Stevenson,Andrew	L	16	22	CF	aa	WAS	256	34	60	11	1	2	14	18	53	11	5	233	284	304	588	7%	79%	0.34	49	112	2.36	4
		17	23	CF	a/a	WAS	389	43	95	11	3	2	32	25	101	9	4	245	290	302	592	6%	74%	0.25	37	106	2.51	-28
Stewart,Christin	L	16	23	LF	aa	DET	87	14	17	2	0	5	15	10	27	0	0	192	275	375	650	10%	69%	0.36	112	42	3.08	-1
		17	24	LF	aa	DET	485	55	109	25	3	23	71	47	151	2	0	225	293	433	726	9%	69%	0.31	130	76	3.58	22
Stewart,D.J.	L	17	24	LF	aa	BAL	457	65	104	14	1	17	64	57	105	16	5	229	314	379	693	11%	77%	0.55	82	101	3.60	28
Straw,Myles	R	17	23	CF	aa	HOU	46	8	10	0	0	0	3	6	10	2	0	214	303	214	516	11%	77%	0.56	0	86	2.30	-40
Stubbs,Garrett	L	16	23	C	aa	HOU	120	18	35	8	1	3	13	11	13	4	0	289	349	457	805	8%	89%	0.87	93	105	4.91	82
		17	24	C	a/a	HOU	340	34	65	15	0	3	27	31	71	8	0	191	258	261	519	8%	79%	0.43	47	86	1.87	-1
Tatis,Fernando	R	17	18	SS	aa	SD	55	6	15	1	0	1	6	2	16	3	0	268	294	341	634	3%	71%	0.12	45	81	3.60	-48
Taylor,Chuck	B	16	23	LF	aa	ARI	84	10	19	6	0	1	10	5	16	1	0	225	271	328	600	6%	81%	0.32	74	61	2.35	14
		17	24	LF	aa	SEA	471	63	113	22	2	8	49	55	106	8	2	239	319	344	663	11%	77%	0.52	65	90	3.14	12
Tellez,Rowdy	L	16	21	1B	aa	TOR	438	63	126	30	2	22	72	56	100	4	3	288	369	518	887	11%	77%	0.56	141	59	5.72	63
		17	22	1B	aaa	TOR	445	44	99	31	1	6	55	46	100	6	1	223	296	339	635	9%	78%	0.46	78	73	2.62	15
Thompson,David	R	17	24	3B	aa	NYM	476	59	114	26	1	16	65	42	109	8	7	240	301	400	701	8%	77%	0.39	95	66	3.33	23
Tilson,Charlie	L	14	22	CF	aa	STL	139	15	29	4	1	1	13	5	30	2	3	208	235	276	510	3%	78%	0.16	49	89	1.63	-13
		15	23	CF	aa	STL	539	63	137	18	6	3	24	33	80	34	21	255	298	328	626	6%	85%	0.42	46	135	2.58	32
		16	24	CF	aaa	STL	351	39	83	13	6	3	25	25	62	11	3	236	287	329	616	7%	82%	0.40	55	133	2.54	29
Tobias,Josh	B	17	25	2B	aa	BOS	332	24	80	19	0	2	26	15	79	3	3	242	274	321	595	4%	76%	0.19	58	43	2.35	-26
Torres,Gleyber	R	17	21	SS	a/a	NYY	201	29	56	13	1	8	32	29	50	7	6	280	372	476	847	13%	75%	0.59	117	87	4.84	48
Trahan,Blake	R	17	24	SS	aa	CIN	455	56	98	17	0	2	28	55	93	12	8	215	299	268	567	11%	79%	0.58	37	76	2.20	-6
Travis,Sam	R	15	22	1B	aa	BOS	243	29	70	18	2	3	31	27	36	7	6	287	359	413	772	10%	85%	0.76	88	85	3.94	59
		16	23	1B	aaa	BOS	173	25	47	11	0	5	28	15	43	1	0	272	328	431	759	8%	75%	0.34	106	53	4.23	20
		17	24	1B	aaa	BOS	304	35	79	15	0	5	21	33	61	5	2	260	333	361	694	10%	80%	0.55	63	60	3.57	10
Trevino,Jose	R	17	25	C	aa	TEX	402	33	86	10	0	6	35	16	49	1	2	215	245	285	531	4%	88%	0.33	37	33	2.01	1

BATTER	B	Yr	Age	Pos	Lvl	Tm	AB	R	H	D	T	HR	RBI	BB	K	SB	CS	BA	OB	Slg	OPS	bb%	ct%	Eye	PX	SX	RC/G	BPV
Tucker,Cole	B	17	21	SS	aa	PIT	167	23	42	4	5	2	17	19	31	10	3	251	330	364	694	10%	81%	0.62	55	142	3.28	34
Tucker,Kyle	L	17	20	CF	aa	HOU	287	35	72	20	1	15	42	19	71	7	4	251	299	481	780	6%	75%	0.28	136	83	3.97	50
Urena,Jhoan	B	17	23	1B	aaa	NYM	44	4	8	0	1	2	6	3	19	1	0	185	239	362	601	7%	57%	0.16	113	84	2.60	-43
Urena,Richard	B	16	20	SS	aa	TOR	124	13	32	6	4	0	16	4	20	0	2	262	283	383	666	3%	84%	0.18	69	96	2.35	26
		17	21	SS	aa	TOR	510	39	122	37	3	5	53	26	107	0	1	238	276	349	625	5%	79%	0.25	75	42	2.43	1
Urias,Luis	R	17	20	SS	aa	SD	442	74	130	20	3	3	36	63	66	7	5	294	382	373	756	13%	85%	0.96	48	89	4.23	32
Valera,Breyvic	B	14	22	2B	aa	STL	227	25	58	7	1	0	16	12	24	3	6	254	292	298	590	5%	89%	0.51	33	79	2.33	20
		15	23	2B	aa	STL	360	27	72	8	1	2	23	24	30	1	4	201	252	249	501	6%	92%	0.83	29	51	1.67	20
		16	24	2B	a/a	STL	395	37	102	16	1	0	33	32	48	9	6	259	314	307	621	7%	88%	0.66	34	78	2.75	19
		17	25	2B	aaa	STL	424	54	116	19	5	6	32	30	38	9	13	273	320	383	703	7%	91%	0.79	57	92	3.21	53
Verdugo,Alex	L	16	20	CF	aa	LA	477	56	126	23	1	13	61	39	71	2	6	264	320	398	718	8%	85%	0.55	77	39	3.65	31
		17	21	CF	aaa	LA	433	56	123	26	2	5	52	40	56	8	3	285	345	392	737	8%	87%	0.72	63	87	3.94	44
Vogelbach,Dan	L	15	23	1B	aa	CHC	254	32	61	15	1	5	31	46	69	1	1	241	357	370	727	15%	73%	0.66	98	50	3.63	17
		16	24	1B	aaa	SEA	459	61	113	21	1	17	74	73	121	0	0	246	349	411	761	14%	74%	0.60	104	38	4.25	19
		17	25	1B	aaa	SEA	459	51	112	21	0	14	67	60	119	2	1	244	331	380	710	11%	74%	0.50	83	40	3.72	0
Wade,LaMonte	L	17	23	LF	aa	MIN	424	68	118	21	3	6	61	67	73	8	2	278	377	386	763	14%	83%	0.92	63	98	4.36	40
Wade,Tyler	L	15	21	SS	aa	NYY	113	6	22	4	0	1	3	2	26	2	1	194	207	254	461	2%	77%	0.07	46	50	1.42	-35
		16	22	SS	aa	NYY	505	89	128	15	6	6	27	66	111	27	8	254	340	340	679	12%	78%	0.59	52	143	3.43	21
		17	23	SS	aaa	NYY	339	61	97	20	3	7	28	34	84	23	6	287	352	427	779	9%	75%	0.40	88	142	4.60	34
Ward,Drew	L	16	22	3B	aa	WAS	178	17	37	7	0	2	21	20	53	0	1	208	287	288	575	10%	70%	0.37	60	29	2.24	-41
		17	23	3B	aa	WAS	413	39	87	18	0	8	44	46	145	0	0	210	289	311	600	10%	65%	0.32	75	21	2.49	-52
Ward,Taylor	R	17	24	C	aa	LAA	119	13	31	3	0	3	18	20	20	0	0	260	367	351	719	14%	83%	1.02	47	17	4.16	7
Wendle,Joey	L	14	24	2B	aa	CLE	336	36	72	18	3	6	39	20	65	3	2	216	259	340	600	6%	81%	0.31	91	91	2.23	36
		15	25	2B	aaa	OAK	577	64	144	37	7	7	45	18	129	10	2	250	273	378	651	3%	78%	0.14	92	127	2.71	30
		16	26	2B	aaa	OAK	491	69	121	28	9	9	52	22	126	12	5	247	279	396	676	4%	74%	0.17	98	148	2.86	31
		17	27	2B	aaa	OAK	478	49	111	24	6	5	40	14	95	10	5	232	254	343	596	3%	80%	0.14	66	120	2.21	16
Westbrook,Jamie	R	16	21	2B	aa	ARI	435	46	111	22	1	5	33	24	63	9	5	256	294	343	637	5%	85%	0.37	56	81	2.85	23
		17	22	LF	aa	ARI	377	32	96	19	4	7	47	13	46	2	2	255	281	380	661	3%	88%	0.29	66	67	2.94	33
Wilkerson,Steve	B	17	25	3B	aa	BAL	245	27	59	7	0	5	24	17	65	4	2	239	289	327	616	7%	73%	0.26	54	61	2.85	-30
Williams,Justin	L	16	21	RF	aa	TAM	148	17	32	5	2	5	23	4	33	0	1	219	241	377	618	3%	77%	0.13	91	82	2.41	15
		17	22	RF	aa	TAM	366	47	100	19	2	12	64	33	78	5	2	274	335	437	771	8%	79%	0.43	93	85	4.36	33
Winker,Jesse	L	15	22	LF	aa	CIN	443	60	117	22	2	14	48	65	95	7	4	264	359	414	773	13%	79%	0.69	99	73	4.37	43
		16	23	RF	aaa	CIN	380	35	108	21	0	3	41	55	68	0	0	284	375	363	738	13%	82%	0.81	56	16	4.10	5
		17	24	RF	aaa	CIN	299	27	83	19	0	2	34	32	54	2	5	277	347	361	708	10%	82%	0.59	58	29	3.44	4
Young,Chesny	R	16	24	2B	aa	CHC	491	47	130	23	2	3	28	45	74	12	16	265	326	337	664	8%	85%	0.61	48	65	2.94	16
		17	25	2B	aaa	CHC	425	42	90	17	0	1	25	25	83	5	7	211	255	255	510	6%	80%	0.30	33	60	1.69	-21
Zagunis,Mark	R	16	23	LF	a/a	CHC	358	47	91	22	4	8	38	41	89	4	2	255	332	407	739	10%	75%	0.46	100	93	3.65	31
		17	24	LF	aaa	CHC	330	45	74	18	1	10	42	55	109	3	3	225	335	373	708	14%	67%	0.50	102	57	3.38	-2

PITCHER	Th	Yr	Age	LvL	Org	W	L	G	Sv	IP	H	ER	HR	BB	K	ERA	WHIP	BF/G	OBA	bb/9	k/9	Cmd	hr/9	H%	S%	BPV
Acevedo,Domingo	R	17	23	a/a	NYY	6	2	16	0	92	95	37	12	27	78	3.68	1.33	23.8	269	2.7	7.6	2.9	1.2	32%	77%	72
Adams,Chance	R	16	22	aa	NYY	8	1	13	0	70	44	23	8	27	63	3.01	1.01	20.5	182	3.4	8.1	2.4	1.0	21%	75%	87
		17	23	a/a	NYY	15	5	27	0	150	129	57	16	63	117	3.41	1.27	22.8	233	3.8	7.0	1.9	1.0	27%	77%	60
Adams,Spencer	R	16	20	aa	CHW	2	5	9	0	55	64	27	2	10	24	4.39	1.34	25.6	291	1.7	3.9	2.4	0.4	32%	66%	59
		17	21	aa	CHW	7	15	26	0	153	206	102	25	45	103	6.03	1.65	26.2	324	2.7	6.0	2.3	1.5	36%	66%	30
Alcantara,Sandy	R	17	22	aa	STL	7	5	25	0	125	146	76	14	55	88	5.43	1.60	22.1	292	3.9	6.3	1.6	1.0	33%	67%	38
Alexander,Tyler	L	16	22	aa	DET	2	1	6	0	34	41	14	4	4	19	3.73	1.30	23.6	296	1.1	4.9	4.6	1.1	32%	75%	89
		17	23	aa	DET	8	9	27	0	138	208	97	23	24	99	6.32	1.68	23.0	348	1.5	6.4	4.1	1.5	39%	64%	67
Allard,Kolby	L	17	20	aa	ATL	8	11	27	0	150	174	72	13	49	120	4.34	1.49	24.0	292	3.0	7.2	2.4	0.8	35%	72%	68
Almonte,Miguel	R	15	22	a/a	KC	6	6	28	0	104	112	62	7	41	80	5.42	1.48	15.9	276	3.6	6.9	1.9	0.6	33%	62%	62
		16	23	a/a	KC	5	8	32	0	76	101	60	9	46	59	7.14	1.94	11.3	321	5.4	7.0	1.3	1.1	37%	63%	27
		17	24	a/a	KC	1	1	16	0	47	52	12	3	14	42	2.31	1.39	12.4	280	2.6	8.0	3.1	0.6	35%	86%	92
Almonte,Yency	R	16	22	aa	COL	3	1	5	0	30	28	15	6	18	17	4.58	1.53	26.1	250	5.3	5.2	1.0	1.8	25%	77%	2
		17	23	a/a	COL	8	4	22	0	111	124	51	16	57	72	4.15	1.63	22.5	283	4.6	5.9	1.3	1.3	31%	78%	22
Alvarez,Yadier	R	17	21	aa	LA	2	2	7	0	33	32	15	1	22	32	4.02	1.64	21.0	255	6.0	8.7	1.4	0.3	34%	74%	78
Alzolay,Adbert	R	17	22	aa	CHC	0	3	7	0	33	32	14	0	13	26	3.92	1.37	19.5	257	3.5	7.3	2.1	0.0	33%	68%	91
Anderson,Drew	R	17	23	a/a	PHI	9	4	22	0	114	101	55	17	43	82	4.30	1.25	21.2	238	3.4	6.4	1.9	1.3	26%	70%	46
Appel,Mark	R	14	23	aa	HOU	1	2	7	0	39	39	18	2	13	33	4.07	1.31	23.0	260	2.9	7.6	2.6	0.5	32%	68%	89
		15	24	a/a	HOU	10	3	25	0	132	150	71	14	50	94	4.84	1.52	22.9	288	3.4	6.4	1.9	0.9	33%	69%	47
		16	25	aaa	PHI	3	3	8	0	38	53	29	5	23	29	6.85	2.00	23.1	329	5.5	6.7	1.2	1.1	38%	66%	22
		17	26	aaa	PHI	5	4	17	0	82	115	65	12	58	50	7.13	2.11	23.8	331	6.4	5.4	0.8	1.3	36%	67%	0
Arano,Victor	R	16	21	aa	PHI	1	1	11	1	17	12	5	2	4	22	2.54	0.98	5.8	208	2.1	11.8	5.5	1.3	28%	83%	160
		17	22	aa	PHI	1	2	32	9	39	44	21	8	11	34	4.98	1.42	5.1	288	2.5	7.9	3.1	1.9	32%	72%	54
Armenteros,Rogelio	R	16	22	aa	HOU	2	0	3	0	18	19	5	1	4	12	2.23	1.24	24.8	267	1.9	5.7	3.0	0.6	31%	84%	82
		17	23	a/a	HOU	10	4	24	1	124	98	29	8	35	130	2.14	1.07	20.1	219	2.6	9.4	3.7	0.6	29%	83%	129
Ball,Trey	L	17	23	aa	BOS	7	12	25	0	125	193	95	19	60	85	6.87	2.03	24.2	354	4.4	6.1	1.4	1.4	39%	68%	8
Banda,Anthony	L	16	23	a/a	ARI	10	6	26	0	150	165	58	11	55	129	3.49	1.47	24.7	281	3.3	7.7	2.3	0.7	34%	77%	74
		17	24	aaa	ARI	8	7	22	0	122	136	77	15	48	96	5.70	1.51	24.0	284	3.6	7.1	2.0	1.1	33%	63%	49
Barlow,Scott	R	16	24	aa	LA	4	7	24	0	124	153	73	11	51	85	5.30	1.64	23.1	304	3.7	6.2	1.7	0.8	35%	68%	42
		17	25	a/a	LA	7	6	26	0	140	113	61	17	57	132	3.92	1.22	21.7	224	3.6	8.5	2.3	1.1	27%	71%	78
Barria,Jaime	R	17	21	a/a	LAA	3	6	15	0	76	79	29	8	17	54	3.38	1.26	20.7	269	2.0	6.4	3.2	0.9	31%	76%	81
Beede,Tyler	R	15	22	aa	SF	3	8	13	0	72	73	54	4	37	43	6.67	1.52	24.1	263	4.6	5.3	1.2	0.5	30%	53%	44
		16	23	aa	SF	8	7	24	0	147	165	63	9	57	117	3.82	1.51	26.6	284	3.5	7.1	2.0	0.6	34%	75%	67
		17	24	aaa	SF	6	7	19	0	109	140	70	13	40	70	5.74	1.66	25.7	314	3.3	5.7	1.7	1.0	35%	66%	31
Beeks,Jalen	L	16	23	aa	BOS	5	4	13	0	65	86	44	7	29	47	6.06	1.76	23.0	318	4.0	6.5	1.6	0.9	37%	66%	38
		17	24	a/a	BOS	11	8	26	0	145	153	76	16	62	125	4.69	1.48	24.0	272	3.8	7.7	2.0	1.0	33%	70%	60
Bernardino,Brennan	L	17	25	aa	CIN	2	4	38	0	40	58	34	8	24	35	7.52	2.04	5.2	339	5.3	7.9	1.5	1.9	39%	66%	9
Bieber,Shane	R	17	22	aa	CLE	2	1	9	0	54	66	18	2	5	38	2.99	1.31	25.0	301	0.9	6.3	7.2	0.4	36%	77%	171
Blackburn,Clayton	R	14	21	aa	SF	5	6	18	0	93	101	37	1	19	74	3.56	1.29	21.2	278	1.8	7.2	3.9	0.1	35%	70%	123
		15	22	aaa	SF	10	4	23	0	123	130	37	5	30	85	2.69	1.30	22.1	273	2.2	6.3	2.9	0.3	33%	79%	88
		16	23	aaa	SF	7	10	25	0	136	158	75	16	35	87	4.92	1.42	23.1	292	2.3	5.8	2.5	1.0	32%	67%	53
		17	24	aaa	TEX	6	2	20	0	96	123	65	6	27	64	6.09	1.57	21.1	313	2.6	6.0	2.3	0.5	36%	59%	61
Borucki,Ryan	L	17	23	a/a	TOR	2	3	8	0	52	46	14	3	10	41	2.42	1.07	25.4	238	1.7	7.1	4.2	0.5	29%	79%	124
Buehler,Walker	R	17	23	a/a	LA	3	3	23	1	72	66	35	6	23	85	4.41	1.24	12.8	245	2.9	10.5	3.6	0.8	33%	65%	121
Bummer,Aaron	L	17	24	a/a	CHW	1	3	20	3	38	41	16	2	19	34	3.70	1.59	8.4	277	4.6	8.0	1.7	0.6	34%	77%	66
Burdi,Nick	R	15	22	aa	MIN	3	4	30	2	44	44	25	3	30	45	5.06	1.70	6.6	263	6.3	9.3	1.5	0.6	34%	70%	72
		17	24	aa	MIN	2	0	14	1	17	12	1	1	4	16	0.77	0.93	4.6	194	2.3	8.3	3.6	0.7	24%	99%	122
Burdi,Zack	R	16	21	a/a	CHW	2	0	42	2	64	35	25	4	42	83	3.56	1.20	6.1	164	5.8	11.7	2.0	0.6	24%	71%	116
		17	22	aaa	CHW	0	4	29	7	33	33	17	2	18	46	4.64	1.53	5.0	262	4.8	12.4	2.6	0.6	39%	69%	113
Burnes,Corbin	R	17	23	aa	MIL	3	3	16	0	86	86	31	3	23	73	3.22	1.26	21.9	262	2.4	7.6	3.2	0.3	33%	74%	105
Burrows,Beau	R	17	21	aa	DET	6	4	15	0	76	90	48	5	33	63	5.70	1.61	22.5	294	3.9	7.5	1.9	0.6	36%	64%	62
Buttrey,Ty	R	16	23	aa	BOS	1	10	33	0	79	95	50	7	48	44	5.75	1.82	11.1	300	5.5	5.0	0.9	0.7	33%	68%	22
		17	24	a/a	BOS	2	5	40	4	64	76	48	4	37	60	6.85	1.77	7.3	297	5.2	8.4	1.6	0.5	38%	59%	64
Cabrera,Genesis	L	17	21	aa	TAM	5	4	12	0	65	85	31	6	27	46	4.36	1.74	24.6	318	3.8	6.4	1.7	0.9	37%	76%	39
Callahan,Jamie	R	17	23	a/a	NYM	6	3	41	7	52	56	21	5	19	59	3.58	1.43	5.4	275	3.3	10.2	3.1	0.8	37%	77%	103
Carroll,Cody	R	17	25	aa	NYY	2	5	26	5	47	47	21	6	25	49	3.98	1.53	7.9	261	4.8	9.3	1.9	1.2	33%	78%	63
Castellani,Ryan	R	17	21	aa	COL	9	12	27	0	157	207	127	24	52	106	7.29	1.65	26.1	319	3.0	6.1	2.0	1.4	35%	56%	28
Castillo,Jesus	R	17	22	aa	LAA	0	2	5	0	24	32	11	2	6	20	4.07	1.63	21.1	327	2.3	7.5	3.2	0.9	39%	77%	75
Chargois,J.T.	R	15	25	aa	MIN	1	1	32	11	33	30	12	1	20	27	3.24	1.53	4.5	246	5.5	7.3	1.3	0.3	31%	78%	69
		16	26	a/a	MIN	2	1	39	16	47	45	10	2	14	42	1.87	1.26	4.9	253	2.7	8.1	3.0	0.5	32%	87%	101
Chirinos,Yonny	R	16	23	aa	TAM	5	3	14	0	67	85	39	5	12	37	5.28	1.45	20.3	310	1.6	5.1	3.1	0.7	34%	63%	68
		17	24	a/a	TAM	13	5	27	0	168	168	67	17	28	122	3.58	1.16	24.8	261	1.5	6.5	4.3	0.9	30%	72%	105
Clarke,Taylor	R	16	23	aa	ARI	8	6	17	0	98	123	54	12	23	61	5.00	1.49	24.7	308	2.1	5.6	2.7	1.1	34%	68%	52
		17	24	a/a	ARI	12	9	27	0	145	143	65	17	52	114	4.03	1.35	22.4	259	3.3	7.1	2.2	1.1	30%	73%	60

PITCHER	Th	Yr	Age	LvL	Org	W	L	G	Sv	IP	H	ER	HR	BB	K	ERA	WHIP	BF/G	OBA	bb/9	k/9	Cmd	hr/9	H%	S%	BPV
Clifton,Trevor	R	17	22	aa	CHC	5	8	21	0	100	132	75	9	48	76	6.73	1.80	22.1	319	4.3	6.8	1.6	0.8	37%	62%	40
Conlon,PJ	L	17	24	aa	NYM	8	9	28	1	136	169	77	20	48	95	5.09	1.59	21.4	306	3.2	6.3	2.0	1.3	34%	71%	33
Cooney,Tim	L	13	23	aa	STL	7	10	20	0	118	142	53	7	17	105	4.02	1.35	24.7	299	1.3	8.0	6.0	0.5	37%	70%	153
		14	24	aaa	STL	14	6	26	0	158	170	63	18	45	98	3.57	1.36	25.4	276	2.5	5.6	2.2	1.0	30%	77%	48
		15	25	aaa	STL	6	4	14	0	89	70	31	9	16	50	3.10	0.96	23.9	218	1.6	5.1	3.2	0.9	23%	72%	82
Coonrod,Sam	R	16	24	aa	SF	4	3	13	0	77	73	35	7	42	44	4.11	1.48	25.6	251	4.9	5.1	1.0	0.8	27%	74%	32
		17	25	aa	SF	4	11	24	0	104	121	75	7	47	77	6.47	1.62	19.2	292	4.1	6.7	1.6	0.6	35%	58%	52
Cosart,Jake	R	17	23	aa	BOS	5	2	38	2	49	34	22	6	43	43	4.05	1.56	5.7	194	7.9	7.8	1.0	1.0	22%	77%	53
Crichton,Stefan	R	16	24	aa	BAL	2	6	48	1	72	87	38	5	27	50	4.71	1.57	6.6	299	3.3	6.2	1.8	0.6	35%	70%	52
		17	25	aaa	BAL	7	2	29	2	48	59	22	3	13	42	4.19	1.52	7.1	306	2.5	8.0	3.2	0.5	38%	72%	95
Curtiss,John	R	17	24	a/a	MIN	2	0	39	19	49	30	10	0	24	54	1.91	1.10	5.0	177	4.4	9.8	2.2	0.0	26%	81%	125
Davis,Rookie	R	15	22	aa	NYY	2	1	6	0	33	45	21	1	9	21	5.71	1.62	24.6	325	2.3	5.7	2.5	0.4	38%	62%	65
		16	23	a/a	CIN	10	5	24	0	125	158	76	19	42	69	5.48	1.60	23.0	310	3.0	5.0	1.6	1.4	33%	69%	16
		17	24	a/a	CIN	4	4	14	0	74	102	56	17	22	56	6.83	1.67	23.7	328	2.6	6.8	2.6	2.1	36%	63%	21
De Jong,Chase	R	16	23	a/a	LA	15	5	26	0	147	130	56	17	37	114	3.46	1.14	22.4	239	2.3	7.0	3.0	1.1	27%	74%	81
		17	24	a/a	SEA	4	9	20	0	113	152	90	24	37	68	7.19	1.68	25.4	324	3.0	5.4	1.8	1.9	34%	60%	5
De Leon,Jose	R	15	23	aa	LA	2	6	16	0	77	71	39	13	28	91	4.54	1.30	19.7	248	3.3	10.6	3.2	1.6	32%	71%	90
		16	24	aaa	LA	7	1	16	0	86	71	33	10	19	93	3.45	1.04	20.8	227	1.9	9.7	5.0	1.1	29%	71%	141
De Los Santos,Enyel	R	17	22	aa	SD	10	6	26	0	150	159	86	14	49	117	5.16	1.39	24.3	273	3.0	7.0	2.4	0.8	32%	63%	67
Deetz,Dean	R	17	24	a/a	HOU	7	6	25	0	85	80	43	8	47	84	4.56	1.50	14.6	251	5.0	8.9	1.8	0.8	32%	71%	70
Diaz,Jairo	R	14	23	aa	LAA	2	1	27	11	33	35	10	2	10	41	2.73	1.37	5.1	275	2.7	11.3	4.1	0.6	39%	82%	137
		15	24	aaa	COL	3	5	47	8	55	60	35	8	38	40	5.73	1.79	5.4	280	6.2	6.5	1.0	1.3	31%	70%	22
		17	26	aaa	COL	0	1	20	3	18	20	14	1	8	12	6.99	1.57	4.0	288	3.9	6.2	1.6	0.7	33%	53%	47
Ecker,Mark	R	17	22	aa	DET	0	0	15	3	18	17	5	2	8	15	2.44	1.41	5.1	253	4.1	7.5	1.9	1.1	30%	88%	55
Evans,Jacob	L	17	24	aa	STL	1	3	14	0	18	24	7	2	8	17	3.34	1.85	5.9	328	4.3	8.5	2.0	1.2	40%	86%	47
Farris,James	R	16	24	aa	CHC	1	3	26	5	36	31	13	2	10	32	3.31	1.16	5.5	236	2.6	8.0	3.1	0.6	30%	72%	104
		17	25	a/a	COL	1	3	48	11	58	67	34	13	19	52	5.34	1.49	5.2	291	3.0	8.0	2.7	2.1	32%	71%	38
Fedde,Erick	R	16	23	aa	WAS	2	1	5	0	29	40	17	1	11	23	5.30	1.73	26.7	325	3.3	7.1	2.2	0.3	39%	67%	68
		17	24	a/a	WAS	4	5	29	0	90	98	47	8	24	65	4.70	1.36	13.0	278	2.4	6.5	2.7	0.8	32%	66%	72
Fillmyer,Heath	R	16	22	aa	OAK	2	0	8	0	39	34	12	3	8	24	2.85	1.07	19.0	237	1.8	5.6	3.1	0.6	27%	76%	88
		17	23	aa	OAK	11	5	29	0	150	178	67	18	49	93	4.04	1.52	22.4	297	3.0	5.6	1.9	1.1	33%	77%	36
Flaherty,Jack	R	17	22	a/a	STL	14	4	25	0	149	138	44	13	35	122	2.66	1.16	23.7	247	2.1	7.4	3.5	0.8	30%	80%	100
Flexen,Chris	R	17	23	aa	NYM	6	1	7	0	49	36	13	6	9	45	2.46	0.91	25.9	206	1.6	8.3	5.2	1.1	25%	80%	142
Fried,Max	L	17	23	a/a	ATL	2	11	21	0	93	108	76	9	50	81	7.42	1.71	20.0	293	4.9	7.9	1.6	0.9	35%	55%	51
Fulmer,Carson	R	16	23	a/a	CHW	6	10	21	0	103	110	63	9	60	92	5.49	1.65	21.9	274	5.2	8.0	1.5	0.8	34%	67%	56
		17	24	aaa	CHW	7	9	25	0	126	153	97	21	70	83	6.90	1.77	23.1	301	5.0	5.9	1.2	1.5	33%	62%	11
Gallegos,Giovanny	R	16	25	a/a	NYY	7	2	42	4	78	63	18	8	20	88	2.11	1.07	7.2	224	2.3	10.1	4.4	0.9	30%	86%	137
		17	26	aaa	NYY	4	2	28	5	43	36	14	6	12	56	2.97	1.12	6.1	229	2.6	11.6	4.5	1.3	31%	81%	135
Garcia,Bryan	R	17	22	a/a	DET	2	1	31	8	32	20	10	2	17	30	2.89	1.15	4.1	182	4.7	8.5	1.8	0.7	23%	77%	88
Garcia,Elniery	L	17	23	aa	PHI	2	1	5	0	26	20	6	0	17	9	2.13	1.44	21.8	213	6.0	3.1	0.5	0.0	24%	84%	42
Gardewine,Nick	R	17	24	aa	TEX	1	2	33	6	37	44	13	3	14	43	3.14	1.57	4.9	300	3.3	10.5	3.1	0.6	41%	82%	105
German,Domingo	R	17	25	a/a	NYY	8	6	20	0	109	117	51	14	36	99	4.17	1.40	23.1	276	3.0	8.1	2.7	1.1	33%	74%	71
Gohara,Luiz	L	17	21	a/a	ATL	4	3	19	0	87	86	36	7	37	99	3.75	1.41	19.4	259	3.8	10.2	2.7	0.7	35%	74%	101
Gomber,Austin	L	16	23	aa	STL	1	0	4	0	19	13	4	0	9	13	1.69	1.14	19.1	189	4.3	6.2	1.4	0.0	24%	83%	85
		17	24	aa	STL	10	7	26	0	143	141	70	19	54	111	4.38	1.36	23.0	259	3.4	7.0	2.1	1.2	29%	71%	52
Gonsalves,Stephen	L	16	22	aa	MIN	8	1	13	0	74	49	18	1	36	74	2.19	1.14	22.7	190	4.3	8.9	2.1	0.1	26%	80%	110
		17	23	a/a	MIN	9	5	20	0	110	119	59	15	33	95	4.80	1.39	23.2	278	2.7	7.8	2.8	1.2	33%	68%	70
Greene,Conner	R	15	20	aa	TOR	3	1	5	0	25	28	16	1	12	14	5.78	1.61	22.2	287	4.3	5.0	1.2	0.4	32%	62%	39
		16	21	aa	TOR	6	5	12	0	69	66	40	6	34	43	5.31	1.45	24.5	255	4.4	5.7	1.3	0.8	28%	63%	40
		17	22	aa	TOR	5	10	26	0	133	166	101	9	86	80	6.84	1.90	24.1	308	5.8	5.4	0.9	0.6	35%	62%	28
Gregorio,Joan	R	15	23	aa	SF	3	2	37	1	79	77	35	6	35	62	4.02	1.41	9.0	257	4.0	7.0	1.8	0.7	31%	72%	63
		16	24	a/a	SF	6	10	26	0	134	150	87	13	52	129	5.85	1.50	22.3	284	3.5	8.6	2.5	0.9	35%	61%	75
		17	25	aaa	SF	4	4	13	0	74	75	31	8	37	50	3.72	1.51	24.6	263	4.5	6.1	1.4	1.0	29%	78%	37
Griffin,Foster	L	17	22	aa	KC	11	5	18	0	105	131	57	12	35	68	4.90	1.59	25.6	307	3.0	5.8	1.9	1.1	34%	71%	37
Guerrero,Jordan	L	16	22	aa	CHW	7	8	25	0	136	149	85	15	76	97	5.60	1.66	24.3	279	5.1	6.4	1.3	1.0	32%	67%	35
		17	23	aa	CHW	7	12	25	0	146	187	96	11	50	120	5.88	1.62	26.0	311	3.1	7.4	2.4	0.7	38%	62%	67
Guerrieri,Taylor	R	15	23	aa	TAM	3	1	8	0	36	31	7	2	8	24	1.69	1.09	17.6	235	2.0	6.0	3.1	0.5	27%	87%	94
		16	24	aa	TAM	12	6	28	1	146	152	74	12	47	77	4.55	1.36	21.8	269	2.9	4.7	1.6	0.7	29%	67%	42
Gustave,Jandel	R	15	23	aa	HOU	5	2	46	20	59	57	16	2	25	43	2.45	1.40	5.4	257	3.8	6.6	1.7	0.3	31%	83%	69
		16	24	aaa	HOU	3	3	47	3	57	51	26	1	22	47	4.17	1.29	5.0	241	3.5	7.4	2.1	0.2	31%	65%	90
Hall,Matt	L	17	24	aa	DET	1	0	6	0	35	36	15	2	22	31	3.92	1.66	26.1	266	5.7	8.1	1.4	0.6	33%	77%	62
Hamilton,Ian	R	17	22	aa	CHW	1	3	14	1	19	32	15	0	9	20	7.18	2.15	6.7	372	4.3	9.4	2.2	0.0	48%	63%	82
Harris,Greg	R	17	23	aa	TAM	3	8	29	0	97	109	66	16	44	82	6.09	1.57	14.7	284	4.1	7.6	1.9	1.5	32%	64%	37
Harris,Jon	R	17	24	aa	TOR	7	11	26	0	143	208	116	26	51	95	7.28	1.81	25.4	340	3.2	6.0	1.9	1.6	37%	61%	13

PITCHER	Th	Yr	Age	LvL	Org	W	L	G	Sv	IP	H	ER	HR	BB	K	ERA	WHIP	BF/G	OBA	bb/9	k/9	Cmd	hr/9	H%	S%	BPV
Heller,Ben	R	16	25	a/a	NYY	3	3	49	13	48	34	14	3	16	46	2.57	1.06	3.8	202	3.1	8.5	2.8	0.6	26%	78%	107
		17	26	aaa	NYY	5	4	41	6	56	44	26	9	24	66	4.11	1.20	5.5	217	3.8	10.6	2.8	1.5	27%	72%	90
Helsley,Ryan	R	17	23	a/a	STL	3	1	7	0	39	37	15	4	18	37	3.48	1.44	23.5	256	4.3	8.7	2.0	1.0	32%	79%	69
Heredia,Luis	R	17	23	aa	PIT	3	3	36	2	52	50	24	3	33	35	4.15	1.59	6.4	252	5.7	6.0	1.0	0.6	29%	74%	45
Herget,Jimmy	R	17	24	a/a	CIN	4	4	52	25	62	66	29	7	24	62	4.18	1.46	5.1	274	3.5	9.0	2.6	1.0	34%	74%	77
Hernandez,Ariel	R	17	25	a/a	CIN	3	2	39	1	50	42	26	1	46	49	4.76	1.74	5.9	228	8.2	8.8	1.1	0.3	30%	71%	77
Hess,David	R	16	23	aa	BAL	5	13	25	0	127	189	94	24	39	71	6.65	1.79	23.5	345	2.8	5.0	1.8	1.7	36%	66%	3
		17	24	aa	BAL	11	9	27	0	154	163	83	18	60	106	4.85	1.44	24.4	272	3.5	6.2	1.8	1.1	30%	68%	43
Holmes,Clay	R	16	23	aa	PIT	10	9	26	0	136	160	78	10	63	82	5.13	1.64	23.4	293	4.2	5.4	1.3	0.7	33%	68%	36
		17	24	aaa	PIT	10	5	25	0	113	118	57	5	64	79	4.54	1.62	20.0	271	5.1	6.3	1.2	0.4	32%	71%	53
Holmes,Grant	R	17	21	aa	OAK	11	12	29	0	148	163	83	14	57	126	5.05	1.49	22.0	281	3.5	7.6	2.2	0.8	34%	66%	65
Honeywell,Brent	R	16	21	aa	TAM	3	2	10	0	59	57	17	4	14	48	2.62	1.18	23.7	253	2.1	7.2	3.5	0.6	30%	80%	103
		17	22	a/a	TAM	13	9	26	0	137	156	67	13	36	154	4.40	1.41	22.2	288	2.4	10.2	4.2	0.9	38%	70%	121
Houser,Adrian	R	15	22	aa	MIL	5	3	14	0	70	88	48	15	23	48	6.14	1.57	22.1	306	3.0	6.2	2.1	1.9	33%	65%	18
		16	23	aa	MIL	3	7	13	0	70	96	59	7	25	47	7.59	1.72	24.5	326	3.2	6.1	1.9	0.9	37%	54%	41
Howard,Sam	L	16	23	aa	COL	5	6	16	0	90	148	62	17	32	52	6.20	1.99	27.1	367	3.2	5.1	1.6	1.7	39%	72%	-4
		17	24	a/a	COL	5	8	24	0	127	145	68	16	48	79	4.84	1.51	23.0	287	3.4	5.6	1.6	1.1	31%	70%	32
Hu,Chih-Wei	R	16	23	a/a	TAM	7	9	25	0	147	157	57	9	39	99	3.46	1.33	24.5	274	2.4	6.1	2.6	0.5	32%	74%	74
		17	24	aaa	TAM	4	1	31	2	62	73	29	11	13	49	4.17	1.40	8.4	295	1.9	7.2	3.7	1.6	33%	76%	70
Hudson,Dakota	R	17	23	a/a	STL	10	5	25	0	153	172	64	8	50	78	3.75	1.45	26.1	286	2.9	4.6	1.6	0.4	32%	74%	45
Irvin,Cole	L	17	23	aa	PHI	5	3	13	0	84	83	46	14	24	58	4.92	1.27	26.6	259	2.6	6.2	2.4	1.5	28%	66%	45
Jerez,Williams	L	15	23	aa	BOS	1	2	22	1	37	40	19	2	18	26	4.59	1.56	7.4	277	4.3	6.3	1.5	0.5	33%	70%	53
		16	24	aa	BOS	1	6	40	0	65	85	45	7	32	54	6.21	1.80	7.5	317	4.4	7.5	1.7	0.9	38%	65%	44
		17	25	a/a	BOS	2	2	38	4	63	76	33	8	26	45	4.76	1.62	7.4	299	3.7	6.4	1.7	1.1	34%	73%	37
Jewell,Jake	R	17	24	aa	LAA	7	8	24	0	125	170	93	17	44	70	6.73	1.72	23.6	326	3.2	5.0	1.6	1.2	35%	61%	16
Jimenez,Joe	R	16	21	a/a	DET	3	3	38	20	36	24	11	1	12	41	2.77	1.01	3.7	191	3.1	10.3	3.3	0.3	27%	72%	140
		17	22	aaa	DET	1	1	26	4	25	23	5	1	13	30	1.96	1.43	4.1	246	4.6	10.9	2.3	0.4	35%	88%	107
Johnson,Brian	L	14	24	aa	BOS	10	2	20	0	118	94	30	7	33	81	2.29	1.08	23.0	221	2.5	6.2	2.4	0.5	26%	81%	84
		15	25	aaa	BOS	9	6	18	0	96	96	40	8	37	72	3.71	1.38	22.4	262	3.4	6.8	2.0	0.7	31%	74%	64
		16	26	aaa	BOS	5	6	15	0	77	104	58	13	44	43	6.83	1.92	24.3	323	5.2	5.0	1.0	1.5	34%	66%	-3
		17	27	aaa	BOS	3	4	17	0	90	115	51	14	35	53	5.05	1.65	23.8	311	3.5	5.3	1.5	1.4	33%	73%	14
Johnson,Jordan	R	17	24	aa	SF	4	6	21	0	92	110	62	12	41	54	6.06	1.63	19.6	296	4.0	5.3	1.3	1.2	32%	64%	20
Jorge,Felix	R	16	22	aa	MIN	3	5	11	0	74	95	41	7	12	27	4.96	1.43	28.7	311	1.4	3.2	2.3	0.9	32%	66%	33
		17	23	a/a	MIN	10	4	25	0	149	205	89	18	43	87	5.40	1.66	26.7	327	2.6	5.2	2.0	1.1	36%	69%	30
Jurado,Ariel	R	16	20	aa	TEX	1	4	8	0	44	50	20	3	10	31	4.10	1.39	23.0	290	2.1	6.3	2.9	0.7	34%	71%	76
		17	21	aa	TEX	9	11	27	0	157	226	108	20	40	80	6.19	1.69	26.2	338	2.3	4.6	2.0	1.1	36%	64%	23
Keller,Brad	R	17	22	aa	ARI	10	9	26	0	131	171	91	9	59	96	6.27	1.76	23.0	316	4.1	6.6	1.6	0.6	37%	63%	47
Keller,Mitch	R	17	21	aa	PIT	2	2	6	0	35	29	16	2	11	38	4.05	1.18	23.1	232	3.0	9.8	3.3	0.6	31%	65%	119
Kilome,Franklyn	R	17	22	aa	PHI	1	3	5	0	30	28	14	2	15	18	4.33	1.46	25.4	253	4.5	5.4	1.2	0.7	28%	71%	41
Kingham,Nick	R	14	23	a/a	PIT	6	11	26	0	159	152	62	8	47	96	3.51	1.25	24.9	253	2.7	5.4	2.0	0.4	29%	72%	66
		15	24	aaa	PIT	1	2	6	0	31	40	19	3	7	25	5.43	1.51	22.6	314	2.0	7.3	3.7	0.8	37%	64%	88
		17	26	aaa	PIT	9	6	20	0	113	153	73	10	33	71	5.83	1.64	25.3	324	2.6	5.6	2.2	0.8	37%	64%	46
Kopech,Michael	R	17	21	a/a	CHW	9	8	25	0	134	106	53	7	70	156	3.57	1.31	22.2	218	4.7	10.5	2.2	0.5	31%	73%	107
Labourt,Jairo	L	17	23	a/a	DET	1	1	37	4	53	42	20	5	32	47	3.36	1.40	6.0	221	5.4	8.0	1.5	0.8	27%	78%	65
Lakins,Travis	R	17	23	aa	BOS	0	4	8	0	30	41	27	2	22	16	8.13	2.08	18.6	323	6.6	4.6	0.7	0.7	35%	59%	13
Lauer,Eric	L	17	22	aa	SD	4	3	10	0	55	63	33	7	18	41	5.36	1.46	23.6	289	2.9	6.6	2.3	1.2	33%	65%	51
Lee,Chris	L	15	23	aa	BAL	4	2	7	0	38	39	17	0	21	22	4.06	1.58	23.9	265	5.0	5.2	1.0	0.0	31%	71%	54
		16	24	aa	BAL	5	0	8	0	51	49	21	5	13	15	3.76	1.21	25.9	252	2.4	2.7	1.2	0.9	25%	71%	18
		17	25	aaa	BAL	5	6	27	0	116	182	91	14	64	70	7.08	2.11	21.3	356	5.0	5.4	1.1	1.1	39%	67%	7
Liranzo,Jesus	R	16	21	aa	BAL	1	1	11	0	19	9	8	4	12	17	4.05	1.12	6.7	147	5.7	8.2	1.5	1.8	13%	72%	53
		17	22	aa	BAL	3	4	31	2	65	62	42	13	46	67	5.86	1.66	9.4	252	6.4	9.3	1.5	1.8	29%	69%	36
Littell,Zack	R	17	22	aa	MIN	10	0	14	0	86	86	32	5	27	70	3.38	1.32	25.3	262	2.8	7.3	2.6	0.5	32%	75%	85
Long,Grayson	R	17	23	aa	DET	8	7	24	0	126	126	50	10	40	94	3.57	1.33	21.7	263	2.9	6.7	2.3	0.7	31%	75%	69
Lopez,Jose	R	17	24	aa	CIN	7	2	17	0	96	87	43	15	43	82	4.01	1.35	23.6	243	4.0	7.7	1.9	1.4	28%	76%	51
Lovelady,Richard	L	17	22	aa	KC	3	2	21	3	33	34	11	1	13	30	2.93	1.42	6.7	265	3.6	8.1	2.2	0.3	34%	79%	89
Lucchesi,Joey	L	17	24	aa	SD	5	3	10	1	60	58	17	4	15	43	2.54	1.21	24.3	255	2.2	6.4	2.9	0.5	30%	81%	86
Maddox,Austin	R	16	25	a/a	BOS	3	3	26	0	43	43	27	5	19	32	5.52	1.44	7.1	260	4.0	6.7	1.7	1.0	30%	62%	48
		17	26	a/a	BOS	2	3	37	8	49	41	24	3	30	35	4.34	1.45	5.7	227	5.5	6.5	1.2	0.5	27%	69%	59
Mader,Michael	L	16	22	aa	ATL	0	3	5	0	30	33	11	0	7	24	3.37	1.33	24.9	282	2.0	7.1	3.6	0.0	35%	72%	116
		17	23	aa	ATL	5	5	35	4	65	72	43	6	47	51	5.99	1.84	8.6	282	6.6	7.0	1.1	0.8	33%	67%	38
Mahle,Tyler	R	16	22	aa	CIN	6	3	14	0	71	98	56	18	23	60	7.00	1.69	23.0	327	2.9	7.5	2.6	2.3	36%	63%	22
		17	23	a/a	CIN	10	7	24	0	144	136	47	13	34	121	2.90	1.17	24.0	250	2.1	7.6	3.6	0.8	30%	78%	102
Maples,Dillon	R	17	25	a/a	CHC	2	3	31	10	32	28	11	1	24	46	3.16	1.60	4.6	234	6.7	13.0	2.0	0.3	38%	80%	118
Martinez,Rodolfo	R	16	22	aa	SF	0	3	25	3	23	34	22	1	16	15	8.67	2.19	4.6	347	6.2	5.9	0.9	0.4	40%	57%	29

PITCHER	Th	Yr	Age	LvL	Org	W	L	G	Sv	IP	H	ER	HR	BB	K	ERA	WHIP	BF/G	OBA	bb/9	k/9	Cmd	hr/9	H%	S%	BPV
Means,John	L	16	23	aa	BAL	4	8	18	0	96	132	62	9	25	42	5.80	1.64	23.8	328	2.4	4.0	1.7	0.8	35%	64%	24
		17	24	aa	BAL	9	9	26	0	142	188	82	18	40	107	5.17	1.60	24.2	319	2.6	6.8	2.6	1.2	37%	70%	52
Meisner,Casey	R	17	22	aa	OAK	4	4	12	0	59	61	31	4	26	31	4.68	1.47	21.1	268	3.9	4.7	1.2	0.6	30%	67%	37
Mella,Keury	R	17	24	aa	CIN	4	10	27	1	134	184	106	23	53	94	7.09	1.77	22.8	327	3.5	6.3	1.8	1.6	36%	61%	18
Mendez,Yohander	L	16	21	a/a	TEX	8	2	17	0	78	58	22	2	31	58	2.55	1.15	18.2	210	3.6	6.7	1.9	0.3	26%	77%	85
		17	22	aa	TEX	7	8	24	0	138	138	79	29	47	104	5.17	1.34	23.9	263	3.0	6.8	2.2	1.9	28%	68%	33
Merritt,Ryan	L	15	23	a/a	CLE	12	7	27	0	171	220	91	11	22	91	4.77	1.42	26.8	313	1.2	4.8	4.0	0.6	35%	66%	89
		16	24	aaa	CLE	11	8	24	0	143	193	80	19	24	74	5.05	1.52	25.9	323	1.5	4.6	3.0	1.2	35%	69%	46
		17	25	aaa	CLE	10	5	19	0	116	147	55	25	29	62	4.23	1.51	26.5	310	2.2	4.8	2.2	1.9	31%	80%	9
Merryweather,Julian	R	16	25	aa	CLE	5	4	13	0	74	94	44	8	18	48	5.33	1.52	24.7	311	2.2	5.8	2.6	0.9	35%	65%	55
		17	26	a/a	CLE	7	9	25	0	129	183	108	21	41	92	7.52	1.74	23.5	335	2.8	6.4	2.3	1.5	37%	57%	29
Miller,Jared	L	16	23	a/a	ARI	0	1	24	2	33	27	18	3	15	33	5.01	1.27	5.6	224	4.1	9.1	2.2	0.9	28%	61%	83
		17	24	a/a	ARI	3	6	53	3	71	57	28	5	28	78	3.53	1.21	5.4	222	3.6	9.9	2.8	0.6	30%	71%	111
Mills,Alec	R	16	25	a/a	KC	5	5	24	0	126	144	58	11	32	96	4.13	1.41	22.1	289	2.3	6.9	3.0	0.8	34%	72%	78
Minter,AJ	L	16	23	aa	ATL	1	0	18	0	19	16	7	0	7	28	3.46	1.24	4.2	237	3.2	13.3	4.1	0.0	39%	69%	173
		17	24	a/a	ATL	1	2	20	0	18	20	11	1	14	17	5.37	1.83	4.3	277	6.7	8.5	1.3	0.6	35%	70%	61
Molina,Marcos	R	17	22	aa	NYM	3	7	13	0	78	96	49	7	25	58	5.68	1.56	26.3	304	2.9	6.7	2.3	0.8	35%	63%	58
Moreno,Gerson	R	17	22	aa	DET	0	3	20	0	28	26	24	4	17	30	7.84	1.56	6.1	250	5.5	9.7	1.7	1.4	31%	49%	57
Morimando,Shawn	L	14	22	aa	CLE	2	6	10	0	56	69	27	2	16	33	4.24	1.50	24.4	302	2.5	5.3	2.1	0.3	35%	70%	61
		15	23	aa	CLE	10	12	28	0	159	168	75	11	67	111	4.23	1.48	24.4	273	3.8	6.3	1.7	0.6	32%	72%	54
		16	24	a/a	CLE	15	5	27	0	152	174	74	13	60	96	4.40	1.54	24.6	288	3.6	5.7	1.6	0.7	33%	72%	42
		17	25	aaa	CLE	10	9	26	0	159	224	109	29	65	94	6.16	1.82	28.4	333	3.7	5.3	1.4	1.6	35%	69%	1
Moronta,Reyes	R	17	24	a/a	SF	3	1	32	5	35	33	15	2	21	36	3.92	1.57	4.8	253	5.5	9.3	1.7	0.5	33%	75%	81
Morris,Akeel	R	15	23	aa	NYM	0	1	23	0	29	19	9	1	15	31	2.89	1.17	5.1	190	4.6	9.4	2.0	0.3	26%	75%	106
		16	24	aa	ATL	5	3	47	6	61	59	32	5	42	75	4.75	1.66	5.8	255	6.3	11.0	1.8	0.7	36%	72%	85
		17	25	a/a	ATL	1	3	36	5	54	51	22	4	29	53	3.70	1.47	6.5	248	4.8	8.8	1.8	0.6	32%	75%	78
Moya,Gabriel	L	17	22	aa	MIN	6	1	47	24	58	37	7	3	16	71	1.08	0.90	4.6	183	2.4	11.0	4.6	0.4	27%	91%	169
Neidert,Nick	R	17	21	aa	SEA	1	3	6	0	23	37	20	4	5	12	7.70	1.79	17.9	360	1.9	4.5	2.4	1.7	38%	58%	11
Nix,Jacob	R	17	21	aa	SD	1	2	6	0	28	38	23	0	9	19	7.47	1.72	20.9	330	3.0	6.1	2.0	0.0	39%	52%	69
Oaks,Trevor	R	16	23	a/a	LA	13	2	20	0	126	139	44	9	17	74	3.16	1.24	25.6	282	1.2	5.3	4.4	0.7	32%	76%	102
		17	24	aaa	LA	4	3	15	0	84	99	39	5	16	61	4.16	1.37	23.5	294	1.8	6.5	3.7	0.6	35%	69%	96
Ortiz,Luis	R	16	21	aa	MIL	3	6	15	1	63	89	32	6	19	44	4.61	1.71	19.0	335	2.7	6.2	2.3	0.9	38%	75%	47
		17	22	aa	MIL	4	7	22	0	94	100	63	19	41	70	6.01	1.50	18.5	274	3.9	6.6	1.7	1.8	29%	64%	21
Oswalt,Corey	R	17	24	aa	NYM	12	5	24	0	134	154	51	13	50	105	3.43	1.52	24.3	288	3.4	7.0	2.1	0.9	34%	80%	57
Pannone,Thomas	L	17	23	aa	TOR	7	3	20	0	117	118	50	18	31	94	3.85	1.27	23.9	263	2.4	7.2	3.1	1.4	30%	75%	70
Paredes,Eduardo	R	16	21	aa	LAA	0	3	35	8	48	54	23	7	14	39	4.36	1.42	5.9	284	2.7	7.2	2.7	1.2	33%	73%	61
		17	22	a/a	LAA	1	0	34	3	50	42	16	3	20	49	2.83	1.24	5.9	229	3.6	9.0	2.5	0.5	30%	78%	99
Paulino,David	R	16	22	a/a	HOU	5	4	17	1	78	68	21	4	16	82	2.40	1.09	17.9	237	1.9	9.4	5.1	0.5	32%	79%	155
Payano,Pedro	R	17	23	aa	TEX	4	5	17	0	84	94	47	5	46	63	5.05	1.67	22.3	283	5.0	6.7	1.4	0.5	34%	69%	51
Peralta,Freddy	R	17	21	aa	MIL	2	5	13	1	64	48	24	3	34	81	3.36	1.29	20.1	210	4.8	11.4	2.4	0.4	31%	74%	118
Perez,Franklin	R	17	20	aa	HOU	2	1	7	1	32	37	13	2	10	23	3.62	1.47	19.6	288	2.9	6.6	2.2	0.6	34%	76%	66
Peters,Dillon	L	16	24	aa	MIA	3	0	4	0	23	21	7	2	4	13	2.70	1.12	22.3	247	1.7	5.2	3.0	0.8	27%	80%	74
		17	25	aa	MIA	6	2	9	0	46	42	14	1	12	33	2.77	1.19	20.3	245	2.4	6.6	2.7	0.2	30%	76%	95
Peterson,David	R	15	25	a/a	ATL	4	0	23	5	29	32	8	2	9	14	2.50	1.41	5.3	283	2.7	4.5	1.7	0.7	31%	85%	38
		16	26	a/a	ATL	2	5	42	10	52	85	47	4	28	36	8.06	2.16	6.2	367	4.8	6.2	1.3	0.6	42%	61%	27
		17	27	aaa	ATL	2	4	50	7	68	96	42	5	18	43	5.65	1.68	6.1	335	2.3	5.8	2.4	0.6	38%	65%	56
Pfeifer,Phillip	L	17	25	a/a	ATL	1	5	41	4	59	60	32	2	49	66	4.87	1.83	6.7	262	7.4	10.0	1.3	0.4	36%	72%	80
Phillips,Evan	R	16	22	aa	ATL	6	3	22	2	34	41	24	2	18	39	6.26	1.70	7.0	296	4.6	10.2	2.2	0.6	40%	62%	85
		17	23	a/a	ATL	3	4	40	3	51	63	47	7	38	47	8.22	1.97	6.1	304	6.7	8.3	1.2	1.2	37%	57%	34
Pike,Tyler	L	14	20	aa	SEA	3	4	13	0	49	60	43	5	30	30	7.83	1.85	17.6	304	5.6	5.6	1.0	0.8	34%	56%	23
		17	23	aa	ATL	0	9	15	0	75	78	54	4	73	76	6.57	2.02	24.1	270	8.8	9.2	1.1	0.4	36%	65%	65
Plutko,Adam	R	15	24	aa	CLE	9	5	19	0	116	119	50	11	24	76	3.89	1.23	24.8	265	1.9	5.9	3.2	0.9	30%	70%	78
		16	25	a/a	CLE	9	8	28	0	162	190	93	17	50	102	5.15	1.48	24.8	294	2.8	5.7	2.1	0.9	33%	66%	46
		17	26	aaa	CLE	7	12	24	0	136	198	127	32	62	74	8.43	1.92	26.8	341	4.1	4.9	1.2	2.2	35%	58%	-23
Ponce,Cody	R	17	23	aa	MIL	2	1	3	0	18	13	5	0	6	8	2.34	1.06	22.8	207	2.9	4.0	1.4	0.0	24%	75%	66
Povse,Max	R	16	23	aa	ATL	4	1	11	0	71	77	33	5	13	43	4.20	1.27	26.3	278	1.7	5.4	3.2	0.6	31%	67%	80
		17	24	a/a	SEA	4	6	22	0	71	87	49	4	26	53	6.27	1.60	14.2	304	3.3	6.7	2.0	0.6	36%	59%	59
Puk,A.J.	L	17	22	aa	OAK	2	5	13	0	64	71	35	2	24	71	4.95	1.48	21.2	282	3.3	10.0	3.0	0.3	39%	64%	114
Quantrill,Cal	R	17	22	aa	SD	1	5	8	0	42	63	26	6	16	29	5.51	1.88	24.9	346	3.5	6.1	1.7	1.3	39%	73%	22
Rainey,Tanner	R	17	25	aa	CIN	1	1	14	4	17	11	5	3	14	23	2.68	1.47	5.2	188	7.3	12.1	1.7	1.8	24%	92%	71
Ramirez,Carlos	R	17	26	a/a	TOR	3	0	25	3	38	21	0	0	12	36	0.00	0.87	5.6	166	2.8	8.6	3.1	0.0	23%	100%	139
Ramirez,Nick	L	17	28	a/a	MIL	7	4	49	3	79	73	17	6	27	43	1.88	1.26	6.6	246	3.1	4.9	1.6	0.7	27%	89%	49
Ravenelle,Adam	R	16	24	aa	DET	1	1	27	1	30	35	20	4	17	18	6.00	1.76	5.0	297	5.2	5.5	1.1	1.3	32%	68%	11
		17	25	aa	DET	0	5	42	1	52	72	39	9	23	39	6.69	1.81	5.8	328	3.9	6.6	1.7	1.6	36%	65%	16

PITCHER	Th	Yr	Age	LvL	Org	W	L	G	Sv	IP	H	ER	HR	BB	K	ERA	WHIP	BF/G	OBA	bb/9	k/9	Cmd	hr/9	H%	S%	BPV
Reed,Cody	L	15	22	aa	CIN	8	4	13	0	78	76	29	6	25	72	3.32	1.28	24.7	255	2.9	8.2	2.9	0.6	32%	75%	95
		16	23	aaa	CIN	6	4	13	0	73	88	35	8	22	58	4.27	1.51	24.3	299	2.7	7.2	2.6	1.0	35%	74%	62
		17	24	aaa	CIN	4	9	21	0	106	126	54	9	66	88	4.54	1.80	23.4	295	5.6	7.4	1.3	0.8	36%	76%	46
Reed,Jake	R	15	23	aa	MIN	4	4	35	1	47	62	38	3	20	32	7.19	1.74	6.1	317	3.9	6.1	1.6	0.6	37%	56%	44
		16	24	a/a	MIN	4	4	50	3	71	72	37	2	25	57	4.74	1.37	5.9	266	3.2	7.2	2.3	0.3	33%	63%	84
		17	25	a/a	MIN	2	0	27	6	38	37	14	1	19	25	3.26	1.48	6.1	257	4.5	6.0	1.3	0.3	30%	77%	58
Reid-Foley,Sean	R	17	22	aa	TOR	10	11	27	0	133	171	96	27	55	106	6.49	1.70	22.2	314	3.7	7.2	1.9	1.8	35%	66%	21
Reyes,Alex	R	16	22	aaa	STL	2	3	14	0	65	68	39	6	31	84	5.33	1.51	20.2	269	4.2	11.6	2.7	0.8	38%	64%	105
Rhame,Jacob	R	15	22	aa	LA	3	3	39	2	50	39	21	6	18	50	3.74	1.14	5.1	217	3.3	9.0	2.8	1.1	27%	71%	92
		16	23	aaa	LA	1	7	54	7	63	60	27	6	25	60	3.81	1.35	4.9	252	3.6	8.5	2.4	0.8	32%	74%	82
		17	24	aaa	NYM	0	3	45	2	54	59	25	6	10	58	4.23	1.28	4.9	279	1.7	9.7	5.5	1.0	36%	70%	143
Richards,Trevor	R	17	24	aa	MIA	5	7	14	0	75	83	33	5	20	66	3.94	1.37	22.5	282	2.4	7.9	3.3	0.6	35%	71%	99
Rios,Francisco	R	17	22	aa	TOR	3	9	23	0	86	106	53	12	40	55	5.54	1.70	16.9	305	4.2	5.8	1.4	1.3	33%	70%	19
Romero,Fernando	R	17	23	aa	MIN	11	9	24	0	125	155	70	5	48	96	5.03	1.63	23.2	306	3.4	6.9	2.0	0.4	37%	67%	67
Sadzeck,Connor	R	15	24	aa	TEX	1	1	7	0	20	26	25	1	17	13	11.55	2.19	14.1	316	8.0	6.0	0.8	0.5	37%	42%	29
		16	25	aa	TEX	10	8	25	0	141	159	89	22	59	106	5.67	1.55	24.6	286	3.8	6.8	1.8	1.4	32%	66%	34
		17	26	aa	TEX	4	8	38	0	94	137	96	18	46	86	9.26	1.95	11.8	342	4.4	8.2	1.9	1.7	40%	52%	24
Santana,Dennis	R	17	21	aa	LA	3	1	7	0	33	35	23	2	20	33	6.25	1.70	21.1	277	5.6	9.1	1.6	0.6	36%	62%	70
Sborz,Josh	R	16	23	aa	LA	0	1	10	1	17	20	9	2	6	15	4.93	1.57	7.3	302	3.1	7.8	2.5	1.3	36%	72%	54
		17	24	aa	LA	8	8	24	0	117	123	60	9	52	68	4.61	1.50	21.0	272	4.0	5.3	1.3	0.7	30%	69%	39
Schultz,Jaime	R	15	24	aa	TAM	9	5	27	0	135	119	63	11	91	142	4.22	1.56	21.9	239	6.0	9.5	1.6	0.7	31%	74%	76
		16	25	aaa	TAM	5	7	27	0	131	140	69	14	74	136	4.77	1.63	21.5	275	5.1	9.4	1.9	1.0	35%	72%	66
Scott,Tanner	L	16	22	aa	BAL	1	2	14	0	16	21	12	0	15	15	6.82	2.22	5.8	313	8.4	8.6	1.0	0.0	41%	66%	65
		17	23	aa	BAL	0	2	24	0	69	52	21	2	51	77	2.73	1.49	12.4	212	6.6	10.0	1.5	0.3	30%	81%	95
Sheffield,Justus	L	17	21	aa	NYY	7	6	17	0	93	115	46	21	35	73	4.43	1.61	24.3	303	3.4	7.0	2.1	2.0	33%	81%	20
Shepherd,Chandler	R	16	24	a/a	BOS	2	3	40	7	64	54	29	7	20	51	4.07	1.15	6.4	229	2.8	7.2	2.6	1.0	26%	67%	76
		17	25	aaa	BOS	1	5	34	2	60	79	42	7	21	54	6.38	1.68	7.9	320	3.2	8.1	2.5	1.0	39%	62%	61
Sherfy,Jimmie	R	14	23	aa	ARI	3	1	37	1	38	40	26	5	18	38	6.16	1.52	4.5	270	4.3	8.9	2.1	1.1	34%	60%	65
		15	24	aa	ARI	1	6	44	2	50	61	48	4	29	41	8.75	1.83	5.2	305	5.3	7.5	1.4	0.7	37%	49%	47
		16	25	a/a	ARI	3	4	40	22	43	31	21	7	19	47	4.50	1.16	4.3	205	3.9	9.9	2.5	1.5	25%	66%	82
		17	26	aaa	ARI	2	1	44	20	49	42	19	6	10	48	3.45	1.06	4.3	234	1.8	8.9	4.9	1.2	29%	73%	130
Skoglund,Eric	L	16	24	aa	KC	7	10	27	0	156	167	82	22	40	108	4.70	1.33	24.0	275	2.3	6.2	2.7	1.3	30%	68%	56
		17	25	a/a	KC	4	5	20	0	104	144	64	16	34	81	5.57	1.72	23.6	330	3.0	7.0	2.4	1.4	38%	70%	40
Smith,Caleb	L	15	24	a/a	NYY	10	7	26	0	135	152	71	11	62	81	4.71	1.58	22.9	285	4.1	5.4	1.3	0.7	32%	71%	36
		16	25	aa	NYY	3	5	27	3	64	88	43	6	24	58	6.13	1.75	10.8	329	3.3	8.2	2.5	0.9	40%	65%	63
		17	26	a/a	NYY	9	1	19	0	101	100	40	13	36	83	3.57	1.35	22.1	261	3.2	7.4	2.3	1.1	30%	78%	62
Smith,Nate	L	14	23	aa	LAA	5	3	11	0	62	56	25	3	30	57	3.57	1.38	23.8	242	4.3	8.3	1.9	0.5	31%	74%	83
		15	24	a/a	LAA	10	8	24	0	138	144	64	15	40	88	4.21	1.33	23.8	270	2.6	5.7	2.2	1.0	30%	71%	52
		16	25	aaa	LAA	8	9	26	0	150	181	80	16	42	102	4.80	1.48	24.9	300	2.5	6.1	2.4	1.0	34%	69%	54
Soroka,Mike	R	17	20	aa	ATL	11	8	26	0	154	159	64	11	37	117	3.75	1.28	24.2	268	2.2	6.8	3.1	0.7	32%	72%	88
Stanek,Ryne	R	15	24	aa	TAM	4	3	16	1	62	59	32	7	31	35	4.71	1.46	16.5	254	4.5	5.1	1.1	1.0	27%	70%	28
		16	25	a/a	TAM	4	10	34	3	103	104	63	10	51	94	5.51	1.51	13.1	265	4.5	8.3	1.9	0.9	33%	64%	64
		17	26	aaa	TAM	3	0	37	8	45	34	9	0	18	50	1.72	1.16	4.8	210	3.7	10.0	2.7	0.0	31%	84%	129
Staumont,Josh	R	16	23	aa	KC	2	1	11	0	50	51	23	2	38	60	4.05	1.77	21.0	264	6.9	10.7	1.6	0.4	37%	77%	87
		17	24	a/a	KC	6	12	26	0	125	130	103	18	102	111	7.45	1.86	22.5	270	7.4	8.0	1.1	1.3	32%	60%	34
Stephens,Jordan	R	17	25	aa	CHW	3	7	16	0	92	109	47	6	43	70	4.60	1.65	25.6	296	4.2	6.9	1.6	0.6	35%	72%	55
Stewart,Kohl	R	16	22	aa	MIN	9	6	16	0	92	104	37	4	43	39	3.66	1.59	25.4	286	4.2	3.8	0.9	0.4	31%	77%	28
		17	23	a/a	MIN	6	6	17	0	82	100	57	7	50	46	6.28	1.83	22.4	303	5.4	5.0	0.9	0.7	34%	65%	22
Suarez,Andrew	L	16	24	aa	SF	7	7	19	0	114	159	68	11	26	76	5.36	1.63	26.7	331	2.1	6.0	2.9	0.9	38%	68%	58
		17	25	a/a	SF	10	10	26	0	156	203	74	10	46	111	4.28	1.59	26.4	316	2.6	6.4	2.4	0.6	37%	73%	64
Tate,Dillon	R	17	23	aa	NYY	1	2	4	0	25	29	13	5	10	15	4.65	1.55	27.3	291	3.6	5.3	1.5	1.7	30%	76%	10
Taveras,Jose	R	17	24	a/a	PHI	3	2	9	0	52	43	14	9	17	41	2.40	1.14	23.0	225	2.9	7.1	2.5	1.5	24%	90%	60
Taylor,Ben	R	16	25	aa	BOS	1	0	21	5	34	35	18	5	13	34	4.64	1.41	6.8	266	3.5	9.0	2.6	1.2	33%	70%	75
Taylor,Corey	R	17	24	aa	NYM	5	5	42	3	62	90	38	4	18	41	5.44	1.72	6.7	338	2.5	6.0	2.4	0.6	39%	68%	54
Taylor,Cory	R	17	24	aa	SF	4	11	25	0	128	154	82	9	64	84	5.81	1.71	23.1	300	4.5	5.9	1.3	0.6	34%	65%	39
Thompson,Jake	R	14	20	aa	TEX	4	1	9	0	47	43	19	4	22	44	3.74	1.39	21.8	245	4.3	8.6	2.0	0.7	31%	74%	79
		15	21	aa	PHI	11	7	24	0	133	137	60	11	41	102	4.09	1.34	23.0	269	2.8	6.9	2.5	0.8	32%	71%	73
		16	22	aaa	PHI	11	5	21	0	130	131	52	15	41	78	3.61	1.33	25.6	264	2.8	5.4	1.9	1.0	29%	76%	44
		17	23	aaa	PHI	5	14	22	0	118	161	88	15	49	79	6.67	1.77	24.7	325	3.7	6.0	1.6	1.1	36%	63%	26
Torrez,Daury	R	17	24	aa	CHC	6	4	43	1	77	71	16	7	14	47	1.88	1.11	7.1	246	1.7	5.5	3.3	0.9	27%	89%	82
Toussaint,Touki	R	17	21	aa	ATL	3	4	7	0	40	37	19	4	25	40	4.42	1.54	24.7	246	5.6	9.1	1.6	0.8	32%	72%	71
Tseng,Jen-Ho	R	16	22	aa	CHC	6	8	22	0	113	154	62	13	32	61	4.96	1.64	23.0	325	2.5	4.8	1.9	1.1	35%	72%	27
		17	23	a/a	CHC	13	4	24	0	145	146	49	13	39	105	3.04	1.27	24.8	262	2.4	6.5	2.7	0.8	30%	79%	74
Turnbull,Spencer	R	17	25	aa	DET	0	3	4	0	20	27	18	1	9	17	8.04	1.74	23.2	319	3.8	7.7	2.0	0.5	39%	50%	64

PITCHER	Th	Yr	Age	LvL	Org	W	L	G	Sv	IP	H	ER	HR	BB	K	ERA	WHIP	BF/G	OBA	bb/9	k/9	Cmd	hr/9	H%	S%	BPV
Unsworth,Dylan	R	15	23	aa	SEA	4	7	13	0	66	89	38	6	13	44	5.09	1.52	22.2	321	1.7	6.0	3.5	0.9	37%	67%	76
		16	24	aa	SEA	3	1	9	0	47	51	8	2	7	30	1.54	1.25	21.1	280	1.4	5.8	4.2	0.5	33%	90%	108
		17	25	a/a	SEA	9	9	22	0	128	145	58	10	23	76	4.04	1.30	24.1	286	1.6	5.3	3.4	0.7	32%	70%	79
Valdez,Framber	L	17	24	aa	HOU	5	5	12	0	49	71	40	5	23	46	7.38	1.93	19.4	340	4.3	8.5	2.0	0.8	42%	61%	54
Vieira,Thyago	R	17	24	a/a	SEA	2	4	41	4	54	56	29	2	22	40	4.80	1.44	5.6	268	3.7	6.6	1.8	0.4	32%	65%	67
Voth,Austin	R	15	23	aa	WAS	6	7	28	0	157	158	65	11	41	122	3.70	1.27	23.0	263	2.3	7.0	3.0	0.6	31%	71%	88
		16	24	aaa	WAS	7	9	27	0	157	176	79	13	65	108	4.55	1.53	25.3	284	3.7	6.2	1.7	0.8	33%	71%	48
		17	25	a/a	WAS	4	11	23	0	121	181	101	23	51	70	7.57	1.92	24.9	347	3.8	5.2	1.4	1.7	37%	62%	-5
Waddell,Brandon	L	16	22	aa	PIT	7	9	22	0	118	138	64	9	59	78	4.90	1.67	24.1	294	4.5	5.9	1.3	0.7	34%	71%	39
		17	23	aa	PIT	3	3	15	0	66	73	35	3	29	46	4.75	1.54	19.2	281	4.0	6.2	1.6	0.5	33%	68%	55
Wahl,Bobby	R	15	23	aa	OAK	2	0	24	4	32	39	16	2	14	30	4.37	1.61	6.0	298	3.8	8.3	2.2	0.5	38%	72%	77
		16	24	a/a	OAK	1	1	42	14	50	39	16	3	24	50	2.93	1.26	4.9	217	4.3	8.9	2.1	0.6	28%	78%	92
Weigel,Patrick	R	16	22	aa	ATL	1	2	3	0	21	11	7	2	9	15	3.06	0.96	26.1	160	3.8	6.7	1.8	1.1	17%	74%	68
		17	23	a/a	ATL	6	2	15	0	78	90	48	8	31	60	5.54	1.55	22.8	289	3.6	6.9	1.9	0.9	34%	64%	52
Whalen,Rob	R	16	22	a/a	ATL	7	6	21	0	120	117	42	5	46	102	3.12	1.36	23.9	257	3.5	7.6	2.2	0.3	32%	77%	85
		17	23	aaa	SEA	0	7	10	0	53	68	45	10	19	38	7.52	1.65	23.8	313	3.3	6.4	1.9	1.6	34%	55%	23
White,Mitchell	R	17	23	aa	LA	1	1	7	0	28	19	9	2	12	27	3.01	1.11	15.7	196	3.8	8.6	2.3	0.7	25%	75%	93
Wood,Hunter	R	16	23	aa	TAM	6	2	10	0	49	41	21	5	20	43	3.89	1.24	20.0	228	3.6	7.8	2.1	1.0	27%	71%	72
		17	24	a/a	TAM	7	5	31	0	123	148	83	17	48	99	6.04	1.59	17.5	299	3.5	7.2	2.1	1.3	34%	63%	44
Woodruff,Brandon	R	16	23	aa	MIL	10	8	20	0	114	111	55	5	34	105	4.35	1.27	23.3	257	2.7	8.3	3.1	0.4	33%	64%	106
		17	24	aaa	MIL	6	5	16	0	75	85	38	9	24	59	4.57	1.45	20.1	286	2.9	7.1	2.5	1.1	33%	71%	60
Yacabonis,Jimmy	R	16	24	aa	BAL	2	2	34	6	44	41	13	3	14	37	2.56	1.24	5.3	245	2.9	7.6	2.6	0.5	30%	81%	90
		17	25	aaa	BAL	4	0	41	11	61	38	12	0	33	41	1.83	1.16	6.0	179	4.9	5.9	1.2	0.0	22%	82%	80
Yarbrough,Ryan	L	16	25	aa	SEA	12	4	25	0	128	138	57	8	33	84	3.99	1.33	21.3	277	2.3	5.9	2.5	0.6	32%	70%	71
		17	26	aaa	TAM	13	6	26	0	157	186	85	25	45	131	4.87	1.47	25.9	295	2.6	7.5	2.9	1.4	34%	71%	60
Young,Alex	L	17	24	aa	ARI	9	9	27	0	137	156	78	16	63	85	5.13	1.60	22.4	288	4.1	5.6	1.4	1.0	32%	69%	28
Zastryzny,Rob	L	15	23	aa	CHC	2	5	14	0	61	88	50	10	29	41	7.38	1.92	20.6	339	4.3	6.1	1.4	1.4	38%	63%	11
		16	24	a/a	CHC	10	5	24	0	136	135	77	15	52	101	5.10	1.38	23.7	261	3.5	6.7	1.9	1.0	30%	64%	54
		17	25	aaa	CHC	2	3	14	1	47	57	35	7	14	33	6.78	1.53	14.6	302	2.8	6.3	2.3	1.4	33%	56%	39
Zimmer,Kyle	R	15	24	aa	KC	2	5	15	3	48	49	18	4	14	41	3.46	1.33	13.3	267	2.7	7.6	2.8	0.8	32%	76%	83
		17	26	a/a	KC	0	0	21	3	37	53	31	5	18	31	7.55	1.91	8.3	337	4.3	7.6	1.8	1.1	40%	60%	36

Organization Ratings/Rankings

Each organization is graded on a standard A-F scale in four separate categories, and then after weighing the categories and adding some subjectivity, a final grade and ranking are determined. The four categories are the following:

Hitting: The quality and quantity of hitting prospects, the balance between athleticism, power, speed, and defense, and the quality of player development.

Pitching: The quality and quantity of pitching prospects and the quality of player development.

Top-End Talent: The quality of the top players within the organization. Successful teams are ones that have the most star-quality players. These are the players who are a teams' above average regulars, front-end starters, and closers.

Depth: The depth of both hitting and pitching prospects within the organization.

Overall Grade: The four categories are weighted, with top-end talent being the most important and depth being the least.

TEAM	Hitting	Pitching	Top-End Talent	Depth	Overall
Atlanta Braves	B+	A+	A+	B+	A
San Diego Padres	A-	A	A	A	A-
Chicago White Sox	A-	B+	A	B-	A-
New York Yankees	B+	A-	A-	A-	A-
Tampa Bay Rays	A-	B	A-	A-	A-
Los Angeles Dodgers	B	B+	A-	A-	B+
Milwaukee Brewers	A	B-	B+	A-	B+
Philadelphia Phillies	B	A-	B+	A	B+
Toronto Blue Jays	A-	B	B+	B+	B+
Cincinnati Reds	B+	B	B+	B	B
Oakland Athletics	B	B	B+	B	B
Minnesota Twins	B+	B-	B	B+	B
St. Louis Cardinals	B+	B-	B	B	B
Texas Rangers	B	C	B	B+	B
Pittsburgh Pirates	B	B	B-	B-	B-
Detroit Tigers	C	B	B-	B	B-
Houston Astros	B-	C+	B+	C+	B-
Colorado Rockies	A-	C+	C+	C+	B-
Washington Nationals	B+	C-	A-	D	C+
Arizona Diamondbacks	C	B-	C+	B-	C+
Baltimore Orioles	C	C+	C	C-	C
Miami Marlins	C	C+	C-	C-	C-
Chicago Cubs	D	B	C-	C-	C-
Los Angeles Angels	C-	D	C+	D+	C-
San Francisco Giants	C-	C-	D	C-	C-
Cleveland Indians	C+	D-	C-	D	D+
Boston Red Sox	D	C-	D	C-	D+
Kansas City Royals	C-	D	D	C-	D+
New York Mets	D+	C-	D-	C	D+
Seattle Mariners	D-	D-	D	D-	D-

This section of the book may be the smallest as far as word count is concerned, but may be the most important, as this is where players' skills and potential are tied together and ranked against their peers. The rankings that follow are divided into long-term potential in the major leagues and shorter-term fantasy value.

ORGANIZATIONAL: Lists the top 15 minor league prospects within each organization in terms of long-range potential in the major leagues.

POSITIONAL: Lists the top 15 prospects, by position, in terms of long-range potential in the major leagues.

TOP POWER: Lists the top 25 prospects that have the potential to hit for power in the major leagues, combining raw power, plate discipline, and at the ability to make their power game-usable.

TOP BA: Lists the top 25 prospects that have the potential to hit for high batting average in the major leagues, combining contact ability, plate discipline, hitting mechanics and strength.

TOP SPEED: Lists the top 25 prospects that have the potential to steal bases in the major leagues, combining raw speed and base-running instincts.

TOP FASTBALL: Lists the top 25 pitchers that have the best fastball, combining velocity and pitch movement.

TOP BREAKING BALL: Lists the top 25 pitchers that have the best breaking ball, combining pitch movement, strikeout potential, and consistency.

2017 TOP FANTASY PROSPECTS: Lists the top 40 minor league prospects likely to have the most value to their respective fantasy teams in 2017, then 35 more players to consider who could get the call and have the skills to produce. Remember that this section addresses 2018 value, not long-term value.

TOP 100 ARCHIVE: Takes a look back at the top 100 lists from the past eight years.

The rankings in this book are the creation of the minor league department at BaseballHQ.com. While several baseball personnel contributed player information to the book, no opinions were solicited or received in comparing players.

Top Prospects by Organization

AL EAST

BALTIMORE ORIOLES

1. Austin Hays, OF
2. Ryan Mountcastle, 3B/SS
3. Chance Sisco, C
4. D.L. Hall, LHP
5. Hunter Harvey, RHP
6. Tanner Scott, LHP
7. D.J. Stewart, OF
8. Cody Sedlock, RHP
9. Keegan Akin, LHP
10. Anthony Santander, OF
11. Cedric Mullins, OF
12. Jomar Reyes, 3B
13. Cameron Bishop, LHP
14. Michael Baumann, RHP
15. Adam Hall, SS

BOSTON RED SOX

1. Jason Groome, LHP
2. Tanner Houck, RHP
3. Sam Travis, 1B
4. Michael Chavis, 3B
5. Alex Scherff, RHP
6. Darwinzon Hernandez, LHP
7. Bryan Mata, RHP
8. Josh Ockimey, 1B
9. Travis Lakins, RHP
10. Mike Shawaryn, RHP
11. Jalen Beeks, LHP
12. C.J. Chatham, SS
13. Cole Brannen, OF
14. Bobby Dalbec, 3B
15. Jake Thompson, RHP

NEW YORK YANKEES

1. Gleyber Torres, 2B/3B/SS
2. Chance Adams, RHP
3. Estevan Florial, OF
4. Domingo Acevedo, RHP
5. Clarke Schmidt, RHP
6. Justus Sheffield, LHP
7. Dillon Tate, RHP
8. Albert Abreu, RHP
9. Miguel Andujar, 3B
10. Matt Sauer, RHP
11. Tyler Austin, 1B/OF
12. Freicer Perez, RHP
13. Tyler Wade, 2B/3B/SS/OF
14. Luis Medina, RHP
15. Nick Solak, 2B

TAMPA BAY RAYS

1. Willy Adames, SS
2. Brent Honeywell, RHP
3. Jesus Sanchez, OF
4. Brendan McKay, 1B
5. Jake Bauers, 1B/OF
6. Jose De Leon, RHP
7. Christian Arroyo, 2B/3B/SS
8. Joshua Lowe, OF
9. Justin Williams, OF
10. Wander Franco, SS
11. Garrett Whitley, OF
12. Michael Mercado, RHP
13. Brandon Lowe, 2B
14. Jaime Schultz, RHP
15. Austin Franklin, RHP

TORONTO BLUE JAYS

1. Vladimir Guerrero, 3B
2. Bo Bichette, 2B/SS
3. Sean Reid-Foley, RHP
4. Anthony Alford, OF
5. T.J. Zeuch, RHP
6. Logan Warmoth, SS
7. Conner Greene, RHP
8. Nate Pearson, RHP
9. Max Pentecost, C/1B
10. Justin Maese, RHP
11. Ryan Borucki, LHP
12. Rowdy Tellez, 1B
13. Lourdes Gurriel, 2B/3B/SS
14. Richard Urena, 2B/SS
15. Danny Jansen, C

AL CENTRAL

CHICAGO WHITE SOX

1. Eloy Jimenez, OF
2. Michael Kopech, RHP
3. Luis Robert, OF
4. Alec Hansen, RHP
5. Dylan Cease, RHP
6. Blake Rutherford, OF
7. Micker Adolfo, OF
8. Jake Burger, 1B/3B
9. Zack Collins, C
10. Dane Dunning, RHP
11. Carson Fulmer, RHP
12. Zack Burdi, RHP
13. Gavin Sheets, 1B
14. Thyago Vieira, RHP
15. Luis Alexander Basabe, OF

CLEVELAND INDIANS

1. Triston McKenzie, RHP
2. Francisco Mejia, C
3. Bobby Bradley, 1B
4. Yu-Cheng Chang, SS
5. Nolan Jones, 3B
6. Willi Castro, SS
7. Will Benson, OF
8. Greg Allen, OF
9. Quentin Holmes, OF
10. Julian Merryweather, RHP
11. Shane Bieber, RHP
12. Conner Capel, OF
13. Aaron Civale, RHP
14. Juan Hillman, LHP
15. Brady Aiken, RHP

DETROIT TIGERS

1. Franklin Perez, RHP
2. Alex Faedo, RHP
3. Matt Manning, RHP
4. Beau Burrows, RHP
5. Christin Stewart, OF
6. Kyle Funkhouser, RHP
7. Daz Cameron, OF
8. Isaac Paredes, SS
9. Bryan Garcia, RHP
10. Dawel Lugo, 3B
11. Derek Hill, OF
12. Gregory Soto, LHP
13. Jairo Labourt, LHP
14. Michael Gerber, OF
15. Jake Rogers, C

KANSAS CITY ROYALS

1. Nick Pratto, 1B
2. Hunter Dozier, 1B/3B/OF
3. Josh Staumont, RHP
4. Eric Skoglund, LHP
5. M.J. Melendez, C
6. Khalil Lee, OF
7. Foster Griffin, LHP
8. Seuly Matias, OF
9. Scott Blewett, RHP
10. Chase Vallot, C
11. Nicky Lopez, 2B/SS
12. Kyle Zimmer, RHP
13. Miguel Almonte, RHP
14. Emmanuel Rivera, 3B
15. Michael Gigliotti, OF

MINNESOTA TWINS

1. Royce Lewis, SS
2. Nick Gordon, SS
3. Fernando Romero, RHP
4. Wander Javier, SS
5. Stephen Gonsalves, LHP
6. Alex Kirilloff, OF
7. Tyler Jay, LHP
8. Blayne Enlow, RHP
9. Brent Rooker, 1B/OF
10. Brusdar Graterol, RHP
11. John Curtiss, RHP
12. Felix Jorge, RHP
13. Travis Blankenhorn, 2B/3B
14. Andrew Bechtold, 3B
15. Mitch Garver, C/1B/OF

AL WEST

HOUSTON ASTROS

1. Kyle Tucker, OF
2. Forrest Whitley, RHP
3. Yordan Alvarez, 1B/OF
4. J.B. Bukauskas, RHP
5. Freudis Nova, SS
6. David Paulino, RHP
7. Colin Moran, 1B/3B
8. J.D. Davis, 3B
9. Corbin Martin, RHP
10. Cionel Perez, LHP
11. Hector Perez, RHP
12. Gilberto Celestino, OF
13. Garrett Stubbs, C
14. Jandel Gustave, RHP
15. Jason Martin, OF

LOS ANGELES ANGELS

1. Jahmai Jones, OF
2. Jo Adell, OF
3. Kevin Maitan, 3B/SS
4. Matt Thaiss, 1B
5. Jaime Barria, RHP
6. Griffin Canning, RHP
7. Brandon Marsh, OF
8. Chris Rodriguez, RHP
9. Taylor Ward, C
10. Jesus Castillo, RHP
11. David Fletcher, 2B/SS
12. Joe Gatto, RHP
13. Cole Duensing, RHP
14. Jared Foster, OF
15. Eduardo Paredes, RHP

OAKLAND ATHLETICS

1. Franklin Barreto, 2B/SS
2. A.J. Puk, LHP
3. Jorge Mateo, 2B/SS/OF
4. Austin Beck, OF
5. Grant Holmes, RHP
6. James Kaprielian, RHP
7. Jesus Luzardo, LHP
8. Dustin Fowler, OF
9. Logan Shore, RHP
10. Sean Murphy, C
11. Renato Nunez, 3B/OF
12. Daulton Jefferies, RHP
13. Lazaro Armenteros, OF
14. Dakota Chalmers, RHP
15. Nick Allen, SS

SEATTLE MARINERS

1. Kyle Lewis, OF
2. Evan White, 1B
3. Sam Carlson, RHP
4. Braden Bishop, OF
5. Julio Rodriguez, OF
6. Max Povse, RHP
7. Dan Vogelbach, 1B
8. Rob Whalen, RHP
9. Anthony Jimenez, OF
10. Luis Liberato, OF
11. Seth Elledge, RHP
12. Greifer Andrade, OF
13. Joe Rizzo, 3B
14. Bryson Brigman, 2B/SS
15. Wyatt Mills, RHP

TEXAS RANGERS

1. Leody Taveras, OF
2. Willie Calhoun, 2B/OF
3. Hans Crouse, RHP
4. Yohander Mendez, LHP
5. Cole Ragans, LHP
6. Bubba Thompson, OF
7. Chris Seise, SS
8. Ronald Guzman, 1B
9. Kyle Cody, RHP
10. Alex Speas, RHP
11. Pedro Gonzalez, OF
12. Yanio Perez, 1B/3B/OF
13. A.J. Alexy, RHP
14. Ariel Jurado, RHP
15. Matt Whatley, C

Top Prospects by Organization

NL EAST

ATLANTA BRAVES
1. Ronald Acuna, OF
2. Luiz Gohara, LHP
3. Kyle Wright, RHP
4. Kolby Allard, LHP
5. Joey Wentz, LHP
6. Mike Soroka, RHP
7. Ian Anderson, RHP
8. Austin Riley, 3B
9. AJ Minter, LHP
10. Cristian Pache, OF
11. Bryse Wilson, RHP
12. Alex Jackson, C
13. Max Fried, LHP
14. Touki Toussaint, RHP
15. Tucker Davidson, LHP

MIAMI MARLINS
1. Trevor Rogers, LHP
2. Braxton Garrett, LHP
3. Magneuris Sierra, OF
4. Brian Anderson, 3B
5. Sandy Alcantara, RHP
6. Merandy Gonzalez, RHP
7. Nick Neidert, RHP
8. Jorge Guzman, RHP
9. Brian Miller, OF
10. Dillon Peters, LHP
11. James Nelson, 3B
12. Joe Dunand, 3B
13. Brayan Hernandez, OF
14. Christopher Torres, SS
15. Edward Cabrera, RHP

NEW YORK METS
1. Andres Gimenez, SS
2. Thomas Szapucki, LHP
3. Peter Alonso, 1B
4. David Peterson, LHP
5. Mark Vientos, 3B/SS
6. Justin Dunn, RHP
7. Desmond Lindsay, OF
8. Marcos Molina, RHP
9. David Thompson, 1B/3B
10. Luis Guillorme, 2B/3B/SS
11. Corey Oswalt, RHP
12. Anthony Kay, LHP
13. Jordan Humphreys, RHP
14. Patrick Mazeika, C/1B
15. Tomas Nido, C

PHILADELPHIA PHILLIES
1. Sixto Sanchez, RHP
2. Scott Kingery, 2B
3. J.P. Crawford, SS
4. Adonis Medina, RHP
5. Jorge Alfaro, C
6. Jhailyn Ortiz, OF
7. Franklyn Kilome, RHP
8. Adam Haseley, OF
9. Seranthony Dominguez, RHP
10. Francisco Morales, RHP
11. Daniel Brito, 2B
12. Mickey Moniak, OF
13. JoJo Romero, LHP
14. Spencer Howard, RHP
15. Enyel De Los Santos, RHP

WASHINGTON NATIONALS
1. Victor Robles, OF
2. Juan Soto, OF
3. Carter Kieboom, SS
4. Erick Fedde, RHP
5. Seth Romero, LHP
6. Luis Garcia, 2B
7. Daniel Johnson, OF
8. Yasel Antuna, SS
9. Wil Crowe, RHP
10. Raudy Read, C
11. Blake Perkins, OF
12. Kelvin Gutierrez, 3B
13. Andrew Stevenson, OF
14. Rhett Wiseman, OF
15. Brigham Hill, RHP

NL CENTRAL

CHICAGO CUBS
1. Jose Albertos, RHP
2. Oscar De La Cruz, RHP
3. Alex Lange, RHP
4. Adbert Alzolay, RHP
5. Victor Caratini, C/1B
6. Brendon Little, LHP
7. Aramis Ademan, SS
8. Thomas Hatch, RHP
9. Justin Steele, LHP
10. Mark Zagunis, OF
11. Trevor Clifton, RHP
12. Dillon Maples, RHP
13. Jen-Ho Tseng, RHP
14. Duane Underwood, RHP
15. Eddy Martinez, OF

CINCINNATI REDS
1. Nick Senzel, 3B
2. Hunter Greene, RHP
3. Taylor Trammell, OF
4. Jesse Winker, OF
5. Tony Santillan, RHP
6. Tyler Mahle, RHP
7. Shed Long, 2B
8. Jeter Downs, SS
9. Keury Mella, RHP
10. Vladimir Gutierrez, RHP
11. Tyler Stephenson, C
12. Stuart Fairchild, OF
13. Ariel Hernandez, RHP
14. Jacob Heatherly, LHP
15. Jose Siri, OF

MILWAUKEE BREWERS
1. Lewis Brinson, OF
2. Keston Hiura, 2B
3. Monte Harrison, OF
4. Brett Phillips, OF
5. Isan Diaz, 2B/SS
6. Corbin Burnes, RHP
7. Corey Ray, OF
8. Brandon Woodruff, RHP
9. Lucas Erceg, 3B
10. Luis Ortiz, RHP
11. Freddy Peralta, RHP
12. Mauricio Dubon, 2B/SS
13. Trent Grisham, OF
14. Caden Lemons, RHP
15. Tristen Lutz, OF

PITTSBURGH PIRATES
1. Mitch Keller, RHP
2. Austin Meadows, OF
3. Shane Baz, RHP
4. Ke'Bryan Hayes, 3B
5. Cole Tucker, SS
6. Kevin Newman, 2B/3B/SS
7. Luis Escobar, RHP
8. Will Craig, 3B
9. Taylor Hearn, LHP
10. Nick Kingham, RHP
11. Clay Holmes, RHP
12. Steven Jennings, RHP
13. Lolo Sanchez, OF
14. Jordan Luplow, OF
15. Conner Uselton, OF

ST. LOUIS CARDINALS
1. Alex Reyes, RHP
2. Jack Flaherty, RHP
3. Carson Kelly, C
4. Tyler O'Neill, OF
5. Jose Adolis Garcia, OF
6. Jordan Hicks, RHP
7. Harrison Bader, OF
8. Ryan Helsley, RHP
9. Yairo Munoz, 2B/3B/SS/OF
10. Dakota Hudson, RHP
11. Max Schrock, 2B
12. Delvin Perez, SS
13. Junior Fernandez, RHP
14. Randy Arozarena, OF
15. Andrew Knizner, C

NL WEST

ARIZONA DIAMONDBACKS
1. Jon Duplantier, RHP
2. Pavin Smith, 1B
3. Marcus Wilson, OF
4. Drew Ellis, 1B/3B
5. Jasardo Chisholm, SS
6. Jose Almonte, RHP
7. Anthony Banda, LHP
8. Cody Reed, LHP
9. Matt Tabor, RHP
10. Jimmie Sherfy, RHP
11. Jared Miller, LHP
12. Daulton Varsho, C
13. Taylor Clarke, RHP
14. Domingo Leyba, 2B/SS
15. Socrates Brito, OF

COLORADO ROCKIES
1. Brendan Rodgers, SS
2. Ryan McMahon, 1B/2B/3B
3. Riley Pint, RHP
4. Colton Welker, 3B
5. Ryan Castellani, RHP
6. Peter Lambert, RHP
7. Ryan Vilade, SS
8. Garrett Hampson, 2B/SS
9. Yency Almonte, RHP
10. Tom Murphy, C
11. Sam Howard, LHP
12. Tyler Nevin, 1B/3B
13. Sam Hilliard, OF
14. Dom Nunez, C
15. Jordan Patterson, OF

LOS ANGELES DODGERS
1. Walker Buehler, RHP
2. Alex Verdugo, OF
3. Yadier Alvarez, RHP
4. Keibert Ruiz, C
5. Dustin May, RHP
6. Mitchell White, RHP
7. Yusniel Diaz, OF
8. Jeren Kendall, OF
9. Starling Heredia, OF
10. Jordan Sheffield, RHP
11. Gavin Lux, SS
12. Dennis Santana, RHP
13. DJ Peters, OF
14. Edwin Rios, 1B/3B
15. Will Smith, C/2B/3B

SAN DIEGO PADRES
1. Mackenzie Gore, LHP
2. Fernando Tatis, SS
3. Cal Quantrill, RHP
4. Luis Urias, 2B/SS
5. Anderson Espinoza, RHP
6. Michel Baez, RHP
7. Esteury Ruiz, 2B/SS
8. Jeisson Rosario, OF
9. Adrian Morejon, LHP
10. Eric Lauer, LHP
11. Mason Thompson, RHP
12. Joey Lucchesi, LHP
13. Jacob Nix, RHP
14. Logan Allen, LHP
15. Jorge Ona, OF

SAN FRANCISCO GIANTS
1. Chris Shaw, 1B/OF
2. Tyler Beede, RHP
3. Heliot Ramos, OF
4. Bryan Reynolds, OF
5. Steven Duggar, OF
6. Andrew Suarez, LHP
7. Jacob Gonzalez, 3B
8. Garrett Williams, LHP
9. Reyes Moronta, RHP
10. Austin Slater, OF
11. Sandro Fabian, OF
12. Aramis Garcia, C/1B
13. Shaun Anderson, RHP
14. Melvin Adon, RHP
15. Seth Corry, LHP

TOP PROSPECTS BY POSITION

CATCHER
1 Francisco Mejia, CLE
2 Keibert Ruiz, LA
3 Carson Kelly, STL
4 Jorge Alfaro, PHI
5 Chance Sisco, BAL
6 Zack Collins, CHW
7 Sean Murphy, OAK
8 Alex Jackson, ATL
9 Jake Rogers, DET
10 M.J. Melendez, KC
11 Max Pentecost, TOR
12 Chase Vallot, KC
13 Garrett Stubbs, HOU
14 Victor Caratini, CHC
15 Tyler Stephenson, CIN

FIRST BASEMEN
1 Ryan McMahon, COL
2 Brendan McKay, TAM
3 Pavin Smith, ARI
4 Yordan Alvarez, HOU
5 Chris Shaw, SF
6 Bobby Bradley, CLE
7 Ronald Guzman, TEX
8 Peter Alonso, NYM
9 Evan White, SEA
10 Josh Naylor, SD
11 Sam Travis, BOS
12 Nick Pratto, KC
13 Gavin Sheets, CHW
14 Matt Thaiss, LAA
15 Rowdy Tellez, TOR

SECOND BASEMEN
1 Keston Hiura, MIL
2 Scott Kingery, PHI
3 Luis Urias, SD
4 Isan Diaz, MIL
5 Esteury Ruiz, SD
6 Garrett Hampson, COL
7 Brandon Lowe, TAM
8 Mauricio Dubon, MIL
9 Yairo Munoz, STL
10 Nick Solak, NYY
11 Luis Garcia, WAS
12 Tyler Wade, NYY
13 Daniel Brito, PHI
14 Shed Long, CIN
15 Max Schrock, STL

SHORTSTOP
1 Gleyber Torres, NYY
2 Brendan Rodgers, COL
3 Fernando Tatis, Jr., SD
4 Bo Bichette, TOR
5 Willy Adames, TAM
6 Royce Lewis, MIN
7 Franklin Barreto, OAK
8 J.P. Crawford, PHI
9 Nick Gordon, MIN
10 Jorge Mateo, OAK
11 Carter Kieboom, WAS
12 Wander Javier, MIN
13 Cole Tucker, PIT
14 Andres Gimenez, NYM
15 Ryan Vilade, COL

THIRD BASEMEN
1 Vladimir Guerrero, Jr., TOR
2 Nick Senzel, CIN
3 Kevin Maitan, LAA
4 Ryan Mountcastle, BAL
5 Austin Riley, ATL
6 Michael Chavis, BOS
7 Christian Arroyo, TAM
8 Miguel Andujar, NYY
9 Colton Welker, COL
10 Ke'Bryan Hayes, PIT
11 Colin Moran, HOU
12 Lucas Erceg, MIL
13 Nolan Jones, CLE
14 Brian Anderson, MIA
15 J.D. Davis, HOU

OUTFIELDERS
1 Ronald Acuna, ATL
2 Victor Robles, WAS
3 Eloy Jimenez, CHW
4 Kyle Tucker, HOU
5 Lewis Brinson, MIL
6 Leody Taveras, TEX
7 Juan Soto, WAS
8 Alex Verdugo, LA
9 Luis Robert, CHW
10 Willie Calhoun, TEX
11 Austin Hays, BAL
12 Anthony Alford, TOR
13 Austin Meadows, PIT
14 Kyle Lewis, SEA
15 Taylor Trammell, CIN
16 Estevan Florial, NYY
17 Jesus Sanchez, TAM
18 Monte Harrison, MIL
19 Austin Beck, OAK
20 Blake Rutherford, CHW
21 Jake Bauers, TAM
22 Heliot Ramos, SF
23 Dustin Fowler, OAK
24 Mickey Moniak, PHI
25 Yusniel Diaz, LA
26 Jesse Winker, CIN
27 Tyler O'Neill, STL
28 Jo Adell, LAA
29 Corey Ray, MIL
30 Jahmai Jones, LAA
31 Adam Haseley, PHI
32 Jhailyn Ortiz, PHI
33 Brett Phillips, MIL
34 Harrison Bader, STL
35 Starling Heredia, LA
36 Jeren Kendall, LA
37 Daz Cameron, DET
38 Cristian Pache, ATL
39 Daniel Johnson, WAS
40 Franchy Cordero, SD
41 Akil Baddoo, MIN
42 Jeisson Rosario, SD
43 Lazaro Armenteros, OAK
44 Joshua Lowe, TAM
45 Justin Williams, TAM

STARTING PITCHERS
1 Alex Reyes, STL
2 Walker Buehler, LA
3 Michael Kopech, CHW
4 Brent Honeywell, TAM
5 MacKenzie Gore, SD
6 Forrest Whitley, HOU
7 Mitch Keller, PIT
8 Kyle Wright, ATL
9 A.J. Puk, OAK
10 Sixto Sanchez, PHI
11 Hunter Greene, CIN
12 Triston McKenzie, CLE
13 Luiz Gohara, ATL
14 Franklin Perez, DET
15 Mike Soroka, ATL
16 Kolby Allard, ATL
17 Jack Flaherty, STL
18 Yadier Alvarez, LA
19 Jay Groome, BOS
20 Cal Quantrill, SD
21 Chance Adams, NYY
22 Ian Anderson, ATL
23 Michel Baez, SD
24 Alec Hansen, CHW
25 Riley Pint, COL
26 Anderson Espinoza, SD
27 Matt Manning, DET
28 Dylan Cease, CHW
29 Justus Sheffield, NYY
30 Corbin Burnes, MIL
31 Adonis Medina, PHI
32 Jon Duplantier, ARI
33 Adrian Morejon, SD
34 Shane Baz, PIT
35 Stephen Gonsalves, MIN
36 Joey Wentz, ATL
37 Alex Faedo, DET
38 Brandon Woodruff, MIL
39 Mitchell White, LA
40 Jose De Leon, TAM
41 Luis Ortiz, MIL
42 Sean Reid-Foley, TOR
43 Beau Burrows, DET
44 James Kaprielian, OAK
45 Erick Fedde, WAS
46 Tyler Mahle, CIN
47 Max Fried, ATL
48 Domingo Acevedo, NYY
49 Dustin May, LA
50 Braxton Garrett, MIA
51 Trevor Rogers, MIA
52 Fernando Romero, MIN
53 Jesus Luzardo, OAK
54 Grant Holmes, OAK
55 Sandy Alcantara, MIA
56 Tyler Beede, SF
57 Jorge Guzman, MIA
58 Nick Neidert, MIA
59 Jose Albertos, CHC
60 Oscar de la Cruz, CHC
61 Clarke Schmidt, NYY
62 Bryse Wilson, ATL
63 Cole Ragans, TEX
64 Hans Crouse, TEX
65 Hunter Harvey, BAL
66 T.J. Zeuch, TOR
67 Freicer Perez, NYY
68 Tony Santillan, CIN
69 Anthony Banda, ARI
70 Adbert Alzolay, CHC
71 J.B. Bukauskas, HOU
72 Joey Lucchesi, SD
73 Seth Romero, WAS
74 Jordan Sheffield, LA
75 Jordan Hicks, STL

RELIEF PITCHERS
1 Zack Burdi, CHW
2 A.J. Minter, ATL
3 Tanner Scott, BAL
4 Dillon Maples, CHC
5 Tyler Jay, MIN
6 Jimmie Sherfy, ARI
7 Bryan Garcia, DET
8 Jairo Labourt, DET
9 Ryne Stanek, TAM
10 Thyago Vieira, CHW
11 John Curtiss, MIN
12 Reyes Moronta, SF
13 Chih-Wei Hu, TAM
14 Jimmy Herget, CIN
15 Ariel Hernandez, CIN

TOP PROSPECTS BY SKILLS

TOP POWER
Dylan Cozens, OF, PHI
Eloy Jimenez, OF, CHW
Bobby Bradley, 1B, CLE
Brendan Rodgers, SS, COL
Christin Stewart, OF, DET
Vladimir Guerrero, Jr., 3B, TOR
Chris Shaw, 1B, SF
Renato Nunez, 3B, OAK
Tyler O'Neill, OF, STL
Will Benson, OF, CLE
Willie Calhoun, OF, TEX
Michael Chavis, 3B, BOS
Austin Riley, 3B, ATL
D.J. Peters, OF, LA
Ronald Acuna, OF, ATL
Nick Senzel, 3B, CIN
Ryan McMahon, 1B, COL
Scott Kingery, 2B, PHI
J.D. Davis, 3B, HOU
Brent Rooker, OF, MIN
Kyle Lewis, OF, SEA
Lewis Brinson, OF, MIL
Austin Hays, OF, BAL
Isan Diaz, 2B, MIL
Kyle Tucker, OF, HOU

TOP BA
Bo Bichette, SS, TOR
Keston Hiura, 2B, MIL
Vladimir Guerrero, Jr., 3B, TOR
Victor Robles, OF, WAS
Brendan Rodgers, SS, COL
Ronald Acuna, OF, ATL
Luis Urias, 2B/SS, SD
Nick Senzel, 3B, CIN
Kevin Newman, SS, PIT
Alex Verdugo, OF, LA
Chance Sisco, C, BAL
Pavin Smith, 1B, ARI
Eloy Jimenez, OF, CHW
Francisco Mejia, C, CLE
Christian Arroyo, 3B, TAM
Gleyber Torres, SS, NYY
Austin Hays, OF, BAL
Kyle Tucker, OF, HOU
Juan Soto, OF, WAS
Heliot Ramos, OF, SF
Jesus Sanchez, OF, TAM
Nick Solak, 2B, NYY
Jesse Winker, OF, CIN
Garrett Hampson, 2B, COL
Sheldon Neuse, 3B, OAK

TOP SPEED
Jorge Mateo, SS, NYY
Roman Quinn, OF, PHI
Rafael Bautista, OF, WAS
Derek Hill, OF, DET
Victor Robles, OF, WAS
Greg Allen, OF, CLE
Jahmai Jones, OF, LAA
Anthony Alford, OF, TOR
Garrett Whitley, OF, TAM
Ronald Acuna, OF, ATL
Dustin Fowler, OF, OAK
Mauricio Dubon, SS, MIL
Lucius Fox, SS, TAM
Zack Granite, OF, MIN
Cole Tucker, SS, PIT
Magneuris Sierra, OF, MIA
Garrett Hampson, 2B, COL
Taylor Trammell, OF, CIN
Luis Alexander Basabe, OF, CHW
Cristian Pache, OF, ATL
Trent Grisham, OF, MIL
Jose Siri, OF, CIN
Quentin Holmes, OF, CLE
Bubba Thompson, OF, TEX
Charlie Tilson, OF, CHW

TOP FASTBALL
Alex Reyes, RHP, STL
Domingo Acevedo, RHP, NYY
Michael Kopech, RHP, CHW
Walker Buehler, RHP, LA
Hunter Greene, RHP, CIN
Yadier Alvarez, RHP, LA
Dylan Cease, RHP, CHW
Taylor Hearn, RHP, PIT
Josh Staumont, RHP, KC
Shane Baz, RHP, PIT
Dillon Maples, RHP, CHC
Riley Pint, RHP, COL
Ariel Hernandez, RHP, CIN
Zack Burdi, RHP, CHW
Sixto Sanchez, RHP, PHI
Sandy Alcantara, RHP, MIA
A.J. Puk, LHP, OAK
Mitch Keller, RHP, PIT
Triston McKenzie, RHP, CLE
Luiz Gohara, LHP, ATL
Thyago Vieira, RHP, CHW
Forrest Whitley, RHP, HOU
Kolby Allard, LHP, ATL
MacKenzie Gore, LHP, SD
Kyle Wright, RHP, ATL

TOP BREAKING BALL
Touki Toussaint, RHP, ATL
Josh Staumont, RHP, KC
Jay Groome, LHP, BOS
Alex Reyes, RHP, STL
Max Fried, LHP, ATL
Dylan Cease, RHP, CHW
Walker Buehler, RHP, LA
Luis Ortiz, RHP, MIL
Kolby Allard, LHP, ATL
Yadier Alvarez, RHP, LA
Erick Fedde, RHP, WAS
Cal Quantrill, RHP, SD
A.J. Puk, LHP, OAK
Luiz Gohara, LHP, ATL
Michael Kopech, RHP, CHW
MacKenzie Gore, LHP, SD
Dillon Maples, RHP, CHC
Chance Adams, RHP, NYY
Joey Wentz, LHP, ATL
Forrest Whitley, RHP, HOU
Kodi Medeiros, LHP, MIL
Tyler Jay, LHP, MIN
Ariel Hernandez, RHP, CIN
Zack Burdi, RHP, CHW
Zach Jackson, RHP, TOR
L

2018 TOP FANTASY IMPACT

THE TOP 40 • RANKED
1 Ronald Acuna (OF, ATL)
2 Dustin Fowler (OF, OAK)
3 Willie Calhoun (LF, TEX)
4 Victor Robles (OF, WAS)
5 Nick Senzel (3B, CIN)
6 J.P. Crawford (SS, PHI)
7 Brian Anderson (3B, MIA)
8 Christian Arroyo (SS, TAM)
9 Jeimer Candelario (3B, DET)
10 Ryan McMahon (1B/2B, COL)

11 Brett Phillips (OF, MIL)
12 Alex Verdugo (OF, LA)
13 Lewis Brinson (OF, MIL)
14 Greg Allen (OF, CLE)
15 Franklin Barreto (SS/2B, OAK)
16 Alex Reyes (RHP, STL)
17 Jorge Alfaro (C, PHI)
18 Anthony Alford (OF, TOR)
19 Harrison Bader (OF, STL)
20 Jake Bauers (OF/1B, TAM)

21 Jack Flaherty (RHP, STL)
22 Scott Kingery (2B, PHI)
23 Francisco Mejia (C, CLE)
24 Brent Honeywell (RHP, TAM)
25 Austin Meadows (OF, PIT)
26 Tyler O'Neill (OF, STL)
27 Fernando Tatis Jr. (SS, SD)
28 Willy Adames (INF, TAM)
29 Jordan Luplow (OF, PIT)
30 Tom Murphy (C, COL)

31 Gleyber Torres (INF, NYY)
32 Brandon Woodruff (RHP, MIL)
33 Austin Hays (OF, BAL)
34 Michael Kopech (RHP, CHW)
35 Tyler Mahle (RHP, CIN)
36 Colin Moran (3B, HOU)
37 Brendan Rodgers (SS, COL)
38 Chance Sisco (C, BAL)
39 Luiz Gohara (LHP, ATL)
40 Carson Kelly (C, STL)

THE NEXT 35 • ALPHA ORDER
Chance Adams (RHP, NYY)
Sandy Alcantara (RHP, STL)
Kolby Allard (LHP, ATL)
Miguel Andujar (3B, NYY)
Bobby Bradley (1B, CLE)
Walker Buehler (RHP, LA)
Beau Burrows (RHP, DET)
Michael Chavis (3B, BOS)
Zack Collins (C, CHW)
Jose De Leon (RHP, TAM)
Mauricio Dubon (SS, MIL)
Hunter Dozier (3B, KC)
Lucas Erceg (3B, MIL)
Erick Fedde (RHP, WAS)
Stephen Gonsalves (LHP, MIN)
Nick Gordon (SS, MIN)
Eloy Jimenez (OF, CHW)
Mitch Keller (RHP, PIT)
Jorge Mateo (SS, OAK)
Yohander Mendez (LHP, TEX)
Ryan Mountcastle (3B, BAL)
Sheldon Neuse (3B, OAK)
Kevin Newman (SS, PIT)
A.J. Puk (LHP, OAK)
Cal Quantrill (RHP, SD)
Edwin Rios (3B/OF/1B, LAD)
Chris Shaw (OF/1B, SF)
Justus Sheffield (LHP, NYY)
Magneuris Sierra (OF, MIA)
Mike Soroka (RHP, ATL)
D.J. Stewart (OF, BAL)
Christin Stewart (OF, DET)
Rowdy Tellez (1B, TOR)
Kyle Tucker (OF, HOU)
Luis Urias (SS/2B, SD)

Top 100 Prospects Archive

2017

1. Yoan Moncada (2B, CHW)
2. Andrew Benintendi (OF, BOS)
3. Dansby Swanson (SS, ATL)
4. Alex Reyes (RHP, STL)
5. Lucas Giolito (RHP, CHW)
6. Victor Robles (OF, WAS)
7. J.P. Crawford (SS, PHI)
8. Tyler Glasnow (RHP, PIT)
9. Brendan Rodgers (SS, COL)
10. Austin Meadows (OF, PIT)
11. Gleyber Torres (SS, NYY)
12. Amed Rosario (SS, NYM)
13. Rafael Devers (3B, BOS)
14. Lewis Brinson (OF, MIL)
15. Anderson Espinoza (RHP, SD)
16. Willy Adames (SS, TAM)
17. Eloy Jimenez (OF, CHC)
18. Manuel Margot (OF, SD)
19. Ozzie Albies (2B, ATL)
20. Clint Frazier (OF, NYY)
21. Bradley Zimmer (OF, CLE)
22. Franklin Barreto (SS, OAK)
23. Brent Honeywell (RHP, TAM)
24. Cody Bellinger (1B, LAD)
25. Francis Martes (RHP, HOU)
26. Reynaldo Lopez (RHP, CHW)
27. Jose De Leon (RHP, LAD)
28. Mickey Moniak (OF, PHI)
29. Ian Happ (2B, CHC)
30. Kyle Tucker (OF, HOU)
31. Nick Senzel (3B, CIN)
32. Michael Kopech (RHP, CHW)
33. Aaron Judge (OF, NYY)
34. Josh Bell (1B, PIT)
35. Kyle Lewis (OF, SEA)
36. Hunter Renfroe (OF, SD)
37. Jorge Mateo (SS, NYY)
38. Amir Garrett (LHP, CIN)
39. Corey Ray (OF, MIL)
40. Jeff Hoffman (RHP, COL)
41. Tyler O'Neill (OF, SEA)
42. Josh Hader (LHP, MIL)
43. Kolby Allard (LHP, ATL)
44. Jason Groome (LHP, BOS)
45. Jorge Alfaro (C, PHI)
46. Nick Williams (OF, PHI)
47. Nick Gordon (SS, MIN)
48. Sean Newcomb (LHP, ATL)
49. Alex Verdugo (OF, LAD)
50. Blake Rutherford (OF, NYY)
51. Carson Fulmer (RHP, CHW)
52. Vladimir Guerrero, Jr. (3B, TOR)
53. David Paulino (RHP, HOU)
54. Mitch Keller (RHP, PIT)
55. Riley Pint (RHP, COL)
56. Francisco Mejia (C, CLE)
57. Brady Aiken (LHP, CLE)
58. Yulieski Gurriel (3B, HOU)
59. Braxton Garrett (LHP, MIA)
60. Tyler Jay (LHP, MIN)
61. A.J. Puk (LHP, OAK)
62. Kevin Newman (SS, PIT)
63. Robert Stephenson (RHP, CIN)
64. Sean Reid-Foley (RHP, TOR)
65. Matt Manning (RHP, DET)
66. Anthony Alford (OF, TOR)
67. Jesse Winker (OF, CIN)
68. Dominic Smith (1B, NYM)
69. Raimel Tapia (OF, COL)
70. Zack Collins (C, CHW)
71. James Kaprielian (RHP, NYY)
72. Erick Fedde (RHP, WAS)
73. Luis Ortiz (RHP, MIL)
74. Phil Bickford (RHP, MIL)
75. Jake Bauers (OF, TAM)
76. Justus Sheffield (LHP, NYY)
77. Matt Chapman (3B, OAK)
78. Luke Weaver (RHP, STL)
79. Grant Holmes (RHP, OAK)
80. Bobby Bradley (1B, CLE)
81. Ronald Acuna (OF, ATL)
82. Derek Fisher (OF, HOU)
83. Brett Phillips (OF, MIL)
84. Yadier Alvarez (RHP, LAD)
85. Leody Taveras (OF, TEX)
86. Yohander Mendez (LHP, TEX)
87. Kevin Maitan (SS, ATL)
88. Triston McKenzie (LHP, CLE)
89. Willie Calhoun (2B, LAD)
90. Ryan McMahon (3B, COL)
91. Isan Diaz (2B, MIL)
92. Ian Anderson (RHP, ATL)
93. Trent Clark (OF, MIL)
94. Alex Kirilloff (OF, MIN)
95. Harrison Bader (OF, STL)
96. Tyler Beede (RHP, SF)
97. Richard Urena (SS, TOR)
98. Mike Soroka (RHP, ATL)
99. Dylan Cease (RHP, CHC)
100. Stephen Gonsalves (LHP, MIN)

2016

1. Byron Buxton (OF, MIN)
2. Corey Seager (SS, LAD)
3. Lucas Giolito (RHP, WAS)
4. J.P. Crawford (SS, PHI)
5. Alex Reyes (RHP, STL)
6. Julio Urias (LHP, LAD)
7. Yoan Moncada (2B, BOS)
8. Tyler Glasnow (RHP, PIT)
9. Joey Gallo (3B, TEX)
10. Steven Matz (LHP, NYM)
11. Rafael Devers (3B, BOS)
12. Jose Berrios (RHP, MIN)
13. Orlando Arcia (SS, MIL)
14. Blake Snell (LHP, TAM)
15. Trea Turner (SS, WAS)
16. Bradley Zimmer (OF, CLE)
17. Jose De Leon (RHP, LAD)
18. Brendan Rodgers (SS, COL)
19. Dansby Swanson (SS, ATL)
20. Robert Stephenson (RHP, CIN)
21. Nomar Mazara (OF, TEX)
22. Victor Robles (OF, WAS)
23. Aaron Judge (OF, NYY)
24. Manuel Margot (OF, SD)
25. Clint Frazier (OF, CLE)
26. Lewis Brinson (OF, TEX)
27. Alex Bregman (SS, HOU)
28. Jon Gray (RHP, COL)
29. Ryan McMahon (3B, COL)
30. Austin Meadows (OF, PIT)
31. Nick Williams (OF, PHI)
32. Franklin Barreto (SS, OAK)
33. David Dahl (OF, COL)
34. Brett Phillips (OF, MIL)
35. Gleyber Torres (SS, CHC)
36. Sean Newcomb (LHP, ATL)
37. Carson Fulmer (RHP, CHW)
38. Ozhaino Albies (SS, ATL)
39. Dillon Tate (RHP, TEX)
40. Andrew Benintendi (OF, BOS)
41. Jameson Taillon (RHP, PIT)
42. Raul Mondesi (SS, KC)
43. Archie Bradley (RHP, ARI)
44. Tim Anderson (SS, CHW)
45. Kolby Allard (LHP, ATL)
46. Jake Thompson (RHP, PHI)
47. Dylan Bundy (RHP, BAL)
48. Willy Adames (SS, TAM)
49. Anderson Espinoza (RHP, BOS)
50. Aaron Blair (RHP, ATL)
51. A.J. Reed (1B, HOU)
52. Jeff Hoffman (RHP, COL)
53. Jesse Winker (OF, CIN)
54. Brent Honeywell (RHP, TAM)
55. Josh Bell (1B, PIT)
56. Anthony Alford (OF, TOR)
57. Tyler Kolek (RHP, MIA)
58. Max Kepler (OF, MIN)
59. Hunter Renfroe (OF, SD)
60. Mark Appel (RHP, PHI)
61. Kyle Zimmer (RHP, KC)
62. Jose Peraza (2B, CIN)
63. Kyle Tucker (OF, HOU)
64. Cody Reed (LHP, CIN)
65. Billy McKinney (OF, CHC)
66. Nick Gordon (SS, MIN)
67. Braden Shipley (RHP, ARI)
68. Jorge Lopez (RHP, MIL)
69. Touki Toussaint (RHP, ATL)
70. Hector Olivera (3B, ATL)
71. Derek Fisher (OF, HOU)
72. Jorge Alfaro (C, PHI)
73. Raimel Tapia (OF, COL)
74. Grant Holmes (RHP, LAD)
75. Dominic Smith (1B, NYM)
76. Daz Cameron (OF, HOU)
77. Alex Jackson (OF, SEA)
78. Sean Manaea (LHP, OAK)
79. Amed Rosario (SS, NYM)
80. Reynaldo Lopez (RHP, WAS)
81. Javier Guerra (SS, SD)
82. Hunter Harvey (RHP, BAL)
83. Luis Ortiz (RHP, TEX)
84. Brady Aiken (LHP, CLE)
85. Matt Olson (1B, OAK)
86. Jorge Mateo (SS, NYY)
87. Daniel Robertson (SS, TAM)
88. Taylor Guerrieri (RHP, TAM)
89. Amir Garrett (LHP, CIN)
90. Willson Contreras (C, CHC)
91. Renato Nunez (3B, OAK)
92. Tyler Jay (LHP, MIN)
93. Tyler Stephenson (C, CIN)
94. Christian Arroyo (SS, SF)
95. Josh Naylor (1B, MIA)
96. Brian Johnson (LHP, BOS)
97. Tyler Beede (RHP, SF)
98. Garrett Whitley (OF, TAM)
99. Cody Bellinger (1B, LAD)
100. Michael Fulmer (RHP, DET)

Top 100 Prospects Archive

2015

1. Kris Bryant (3B, CHC)
2. Byron Buxton (OF, MIN)
3. Carlos Correa (SS, HOU)
4. Addison Russell (SS, CHC)
5. Corey Seager (SS, LAD)
6. Francisco Lindor (SS, CLE)
7. Joc Pederson (OF, LAD)
8. Miguel Sano (3B, MIN)
9. Lucas Giolito (P, WAS)
10. Joey Gallo (3B, TEX)
11. Dylan Bundy (P, BAL)
12. Jorge Soler (OF, CHC)
13. Archie Bradley (P, ARI)
14. Julio Urias (P, LAD)
15. Jon Gray (P, COL)
16. Daniel Norris (P, TOR)
17. Carlos Rodon (P, CHW)
18. Tyler Glasnow (P, PIT)
19. Noah Syndergaard (P, NYM)
20. Blake Swihart (C, BOS)
21. Aaron Sanchez (P, TOR)
22. Henry Owens (P, BOS)
23. Jameson Taillon (P, PIT)
24. Robert Stephenson (P, CIN)
25. Andrew Heaney (P, LAA)
26. David Dahl (OF, COL)
27. Jose Berrios (P, MIN)
28. Jorge Alfaro (C, TEX)
29. Hunter Harvey (P, BAL)
30. Alex Meyer (P, MIN)
31. Kohl Stewart (P, MIN)
32. J.P. Crawford (SS, PHI)
33. Alex Jackson (OF, SEA)
34. Jesse Winker (OF, CIN)
35. Raul Mondesi (SS, KC)
36. D.J. Peterson (3B, SEA)
37. Austin Meadows (OF, PIT)
38. Josh Bell (OF, PIT)
39. Kyle Crick (P, SF)
40. Luis Severino (P, NYY)
41. Nick Gordon (SS, MIN)
42. Kyle Schwarber (OF, CHC)
43. Aaron Nola (P, PHI)
44. Kyle Zimmer (P, KC)
45. Alex Reyes (P, STL)
46. Braden Shipley (P, ARI)
47. Albert Almora (OF, CHC)
48. Clint Frazier (OF, CLE)
49. Tyler Kolek (P, MIA)
50. Mark Appel (P, HOU)
51. Rusney Castillo (OF, BOS)
52. Sean Manaea (P, KC)
53. A.J. Cole (P, WAS)
54. Matt Wisler (P, SD)
55. Raimel Tapia (OF, COL)
56. C.J. Edwards (P, CHC)
57. Dalton Pompey (OF, TOR)
58. Hunter Renfroe (OF, SD)
59. Hunter Dozier (3B, KC)
60. Brandon Nimmo (OF, NYM)
61. Tim Anderson (SS, CHW)
62. Maikel Franco (3B, PHI)
63. Mike Foltynewicz (P, HOU)
64. Nick Kingham (P, PIT)
65. Eddie Butler (P, COL)
66. Steven Matz (P, NYM)
67. Domingo Santana (OF, HOU)
68. Aaron Judge (OF, NYY)
69. Daniel Robertson (SS, OAK)
70. Stephen Piscotty (OF, STL)
71. Kyle Freeland (P, COL)
72. Kevin Plawecki (C, NYM)
73. Lucas Sims (P, ATL)
74. Yasmany Tomas (OF, ARI)
75. Jose Peraza (2B, ATL)
76. Eduardo Rodriguez (P, BOS)
77. Max Fried (P, ATL)
78. Manuel Margot (OF, BOS)
79. Matt Olson (1B, OAK)
80. Ryan McMahon (3B, COL)
81. Alex Gonzalez (P, TEX)
82. Tyler Beede (P, SF)
83. Alen Hanson (SS, PIT)
84. Grant Holmes (P, LAD)
85. Aaron Blair (P, ARI)
86. Michael Taylor (OF, WAS)
87. Trea Turner (SS, SD/WAS)
88. Christian Bethancourt (C, ATL)
89. Marco Gonzales (P, STL)
90. Michael Conforto (OF, NYM)
91. Sean Newcomb (P, LAA)
92. Alex Colome (P, TAM)
93. Jeff Hoffman (P, TOR)
94. Luke Jackson (P, TEX)
95. Lewis Brinson (OF, TEX)
96. Willy Adames (SS, TAM)
97. Jake Thompson (P, TEX)
98. Nick Williams (OF, TEX)
99. Colin Moran (3B, HOU)
100. Bradley Zimmer (OF, CLE)

2014

1. Byron Buxton (OF, MIN)
2. Oscar Taveras (OF, STL)
3. Xander Bogaerts (SS, BOS)
4. Taijuan Walker (RHP, SEA)
5. Miguel Sano (3B, MIN)
6. Francisco Lindor (SS, CLE)
7. Javier Baez (SS, CHC)
8. Archie Bradley (RHP, ARI)
9. Carlos Correa (SS, HOU)
10. Gregory Polanco (OF, PIT)
11. Addison Russell (SS, OAK)
12. Jameson Taillon (RHP, PIT)
13. Kris Bryant (3B, CHC)
14. Dylan Bundy (RHP, BAL)
15. George Springer (OF, HOU)
16. Nick Castellanos (3B, DET)
17. Noah Syndergaard (RHP, NYM)
18. Kevin Gausman (RHP, BAL)
19. Carlos Martinez (RHP, STL)
20. Robert Stephenson (RHP, CIN)
21. Yordano Ventura (RHP, KC)
22. Jonathan Gray (RHP, COL)
23. Kyle Zimmer (RHP, KC)
24. Albert Almora (OF, CHC)
25. Mark Appel (RHP, HOU)
26. Aaron Sanchez (RHP, TOR)
27. Travis d'Arnaud (C, NYM)
28. Kyle Crick (RHP, SF)
29. Joc Pederson (OF, LA)
30. Alex Meyer (RHP, MIN)
31. Garin Cecchini (3B, BOS)
32. Jorge Soler (OF, CHC)
33. Jonathan Singleton (1B, HOU)
34. Maikel Franco (3B, PHI)
35. Lucas Giolito (RHP, WAS)
36. Eddie Butler (RHP, COL)
37. Andrew Heaney (LHP, MIA)
38. Jackie Bradley (OF, BOS)
39. Taylor Guerrieri (RHP, TAM)
40. Corey Seager (SS, LA)
41. Adalberto Mondesi (SS, KC)
42. Billy Hamilton (OF, CIN)
43. Clint Frazier (OF, CLE)
44. Tyler Glasnow (RHP, PIT)
45. Kolten Wong (2B, STL)
46. Henry Owens (LHP, BOS)
47. Gary Sanchez (C, NYY)
48. Jorge Alfaro (C, TEX)
49. Austin Meadows (OF, PIT)
50. Austin Hedges (C, SD)
51. Alen Hanson (SS, PIT)
52. Marcus Stroman (RHP, TOR)
53. Kohl Stewart (RHP, MIN)
54. Max Fried (LHP, SD)
55. Jake Odorizzi (RHP, TAM)
56. Michael Choice (OF, TEX)
57. C.J. Edwards (RHP, CHC)
58. Trevor Bauer (RHP, CLE)
59. Julio Urias (LHP, LA)
60. Jake Marisnick (OF, MIA)
61. Jesse Biddle (LHP, PHI)
62. Eddie Rosario (2B, MIN)
63. Lucas Sims (RHP, ATL)
64. Lance McCullers (RHP, HOU)
65. A.J. Cole (RHP, WAS)
66. Rougned Odor (2B, TEX)
67. Colin Moran (3B, MIA)
68. Mike Foltynewicz (RHP, HOU)
69. Allen Webster (RHP, BOS)
70. Chris Owings (SS, ARI)
71. Eduardo Rodriguez (LHP, BAL)
72. Miguel Almonte (RHP, KC)
73. Blake Swihart (C, BOS)
74. Jose Abreu (1B, CHW)
75. Zach Lee (RHP, LA)
76. Danny Hultzen (LHP, SEA)
77. Matt Wisler (RHP, SD)
78. Matt Barnes (RHP, BOS)
79. James Paxton (LHP, SEA)
80. Rosell Herrera (SS, COL)
81. Erik Johnson (RHP, CHW)
82. David Dahl (OF, COL)
83. Hak-Ju Lee (SS, TAM)
84. D.J. Peterson (3B, SEA)
85. Luke Jackson (RHP, TEX)
86. Delino DeShields (OF, HOU)
87. Brian Goodwin (OF, WAS)
88. Hunter Dozier (SS, KC)
89. Matt Davidson (3B, CHW)
90. Anthony Ranaudo (RHP, BOS)
91. Jimmy Nelson (RHP, MIL)
92. Bubba Starling (OF, KC)
93. Christian Bethancourt (C, ATL)
94. Courtney Hawkins (OF, CHW)
95. Domingo Santana (OF, HOU)
96. Kaleb Cowart (3B, LAA)
97. Jose Berrios (RHP, MIN)
98. Braden Shipley (RHP, ARI)
99. Justin Nicolino (LHP, MIA)
100. Alex Colome (RHP, TAM)

Top 100 Prospects Archive

2013

1. Jurickson Profar (SS, TEX)
2. Dylan Bundy (RHP, BAL)
3. Wil Myers (OF, TAM)
4. Gerrit Cole (RHP, PIT)
5. Oscar Taveras (OF, STL)
6. Taijuan Walker (RHP, SEA)
7. Trevor Bauer (RHP, CLE)
8. Jose Fernandez (RHP, MIA)
9. Travis d'Arnaud (C, NYM)
10. Miguel Sano (3B, MIN)
11. Zack Wheeler (RHP, NYM)
12. Christian Yelich (OF, MIA)
13. Tyler Skaggs (LHP, ARI)
14. Francisco Lindor (SS, CLE)
15. Javier Baez (SS, CHC)
16. Shelby Miller (RHP, STL)
17. Nick Castellanos (OF, DET)
18. Xander Bogaerts (SS, BOS)
19. Jameson Taillon (RHP, PIT)
20. Danny Hultzen (LHP, SEA)
21. Jonathan Singleton (1B, HOU)
22. Mike Zunino (C, SEA)
23. Billy Hamilton (OF, CIN)
24. Anthony Rendon (3B, WAS)
25. Mike Olt (3B, TEX)
26. Byron Buxton (OF, MIN)
27. Nolan Arenado (3B, COL)
28. Carlos Correa (SS, HOU)
29. Archie Bradley (RHP, ARI)
30. Julio Teheran (RHP, ATL)
31. Matt Barnes (RHP, BOS)
32. Gary Sanchez (C, NYY)
33. Jackie Bradley (OF, BOS)
34. Carlos Martinez (RHP, STL)
35. Bubba Starling (OF, KC)
36. Jake Odorizzi (RHP, TAM)
37. Jedd Gyorko (3B, SD)
38. Alen Hanson (SS, PIT)
39. George Springer (OF, HOU)
40. Nick Franklin (2B, SEA)
41. Aaron Sanchez (RHP, TOR)
42. Albert Almora (OF, CHC)
43. Kaleb Cowart (3B, LAA)
44. Taylor Guerrieri (RHP, TAM)
45. Kyle Zimmer (RHP, KC)
46. Noah Syndergaard (RHP, NYM)
47. Kolten Wong (2B, STL)
48. Tyler Austin (OF, NYY)
49. James Paxton (LHP, SEA)
50. Rymer Liriano (OF, SD)
51. Jake Marisnick (OF, MIA)
52. Trevor Story (SS, COL)
53. Kevin Gausman (RHP, BAL)
54. Trevor Rosenthal (RHP, STL)
55. Alex Meyer (RHP, MIN)
56. Jorge Soler (OF, CHC)
57. Matt Davidson (3B, ARI)
58. Brett Jackson (OF, CHC)
59. Michael Choice (OF, OAK)
60. David Dahl (OF, COL)
61. Mason Williams (OF, NYY)
62. Robert Stephenson (RHP, CIN)
63. Chris Archer (RHP, TAM)
64. Oswaldo Arcia (OF, MIN)
65. Zach Lee (RHP, LA)
66. Tony Cingrani (LHP, CIN)
67. Jesse Biddle (LHP, PHI)
68. Gregory Polanco (OF, PIT)
69. Addison Russell (SS, OAK)
70. Robbie Erlin (RHP, SD)
71. Courtney Hawkins (OF, CHW)
72. Brian Goodwin (OF, WAS)
73. Martin Perez (LHP, TEX)
74. Luis Heredia (RHP, PIT)
75. Yasiel Puig (OF, LA)
76. Wilmer Flores (3B, NYM)
77. Justin Nicolino (LHP, MIA)
78. Max Fried (LHP, SD)
79. Adam Eaton (OF, ARI)
80. Gary Brown (OF, SF)
81. Casey Kelly (RHP, SD)
82. Lucas Giolito (RHP, WAS)
83. Wily Peralta (RHP, MIL)
84. Michael Wacha (RHP, STL)
85. Austin Hedges (C, SD)
86. Kyle Gibson (RHP, MIN)
87. Hak-Ju Lee (SS, TAM)
88. Dan Straily (RHP, OAK)
89. Kyle Crick (RHP, SF)
90. Avisail Garcia (OF, DET)
91. Cody Buckel (RHP, TEX)
92. Tyler Thornburg (RHP, MIL)
93. Allen Webster (RHP, BOS)
94. Jarred Cosart (RHP, HOU)
95. Bruce Rondon (RHP, DET)
96. Delino DeShields (2B, HOU)
97. A.J. Cole (RHP, OAK)
98. Manny Banuelos (LHP, NYY)
99. Yordano Ventura (RHP, KC
100. Trevor May (RHP, MIN)

2012

1. Bryce Harper (OF, WAS)
2. Matt Moore (LHP, TAM)
3. Mike Trout (OF, LAA)
4. Julio Teheran (RHP, ATL)
5. Jesus Montero (C, NYY)
6. Jurickson Profar (SS, TEX)
7. Manny Machado (SS, BAL)
8. Gerrit Cole (RHP, PIT)
9. Devin Mesoraco (C, CIN)
10. Wil Myers (OF, KC)
11. Miguel Sano (3B, MIN)
12. Jacob Turner (RHP, DET)
13. Anthony Rendon (3B, WAS)
14. Trevor Bauer (RHP, ARI)
15. Nolan Arenado (3B , COL)
16. Jameson Taillon (RHP, PIT)
17. Shelby Miller (RHP, STL)
18. Dylan Bundy (RHP, BAL)
19. Brett Jackson (OF, CHC)
20. Drew Pomeranz (LHP, COL)
21. Martin Perez (LHP, TEX)
22. Yonder Alonso (1B, SD)
23. Taijuan Walker (RHP, SEA)
24. Danny Hultzen (LHP, SEA)
25. Gary Brown (OF, SF)
26. Anthony Rizzo (1B, CHC)
27. Bubba Starling (OF, KC)
28. Travis d'Arnaud (C, TOR)
29. Mike Montgomery (LHP, KC)
30. Jake Odorizzi (RHP, KC)
31. Hak-Ju Lee (SS, TAM)
32. Jonathan Singleton (1B, HOU)
33. Garrett Richards (RHP, LAA)
34. Manny Banuelos (LHP, NYY)
35. James Paxton (LHP, SEA)
36. Jarrod Parker (RHP, OAK)
37. Carlos Martinez (RHP, STL)
38. Jake Marisnick (OF, TOR)
39. Yasmani Grandal (C, SD)
40. Trevor May (RHP, PHI)
41. Gary Sanchez (C, NYY)
42. Mike Olt (3B, TEX)
43. Wilin Rosario (C, COL)
44. John Lamb (LHP, KC)
45. Francisco Lindor (SS, CLE)
46. Dellin Betances (RHP, NYY)
47. Michael Choice (OF, OAK)
48. Arodys Vizcaino (RHP, ATL)
49. Trayvon Robinson (OF, SEA)
50. Matt Harvey (RHP, NYM)
51. Will Middlebrooks (3B, BOS)
52. Jedd Gyorko (3B, SD)
53. Randall Delgado (RHP, ATL)
54. Zack Wheeler (RHP, NYM)
55. Zach Lee (RHP, LA)
56. Tyler Skaggs (LHP, ARI)
57. Nick Castellanos (3B, DET)
58. Robbie Erlin (LHP, SD)
59. Christian Yelich (OF, MIA)
60. Anthony Gose (OF, TOR)
61. Addison Reed (RHP, CHW)
62. Javier Baez (SS, CHC)
63. Starling Marte (OF, PIT)
64. Kaleb Cowart (3B, LAA)
65. George Springer (OF, HOU)
66. Jarred Cosart (RHP, HOU)
67. Jean Segura (2B, LAA)
68. Kolten Wong (2B, STL)
69. Nick Franklin (SS, SEA)
70. Alex Torres (RHP, TAM)
71. Rymer Liriano (OF, SD)
72. Josh Bell (OF, PIT)
73. Leonys Martin (OF, TEX)
74. Joe Wieland (RHP, SD)
75. Joe Benson (OF, MIN)
76. Wily Peralta (RHP (MIL)
77. Tim Wheeler (OF, COL)
78. Oscar Taveras (OF, STL)
79. Xander Bogaerts (SS, BOS)
80. Archie Bradley (RHP, ARI)
81. Kyle Gibson (RHP, MIN)
82. Allen Webster (RHP, LA)
83. C.J. Cron (1B, LAA)
84. Grant Green (OF, OAK)
85. Brad Peacock (RHP, OAK)
86. Chris Dwyer (LHP, KC)
87. Billy Hamilton (SS, CIN)
88. A.J. Cole (RHP, OAK)
89. Aaron Hicks (OF, MIN)
90. Noah Syndergaard (RHP, TOR)
91. Tyrell Jenkins (RHP, STL)
92. Anthony Ranaudo (RHP, BOS)
93. Jed Bradley (LHP, MIL)
94. Nathan Eovaldi (RHP, LA)
95. Andrelton Simmons (SS, ATL)
96. Taylor Guerrieri (RHP, TAM)
97. Cheslor Cuthbert (3B, KC)
98. Edward Salcedo (3B, ATL)
99. Domingo Santana, OF, HOU)
100. Jesse Biddle (LHP, PHI)

Top 100 Prospects Archive

2011

1. Bryce Harper (OF, WAS)
2. Domonic Brown (OF, PHI)
3. Jesus Montero (C, NYY)
4. Mike Trout (OF, LAA)
5. Jeremy Hellickson (RHP, TAM)
6. Aroldis Chapman (LHP, CIN)
7. Eric Hosmer (1B, KC)
8. Dustin Ackley (2B, SEA)
9. Desmond Jennings (OF, TAM)
10. Julio Teheran (RHP, ATL)
11. Mike Moustakas (3B, KC)
12. Brandon Belt (1B, SF)
13. Freddie Freeman (1B, ATL)
14. Michael Pineda (RHP, SEA)
15. Matt Moore (LHP, TAM)
16. Mike Montgomery (LHP, KC)
17. Brett Jackson (OF, CHC)
18. Nick Franklin (SS, SEA)
19. Jameson Taillon (RHP, PIT)
20. Jacob Turner (RHP, DET)
21. Shelby Miller (RHP, STL)
22. Martin Perez (LHP, TEX)
23. Wil Myers (C, KC)
24. Kyle Gibson (RHP, MIN)
25. Lonnie Chisenhall (3B, CLE)
26. Tyler Matzek (LHP, COL)
27. Brett Lawrie (2B, TOR)
28. Yonder Alonso (1B, CIN)
29. Jarrod Parker (RHP, ARI)
30. Jonathan Singleton (1B, PHI)
31. Tanner Scheppers (RHP,TEX)
32. Kyle Drabek (RHP, TOR)
33. Jason Knapp (RHP, CLE)
34. Manny Banuelos (LHP, NYY)
35. Alex White (RHP, CLE)
36. Jason Kipnis (2B, CLE)
37. Wilin Rosario (C, COL)
38. Manny Machado (SS, BAL)
39. Chris Sale (LHP, CHW)
40. Devin Mesoraco (C, CIN)
41. Tyler Chatwood (RHP, LAA)
42. John Lamb (LHP, KC)
43. Danny Duffy (LHP, KC)
44. Trevor May (RHP, PHI)
45. Mike Minor (LHP, ATL)
46. Jarred Cosart (RHP, PHI)
47. Tony Sanchez (C, PIT)
48. Brody Colvin (RHP, PHI)
49. Zach Britton (LHP, BAL)
50. Dee Gordon (SS, LA)
51. Miguel Sano (3B, MIN)
52. Grant Green (SS, OAK)
53. Danny Espinosa (SS, WAS)
54. Simon Castro (RHP, SD)
55. Derek Norris (C, WAS)
56. Chris Archer (RHP, CHC)
57. Jurickson Profar (SS, TEX)
58. Zack Cox (3B, STL)
59. Billy Hamilton (2B, CIN)
60. Gary Sanchez (C, NYY)
61. Zach Lee (RHP, LA)
62. Drew Pomeranz (LHP, CLE)
63. Randall Delgado (RHP, ATL)
64. Michael Choice (OF, OAK)
65. Nick Weglarz (OF, CLE)
66. Nolan Arenado (3B, COL)
67. Chris Carter (1B/OF, OAK)
68. Arodys Vizcaino (RHP, ATL)
69. Trey McNutt (RHP, CHC)
70. Dellin Betances (RHP, NYY)
71. Aaron Hicks (OF, MIN)
72. Aaron Crow (RHP, KC)
73. Jake McGee (LHP, TAM)
74. Lars Anderson (1B, BOS)
75. Fabio Martinez (RHP, LAA)
76. Ben Revere (OF, MIN)
77. Jordan Lyles (RHP, HOU)
78. Casey Kelly (RHP, SD)
79. Trayvon Robinson (OF, LA)
80. Craig Kimbrel (RHP, ATL)
81. Jose Iglesias (SS, BOS)
82. Garrett Richards (RHP, LAA)
83. Allen Webster (RHP, LA)
84. Chris Dwyer (LHP, KC)
85. Alex Colome (RHP, TAM)
86. Zack Wheeler (RHP, SF)
87. Andy Oliver (LHP, DET)
88. Andrew Brackman (RHP,NYY)
89. Wilmer Flores (SS, NYM)
90. Christian Friedrich (LHP, COL)
91. Anthony Ranaudo (RHP, BOS)
92. Aaron Miller (LHP, LA)
93. Matt Harvey (RHP, NYM)
94. Mark Rogers (RHP, MIL)
95. Jean Segura (2B, LAA)
96. Hank Conger (C, LAA)
97. J.P. Arencibia (C, TOR)
98. Matt Dominguez (3B, FLA)
99. Jerry Sands (1B, LA)
100. Nick Castellanos (3B, DET)

2010

1. Stephen Strasburg (RHP, WAS)
2. Jason Heyward (OF, ATL)
3. Jesus Montero (C, NYY)
4. Buster Posey (C, SF)
5. Justin Smoak (1B, TEX)
6. Pedro Alvarez (3B, PIT)
7. Carlos Santana (C, CLE)
8. Desmond Jennings (OF, TAM)
9. Brian Matusz (LHP, BAL)
10. Neftali Feliz (RHP, TEX)
11. Brett Wallace (3B, TOR)
12. Mike Stanton (OF. FLA)
13. M. Bumgarner (LHP, SF)
14. J. Hellickson (RHP, TAM)
15. Dustin Ackley (1B/OF, SEA)
16. Aroldis Chapman (LHP, CIN)
17. Yonder Alonso (1B, CIN)
18. Alcides Escobar (SS, MIL)
19. Brett Lawrie (2B, MIL)
20. Starlin Castro (SS, CHC)
21. Logan Morrison (1B, FLA)
22. Mike Montgomery (LHP, KC)
23. Domonic Brown (OF, PHI)
24. Josh Vitters (3B, CHC)
25. R. Westmoreland (OF, BOS)
26. Todd Frazier (3B/OF, CIN)
27. Eric Hosmer (1B, KC)
28. Freddie Freeman (1B, ATL)
29. Derek Norris (C, WAS)
30. Martin Perez (LHP, TEX)
31. Wade Davis (RHP, TAM)
32. Trevor Reckling (LHP, LAA)
33. Jordan Walden (RHP, LAA)
34. Mat Gamel (3B, MIL)
35. Tyler Flowers (C, CHW)
36. T. Scheppers (RHP, TEX)
37. Casey Crosby (LHP, DET)
38. Austin Jackson (OF, DET)
39. Devaris Gordon (SS, LA)
40. Kyle Drabek (RHP, TOR)
41. Ben Revere (OF, MIN)
42. Michael Taylor (OF, OAK)
43. Jacob Turner (RHP, DET)
44. Tim Beckham (SS, TAM)
45. Carlos Triunfel (SS, SEA)
46. Aaron Crow (RHP, KC)
47. Matt Moore (LHP, TAM)
48. Jarrod Parker (RHP, ARI)
49. F. Martinez (OF, NYM)
50. C. Friedrich (LHP, COL)
51. Jenrry Mejia (RHP, NYM)
52. Tyler Matzek (LHP, COL)
53. Brett Jackson (OF, CHC)
54. Aaron Hicks (OF, MIN)
55. Jhoulys Chacin (RHP, COL)
56. Josh Bell (3B, BAL)
57. Brandon Allen (1B, ARI)
58. Chris Carter (1B, OAK)
59. Jason Knapp (RHP, CLE)
60. Danny Duffy (LHP, KC)
61. Tim Alderson (RHP, PIT)
62. Matt Dominguez (3B, FLA)
63. Mike Moustakas (3B, KC)
64. Jake Arrieta (RHP, BAL)
65. Carlos Carrasco (RHP, CLE)
66. Wilmer Flores (SS, NYM)
67. Drew Storen (RHP, WAS)
68. Lonnie Chisenhall (3B, CLE)
69. Aaron Poreda (LHP, SD)
70. A. Cashner (RHP, CHC)
71. Tony Sanchez (C, PIT)
72. Julio Teheran (RHP, ATL)
73. Jose Tabata (OF, PIT)
74. Jason Castro (C, HOU)
75. Casey Kelly (RHP, BOS)
76. Alex White (RHP, CLE)
77. Jay Jackson (RHP, CHC)
78. Dan Hudson (RHP, CHW)
79. Brandon Erbe (RHP, BAL)
80. Zack Wheeler (RHP, SF)
81. Shelby Miller (RHP, STL)
82. Jordan Lyles (RHP, HOU)
83. Simon Castro (RHP, SD)
84. Aaron Miller (LHP, LA)
85. Michael Ynoa (RHP, OAK)
86. Ethan Martin (RHP, LA)
87. Scott Elbert (LHP, LA)
88. Nick Weglarz (OF, CLE)
89. Donavan Tate (OF, SD)
90. Jordan Danks (OF, CHW)
91. Hector Rondon (RHP, CLE)
92. Chris Heisey (OF, CIN)
93. Kyle Gibson (RHP, MIN)
94. Mike Leake (RHP, CIN)
95. Mike Trout (OF, LAA)
96. Jake McGee (LHP, TAM)
97. Chad James (LHP, FLA)
98. C. Bethancourt (C, NYY)
99. Miguel Sano (SS, MIN)
100. Noel Arguelles (LHP, KC)

AVG: Batting Average (see also BA)

BA: Batting Average (see also AVG)

Base Performance Indicator (BPI): A statistical formula that measures an isolated aspect of a player's situation-independent raw skill or a gauge that helps capture the effects of random chance has on a skill. Although there are many such formulas, there are only a few that we are referring to when the term is used in this book. For pitchers, our BPI's are control (bb%), dominance (k/9), command (k/bb), opposition on base average (OOB), ground/line/fly ratios (G/L/F), and expected ERA (xERA). Random chance is measured witih the hit rate (H%) and strand rate (S%).

***Base Performance Value (BPV):** A single value that describes a pitcher's overall raw skill level. This is more useful than any traditional statistical gauge to track performance trends and project future statistical output. The BPV formula combines and weights several BPIs:

(Dominance Rate x 6) + (Command ratio x 21) – Opposition HR Rate x 30) – ((Opp. Batting Average - .275) x 200)

The formula combines the individual raw skills of power, command, the ability to keep batters from reaching base, and the ability to prevent long hits, all characteristics that are unaffected by most external team factors. In tandem with a pitcher's strand rate, it provides a complete picture of the elements that contribute to a pitcher's ERA, and therefore serves as an accurate tool to project likely changes in ERA. **BENCHMARKS:** We generally consider a BPV of 50 to be the minimum level required for long-term success. The elite of bullpen aces will have BPV's in the excess of 100 and it is rare for these stoppers to enjoy long-term success with consistent levels under 75.

Batters Faced per Game *(Craig Wright)*

((IP x 2.82) + H + BB) / G

A measure of pitcher usage and one of the leading indicators for potential pitcher burnout.

Batting Average (BA, or AVG)

(H/AB)

Ratio of hits to at-bats, though it is a poor evaluative measure of hitting performance. It neglects the offensive value of the base on balls and assumes that all hits are created equal.

Batting Eye (Eye)

(Walks / Strikeouts)

A measure of a player's strike zone judgment, the raw ability to distinguish between balls and strikes. **BENCHMARKS:** The best hitters have eye ratios over 1.00 (indicating more walks than strikeouts) and are the most likely to be among a league's .300 hitters. At the other end of the scale are ratios less than 0.50, which represent batters who likely also have lower BAs.

bb%: Walk rate (hitters)

bb/9: Opposition Walks per 9 IP

BF/Gm: Batters Faced Per Game

BPI: Base Performance Indicator

***BPV:** Base Performance Value

Cmd: Command ratio

Command Ratio (Cmd)

(Strikeouts / Walks)

This is a measure of a pitcher's raw ability to get the ball over the plate. There is no more fundamental a skill than this, and so it is accurately used as a leading indicator to project future rises and falls in other gauges, such as ERA. Command is one of the best gauges to use to evaluate minor league performance. It is a prime component of a pitcher's base performance value. **BENCHMARKS:** Baseball's upper echelon of command pitchers will have ratios in excess of 3.0. Pitchers with ratios under 1.0 — indicating that they walk more batters than they strike out — have virtually no potential for long term success. If you make no other changes in your approach to drafting a pitching staff, limiting your focus to only pitchers with a command ratio of 2.0 or better will substantially improve your odds of success.

Contact Rate (ct%)

((AB - K) / AB)

Measures a batter's ability to get wood on the ball and hit it into the field of play. BENCHMARK: Those batters with the best contact skill will have levels of 90% or better. The hackers of society will have levels of 75% or less.

Control Rate (bb/9), or Opposition Walks per Game

BB Allowed x 9 / IP

Measures how many walks a pitcher allows per game equivalent. **BENCHMARK:** The best pitchers will have bb/9 levels of 3.0 or less.

ct%: Contact rate

Ctl: Control Rate

Dom: Dominance Rate

Dominance Rate (k/9), or Opposition Strikeouts per Game

(K Allowed x 9 / IP)

Measures how many strikeouts a pitcher allows per game equivalent. **BENCHMARK:** The best pitchers will have k/9 levels of 6.0 or higher.

***Expected Earned Run Average** *(Gill and Reeve)*

(.575 x H [per 9 IP]) + (.94 x HR [per 9 IP]) + (.28 x BB [per 9 IP]) - (.01 x K [per 9 IP]) - Normalizing Factor

"xERA represents the expected ERA of the pitcher based on a normal distribution of his statistics. It is not influenced by situation-dependent factors." xERA erases the inequity between starters' and relievers' ERA's, eliminating the effect that a pitcher's success or failure has on another pitcher's ERA.

Similar to other gauges, the accuracy of this formula changes with the level of competition from one season to the next. The normalizing factor allows us to better approximate a pitcher's actual ERA. This value is usually somewhere around 2.77 and varies by league and year. **BENCHMARKS:** In general, xERA's should approximate a pitcher's ERA fairly closely. However, those pitchers who have large variances between the two gauges are candidates for further analysis.

Extra-Base Hit Rate (X/H)

(2B + 3B + HR) / Hits

X/H is a measure of power and can be used along with a player's slugging percentage and isolated power to gauge a player's ability to drive the ball. **BENCHMARKS:** Players with above average power will post X/H of greater than 38% and players with moderate power will post X/H of 30% or greater. Weak hitters with below average power will have a X/H level of less than 20%.

Eye: Batting Eye

h%: Hit rate (batters)

H%: Hits Allowed per Balls in Play (pitchers)

Hit Rate (h% or H%)

(H—HR) / (AB – HR - K)

The percent of balls hit into the field of play that fall for hits.

hr/9: Opposition Home Runs per 9 IP

ISO: Isolated Power

Isolated Power (ISO)

(Slugging Percentage - Batting Average)

Isolated Power is a measurement of power skill. Subtracting a player's BA from his SLG, we are essentially pulling out all the singles and single bases from the formula. What remains are the extra-base hits. ISO is not an absolute measurement as it assumes that two doubles is worth one home run, which certainly is not the case, but is another statistic that is a good measurement of raw power. **BENCHMARKS:** The game's top sluggers will tend to have ISO levels over .200. Weak hitters will be under .100.

k/9: Dominance rate (opposition strikeouts per 9 IP)

Major League Equivalency *(Bill James)*

A formula that converts a player's minor or foreign league statistics into a comparable performance in the major leagues. These are not projections, but conversions of current performance. Contains adjustments for the level of play in individual leagues and teams. Works best with Triple-A stats, not quite as well with Double-A stats, and hardly at all with the lower levels. Foreign conversions are still a work in process. James' original formula only addressed batting. Our research has devised conversion formulas for pitchers, however, their best use comes when looking at BPI's, not traditional stats.

MLE: Major League Equivalency

OBP: On Base Percentage (batters)

OBA: Opposition Batting Average (pitchers)

On Base Percentage (OBP)

(H + BB) / (AB + BB)

Addressing one of the two deficiencies in BA, OBP gives value to those events that get batters on base, but are not hits. By adding walks (and often, hit batsmen) into the basic batting average formula, we have a better gauge of a batter's ability to reach base safely. An OBP of .350 can be read as "this batter gets on base 35% of the time."

Why this is a more important gauge than batting average? When a run is scored, there is no distinction made as to how that runner reached base. So, two thirds of the time—about how often a batter comes to the plate with the bases empty—a walk really is as good as a hit. **BENCHMARKS:** We all know what a .300 hitter is, but what represents "good" for OBP? That comparable level would likely be .400, with .275 representing the level of futility.

On Base Plus Slugging Percentage (OPS): A simple sum of the two gauges, it is considered as one of the better evaluators of overall performance. OPS combines the two basic elements of offensive production — the ability to get on base (OBP) and the ability to advance baserunners (SLG). **BENCHMARKS:** The game's top batters will have OPS levels over .900. The worst batters will have levels under .600.

Opposition Batting Average (OBA)

(Hits Allowed / ((IP x 2.82) + Hits Allowed))

A close approximation of the batting average achieved by opposing batters against a particular pitcher. **BENCHMARKS:** The converse of the benchmark for batters, the best pitchers will have levels under .250; the worst pitchers levels over .300.

Opposition Home Runs per Game (hr/9)

(HR Allowed x 9 / IP)

Measures how many home runs a pitcher allows per game equivalent. **BENCHMARK:** The best pitchers will have hr/9 levels of under 1.0.

Opposition On Base Average (OOB)

(Hits Allowed + BB) / ((IP x 2.82) + H + BB)

A close approximation of the on base average achieved by opposing batters against a particular pitcher. **BENCHMARK:** The best pitchers will have levels under .300; the worst pitchers levels over .375.

Opposition Strikeouts per Game: See Dominance Rate.

Opposition Walks per Game: See Control Rate.

OPS: On Base Plus Slugging Percentage

RC: Runs Created

RC/G: Runs Created Per Game

Runs Created *(Bill James)*

(H + BB - CS) x (Total bases + (.55 x SB)) / (AB + BB)

A formula that converts all offensive events into a total of runs scored. As calculated for individual teams, the result approximates a club's actual run total with great accuracy.

Runs Created Per Game *(Bill James)*

Runs Created / ((AB - H + CS) / 25.5)

RC expressed on a per-game basis might be considered the hypothetical ERA compiled against a particular batter. **BENCHMARKS:** Few players surpass the level of a 10.00 RC/G in any given season, but any level over 7.50 can still be considered very good. At the bottom are levels below 3.00.

S%: Strand Rate

Save: There are six events that need to occur in order for a pitcher to post a single save...

1. The starting pitcher and middle relievers must pitch well.
2. The offense must score enough runs.
3. It must be a reasonably close game.
4. The manager must choose to put the pitcher in for a save opportunity.
5. The pitcher must pitch well and hold the lead.
6. The manager must let him finish the game.

Of these six events, only one is within the control of the relief pitcher. As such, projecting saves for a reliever has little to do with skill and a lot to do with opportunity. However, pitchers with excellent skills sets may create opportunity for themselves.

Situation Independent: Describing a statistical gauge that measures performance apart from the context of team, ballpark, or other outside variables. Strikeouts and Walks, inasmuch as they are unaffected by the performance of a batter's surrounding team, are considered situation independent stats.

Conversely, RBIs are situation dependent because individual performance varies greatly by the performance of other batters on the team (you can't drive in runs if there is nobody on base). Similarly, pitching wins are as much a measure of the success of a pitcher as they are a measure of the success of the offense and defense performing behind that pitcher, and are therefore a poor measure of pitching performance alone.

Situation independent gauges are important for us to be able to separate a player's contribution to his team and isolate his performance so that we may judge it on its own merits.

Slg: Slugging Percentage

Slugging Percentage (Slg)

(Singles + (2 x Doubles) + (3 x Triples) + (4 x HR)) / AB

A measure of the total number of bases accumulated per at bat. It is a misnomer; it is not a true measure of a batter's slugging ability because it includes singles. SLG also assumes that each type of hit has proportionately increasing value (i.e. a double is twice as valuable as a single, etc.) which is not true. **BENCHMARKS:** The top batters will have levels over .500. The bottom batters will have levels under .300.

Strand Rate (S%)

(H + BB - ER) / (H + BB - HR)

Measures the percentage of allowed runners a pitcher strands, which incorporates both individual pitcher skill and bullpen effectiveness. **BENCHMARKS:** The most adept at stranding runners will have S% levels over 75%. Once a pitcher's S% starts dropping down below 65%, he's going to have problems with his ERA. Those pitchers with strand rates over 80% will have artificially low ERAs, which will be prone to relapse.

Strikeouts per Game: See Opposition Strikeouts per game.

Walks + Hits per Innings Pitched (WHIP): The number of baserunners a pitcher allows per inning. **BENCHMARKS:** Usually, a WHIP of under 1.20 is considered top level and over 1.50 is indicative of poor performance. Levels under 1.00 — allowing fewer runners than IP — represent extraordinary performance and are rarely maintained over time.

Walk rate (bb%)

(BB / (AB + BB))

A measure of a batter's eye and plate patience. BENCHMARKS: The best batters will have levels of over 10%. Those with the least plate patience will have levels of 5% or less.

Walks per Game: See Opposition Walks per Game.

WHIP: Walks + Hits per Innings Pitched

Wins: There are five events that need to occur in order for a pitcher to post a single win...

1. He must pitch well, allowing few runs.
2. The offense must score enough runs.
3. The defense must successfully field all batted balls.
4. The bullpen must hold the lead.
5. The manager must leave the pitcher in for 5 innings, and not remove him if the team is still behind.

X/H: Extra-base Hit Rate

***xERA:** Expected ERA

** Asterisked formulas have updated versions in the* Baseball Forecaster. *However, those updates include statistics like Ground Ball Rate, Fly Ball Rate or Line Drive Rate, for which we do not have reliable data for minor leaguers. So we use the previous version of those formulas, as listed here, for the players in this book.*

Team Affiliations

TEAM	ORG	LEAGUE	LEV
Aberdeen	BAL	New York-Penn League	SS
Akron	CLE	Eastern League	AA
Albuquerque	COL	Pacific Coast League	AAA
Altoona	PIT	Eastern League	AA
Arkansas	SEA	Texas League	AA
Asheville	COL	South Atlantic League	A-
Auburn	WAS	New York-Penn League	SS
Augusta	SF	South Atlantic League	A-
AZL Angels	LAA	Arizona League	Rk
AZL Athletics	OAK	Arizona League	Rk
AZL Brewers	MIL	Arizona League	Rk
AZL Cubs	CHC	Arizona League	Rk
AZL Diamondbacks	ARI	Arizona League	Rk
AZL Dodgers	LAD	Arizona League	Rk
AZL Giants	SF	Arizona League	Rk
AZL Indians	CLE	Arizona League	Rk
AZL Mariners	SEA	Arizona League	Rk
AZL Padres	SD	Arizona League	Rk
AZL Rangers	TEX	Arizona League	Rk
AZL Reds	CIN	Arizona League	Rk
AZL Royals	KC	Arizona League	Rk
AZL White Sox	CHW	Arizona League	Rk
Batavia	MIA	New York-Penn League	SS
Beloit	OAK	Midwest League	A-
Billings	CIN	Pioneer League	Rk
Biloxi	MIL	Southern League	AA
Binghamton	NYM	Eastern League	AA
Birmingham	CHW	Southern League	AA
Bluefield	TOR	Appalachian League	Rk
Boise	COL	Northwest League	SS
Bowie	BAL	Eastern League	AA
Bowling Green	TAM	Midwest League	A-
Bradenton	PIT	Florida State League	A+
Bristol	PIT	Appalachian League	Rk
Brooklyn	NYM	New York-Penn League	SS
Buffalo	TOR	International League	AAA
Buies Creek	HOU	Carolina League	A+
Burlington	KC	Appalachian League	Rk
Burlington	LAA	Midwest League	A-
Carolina	MIL	Carolina League	A+
Cedar Rapids	MIN	Midwest League	A-
Charleston	NYY	South Atlantic League	A-
Charlotte	CHW	International League	AAA
Charlotte	TAM	Florida State League	A+
Chattanooga	MIN	Southern League	AA
Clearwater	PHI	Florida State League	A+
Clinton	SEA	Midwest League	A-
Colorado Springs	MIL	Pacific Coast League	AAA

TEAM	ORG	LEAGUE	LEV
Columbia	NYM	South Atlantic League	A-
Columbus	CLE	International League	AAA
Connecticut	DET	New York-Penn League	SS
Corpus Christi	HOU	Texas League	AA
Danville	ATL	Appalachian League	Rk
Dayton	CIN	Midwest League	A-
Daytona	CIN	Florida State League	A+
Delmarva	BAL	South Atlantic League	A-
Down East	TEX	Carolina League	A+
Dunedin	TOR	Florida State League	A+
Durham	TAM	International League	AAA
El Paso	SD	Pacific Coast League	AAA
Elizabethton	MIN	Appalachian League	Rk
Erie	DET	Eastern League	AA
Eugene	CHC	Northwest League	SS
Everett	SEA	Northwest League	SS
Florida	ATL	Florida State League	A+
Fort Myers	MIN	Florida State League	A+
Fort Wayne	SD	Midwest League	A-
Frederick	BAL	Carolina League	A+
Fresno	HOU	Pacific Coast League	AAA
Frisco	TEX	Texas League	AA
GCL Astros	HOU	Gulf Coast League	Rk
GCL Blue Jays	TOR	Gulf Coast League	Rk
GCL Braves	ATL	Gulf Coast League	Rk
GCL Cardinals	STL	Gulf Coast League	Rk
GCL Marlins	MIA	Gulf Coast League	Rk
GCL Mets	NYM	Gulf Coast League	Rk
GCL Nationals	WAS	Gulf Coast League	Rk
GCL Orioles	BAL	Gulf Coast League	Rk
GCL Phillies East	PHI	Gulf Coast League	Rk
GCL Phillies West	PHI	Gulf Coast League	Rk
GCL Pirates	PIT	Gulf Coast League	Rk
GCL Rays	TAM	Gulf Coast League	Rk
GCL Red Sox	BOS	Gulf Coast League	Rk
GCL Tigers East	DET	Gulf Coast League	Rk
GCL Tigers West	DET	Gulf Coast League	Rk
GCL Twins	MIN	Gulf Coast League	Rk
GCL Yankees East	NYY	Gulf Coast League	Rk
GCL Yankees West	NYY	Gulf Coast League	Rk
Grand Junction	COL	Pioneer League	Rk
Great Falls	CHW	Pioneer League	Rk
Great Lakes	LAD	Midwest League	A-
Greeneville	HOU	Appalachian League	Rk
Greensboro	MIA	South Atlantic League	A-
Greenville	BOS	South Atlantic League	A-
Gwinnett	ATL	International League	AAA
Hagerstown	WAS	South Atlantic League	A-

TEAM	ORG	LEAGUE	LEV
Harrisburg	WAS	Eastern League	AA
Hartford	COL	Eastern League	AA
Helena	MIL	Pioneer League	Rk
Hickory	TEX	South Atlantic League	A-
Hillsboro	ARI	Northwest League	SS
Hudson Valley	TAM	New York-Penn League	SS
Idaho Falls	KC	Pioneer League	Rk
Indianapolis	PIT	International League	AAA
Inland Empire	LAA	California League	A+
Iowa	CHC	Pacific Coast League	AAA
Jackson	ARI	Southern League	AA
Jacksonville	MIA	Southern League	AA
Johnson City	STL	Appalachian League	Rk
Jupiter	MIA	Florida State League	A+
Kane County	ARI	Midwest League	A-
Kannapolis	CHW	South Atlantic League	A-
Kingsport	NYM	Appalachian League	Rk
Lake County	CLE	Midwest League	A-
Lake Elsinore	SD	California League	A+
Lakeland	DET	Florida State League	A+
Lakewood	PHi	South Atlantic League	A-
Lancaster	COL	California League	A+
Lansing	TOR	Midwest League	A-
Las Vegas	NYM	Pacific Coast League	AAA
Lehigh Valley	PHI	International League	AAA
Lexington	KC	South Atlantic League	A-
Louisville	CIN	International League	AAA
Lowell	BOS	New York-Penn League	SS
Lynchburg	CLE	Carolina League	A+
Mahoning Valley	CLE	New York-Penn League	SS
Memphis	STL	Pacific Coast League	AAA
Midland	OAK	Texas League	AA
Mississippi	ATL	Southern League	AA
Missoula	ARI	Pioneer League	Rk
Mobile	LAA	Southern League	AA
Modesto	SEA	California League	A+
Montgomery	TAM	Southern League	AA
Myrtle Beach	CHC	Carolina League	A+
Nashville	OAK	Pacific Coast League	AAA
New Hampshire	TOR	Eastern League	AA
New Orleans	MIA	Pacific Coast League	AAA
Norfolk	BAL	International League	AAA
Northwest Arkansas	KC	Texas League	AA
Ogden	LAD	Pioneer League	Rk
Oklahoma City	LAD	Pacific Coast League	AAA
Omaha	KC	Pacific Coast League	AAA
Orem	LAA	Pioneer League	Rk
Palm Beach	STL	Florida State League	A+

TEAM	ORG	LEAGUE	LEV
Pawtucket	BOS	International League	AAA
Pensacola	CIN	Southern League	AA
Peoria	STL	Midwest League	A-
Portland	BOS	Eastern League	AA
Potomac	WAS	Carolina League	A+
Princeton	TAM	Appalachian League	Rk
Pulaski	NYY	Appalachian League	Rk
Quad Cities	HOU	Midwest League	A-
Rancho Cucamonga	LAD	California League	A+
Reading	PHI	Eastern League	AA
Reno	ARI	Pacific Coast League	AAA
Richmond	SF	Eastern League	AA
Rochester	MIN	International League	AAA
Rome	ATL	South Atlantic League	A-
Round Rock	TEX	Pacific Coast League	AAA
Sacramento	SF	Pacific Coast League	AAA
Salem	BOS	Carolina League	A+
Salem-Keizer	SF	Northwest League	SS
Salt Lake	LAA	Pacific Coast League	AAA
San Antonio	SD	Texas League	AA
San Jose	SF	California League	A+
Scranton/Wilkes-Barre	NYY	International League	AAA
South Bend	CHC	Midwest League	A-
Spokane	TEX	Northwest League	SS
Springfield	STL	Texas League	AA
St. Lucie	NYM	Florida State League	A+
State College	STL	New York-Penn League	SS
Staten Island	NYY	New York-Penn League	SS
Stockton	OAK	California League	A+
Syracuse	WAS	International League	AAA
Tacoma	SEA	Pacific Coast League	AAA
Tampa	NYY	Florida State League	A+
Tennessee	CHC	Southern League	AA
Toledo	DET	International League	AAA
Trenton	NYY	Eastern League	AA
Tri-City	HOU	New York-Penn League	SS
Tri-City	SD	Northwest League	SS
Tulsa	LAD	Texas League	AA
Vancouver	TOR	Northwest League	SS
Vermont	OAK	New York-Penn League	SS
Visalia	ARI	California League	A+
West Michigan	DET	Midwest League	A-
West Virginia	PIT	New York-Penn League	SS
West Virginia	PIT	South Atlantic League	A-
Williamsport	PHI	New York-Penn League	SS
Wilmington	KC	Carolina League	A+
Winston-Salem	CHW	Carolina League	A+
Wisconsin	MIL	Midwest League	A-

2.4	46	5.8
	51	5.8
	63	5.8
	64	5.8
5	16.9	5.2
	112	5.8
	109	5.8
	110	5.8